A Bride for the Tsar

A BRIDE FOR THE TSAR

Bride-Shows and Marriage Politics in Early Modern Russia

Russell E. Martin

NIU
PRESS
DeKalb, IL

Published by the Northern Illinois University Press, DeKalb, Illinois 60115

Manufactured in the United States using acid-free paper.

Design by Julia Fauci

Library of Congress Cataloging-in-Publication Data

Martin, Russell, 1963—

A bride for the Tsar: bride-shows and marriage politics in early modern Russia / Russell E. Martin.

pages ; cm

Includes bibliographical references and index.

ISBN 978-0-87580-448-4 (hardcover : alkaline paper) —

ISBN 978-1-60909-054-8 (electronic)

1. Marriages of royalty and nobility—Russia—History—16th century. 2. Marriages of royalty and nobility—Russia—History—17th century. 3. Marriages of royalty and nobility—Political aspects—Russia. 4. Bride shows—Russia—History—16th century. 5. Bride shows—Russia—History—17th century. 6. Marriage customs and rites—Russia—History—16th century. 7. Marriage customs and rites—Russia—History—17th century. I. Title.

GT2756.A2M37 2012

392.5086'210947—dc2

2011043203

Photo section images courtesy of Wikimedia Commons.

Contents

Charts and Tables

CHARTS

TABLES

Acknowledgments

The happiest, easiest, and most gratifying part of this project has been to compose these paragraphs thanking the many institutions and people that have assisted me in researching and writing this book. I have received grants from the Social Science Research Council (SSRC), the International Research and Exchanges Board (IREX), and Westminster College (including endowed funds from the Henderson, McCandless, and Watto families), which supported my lengthy and numerous trips to archives in Russia. I am deeply grateful to these agencies and to my employer for their financial support.

My interest in Muscovite royal weddings began in the archives when I opened a folder at the Russian State Archive of Ancient Acts (RGADA) in Moscow, which contained a jumbled collection of random phrases and bits of unedited text from the ceremonial (*svadebnyi chin*) for Tsar Mikhail Romanov's first wedding in 1624 (RGADA, *fond* 135, section IV, rubric II, number 14). The rich and untapped potential of this source was plain to me at first glance, and so I immediately set out to collect every original and early copy of royal wedding documentation I could lay my hands on. I succeeded in finding and handling what I believe is the full corpus of extant original wedding texts thanks to the help of the capable and selfless staff of RGADA, the primary repository for these materials. I acquired a deep affection for this archive—the creaking floorboards, the grooves worn into the stone staircases, the wood and glass cases full of well-worn typed or handwritten inventories, the ubiquitous cats. I found it the most convivial place to work and, just as important, to establish friendships and collaborations with Russian colleagues. I particularly thank Iurii Moiseevich Eskin, Ideia Andreevna Balakaeva, and Svetlana Romanovna Dolgova. I also acknowledge and am grateful for the assistance offered to me by RGADA's former director, the greatly missed Mikhail Petrovich

Lukichev, who was taken from us far too soon. I spent many months working in or obtaining materials from other manuscript repositories as well, including the Manuscript Division of the Russian State Library (RGB, Moscow), the State Historical Museum (GIM, Moscow), the Archive of the Russian Academy of Sciences (ARAN, Moscow), the Russian State Historical Archive (RGIA, St. Petersburg), the Manuscript Division of the Russian National Library (RNB, St. Petersburg), the Library of the Academy of Sciences (BAN, St. Petersburg), the Military-Historical Museum of Artillery, Engineers, and Communications Forces (VIMAIViVS, St. Petersburg), and the Iaroslav' Regional Library (IaOB, Iaroslav'). I thank the professional staffs of all these institutions, who offered me assistance and advice happily, efficiently, and unstintingly.

Many others—colleagues, friends, and family—also played a role in the completion of this project, and I hasten to add their names to this *tabula gratiarum*. I must thank first and foremost my dear friend Boris Nikolaevich Morozov (Archeographical Commission, Moscow), who lent me his time and expertise again and again over the course of many years. If there is anything new and useful in this book, it is because of his unmatched familiarity with the archives and his willingness to share, advise, encourage, and assist. Ol'ga Evgen'evna Kosheleva (RGADA) has also been for many years a dear and esteemed friend, whose sound advice, expertise with archival materials, critical eye, and sense of humor I have come to rely upon during my research on this and many other projects. Others in various ways also lent me their advice and assistance, for which I am deeply grateful: Nancy Shields Kollmann, Sergei Bogatyrev, Michael Flier, Daniel Rowland, Chester Dunning, Charles Halperin, David Goldfrank, Robert Crummey, Aleksei Ivanovich Alekseev, Vladislav Dmitreevich Nazarov, Andrei Pavlovich Pavlov, Iurii Vladimirovich Ankhimiuk, Irina Aleksandrovna Voznesenskaia, Ludwig Steindorff, Jennifer Spock, Marina Swoboda, Ernest Zitser, Marshall Poe, Orysia Karapinka, A. Dwight Castro, Bryan Rennie, Connie Davis, Eric Forster, Nathan Carlin, Jillian Maniscarco, Sandra Webster, Robert Monyak, John Deegan, Brien Horan, and of blessed memory, Richard Hellie and Oscar Remick. I also thank Amy Farranto and Susan Bean of Northern Illinois University Press, whose professionalism and skill have made the entire experience of producing this book an utter pleasure.

This project plainly displays the influence of two of my intellectual mentors. The first is Edward Keenan, with whom I worked as a graduate student and whose ideas about power and political culture continue to influence my own thinking about the way Muscovy worked. Ned's provocative heresies have inspired and emboldened me to make my own venturesome claims about court politics in Muscovy; and while he may not agree with every argument advanced in the pages that follow, I hope this work meets his own high standards of erudition. The other is Donald Ostrowski. Our hours at Peet's Coffee House in Harvard Square discussing early Russian history have been among my most satisfying intellectual experiences since leaving Harvard fifteen years ago. During one of these intense sessions, Don suggested: "You've done so much on bride-shows, why don't you just write a book about them?" I had not thought to pull together the many strands of my thinking into a focused book-length work until that moment, but I was hard at work on it within hours of that meeting. I am grateful for Don's constant support and advice over the years, but mostly for his generous and warm friendship. I am hardly the only one who has benefited from his advice and encouragement, but I am among the most grateful for it.

Finally, but most importantly, I thank my children, Alexandra, Peter, and Juliana, and my wife, Sarah Kellogg. They have tolerated several years of my blinkered devotion to this book, which, for practical purposes, has meant sequestering myself in my office to work at odd times of the day and night, on weekends, and during family and other holidays. Their patience has enabled every word and idea in the pages that follow. To my children, I offer my heartfelt thanks and earnest promise to emerge more often from my walled-off office. To my wife, Sarah, I dedicate this book and offer the words of the bard: "I would not wish // Any companion in the world but you" (*The Tempest*, 3.1.54–55).

Notes on Dates, Names, and Transliteration

Dates cited in this book are drawn from the manuscript sources upon which this study is predominantly based, which reflect the use of the Julian calendar in Russia during the early modern period (and up until 1918). That calendar numbered years from the traditional date for the creation of the world—5508 B.C.—and ran from September 1 to August 31. These dates are in this book normally converted from *anno mundi* to *anno domini*. On occasions when the day and month were not indicated in the sources, these conversions are presented with a slash: for example, 7083 (the year Ivan IV married for the fifth time) is rendered 1574/75. The sources themselves also dictate the format of names in this book. Variant spellings of names are preserved, as are patronymics, which varied based on the social rank of the individual. The highest ranking servitors had patronymics in "-ovich" (for males) and "-ovna" (for females), as all Russians have today. Lesser servitors had patronymics in syn and doch': Ivan Vasil'ev syn Radilov (i.e., Ivan, the son of Vasilii, of the Radilov family), and Ovdot'ia Ondreeva doch' Gundorova (Ovdot'ia, the daughter of Andrei, of the Gundorov family). These names, as well as occasional brief explanatory passages drawn from original sources, are presented in the Library of Congress system of transliteration. Names for the period during and after Peter the Great's reign (1682–1725) appear in the usual English equivalents (Peter for Pëtr, Catherine for Ekaterina, and so on). Finally, in the case of ranks and terminology that do not translate usefully into English (e.g., *okol'nichii*, the second-highest Duma court rank, or *stol'nik,* "tableman"), the original term is used with a definition at first occurrence.

A BRIDE FOR THE TSAR

Introduction

Sometime between April and September 1776, Prince Mikhail Mikhailovich Shcherbatov—philosopher, courtier, senator, publisher, historian, "pupil of the western Enlightenment," and a "rationalist *par excellence*"[1]—wrote an essay entitled "On the Marriage of the Russian Tsars." In it, he imagines a conversation between a government minister (*ministr*) and an ordinary citizen (*grazhdanin*). The two old acquaintances happen upon each other and begin debating the remarriage of the heir to the throne, Tsarevich Pavel Petrovich (the future Emperor Paul I).[2] The dialog is set just after the death of the tsarevich's first wife, Natal'ia Alekseevna (born Wilhelmina Louisa of Hesse-Darmstadt), on April 15, 1776, in childbirth. Her death, and the still-birth of her child, came as a blow to the young tsarevich, who was smitten with his wife, and as a disappointment to his mother, Catherine II the Great, who had hoped the couple would quickly produce children to repopulate the nearly extinct Romanov dynasty. Obviously, the grieving heir would have to pull himself together and remarry. The tsarevich's sad predicament prompted the question that Shcherbatov's interlocutors discuss in the essay: who makes for a better bride for a Russian tsar, a foreign princess or a native-born maiden?

Shcherbatov's government minister and citizen waste no time getting to the point:

> MINISTER—It seems to me that you have something pressing on your mind today?
>
> CITIZEN—You are right, dear sir. And, moreover, I think that every citizen should share my concerns at this sorrowful time, brought on by the death of the grand princess.

> MINISTER—Your sorrow and concern are very appropriate; and whilst we all share this sorrow, we should all likewise hope for the health of the grand prince, and that his second marriage should be happier and a source of rejoicing for Russia.
>
> CITIZEN—And it is precisely about this second marriage that I am thinking.
>
> MINISTER—And what are you thinking?
>
> CITIZEN—About this, dear sir: is it good for Russian sovereigns to marry foreign princesses, or would it be better to revive the ancient custom of taking brides from among their own subjects?
>
> MINISTER—Your question surprises me, since it has long been settled that great harm would result if Russian sovereigns married their subjects.
>
> CITIZEN—This, dear sir, is precisely the thing that troubles me, because I, unlike you, believe that it is harmful for them to marry foreign princesses.
>
> MINISTER—No, my dear sir, I can give you 40 reasons to show the advantage of marriages with foreign princesses.
>
> CITIZEN—And I could lay before you 400 reasons to prove the advantage of marriages with their own subjects and avoiding foreign-born princesses, and the very proof you offer I can turn around to help me make my case.[3]

The two men maintain a cordial and courteous tone throughout the exchange, even as tensions slowly rise between them. But the minister is clearly Shcherabatov's straw man, whose arguments get space on the page merely so the citizen can debunk them one by one.

The first of the government minister's "40 reasons" is diplomacy. Marriages between the rulers of Russia and those of foreign principalities are essential for building alliances that strengthen the state internationally. "No state can be without alliances," the minister declares, "and the easiest way to establish such alliances is through marriages."[4] Before the minister can move on to his second point, however, the citizen interrupts to remind him that even states that enjoy close kinship ties between their ruling dynasties nonetheless go to war with each other. Moreover, the citizen continues, religion often gets in the way of useful diplomatic matches:

> Princesses from powerful states do not want to change their religion to the Greek faith, which we confess and which no other ruler confesses, just so

> they can marry the heir to the throne of Russia. We are therefore required to search for a bride for the heir from among the smaller German ruling houses, such as Anhalt-Zerbst and Darmstadt. So can you really tell me that an alliance with these houses contributes to the significance of Russia in Europe? Is it not rather the case that Russia is sometimes compelled to defend in Germany the interests of these insignificant princes in their quarrels with other insignificant princes, and against larger powers—without any obvious advantage to Russia for all its trouble?[5]

The diplomacy argument having been blunted, the minister next turns to the social background of foreign princesses. "Your ideas have merit," he admits, "but in marriage, shouldn't each person search, as much as is possible, for someone of equal status to marry; and, of course, are not the princesses of these German ruling houses closer in rank to the grand prince than any of his subjects in Russia?" The citizen responds by getting the minister first to agree that the "sovereign should be happy in his marriage, always be true to his spouse, and with joy maintain forever his love for her." The citizen then asserts that it is impossible to have this kind of close and loving relationship with a bride whose appearance he knows only from a portrait and whose personality he knows only from the reports of diplomats and courtiers. The government minister responds by pointing to the grand princess who has just died—Natal'ia Alekseevna—and the deep love her husband, Tsarevich Pavel Petrovich, had for her. But the citizen calls this "the exception, not the rule," and asserts that there would be "no surprises" when marrying a native-born Russian maiden.[6] The royal groom would have investigated her background, her parents and relatives, and her friends. He would be able to look upon her face with his own eyes and quiz her to assess the depth of her intellect and quality of her morals. "The entire story of her life from the very beginning and the manner of her upbringing would be impossible to conceal," the citizen concludes.[7]

But are there any Russian maidens who are worthy of marrying the future emperor, the government minister asks, now beginning to reveal his growing irritation with his interlocutor: "Can one born a slave acquire the majesty required to occupy the throne?" The citizen responds by asking who can really know how a German princess born in a remote town in central Europe has been raised: "God would be unjust if it were the case that grace and virtue were the sole possession only of noble and royal houses, and the rest of humanity were just so much livestock, without any spiritual gifts."[8] Moreover, the citizen continues, the commoner origins of a Russian bride would make the ruler all the more sensitive to the needs and daily struggles of the ordinary people of the empire. After all, "the wife of the sovereign has the duty to please her husband; and inasmuch as she is his subject and is duty-bound to advance his welfare, she can fulfill that duty far better than a foreign princess." The wife of a sovereign "has the role of turning the heart of her sovereign and husband toward mercy, a role she can fulfill better [than foreign-born princesses] because she understands from her own experience the hardships of ordinary people."[9]

Finally, the two men reach what is for the government minister perhaps the greatest danger of native-born brides: the in-laws they bring with them to court. These in-laws come to occupy high offices and enjoy every social advantage after the marriage. They are parasitical and self-interested. But in-laws are precisely the one thing that foreign-born brides never have in tow. They come to Russia more or less alone, and their fathers, uncles, and brothers therefore can never join or form a faction or otherwise disrupt the balance of families at court, as the relatives of native-born brides invariably did. The citizen attempts a brief and romanticized (and utterly ridiculous) response, claiming that the influence of royal in-laws would be benign because the emperor "by virtue of his imperial title" is already a "father" to all his people, not just his new in-laws. Royal in-laws, he claims, would therefore never enjoy any advantage over ordinary Russian citizens.

The citizen's flimsy riposte launches the minister on a lengthy litany of criticisms of traditional marriage customs in early modern Russia. The minister's description is meant to be a gloomy prophecy of what might transpire if the emperor married a Russian maiden, but it reads more like an indictment of the way things actually worked in pre-Petrine Russia, when most of the rulers' brides were native-born:

> As soon as the common people understood that the sovereign was going to pick a bride from among their daughters or other female relatives, fathers of young girls, as well as other relatives and the girls themselves, would all start scheming—motivated not by love for the sovereign but by ambition. Various parties would form at court, competing with each other and each trying to ruin the other. Many relatives from the bride's network of kin would be established at court, controlling the sovereign.[10]

The minister then draws the distinction between the way things were before Peter I, and the way things are afterward:

> This custom could be tolerated in ancient times in Russia, when the maidens were secluded in the depths of their homes unseen and unknown to anyone, when their charms could not act on the heart of the sovereign and, finally, when their relatives were making all the decisions on the basis of their own family's interests. But those times and those morals have faded into the past: what in those days could be tolerated, has today been rendered obsolete by the insight of Peter the Great, who foresaw all the problems that would naturally follow were this custom to be continued.[11]

The minister has a point. In the sixteenth and seventeenth centuries, when Russia's rulers took native-born brides, royal in-laws entered the court in droves and rose quickly through the court ranks. They established ties of kinship and patronage with the leading boyar clans. They conspired and cavorted with some of the boyars to control the marriages of other members of the dynasty, especially in the next generation. The relatives of native-born brides were necessarily and always a powerful force to be reckoned with in early modern Russia.

And it seems that the citizen—which is to say Shcherbatov, who is putting the words in his mouth—knew that the in-laws were the weak link in his argument. The longest speeches in the dialog come now, as the citizen attempts to minimize or deny the influence of royal in-laws. But here the thrust of the essay moves away from parrying the minister's arguments to elucidating one of Shcherbatov's favorite and recurring themes in much of his writings: his advocacy for a new kind of monarchy, where the emperor ruled in collaboration with the best elements of society. For Shcherbatov, that element was, not surprisingly, the ancient aristocracy, of which Shcherbatov was himself a member. The first and essential step to constituting that new, earthy kind of monarchy was the revival of marriage between the Russian ruler and a maiden from home—Orthodox, Russian, bound by love and a sense of duty to the monarch, and selected to be the ruler's bride from all ranks of society, without regard for social background.[12]

By advocating domestic brides for Russian emperors, Shcherbatov was unwittingly calling for a return to the ancient (and by his time long-defunct) Muscovite bride-show: the gathering of young, native-born maidens from across Muscovy, from which the tsar chose his bride. Shcherbatov describes the advantages of the bride-show without ever using the term or otherwise referring to the specific customs and rituals that constituted it. The irony here is that Shcherbatov had a recent model of the bride-show right at hand in the person of the very princess whose death prompted the writing of his essay. Natal'ia Alekseevna, Tsarevich Pavel Petrovich's first bride, had been sent to Russia in 1773 along with her two sisters (all daughters of Ludwig IX of Hesse-Darmstadt) on Frederick the Great's recommendation, as potential brides for the young heir. In what was surely an unintended echo of the former Muscovite bride-show, the tsarevich was presented with all three candidates and allowed to pick his bride from among them. He chose Wilhelmina Louisa, the middle daughter, who was renamed Natal'ia Alekseevna upon her conversion to Orthodoxy.[13]

Shcherbatov's essay "On the Marriage of the Russian Tsars" never appeared in print at the time, and so it had no influence on the outcome of the search for a new bride for Pavel Petrovich in the summer of 1776. It would not have mattered even if it had appeared in print. No one in Catherine II's court was in the mood for relinquishing the clear diplomatic advantages that inter-dynastic marriages offered Russia. The future Paul I dutifully married Sophie-Dorothea-Auguste-Luise of Württemberg (who took the name Mariia Feodorovna in Orthodox baptism) and refounded the withered Romanov dynasty with their ten children.[14] At the end of the day, it is the government minister—not Shcherbatov's prolocutor, the citizen—whose argument prevailed.

This book is about the bride-show in early modern Russia. It examines the cluster of customs and rituals by which the tsar selected a bride from a pool of native-born candidates. For nearly two centuries, from the turn of the sixteenth to the last decades of the seventeenth, foreign-born brides were almost unknown in the Kremlin. So were brides from the most illustrious Muscovite boyar and princely clans. From 1505 to 1689, the rulers of Muscovy and their brothers, uncles, and sons married almost exclusively into the middle ranks of the aristocracy (and their daughters and sisters mostly did not marry at all). It was not so before 1505, when Muscovite rulers married freely among the daughters of other princely houses of northeastern Rus', the daughters of foreign rulers, and the daughters of the great boyar clans. And it would not be so after 1689, when the ruling dynasty would again turn to foreign-born brides, the other Rus' principalities by then having fallen extinct and the boyar elite having transformed itself into a western-style court aristocracy. The years examined in this book, then, constitute a discrete period of early modern Russian history defined by the marriage and dynastic policy of the ruling dynasties and by a political culture that rested on the bride-show.

This book is also about royal marriage politics. The selection of the bride at a bride-show was not so random or capricious a choice as foreign travelers or even the official documentation from Muscovite royal weddings claimed it to be. Ostensibly a free choice on the part of the royal groom, the bride-show was in fact a carefully choreographed ritual that flexibly served many purposes. First and foremost, and very simply, the bride-show was the way the tsar chose his bride. Until the end of the seventeenth century, nearly every native-born bride of the Muscovite tsar had participated in a bride-show, even when the choice was decided beforehand. Nevertheless, enormous energies and resources were expended by the rulers' court to search the entire realm for candidates that might be brought to Moscow to be presented to the tsar. The bride-show was not a mere literary story-motif, nor an empty ritual. It was an essential element of the Muscovite political system.

In that political system, it was the hefty task of the bride-show to attenuate the competition among boyar clans at court. However one understands the nature of monarchical power in Muscovy (and the views on this topic vary greatly, as we will see), it is nonetheless well established that kinship and politics interacted dynamically in the Kremlin. Boyars married into each other's clans in a calculated fashion, building and reinforcing networks of patronage and clientage that coalesced into factions and parties around the ruler. But these calculated marriage alliances were merely the echo of the most important wedding in each generation: the wedding of the ruler. The ruler's marriage determined who the royal in-laws would be, of course, but also what new blood would enter the informal inner circle of advisors around the ruler, because the bride's family, as Shcherbatov rightly noted, would quickly be promoted to the highest ranks in the court elite. The bride-show was devised in large part to make picking a native-born bride safe: it removed the selection of a bride for the ruler from open politicking among boyar clans and neutralized potential conflict by burying it deep in a ritual; it presupposed and made possible the selection of a candidate from the lower ranks of the landed, *pomest'e*-holding elite, not from the boyar aristocracy, by arranging that, for the most part, only candidates from this background were included in the selection pool; and it put the job of vetting candidates in the hands of the great families—the boyars and, just as important, their wives. This is not to say that the tsar did not pick his own bride. The bride-show gave the tsar the last word. Even so, the tsar picked his consort from among a hand-selected pool of candidates. Thus, while the bride-show might project an image of a free and unfettered choice, it was in fact a ritualized process that simultaneously concealed and expanded boyar control of royal marriage in Muscovy.

The bride-show was also a key means for projecting another image: an image of Muscovite monarchical power as autocratic. Here again, image and reality part ways. The bride-show custom presented an autocratic ruler whose majesty and power were boundless. The ruler scoured the countryside, the provincial towns, and the capital in search of a bride from among all young and beautiful women, regardless of their social background. The only real criterion for selection was being selected: that is, the royal groom got his way irrespective of any looming dynastic, political, or economic concerns that may have restricted or guided the nuptial choices of foreign royalty in places where there were no bride-shows. The ruler's power in Muscovy outwardly appeared to be as absolute as it was capricious: autocratic power penetrated and pervaded even the royal bedroom. But behind this image—aptly, if somewhat vaguely, called by some a "façade of autocracy"—lay, as we shall see, a very different reality. The ruler selected his bride only from a hand-picked assembly of candidates provided for him by his boyars and their wives, who oversaw the entire selection process up until the final choice was made. The groom took the stage only at the very end—after others (the boyars and their wives and relatives) had finished combing through the lists of candidates, inspecting their medical histories, and investigating thoroughly the kinship connections of each and every potential tsaritsa. The bride-show was not so much an exotic and symbolic exercise of boundless monarchical power as a ritualized and rigged device for projecting the "façade of autocracy."

This study of bride-shows is therefore also about power. It argues that the nature and extent of the ruler's power is revealed by the set of rituals surrounding and enabling the selection of a bride for the tsar—the bride-show, especially, but also other nuptial customs that arose around it, including the wedding ritual itself. This study exposes the monarch's power to be highly collaborative and so builds upon the view, advanced by others, that the political culture of Muscovy evolved from its outset in the mid-fourteenth century as a *con*dominium of rulership: the dynastic, hereditary grand prince or tsar ruling best when ruling with his boyars, who over time came to be related to him by marriage and blood.

This study sheds light on symbols and rituals, on court politics, and on the very nature of monarchical power in early modern Russia, and it is the central claim of this book that the bride-show reveals this political culture especially vividly and directly. The collaborative nature of Muscovite monarchical power has been revealed in other recent studies: of factions at court and among the provincial aristocracy, of the relations between tsars and boyars, of court rituals and decorative motifs in the Kremlin palaces, of literary story-motifs, of the church's admonitory texts, and even in studies of Muscovite laws. This book is a contribution to that growing scholarship on power, court politics, and royal marriage, unveiling the bride-show as a vital and necessary element of the political culture of early modern Russia.

Historiography

Power, court politics, and royal marriage are not new topics, but the bride-show is. This is not to say that it was unknown. Bride-shows provided subject material for nineteenth-century historical artists, playwrights, and composers, popular historians and biographers, and historical novelists.[15] They were also noticed by historians. The custom is well-enough documented in the sources to find its way into the works of historians from Vasilii Nikitich Tatishchev, Nikolai Mikhailovich Karamzin, and Sergei Mikhailovich Solov'ev (and other pre-revolutionary scholars) to Stepan Borisovich Veselovskii, Aleksandr Aleksandrovich Zimin, and Ruslan Grigor'evich Skrynnikov (among other Soviet-era scholars).[16] Still, the bride-show has hovered in a historiographical no man's land, treated either as a defunct custom whose oddness serves only to underscore dramatically how strange and exotic the political culture of pre-Petrine Russia was or as the clearest proof possible of the autocratic nature of the Muscovite monarchy. In either case, the narratives largely roll past the bride-shows without much pause or comment.

The exception is the work of Ivan Egorovich Zabelin, the first scholar to study at length the domestic lives and family relations of the tsars and tsaritsas.[17] Zabelin was the first to look at the bride-show as something more than a curiosity from the distant Muscovite past but, rather, as an important and emblematic custom of the political culture. The tsar chose his bride, according to Zabelin, as a proper autocrat should: without regard to the candidate's social origins, her wealth, or her pedigree. He chose his bride on the basis of her physical appearance, which was cause enough to transform a young woman of even the humblest origins into a tsaritsa. In fact, Zabelin argued that the selection of the bride from the entire population only served to elevate the prestige of the monarchy. The ruler's dignity and the bloodline of the ruling house were not in the slightest sullied by these unequal marriages. Instead, Zabelin understood bride-shows to be one of the creative and formative devices that the Muscovite grand princes and tsars used to forge a single, centralized Russian state: "The sovereign, entering a marriage with a bride chosen from the entire country, from the ranks of his subjects, did not diminish his majesty but, on the contrary, he elevated it, giving it a 'national' significance; for who but the sovereign had the right to pick his bride from all the land?"[18] And, more to the point, the ruler chose his spouse himself. Despite all the influence of family and favorites that surrounded the marriage of the Muscovite ruler and the bride-show custom—and Zabelin richly describes how these influences played out among the personalities at court—it was nonetheless the tsar who had the final say in the matter. For Zabelin, Muscovy was a glistening autocracy.

Among the heirs to Zabelin's work are those scholars who have offered important new studies of royal and elite women in early modern Russia. Works by Natalia Pushkareva, Nancy Shields Kollmann, Eve Levin, Daniel Kaiser, Christine Worobec, and especially Isolde Thyrêt, among others, have built on the solid posts and beams that Zabelin had erected nearly a century earlier.[19] They have together explored the role of women in religious culture and observance, the seclusion of elite women, inheritance and landholding, conceptions of female honor, and the active and essential role women played in court politics. Zabelin himself had pointed to the wives of boyars (the *boiaryni*) as having played a fundamental role in bride-shows. He demonstrated that the *boiaryni* were intimately involved in composing the list of bridal candidates and plausibly speculated that they performed many of the physical inspections of candidates aimed at assuring their health and virtue. This book also places the lives of royal women prominently at the center of the *Problematik*. It fleshes out the skeletal biographies of several royal women and bride-show participants and offers a source-based glimpse of the impact that the political culture had on the lives of young women who found themselves face-to-face with the tsar.

Many of the sources that provide that glimpse have been available for some time, but others have come to light only recently. Zabelin's study of the tsaritsas includes many important primary sources that were published for the first time in the pages of his books.[20] More recently, Vladislav Dmitreevich Nazarov has produced helpful and thoroughly modern editions of crucial documents related to the organization of royal weddings and the search for brides in the sixteenth century.[21] On the basis of these newly published sources, Nazarov offered an update to Zabelin's speculations about how the bride-show may have worked in the sixteenth century. Margarita Evgen'evna Bychkova has similarly made a valuable contribution with her publication of Ivan IV's wedding texts, and her study of seventeenth-century wedding manuscript sources has paved the way for this study.[22] There have been other recent publications and codicological studies of original wedding documents;[23] and even though there remain many sources that have yet to be published, it is probably fair to say that the greatest progress in the study of bride-shows has up to now been made by textual scholars (*istochnikovedy*).

This book builds upon prior studies of Muscovite court politics and monarchical power. According to Kollmann's useful sketch of the historiography of Muscovite court politics, there have been two approaches to the topic: "the 'rational' and the 'patrimonial.'"[24] The "rational" school emphasizes the "abstract entities that were impersonally defined, were safeguarded by law, and were accorded a share in public authority." These "entities" included the "'Boyar Duma,' the state, and corporate estates such as the high aristocracy and lesser gentry." This school also envisions a powerful autocrat dominating these "entities" in an essentially adversarial and interminable contest for power: "one's gain was," as Kollmann put it, "the other's loss." The formation of Muscovy, then, followed a familiar, western trajectory—even if its political institutions, as compared to western corollaries, were primitive or ineffectual. This rational model has been embraced by such divergent schools of thought as the liberal "statist" school, the "juridical" school, and by Soviet Marxist historians. The "patrimonial" school, by contrast, emphasizes "premodern political relationships" that were structured by tradition, self-interest, and loyalty, where groupings and factions at court "formed around principles of kinship, friendship, and dependence."[25] One shade of interpretation in this model emphasizes the autocratic power of the ruler and "denies the real political interaction of other political groups"—a view not very different from the rational school, at least as far as monarchical power is concerned.[26] Another shade of interpretation argues something quite different: that consensus, not conflict, characterized the political culture; that the ruler, following the traditional formula that "the tsar commanded and the boyars assented," operated within a traditional, even oligarchical, political system; and, finally, that marriage between and among boyar clans was not only the glue that held the entire structure together, it was the very goal of court politics.

This last view, it must be disclosed at the outset, is the one best supported by the analysis of the bride-show on the pages that follow. This book therefore joins the company of studies by Edward Keenan, Nancy Shields Kollmann, Valerie Kivelson, Daniel Rowland, Donald Ostrowski, George Weickhardt, and others—sometimes collectively called the structural or anthropological school, but nowadays better known by Marshall Poe's parricidal label: the "Harvard School."[27] However labeled, this school sees, as Kivelson put it, "a monarch ruling in council with his boyars and elites, constrained to rule according to custom, tradition, piety, and even law, and enjoying a high degree of legitimacy in the eyes of his subjects."[28] This school owes most of its original insights to the path-breaking work of Veselovskii and to the theoretical refinements introduced by Edward Keenan and developed further by "Keenan's Cambridge Clones" (whence the label Harvard School).[29] It has probably been the most productive of the various models of power in Muscovy in the last several decades, even influencing works that do not wholly adopt the anthropological approach or the centrality of marriage politics.[30]

The Harvard School has had a lot to say about marriage politics and monarchical power, but somewhat less about the ruler's marriage and nearly nothing about the bride-show. Yet, if it is true, as the noted anthropologist and folklorist Arnold van Gennep wrote, that marriage is a "disturbance of equilibrium" and a "social disturbance,"[31] then the marriage that generated the greatest disturbance was the ruler's. His marriage and also sometimes the marriages of his kinsmen and kinswomen were the linchpin of the entire political system as it came into being from the 1450s on; and the political system, including the bride-show, was conjured with the goal of minimizing that "disturbance of equilibrium" among the factions of boyar clans at court. It is therefore curious that the Harvard School has approached the question of monarchical power from the other direction: by examining the marriage politics of the boyar clans, rather than of the tsars. This study reexamines the problem from the more intuitive perspective by focusing on the one wedding that held together all the others: the tsar's. That reexamination of the problem takes us directly to the bride-show.

Sources

The bride-show and its role in the political culture in Muscovy can be reconstructed on the basis of four sets of primary sources, many of which are unpublished and archival: royal wedding descriptions, chancellery documentation for bride-shows, foreigners' accounts, and narrative sources. The most important source for the bride-show and marriage politics is by far the official wedding descriptions, compiled by scribes in the grand princely chancellery and, later, the Foreign Office (*Posol'skii prikaz*). From perhaps 1495 on, the scribes in the chancellery began recording detailed descriptions of all weddings in the dynasty. The most important documents generated by the chancelleries were the wedding musters (*svadebnye razriady*), which listed the names of courtiers and other servitors who held honorific posts at royal weddings, and the wedding ceremonials (*svadebnye chiny*), which described the ritual itself: the processions, banquets, nuptial baths, gift exchanges, texts of speeches, and other happenings over the course of three or more days of celebrations. The two sources were related—the names listed in the muster were plugged into the descriptions of rituals in the ceremonial—but they were used for different purposes. While the ceremonial functioned simultaneously as the official record of the wedding and, more practically, as an instruction manual for how to choreograph royal weddings, the muster served as a permanent record of the participation of individual boyars and other courtiers. Musters were also the documents that scribes, acting as Muscovite wedding planners, held in their hands as they herded courtiers into their positions at the various ceremonies and verified that everyone was where they were supposed to be. In addition to these official documents, the scribes also produced a range of supporting documentation that is vital for this study, including lists of gifts exchanged at weddings, dowry inventories, and various memoranda and instructions pertaining to the preparations for the celebrations. Ceremonials and musters survive for twenty-four weddings between 1500 and 1682. Most of these sources are original manuscripts, many of them in draft form, with a few early copies also surviving. The bulk of this material remains unpublished.

Unlike royal weddings, the bride-show apparently generated no official record: no ceremonial (*chin*) describing the ritualized inspections of prospective brides, though there may have been a muster (*razriad*) listing the candidates, if only to match names to faces and help the boyars and their wives keep track of their investigations and findings. We say "may have been" because, in the nearly two centuries of bride-shows, there is only one extant list of bridal candidates: for Aleksei Mikhailovich's search for a second wife in 1669–1670. It is easy to imagine why rosters of potential brides were not retained. The tsar and his advisors—including now the newly promoted relatives of the new royal bride—might not want to create or retain any form of permanent record of the ruler's other potential matrimonial choices. Doing so would only erode the fiction that the tsar's choice was inevitable and approved by Heaven. Moreover, it is easy to imagine how interest in the bride-show would have quickly faded once the selection was made, as scribal energies were redirected to the enormous task of compiling the wedding muster and revising the wedding ceremonial—documents everyone at court recognized as vitally important because they memorialized for posterity's sake who was present and participated in the wedding ceremonies, and who therefore gleaned honors and rewards for their service.

Despite the lack of a discrete textual source tradition emerging from the bride-show, the historicity of the custom is nonetheless well established in Muscovy. The bride-show is sometimes mentioned in wedding ceremonials, but even more important is the small but coherent set of chancellery documents related to the search for royal brides. This important and unique material includes memoranda (*pamiati*), instructions (*ukaznye gramoty*), and other correspondence related to the bride search; rosters of courtiers sent to the regions in search of candidates; lists of gifts given to finalists in the bride-show; and in one instance, the results of a background investigation and physical description of a potential bride for the young Ivan IV.[32] This treasure trove of sources tells a story of the bride-show that contrasts starkly with the way the custom has been understood in previous treatments.

This story is fleshed out with the aid of the numerous and colorful accounts of foreign travelers, who had quite a lot to say about bride-shows. These travelers—mostly diplomats, but also some mercenaries, merchants, explorers, and churchmen—came to Muscovy and wrote down what they saw, providing some of the most vivid and useful descriptions of how the bride-show worked. Their accounts tell us how the custom was introduced to Muscovy, who the candidates were, how the selections were made, and even what politicking lay behind the selection. To be sure, these are not flawlessly accurate descriptions written by neutral observers: their authors necessarily observed their surroundings through the distorting lens of their own cultures and experiences, and many of them slanted their accounts toward the inevitable conclusion that Muscovy was a "rude and barbarous kingdom." But these foreigners' accounts nevertheless provide insights that richly supplement the skeletal story told by the domestic sources, and these rich, albeit sometimes problematical, accounts are used extensively in this book.

Chronicles, literary tales, and other varieties of narrative texts make up the fourth major set of sources that help to reconstruct the story of the bride-show, though it often appears only as flashes and blurbs in these texts. One chronicle account describing the young Ivan IV's first (and failed) venture into the European marriage market contains only a passing—but vitally important—mention of the custom. Grigorii Kotoshikhin's account of the life of the Muscovite court of the mid-seventeenth century, *O Rossii tsaria Alekseia Mikhailovicha* (*On Russia in the Reign of Aleksei Mikhailovich*), oddly omits any mention of the bride-show custom, though it does offer details on the seventeenth-centuries scandals they spawned. By contrast, the first secular play ever performed in Russia—*Artakserksovo Deistvo* (*The Comedy of Artaxerxes*, 1672), based on the biblical book of Esther—prominently included a bride-show, and mimicked how the bride-show worked in Muscovy (not ancient Persia). Narrative sources, then, run the range; but they do provide in varying measures vital and sometimes unique insights into how the bride-show—and, more generally, marriage politics—worked in early modern Russia.

The story of the bride-show therefore can be recovered from the sources and situated inside the larger political culture in Muscovy; and, like most stories, it is one best told chronologically. The first of the following chapters situates Muscovite bride-shows in the Eurasian space and sorts through the multiple possible origins of the custom in Muscovy. This chapter makes the case that the Muscovite court at the turn of the sixteenth century was inspired by the example of Byzantine bride-shows in the eighth and ninth centuries. The timing is important. It was about then—at the turn of the sixteenth century—that the primary and favored source of royal spouses disappeared as Moscow acquired control of the west Eurasian space and absorbed, dethroned, or exterminated the local princely dynasties. It was also about then that the Muscovites soured on foreign diplomatic unions: the disastrous marriage between the daughter of Grand Prince Ivan III and the grand duke of Lithuania in 1495 proved that the limited and uncertain benefits of inter-dynastic marriages did not outweigh their exorbitant costs and the troubling questions raised by marriage to the Heterodox. Finally, a dispute over the succession to the throne in Muscovy that erupted between 1497 and 1502 exposed the dangers of the ruler marrying the daughter of a prominent boyar, which risked the disruption of the delicate balance of factions at court. The bride-show was introduced in response to all these problems. It was the centerpiece of a system of rituals by which the ruler could pick a domestic bride, not a foreigner, who came from the middle ranks of the provincial aristocracy, not the great boyar families.

In Chapter 2, the bride-show is examined in cross-section over the span of the sixteenth and seventeenth centuries. The chapter dissects and analyzes the three stages of the bride-show, beginning with the regional searches for bridal candidates, then the second round of inspections in Moscow, and ending with the presentation of finalists to the tsar. This chapter also examines the selection criteria. While the official descriptions and foreigners' accounts of royal weddings often stressed beauty and piety and other elements of the candidates' appearance and personality, original chancellery documents emphasized as well the candidates' genealogical connections. Kinship thus emerges as a selection criterion as important as any other. Finally, the chapter explores the way a set of new rituals reinvented the bride's identity in order to compensate for the fact that the tsar was marrying someone of relatively low birth. The chapter describes how the bride-show helped to project an image of an autocratic ruler whose majesty was exalted and power unlimited. It also describes the reality behind this image: that the ruler selected his bride only from a hand-picked lineup of candidates provided for him by his boyars and their wives and other relatives. The bride-show custom, as performed in Muscovy for nearly two centuries, was simply incompatible with an autocratic or despotic monarchy.

In Chapters 3 and 4 the story of the bride-show moves chronologically through the sixteenth century. Chapter 3 begins with Vasilii III's second marriage and ends with Ivan IV's second marriage. The chapter shows the way the bride-show evolved into an essential fixture of the political culture in Muscovy both symbolizing and enabling a political system that revolved around the marriage of the ruler. The chapter explores the questions that the Muscovites themselves appear to have raised and answered about this new custom: Was the bride-show only for tsars, or could it be arranged also for other male members of the dynasty? Was the bride-show only for first marriages, or could it be used for subsequent royal marriages? How free was the tsar's choice, and what role did the boyars and royal favorites play in the selection? Chapter 4 focuses specifically on the marital excesses of Ivan IV. It shows how the "Terrible Tsar" continued to use the bride-show as he married again and again, and it explores the politics and dynastic goals behind the tsar's numerous marriages, as well as the connections between his own remarriages and his sons' marriages. The chapter offers answers to the often-asked questions of how many wives Ivan actually had (4, 5, 7, or 8?) and how legitimate or canonical his marriages were perceived to be. These two chapters bring new archival discoveries to bear on the story of Ivan IV's private life, offering new perspectives on the interaction between the tsar's marriages and Muscovy's foreign and dynastic policies.

In Chapter 5 we follow the chronology into the seventeenth century to the bride-shows arranged for the first two Romanov tsars. The focus here is on the well-documented and notorious scandals that foiled the tsars' wedding plans: two prospective brides who were poisoned, one whose hair was deliberately braided too tightly, causing her to faint; still another who had scandalous rumors spread about her—all victims of plots by boyars and royal favorites who believed the tsar's choice of bride posed an immediate threat to their own positions in court. Thanks to the chance survival of archival sources, this chapter exposes to view the ways marriage and politics intersected in seventeenth-century Muscovy.

The book ends with an examination of the bride-show's gradual slide into obsolescence and the reestablishment of inter-dynastic marriage as a tool in diplomacy during the reign of Peter I. Bride-shows were arranged for the last time in the 1680s. It was precisely then that the political culture was undergoing a fundamental transformation, rendering the bride-show an artifact of a political culture that was being created anew, even before

Peter I began his revolutionary reforms. As the court shed a range of outmoded rituals and ranks, the bride-show became devoid of cultural meaning and divorced from the politics of the court. With the demise of the bride-show, dynastic marriage reentered the realm of diplomacy and foreign relations. Peter the Great married his relatives and children off to foreign rulers with a view to his own diplomatic needs; and unlike the rulers of the early sixteenth century, he was willing to stretch and modify the church's canonical and liturgical rubrics to make marriages happen between Orthodox and non-Orthodox dynasts. By the end of Peter's reign, Russia had fully reentered the European royal marriage market, and the era of the bride-show was over.

Shcherbatov knew and wrote about Peter I's marital upheavals, and he did not approve. In one of his best-known essays, "On the Corruption of Morals in Russia," he wrote, "I cannot refrain from censuring his divorce from his first wife, born Lopukhin, and his second marriage (with the prisoner, Catherine Alexeevna) after sending his first wife to a convent."[33] For Shcherbatov, Peter I's second marriage was doubly disgraceful: not only had he abandoned his Russian-born wife for a foreigner, but his new wife came from a base background. This kind of behavior set a bad precedent, "for this example of the infringement of the sacrament of marriage, which is indissoluble in its essence, showed that it could be infringed with impunity."[34] For Shcherbatov, the second marriage of the first Russian emperor raised the problem of unequal unions. It renewed the old debate over royal remarriages. It displayed a lackadaisical attitude toward the sacrament of matrimony. It brushed aside long-standing concerns about the cultural differences between Russian grooms and non-Russian brides. And it reintroduced foreigners into the Kremlin after nearly two centuries of effectual exile. All these themes, and some others, are taken up in the chapters below. But it is not at all clear, on reading them, that Shcherbatov would approve.

Chapter 1

"It Would Be Best to Marry the Daughter of One of His Subjects"

The Origins of the Bride-Show in Muscovy

> While deliberating and discussing his marriage, Vasilii Ivanovich decided in the end that it would be best to marry the daughter of one of his subjects rather than to marry a foreigner, in part so as to escape the exorbitant costs of a foreign match, in part to avoid taking a wife raised with different customs and in a different religion. This decision was taken on the advice of the sovereign's treasurer and chief advisor, Iurii, who was called Parvus. He had hoped that the sovereign would marry his own daughter. But, finally, as a result of a broader consultation, 1,500 daughters of boyars were assembled together so that the sovereign might choose from them the one he wanted for his bride. Contrary to Iurii's expectations, the sovereign picked Salomea, the daughter of the boyar Ivan Sapur.[1]

With these words from *Rerum Moscoviticarum Commentarii*, the Habsburg emissary Sigismund von Herberstein described the circumstances surrounding the first attested bride-show in Muscovy, arranged in 1505 for Vasilii Ivanovich, the future Vasilii III (1505–1533). It is, admittedly, a very short passage. It nonetheless provides a vital and, it turns out, quite accurate glimpse of how the bride-show made its appearance in Muscovy, who was involved in its invention, and the reasons it became the principal means for picking a bride for the tsar in the sixteenth and seventeenth centuries.

According to Herberstein, the idea of a bride-show in 1505 emerged from two consultations between Vasilii and his advisors. Herberstein does not ascribe any role in this decision to Ivan III, Vasilii's father, probably because he was in the last months of his life and in declining health.[2] The first consultation was between Vasilii and Iurii Trakhaniotov, a Greek who had accompanied Sofiia (Zoë) Paleologa (Ivan III's second wife and Vasilii's mother) to Moscow in 1572 and had become one of Ivan III's (and later one of Vasilii III's) chief advisors.[3] Trakhaniotov suggested that Vasilii take a domestic bride, not a foreigner, and probably also raised the idea of arranging a bride-show. Vasilii evidently took Trakhaniotov's idea to his other advisors, who go unnamed in the account. It was out of this second, larger consultation that the final decision was made to convene a bride-show, which, as Herberstein reports, may have included Trakhaniotov's daughter. Trakhaniotov must have been sorely disappointed by Vasilii's choice of Solomoniia Saburova, but he accomplished more than he may have intended in that the bride-show he proposed to Vasilii—perhaps originally only a scheme to get Vasilii to marry his daughter—launched a nearly two-centuries-long custom of selecting a bride for the tsar in a bride-show.[4]

Herberstein was not himself present at the time the events he describes took place (he gathered his information during diplomatic missions to Moscow in 1517 and 1526), and as a foreigner he undoubtedly understood these events from the perspective of an outsider. He therefore gets some of the details wrong: the bride's name is Solomoniia, not Salomea; her father's name is Iurii Konstantinovich Saburov, not Ivan Sapur; and he attained boyar rank only after, and surely because of, his daughter's marriage to Vasilii, not before.[5] These errors notwithstanding, Herberstein's account is wholly plausible.[6] As this chapter will show, Trakhaniotov's suggestion of a bride-show was the right idea at the right time. Precisely at the turn of the sixteenth century, the Muscovite grand-princely dynasty found itself confronting a vexing conundrum over marriage. The pools from which the ruling dynasty usually drew its spouses had either disappeared entirely or had abruptly become undesirable. This conundrum helped to transform Trakhaniotov's self-serving suggestion into a custom that for nearly two centuries facilitated royal marriage, modulated court politics, and projected a carefully contrived image of monarchical power in Muscovy.[7]

Muscovite and Byzantine Bride-Shows

If, as Herberstein says, Iurii Trakhaniotov was the one who suggested the bride-show to the future Vasilii III, where did he get the idea? Trakhaniotov was likely very young when he accompanied his father, Dmitrii Trakhaniot, and his uncle Iurii "the Elder" to Muscovy in 1472 in the entourage of Sofiia Paleologa.[8] Could he have been familiar enough with Byzantine history and the common story-motifs of Byzantine literature to draw on them for inspiration? Were there other models of the bride-show beyond Byzantium that might have inspired him? Were there Muscovite sources of inspiration? Did Trakhaniotov conjure the idea out of thin air?

There is considerable debate among scholars today about the bride-show in the Byzantine Empire. This debate is a fairly recent one—prompted by Warren Treadgold's 1979 article, which made the case for the historicity of five Byzantine bride-shows between 788 and 882.[9] The Swedish philologist Lennart Rydén fired back with his own study of Byzantine bride-shows, arguing that all five identified by Treadgold were entirely fictitious—nothing more than a common story-motif in Byzantine literature.[10] Soon, prominent Byzantinists were taking sides on the question—some rallying to Treadgold's defense,[11] others agreeing with Rydén, often on the basis of the skimpiness of the source base (three saints' lives, three chronicle entries, and a funeral oration).[12] Treadgold has recently reentered the fray with a persuasive and updated restatement of his case for the historicity of bride-shows in Byzantium,[13] but the debate rages on, both sides still very much entrenched in their views.

Among those who do accept the historicity of Byzantine bride-shows, there is significant disagreement over the question of their origin. Steven Runciman and Romilly Jenkins assigned credit for Byzantine bride-shows to the Khazars, whose empire in the seventh through tenth centuries stretched across the Qipchaq Steppe and north Caucasus and whose rulers, the qaγans, intermarried with Byzantine and, probably, early Rus' dynasties.[14] The first Byzantine bride-shows were organized by Empress Irene, "the Athenian" (ca. 752–802), for her son Constantine VI (ruled 780–797). According to Runciman and Jenkins, Empress Irene drew her inspiration from her mother-in-law, Tzitzak, the daughter of Khazar Qaγan Bihar, who was baptized with the name Irene before her marriage to the future Constantine V (r. 741–775), and who, like her son Leo IV (r. 775–780), was called "the Khazar" (see chart 1.1). But, as Treadgold points out, "this conjecture is too rickety to stand." Tzitzak/Irene the Khazar (died ca. 750) was probably already dead by the time her grandson Constantine VI picked his bride, Maria of Amnia, in a bride-show in 788.[15] For this transmission from Khazaria to the Byzantine Empire to have worked as Runicman and Jenkins have suggested, a long sequence of uncertainties would have had to fall perfectly into place. As Treadgold incredulously put it: "Irene the Khazar may have told her son Leo [IV] who may have told his wife Irene [the Athenian] about the bride-shows that may have been held by the Khazars."[16] Treadgold's skepticism is warranted, especially since it is far from certain that the Khazars themselves ever employed the bride-show custom.

CHART 1.1. Five Byzantine Bride-Shows

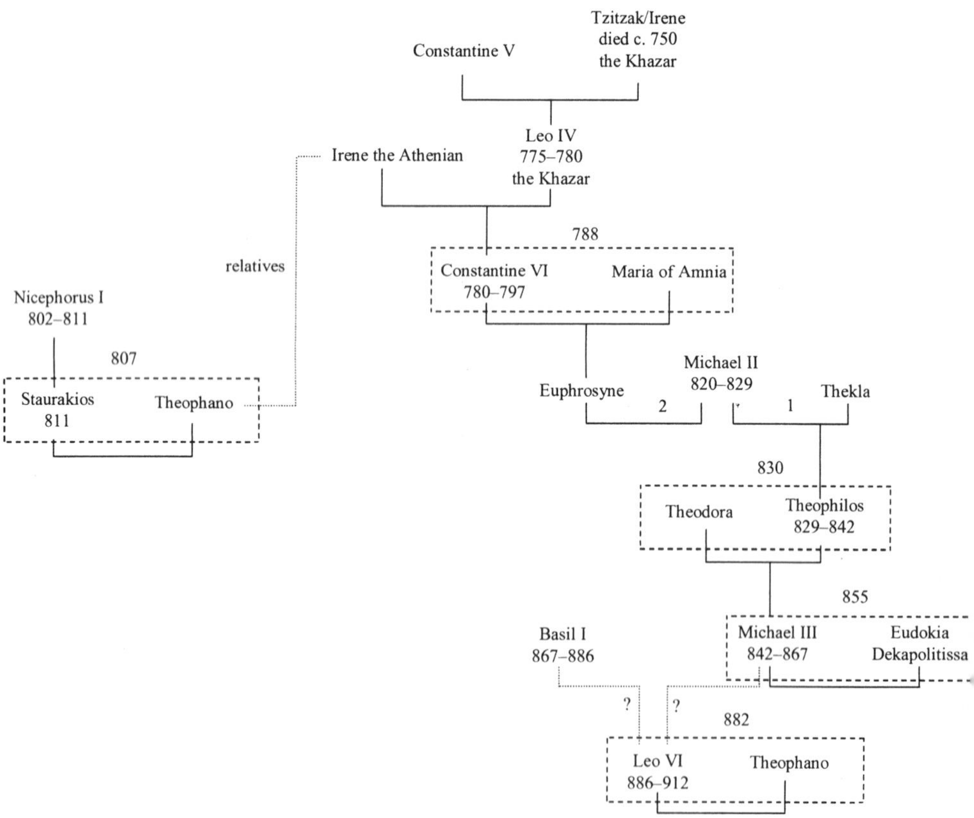

Treadgold suggested two possible alternative inspirations for Byzantine bride-shows, both homegrown. First, he argued that the Byzantine empress Irene the Athenian adopted the custom in 788 in response to Charlemagne's decision to break the engagement between his daughter Rotrud and Irene's son Constantine VI. As Treadgold put it, the bride-show functioned as an "assertion of imperial pride and self-sufficiency, to show that [Irene's] son could marry well without help from the untrustworthy and barbaric Franks."[17] Second, Treadgold speculated, somewhat in passing, that Irene may also (or instead) have been inspired by the biblical Book of Esther, which contains a bride-show in Chapter 2. In either case, Treadgold credits the introduction of the bride-show in the Byzantine Empire to Irene the Athenian, not Irene the Khazar, and therefore sees the bride-show as an indigenous invention, not a borrowing from abroad. As Treadgold concluded: "The idea of choosing the best and most beautiful wife for an emperor through a competition is not so ingenious that Irene and her advisers could not have thought it up for themselves."[18]

One might hasten to add other possible inspirations not considered by Treadgold. One inspiration may have been the accounts of the marriage of Emperor Theodosius II to Athenais/Eudokia in 421. In the account of the marriage preserved in the *Chronicle of John Malalas*, written about 150 years after the wedding, Theodosius II's sister Pulcheria conducts the search for the emperor's bride, inspecting the daughters of notables in the capital and thereafter widening the search to include commoners. Eventually Pulcheria meets and settles on a low-born but stunningly beautiful girl, Athenais, the daughter of a pagan "philosopher." Theodosius II is struck by her incomparable beauty and chooses her for his bride. Athenais is baptized a Christian, given the name Eudokia, and married to the very pleased emperor. In another version of the story, found in the *Parastaseis syntomoi chronikai* and probably written in the late eighth century, Athenais's intelligence (in addition to her beauty) is emphasized, as well as the intelligence of her brothers, who earn the emperor's favor by translating for him several confounding inscriptions etched on ancient ruins.[19] While these versions of the story both present a twist on the familiar narrative of the bride-show (the groom is presented with only one choice), they nonetheless illustrate, quoting Judith Herrin, the "central elements of the beauty contest and the selection criteria: the extreme beauty of the young girl, and the complete insignificance of her background."[20*]

Yet another domestic inspiration for the Byzantine bride-show may have been the well-known ancient Greek myth of the Judgment of Paris. The story evolved over the centuries in both Greek and Latin iterations, but by the second century C.E. had become the familiar tale of the beauty contest held by Zeus at the wedding of Peleus and Thetis. All of the Olympian gods had been invited to the wedding, except Eris. Angry over the slight, she sought to disrupt the wedding by casting into the midst of the attendees a golden apple with the word καλλίστῃ (*kallistē(i)*—"to the most fair") inscribed on it, anticipating rightly that it would ignite a dispute between the goddesses over who among them actually was "the most fair." Three of the goddesses present—Aphrodite, Athena, and Hera—took the bait and immediately began squabbling over the apple. Zeus, seizing the opportunity to entertain his own mischievousness, chose Paris (sometimes called Alexandros), the son of King Priam of Troy, to settle the matter by having him pick which of the three was the most beautiful. The three goddesses each tried to buy Paris's vote, but only Aphrodite knew the bribe that would sway him: the hand of the beautiful Helen, the one Paris believed truly was "the most fair." Paris bestows the golden apple on Aphrodite, and the story moves on to the familiar set of narratives about the Trojan War.[21]

Byzantine bride-shows may therefore have been, as Herrin put it, a "Byzantine adaptation of the Judgement of Paris."[22] The golden apple motif reappears in a chronicle account by Symeon the Logothete describing the third (according to Treadgold) Byzantine bride-show, which was arranged in 830 for Emperor Theophilos.[23] At that bride-show, Theophilus preferred the beautiful and intelligent Cassia, but he rejected her when, in response to Theophilos's melancholy reflection "Yet through a woman evils came to man," she impertinently responded, "But through a woman better things began." The emperor drew back the apple he was about to give her as a token of his choice and instead handed it to another candidate, Theodora. The association between the golden apple and the story of the Judgment of Paris can also be found indirectly in references to Muscovite bride-shows. Writing about Tsar Aleksei Mikhailovich's selection of his second wife in a bride-show in 1671, the Polish diplomat Jacob Reutenfels referred to the tsar as "the judicious Paris."[24]

Whatever their origin—the myth of the Judgment of Paris, the book of Esther, or the imagination of Empress Irene the Athenian—Byzantine bride-shows were probably more than mere "literary fictions" or "motifs."

As the eminent Byzantinist Gilbert Dagron put it, "For a period in the eighth and ninth centuries, the choice of the wife of a porphyrogenitus, or more generally of a young 'prince heir,' was the occasion for a curious 'beauty contest,' which is described in a dozen or so independent sources. These accounts, though they turn readily into moral fables and borrow all sorts of symbolic elements from universal folklore, seem largely to be true. When the sources are compared, it becomes impossible to dismiss them as pure fiction, and the reported episodes form a coherent series from 788 to 882."[25] Like most good yarns, there is a kernel of historical truth behind the subsequent myth.[26]

The Muscovites may not have been the only ones to borrow the idea of the bride-show from the Byzantines. There is good reason to think that the Carolingian emperor Louis the Pious was imitating Byzantine practice when in 819, according to the *Royal Frankish Annals*, he selected Judith, the daughter of Count Welf, "after having carefully inspected many of the daughters of the nobility."[27] The *Vita Hludowici*, written shortly after Louis's death in 840, describes a bride-show even more clearly, reporting that "after inspecting the daughters of the nobles who had been brought in from everywhere he married Judith, the daughter of the most noble count Welf."[28] While this evidence has been dismissed by some, recent work on the Byzantine influence on the Carolingian court suggests not only that these texts describe a bride-show in Aachen but also that it was inspired by contemporary Byzantine practice.[29]

Bride-shows also existed beyond the sphere of Byzantine influence. Chinese emperors employed bride-shows, starting perhaps as early as the Yuan, or Mongol, dynasty (1271–1368) but certainly during the Ming (1368–1644) and Qing dynasties (1644–1911). Yuan emperors preferred to marry into elite Mongol families, but they used a procedure that looked very much like a bride-show to fill the emperor's harem with concubines.[30] Marco Polo (ca. 1254–1324) described the bride-shows (or concubine-shows) arranged for the sons of Kublai Khan (Yuan dynasty): "Every second year, or sometimes more often, as it may happen to be his pleasure, the Great Khan sends out his officers, who collect for him one hundred or more of the most beautiful young women."[31] Things changed under the Ming. According to Ellen Soullière: "In a radical departure from earlier precedents, the Ming dynasty consciously and consistently adopted a policy of selecting marriage partners for the imperial family from families of no social consequence."[32] Their method for finding these middling-born brides was the bride-show. Juan González de Mendoza (ca. 1540–1617) described one of these bride-shows for the sons of emperors during the Ming dynasty. According to Mendoza, the emperor held a banquet

> to which he did invite all the principallest lords and gentlemen of his court, commanding to bring with them their sonnes and daughters, who did accomplish the same, striving who should apparell their children most richest and most gallantest. The banket being done, the young princes do go whereas are these the young ladies, every one placed in order according to their age, and there he doth chuse his wife according to his own will or desire, and where he liketh best.[33]

Indigenous Chinese sources confirm these travelers' accounts. Although the procedure varied over time, usually a decree was circulated summoning all those with eligible daughters to appear with them for inspection in the capital. By an imperial (Ming) edict of 1381, for example, the pool of candidates was to include women from "good families," but none from the highest ranks of the court or provincial service. Although subsequent summonses would be addressed to a somewhat broader pool (including "great and small officials"), the highest-ranking families were normally excluded from the pool of candidates.[34] The Ming also held bridegroom-shows: kingdom-wide searches for young men, again from modest social backgrounds, who were presented as potential husbands for the daughters of Chinese emperors, evidently selected solely on the basis of looks. The Portuguese Jesuit missionary Álvaro Semedo (1585–1658) described these bridegroom-shows as proceeding through several steps: a search for the "lustiest and handsomest" young men in the kingdom aged seventeen or eighteen years old; an initial inspection reducing the original number to twelve candidates; an inspection by the princess, further reducing the number to two finalists; and then the final selection by the emperor himself.[35] Under the Ming, the purpose of excluding the sons and daughters of the highest-ranking officials from the pool of potential imperial spouses was to curb and control the power of in-laws, who, as prior Chinese history had shown, could at times exert a corrosive influence on affairs at court.[36]

These same concerns about in-laws shaped imperial marriage policies and bride selection during the Qing dynasty. The Qing abandoned bridegroom-shows for imperial princesses, who again began to take high-born spouses;[37] but Qing bride-shows became more formalized than ever. Every three years (though there were stretches when the practice fell into disuse), a *xiunŭ* (beautiful women) draft was conducted: a kingdom-wide summons to fathers from banner families (elites in one of the eight military units, called banners) to appear in the capital with their daughters, aged thirteen to sixteen *sui* (age counted after the first year) for inspection.[38] The young girls that passed this initial inspection constituted a pool from which the emperor selected his consorts.[39] Evelyn Rawski has calculated that as much as 76 percent of the emperors' consorts entered the palace through the *xiunŭ* draft.[40] In addition, there were annual drafts of young women 13 *sui* and older to fill positions as palace maids. The selection of these candidates was not, however, based on their skill as seamstresses, or in the arts, or in any other useful domestic vocation, but on their sexual appeal. Some of these women—16 percent, according to Rawski—would later be selected by the emperor as consorts and, in a few rare instances, would so please the ruler that they eventually became empresses.[41]

Bride-shows in China, the Byzantine Empire, and Muscovy thus share many of the same priorities and politics, including the kingdom-wide search, the preference for women from outside the orbit of the court, and a concern over the power and influence of royal in-laws.[42] Put another way, in whatever setting it appeared, the bride-show custom seems to have been linked to, and a means to modulate, the anxieties and tensions generated by political systems dominated by kinship politics. From Byzantium to Muscovy, to China, bride-shows and marriage politics went hand in hand.

This is not to say, however, that all bride-shows have the same DNA. Despite several attempts, there has been no successful demonstration of the migration of the bride-show from China, on one end of the continent, to civilizations on the other end or, for that matter, the other way around. Photeine Bourboulis, who noted that the "royal bride-show is by no means an exclusively byzantine custom," attempted to situate Muscovite and Byzantine bride-shows in an expansive Eurasian context, locating the custom among the "Tatars" (she meant the Mongols), the ancient and modern Chinese (as far back as the eighth century), the Ottomans, as well as the ancient Babylonians and, thanks to the Book of Esther, the ancient Persians.[43] Bourboulis's definition of a bride-show was unformulated and expansive, and in the end she threw up her hands on the question of the origins of the bride-show. "We cannot decide," she admits with apparent frustration, "whether the Chinese bride-show is a Tatar importation, owing to the continuous contacts between the two races, even before the beginning of our era, or otherwise."[44] More recently, Donald Ostrowski's work on cross-cultural borrowing between Muscovy and its eastern neighbors led him to examine the origins of Muscovite bride-shows as well. He suggested that the "direct antecedent of the bride-show" in Muscovy "could have been either Byzantium or the steppe." He ventured that the custom, if it existed among the Tatars, might have derived from the steppe practice of presenting women captured in battle to the khan. "All this," Ostrowski admits, "is complete speculation."[45] The point can be made even more forcefully: except for the passage of the custom from Byzantium to Muscovy (through Trakhaniotov) and from Byzantium to the Carolingian court (through cultural and diplomatic contacts at the time of Louis the Pious), there is no evidence of any cross-cultural borrowing of the bride-show over the Eurasian space. Ihor Ševčenko was certainly right when he dismissed as "out of the question" any notion that the Byzantines might have borrowed the custom from the Chinese or anyone else; and as "dubious" any suggestion that the Muscovites may have acquired the custom from the Mongols, or from the Chinese via the Mongols.[46]

Herberstein's testimony about the bride-show makes it more than likely that the Muscovites did not "think it up for themselves," as the Byzantines may have, but that the custom originated with Trakhaniotov's suggestion to Vasilii in 1505. As for Trakhaniotov's inspiration, he had access to a wealth of Byzantine and ancient Greek sources, but he may just as well have drawn on Muscovite versions of some of the same sources that may have independently inspired Irene the Athenian centuries earlier. One possible inspiration may have been the Slavic translations of the *Chronicle of John Malalas*, which was originally translated, probably in Bulgaria, in the tenth century but later came to be included (in parts) in East Slavic chronicles. These translations include Book 14 (the story of Theodosius II and Athenais/Eudokia), so the account of that early bride-show might have been well-known among the handlers of this text.[47]

Another, more likely inspiration for Trakhaniotov in 1505 may have been the biblical Book of Esther, which, as Treadgold believes, may have also inspired Irene the Athenian. The Gennadii Bible, a full Slavonic translation of the canonical Hebrew and Greek scriptures (from the Latin Vulgate), was made available for the first time in 1499, only a few years before the first bride-show in Muscovy. The Gennadii Bible included a Slavonic version of the Book of Esther, which had not previously been widely available in Muscovy. The Gennadii Bible quickly became the standard text for liturgical use, and it is not hard to imagine that Chapter 2 of Esther could have become known beyond the circle of clerics on the east side of the iconostases of monasteries and churches.[48] It has been established that Archbishop Gennadii of Novgorod, who commissioned the Slavonic translation, had contact with both Dmitrii and Iurii Trakhaniotov—father and son—and, furthermore, had in common with them a relationship with the Moscow Kremlin's Chudov Monastery, where Archbishop Gennadii had formerly been archimandrite and where Iurii took monastic vows (with the name Gennadii) in 1520.[49] This relationship might have translated into a greater familiarity with the text of the Gennadii Bible, including Chapter 2 of Esther, than would otherwise have been the case.[50]

Whatever Trakhaniotov's inspiration, the question remains: what did Ivan III, Vasilii, and their circle of advisors find appealing about bride-shows? For Trakhaniotov, the motives were likely very close to home: maneuvering Vasilii to marry his daughter, as Herberstein suggested. As for Ivan III's and Vasilii's motivations, an important clue is imbedded in Herberstein's account. It reports that Vasilii decided that "it would be best to marry the daughter of one of his subjects rather than to marry a foreigner, in part so as to escape the exorbitant costs of a foreign match, in part to avoid taking a wife raised with different customs and in a different religion." Thus, concerns over cost and culture convinced Vasilii and his advisors to restrict the search for a bride to homegrown, Orthodox women. They had good reason to be concerned about foreign matches, as recent experience had shown.

Elena Ivanovna and Alexander of Lithuania

The bride-show as a mechanism for selecting a native-born bride appears for the first time shortly after the disastrous marriage in 1495 between Ivan III's daughter Elena and Grand Duke Alexander of Lithuania. It was a match that both sides hoped would cement a peace treaty between Muscovy and her western neighbor. From at least 1487, Muscovy and Lithuania had been engaged in an almost constant border war. The Muscovites were almost always the aggressors, and their objective was to absorb key border towns inside Lithuania that would position Ivan III's army for an eventual push on Smolensk, the turnstile between Moscow and Vilnius, the Lithuanian capital. By 1492, the Lithuanians were eager for a truce, but the death of King Casimir IV of Poland-Lithuania that summer derailed the effort. Hostilities flared up again that fall and winter and only subsided when the Muscovites captured the strategic town of Viaz'ma, located within striking distance of Smolensk.[51]

It was in this environment of military retreat and political transition at home that the new ruler of Lithuania, Grand Duke Alexander (Casimir IV's son), approached Ivan III for peace. Within months of Casimir IV's death in the summer of 1492, the Lithuanians sent a delegation proposing both a peace treaty and a dynastic marriage between Alexander and Ivan III's daughter Elena.[52] But with his sights still fixed on taking Viaz'ma, Ivan III was in no hurry for a truce. By spring, however, with Viaz'ma and several other key towns firmly in his hands, Ivan III was willing to talk more seriously about peace, especially since he had something to gain from it: recognition of his territorial gains and, perhaps even more important to him, recognition of the new title he had claimed for himself, "sovereign of all Rus'."[53] Formal negotiations between the parties began in the spring of 1493 and inched along into the next year. Although both sides were, for their own reasons, eager for peace, one issue held up the treaty. Ivan III was adamant that his daughter remain Orthodox, and Alexander seemed just as adamant that she convert to Roman Catholicism. The Lithuanians, who may have been dawdling in the desperate hope that the Poles, ruled by Alexander's brother, would intervene militarily on Lithuania's side, finally agreed both to the territorial concessions and to Ivan III's new title. As part of the deal, Alexander was to take Elena as his bride and solemnly pledge not to compel her to convert.

On February 6, 1494, with all the preliminary pledges in place, Elena Ivanovna was betrothed to Alexander of Lithuania. The betrothal service (*obruchenie*) was performed by an Orthodox priest fully to Orthodox rubrics.[54] Alexander was not, of course, present, so the betrothal had to be performed with the Lithuanian nobleman Stanislav Ianovich standing in proxy for the groom. Orthodox priests offered the prayers joining the couple together, and rings were blessed and exchanged, as were gold crosses on chains. For Ivan III, the betrothal was a good start to his long-range plans for this wedding. Elena Ivanovna was to remain Orthodox, and as John Fennell suggested, become a potential "rallying point" for Alexander's Orthodox Ruthenian subjects to "desert to Moscow."[55] For Alexander, the betrothal and marriage was to be the guarantee of at least a temporary peace with Muscovy—a needed breather in an interminable war.

The betrothal was followed in March with an embassy from Ivan III to Vilnius (it arrived in April) to formalize the treaty and discuss the details of the marriage between Alexander and Elena Ivanovna. On both occasions—in February in Moscow, and in April in Vilnius—Ivan III's negotiators requested written assurance of Alexander's pledge not to compel Elena to convert to Catholicism. It came along with the Lithuanian embassy that arrived in Moscow in November 1494: a charter (*gramota*) "from Grand Duke Alexander, given under seal, to his father-in-law Grand Prince Ivan [III] concerning his daughter Princess Elena, that he will not compel her to convert to the Roman faith, but would allow her to retain her faith according to the Greek law."[56] With this firm assurance in hand, the last hurdle to the wedding was cleared.

Elena departed for her new life as Alexander's bride on January 15, 1495. She set off from Dorogomilovo, a small border town, and made her way west via Smolensk, Vitebsk, Polotsk, and half a dozen other towns in between, arriving in Vilnius on February 15.[57] She traveled with a large entourage, including boyar Prince Semen Ivanovich Riapolovskii, boyar Mikhail Iakovlevich Rusalka, the scribe (*d'iak*) Vasilii Kushenin, and "and many other princes and *deti boiarskie* of the court," plus many of their wives.[58] As she traveled westward through the towns of Muscovy and Lithuania, she was greeted by civil and religious leaders, attended church services, and accepted gifts (*pominki*) offered to her, which were added to the already bulging wagons carrying her father's gifts for Alexander and her own dowry.[59]

The contents of the wagons in Elena's caravan are known from unpublished manuscript inventories compiled at the time of her journey west.[60] They contained Elena's dowry, personal belongings, and other items needed for her new household. These included a large number of traditional Muscovite costumes: five fur coats (*shuba*), seven formal women's outer garments (*torlop*), decorative collars (*ozherel'e*), six summer garments (*letnik*), Muscovite-style sandals and shoes, as well as a large number of broaches, rings, earrings, a mirror, and numerous bolts of fabric and loose gems, presumably so that seamstresses could make her new clothes with familiar materials and ornaments. Also among the personal items in Elena's wagons were numerous religious objects, including six crosses and six icons. The icons are worth noting: one of St. George the Victory-Bearer, one of the Savior, one of the Mother of God, another of the archangels Michael and Gabriel, another of St. Fotina the Samaritan, and a triptych icon depicting the Savior, the Mother of God, and St. Menas. Among the articles given to Elena for her wedding bed was a large, gem-encrusted icon of the Mother of God with Child, plus three icons taken "from Prince Andrei's belongings" (presumably Prince Andrei Vasil'evich *Molodoi*, Ivan III's younger brother): a triptych depicting the Savior, the Holy Archangels Michael and Gabriel, and Ss. Nicholas, Peter, and Sergei; an icon of Psalm 148, "Praise the Lord from the Heavens" (*Khvalite Gospoda s nebes*);[61] and another of the Annunciation.[62] Expectations ran high that Elena would be able to carry on as an Orthodox Christian and that her surroundings would be adorned with familiar Orthodox religious objects. Still, one cannot help but see a measure of anxiety in the selection of icons sent with Elena to Vilnius: the symbol of Muscovite sovereignty and of Orthodoxy's victory over the Heterodox (St. George), the third-century Egyptian Christian in the Roman army who refused to renounce Christ and died a martyr's death (St. Menas), and the woman at the well of John 4:1–30, who stands as a model of (in her case, newfound) sexual virtue and who, being a Samaritan, also represents the fidelity of a believer in a foreign land (St. Fotina the Samaritan). Fertility is another theme represented in the icons (the Annunciation, the Mother and Child, the Nativity). The icons sent with Elena therefore served not only as an aid for Elena's prayers but also as poignant reminders of her father's determination to see her remain Orthodox.

Many of the objects Elena brought with her were specifically meant for use at the wedding. For example, Elena brought with her traditional headpieces (*kika*) that were worn by married women, and items specific to the wedding bed: pillows and pillow cases, comforters, bed curtains (presumably for use with a canopy), and three rugs, as was traditional in Muscovy for under the nuptial bed. Elena also brought gifts for her new husband, Alexander, many of which also seem earmarked for use at the wedding: a gold cross with inscriptions of saints, a gold chain (*chep zolota*), and traditional Muscovite costumes—a fur coat (*shuba*), an ornamental belt (*poias'*), and a sheepskin coat (*kozhukh*). Other gifts seem earmarked for the groom's ritual bath on the morning of the second day of the wedding: another fur coat (*shuba*), a kaftan (*terlik*), a light outer garment (*opashen*), a decorative collar (*ozherel'e*), and a drinking goblet (*chashnik*).[63] Ivan III also sent Alexander a stallion, full tack, and saddle blankets, probably for Alexander to ride during the many processions that the bride's father assumed would be part of the wedding celebration. Clearly, Ivan

III expected Alexander to wear traditional Muscovite costume, at least during some points of the wedding celebrations. He expected him to take the ritual bath and dress in the usual garments grooms wore afterward. He expected him to ride in procession, on a stallion, just as was done at royal weddings in Muscovy.[64] These gifts were evidently given to Alexander so that he could play the role that Ivan III expected him to play—the role of a royal groom at a Muscovite, Orthodox wedding.

At the Lithuanian border town of Nemezhy, a delegation from Alexander met Elena and her caravan, and it was there that the first signs of trouble surfaced. Alexander's envoy, Ian Berezenskii, informed the boyars accompanying Elena that the wedding would take place not in the Orthodox church in Vilnius but in the Roman Catholic Cathedral of St. Stanislaw. The boyars accompanying Elena protested, pointing to Alexander's agreements to honor Elena's religion, including the Orthodox rites of marriage, but the Lithuanians would not budge. With emotions likely running high, the procession continued on its way to Vilnius.[65]

The tensions only grew worse when Elena arrived in Vilnius on February 15. Elena proceeded directly to the Russian Orthodox Church of the Nativity of the Mother of God for an intercessory prayer service (*moleben*). Alexander, who had escorted Elena into Vilnius during the last leg of the journey, went directly and separately to the Cathedral of St. Stanislaw. In the Orthodox church, Archimandrite Makarii of the Trinity Monastery in Vilnius (and metropolitan-designate of Kiev) served the liturgy, and afterward Elena performed many of the rituals that were deemed indispensable by the Muscovites. Elena's hair was combed and rewound from the single braid of an unmarried girl to the two braids of a married woman, her head was veiled, a *kika* was placed on her head, she was sprinkled with hops (*osypali khmelem*), and the Orthodox priest, Fr. Foma (Ivan III's own father-confessor), recited nuptial prayers and blessed her with a cross.[66] Next, the bride, dressed in her finest garments brought with her from Moscow, joined a procession led by Fr. Foma from the Orthodox Church to the church of St. Stanislaw, where Alexander waited.

The marriage ceremony in St. Stanislaw Church followed traditional Catholic rubrics, though elements of the Orthodox wedding service were included for Elena's benefit. Since the bride and groom had already been betrothed by proxy in January, that part of wedding ritual was omitted; but the crowning ritual (*venchanie*)—which, to the Orthodox, joined the couple in the sacrament of matrimony—was included.[67] The bride (but not the groom) stood on a blanket of velvet adorned with forty sables (brought with her from Moscow for the wedding); the Priest Foma recited nuptial prayers only for Elena, while the Catholic bishop said the prayers for Alexander; and a crown was held over Elena (but not over Alexander).[68]

Then there was an incident. While the nuptial crown was still being held over her head, Elena was offered a cup of wine to drink, a customary part of Orthodox weddings.[69] Consistent with the rest of the service, the cup seems only to have been offered to Elena. After she had drunk from the cup, the Priest Foma took it and smashed it on the floor. Smashing the cup with one's feet was an old nuptial custom, and it is recorded in other Muscovite royal weddings in the sixteenth century.[70] In all those cases, the smashing was performed by the groom, who, again, would normally have also drunk from the cup. In Elena's and Alexander's case, the groom was not Orthodox and so was therefore not offered the wine or the privilege of smashing the cup afterward. The groom and the Catholic bishop were so astonished by this display that they immediately stopped the wedding. (They were evidently not told in advance about this custom.) The crown was pulled down from over Elena's head and the Priest Foma was not permitted to continue reciting the nuptial prayers that came next in the ritual. At length, Prince Semen Riapolovskii prevailed upon the groom to let the service continue; and though we do not know what he said to persuade Alexander, the crown was restored over Elena's head and the Priest Foma was permitted to resume the sequence of prescribed prayers.[71]

Frustrations mounted after the wedding. Later in the day there was a banquet where gifts were exchanged, but some on the Lithuanian side complained that Elena was still wearing traditional Muscovite costumes even after the wedding ceremony. The complaints persisted for the next several days as Elena continued to wear the garments of a Muscovite princess. Given all the clothing she had brought with her, it appears she (or her father) intended all along that she would dress in Muscovite garb rather than adopt the fashions of her new homeland. Alexander, for his part, had no intention of adopting Muscovite ways. He may have never worn any of the sumptuous costumes brought by Elena for him, or ridden the stallion, or taken his ritual bath on the morning of the second day of the wedding.[72] Grand Duke Alexander seems to have been entirely unwilling to play the role of a Muscovite groom, even for a few days.

Not only was the wedding ceremony a source of frustration (for both sides), the marriage failed in every aspect of its diplomatic purpose. First, the union was relatively short-lived. Alexander died prematurely in August 1506, and Elena followed him to the grave in January 1513. Although the couple was married for nearly eleven years, they left no heir to the thrones of Lithuania and Poland (which Alexander had inherited in 1501 on the death of his brother King Jan I Albrecht). Second, the marriage failed to bring peace. War between Muscovy and Lithuania had resumed by 1500, lasted until 1503, ignited again for a year in 1507, and thereafter continued off and on until 1537. Third, although Ivan III's desire for his daughter to remain Orthodox was evidently born of a sincere concern for her soul, he seems also to have wanted her to flaunt her Muscovite origins and Orthodox faith so that she might serve as a beacon of Muscovite influence in the religiously split (Catholic and Orthodox) grand duchy. But Elena proved unwilling to be her father's missionary, and she never became any kind of "rallying point" for the revolt of Orthodox Ruthenians against Catholic rule. Finally, Alexander reneged on his pledge not to attempt to convert Elena to Roman Catholicism, forcing Ivan III to remind his son-in-law again and again to respect her religion.[73]

The memory of this failed alliance lingered long. The diplomatic correspondence between Vilnius and Moscow and other marriage-related chancellery documents reveal an increasingly contentious relationship between the two dynasties.[74] The wedding may also have left its mark on the treasury. Weddings were expensive affairs anyway, but this one in particular was exorbitant. According to one of the two surviving copies of Elena's dowry inventory, the value of the objects dispatched with her to Vilnius was 61,898 rubles—a simply astronomical sum.[75] By way of comparison, the value of the dowry for Evdokiia Ivanovna, Ivan III's other daughter who married the converted Tatar Tsarevich Peter (Kudai Kul) in 1506, was calculated to be 2,580 rubles, and the value of the dowry of Mariia Saburova, Vasilii III's sister-in-law, who married Prince Vasilii Semenovich Starodubskii, Vasilii III's agnatic kinsman, was 2,063 rubles, 20 altyn.[76] If these sums are accurate, the wedding of Elena and Alexander must have put a pinch on finances for quite some time. It is hard not to imagine that Ivan III thought he had thrown away his money and his daughter in a wedding that yielded him nothing but headaches over religion and empty coffers.

The Succession Crisis of 1497–1502

If the 1495 wedding of Elena Ivanovna and Grand Duke Alexander soured the Muscovites on marriages to foreigners, the struggle over succession in the last years of Ivan III's reign likewise underscored the high risks of picking a domestic bride. The succession crisis of 1497–1502 was rooted in the two marriages of Ivan III. By his first wife, Mariia Borisovna of Tver', Ivan III had one son, Ivan Ivanovich, called *Molodoi* (the Younger), who in 1482 married Elena Stepanovna, the daughter of the Moldavian despot Stephan III the Great (r. 1457–1504).[77] They had one son, Dmitrii, called *Vnuk* (the Grandson).[78] Ivan III's second marriage was to the Byzantine princess Sofiia Paleologa, the niece of the last Byzantine emperor, Constantine XI (r. 1449–1453). Sofiia bore Ivan III at least twelve children, eight of whom survived to adulthood. Among these children was a son, Vasilii Ivanovich, the future Vasilii III, for whom the first bride-show was arranged in 1505; and a daughter, Elena, who married Grand Duke Alexander in 1495.[79]

The death of Ivan Molodoi in 1490 set the stage for the crisis.[80] As the eldest son, Ivan Molodoi was the designated heir. He had been given the title of grand prince and, after its absorption into Muscovy in 1485, the principality of Tver' as his appanage. His untimely death left Ivan III with two choices for his successor—Dmitrii Vnuk, the son of Ivan Molodoi, or Vasilii, Ivan III's eldest son by his second wife. Both were still children: Dmitrii was six-and-a-half years old, and Vasilii was just a few weeks short of his eleventh birthday. Each was supported by a different boyar faction at Ivan III's court. Dmitrii Vnuk had the support of the leading boyar clan of the age—the Patrikeevs. Patrikei Narimuntovich and his son Iurii Patrikeevich, the founders of the clan, had immigrated to Muscovy in 1408 and enjoyed immediate clout at the Muscovite court. Patrikei was a scion of the Lithuanian ruling dynasty and the first cousin once removed of Vasilii I's wife. Iurii Patrikeevich was made a boyar by 1417, and in 1418 he married the daughter of Vasilii I (r. 1389–1425).[81] From then on, the Patrikeevs masterfully built a leading coalition within the ranks of the boyars, using marriage to solidify their first position at the courts of Vasilii I, Vasilii II, and Ivan III. Iurii Patrikeev's son, Ivan Iur'evich, Ivan III, and Elena Stepanovna of Moldova (Ivan Molodoi's widow) were all first cousins to each other, and it is probably this close bond that made the Patrikeev clan the chief advocates of Dmitrii Vnuk's claims to the throne when Ivan Molodoi died in 1490.[82] The other possible heir, Vasilii, also had supporters, including his mother and many of the boyars outside the Patrikeev faction. Ivan Molodoi's death, then, came at a moment when the court was already divided into at least two camps formed around the grand prince's two potential heirs.

Ivan III did not immediately designate his grandson his heir on the death of Ivan Molodoi. Why he did not do so is not clear; but an early indication that Ivan III was favoring Dmitrii—and his Patrikeev kin—was the marriage he permitted in 1497 between Prince Fedor Ivanovich Bel'skii and Anna Vasil'evna, the daughter of Prince Vasilii Ivanovich of Riazan' and the granddaughter of Vasilii II. Bel'skii was, like the Patrikeevs, a scion of the Lithuanian ruling house and a relative of Elena Stepanovna of Moldavia, Dmitrii Vnuk's mother. Bel'skii had come to Muscovy in 1481/82. He had left behind a wife who never joined him in Moscow, despite numerous attempts to lure her to come; and so in 1497 when he sought to remarry, he had to obtain, as Herberstein reports, a blessing from the metropolitan to do so. As Kollmann put it, Bel'skii's marriage "bolstered the side of the succession struggle that supported Prince Dmitrii and the Patrikeevy."[83]

By late 1497 Ivan III had come to the decision to choose Dmitrii over Vasilii, whose supporters learned of Ivan III's decision and decided to strike against Dmitrii and his camp. In December 1497, a brief and unsuccessful rebellion against Dmitrii erupted, and Vasilii and his mother, Sofiia Paleologa, who supported the uprising and the planned assassination of Dmitrii found themselves in disgrace. Things were much worse for Vasilii's supporters, many of whom were executed, including Vladimir Gusev Dubrynskii, Prince Ivan Khrul' Ivanovich Paletskii, Shchevel' Timofeevich Travin, Poiarok Runov, the scribe Fedor Stromilov, and Afanasii Eropkin.[84] In February 1498, Dmitrii, aged fourteen years, was crowned grand prince in a coronation ceremony borrowed from Byzantine antecedents, nominally becoming co-ruler with his father.[85]

The victory was total—but short-lived. In January 1499, the Patrikeevs and their kinsmen were suddenly and ruthlessly deposed. Prince Ivan Iur'evich Patrikeev and his two unmarried sons, Vasilii and Ivan, were initially sentenced to death, but their sentences were later reduced to forced monastic tonsure, the political equivalent of death. Prince Ivan Iur'evich's son-in-law, Prince Semen Ivanovich Riapolovskii the Younger (Molodoi)—the same Riapolovskii who had accompanied Elena Ivanovna to Vilnius back in 1495 and defused the crisis during her wedding caused by the ceremonial smashing of the common cup—was executed.[86] The final shift in favor from Dmitrii Vnuk to Vasilii occurred in late winter or spring 1499 when Vasilii received the title of grand prince of Novgorod and Pskov.[87]

Why the Patrikeevs were deposed has for decades been debated by historians. Several scholars have argued that the downfall of the Patrikeevs was entirely unrelated to the dynastic crisis of 1497–1502, though the alternate explanations for it run a wide range. Some explain the crisis as an episode in the struggle of the centralizing state against boyars defending feudal fragmentation; others as a foreign-policy move, clearing the Muscovite leadership of elements that were not fully behind Ivan III's war plans against Lithuania; and still others as a chapter in the so-called Judaizer heresy.[88] Kollmann, however, argued that the crisis was very directly related to the succession crisis, which played out against an underlying contest between boyar factions at court. "The fatal error of the Patrikeevy," she suggests, "was that they had monopolized too much power at the expense of other families in the political elite. They had made numerous of their kinsmen boyars, they had seized significant economic resources, they had supported a man for the grand-princely throne [Dmitrii] who had no kin to marry to other boyar families."[89] To this can be added the affront of the 1497 marriage between Bel'skii and Ivan III's niece, which, however much it looked like a good idea beforehand, only strengthened Patrikeev interests in the court and further antagonized their boyar rivals. It may well be that the Bel'skii marriage of 1497 tipped the balance so much in favor of the Patrikeevs that it prompted the failed uprising in favor of Vasilii later that year, precipitating the succession crisis.

That these events pertain to dynastic marriage politics and bride-shows is demonstrated by a close examination of the muster for the marriage of Feodosiia Ivanovna, another daughter of Ivan III, and Prince Vasilii Daniilovich Kholmskii on February 13, 1500. The wedding muster (*svadebnyi razriad*)—the earliest extant wedding muster—survives only in later copies and in two redactions, short and long. The long redaction includes far more names for many more and different duties at the wedding than the short redaction, as well as several references to the wedding's choreography that are important for this study.[90] Coming in the very midst of the succession crisis (though, of course, no one at the time could possibly have known this), the composition of the wedding roster and the choreography of rituals reflect a very conscious effort to make peace between the two warring factions. What is more, the thoughtful selection of Kholmskii, and not a foreigner, shows that the Muscovite court was grappling with the challenges and opportunities presented by the right choice of a domestic spouse for maintaining stability at court.

The wedding muster (in either redaction) focuses almost exclusively on the composition of the wedding cortège (*poezd*) and provides only a partial listing of the other important duties at the wedding. Indeed, Ivan III himself is mentioned only in the opening lines, and even then only as the father of the bride, not as performing any role or appearing in any venue, though he must have done so. The wedding cortège comprised two sections, one centered around the sled carrying the mother of the bride, Sofiia Paleologa, and the other around the groom, Prince Vasilii Daniilovich Kholmskii. The composition of the cortège seems deliberately designed to place together in a very public way the kin of the victims of the 1497 pro-Vasilii uprising and the kin of the Patrikeevs, who had just been deposed the previous year. Thus, in the groom's cortège we find the brothers Prince Fedor "Striga" and Prince Petr "Loban" (of the Obolenskii clan), the first cousins of Prince Semen Ivanovich Riapolovskii—the sole member of the Patrikeev faction to lose his life when the Patrikeevs fell.[91] Also listed were the brothers Princes Mikhail "Golitsa," Andrei "Kuraka," and Dmitrii Ivanovich Bulgak Patrikeev, the grandnephews of Prince Ivan Iur'evich Patrikeev, the leader of the Patrikeev faction;[92] and Princes Iurii, Mikhail, and Boris Vasil'evich Romodanovskii, who were related to the Riapolovskii and Paletskii princes and were the brothers of Prince Vasilii Romodanovskii, who had been arrested in 1499, probably in connection with the fall of the Patrikeevs.[93] In the cortège right next to these partisans of the Patrikeevs was Ivan "Gundor" Fedorovich Pestryi Paletskii, whose first cousin once removed, Ivan "Khrul'" Ivanovich Paletskii, had been executed in 1497.[94] Grand Princess Sofiia's cortège also included the kin of those who had seen the executioner's block. Timofei Grigor'evich "Skriaba" Travin is listed, whose son Shchavel' had been executed in the 1497 conspiracy,[95] as is Ivan Mikhailovich "Kliapik" Eropkin (a Travin kinsman), whose first cousin Afanasii had been executed in 1497.[96]

Perhaps the most significant and telling evidence of the peacemaking role of this wedding is the placement of the mothers of the two rival candidates: Elena Stepanovna, Dmitrii Vnuk's mother, and Sofiia Paleologa, Vasilii's mother. According to the last line of the muster (long redaction), "The Grand Princess Elena is to be with the Grand Princess Sofiia in the same sled [*A velikoi kniagine Elene byti s velikoiu kniagineiu Sof'eiu v odnekh sanekh*]."[97] Descriptions of subsequent royal weddings focus, naturally enough, on the bride and the groom, not the mother of bride or groom, nor even on other members of the dynasty. The choreography of this wedding, however, broadcast a clear message: it signaled a new equilibrium among and between the boyar factions at court that resulted from, and was the very purpose of, the disgrace of the Patrikeevs the year before. Having the mothers of Ivan III's potential heirs riding in the same sled was clearly meant as a public, if surely fictive, demonstration of harmony and peace between them and their rival camps. All vendettas, grudges, and offenses were reconciled in one ritual moment.

If the choreography of reconciliation so evident in this wedding was meant to symbolize and help bring about internal peace at court, the selection of the groom even more reveals how fully marriage within the dynasty had become a matter of court politics. It is never, one supposes, a small matter when the daughter of the ruler, or any member of the dynasty, marries. Feodosiia Ivanovna's marriage to Kholmskii, however, so perfectly reflects the changing composition of the court resulting from the new concerns about dynastic marriage, following the 1495 marriage of Elena Ivanovna and the Patrikeev disgrace in 1499, that it was neither a random pick nor a love match. The Kholmskii match was a deliberate use of marriage by Ivan III and his advisors to establish a "broad distribution of power" at the court in the vacuum left behind by the fall of the Patrikeevs. Kollmann has indentified three factions that shared power and position at Ivan III's and Vasilii III's court: the "Kholmskii-Cheliadnin-Obolenskii faction, the Zakhar'in faction, and the Bulgakov-Shcheniatev faction."[98] The Kholmskii wedding, then, did not create a new dominant faction around Vasilii Daniilovich Kholmskii, the groom in 1500 (merely exchanging the Kholmskii-Cheliadnin-Obolenskii for the ousted Patrikeevs). Rather, the wedding created balance in the inner circle at court by elevating to the status of royal in-laws a clan whose own prominence was inextricably linked to other clans (the Cheliadnins and Obolenskiis)—in effect, diffusing the royal favor over several boyar clans, which might, in other circumstances, have vaulted the groom's kin to the first position in court, as the Patrikeev wedding in 1418 had done. Nothing proves the imperative to create balance at court better than the fact that two months after the Kholmskii wedding, in April 1500, the inner circle welcomed into its fold old enemies: Prince Ivan Andreevich of Mozhaisk and Vasilii

Ivanovich Shemiachich (old opponents of the Muscovite house from the days of the dynastic wars of the 1420s, 1430s, and 1440s); and Prince Semen Ivanovich Bel'skii (Fedor's brother and the kinsman of Elena Stepanovna and the Patrikeevs).[99]

The Kholmskii wedding did not, it turned out, resolve the succession crisis. By the end of 1500, unknown motivations compelled or enticed Vasilii to threaten to withdraw his own forces from the Lithuanian war that had just reignited (perhaps even threatening to join his father's Lithuanian enemies). Faced with the potential revolt of his son, Ivan III finally and fully acquiesced. In 1502, Dmitrii Vnuk and Elena Stepanovna were imprisoned, Elena dying in 1505 and Dmitrii Vnuk in 1509.[100] As for the newly married Kholmskii couple, despite the high hopes for this union, the outcome could not have been more disappointing. The bride promptly died in 1501;[101] and Prince Vasilii Daniilovich, though made a boyar in 1502, was disgraced in 1508 and died in prison.[102] The lessons of the succession crisis can only have reinforced the lessons learned from Elena and Alexander's marriage a few years earlier—if there were going to be domestic matches, then some procedure needed to be devised to make sure the choice of spouse did not create a disequilibrium at court. Picking a bride for the ruler quickly became the goal of Muscovite high politics.

The First Bride-Show—Vasilii III and Solomoniia Saburova

In 1503, before he was persuaded by Trakhaniotov to organize the first bride-show, Vasilii Ivanovich was actively engaged in the search for a bride abroad. It was about time. At twenty-four, he was well past the age rulers and heirs married—a delay very likely linked to the uncertainties in the succession of the previous six or seven years.[103] Perhaps out of habit, the first thought of his father and advisors was to look for a bride abroad. The advantages of a foreign-born bride were obvious, especially in the wake of the upheavals that the court had just experienced. Foreign-born princesses in the Terem preserved the status quo: they introduced no new royal in-laws, or in-laws of in-laws, into the court. The foreign-born queen would come alone, or nearly alone, to her new realm, and so the court was not exposed to the destabilization that a marriage to one of the great boyar clans would risk. On the other hand, the obstacles to foreign matches that manifested themselves in the experience of the marriage of

Elena Ivanovna and Alexander of Lithuania in 1495 were likely still in the minds of the advisors to Ivan III and Vasilii. The definitive turn in marriage patterns in the Muscovite dynasty—away from both foreigners and prominent domestic brides—came together in the failure to find for Vasilii an appropriate bride abroad, where religion and cultural difference again appeared as insurmountable hurdles to forming an inter-dynastic alliance.

The first attempt to find Vasilii a foreign bride focused on Elisabeth (1485–1555), daughter of King Hans of Denmark (r. 1481–1513), who also ruled Norway (1483–1513) and Sweden (1497–1513) in the on-again-off-again Kalmar Union between the three Scandinavian kingdoms. Between 1499 and 1503, the Muscovites made earnest and repeated overtures to the Danes, which were roundly snubbed, evidently because they viewed the requirement for the bride to convert to Orthodoxy as an intolerable imposition. In fact, so dismissive of the Muscovite proposal were the Danes that the Muscovites were still actively seeking Elisabeth's hand when, unbeknownst to them, she married Joachim I Nestor, the Hohenzollern Elector of Brandenburg, in 1502.[104]

Ivan III and Vasilii next turned for help to Elena Ivanovna, whose position as grand duchess of Lithuania and (since 1501) queen of Poland might, they reasonably believed, allow her more easily and less conspicuously to survey the field of suitable candidates than they could in distant Moscow. In May 1503, the Muscovite delegation sent by Ivan III to Grand Duke Alexander of Lithuania to sign the treaty of peace between Moscow and Vilnius was also charged with discreetly discussing with Elena possible marriage candidates for her brother Vasilii. This first inquiry was general and unfocused: "What Orthodox rulers, or Catholic rulers, even of small principalities, have daughters that are suitable for my son, Vasilii, to marry?"[105] The only specific inquiry centered on the daughters of Đurađ Branković, the son of the Orthodox Serbian despot Stefan Branković (ca. 1417–1476). But Ivan III was not even sure that Đurađ was still alive, or if he had any daughters who were available for marriage: "Is Iurii [i.e., Đurađ Branković] in Hungary still alive? Does he have children, sons or daughters? Are they married and have the daughters been married off, or are they still unmarried?"[106]

Elena did not respond to this first inquiry, so far as we know, but a second embassy departed from Moscow for Vilnius in November 1503, and this time Elena was pressed more firmly for information. In the memorandum (*pamiat'*) given to the scribe Nikita Guba Moklokov (who had been a member of the embassy in May), he is instructed "to ask the grand duchess [Elena]: Which rulers have daughters and how old are they? Ask also about their mothers, if there is any information about them." The instructions to Moklokov reveal particular interest in the daughters of the despots of Serbia, probably because, being Orthodox, they presented no confessional obstacles to any proposed match: "They say that in Hungary [*Ugorskaia zemlia*] the Serbian despots have daughters; and have you [Elena] inquired [*posylyvala*] in Hungary about the daughters of the Serbian despots, or not? And if you have not, what have you heard, O queen [*gospozhe*]—which despot has daughters, and what are they like, and how old are they?"[107]

Elena did not, in fact, conduct an extensive investigation of European royal houses prior to Moklokov's arrival, as she had been asked to do by her father. Except for one line on the Serbian despots, she confines her comments to royal families related to her husband, Alexander—information that must have been fairly easy for her to obtain:

> I inquired about the daughters of Stefan, the Serbian despot, but I could not get any information. They say that the margrave has five daughters: the eldest is 18 years old, lame and ugly [*khroma i nekhorosha*]; the next oldest is 14 years old and has, they say, an attractive appearance.[108] The Bavarian prince, the brother-in-law [*ziat'*] of the king [i.e., King Alexander, Elena's husband], has daughters, but they would not say how old they are, and their mother is deceased.[109] They say that the Stettin prince, the king's brother-in-law, has daughters, but they again would not say how old they are; and their mother is deceased, but they say positive things about her.[110] The French king's sister, the kinswoman [*svoiakina*] of the Hungarian king, was promised to [Jan] Albrecht the king. They say she is attractive in appearance but lame, and now she has taken the veil and joined a cloister.[111] The Danish king will himself tell you better than I can that he has a daughter.[112]

Moklokov requested Elena to inquire further, but she demurred, responding that her father and brother could inquire better themselves through emissaries. She warned them, however, that western European kingdoms were "so staunchly Catholic that none of these rulers would give their daughters in marriage and convert to the Greek faith without the blessing of the pope [*bez papina vedoma*]."[113] Her message could not have been clearer. If Ivan III or Vasilii Ivanovich thought these rulers would permit their daughters to convert to Orthodoxy for the purposes of a dynastic marriage, they had another think coming. It was one thing for Elena (and other Muscovite royal women in the fifteenth century) to marry non-Orthodox foreigners, themselves remaining Orthodox. It was another thing altogether to expect non-Orthodox foreign royal women to convert "to the Greek faith," even for the sake of an advantageous diplomatic match with the heir to the Muscovite throne.

Although Elena's report was limited and perhaps perfunctory, it touched on the issues that mattered most to Ivan III, Vasilii, and their advisors. Her report suggests that the first objective was to find a healthy pool of candidates. This explains the references in the memorandum to Moklokov to the health of both the young girl and, if obtainable, her mother. These inquiries were necessary because any royal bride in that time of high infant mortality would be expected to be pregnant continuously, to assure as many live and healthy births as possible. Appearance also figures in her report, as does the age of the candidates—probably to ascertain their reproductive readiness. Last, Elena's report suggests that the Muscovites expected their ruler's consort to be Orthodox. When Elena Ivanovna married Alexander in 1495, a sticking point had been, as we have seen, the staunch insistence of Ivan III that his daughter Elena remain Orthodox, but there was no evidence of concern for the fact that she was entering into a mixed marriage with a Catholic.[114] But here, the search was for a foreign bride, not a groom. The bride would come to Muscovy and become, as Isolde Thyrêt has put it, the "blessed womb" of the dynasty.[115] A Heterodox tsaritsa was likely as inconceivable as it was inconsistent with the intercessory function the bride fulfilled in Muscovite political culture.

What is absent from Elena's report is any serious concern for the noble ancestry of the potential bridal candidates. The genealogical notations in Elena's report serve only to help identify the relationship of the potential bridal candidates to Elena's husband, Alexander. There is no mention or suggestion that an illustrious parentage was in any way sought or deemed advantageous. In fact, religion seems to have trumped genealogy even to the extent that the daughters of the Serbian despots were considered seriously—not because of their ancestry, which, in European terms, was far from illustrious but because of their Orthodoxy. The Muscovites had been very pleased in 1472 to welcome Sofiia Paleologa, a Byzantine princess, into the royal family as the wife of Ivan III—a union that accounted for the importation of much of the imperial style adopted or improvised by the Muscovite court in the last quarter of the fifteenth century. But even in this case, there was no effort to trace Sofiia's genealogy or to add her ancestors to those of the Daniilovichi. Muscovite genealogical consciousness remained fundamentally agnatic. Similarly, when Ivan IV married a second time in 1561, the relative obscurity of Mariia Temriukovna Cherkasskaia's background was in no way an impediment to her selection. And when in 1643–1645 Mikhail Romanov sought to marry his daughter Irina to Valdemar of Denmark-Norway, it did not in the slightest trouble the tsar and his advisors that Valdemar was the son of a morganatic second marriage between King Christian IV and Kristen Munk. This practical attitude toward ancestry contrasts dramatically with the heightened genealogical consciousness of early modern European dynasties in these centuries, which were obsessed with demonstrating, or fabricating, their descent from august historical personages—from Charlemagne to, in the most fanciful cases, Homer's and Virgil's King Priam of Troy, the biblical King David, or Alexander the Great.[116]

This lack of concern for ancestry also contrasts with the heightened focus on genealogy that runs through domestic bride searches. Bride-shows included investigations that ascertained medical histories (the prospective bride's and her parents'), verified the age and virtue of candidates, appraised the physical beauty of each candidate, and attempted to predict, using the folksy means available then for assessing it, the candidates' prospects for bearing healthy and numerous children. But the investigations of prospective brides also involved an extensive investigation into the candidate's genealogy: not to find the candidate with the most illustrious family tree (since all the candidates were domestic, no one's family tree could compare with the tsar's), but for the purpose of compiling a list of relatives. Genealogy became a fundamental concern in domestic bride searches in order to find a bride who would not disrupt the delicate balance of factions at court—a lesson that could not have been missed from the dynastic crisis of 1497–1502.

When Iurii Trakhaniotov and the other advisors suggested that the future Vasilii III choose his wife from a bride-show, they cannot have been unaware of the pitfalls incumbent on foreign and domestic searches. Foreigners were, as Herberstein notes, eliminated as an option because of the cost and because of religious and other cultural differences. But domestic brides offered risks, too. As a result, restrictions had to be placed on the domestic pool of bridal candidates, as well.

These restrictions are directly mentioned in several accounts of foreigners who described Muscovite bride-shows. The papal official Paolo Giovio provides a rich description of the Muscovite bride-show in his *Pauli Iovii Novocomensis libellus de legatione Basilij magni prinicipis Moscoviae ad Clementem VII* of 1525. While Giovio never traveled to Muscovy himself, his account is worth considering seriously because he was a noted Renaissance-era historian whose works (largely on Italian history and historical biographies) are still regarded today as significant early examples of scholarly humanistic historical writing. Giovio's work is important also because he based his research on Muscovy in large part on a solid primary source: an interview with Dmitrii Gerasimov, the Muscovite diplomat and translator who was in Rome in 1525 on a mission to Pope Clement VII.[117] Gerasimov was a good choice for interviewee since his involvement in diplomacy brought him close to all manner of dynastic matters, including royal weddings.[118] Both diplomacy and weddings were managed by a small group of scribes with increasingly specialized knowledge inside the royal scriptorium. It would be out of this royal scriptorium that the Foreign Office and its archive would emerge in the first half of the sixteenth century. This archive and its staff of scribes would be responsible for composing, editing, and preserving wedding documents throughout the sixteenth and seventeenth centuries.[119] That Gerasimov was a highly placed diplomat therefore means he knew well and worked with the scribes and other courtiers who arranged Vasilii III's bride-show and wedding.

Ever the historian, Giovio takes Gerasimov's information and repackages it in a general descriptive tone, never actually referring to Vasilii III by name, but describing how bride-shows worked generally.[120] "Having decided to marry," Giovio begins,

> Muscovite sovereigns, as usual, select from among all young virgins of the entire realm; they order that all [maidens], especially those with distinguishing physical and spiritual qualities, be summoned before them. Then they order knowledgeable persons and trusted women-folk to examine them with great care, even such that they are permitted to perform physical examinations of the most private parts. And then only after a long and agonizing wait for the parents [of the candidates], one from their number is chosen as worthy to wed the king, one who is to the liking of the sovereign. The remaining maidens who have competed in this contest of beauty, wisdom, and morality are married, often on this same day, to prominent men and military leaders,

> as the sovereigns see fit. In this way, the sovereigns avoid the great scions of the royal house, and marry for no other reason than beauty, elevating to the heights of the royal bed only maidens from undistinguished families, as is also the custom among the Turkish Ottomans.[121]

This extraordinary account points out plainly that the Muscovites devised and used the bride-show as a means to avoid bridal candidates from the great clans at court. Giovio tells us that the bride-show was created precisely as a means to "avoid the great scions of the royal house"—which surely means the great boyar clans that dominated politics and were themselves related to the ruler by marriage and sometimes by blood. In this way, Giovio reinforces Herbertein's account that Ivan III, Vasilii, and their advisors all agreed that "it would be best to marry the daughter of one of his subjects rather than to marry a foreigner."

The Swedish diplomat Peter Petreius's (1570–1622) important description of Vasilii III's 1505 bride-show (published in 1615) mirrors much of what Herberstein reported, especially the concerns for cost and culture:

> Having lived for quite some time in great profligacy and weakness of the flesh with depraved women and trollops, and not wanting that the grand princely power should pass to his brother and his children, [Vasilii III] decided to take a wife. And he assembled the entire boyar duma, so that the boyars could discuss the matter thoroughly and so that they could decide if it would be better for him to marry a domestic or a foreign princess.
>
> They advised him at length, and it was finally decided in the duma that he should marry a domestic girl and abandon the idea of marrying foreigners, and they did not long worry about the loss of kinship ties with foreign rulers, because they are perfidious, prideful, and arrogant, and because they do not give away in marriage nor send their daughters to any barbarian land, much less to the Muscovite ruler. In addition, a foreign bride and a new princess would usually bring with her new and strange customs, many foreign attendants, and foreign dress; and a foreign marriage would entail extraordinary expense. And they have a different faith, which Russians cannot abide, even to hear of it, and this would lead to extraordinary changes and discord in the government.
>
> This view and suggestion was introduced by another duma boyar and courtier, the well-known Greek-born Georgii Mikrus, who was in favor and respected by the grand prince. To him everyone was well disposed, all

> the nobles and non-nobles, on account of his honor and humility. He said that in Moscow one could find maidens who were equal in their beauty, goodness, and nobility to European women; that the grand prince could pick the one who seemed to him to be the best; and that the country could benefit more from such a marriage than from a marriage to a foreigner. In point of fact, [Georgii Mikrus] thought that he was so much honored by the grand prince that he would pick his daughter, who exceeded all others in beauty, figure, virtue, and goodness.[122]

Later accounts repeat this ongoing concern about foreign entanglements. Philip John von Strahlenberg (1676–1747), a Swedish soldier who was captured after the battle of Poltava and lived in Russia for thirteen years, wrote (before 1730):

> It is well-known that the Russian Monarchs seldom marry Foreign Princesses; But, on the contrary, chuse one of their own Subjects; And that the Russian Princesses have been generally married to Russian Knieses; Occasion'd partly on Account of Religion, and partly because they have had no great Correspondence with other Courts. Nay, these mighty Princes have seldom married into a great Family; As well out of Policy, that by such marriages, the Rich might not have an Opportunity to increase their Wealth; As also, because the Czar wants neither Riches nor great Relations, but a beautiful and virtuous Consort only.[123]

Johann Georg Korb (1670–1741), the secretary to the Habsburg envoy to Peter I, similarly wrote (in 1700):

> To seek for a wife among foreign princes has up to this, been a perilous experiment for a Czar, the Boyars and leading people holding out vain apprehensions that by foreign marriages foreign and new-fangled manners would be most perniciously substituted in their country, that ancient usages would be corrupted, the purity of the religion of their fathers be imperiled, and in short, all Muscovy be exposed to the utmost danger.[124]

We encounter perhaps the most direct statement of Muscovite apprehensions about foreign matches in the account by the Polish diplomat Jacob Reutenfels, who wrote in 1671 (at the time of Tsar Aleksei Mikhailovich's second bride-show and marriage):

> Of the various peculiarities that distinguish the Muscovite tsars from other European sovereigns, one must make special mention, certainly, of the fact that they in no way will agree to search for a bride abroad. Since a hindrance or obstacle to this is nothing other than the difference in religion, and so, as a consequence, they do not give away their daughters to marry foreigners abroad....And so, the tsars select their spouses from among their own subjects, just as the eastern Emperor Nicephorus [I] summoned, they say, the most beautiful girls to his palace with the intention of picking a wife for his son, Stauracius. And they presently very strictly follow this ancestral custom, mainly so as not to give rise among their subjects to the desire to intermarry and excessively mix with foreigners, for they have sufficiently learned how badly this can go, when they at one time gave their princesses [*tsarevny*] in marriage to the Poles and other kings, and to the Lithuanian grand dukes, or when they took their wives from Georgia, or some other country.[125]

In this late but extraordinary account, we have many of the themes that have been traced above: the exclusion of foreign candidates because of religion, the bad experiences of foreign marriages in the past (including a likely reference to Elena and Alexander), and the historical precedent set by Byzantine bride-shows (Stauracius and Theophano in 807—the second on Treadgold's list of bride-shows).

Most sources agree that the wedding of Vasilii and Solomoniia Saburova took place on September 4, 1505, probably shortly after Vasilii picked her in the bride-show.[126] According to one chronicle account, "Grand Prince Vasilii Ivanovich decided [*pomysli*] to marry and began to gather the daughters of princes and boyars [*nacha izbirati kniazh'ny i boiarchiny*]."[127] The placement of this reference to this bride-show in the chronicle suggests that the selection was made no later than August 1505. It is easy to imagine, however, that the monumental work of arranging the first ever bride-show may have required some weeks of preparation and so may have begun earlier in the summer.[128]

According to Kollmann, the bride's family, the Saburovs, "were a safe choice for Vasilii III." They were not, Kollmann continues, "sufficiently strong politically to threaten the balance of power among the Kholmskii, Zakhar'in (Koshkin), Bulgakov-Shcheniatev, Obolenskii, and Cheliadnin families." The Saburovs were, to be sure, an old boyar clan, but one that had largely lost its luster in the years since their heyday during the reign of Vasilii I. Moreover, Solomoniia came from a branch of the Saburov clan that was, by the customary rules observed at court, excluded from boyar rank. Solomoniia's father, Iurii Konstantinovich Saburov, was made a boyar in 1509, but his promotion was "apparently honorific, not hereditary." Kollmann is therefore right to suggest that "the marriage of Grand Prince Vasilii III into a non-boyar line of a lesser clan represented a break with the custom of grand princes marrying into prominent boyar families."[129]

More than a break, Vasilii III's selection of Solomoniia established a "new pattern in marriage politics." According to Kollmann, it was the "first time a Daniilovich bride had been chosen from a relatively insignificant clan, rather than a leading foreign, appanage princely, or boyar family."[130] This insight is easily confirmed by a statistical analysis of the weddings of the descendants of Prince Daniil Aleksandrovich, the first prince of Moscow. Over the course of the fourteenth, fifteenth, and sixteenth centuries, Kollmann's three sources of Muscovite spouses—"a leading foreign, appanage princely, or boyar family"—were drawn from in different proportions and followed different trends (see table 1.1).[131] By far, the Daniilovichi's favorite sources for brides and grooms in the fourteenth and fifteenth centuries were other appanage princes, second were foreigners (mostly the Lithuanian Gedyminids), and third were matches with prominent boyar clans. In the sixteenth century, marriages with appanage houses disappeared entirely (along with the appanage principalities themselves) and the space was filled by a dramatic leap in the number of marriages to domestic brides and grooms.

The decline in marriages to foreigners appears after the 1495 marriage of Ivan III's daughter Elena Ivanovna and Alexander of Lithuania. Elena's marriage with Alexander soured the Muscovite court against foreign diplomatic matches for precisely the reason Herberstein says: the "exorbitant costs of a foreign match" and the risks and complications involved in "taking a wife raised with different customs and in a different religion." After 1495, there are only four weddings to foreigners in the next century: Evdokiia and Tsarevich Peter (1506), Grand Prince Vasilii III and Elena Glinskaia (1526), Ivan IV and Mariia/Kochenei Cherkasskaia (1561), and Mariia Vladimirovna Staritskaia and Magnus, the "king" of Livonia (1573). But these marriages hardly qualify as true diplomatic matches. In each of these cases, the foreign spouse moved to and resided in Muscovy, sometimes well before the wedding. Tsarevich Peter was a converted Chinggisid prince who resided—or, better, was held captive—in Muscovy even

TABLE 1.1.

PATTERNS OF DYNASTIC MARRIAGE IN MUSCOVY, ORIGINS OF MUSCOVITE SPOUSES, FOURTEENTH TO EIGHTEENTH CENTURIES

Century	Foreign, N (%)	Appanage, N (%)	Domestic, N (%)	Total, N
Fourteenth	6 (32%)	12 (63%)	1 (5%)	19
Fifteenth	8 (30%)	13 (48%)	6 (22%)	27
Sixteenth	6 (25%)	0	18 (75%)	24
Seventeenth	1 (12%)	0	8 (88%)	9
Eighteenth	10 (91%)	0	1 (9%)	11

Source: Baumgarten, "Généalogies des branches régnantes de Rurikides, XIII–XVI s.," 10–35 (Tables II, III, IV, and V).

before his conversion and marriage to Ivan III's daughter. Elena Glinskaia and members of her family had immigrated to Muscovy in 1508.[132] Mariia/Kochenei Cherkasskaia was a genuine foreign bride, but her family had already established itself in Muscovy, where her brothers were serving at Ivan IV's court. And Magnus, the son of King Christian III of Denmark, was tapped to rule the puppet state of Livonia in Ivan IV's grand scheme to become a player in the Baltic.[133]

In all four cases, the foreign spouse already had some preexisting connection to the court in Moscow. If we disregard these, there are no other marriages contracted between a Muscovite dynast and a foreign prince or princess after 1495 until the 1710 wedding of Peter the Great's niece Anna Ioannovna (the future Empress Anna) with Friedrich Wilhelm of Courland. (We omit the marriages of the First False Dmitrii and Marina Mnishek in 1606 and of Peter the Great with Marfa Skavronka in 1712 since these were each idiosyncratic bride selections.) This was not for lack of trying: Muscovite rulers continued to attempt to contract marriage alliances with other states, particularly western powers. But the catastrophic failure of Elena Ivanovna and Alexander's marriage seems only to have made the grand princes and tsars and their advisors at court more, not less, reluctant to exploit the marriage of the ruler as an instrument of diplomacy. Only Peter the Great, at the outset of the eighteenth century, was willing to make the necessary compromises in the wedding ritual and in the requirement to convert to Orthodoxy that allowed dynastic marriage again to be used in the diplomatic arena.[134]

Marriages after the turn of the sixteenth century showed not only a marked preference for domestic spouses, they showed an equally dramatic shift in the backgrounds of these domestic spouses from previous centuries. No longer were spouses drawn from prominent boyar clans like the Patrikeevs but, rather, from "relatively insignificant" clans like the Saburovs, the Sobakins, the Koltovskiis, and most of the other families that gave a daughter to a Muscovite ruler in the sixteenth and seventeenth centuries. There were exceptions, of course, but by and large, these centuries are noteworthy for the conspicuous absence from the Terem of brides from illustrious families.

This "new pattern" in Daniilovich marriages was the direct and intentional result of the introduction of the bride-show. Between 1505 (Vasilii III's first wedding) and 1689 (Tsar Peter I's first wedding), bride-shows were organized for nearly every marriage of a male Muscovite dynast (see table 1.2). The Muscovite court found in the marriages arranged by bride-shows nearly all the advantages of foreign matches. Foreign brides and grooms came to Muscovy with few retainers and so tended not to disrupt the balance of factions at court. The bride was an outsider, and this suited all the insiders who wanted more than anything else to remain insiders. The winner of a bride-show was, functionally, a foreigner, but without either the high costs or cultural barriers foreigners brought. This explains why (as we shall see in Chapter 2) the bride-show spawned a set of new and associated rituals that helped to concoct a new, fictive identity for the bride.

That the bride-show and this "new pattern" in dynastic marriages should appear on the scene at the same time was not coincidental. However the idea may have been proposed (as an echo of Byzantine bride-shows, as a Muscovite adaptation of Esther, as a ploy by Trakhaniotov to get the ruler to marry his daughter), the bride-show perfectly resolved the matrimonial dilemma that Vasilii III and his advisors found themselves in. The bride-show was devised in reaction to the new matrimonial environment prompted by the successful "gathering of Rus'" under Moscow (the loss of the appanage pool of spouses), the turning away from foreigners (after the Elena Ivanovna debacle), and the broad recognition, probably by ruler and boyars alike, that marrying the daughters of prominent boyars was not a good idea (after the succession crisis of 1497–1502). The bride-show was the instrument devised for finding brides from "relatively insignificant" clans—the perfect new pool of candidates that provided all the benefits of foreign brides without the trouble and cost, and all the advantages of domestic brides without the destabilizing favoritism that past marriages to the daughters of powerful courtiers had produced.

TABLE 1.2.

BRIDE-SHOWS IN MUSCOVY, 1505–1689

Date of Wedding	Documented Bride-Shows	Probable Bride-Shows	Unknown	No Bride-Show
September 4, 1505	Vasilii III and Solomoniia Saburova			
January 21, 1526	Vasilii III and Elena Glinskaia			
February 2, 1533		Andrei Staritskii and Efrosiniia Khovanskaia		
February 3, 1547	Ivan IV and Anastasiia Iur'eva			
November 3, 1547	Iurii Vasil'evich and Ul'iana Paletskaia			
May 31, 1549	Vladimir Staritskii and Evdokiia Nagaia			
August 21, 1561				Ivan IV and Mariia Cherkasskaia
No later than 1578				Boris Godunov
)ctober 28, 1571	Ivan IV and Marfa Sobakina			
Jovember 4, 1571	Ivan Ivanovich and Evdokiia Saburova			
April or May 1572		Ivan IV and Anna Koltovskaia		
eptember or)ctober 1574, anuary 1575		Ivan IV and or Anna Vasil'chikova		
575			Ivan Ivanovich and Pelageia Solovaia	
575			Fedor Ivanovich and Irina Godunova	
577?		Ivan IV and Vasilissa Radilova (Melent'eva)		

TABLE 1.2.

CONTINUED

Date of Wedding	Documented Bride-Shows	Probable Bride-Shows	Unknown	No Bride-Show
September 6, 1580		Ivan IV and Mariia Nagaia		
1580			Ivan Ivanovich and Elena Sheremeteva	
May 8, 1606				First False Dmitrii
January 17, 1608				Vasilii Shuiskii
Proposed for July 1616	Mikhail Romanov and Mariia Khlopova			
September 19, 1624	Mikhail Romanov and Mariia Dolgorukova			
February 5, 1626	Mikhail Romanov and Evdokiia Streshneva			
Proposed for February 14, 1648	Aleksei Mikhailovich and Efimiia Vsevolozhskaia			
January 16, 1648	Aleksei Mikhailovich and Mariia Miloslavskaia			
January 22, 1671	Aleksei Mikhailovich and Natal'ia Naryshkina			
July 18, 1680	Fedor Alekseevich and Agafiia Grushetskaia			
February 5, 1682	Fedor Alekseevich and Marfa Apraksina			
January 9, 1684	Ivan Alekseevich and Praskov'ia Saltykova			
January 27, 1689	Peter I and Evdokiia Lopukhina			

Chapter 2

"Without Any Regard for Noble Ancestry"

Picking a Bride for the Tsar

The selection of a bride for the tsar was a lengthy and complex affair. The fact is that the tsar picked his bride himself and was governed in his selection solely by his own judgment. The bride did not have to be from a prominent family, nor close to the tsar's court, nor even rich. The pleasure of being the tsar's bride was determined entirely by the candidate's beauty, by her physical characteristics. The only thing required was that the tsar found her appealing in his heart, and her family origins and her status and all other considerations were not taken into account. Therefore the tsar did not limit his choice only to the daughters of his closest princes and boyars or to the families of other intimate Moscow boyars, but he searched for his bride throughout the entire realm, in all Russia.

This kind of selection required, of course, an expansive search of all maidens in Muscovy. For this purpose, an edict was drawn up in Moscow and disseminated to all the landowners of Russia, in multiple copies for convenience sake, to all regions, to bring their maiden daughters to the town for a bride-show. To these regional and other towns, the tsar had sent trusted people from among the *okol'nichie* and courtiers, with scribes, who, together with the local *namestnik* and *voevoda*, were supposed to examine all the maidens from their given district…

> At that [regional] bride-show, the tsar's trusted servitors were to select the most beautiful maidens and compile a special list. These beautiful maidens were then supposed to appear in Moscow within a specified period, where they would undergo yet another, more detailed and careful inspection, at which would be present those closest to the tsar, and the tsar himself...
>
> From those beautiful maidens gathered, the tsar himself selected the best one, the one that most touched his heart. The tsar made his decision known by giving to the one he selected a kerchief [*platok*] and ring. Immediately after the choice was made, the royal bride-to-be entered the royal apartments with great ceremony and she remained there until the wedding, under the care and supervision of the *boiaryni* and her own and the tsar's relatives.[1]

This image of selecting a bride for the tsar appears again and again in the popular and scholarly historical literature alike. The narrative above is from a popular late-nineteenth-century history, and it gathers all the common myths about the bride-show in Muscovy. The tsar "picked his bride himself and was governed in his selection solely by his own judgment." The tsar's choice was motivated by the candidates' beauty, not their high birth or pedigree. The bride-show was an "expansive," kingdom-wide search and involved courtiers who were dispatched to the regions to gather candidates they thought might be pleasing to the tsar. And when those candidates were finally presented to the tsar, he signaled his choice by bestowing a ring and kerchief to "the one that most touched his heart." While a "lengthy and complex affair," all of it was directed and decided by the ruler himself. The bride-show was the quintessential expression of autocratic power.

The idealized view of the bride-show found in this passage and in many scholarly treatments presents the modern reader with many problems of interpretation. First, it is based on a conflation of sources of very different kinds and quality, including foreigners' accounts and official wedding descriptions, which frequently conflict with each other and tend to blur the changes in the bride-show custom over time. Second, this rendition of the bride-show emphasizes beauty as the sole selection criterion, but other sources emphasize other factors, including genealogy: not a search for the best-born but for bridal candidates without direct connections to the illustrious names in the Muscovite court. Finally, this depiction of the bride-show misrepresents both the purpose and meaning of the custom. While the bride-show certainly did broadcast an image of an all-powerful and autocratic ruler, that image concealed a very different reality. As chancellery sources reveal, boyars, courtiers of varying ranks, and royal relatives played a very direct and determinative role in the choice of bride. Picking the bride for the tsar was a collaborative decision.

This chapter deconstructs the conventional narrative of Muscovite bride-shows and examines their three principal stages: assembling a pool of candidates, narrowing the pool to a small group of finalists through physical inspections and background investigations, and the selection. The chapter reveals bride-shows to be less about the tsar's free "judgment" than about the sober and calculated selection of a healthy, beautiful, and (it was hoped) fertile bride who had the right kin: or better, did not have the wrong kin. Kinship, then, emerges as a vital selection criterion, one that is muted in foreigners' descriptions and entirely ignored in Muscovite official descriptions of weddings. Finally, this chapter examines the brides themselves and how their identities were remade after being picked in a bride-show. The chapter offers the building materials for constructing a new narrative description of the bride-show that is firmly rooted in the sources, accounts for the changes that the custom underwent over the course of nearly two centuries, and is sensitive to the vital role played by the women, both winners and losers, in the bridal pageant.

How the Bride-Show Worked

The traditional narrative of the bride-show is largely based on the cobbled-together accounts of foreigners and official descriptions of Muscovite weddings. The foreigners' accounts are, to be sure, rich in detail and have therefore been the most-often-cited source of information about bride-shows. But, as W. F. Ryan admonished, "It is precisely the traveller's encounter with what is to him unfamiliar and alien, even repulsive, that may make his story interesting and useful, and it is the task of the later reader of that story, and the responsibility of the historian, to disentangle the threads, to assess the trustworthiness of the story, to take into account the beliefs, gullibility, and preconceptions of the traveler, his competence as an observer, his knowledge of local language and custom, and the reliability of his informants."[2] When the foreigners' accounts of the bride-show are "disentangled" and "assessed" in the way Ryan suggests, much of the traditional narrative crumples into a pile of loose threads. Official wedding descriptions do little to clarify things. The true purpose of bride-shows is revealed by setting foreigners' accounts and official descriptions of weddings side by side with the chancellery documents that were composed in connection with the search for a bride. These documents are the remnants of a paper trail left from what clearly were enormous scribal undertakings, and they help to construct a new and more accurate image of how bride-shows worked.

Assembling the Pool of Candidates

Most Muscovite court rituals were performed within the isolating walls of the Kremlin. Only a few court happenings—the Palm Sunday procession, the Blessing of the Waters at Epiphany, religious pilgrimages, to cite the best studied examples—ever took the tsar and his entourage outside the Kremlin into full view of his subjects.[3] As the historian Paul Kléber Monod aptly noted about the pre-Reformation west: "Before the age of religious reform, European monarchs had played out the hieratic gestures of rulership before tiny audiences of courtiers. Their sacred bodies were seldom seen and were never meant to be comprehended by their subjects."[4] In Muscovy, the audiences for most royal rituals—coronations, baptisms, name day celebrations, and so on—were, if anything, even tinier. But the bride-show was different. Its opening act was performed necessarily in the public spaces outside the Kremlin. It was a ritual that, quoting Monod again, functioned as "public enunciations of the theme of authority," or what Michèle Fogel called "les cérémonies de l'information."[5] Few royal rituals—not coronations, not even the wedding service—could be appropriated to project a predetermined image of majesty and power as effectively as a bride-show.

Bride-shows were arranged in various ways over the course of the nearly two centuries of their existence in Muscovy, but some elements of the custom run across the period. The first step in arranging a bride-show was the dispatching of courtiers from the ruler's court in Moscow to the principal towns of European Russia in order to conduct regional inspections of prospective candidates. Foreign travelers variously hint at these preliminary bride-shows in their accounts. Peter Petreius (1615) wrote of how Vasilii III "summoned" young women "from the entire land."[6] Francesco da Collo (1518) reported that "Grand Prince Vasilii—or so I was informed—decided to take a wife in order to have children and give himself a legitimate heir and successor to the realm," and so he "commanded it be proclaimed in all parts of his realm, that the most beautiful virgins were to be found, without any regard for their noble ancestry, but only with regard to their beauty [*che non hauutosi riguardo à nobiltà di sangue, ma à beltà sola fossero elete più belle Vergini*]."[7] Jerome Horsey (1571) described how Ivan IV "sends for all his nobles' and gentlemen's fairest daughters, maidens, throughout his kingdoms."[8] Johann Taube and Elbert Kruse (1571) went into greater detail, explaining that, in 1570, Tsar Ivan IV "dispatched several people to all the regions, even to territories that had only just become part of this giant country, to examine all girls, young and old, of high and low estate, to note and describe their names, height, and build so there would be no substitutions nor deceit, and he ordered all of them, numbering 2,000, to come to Alexandrovo Sloboda."[9] Strahlenberg (1730) also suggested that there were delegations dispatched to assemble a pool of candidates: "The Czar having declared his Intension of marrying, to the Senate, the Bojari look'd out for the most beautiful Ladies that were to be found, and sent them to Court."[10] Samuel Collins (1667) described how the Tsar Aleksei Mikhailovich "gathered many young girls."[11] Foy de la Neuville (1689) generally reported how the rulers of Russia "order[ed] the most beautiful girls from all over Russia to be brought to the court."[12]

Firm evidence of tsardom-wide searches also appears in the extant chancellery documentation from sixteenth-century bride-shows. Two original chancellery drafts contain lists of courtiers dispatched far and wide in search of candidates for the bride-show for Tsar Ivan IV's first marriage—one dated by Vladislav Nazarov to December 12–18, 1546, and the other to around January 9, 1547 (see table 2.1).[13] These lists, while incomplete, contain the names of twenty-nine courtiers who formed thirteen groups dispatched to twenty-seven regional towns for the initial inspection of bridal candidates for Ivan IV. Each courtier was accompanied by a scribe (*d'iak*), sometimes by both a scribe and a clerk (*pod'iachii*). Each delegation was assigned anywhere from one to four towns to canvass, depending, one assumes, on the population of the towns.[14] For example, *okol'nichii* Ivan Ivanovich Bezzubtsov and the *d'iak* Posnik Putiatin were sent due south from Moscow to Kolomna, Kashira, Serpukhov, and Tarusa.[15] Prince Petr Andreevich Bulgakov and *d'iak* Gavrilo Tyrtov were sent due east, to Vladimir, Suzdal', and Iur'ev.[16] Novgorod, Pereslavl', and Kostroma appeared to have been sufficiently large enough towns to merit their own delegations.[17]

TABLE 2.1

List of Towns Visited by Courtiers to Identify Candidates for the Bride-Show for Ivan IV, December 1546 and January 1547

Town(s) Visited	Courtiers Sent (December List)	Courtiers Sent (January List)
Kolomna, Kashira, Serpukhov, Tarusa	*okol'nichii* Ivan Ivanovich Bezzubtsov *d'iak* Posnik Putiatin	
Borovsk, Kaluga, Kozelsk, Vorotynsk	Prince Fedor Andreevich Kurakin *d'iak* Shershen' Bilibin	
Mozhaisk, Volok	Prince Semen Fedorovich Alabyshev *d'iak* Istoma Chertovskii	
Viaz'ma, Dorogobuzh	Prince Ivan Semenovich Mezetskii *d'iak* Gavrilo Shchenok	
Tver', Torzhok	Boris Ivanovich Saltykov *d'iak* Gavrilo Severitsyn	
Kostroma	Prince Boris Dmitreevich Shchepin *d'iak* Nevezha Kopnin	
Pereslavl'	Prince Dmitrii Dmitreevich Shchepin *d'iak* Pospel Lebedev	Prince Dmitrii Dmitreevich Shchepin *d'iak* Pospel Lebedev *pod'iachii* Ontipa Gridin
Rostov, Iaroslavl'	Prince Fedor Semenovich Mezetskii *d'iak* Dmitrii Gorin	Prince Fedor Semenovich Mezetskii *d'iak* Dmitrii Gorin *pod'iachii* Ontipa Gridin
Vladimir, Suzdal', Iur'ev	Prince Petr Andreevich Kurakin *d'iak* Gavrilo Tyrtov	Prince Petr Andreevich Bulgakov *d'iak* Gavrilo Tyrtov *pod'iachii* Vasilii Nechaev
Murom, Nizhnii Novgorod	Prince Petr Semenovich Ianov-Rostovskii Ivan Kuz'min	Prince Petr Semenovich Ianov-Rostovskii Ivan Kuz'min Arbuz Treskin

TABLE 2.1,

CONTINUED

Town(s) Visited	Courtiers Sent (December List)	Courtiers Sent (January List)
Uglich, Bezhetskii Verkh	Vladimir Vasil'evich Morozov *d'iak* Stepan Skrypov	Vladimir Vasil'evich Morozov *d'iak* Stepan Skrypov Molchan Sudokov
Novgorod	*okol'nichii* Ivan Dmitreevich Shein	*okol'nichii* Ivan Dmitreevich Shein Ovram (Orap?) Kacharov syn Pogozhevo
Toropets		

Source: RGADA, *fond* 135, sec. IV, rub. II, no. 2, fols. 6–7 and 8.

The courtier and his small scribal staff did not sort through prospective candidates alone. The servitors who had been dispatched from Moscow worked with the local *namestniki*, or governors, who typically were boyars or *okol'nichie*, and together they formed panels—or, as Nazarov called them, "commissions"—that would run the regional bride-shows.[18] For example, the summons circulated by Tsar Ivan IV in *Bezhetskaia piatina* in December 1547 identifies precisely who was to serve on the selection commission for the various districts (*piatiny*) of Novgorod:

> From Grand Prince Ivan Vasil'evich of all Russia to our patrimony, to Novgorod the Great, to the *Bezhetskaia piatina*, 100, 150, and 200 versts outside Novgorod, to our princes and *deti boiarskie*. We have dispatched to our patrimony, to Novgorod the Great, our *okol'nichii* Ivan Dmitreevich Shein, and we have commanded Our boyars and governor [*namestnik*] Prince Iurii Mikhailovich Bulgakov and Vasilii Dmitreevich [Shein, evidently the brother of the envoy—*REM*][19] and Our *okol'nichii* Ivan to view your unwed daughters for Our bride. And when you will have received this edict, those of you who have unwed daughters shall immediately come with them to Novgorod the Great; and you shall not conceal your unwed daughters, but escort them to Novgorod the Great without delay. And if anyone has a daughter and attempts to conceal her and not bring her to Our boyars and Our governor, to Prince Iur'ii Mikhailovich and to Vasilii Dmitreevich, and to Our *okol'nichii* Ivan—he will be disgraced [*v opale*] and punished [*v kazni*].[20]

Clearly, in Novgorod, the selection of candidates was made by a panel of three: the *okol'nichii* Ivan Dmitreevich Shein (who was sent from Moscow for this purpose), the boyar Prince Iurii Mikhailovich Bulgakov (the governor), and boyar Vasilii Dmitreevich Shein (who seems already to have been in Novgorod). These three were assisted by at least one scribe, Ovram (or Orap) Kachabarov syn Pogozhevo.[21] The formation of commissions in large- and medium-sized towns throughout Muscovy and the highly visible work they engaged in would have been hard for the surrounding population to ignore, or to misread its political message: the tsar's majesty and power must truly be boundless and divinely ordained if his marriage was to warrant so grand a spectacle as this.

Other weddings followed similar procedures. The ceremonial (*svadebnyi chin*) for the wedding in 1547 of Ivan IV's younger brother Prince Iurii Vasil'evich and Iulianiia Paletskaia states that candidates were summoned to Moscow—perhaps by the circulation of an edict (*ukaz*)—where the inspections took place: "And Tsar and Grand Prince Ivan Vasil'evich of all Russia ordered the boyars and princes to bring their daughters to his [Ivan IV's] royal court; and when they had brought them, Tsar and Grand Prince Ivan Vasil'evich and Prince Iurii Vasil'evich inspected [*smotreli*] the virgins; and Prince Iur'ii Vasil'evich preferred [*poliubil*] Princess Ul'iana, the daughter of Dmitrii Fedorovich Paletskii."[22] Similarly, the ceremonial for the wedding in 1549 of Prince Vladimir Staritskii and Evdokiia Nagaia hints at a circulated summons to the bride-show in Moscow:

> And the tsar and grand prince ordered the boyars and princes to list their unwed daughters, and at the appropriate time, to view them; but then the tsar and grand prince postponed the wedding on account of the expedition to Kazan'; and [he] ordered [the girls] to be viewed after the Kazan' affair. And on May 24, on Sunday, Tsar and Grand Prince Ivan Vasil'evich of all Russia and Prince Vladimir Andreevich inspected the virgins [*smotreli... devok*], and he [presumably Vladimir] preferred [*poliubil*] the virgin Avdot'ia, the daughter of Aleksandr Mikhailovich Nagoi.[23]

Regional, preliminary bride-shows seem also to have survived into the seventeenth century, but the circumstances of the new dynasty prompted changes to the procedure. When Tsar Aleksei Mikhailovich sought in 1669–1671 to marry a second time, he summoned prospective brides to him—most from Moscow, but others from Kostroma, Suzdal', Riazan',

Vladimir, and Novgorod.[24] As we will see below, the bridal candidates were presented to the tsar in installments over many months—usually two or three or four at a time, rather than all at once at a single bride-show. The marriages of Tsar Fedor III in 1680 and 1682 and of Tsar Ivan V in 1684 were so influenced and affected by the grooms' different illnesses (physical and mental), by the decisive influence of relatives and favorites, and by the general changes in political culture at court, that these last bride-shows seem to have been far smaller affairs, probably omitting the extensive searching of the provinces for the "fairest in the land." The seventeenth-century bride-shows, like so many other things, represent variations on earlier themes.[25]

Who made up the pool of candidates targeted by these commissions? Were they the daughters of "boyars and princes," as official wedding descriptions and some foreigners' accounts say? Or were they, as Da Collo reports, the "most beautiful virgins" who were selected "without any regard for noble ancestry"?[26]

Were we to rely on foreigners' accounts alone, we might be led to think that bride-shows were an entirely open contest, including candidates drawn from all social layers of society and from all corners of tsardom, so long as they were beautiful, pious, and virtuous. Were we to rely only on official documents, we might think just the opposite, that the bride-show was not an open contest at all and that the pool of candidates was composed entirely of the daughters of prominent princely families and boyar clans. The chancellery sources make it clear, however, that these were neither open contests nor pageants of aristocracy. Bride-shows over the sixteenth and seventeenth centuries included no daughters of peasants, no daughters of priests, and very few daughters of princes (at least until the very end of the seventeenth century). The edicts circulated by the selection commissions had an addressee: servitor princes holding posts in the regional administration or cavalry, and the *deti boiarskie* (middle-ranking servitors) who garrisoned the towns. When in 1547 Ivan IV issued a call for preliminary bride-shows in Viaz'ma, Dorogobuzh, Rostov, Novgorod, and (probably) elsewhere, he addressed his edicts uniformly to the "princes and to the court and town [*dvorovym i gorodovym*] *deti boiarskie*," not to the entire population.[27] By "princes," the text does not mean families of great power and position, or else there would be some mention of their ranks (boyar, *okol'nichii*, *voevoda*, *namestnik*). Rather, these were Riurikovich princes who had slipped into relative obscurity in the regional administrative ranks, serving as leaders in the local cavalry or provincial (*uezd*) administration. This expression then—"princes and the court and town *deti boiarskie*"—probably served as a catch-all phrase for families who enjoyed a measure of exclusively local privilege but were hardly known in Moscow. These are the families that Valerie Kivelson studied and called the "provincial gentry": the "lowest rung of the privileged elite within a highly stratified, explicitly ordered society."[28]

Despite what might outwardly seem to have been an enticing opportunity for fathers with eligible daughters, it appears from the surviving evidence that the "princes and *deti boiarskie*" were not always eager to send their daughters off to participate in these preliminary regional bride-shows. Royal summonses were sometimes very stubbornly resisted by the "provincial gentry." Again, the bride search for Ivan IV's first wedding provides us with vital evidence. As we already saw in the edict sent to Novgorod in December 1546, Ivan the Terrible had warned the princes and *deti boiarskie* "not [to] conceal your unwed daughters."[29] It was a well-advised warning. Prince Fedor Semenovich Mezetskii, who had been dispatched to Rostov in December 1546, reported to Ivan IV at the end of the month how, after having circulated the royal summons to all the princes and *deti boiarskie* in the district, there had not been any response: "And the messengers whom we sent out with Your royal letters and with our letters, these messengers, sovereign, have all returned to Rostov. And after that, sovereign, we stayed in Rostov for a week, and no one from the Rostov district appeared [before us]." In the end, Mezetskii was reduced to having to track down eligible young girls himself: "And, sovereign, we were told, '[Prince] Petr and Ivan [Semenovich] Ianov have daughters.' And we [went and] viewed them. And some of the Archbishop's *deti boiarskie* and town elite [*gorodtskie liudi*] have daughters, and we viewed them." (The daughters of Petr and Ivan Ianov-Rostovskii mentioned in this text were likely not withheld from the bride-show since one of the two brothers, Prince Petr, was himself involved in the search for a bride for the tsar, having been dispatched to organize regional bride-shows in Murom and Nizhnii Novgorod.)[30] Nothing came of Mezetskii's efforts in Rostov, so he and his scribe, Dmitrii Gorin, set off for Iaroslavl', their next assignment.[31]

Similar reluctance to participate in the regional bride-show was encountered by Prince Fedor's brother Ivan Semenovich Mezetskii, who had been dispatched to Viaz'ma. He wrote complaining to the tsar:

> To the sovereign, Grand Prince Ivan Vasil'evich of all Russia, your servants Ivan Mezetskii and Shchenok salute. You sent us, sovereign, to Viaz'ma, and we, sovereign, having arrived in Viaz'ma, circulated your royal edict to the princes and *deti boiarskie* of the Viaz'ma province, into the settlements and districts [*volosty*]; and according to your royal command, we circulated your royal edicts to the princes and *deti boiarskie*. And we, sovereign, have been residing in Viaz'ma for two weeks, but not one prince or *syn boiarskii* has come to us and brought his daughter to us. And among the town elite [*u gorodtskikh liudei*], sovereign, there are no suitable daughters; they are all young and skinny. And we viewed the daughter of Prince Vasilii, the son of Ivan Gundorov. And regarding the princess's appearance and age, we, sovereign, have sent to you a description under your seal with the clerk Ustiug. And we ourselves, sovereign, have departed for Dorogobuzh.[32]

Reluctance to participate was not limited to Ivan IV's bride-show. The same resistance from provincial servitors was expressed about the bride-show that had been organized for Ivan IV's unstable brother, Prince Iurii Vasil'evich. Princess Anna Penkova had been ordered to present her daughter in Moscow but instead sent a letter to the tsar in October 1547 declining to do so. In her letter Penkova claimed her daughter was ill, which Nazarov plausibly speculated was merely an excuse to avoid presenting her. She wrote: "To the Sovereign, Tsar, and Grand Prince Ivan Vasil'evich of all Rus', Princess Anna, the wife of Prince Vasilii Penkov, petitions. You have ordered, sovereign, that I appear in Moscow with my virgin daughter on the eve of St. Dmitrii's Day. But, sovereign, on account of my sins my daughter is ill, and my daughter cannot, sovereign, appear."[33] Penkova evidently shuddered at the thought of having her daughter united with the weak-minded Prince Iurii.[34] Penkova had her daughter, in effect, play hooky from the bride-show.

Nazarov attributed the resistance to bride-shows to a number of reasons. He speculated that fathers of eligible daughters may have been discouraged by the small chances of success; that there were logistical difficulties that burdened many candidates (bad roads and the cost of properly outfitting their daughters for the bride-show); that some fathers may have been away in service (like Petr Ianov-Rostovskii was) or ill; and finally, that the most serious and determined candidates would go directly to Moscow, and not rely on the opinion of the local governor or other servitors who happened to form the ad hoc commission at the regional bride-shows.[35]

But Ivan IV did not believe that his princes and *deti boiarskie* had such innocent reasons for failing to present their daughters at the regional bride-shows. Prince Ivan Mezetskii's report from Viaz'ma elicited a stern response. Ivan IV told Mezetskii, "We have sent to them [i.e., to the princes and *deti boiarskie* of Viaz'ma province] other edicts threatening disgrace [*opala*], and have ordered them to go to you [i.e., Mezetskii] immediately with their daughters. And you are to circulate Our new edict immediately."[36] A draft copy of Ivan IV's new edict survives and leaves no doubt about the seriousness of the matter at hand:

> Prince Ivan Semenovich Mezetskii and court scribe Gavrilo Shchenok wrote to Us that they, in accordance with Our orders, circulated Our letters to you and sent letters of their own, that you should go to them with your daughters; and We commanded them to examine your daughters as a possible bride for Us. But you have not gone to them and you have not brought your daughters, and Our edicts you have disobeyed. And it is wrong not to obey Our edicts. And you are to go immediately and without fail with your daughters to Prince Ivan Mezetskii and to the court scribe Gavrilo Shchenok. And if any one of you do not immediately go to him, that one will be disgraced and punished.[37]

These letters indicate that, whatever the quality of the roads, the cost of outfitting a young girl for a bride-show, or her father's belief about the odds of success, Ivan IV and his advisors expected provincial servitors to comply with this edict. The resistance to the bride-show in Viaz'ma was hardly unique. This "disobedience" was also reported in Dorogobuzh and Rostov—all very different locales, suggesting that resistance was widespread. Nor was it limited to the marriages of Ivan IV and his brother Iurii. When Tsar Aleksei Mikhailovich conducted a search for his second bride in 1669–1671, a certain Petr Kokorev was heard advising his fellow courtiers not to let their daughters participate: "It would be better if you drowned your maiden daughters in water than to take them to the Terem [*v Verkh*] to the bride-show."[38]

Besides those offered by Nazarov, it is easy to imagine two other reasons that princes and *deti boiarskie* in the regions were so reluctant to join in what surely was a once-in-a-lifetime opportunity to become royal in-laws. First, fathers might have seen more risk than opportunity in the tsar's summons. There was the family's honor to consider. Participation in bride-shows involved taking daughters from their secluded rooms inside the family's living compounds and exposing them, literally, to the view of outsiders—something that, in this culture of elite female seclusion, must have been very discomfiting to fathers, mothers, and probably to the young women themselves. To a provincial servitor whose family's honor depended on the reputation of his womenfolk, the thought of having his young daughter scrutinized so thoroughly—a stranger measuring her height, weight, the length of her nose, the width of her hips, and the color of her eyes, not to mention the potentially humiliating physical examination to assure virtue—might very well have been an intolerable violation of the social norms about the treatment of elite young women.[39]

A second possible reason that the princes and *deti boiarskie* failed to heed the tsar's summonses may have been their sensible hesitancy to join in the "game of politics" that revolved precisely around the marriage of the ruler. Boyar families in Moscow were professionals in this game. Marriage politics and warfare were their only occupations. But, as Valerie Kivelson has shown, lesser courtier families, especially those in the provinces, did not operate in the same circles.[40] They had little or no experience in high court politics and therefore probably had few protectors or patrons in Moscow. Participation in the bride-show would thrust these families into the center of politicking, the dynamics of which—who are allies? who are enemies?—were probably poorly understood by families from outside the inner circle at court. Even the preliminary stages of the bride search—sometimes conducted, as we have seen, in the provincial towns—could be risky, since the selection commissions included members of Muscovy's most important clans. Fathers may not have been willing to risk their daughters, and the fate and fortunes of their entire clan, on the remote chance of becoming royal in-laws. And as we shall see in subsequent chapters, the fears of these fathers for their clans were not without foundation.[41]

Narrowing the Pool

Despite the reluctance among some candidates or their families to participate in the regional bride-shows, the pool of potential brides that appeared in Moscow was large enough that it still needed trimming. Thus, it is a point made in several foreigners' accounts that the number of candidates was progressively reduced until just a handful—12, or 10, or 6—were left. It was these survivors that actually earned an audience with the tsar.

According to Herberstein, the selection process for Vasilii III's first bride-show in 1505 yielded 1,500 "daughters of boyars."[42] Peter Petreius repeats this number in his account of Vasilii III's nuptials, though it is likely that he simply borrowed it from Herberstein.[43] This number is clearly an exaggeration: there were only six boyars (and five *okol'nichie*) in 1505, hardly enough to yield more than a handful of candidates.[44] Francesco da Collo put the number of candidates in 1505 at 500, a number that may also be too high. He went on to report that the pool was then reduced to 300, then 200, then 100, and then, finally, 10.[45] Taube and Kruse described the bride-show for Ivan IV's third marriage (in 1571, to Marfa Sobakina), which also produced the first bride for Ivan IV's son Tsarevich Ivan Ivanovich (Evdokiia Saburova). According to Taube and Kruse, 2,000 prospective bridal candidates were summoned to Alexandrovo Sloboda, Ivan IV's residence during the *oprichnina*. "From all that were gathered," the account reads, "24 were left; then, spending time with each one-on-one, he selected from them 12."[46] Daniel Printz von Buchau (1578), assessing Ivan IV's later marriages just a few years after this, reported that the tsar "summons to himself all the daughters of boyars from all the land and at first he looks at them all, then, after a few days, half are sent away; soon after that the number is again reduced, until there is only one left whom he considers worthy of marrying."[47] That these kinds of progressive reductions also took place in the seventeenth century is suggested by the report of a Swedish diplomat in Muscovy in 1647, which describes the first bride-show organized for Tsar Aleksei Mikhailovich: "To His Majesty in the court in the Great Hall were presented six virgins, chosen from 200 others, who had been designated for this purpose by the nobles [*vel'mozhi*]."[48]

How the numbers were reduced is not divulged in the indigenous sources, but foreigners had a lot to say about it. Many reported that there were physical examinations of the candidates, which were carried out by women in the Kremlin. Da Collo reports that the candidates were "examined by midwives [*ostetrici*] with due attention to verifying their virtue, and to determining if they were healthy enough for childbirth, and if they had any other ailments."[49] Giovio says that the candidates were made available to "knowledgeable persons and trusted womenfolk, to examine them with great care, even such that they are even permitted to perform physical examinations of the most private parts."[50] Reutenfels, writing in 1671, described how these examinations had changed over time: "In former times," he wrote, "three [candidates] who were chosen by the tsar himself from this throng underwent similar investigations of physical and moral qualities by women, who were trusted and experienced in such matters, for only the most outstanding of all [the candidates] was selected for the royal bed. But Aleksei, having a penetrating intellect, for the first time did not suffer any delays, but chose for himself as a consort Natal'ia Kirillovna and soon gained her love through gifts worthy of a great Sovereign."[51]

The identity of these "trusted women-folk" is never revealed in the accounts, but Neuville (1689) is probably on the right track when he identifies them as "the tsars' mothers, sisters and relations together with doctors and surgeons."[52] On four notable occasions, a mother played a vital role in her son's choice: Tsar Mikhail Fedorovich's mother, the nun Kseniia Shestova, sabotaged the tsar's first pick (Mariia Khlopova) in 1616, guided him to his first wife (Mariia Dolgorukova) in 1624, and reluctantly acquiesced to the selection of his second (Evdokiia Streshneva) in 1626. Peter I's mother, Natal'ia Naryshkina, handpicked Evdokiia Lopukhina for her son in 1689. Sisters played the key role on three occasions: Vasilii III consulted with his sister in the search for his first wife in 1505, as described in Chapter 1; Tsar Aleksei Mikhailovich's sister meddled in his bride-shows in 1670 and 1671; and the Regent Sofiia essentially ran the bride search for her brother Tsar Ivan Alekseevich in 1684. Neuville's "relations" probably refers to the *boiaryni*—the wives and female relatives of the boyars, who lived in close proximity to the ruler's consort, had regular and open access to the Terem, and were in many cases related to the royal family by marriage. Zabelin assigned to them the chief role in the inspections of bridal candidates who had progressed in the contest to the penultimate stage, perhaps being assisted in their inspections by the midwives and other child care providers inside the Terem.[53] Given that these were "physical examinations of the most private parts," they simply had to be conducted by women; and given the high stakes involved for everyone at the court, these examinations had to be handled by the tsar's kith and kin. In many cases, this meant the wives of his boyars or, in other words, his in-laws, or in-laws of in-laws. Of course, the fact that doctors—almost certainly all foreigners—were involved makes perfect sense, as well. They appear more than once in both foreign and Muscovite sources describing royal brides and marriages.[54] These rigorous and intrusive inspections reduced the number of candidates to a handful of healthy, virginal, and stunningly beautiful finalists who could now be presented to the tsar.

THE SELECTION

Muscovite sources are nearly silent on how the final selection was actually made, but foreigners, again, often described the process in some detail, though their accounts often disagree. Taube and Kruse, for example, appear most interested in conveying a seedy picture of the bride-show custom, at least the one Ivan IV conducted in 1571. According to them, "When they were all gathered together from all the lengths and distant reaches, [the tsar] viewed them in the following way, which required nearly an entire year to complete." The account continues:

> Each woman or girl was ordered to come to a house where she was to dress in finery. Then he [Ivan IV] entered the room together with two or three trusted persons, who were also dressed up in the most exact way. He bowed to them, spoke with them briefly, looked them over, then departed. This is the way he treated all of the candidates: those he did not like, he used for shameful passions of the flesh, gave them some sort of gift and had them marry his executioners or they were entirely banished in the most pitiless way. From all that were gathered, 24 were left. Then, spending time with each one-on-one, he selected from them 12; and when we on July 26, 1571, were with him at Alexandrovo Sloboda, he selected for himself and for his son the ones he wanted in the following way: They had to remove all their jewelry and clothing and allow themselves to be inspected naked, without any objection and resistance. At this time, his doctor was present, and he was supposed to inspect their urine in a glass and to determine and report on their character, attributes, and health.[55]

The erotic elements of this description are uncorroborated in other sources, but the special "house" mentioned by Taube and Kruse, in which the final stage of the bride-show took place, is mentioned elsewhere. According to Strahlenberg, the Swedish prisoner of war who wrote an important "cosmography" of eastern Europe and Siberia:

> Each of the [candidates] had an Apartment provided suitable to their respective Quality, till the Time of the Election. During this Interval, they all din'd together at one Table, where the Czar had an Opportunity of seeing them in Publick, and incognito, in Order the better to direct his Choice to one of this beautiful Company. However, Recommendation has usually had no small share in this Matter; Because, in so short a Time, it was impossible

> for the Czar perfectly to judge of their Humours and Passions. And tho' he often disguis'd himself, and waited, among others, at Table; Yet, in all Probability, ther could not be done with so much Privacy, but every one might have a Hint to be upon her Guard, and artfully to conceal her natural Temper.[56]

And according to Reutenfels, Tsar Aleksei Mikhailovich in 1671 ordered the candidates in his bride-show

> to gather at Artamon Sergeevich's house (who, as the saying goes, is called the shrewd Artamon), who was the principal man of the court. When they all had gathered, the tsar entered Artamon's house through a secret passage, and having concealed himself in a hiding-place (from which, however, he could observe the candidates), he carefully inspected this troop of beautiful women, evaluating them not only in terms of their physical beauty, but also their spiritual qualities and behavior; and when they one-by-one walked past his little viewing portal, he thoughtfully noted for each how much of their beauty was from makeup and how much was natural.[57]

Finally, two sources—one the account of the Polish diplomat Heidenstein and the other a peculiar Russian chronicle—provide the most striking and detailed descriptions of what went on in one of these special "houses." Heidenstein claimed that his account was based on the report of a "captive noble girl who took part in the bride-show" (which bride-show goes unstated, but the date and context of this passage link it to one of Ivan IV's later marriages, perhaps for the Nagaia wedding in 1580). According to Heidenstein:

> Having circulated the edict, the tsar of Moscow ordered boyars and courtiers with daughters or unmarried relatives, who were distinguished by their beauty, to bring them to him on an appointed day. In advance of this day, a large and lavish house was prepared for this purpose, and in every room there were placed 12 beds and as many girls were assigned to each room. The tsar himself, accompanied by an old man, goes about all the rooms; entering, he immediately sits on a throne placed there beforehand. Then all the girls, dressed in rich clothing and all very much wanting to please the sovereign and be selected, each take their turn in front of him, falling to the ground on their knees; and he casts to their feet a kerchief [*platok*] sewn

> with gold thread and pearls, and they move away. The tsar picks the one he likes most, and the rest get a parcel of land or money, and depart.[58]

This account is repeated almost verbatim in a Russian chronicle (*leto-pischik*) that comes down to us today only in a copy from the second half of the eighteenth century, though it was, according to Sigurd Ottovich Shmidt, assembled in perhaps the third quarter of the seventeenth century from various separate sources that go back to the sixteenth century.[59] The snippet on the bride-show is worth quoting in its entirety:

> I heard it from the very lips of a certain girl who had been with the others at a bride-show for Tsar Ivan Vasil'evich, about how the tsars picked their brides in bride-shows. One of them happened in the following manner: Tsar Ivan Vasil'evich ordered all his princes and boyars to bring their daughters who had reached marriageable age to Moscow on a predetermined date. In advance of their arrival in Moscow, a large and beautiful house with many rooms was prepared, and in each bedroom there were placed 12 beds, each assigned to one of the girls. And they all lived together in one house, waiting for the royal bride-show. And when that time had arrived, his tsarist majesty [*tsarskoe velichestvo*] came to the house with one elderly boyar and entered a room especially prepared for him, and he sat on a beautifully decorated seat prepared for him; and then the daughters of the princes and boyars, all dressed in their finest maiden's costumes, and with expensive clothes, beautifully adorned, entered one after the other before the tsar, and bowed to him at his feet. At that time, the tsar gave each of them a kerchief, sewn with gold and silver thread and with expensive pearls, throwing it at the girl's feet, and then each girl returned to her own room. And the one the tsar favored best of all he took for his bride, and the others were all excused with honor and given land and money.[60]

While the two texts vary in some small details (Shmidt is undoubtedly right in suggesting that the chronicle was reworked as it was compiled and copied, with much of the language modernized),[61] there can be little doubt that the compiler of this strange and unstudied chronicle had Heidenstein's account at hand. But whether there actually ever was an interview with a "captive noble girl who took part in the bride-show," as both this chronicle and Heidenstein claim, can only be guessed. There is no other reference to this or any other interview or commentary from any of the women that participated in Muscovite bride-shows over the course of nearly two centuries. As for the house—where it was (inside the Kremlin?) and whose it was (a royal residence or the house of one of his boyars?) is never explained.[62]

As for the actual selection, Collins reported that the successful candidate was given a kerchief (*platok*) and a ring as a sign that she had been selected.[63] Heidenstein wrote, however, that *all* the finalists received kerchiefs as a token of their participation in the bride-show.[64] He also wrote that they "get a parcel of land or money, and depart." Heidenstein and others further reported that many of the finalists were married off to the tsar's servitors.[65] Strahlenberg explained that the winner received a new and richly ornamented "wedding suit"—the signal that a choice had been made—though the other finalists were given new "cloaths," too:

> "IX. As soon as the Czar was determin'd in his Choice, the Grand Gouvernante only was made acquainted with it, and order'd to get Cloaths made for them all, and for the Bride a Wedding-Suit."
>
> "X. In the mean Time, a Day for the Solemnization of the Nuptials was appointed, tho' none of them knew who was to be the Bride; and that Day being come, the new Cloaths were distributed, and the Bride then receiv'd her Nuptial Robes. Which made it known on whom the Choice was fallen. They then all paid their congratulatory Compliments to the Bride, and as soon as she was proclaim'd, the Rest were sent home.[66]

Did the tsars ever dress as waiters and serve the bridal candidates their meals incognito, as Strahlenberg has it? Did they ever peep at the finalists through hidden spy holes drilled through walls, as Reutenfels says? Did they sit on a throne and watch the bevy of beauties pass by, as Heidenstein says? Are the colorful details from foreigners' accounts to be regarded in the same skeptical way the unknown author of the Shmidt's *letopischik* apparently regarded them: "I do not know if this story about this ceremony [the bride-show] is true or not, because so many libelous things have been fabricated about it to the detriment of Russia's sovereigns and the Russian people"?[67] Or, in perhaps a more measured tone, are these colorful stories to be dismissed as Isabel de Madariaga does, who described Heidenstein's account as "a very fanciful description of the procedure"?[68] How the bride-show was performed and changed over time can still only be described in rough outline, but it is easy to imagine how such accounts might have tickled the ears of foreigners, who saw the bride-show as the epitome of everything despotic and exotic about Muscovy, as well as the ears of Muscovites, who may have found in the bride-show the best means possible to conceal the nature of the political system in Muscovy behind what Kollmann and Kivelson have called the "façade of autocracy."[69]

The Primacy of Kinship

If bride-shows were not open contests, they were also not solely about love or looks, except to the extent that beauty might be regarded popularly as a sign of health, vigor, and the promise of agreeable-looking children. Nazarov, who dated and published many of the chancellery texts from bride-shows of the sixteenth century, found in them four search criteria for potential brides: good health (of the candidate and her parents); age; appearance; and family origins.[70] But these were not all of equal importance. To be sure, the appearance of the candidates is mentioned prominently and described at some length in the sources. The focus on good health and age seem natural enough. Childbirth at this time was a dangerous risk even to the healthiest of young women. Youth and good health held out the promise of many years of fertility; and given the high rates of infant and child mortality, a tsaritsa would be expected to live out her fecund years in a nearly constant state of pregnancy.

The attention paid in the chancellery documents to kinship reveals it to be a vitally important criterion when picking a bride for the tsar. Bridal searches were, in point of fact, complex calculations of candidates' genealogical ties—both agnatic and affinal. Having the wrong connections and kin could wreck a candidacy as fast as a cleft palate or a club foot. A memorandum composed in 1526 regarding the search for Vasilii III's second bride bears out this point.

> A memorandum to the *okol'nichii* Ivan Vasil'evich [Liatskii] and the clerk Timofei Klobukov: He is to take careful precautions and make secret inquiries on his own in order to make sure that they avoid all eligible girls of any description in the Shcheniatev or Pleshcheev families. Ivan and Timofei are to make sure of this. And if a girl is fair [*dobra*] but only slightly related to the Shcheniatevs or Pleshcheevs, then Ivan and Timofei may go and examine this girl, and report in writing to the grand prince what she looks

> like, how old she is, and how tall, and how distant her kinship is to those clans [the Shcheniatevs or Pleshcheevs], and whether she is related through her father or her mother.[71]

Vasilii III was keen to avoid reestablishing dynastic links with the Patrikeev clan (of which the Shcheniatevs were a part) in the wake of the anti-Patrikeev coup of 1499, part of the succession crisis of 1497–1502 discussed in Chapter 1. The reason for avoiding Pleshcheev girls is less clear, though their connections to the appanage court of Prince Iurii Ivanovich, Vasilii III's troublesome younger brother, and to the Patrikeev clan must have placed them in a suspect position in the eyes of the Muscovite ruler and his advisors.[72] Whatever the case, the memorandum makes it clear that, even if all other requirements for candidacy were met, a close kinship tie with either of these two clans was disqualifying. Even if a girl was exceptionally beautiful (*dobra*), she could be considered for the bride-show only if her kinship ties to either of these two clans were very remote.

For each candidate, a comprehensive description was composed by the regional "commissions" and sent to the tsar (and his advisors) to review.[73] By chance, one of these original descriptions survives, from the search conducted in early 1547 for Ivan IV. It is the "description" (*spisok*) of Ovdot'ia Vasil'evna Gundorova, which was mentioned in Prince Ivan Mezetskii's letter to Ivan IV quoted above. It will be remembered that she was the only candidate inspected during a two-week stay in Viaz'ma. It is a remarkable document that, by the sequence of inspections and the apportioning of attention, demonstrates what was foremost in the minds of the men who picked the tsar's bride. The text is translated in full below:

> By order of the Sovereign Grand Prince Ivan Vasil'evich of all Russia, in Viaz'ma Prince Ivan Mezetskii and court scribe Shchenok viewed the daughter of Prince Vasilii, the son of Ivan Gundorov. Princess Ovdot'ia is 12 years old, has a well proportioned figure, is not too thin and not too fat, black eyes, a nose that is not too long for her face, dark brown hair. Concerning illnesses, Prince Vasilii said that his daughter, Ovdot'ia, had been ill with a fever when a child, but now, thank God, was without any ailments.
>
> Her mother was Princess Fetin'ia, the daughter of Grigorii Poluekhtovich Buturlin. Her sister, Stefanida, is married to Goriain, the son of

> Prokofii Dement'ev. Her other sister, Ogrofena, is married to Ofanasii, the son of Ondrei Godunov. Her brothers are Prince Ivan, Prince Davyd, Prince Fedor. Her stepmother is Orina, the daughter of Semen Zvenigorodskii. Her stepmother's brothers are Prince Ivan, Prince Fedor, Prince Golova, the sons of Semen Zvenigorodskii.
>
> Prince Vasilii himself has had an ailment with his foot [*noshkoi bolen*] since the fall, since the Feast of St. Nicholas. The father and mother have had no other ailments or illnesses.[74]

The document begins with a description of the candidate's physical features. The candidate's hair and eye color, the shape of her nose, and figure are briefly noted, then Mezetskii reports on the candidate's medical history, which, but for one childhood bout with a fever, included no noteworthy illnesses. This first paragraph is designed, it seems, to affirm that the candidate meets the base qualifications—acceptable looks and good health.

The next paragraph, the longest one in the document, provides a remarkably detailed description of the candidate's kinship ties. That this report should include this material at all is itself very telling since this is a feature of bridal candidates that is totally ignored by foreign travelers and in official wedding documents. Interesting, too, is the focus of the genealogy. The investigators seem to have been most curious about Ovdot'ia's female kin—her mother, sisters, and affines. Recorded here, for example, are the names of Ovdot'ia's sisters' husbands, and the names of Ovdot'ia's birth-mother's clan and her step-relatives. The fixation on relatives via females contrasts with the genealogies that courtier families compiled and inserted in the Genealogical Books (*Rodoslovnye knigi*), which were arranged rigidly by agnatic lines and which did not include, in the main, the names of wives or daughters.[75] The investigators thus seem to have been charged with supplementing the genealogies of candidates that were already available in the Genealogical Books. That the bridal search panel focused so intently on relatives by marriage suggests that they were interested in assembling a list of families that had connections with the Gundorovs. This particular investigation found links between the Gundorovs and the Zvenigorodskiis, Buturlins, Dement'evs, and Godunovs (see chart 2.1).[76] Since it was assumed and expected that the bride would bring many of her relatives and in-laws with her into the Kremlin, and that many of them would shortly assume prominent positions at the court,[77] it may be that the investigators wanted to know whom a given candidate might bring along with her should she become tsaritsa.

CHART 2.1. Kinship Investigation of Ovdot'ia Gundorova, 1547

(unless otherwise indicated, the chart includes only those listed in the source.)

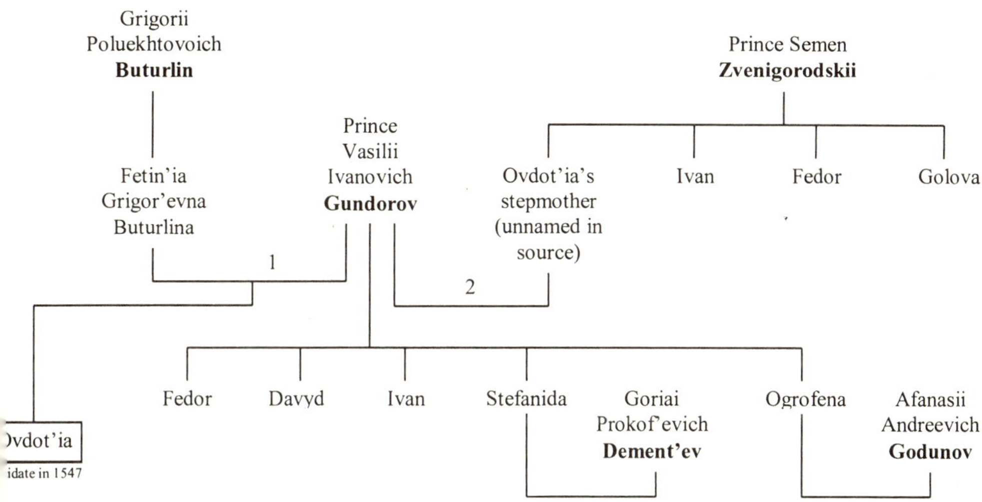

The report on Gundorova closes by returning to the question of health, this time to the health of her parents. The document makes it clear that this information, like the genealogies, was obtained from extensive interviews with the candidate and her relatives. What is remarkable in this report is that, despite all the thoroughness of the interviews, no attempt was made to describe or assess the candidate's character, morals, or religious devotions. This is, of course, in stark contrast to the emphasis we find in many foreigners' accounts and in the official Muscovite descriptions of weddings. Good health, agreeable looks, and the right relatives—these were the priorities of Muscovite royal bride selection.

Seventeenth-century bride-shows displayed the same priorities. While we do not have the same kind of rich documentary evidence that survives for Vasilii III's or Ivan IV's weddings, it is nonetheless clear that the same priorities guided the investigations into potential brides for Tsar Mikhail Romanov in 1624 and 1626. The inventory of the archive of the Foreign Office includes a list of genealogies that appear to have been produced from the background investigations of prospective brides for the first Romanov tsar—investigations very much like the one conducted of Ovdot'ia Gundorova. These genealogies, which are no longer extant, were preserved in and among other wedding documents in the "box" (*iashchik*) of council secretary (*dumnyi d'iak*) Ivan T. Gramotin, the head of the Foreign Office and the organizer of Mikhail Romanov's two weddings.[78] Listed in the inventory are "3 draft rolls (*stolbtsy*), in Ivan Gramotin's hand, and in them are written interviews (*rosprosy*) about the families of Vasilii Barbashin, Vasilii and Grigorii Shestov, Prince Dmitrii Masal'skii and Prince Fedor Eletskii." Also here are a memorandum (*pamiat'*) about the kinship ties (*rodstvo*) of the Streshnevs, also written by Gramotin, and various notes (*vypiski*) and genealogical rosters (*rospistsy* and *rospisi*) about the Pozharskiis, Shchelkalovs, Dolgorukovs, Bolkhovskiis, Volkonskiis, Trakhaniotovs, Eletskiis, and Proestevs—many of which were written or edited by Ivan Gramotin.[79]

That these genealogical reports and rosters should be found next to wedding documents and in the possession of (and often authored or edited by) the "master of ceremonies" for the tsar's weddings suggests that these families had been involved in the bride-shows in 1624 and 1626—either as families with suitable daughters or as families related to families with suitable daughters. Thus, among the documents listed in the inventory are genealogies of the Dolgorukovs, the family of Tsar Mikhail's first wife. Here also are genealogies for the Barbashins, Eletskiis, and Shestovs—families related to the father of the Dolgorukov tsaritsa, Prince Vladimir Timofeevich Dolgorukov, and which may have themselves provided bridal candidates in 1624 or 1626.[80] The Shestovs listed in the inventory are the grandfather (Vasilii) and great-uncle (Grigorii) of Mikhail's mother, Kseniia Ivanovna Shestova (the nun Marfa), who had links with the Dolgorukovs. The genealogy of the Streshnevs—the family of Mikhail Romanov's second wife—was also investigated. The other families mentioned (Pozharskiis, Shchelkalovs, Bolkhovskiis, Volkonskiis, Trakhaniotovs, Proestevs, and so on) may have provided alternative candidates to Dolgorukova and Streshneva, and so they were investigated, as well. The inventory therefore provides a partial list of the families that supplied candidates for one or both of the bride-shows for Tsar Mikhail Fedorovich. Clearly, bride selection was a cold calculus that allowed little room for love or libido. The winner of a bride-show was not necessarily the "fairest in the land" but, rather, the one who had passed rigorous investigations into her kinship ties.

Prospective Bride Lists

While the 1626 archival inventory provides a list of some families that had been investigated as potential royal in-laws, the actual names of the candidates are not included. In fact, except for the chance survival of the report on the investigation of Gundorova in 1547, we know the names of no other sixteenth-century bridal candidates, except, of course, for the winners. The situation is better for the seventeenth century. Two lists of bridal candidates survive. The first is a list of 70 young women from 58 different clans who had been presented to Tsar Aleksei Mikhailovich between November 28, 1669 (just a few months after the death of his first wife), and April 17, 1670 (see Appendix B).[81] The second is a list of gifts presented on August 14, 1680, to the young women who had participated in a bride-show arranged to find the first wife of Tsar Fedor Alekseevich (see Appendix C).[82] It contains the names of 18 young women from 15 different clans. A close analysis of these lists, with particular attention to the social origins, service careers, and kinship ties of the families included in them, reveals the types of families tapped for candidacy in royal bride searches (and those that were not).

The document listing the young women assembled before Tsar Aleksei Mikhailovich is arranged chronologically, with the names of the candidates organized by the date they were presented to the tsar. Between November 1669 and April 1670, Tsar Aleksei conducted eighteen separate sessions, sometimes with as many as eight candidates at a time, sometimes only one. Most of the candidates were drawn from Moscow, but there were candidates also drawn from servitor families from Novgorod, Suzdal', Kostroma, Riazan', and Vladimir (though some of these candidates may have been living with relatives in Moscow at the time). The document also provides the identity of each candidate's father or guardian.

The social background of the prospective brides for Tsar Aleksei is remarkably uniform. Absent from the list are the daughters of any of the 26 men who held boyar rank at the time of the bride-shows, and the daughters of any *okol'nichii* (between 16 and 19 men at the time of the bride-shows). Two-thirds of the families represented on this list (39 of the 58 families listed, representing 44 of the 70 young women) never had a member reach Duma rank in the seventeenth century.[83] To be sure, many of these families are recorded in military muster rolls and court rosters as having members who served as military governors (*voevody*), tablemen (*stol'niki*), adjutants (*striapchie*), Moscow gentry (*Moskovskie dvoriane*), and commanders of musketeer formations (*streletskie golova*). These were not, certainly, unknown families. Some of them, like the Kolychevs, had held high rank in the sixteenth century but had fallen to the political periphery by the seventeenth. Only 10 of the 58 families (representing 16 of the 70 young women) had a family member who had reached Duma rank before 1671, and even here the connection to their prominent ancestor was distant.[84] For example, the list includes Anna and Nastas'ia, granddaughters of Erofei/Almaz Ivanovich Ivanov, a *dumnyi d'iak* and Tsar Aleksei Mikhailovich's keeper of the seal (*pechatnik*).[85] Similarly, it includes a granddaughter of the *dumnyi dvorianin* and treasurer (*kaznachei*) Bogdan Dubrovskii.[86] The only prospective bride represented on this list who had family members in the highest Duma ranks before (and after) the bride-show was the Dolgorukov candidate, Anna.[87] The daughter of Prince Grigorii Daniilovich Dolgorukov, Anna came from a lineage that had been producing boyars since the turn of the seventeenth century.[88] While her father never himself had attained the highest court ranks (he was only a *stol'nik*), Anna's grandfather Daniil and her first cousin Prince Fedor Fedorovich had been *okol'nichie*. More distant relatives Prince Iurii Alekseevich and Prince Dmitrii Alekseevich had attained boyar rank in mid-century and numbered among the most important court figures of the time.[89] Anna Dolgorukova is the only "outlier" on this list of middle-tier families.

The list of young women who received gifts for their participation in the bride-show for Tsar Fedor Alekseevich in 1680 presents a somewhat different field of candidates in terms of social background. Slightly more than half of the families listed (8 of 15 families, representing 10 of the 18 women) had members who had reached Duma rank before the bride-show.[90] Four families (representing 4 women) never attained Duma rank.[91] The remaining 3 families would eventually place a member in the Duma, but only in the years after the bride-show.[92] Three of the 18 young women listed were the daughters of important boyars—Anna and Marfa, the daughters of Prince Fedor Fedorovich Kurakin, and Vasilisa, the daughter of Ivan Bogdanovich Khitrovo. Both men were the young tsar's "tutors," or *diad'ki*.[93] This privileged position may have provided them with the influence to arrange for their daughters' inclusion in the bride-show. It is not the case, however, that the bride-show had been opened up generally to boyars' daughters. Otherwise, we would expect to see candidates put forward by the other 39 boyars in 1680. One of the young women on the list (who is unnamed) was the daughter of *okol'nichii* Prince Daniil Stepanovich Veliko-Gagin. Except for Anna, Marfa, Vasilisa, and the unnamed Veliko-Gagina, the remainder of the candidates (14 girls) were the daughters of *stol'niki*. Thus, as we have seen was the case with Aleksei's list, Fedor's bride-show was dominated by middle-tier families; but it did include a few whose families occupied places in the inner circle at court. Despite the broader choices available to him, Tsar Fedor Alekseevich's choice was nonetheless traditional, falling on Agafiia Grushetskaia, the scion of a rather undistinguished servitor family.[94]

Closer inspection of the two lists of bridal candidates provides clues about the role kinship played in the bride-show. Several families had more than one representative in the bride-shows. Aleksei Mikhailovich's list includes two Gagarin sisters, two Leont'evs, two Eropkins, two Uvarov sisters, two Bunin sisters, two pairs of Tol'stoi sisters, two Kolemin sisters, and three Khotetovskii sisters. Fedor's list similarly includes, in addition to the two Kurakin sisters already mentioned, two Zvenigorodskii first cousins and two Izmailov first cousins. Three families had representatives on both lists. The Poltevs and Verderevskiis each presented a candidate in both 1669–1670 and 1680, and Vikula Fedorovich Izvol'skii had a daughter on both lists.[95]

Many of the families on these lists were related to each other by marriage. Mavra Vasil'evna Kolycheva (the sister of Marfa, a candidate in the 1669–1670 bride-show) married Semen Zvenigorodskii, whose brother Aleksei had a daughter who participated in the 1680 bride-show. Mavra's kinsman Ivan Ivanovich Kolychev was married to Kseniia Khotetovskaia, whose three nieces Nastas'ia, Iulianiia, and Anisiia all participated in the 1669–1670 bride-shows. Semen Zvenigorodskii married a second time around 1649. His bride was Akulina Averkievna Boltina, with whom he had a daughter who was a candidate in 1680 and whose sister Agrafena had been a candidate in the 1669–1670 bride-shows. Thus, seven candidates in these two bride-shows were all linked in a cluster of kinship that joined four clans—the Khotetovskiis, Kolychevs, Zvenigorodskiis, and Boltins. The Kolychevs were the crucial link. They were one of the families on the list that had reached Duma rank in the years before the bride-shows but were not, one would certainly say, a first-tier family anymore. The Kolychevs did, however, have ties to important boyar clans.

Ivan Ivanovich Kolychev, the husband of Kseniia Khotetovskaia, was himself the son of Ivan Kolychev and Kseniia Cherkasskaia, and through this Cherkasskii marriage, the Kolychevs were linked to the Sheremetevs and even the Romanovs themselves (see chart 2.2).[96] The lists contain other related families as well. The Satin and Korenev candidates in the 1669–1670 bride-show were related to each other by marriage.[97] The Polev and Izmailov candidates in the 1680 bride-show were related to the Saltykov and Buturlin boyars, respectively.[98] And indeed, Tsar Aleksei Mikhailovich's pick in 1671, Natal'ia Naryshkina, had ties to the two Leont'ev candidates, the family of Natal'ia's mother, and to Artemon Sergeevich Matveev, the tsar's favorite.[99]

The image of intertwining kinship clusters linking the families on these prospective bride lists suggests how the tsar's choice played out in court politics. Had Tsar Aleksei in 1669–1670 chosen one of the three Khotetovskii women or the Boltina candidate, the new bride would have brought in tow a herd of in-laws to court, all upstarts to be sure. But the real winners would have been the Kolychevs, who had kinship ties to all

CHART 2.2. Kinship Ties of Seven Bridal Candidates

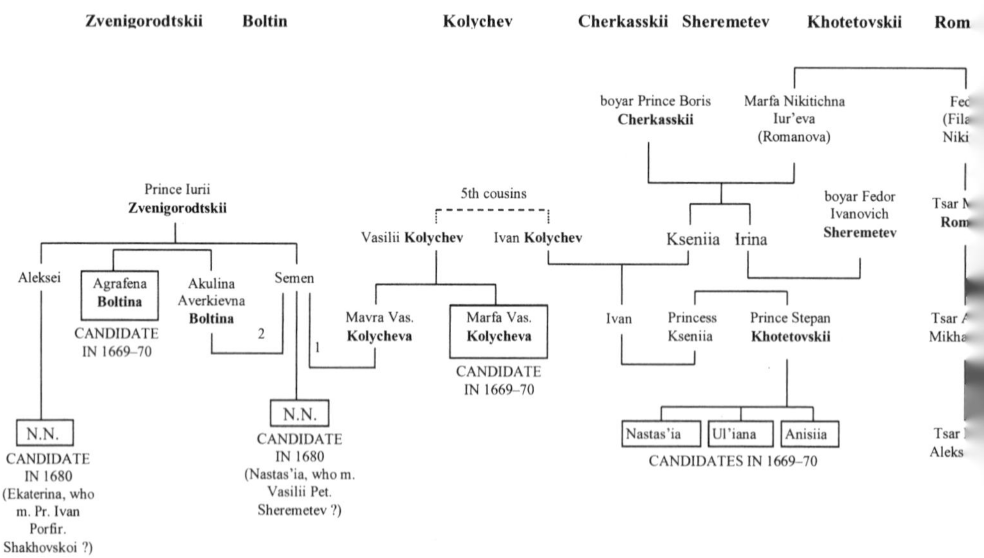

four candidates. It is easy to imagine how Kolychev fortunes, which had lain dormant for nearly a century, might have been entirely turned around by the tsar's marriage to one of these women, and how the Kolychevs' preexisting ties to the Cherkasskiis and Sheremetevs, which had up to then failed to secure very much status or rank at court for them, might all of a sudden become vital links to the inner circle of the ruler's court.

It is likely that at least some of the families on these prospective bridal lists were placed there precisely because of their kinship ties with other clans—or, as we have already seen could be the case, because of an absence of kinship ties with particular families (as in the example from 1526 of the Shcheniatevs and Pleshcheevs). A candidate's kinship ties also explain the appearance in both lists of multiple candidates from one clan. Once a family with the right kinship profile was identified, all its eligible daughters were evidently tapped for the bride-show. The marked increase in representation of high-ranking families in Tsar Fedor's list compared to Tsar Aleksei's a decade before might be related to the "inflation of honors"—the expansion of the rolls of boyars and other Duma ranks—that Crummey found precisely in the 1670s and 1680s.[100] It may also be a symptom of the gradual obsolescence of the bride-show toward the end of the seventeenth century as the court found many of its former rituals ill-suited to the new political environment at court and gradually eliminated them.[101] The old rules were breaking down, including perhaps the most important one for bride-shows, the one that excluded the great clans from participating.

The remarkable thing about both lists, finally, is the way the social backgrounds of the winners (Naryshkina and Grushetskaia) so closely matched the backgrounds of the other candidates in their bride-shows. The candidates—winners and losers alike—were nearly all from the same, fairly narrow social background: mid-level servitor families. Of the 27 brides (or prospective brides) picked by Russian dynasts in the sixteenth and seventeenth centuries, only three were the daughters of boyars (Iulianiia Paletskaia, Elena Sheremeteva, and Mariia Dolgorukova) and only four others were from non-boyar branches of established boyar clans (Solomoniia Saburova, Anastasiia Iur'eva, Evdokiia Saburova, and Praskov'ia Saltykova). The rest were from families whose fame came later, as a result of their status as royal in-laws (see table 2.2).

TABLE 2.2.

THE BACKGROUNDS OF MUSCOVITE ROYAL CONSORTS

Date of Wedding	Groom	Bride	Background of Bride
1505	Vasilii III	Solomoniia Saburova	non-boyar line of boyar clan
1526	Vasilii III	Elena Glinskaia	foreigner/resident alien
1533	Andrei Staritskii	Efrosiniia Khovanskaia	provincial gentry
1547	Ivan IV	Anastasiia Iur'eva	non-boyar line of boyar clan
1547	Iurii Vasil'evich	Iulianiia Paletskaia	daughter of boyar
1549	Vladimir Staritskii	Evdokiia Nagaia	provincial gentry
1555	Vladimir Staritskii	Evdokiia Odoevskaia	provincial gentry
1561	Ivan IV	Mariia Cherkasskaia	foreigner
1571	Ivan IV	Marfa Sobakina	provincial gentry
1571	Ivan Ivanovich	Evdokiia Saburova	non-boyar line of boyar clan
1572	Ivan IV	Anna Koltovskaia	provincial gentry
1575	Ivan IV	Anna Vasil'chikova	provincial gentry
1575	Ivan Ivanovich	Pelageia Petrova-Solovaia	provincial gentry
1575	Fedor Ivanovich	Irina Godunova	sister of high-ranking courtier
1577	Ivan IV	Vasilisa "Melent'eva"	provincial gentry
1580	Ivan IV	Mariia Nagaia	courtiers
1580	Ivan Ivanovich	Elena Sheremeteva	daughter of boyar
1616	Mikhail Fedorovich	Mariia Khlopova	provincial gentry
1626	Mikhail Fedorovich	Mariia Dolgorukova	daughter of boyar
1626	Mikhail Fedorovich	Evdokiia Streshneva	provincial gentry
1647	Aleksei Mikhailovich	Efimiia Vsevolozhskaia	provincial gentry
1648	Aleksei Mikhailovich	Mariia Miloslavskaia	provincial gentry
1671	Aleksei Mikhailovich	Natalia Naryshkina	provincial gentry
1680	Fedor III Alekseevich	Agafiia Grushetskaia	provincial gentry
1682	Fedor III Alekseevich	Marfa Apraksina	provincial gentry
1684	Ivan V Alekseevich	Praskov'ia Saltykova	non-boyar line of boyar clan
1689	Peter I	Evdokiia Lopukhina	provincial gentry

It is no wonder that there is such social uniformity on these prospective bride lists. The daughters of peasants and priests were not represented at these bride-shows because, as we have seen, they were not invited to them. Bride-shows were far from open contests where young women of all social backgrounds vied on equal terms for a shot at the Terem. Brides were plucked out of a specific layer of the elite and drawn into the center of the court by the magnetic pull of the bride-show and subsequent wedding, the way the Sun's gravity plucks new comets out of the Kuiper Belt and into the inner solar system. Thus, Russian tsars married beneath themselves not because they fell in love time and again with women who just happened to be from the middle ranks or the service elite, but because it was by design that they should do so.

Did Russian tsars pick their brides on their own, by themselves? The evidence already presented suggests overwhelmingly that they did not. The fact that it was members of the great clans at court who conducted the regional bride-shows; that they and their wives had vastly reduced the pool of candidates by stages before most royal grooms ever saw a single candidate; that genealogy and kinship figured so centrally in the investigations of bridal candidates; and, finally, that the tsars' choices at bride-shows were largely limited to families of a certain social background—all this points to a collaborative decision. Returning to the preliminary bride-shows held for Ivan IV and to the composition of the selection commissions that oversaw the regional investigations, we find that all of the courtiers sent out from Moscow to the provincial towns were younger members of boyar clans, some of whom would later become boyars themselves (see, again, table 2.1).[102] These younger courtiers worked with the boyars and *okol'nichie* already posted in the towns. The first and second stages of the bride-show—the initial inspection of candidates, their physical examinations, and the reduction of the number to a handful of finalists—were firmly in the hands of the boyar clans. With their power and status so determined by the marriage of the ruler, it is hard to imagine how it could have been otherwise.

Remaking the Bride's Identity

After the bride-show, the next time the bride-to-be is encountered in the sources is when she participates in a set of rituals designed to transform her identity from the daughter of a middle-level servitor into a grand princess or tsaritsa. These rituals are reported in the sources unevenly across the sixteenth and seventeenth centuries, and so, how these rituals might have been performed exactly (processions? a blessing by a priest? speeches?) remains largely concealed from view. But the glimpses and hints in the sources that we do have provide a clear enough image of them to reconstruct at least the purpose of these rituals: the remaking the bride's identity.

The first set of these transformative rituals was the bestowing on the bride-to-be of the title tsarevna (daughter of a tsar) and her formal entry into the Terem. The bestowal of the title tsarevna is recorded for only one sixteenth-century marriage (Tsarevich Ivan Ivanovich and Evdokiia Saburova in 1571), but it is likely that the ritual was performed at other weddings as well.[103] Both the new title and the formal entry into the Terem are recorded for the second wedding of Tsar Mikhail Fedorovich, for both weddings of Tsar Aleksei Mikhailovich, and for the first wedding of Tsar Fedor Alekseevich.[104] The ceremonial (*chin*) for the wedding of Aleksei Mikhailovich and Mariia Miloslavskaia provides a fairly skeletal description of the event, but it illustrates that both rituals seem to have been performed at the same time: "On Friday, two days before the sovereign's wedding, Mariia Il'ichna was, on the sovereign's command, entered into the tsaritsa's apartments and they called her tsarevna [*narekli ee gosudarynoiu tsarevnoiu*]."[105]

It seems likely that the bestowal of the fictive title tsarevna began after 1526. A fragment of the original ceremonial for the 1526 wedding of Grand Prince Vasilii III and Princess Elena Glinskaia consistently refers to the bride as princess (*kniazhna*)—the title she was born with—up until the wedding service, after which she is referred to as grand princess (*velikaia kniaginia*), her title as consort of Vasilii III.[106] Ivan IV's first wedding, to Anastasiia Iur'eva in 1547, makes no mention either of a new title for the bride or a grand entry into the Terem. The three extant draft wedding musters (*razriady*) consistently refer to the bride as grand princess (and, curiously, to the groom, Ivan IV, as grand prince, not tsar).[107] The weddings of collateral members of the dynasty—Andrei Staritskii (in 1533), Iurii Vasil'evich (in 1547), and Vladimir Staritskii (in 1549 and 1555)—likewise omit any mention of the ritual, though this is probably because, as collaterals, the fiction of an equal marriage was less important. Thus, the custom of granting the title tsarevna to the bride may have been developed only around the time of its first clear appearance: in 1571, with the wedding of Tsarevich Ivan Ivanovich (see table 2.3).

TABLE 2.3.

REMAKING THE BRIDE'S IDENTITY

		NEW FIRST NAMES	
itle "Tsarevna"	Entry into the Terem	Of the Bride	Of the Bride's Father
571) Evdokiia Saburova d Tsarevich Ivan Ivanovich			
		(1572) Marfa Sobakina (→ Marfa?) and Ivan IV	
		(1575) Pelageia → Feodosiia Petrova-Solovaia (nun Praskov'ia) and Tsarevich Ivan Ivanovich	
		(1607) Ekaterina → Mariia Buinosova-Rostovskaia (nun Elena) and Vasilii Shuiskii	
516) Mariia/Nastas'ia lopova and Mikhail manov disgraced	In the Kremlin 6 weeks before	Mariia → Nastas'ia	
526) Evdokiia Streshneva d Mikhail Romanov	3 days before wedding		
47) Efimiia evolozhskaia and eksei Mikhailovich	3 days before wedding		Raf → Fedor
48) Mariia Miloslavskaia Aleksei Mikhailovich	2 days (reduced from 3 days)		
71) Natal'ia Naryshkina Aleksei Mikhailovich	1 day before wedding		
80) Agafiia Grushetskaia Fedor Alekseevich	1 day before wedding		
			(1684) Aleksandr → Fedor Saltykov, father of Praskov'ia, wife of Ivan V
			(1689) Illarion → Fedor Lopukhin, father of Evdokiia, wife of Peter I

As for the dating of the ritual of the formal entry into the Terem, we can again only speculate. Attested incidences of the ritual appear only in the seventeenth century, but it may well have sixteenth-century origins. The choreography of Muscovite royal weddings required that the bride and her attendants be in the Kremlin before the beginning of the wedding ritual. The opening scenes of sixteenth- and seventeenth-century weddings all locate the bride having already been installed in the Terem, waiting to be summoned to the Golden Hall or Palace of Facets (depending on the wedding), where the banquets were to take place. Whether the brides and their families got there through a formal entry ritual or otherwise is not stated in the sources, but it is hard to imagine that it would have been done without some procession or other ceremony.

Another ritual that evolved alongside the new title and the formal entry was the bride's adoption of a new, royal name. After the death of Ivan IV's third bride, Marfa Sobakina, on November 13, 1572 (just two weeks after the wedding), the tsar petitioned church hierarchs for permission to marry a fourth time, arguing that "the Devil, who hates the good, incited many of those around me to hate Tsaritsa Marfa while she was still a maiden, the royal name only having been bestowed upon her [*tochiiu imia tsarskoe vozlozheno na nee*], and evil poison was administered to her."[108] No other name for Sobakina is known for her but Marfa; so either Marfa was her royal name and her birth name is unknown to us, or, and this is only speculation, as tsaritsa she took the same royal name as her birth name with, perhaps, a new patron saint, which would provide a real and meaningful differentiation between her old and new identities.

Other cases of name changes are clearer. Tsarevich Ivan Ivanovich's second wife, Pelageia Petrova-Solovaia, took the name Feodosiia at the time of their wedding in 1575. Tsar Vasilii Shuiskii's (second) bride, Ekaterina Buinosova-Rostovskaia, took the name Mariia in 1607; and Tsar Mikhail Fedorovich's first choice for a bride, Mariia Khlopova, took the name Nastas'ia (i.e., Anastasiia) in 1616.[109] When Pelageia/Feodosiia Petrova-Solovaia and Ekaterina/Mariia Buinosova-Rostovskaia were later tonsured nuns, they yet again took new (monastic) names. To be given a new name was part and parcel of becoming a monk or a nun, and the new name was again about the remaking of identity (in this case, from tsaritsa to nun). Usually, monastic names began with the same first letter as one's secular name. It is therefore perhaps significant that both of these royal brides were given monastic names that began with the same letters as their birth names, not their royal names. Thus, Pelageia/Feodosiia became Praskov'ia, and Ekaterina/Mariia became Elena. These two royal women, then, remade their identities twice over the span of their lifetimes (from daughter of a Muscovite courtier to tsaritsa, and from tsaritsa to monastic), and each new identity was signaled by the adoption of a new name (and, presumably, a new patron saint and name day).

The remaking of identities extended, in three known cases, even to the fathers of the brides: Raf Vsevolozhskii, the father of Aleksei Mikhailovich's first choice for a bride, Efimiia; Aleksandr Saltykov, the father of Ivan V's wife, Praskov'ia; and Illarion Lopukhin, the father of Evdokiia, Peter I the Great's first wife. These all took the name Fedor upon the selection of their daughters in bride-shows.[110] It was not, however, the fathers' identities that were remade by these new names so much as it was their daughters'. The actual purpose of the fathers' new names may have been to change the bride's patronymic and thereby distance her fictively from her kin even more than her new title or place of residence would. Zabelin points out that when the bride was given the title tsarevna and entered into the Terem, her relationship with her relatives was symbolically altered forever: "From that moment, the personality of the royal bride-to-be took on royal significance and was separated entirely from the ruler's other subjects and from the midst of her own family such that even her father no longer called her his daughter, and her relatives could not call her their kin."[111] If this is so, then the name Fedor was well chosen, since its meaning—"God's gift" (a Slavicization of Greek Θεόδωρος, "Theodōrus")—might easily confer a generic ancestry upon a tsarevna with the patronymic Fedorovna.[112]

The sources suggest that the selection of a winner in a bride-show, her formal entry into the Terem, and the adoption of her new title and, sometimes, her new name all happened in fairly rapid succession, just days before the wedding. Not more than a month separated Prince Andrei Staritskii's choice of his bride in January 1533 from his wedding on February 2. Sources for Ivan IV's first wedding show that regional bride-shows were taking place in December 1546 through to the end of January 1547, when the selection was made. The wedding followed on February 3. The search for bridal candidates for Ivan IV's brother Iurii Vasil'evich was still going on in October 1547 and the wedding took place on November 3. Ivan IV's cousin Vladimir Staritskii chose his first bride on May 24, 1549, and the wedding took place on May 31, exactly one week later.

The dizzying speed between a bride's selection and her nuptials seems also to have been the case for seventeenth-century weddings. Mikhail Romanov's second bride, Evdokiia Streshneva, was installed in the Terem three days before the wedding. Three days is also the interval found in the documents prepared for Tsar Aleksei Mikhailovich's aborted marriage to Efimiia Vsevolozhskaia in 1647.[113] From this point on, the interval narrows even more. Early drafts of Tsar Aleksei's marriage to Mariia Miloslavskaia in 1648 report that she, too, was supposed to be installed three days before the wedding, but later drafts have her entering the Terem only two days before.[114] Both Natal'ia Naryshkina, Tsar Aleksei's second wife, and Agafiia Grushetskaia, Tsar Fedor III's first, were installed in the Terem and given the title tsarevna only one day before the wedding.[115] It is only a guess, but shortening the time between the bride-show and the wedding was probably a reaction to the conspiracies that came to be routine in the seventeenth century (see Chapter 5). The less time the bride was in the Terem, the less access conspirators had to her. But whether the interval was long or short, the purpose of the rituals surrounding the bride's identity is clear—all of these rituals combined to remake the bride's identity from parvenue to princess.

It remains for us to place the bride-show custom within the larger political context. What does our analysis of the documents pertaining to bride-shows reveal about the nature of the political system in Muscovy and the limits of monarchical power? How did the ritual of the bride-show reflect the unarticulated rules of the "game of politics" at the Muscovite court?

Far from affirming the unlimited and "all-Russian" nature of Muscovite monarchical power, as Zabelin suggested, the bride-show actually reveals more clearly than anything else the "façade of autocracy." It seems that the "trick" of bride selection in Muscovy was the careful compiling of the list of candidates from which the tsar would choose his bride. If the boyars and courtiers in charge of the process had done their homework (and the surviving evidence of extensive interviews and genealogical investigations suggests that they usually had), then the tsar probably could freely choose from the list of young women presented to him, according to his own preferences. Any choice from such well-crafted lists tended already to have the approval of most members of the boyar aristocracy.

That the tsar chose his bride from a pool of candidates handpicked for him, not from all eligible young girls in the kingdom; that this pool of candidates should share such similar profiles and backgrounds; and that kinship should play as much a role as health and good looks in the composition of prospective bride lists—all this requires a modulated view of monarchical power in Muscovy. As Chester Dunning has put it: "Boyars and princes, along with the church, exalted the grand prince of Moscow as a sovereign and an autocrat, but the actual political system they invented may have been, at least in the beginning, far more collegial and oligarchic than any of them ever admitted to foreigners or even to Russians outside the highest court circles."[116] This assertion is certainly buttressed by the analysis of chancellery documents produced for bride-shows. Monarchical power in Muscovy must be viewed within the context of a boyar oligarchy that played a prominent role in the selection of the ruler's consort. And it did so, clearly, not by infringing on royal prerogatives or challenging monarchical power but, rather, as a function of consensus and cooperation in a unified political order where most of the players were already in-laws with each other. In this way, Zabelin was, in a sense, at least half right: the bride-show was a means of projecting the image of the autocratic, All-Russian tsar—though this image had little to do with what was actually going on at bride-shows or with the actual nature of monarchical power in Muscovy.

While there are still many questions about the way the bride-show was performed over the course of the sixteenth and seventeenth centuries, the surviving sources show that the entire spectacle was an extension of the larger kinship-based political system in Muscovy. Kinship calculations were central to the process of finding a bride for the tsar—the chief concern of the boyar advisors of the royal groom, after having first established the health of the candidate pool. Morality and Christian piety played no role in the bride-show, so far as the chancellery documents reveal, probably because any aspects of personality were distant concerns as compared to finding a bride who would produce lots of heirs and not disrupt the balance of factions at court. Bride selection was a cold calculation, where the groom's preferences played second fiddle to the political concerns of his advisors and the good of the dynasty. That being so, picking a bride for the tsar was high politics, a deadly game that settled in large measure who moved in the closest orbits around the tsar as much as it did who occupied the tsar's bed. As Edward Keenan put it so aptly, it was "during the process of betrothal of an heir or royal daughter that one heard the thud of limp bodies in the Kremlin."[117] It is to the marriage politics that produced those "thuds" that we now turn.

Litsevoi letopisnyi svod (*Bride-Show for Ivan the Terrible*).

A. Abramov. *Vybor nevesty tsaria Alekseia Mikhailovicha* [*Selection of a Bride by Tsar Aleksei Mikhailovich*] (1882). Chromolithograph.

Il'ia Efimovich Repin (1844–1930). *Vybor velikokniazheskoi nevestoi* [*The Grand Prince Picks a Bride*] (1884–1887). Oil on canvas.

Konstantin Egorovich Makovskii (1839–1915). *Vybor nevesty tsarem Alekseem Mikhailovichem* [*Tsar Aleksei Mikhailovich Selects a Bride*] (1887). Oil on canvas.

Grigorii Semenovich Sedov (1836–1886). *Vybor nevesty tsarem Alekseem Mikhailovichem* [*Tsar Aleksei Mikhailovich Selects His Bride*] (1882). Oil on canvas.

Engraver El'val'. *Izbranie Natal'i Kirillovny Naryshkinoi nevestoi tsaria Alekseia Mikhailovicha (1670)* [*Selection of Natal'ia Kirillovna Naryshkina as the Bride of Tsar Aleksei Mikhailovich (1670)*] (early 1840s). Engraving. (First published in N. P. Lambin, *Istoriia Petra velikogo* [St. Petersburg: Tip. F. I. El'snera, 1844], 44.)

Chapter 3

"If You Marry a Second Time, You Will Have an Evil Child Born to You"

Bride-Shows and Muscovite Political Culture

> If you do this thing, if you cast aside your first wife and marry a second in order to have a son born to you, you will be committing adultery, I say again, adultery! And if God, Who loves mankind, should give you a son, and if you then should say to yourself, "This is my heir, the sovereign of our *tsarstvo*," do not believe it. Because of your fornication, you will be given children who as tsar will be the destruction of your *tsarstvo*....And your *tsarstvo* will be filled with tears and terror, and in that time there will be killing, and great suffering from the *Sarapadasiistii* [*sic*] people, and unruly youth, and some will be broken on the wheel, and others will have their heads cut off, and those in exile will be shown no mercy, and many cities will be consumed in flames.[1]

It is said that Patriarch Mark of Jerusalem wrote the above words, half prophecy and half curse, when he learned of Vasilii III's intentions to send Solomoniia, his childless wife of twenty years (the winner of the first bride-show) to a monastery so he would be free to remarry in hopes of fathering an heir. In a version of the passage published by Karamzin, the ominous prophecy is put more succinctly: "If you marry a second time, you will have an evil child born to you."[2]

This scathing condemnation of Vasilii III's decision to remarry, taken from the *Extract on the Second Wedding of Vasilii III* (*Vypis' o vtorom brake Vasiliia III*), was but one of many similar denunciations recorded in this text from patriarchs and venerated monastic elders throughout the Orthodox East.[3] This "evil deed," these churchmen warn, will only come back to haunt the grand prince and the whole of Muscovy. Near-apocalyptic conditions will result, as the crimes of the grand prince's bed take on cosmic significance. In fact, these horrific portents will be realized, it is prophesied, at the hand of the very child born of this illicit marriage.

The *Extract* has attracted the attention of many prominent medieval historians and textual scholars, but there remains even now considerable disagreement on its dating. While all agree that the archetype of this text was composed well after the events it describes (making it, in Zimin's words, a "freakish jumble of factual and completely false information"),[4] theories of the text's dating have varied greatly: from the early years of Ivan IV's reign (M. N. Tikhomirov and S. O. Shmidt), to the second half of Ivan IV's reign (S. A. Belokurov, E. E. Golubinskaia, N. A. Kazakova), to the very end of the sixteenth century and beginning of the seventeenth (A. A. Zimin, M. D. Kagan).[5] It is hard not to agree with those who have suggested that the vigorous attacks on remarriage in the *Extract*, though ostensibly aimed at Vasilii III, were in point of fact targeted more at Ivan IV.[6] The text was likely written after Ivan IV's sacking of Novgorod in 1570 and not long after (perhaps during) the controversies over his third and fourth marriages (in 1571 and 1572, respectively). The *Extract* appeared at the moment when the "evil child" of the second bed—Ivan IV, who certainly reigned over a Muscovy "filled with tears and terror"—was himself causing scandal and controversy with his own plans to remarry, just as his father had.

The remarriage controversies of father and son bookend a period when the new dynastic marriage system, based on a preference for domestic brides and the bride-show, was still being parsed out. Vasilii III and his boyars did not, naturally enough, devise in 1505 a new dynastic marriage system in one fell swoop. Questions about how the bride-show fitted in the political culture of the court remained unanswered. Was the bride-show to be a onetime happening, or was it to be adopted as the usual way to find a bride for the tsar? Was the bride-show to be limited to rulers and heirs-apparent, as in the Byzantine Empire, or could it also be used for the tsar's siblings and younger sons? Was a bride-show to be arranged only for first marriages, as again was the case in the Byzantine Empire, or could it be employed for second (and subsequent) weddings, as well? As this chapter will show, the sixteenth century provided ample opportunities to raise and resolve these questions, since it was then that the dynasty had collaterals, younger sons and cousins, as well as a tsar who married and remarried more than any other Christian ruler in Europe, besting even the hexagamous Henry VIII. It was between 1525, in the run-up to Vasilii III's second marriage, and 1571, in the run-up to Ivan IV's third, that the political and symbolic permutations of the bride-show in Muscovite political culture would come into focus.

Vasilii III and Elena Glinskaia

On November 28, 1525, Grand Prince Vasilii III compelled his wife of twenty years, Solomoniia Saburova, to take the veil "because of her infertility" and, evidently, against her will.[7] The move would come at a cost, however. While the numerous and well-founded objections to the divorce and remarriage of the grand prince in the *Extract on the Second Marriage of Vasilii III* appeared much later and were directed more at son than father, there is ample reason to believe that Vasilii III's marital plans produced shock and open opposition in even the closest quarters around the ruler. Maksim Grek, the Greek monk who came to Muscovy in 1518 and produced some of the most important translations of biblical and other texts, earned the grand prince's enmity by opposing the divorce. His uncomfortably logical arguments against Vasilii III's remarriage surely contributed to his downfall—being hauled up on heresy and other (trumped-up) charges in 1525 and again in 1531.[8] Vassian Patrikeev, whose family had been disgraced in 1499 as part of the succession crisis described in Chapter 1, fared no better for his opposition to the divorcing of Solomoniia. Vassian had been a trusted advisor of Vasilii III, even witnessing the grand prince's 1523 will—a tremendous sign of honor and status—but had earned Vasilii III's disfavor by staunchly opposing the divorce of Solomoniia.[9] The remarriage of Grand Prince Vasilii III was thus no minor moment in the life of the Muscovite court. Not only did it potentially violate sacred canons of the church, it would require an exhausting and complex recalculation of the relationships among the boyars at the court—a reestablishment of the always tenuous balance of boyar clans and allies that had been achieved by the selection of Solomoniia Saburova twenty years before.

But Vasilii III got his way anyhow. Having draped Solomoniia in the monastic habit (*mantiia*), Vasilii III considered himself free to remarry for the sake of the succession—his only apparent motive for taking so drastic and soul-endangering a move. Despite the controversy, Vasilii III apparently felt no qualms about turning again to the bride-show to find a new wife. It was a departure from the bride-show customs of the Byzantines, who—as Treadgold put it in the case of the digamous Emperor Michael II (820–829)—held bride-shows only for a first marriage because they did not want to make a "spectacle of a second marriage."[10] That a bride-show took place in advance of Vasilii's second wedding is amply demonstrated by the text of the surviving memorandum, quoted in Chapter 2, written probably in December 1525 or early January 1526, to *okol'nichii* Ivan Vasil'evich Liatskii and the scribe (*d'iak*) Timofei Klobukov, who were admonished to exclude women of the Shcheniatev and Pleshcheev clans from the bride-show.[11] A bride-show is also suggested in the *Tale of the Second Wedding of Vasilii III* (not to be confused with the *Extract*), written, according to Iu. K. Begunov, between 1526 and 1530, shortly after the events it describes, as a justification for Vasilii III's controversial second marriage.[12] The *Tale* describes how courtiers were dispatched far and wide in search of a bride: "The grand prince sent his boyars and his faithful lords [*vernya velmozha*] to all the cities and towns of his autocratic realm so that they choose for him a maiden fitting [*lepu*] and good-looking [*dobrozrachnu*] and of good intellect [*razumnu*]."[13] The boyars and "lords" came back to Vasilii III lauding their lone, unanimous pick: "'O Tsar [*sic*], nowhere have we found, never in our lives have we seen, nor have our minds ever imagined such a maiden as Elena, the daughter of Prince Vasilii L'vovich Glinskii.'"[14] Vasilii ordered the boyars and lords to bring Elena to the palace so he could see her. Vasilii III evidently briefly interviewed Elena, asking her about herself (*o zhitelstve*), and was impressed by her wise responses. As a result, the "prince became deeply enamored with her because of her beautiful face and youth, and even more so because of her wisdom, because both of these were given to her by God: her good looks and her wisdom. And he ordered that she be called tsaritsa and sovereign [*gosudaryniu*] of all Rus'."[15] The wedding was celebrated on January 21, 1526.[16]

Unlike his first bride, Vasilii III's second was foreign-born, though not a true foreigner. Elena Glinskaia was the daughter of Vasilii "Slepoi" L'vovich Glinskii, a rich and high-ranking Ruthenian nobleman of the

Grand Duchy of Lithuania who, along with his three brothers—Ivan "Mamai," Fedor, and Mikhail "Dorodnyi"—had left the grand duchy and had established themselves in Muscovy in 1508.[17] Vasilii III's selection of Glinskaia was therefore unlike subsequent bride-shows over the next two centuries, since foreigners were not, as far as the extant sources indicate, ever included among the candidates who were paraded before the Muscovite ruler. But courtiers like Liatskii and Klobukov treated Elena Glinskaia—a resident alien—as a domestic candidate, because she had lived in Muscovy for many years. At the time of the bride-show and wedding Elena's father, Vasilii "Slepoi," and uncle Ivan "Mamai" were dead, and another uncle, Mikhail "Dorodnyi," was in prison for having tried to flee to Lithuania in 1514.[18] She had three brothers (Iurii, Ivan, and Mikhail) and two sisters, the nun (*staritsa*) Aleksandra and Mariia, but none had yet forged a marriage alliance with any member of the court elite.[19] These marriage alliances would come, but only in the next decade or two, as Elena's relatives intermarried with many of the most important clans at the court of Ivan IV.[20] In 1525, Elena was probably living with her mother and perhaps her aunt Nastasiia (widow of Ivan Mamai), and her family's prospects were hardly very promising.[21]

Elena Glinskaia represented the best of both worlds, offering the benefits of both a foreign and a domestic bride. As for foreign policy motivations, Elena's candidacy benefited from her clan's genealogical ties with neighboring polities. The Glinskiis claimed descent both from Mamai and from Chinggis Khan, and furthermore, Elena Glinskaia's mother was a member of the Serbian ruling dynasty and thus offered Vasilii III a potentially useful dynastic connection with another Orthodox realm.[22] Domestic concerns were also probably very important motivations for this choice. First, the selection of Elena Glinskaia very nicely suited the boyars around Vasilii III—the "boyars and great lords" from the *Tale*—since it was their honor and status at court that was most jeopardized by the marriage of the ruler when room in the inner circle had to be made for the new bride's kin. Since the male members of Elena's family were all either minors, imprisoned, or dead, she posed no threat to Vasilii III's advisors. As Kollmann put it, the Glinskii match was "actually beneficial to the inner circle...Elena Glinskaia was likely a controllable candidate from the point of view of the boyars, who could thus look forward to maintaining their established balance of power."[23] Finally, the Glinskiis were Orthodox (Elena's uncle Mikhail had for a time converted to Catholicism but had converted back to Orthodoxy when he immigrated to Muscovy), which meant that there would be no cultural obstacles to the marriage—no "exorbitant costs of a foreign match," no "wife raised with different customs and in a different religion," to recall Herberstein's account.[24]

Even with all these advantages, Vasilii III still had to find Elena acceptable as a wife. And it appears he did. Sources repeat in a way that may not be purely formulaic that Elena was quite beautiful and that Vasilii III adored her even to the point of shaving off his beard to please her. Vasilii III may also have appreciated her foreign and exuberant manner. Her uncle Mikhail "Dorodnyi" had some formal education in the west and had served in the armies of the empire and Saxony before his arrival in Muscovy. Some of her uncle's western tastes and demeanor may have rubbed off on Elena, which, as Karamzin had suggested, made her all the more appealing to Vasilii III.[25]

The search for Vasilii III's second wife therefore started in the same way the search for his first had—with a scouring of the land for suitable candidates for a bride-show. The *Tale* confirms the bride-show, but probably many of the other details it relays are distorted. It was composed when Elena was already Vasilii III's consort, and its authors scrubbed the narrative of any mention of other potential candidates, portraying Elena as the one and inevitable choice. The same scrubbing of the facts can be found in the way the *Tale* treats Solomoniia, Vasilii III's first wife. It depicts her departure for the convent as her own idea, not Vasilii III's. Vasilii relents to Solomoniia's repeated requests to be allowed to take the veil out of a respect for the sincerity of her piety, and then only reluctantly. Clearly, the crafting of this narrative reflects lingering awkwardness with the whole business of the grand prince's second marriage. Even so, the memorandum to Liatskii and Klobukov shows that this bride-show was very much like the first one—made up of a large number of candidates drawn from many different locations across the realm.

Even after two bride-shows, the custom was still very much a work in progress in the first quarter of the sixteenth century. Some things, however, were clear by 1526. First, bride-shows would be permitted for second marriages of the grand prince, not just the first. Concern over the canonical appropriateness of remarriage was trumped by the larger benefits—political and symbolic—that the bride-show ritual offered: a bride who was unconnected to the inner circle of boyars, and a useful means for projecting an image of boundless monarchical power. Second, the selection of Solomoniia Saburova and Elena Glinskaia in the first two bride-shows served to entrench the preference for domestic spouses—Orthodox, sharing the groom's "culture," and to be sure, extraordinarily beautiful.

Andrei Staritskii and Collaterals in the Dynasty

In February 1533, just ten months before his own death, Vasilii III finally permitted his youngest and least troublesome brother, Andrei Staritskii, to marry. The marriage of a younger brother had long been a rarity in the Muscovite ruling house. Vasilii III's other brothers—Iurii, prince of Dmitrov; Dmitrii, prince of Uglich; and Simeon, prince of Kaluga—lived out their lives without ever being allowed to marry and therefore without leaving legitimate heirs. Simeon had died in 1518 at the age of 31, and Dmitrii had passed in 1521 at age 39. Iurii would die of starvation in prison in 1536 at the age of 56.[26] The decision to prevent these three brothers from marrying was motivated by an effort to control the succession. The youngest brother, Prince Andrei Staritskii, was permitted to marry only after Vasilii III had secured the succession with the birth by his second wife of two sons—Ivan (the future Ivan IV the Terrible, born 1530) and Iurii (born 1532)—and when Vasilii III had reached the relatively ripe age of nearly 54, was perhaps ill, and therefore unlikely to produce any more heirs.[27] Dynastic succession and dynastic marriage merged into a single concern when it came to the dynasty's collateral lines. As Janet Martin aptly summarized the situation, "Younger brothers...remained critical to the perpetuation of the Muscovite dynasty. But once their elder brother sat on the throne and produced his own sons, their value to the dynasty and the political system evaporated."[28]

The harsh treatment of junior members of the dynasty was not unique to Vasilii III—he had learned it at his father's knee. In preventing his brothers from marrying, Vasilii III was merely continuing a tradition practiced by his father, Ivan III. During his lifetime, Ivan III had refused the opportunity to marry off Vasilii's younger brothers, Iurii of Dmitrov, Dmitrii of Ulgich, and Simeon of Kaluga. (Iurii, the eldest of the three, was 25 years old at the time of Ivan III's death; Andrei, the youngest, was 15—all marriageable ages.) Vasilii III's own marriage in 1505 was late in coming: he was 26, a delay likely explained by the uncertainty in the succession up until 1502. Ivan III had been almost as harsh with his own younger siblings. Two of his four brothers—Iurii, prince of Dmitrov and the eldest of Ivan III's siblings, and Andrei "the Younger," prince of Vologda—were never permitted to marry.[29] The second-eldest male sibling, Andrei "the Elder," prince of Uglich, was not allowed to marry until 1469, when he was 27 years old.[30] Ivan III's next brother, Boris, prince of Volokolamsk, married in 1471 at the age of 22 (see Appendix D.1).[31]

Going back still one more generation—to Vasilii II (1425–1462), Ivan III's father and Vasilii III's grandfather—we arrive at the moment when the harsh dynastic policy toward collaterals made its debut. Before Vasilii II's reign, there was little or no infringement on marriage for collateral members of the dynasty. Tracing the line back to its foundations in the early fourteenth century, both of the sons of Vasilii I married, as did all five of the sons of Dmitrii Donskoi, both sons of Ivan II, and all three sons of Ivan I Kalita.[32] The change in policy toward collaterals plainly appears for the first time in the second half of the fifteenth century and was directly related to the establishment and maintenance of succession by primogeniture.

Prior to the reign of Vasilii II, succession within the Daniilovich dynasty had followed a pattern that appears primogeniturial from at least the fourteenth century, but as Janet Martin and Donald Ostrowski have convincingly shown, this was the product more of a biostatistical accident than a deliberate policy.[33] In the first four generations of the Daniilovich dynasty, no collateral candidates were available to contest what was, in effect, de facto succession by primogeniture. St.-Prince Daniil Aleksandrovich's elder son and successor, Iurii, had only a daughter, who of course could not succeed. The succession fell instead to Iurii's younger brother Ivan, called Kalita. Ivan was, in turn, succeeded by his son Simeon, whose own sons died in a plague outbreak in 1353. He was, as a result, succeeded by his younger brother, Ivan II. Ivan II had only one son who lived to maturity, Dmitrii Donskoi, who succeeded him. Dmitrii Donskoi was the father of many long-lived sons, the first of his line to be so prolific. His eldest surviving son, Vasilii I, succeeded him. To be sure, the succession had up to this point twice passed to younger brothers (Ivan I Kalita in 1325 and Ivan II in 1353); but in both cases, the older sibling had not left a male heir. Thus, for the first century and a half of its existence, the principality of Muscovy practiced primogeniture, even if only by the vagaries of births and deaths in the ruling house.

But if biostatistical chance had produced lineal succession, its advantages had at length become plain enough to the court to recommend its continuance when the first opportunity for collateral succession presented itself. This challenge to primogeniture erupted in the 1430s over the succession of Vasilii II, son of Vasilii I. The young heir was only ten years old on his father's death in 1425; and his claim was challenged by the eldest of Vasilii I's surviving brothers, Prince Iurii of Galich. Sparked perhaps by the ruling in 1432 of Khan Ulu Mehmed in Sarai in favor of Vasilii II's claim to the throne, or perhaps by a dispute over the ownership of a golden belt that erupted at Vasilii II's wedding the following year, a bloody dynastic war broke out between Vasilii II of Moscow and Prince Iurii and his armed retinue, then against Iurii's son Prince Dmitrii of Galich, who was called Shemiaka.[34] The war widened to include the Grand Duchy of Lithuania and the Tatars, and it fundamentally shaped political culture at home.[35] These dynastic wars of the mid-fifteenth century provided, in Edward Keenan's phrase, the "catastrophic stimulus" to the twin problems of power and succession.[36] Quoting Keenan:

> After the great civil war of the first half of the fifteenth century, begun by a dynastic dispute, in which all the weaknesses of the former system were revealed, the winning coalition (Vasilii II and his allies) confirmed forever a new dynastic principle, whereby only the eldest son of only one family—that of Vasilii—was clearly designated as successor, his brothers and uncles being effectively excluded from political life, typically by means of imprisonment or exile in the so-called "appanage" centers. By this change the grand-princely family established an unprecedented form of internal organization for itself, and set itself apart...from other princely clans, which continued to practice a modified collateral and collective seniority system.[37]

Put another way, the dynastic wars from 1433 to 1453 transformed the Daniilovichi into a dynasty engaged in a constant struggle against itself, and the outcome of that struggle was a system of succession that favored sons over brothers and uncles.

From the reign of Vasilii II onward, the Muscovite grand prince and his advisors regulated the collateral branches of the Daniilovich dynasty through imprisonment, execution, and the strict control of marriage. By 1453, when the wars finally ended, all of Vasilii II's uncles and cousins were dead or had fled to Lithuania, and only two collateral kin remained.[38] Vasilii II and Vasilii III adopted a calculated and callous but successful dynastic policy aimed at limiting the succession to the son, rather than the younger brother, of the ruling grand prince. The genealogist Nicolas Baumgarten noted just how callous the policy was. His annotated genealogy of the Daniilovichi included a tabulation of the "extraordinary enmity [*l'acharnement*] of the princes of Moscow against their collaterals: two princes were blinded, five poisoned, two killed, two princesses were drowned, one prince died of starvation, and eleven died in prison, often while in irons."[39]

This "extraordinary enmity" did not usually extend to the princesses of the dynasty, however. Princesses were routinely married off, from the early fourteenth century down to the extinction of the Daniilovich dynasty at the end of the sixteenth century. Thus, all three of Dmitrii Donskoi's adult daughters were married, as were all four of Vasilii I's daughters, Vasilii II's lone daughter, and all three of Ivan III's. (Vasilii III had no daughters, and Ivan IV had none who survived to adulthood.) The marriages of royal daughters, moreover, often provided crucial links between the grand-princely house and leading boyar or princely clans. No better example can be provided than the Patrikeev clan in the early fifteenth century. Prince Iurii Patrikeev, the clan's Muscovite founder, married the daughter of Grand Prince Vasilii I in 1418, setting the stage for a generation of Patrikeev domination of the inner circle at court.[40] The marriage of Feodosiia Ivanovna, the daughter of Ivan III, to Prince Vasilii Daniilovich Kholmskii in 1500 also served a political purpose, coming, as it did, in the midst of a succession crisis of 1497–1502. And as we shall explore in the next chapter, the marriage of Evdokiia Ivanovna, another daughter of Ivan III, with Tsarevich Peter (Kudai Kul) in 1506 provided a line of descendants that most likely served as backup successors to the throne in the event of the failure of the senior line of Daniilovichi. While the rules of primogeniture did not allow royal daughters to inherit the throne themselves, their marriages could be exploited by their male kinsmen for profitable political ends. Thus the Daniilovich dynasty can be characterized as consisting of daughters who married and sons who plotted, were murdered or imprisoned, or died bitter bachelors.

Nothing better explains the difference in marriage patterns between the sons and daughters of rulers than anxiety over the succession. The risk of letting younger sons marry was enormous and obvious: collateral lines could (and usually did) end up competing for the succession. Daughters could be married to foreigners or to prominent boyars at home in ways that would, it was hoped, enhance the security of Muscovy's borders or the equilibrium of factions at court. Until Elena Ivanovna's wedding in 1495, all options were open when it came to royal women. Royal men from collateral lines, by contrast, had few.

The practical but callous treatment of collaterals was therefore by Vasilii III's time a well-worn habit of mind among Muscovite grand princes from at least the mid-fifteenth century. The delay in permitting Vasilii's youngest brother, Andrei Staritskii, to marry (he was 43, the oldest at first marriage for anyone in the dynasty)[41] was apparently deliberate and linked to the same habits of mind that kept Vasilii III from letting any of his other three younger brothers—Iurii, Dmitrii, or Simeon—from marrying at all, and that had recommended to Ivan III and Vasilii II that the same prohibitions be applied to their siblings and younger sons. Vasilii III decided the nuptial fates of his siblings while the dynasty was still healing the wounds of the civil war, acting on the hard-learned lessons of his grandfather Vasilii II, the victor of the dynastic wars. The drastic pruning of the family tree had become a three-generations-long Daniilovich custom.

According to the wedding *chin* for Andrei Staritskii's wedding, sometime in January 1533 (the day is not specified in the extant draft original of the wedding *chin*, nor in any of the later copies), Prince Andrei Staritskii petitioned his brother Vasilii III "to be permitted to marry [*chtob emu kniaz' veliki(i) oslobodil zhenitis'*]." Vasilii III granted the request and probably had done so even before the formal, ritualized request was made. The wedding was celebrated on February 2, 1533.[42] How the choice of bride was made is not stated in the text, but there are some edits in the draft at this point in the narrative that suggest a bride-show. Originally, the text stated that the grand prince picked a bride for his brother: Grand Prince Vasilii III "ordered him, the prince, to take Princess Efrosiniia, the daughter of Prince Andrei Khovanskii, as his wife [*a velel emu knia(ziu) poniati kniazh Ondreevu doch' Khovanskogo knizhnu Ofrosin'iu*]." But this phrasing was revised in the final version to assign the choice of bride to both the grand prince and his brother, the groom. It reads that "they preferred the virgin Princess Efrosiniia, the daughter of Prince Andrei Khovanskii [*i poliubili devku kniazhnu Ofrosin'iu kniazh Ondreevu Khovanskogo*]."[43] That Efrosiniia was "preferred" implies that she was preferred over other candidates—as in a bride-show.

The identity of the chosen bride also suggests a bride-show. Efrosiniia was the kind of bridal candidate that bride-shows generated throughout their nearly two-centuries-long run: young and healthy maidens from families that were not at the center of power at the court. The Khovanskiis played a significant role at court later in the century, especially, of course, Efrosiniia; and this marriage spawned the Staritskii cadet line of the dynasty that remained important through Ivan IV's reign until he all but eradicated it in 1569. But in 1533, the Khovanskiis were not unlike other royal in-laws, well-born princes locked in one of the outer orbits around the court.[44]

The marriage of Prince Andrei Staritskii in 1533 was probably a move to rebuild a dynasty that had nearly been obliterated by the efforts to institutionalize primogeniture. Vasilii III permitted his brother Andrei Staritskii to marry because, at the time of the wedding in February 1533, the Moscow line of the Daniilovich dynasty consisted only of Vasilii III's two young sons (Ivan and Iurii) and his two brothers—one who had not been much of a threat to his power over the years (Andrei Staritskii) and the other who was thoroughly distrusted and despised (Iurii of Dmitrov). Were Vasilii III to die, and his declining health may have warned him that death was approaching, the hopes of the dynasty would rest on two toddler boys. Whether Andrei Staritskii's wedding in 1533 was arranged by a bride-show or not (and it probably was), there can be little doubt that its purpose was to restock the pond.

Ivan IV and Rebuilding the Dynasty

After Vasilii III's death in 1533, the first attempt at giving young Ivan IV a role in restocking the pond began in the fall of 1543, when he was just fourteen. The Muscovites were then involved in intense negotiations with Poland-Lithuania to renew the five-year truce between the two neighbors that had ended the most recent war (1534–1537).[45] Among the issues raised during these negotiations was a possible marriage between the young Ivan IV and one of the daughters of the Polish king, Sigismund I (r. 1506–1548), the younger brother and heir of Grand Duke Alexander who, as we have seen, had married Vasilii III's sister Elena. Russian sources do not name the target of these matrimonial negotiations, but Sigismund I had two available daughters—Anna Jagiellon, who was about twenty years old, and Catherine Jagiellon, who was about eighteen. Two older sisters, Hedwig and Isabella, had already married. A surviving memorandum (*pamiat'*) to Boris Ivanov syn Sukin, one of the Muscovite negotiators, describes how he was to suggest to the Poles that the young Ivan IV had already reached adulthood and was contemplating marriage:

> And Boris is to speak with them about things that are not secret, and to survey the situation there. And they will ask certain things about our grand prince: is he yet considering marriage, how old is he, and how tall? And Boris is to say: Our sovereign, the great sovereign Ivan, by the grace of God, has reached manhood, and is as big as a full-grown man already, and in accordance with God's will, has already begun to consider marriage. And our sovereign has not yet sent to have maidens gathered together for his inspection [*i ne v odno mesto poslal sebe nevest pytati*], though such a gathering will take place [*i otkoleva k gosudariu nashemu budet prisylka*], for it is our sovereign's will to be married. And Boris is to write down all that is said about this, and on arriving is to report all to the sovereign grand prince.[46]

These instructions to Sukin indicate that, two years before Ivan IV married, the court was already sure that a bride-show would be held for him. It was assumed that Ivan IV would marry one of his own subjects and use a bride-show to find her, as his father had found his mother. The memorandum reports (perhaps stretching the truth a bit) that Ivan IV was already mature enough for marriage and that the future bride-show could be set aside if the Polish king was willing to give one of his daughters to Ivan IV in marriage—which one probably did not matter much. These first overtures came to nothing, though both Anna and Catherine would again enter into Ivan IV's matrimonial calculations later. The Polish match foiled, Ivan IV's advisors returned to what had already become the traditional method of picking a bride for the tsar: a bride-show.

Two years passed before the topic of Ivan IV's marriage was raised again, at least so far as our sources show. A chronicle account of the deliberations about his first marriage provides important additional insights into Ivan IV's choice of his first wife, Anastasiia Iu'reva, in 1547:

> On Friday, December 17, the grand prince was with the metropolitan and all the boyars, and in the presence of the boyars, he said to the metropolitan: "By the grace of God and His Most-Pure Mother the Queen [*tsaritsa*], and through the grace and prayers of the great miracle-workers Peter and Aleksei, Iona, and Sergei the Miracle-Worker, and all the holy Russian miracle-workers, having put my hope in them, and having received a blessing to marry from you, my [spiritual] father, I have been thinking about marriage and want to marry someone from a place that God and his Most-Pure Mother and the miracle-workers of the Rus'ian land shall bless

> me to choose. I had thought about marrying someone from abroad [*v ynykh tsar'stvakh*], the daughter of some king or the daughter of some tsar, and I, father, have rejected the idea of marrying abroad because I do not want to marry a foreigner on account of the fact that the marriage of my father, Grand Prince Vasilii, and my mother did not work out well. Bring me a wife from abroad and we will have different customs and between us there will be problems. And having considered the matter, I, father, want with your blessing to marry in my own realm [*v svoem gosudarstve*], someone whom God shall appoint for me.[47]

As in the case of Ivan IV's father's nuptials, concern over differences in customs again appear in Ivan IV's deliberations, and so foreigners are quickly ruled out as a source for his bride. What problems his mother and father may have had in their marriage—"it did not work out well" for them—remain unknown, since, as far as the surviving letters between the couple suggest, they were dutifully affectionate with each other and attentive parents to their son.[48]

The wedding of Tsar Ivan IV and Anastasiia Iur'eva on February 2, 1547—less than two months after this audience—came after one of the best-documented bride-shows of the sixteenth century, drawing candidates from many regions of European Russia. The search for bridal candidates began no later than December 1546 and evidently lasted until late January 1547.[49] Anastasiia was probably no stranger to Ivan IV or to the members of the great families in the Kremlin. Many in her clan had held boyar rank from the first mention in the sources of its progenitor, Andrei Ivanovich Kobyla, in 1346/47. Andrei's descendants were numerous and divided into different lines, becoming over time distinct families at court. Anastasiia descended from Andrei's fourth son, Fedor Koshka, who was a boyar between 1389 and his death in 1408. Anastasiia's great-grandfather Zakharii was a boyar, as was her grandfather Iurii. Anastasiia descended from the Iur'ev line of the Koshkin branch of the clan. The names of each of the males in the line provided a surname for the next generation: thus Anastasiia's ancestors were known as Koshkins (after Fedor Koshka), Zakhar'ins (after Zakharii Ivanovich), and Iur'evs (after Iurii Zakhar'evich). Anastasiia's father, Roman (her only ancestor who did not attain boyar rank), gave his name to the subsequent Romanov dynasty, which descends from her brother Nikita Romanovich.[50] Anastasiia thus came from a prominent old boyar family, but one that had recently struck upon some bad luck. Anastasiia's father had died in 1543 before he himself became a boyar, as would have been his right given his place within the clan's hierarchy of seniority and the prevailing customs of succession to boyar rank. Those same customs, however, now rendered Roman's descendants ineligible for the rank because of his premature death. Anastasiia Iur'eva thus came from a non-boyar line of her clan—just as Solomoniia Saburova had done back in 1505—and so, ironically, it was not the illustriousness of her background, as is sometimes claimed, but rather, the bride's relative distance from the most illustrious names at court and in her own clan that offered the twin advantages of familiarity and distance that may have been so appealing to the other boyars. It would be Anastasiia's marriage to the tsar that would restore the fortunes of her branch of the family.[51]

Why Ivan IV's choice fell on Anastasiia has been debated, but the usual explanations stress either her unmatched beauty or the prominence of her family. Karamzin—faithfully rehearsing the post-1613 Romanov propaganda—saw the choice of Anastasiia solely as the result of the bride-show run in 1546 and 1547: "It was not her distinguished background, but the personal qualities of the bride that determined the choice; and contemporaries, describing her qualities, attributed to her all the feminine traits that can be described only in the Russian language: chastity, humility, piety, sensitivity, and goodness, all joined with a good intellect."[52] The more practical-minded Solov'ev suggested that the choice had more to do with the prominence of Anastasiia's clan during Vasilii III's reign than with any qualities of the bridal candidate herself. He also believed that the clan's apparent neutrality during the factional violence of Ivan IV's minority may have offered her an advantage over other candidates.[53] Skrynnikov acknowledged that the tsar almost certainly knew Anastasiia before he married her, but he put the decision more in the hands of the young tsar's boyar handlers than in Ivan IV's: "at the bride-show arranged by the boyars, they selected Anastasiia for the tsar, the daughter of the *okol'nichii* Roman Iur'evich Zakhar'in. The father of the royal bride was no one of great importance. On the other hand, her uncle had risen to prominence during Ivan's youth as one of his guardians, so that the grand prince knew the bride's family since childhood."[54] Madariaga agrees that the decision had been taken in advance and plausibly speculates that "the choice had the advantage of not introducing a new boyar family into the delicate balance at court, since it was already there."[55]

No matter how distinguished the Iur'evs may have been or how beautiful the bride was, deciphering the choice of Anastasiia requires placing the first marriage of the young Ivan IV in the context of the turbulent years of his minority. Ivan IV came to the throne in 1533 at age three, and for the next thirteen years, his life and court were dominated by a succession of boyar families and favorites. On Vasilii III's death, Ivan IV's mother, Elena Glinskaia, held the reins of power until her death in 1538.[56] Kollmann has plotted out the shifting alliances in clans during these years. She shows that, from 1526 to 1533, a shaky but successful balance of power had prevailed at court between three factions—the Shuiskiis, the Cheliadnins and Telepnev-Obolenskiis, and the Iur'evs-Zakharins (Anastasii's family)—with many other prominent clans (the Bel'skiis, Sheniatevs, Morozovs, Vorontsovs, and others) "grouped in flexible networks" around them.[57] In 1534, however, a shake-up at court involving members of the Bel'skii, Vorotynskii, Liatskoi, and Glinskii clans left the Shuiskii and Telepnev-Obolenskii clans preeminent. This new configuration itself collapsed and open violence ensued upon the death of the regent, Elena Glinskaia, in 1538. The Shuiskiis made their grab for power by attacking the Telepnev-Obolenskiis and their allies and by securing the marriage in June 1538 of Prince Vasilii Vasil'evich Shuiskii to Anastasiia Petrovna, the daughter of Tsarevich Peter (the converted Tatar tsarevich Kudai Kul) and his wife Evdokiia Ivanovna, the daughter of Ivan III.[58] This marriage made the Shuiskiis royal in-laws; and even though the groom died just a few months later (in December), the Shuiskiis managed to dominate court politics from 1538 to 1543. Other families had to wait for their opportunity to strike.

That opportunity came in December 1543, when Prince Andrei Mikhailovich Shuiskii was murdered and many of his kinsmen and allies were exiled. The years from 1544 to 1547 show a balance of boyar factions at court, with new appointments to the boyar rank and no single family dominating in numbers the Duma ranks. As Kollmann put it: "No one faction had exclusive power in the two years before Ivan IV's 1547 wedding."[59] On the eve of Ivan IV's wedding, old scores were settled in two ways. First, "measured violence" evened the tally of murders and exiles of the previous decade. Second, exiles and executions just before and after the coronation and wedding of Ivan IV in early 1547 "apparently satisfied the boyars' demand for requital and allowed various political groups to agree on a new distribution of power."[60] In this way, the court had attained a moment of rare equilibrium precisely at the time the young tsar reached a marriageable age. Dynastic marriages and the political climate at court were often linked. Again quoting Kollmann: "Such choices as Aleksandra Vel'iaminova in 1345, Princess Mariia Iaroslavovna (the Koshkin kinswoman) in 1433, Solomoniia Saburova in 1505, Princess Elena Glinskaia in 1526, and Anastasiia Romanovna in 1547 so accurately reflect the court political situation that they could not have been arrived at by chance or motivated by love."[61]

It has become common to think of the timing of Ivan IV's first marriage in terms of his age (that he had by February 1547 reached his "majority"),[62] but surely more important for the timing of his marriage was this temporary equilibrium in the factions at court. The timing of his marriage suggests not so much a young man who had reached his formal majority (there was no legal age of majority in the dynasty until Emperor Paul I established it in 1797)[63] but, rather, a collective decision by the boyars to seize upon the opportunity to marry off Ivan IV (as well as his brother Iurii and cousin Vladimir) before the equilibrium was disrupted. After all, Ivan IV was relatively young for his first marriage. In the history of the Daniilovich dynasty, only three had married younger: Ivan IV's brother Iurii Vasil'evich, at age 14; Ivan III, who was betrothed at age 7 and married at age 12 in 1452 while still "under age";[64] and Ivan II, in 1341/42, at age 15. Only one other married at the same age of 16: Ivan IV's cousin Vladimir Staritskii, his first marriage in 1549. All the other known ages at first marriage (20 cases) were years older.[65] In other words, three of the five marriages in the dynasty in which grooms were youngest occurred within a two-year span in the late 1540s—just when the boyar factions at court had found a moment of calm. The dynastic marriages during this reprieve in the violence appear opportunistic, not normative. The timing of Ivan IV's first wedding (and of those of his brother and cousin) is therefore probably best explained by two factors: the equilibrium at court, which provided a stable and safe environment for the negotiations that lay behind a search for a royal bride; and the need to expand the dynasty's size to offset the risks of extinction. It was the costly impact of the previous three generations of war on collaterals that pushed the adolescent Ivan IV and his collateral kin to the marriage altar.

The restocking of the dynastic pond extended beyond the tsar's own marriage, and so would the bride-show custom. Within months of Ivan IV's marriage, the scribes, boyars, and other ranks of courtiers, plus their wives, were all mobilized again to hold another bride-show, this time for the tsar's brother Prince Iurii Vasil'evich. Within two years, the whole process was repeated yet again, for Ivan IV's first cousin Prince Vladimir Andreevich Staritskii.

Iurii Vasil'evich's bride-show in the fall of 1547 was summoned and held by the tsar, but Iurii is said to have made the choice—though his well-known cognitive incapacities may have required greater involvement of others than the wedding muster (*razriad*) indicates. According to that text, "Prince Iurii Vasil'evich preferred [*poliubil*] Princess Ul'iana, the daughter of Prince Dmitrii Fedorovich Paletskii."[66] Few facts can be brought to bear on the reason for this choice, though the Paletskii clan—a branch of the Starodubskii princes—did have perhaps one of the most distinguished records of service of any of the families of royal brides in the sixteenth and seventeenth centuries. Her uncle Prince Ivan Fedorovich was made an *okol'nichii* between 1526/27 and December 1551, and her father, Prince Dmitrii Fedorovich, was made a boyar between June 1542 and July 1547—not long before his daughter married the tsar's brother.[67] It may not be accidental that Iulianiia was a relative (an agnatic second cousin once removed) of Ovdot'ia Vasil'evna Gundorova, the candidate for Ivan IV's bride-show, whose health, looks, and genealogy were investigated by Prince Ivan Mezetskii while searching for bridal candidates in Viaz'ma (see Chapter 2).[68] It is possible that Iulianiia had been a candidate in both bride-shows, since, as we have seen, candidates often did come from a single family or set of related families. That Iurii was only 14 years old at the time and severely mentally handicapped suggests that the only reason for the nuptials was the potential offspring that the couple might produce, were Iurii physically capable of it. As it turned out, the one known child born of the union—Prince Vasilii Iur'evich—died before his first birthday.[69] Still, Iurii's marriage should be recognized for the unusual event it was. It was the first time a collateral member of the dynasty had married when there had yet to be born an heir in the senior line since Ivan I Kalita (r. 1325–1341) allowed his younger son, the future Ivan II (r. 1353–1359), to marry before his elder son, Simeon (r. 1341–1353), had succeeded in having an heir born to him.[70]

The first of Prince Vladimir Staritskii's two marriages also predates the birth of a male heir to Ivan IV. Vladimir married Evdokiia Aleksandrovna Nagaia on May 31, 1549.[71] The ceremonial (*chin*) for Vladimir Staritskii's wedding reports that both the tsar and the groom inspected candidates at a bride-show in the spring of 1549, though again, Vladimir is described as making the final selection.[72] Two rare manuscript versions of the *chin* provide details not available in the better-known published accounts:

> In the year 7058/1549, on September 10, Tsar and Grand Prince Ivan Vasil'evich of all Rus' commanded Prince Volodimir Andreevich to marry; and he spoke about this with Prince Volodimir's mother, Princess Efrosiniia. And Princess Efrosiniia petitioned the sovereign to permit him to marry. And the tsar and grand prince commanded that all the virgin daughters of the boyars and princes be written down, and that they be examined at the appointed time...And on March 27, the tsar and grand prince ordered that the virgins be brought one by one to the scribe Mikita Funikov, and when they had brought them, for him to examine them one by one.[73]

The involvement of the scribe Funikov in the bride-show suggests that the wedding was handled by the same chancellery staff as had handled the tsar's own wedding just two years before. Funikov had served at Ivan IV's wedding to Anastasiia Iur'eva, tending to the tsar's costumes (*u plat'ia u velikogo kniazia*).[74] The involvement of Vladimir's mother, Efrosiniia, hints that the input of more than just the tsar was at play in this choice of bride. The bride's background is not unlike that of Solomoniia Saburova, Anastasiia Iur'eva, or Iulianiia Paletskaia: they all had boyars in their blood. While Evdokiia's father never held Duma rank, her uncle Fedor Mikhailovich Nagoi appears as an *okol'nichii* in sources as early as September 1533 and through to his last mention in July 1557.[75]

Vladimir Staritskii married again on April 21, 1555, after his first wife's death (probably in 1554).[76] The surviving sources for the wedding—a single folio of the original draft ceremonial, which was later copied, and long and short redactions of the muster—do not report a bride-show, but this does not mean none was held, since the official documentation sometimes omits reference to it. For example, the musters for Ivan IV's first and third weddings omit any mention of a bride-show, though we know from other sources that they took place.[77] Vladimir Staritskii's new bride, Princess Evdokiia Romanovna Odoevskaia, is the first after the introduction of the bride-show custom who did not have some kind of boyar connection prior to her marriage. Her brother Nikita Romanovich, who is identified as having served in the *oprichnina*, received boyar rank only in 1571 and held it only briefly, until his execution in 1573.[78] Even still, the Odoevskiis were, in Robert Crummey's phrase, "no mean family." After their entry into the service of the grand prince of Moscow in the late fifteenth century, "each generation of Odoevskiis produced distinguished servitors over the course of the sixteenth and seventeenth centuries."[79] Vladimir Staritskii's two marriages were fruitful. From the first, he had a son (Vasilii) and daughter (Efimiia); from his second he had two more sons (Iurii and Ivan) and two more daughters (Mariia and Evdokiia).[80] And they must have been a healthy set of children: only one (Evdokiia) of the six is reported to have died young, though their fates, as we shall see, were far from happy ones.

It is likely that the extension of the bride-show custom to collaterals happened first with Andrei Staritskii's 1533 wedding; but whenever it was, the marriages of Prince Andrei Ivanovich, Prince Iurii Vasil'evich, and Prince Vladimir Andreevich were motivated by the need to rebuild the ranks of the dynasty, which had been decimated by the aggressive policy of confinement and eradication of collateral lines in the previous two reigns, and the desire to control the choice of bride. Sergei Bogatyrev agrees that the goal of allowing at least Vladimir Staritskii to marry was, as he put it, the "proliferation of the dynasty," a goal that required the loosening up of the long-standing dynastic policy of forced bachelorhood for collaterals.[81] But Bogatyrev sees the change in dynastic policy toward collaterals (letting them marry) as benign. "Ivan's leniency toward Vladimir," he asserts, "means that in the late 1540s the tsar did not see his cousin as a dynastic rival,"[82] and "contrary to widespread opinion, in the 1550s the main source of concern for Ivan IV was not Vladimir of Staritsa, but his own sons. Prior to the establishment of the *oprichnina,* Ivan IV saw Vladimir more as a guarantor of peace between the tsar's heir, Ivan Ivanovich, and his future brothers than as a dynastic rival."[83] In other words, according to Bogatyrev, Ivan IV feared more the potential conflicts that might arise over the succession between his son Ivan Ivanovich and the as-yet unborn sons he might eventually have than he feared potential conflicts between his heir, the infant Ivan Ivanovich, and his cousin Vladimir Staritskii. In fact, Bogatyrev sees Vladimir Staritskii as the "guarantor" of Ivan IV's son's succession, not a potential competitor for it.[84]

But it is hard not to see in Ivan IV's treatment of Vladimir Staritskii the very same manipulative control and distrust that all grand princes since Vasilii II's time had displayed toward their collaterals. It is not for nothing that Vladimir Staritskii was arrested along with his father in 1537, and on his release in 1540, his servitors were replaced with new ones;

that he was compelled to sign three loyalty treaties in 1553 and 1554 (at the time of Ivan IV's illness); that he was again arrested in 1563 and his servitors again dismissed and replaced with new ones (at the time of Prince Iurii Vasil'evich's death); and that his appanage of Staritsa was confiscated and exchanged for Dmitrov in 1566.[85] Vladimir, his second wife, and a daughter were executed on October 9, 1569;[86] and the quartet of grisly deaths was complete when Vladimir's mother, Efrosiniia, who had been forcibly tonsured in 1563, was herself put to death on October 11, 1569.[87] The treatment of Vladimir was, if anything, worse than what most collaterals had suffered at the hands of previous grand princes. That Vladimir Staritskii was permitted to marry at all was not a sign of friendship between the tsar and the prince, nor, certainly, an outgrowth of Ivan IV's dynastic plan to have Vladimir referee some possible future disputes between sons who had not yet been born. Rather, it is more plausible that Vladimir was permitted to marry only for the purpose of repopulating the dynasty—and even then, only reluctantly.

The Remarriage of Ivan IV

Anastasiia Iur'eva, Ivan IV's first wife, died on August 7, 1560. Almost immediately, Ivan IV's advisors began urging him to remarry.[88] His first marriage had been fertile: six children were born to him and Anastasiia, but four of them (Anna, Mariia, Dmitrii, and Evdokiia) had died as infants.[89] Ivan IV's remaining sons, Ivan Ivanovich and Fedor Ivanovich, were a slender thread from which to hang the future of the dynasty, so remarriage was imperative and urgent.

One source reports that on August 14, Metropolitan Makarii, Archbishop Matvei of Sarskii and Podonskii, and "all the archimandrites and all the boyars" met with Ivan IV to beg him to put aside his apparent anguish over Anastasiia's death and marry again. The tsar was too young to live without a wife, they claimed, and they pleaded that the hopes of the Christian people required the tsar be married. Ivan IV initially rejected the idea firmly, or so it is formulaically reported; but when the topic was raised again two days later, he agreed—for the sake of his children, in obedience to the metropolitan's pleas, and for the good of his realm (*zemlia*).[90] Other sources report that the reason Ivan IV's hierarchs and boyars implored him to remarry was because the tsar's debauchery had reached such intolerable levels that remarriage was thought to be the only means to control the tsar's insatiable and indecent impulses.[91] Whatever the truth, the interval between Anastasiia's death and his remarriage seems unseemly brief (twelve months), so whether he was genuinely distraught over his wife's death or not (and he probably was not), his feelings on the matter one way or the other were irrelevant. The main business at hand for a monarch who was only thirty years old with two small sons (only one of whom may have been in robust health) must have been securing the succession in his own line, even if there were now collaterals (Vladimir Staritskii and his sons) waiting to step in if needed.[92]

From the very beginning of the campaign to get Ivan IV remarried, both he and his advisors had their sights set on marrying a foreigner. No known sources suggest that a bride-show was ever arranged or even contemplated.[93] On the very day that the decision to remarry was finally taken (evidently August 16, 1560), Ivan IV and his advisors dispatched envoys in three directions in search of a bride. He sent *okol'nichii* Fedor Ivanovich Sukin and the scribe (*d'iak*) Grigorii Shapkin to the court of King Sigismund II Augustus of Poland-Lithuania to see the king's two sisters, Anna and Catherine, who had been targeted back in 1543. Even though both were still unmarried in 1560, the Nikonovskii Chronicle suggests that only one was being considered now (subsequent events suggest it was Catherine).[94] Ivan IV must have been fairly serious and sure about the Jagiellon match, because he asked Metropolitan Makarii for a ruling as to whether a marriage with the king's daughter would violate the laws of consanguinity.[95] (The concern was the marriage of Sof'ia Vitovtna and Vasilii I in 1392, which made Ivan IV and Anna and Catherine fourth cousins twice removed.)[96] The metropolitan evidently responded that a match with either sister would not violate the church's canons; and Ivan IV boldly (and prematurely) announced on August 18, 1560, his intention to marry a daughter of the Polish king.[97] In his exuberance, Ivan IV "ordered that, for his wedding, miraculous icons be adorned with gold and silver covers, and that other icons be inlaid with diamonds and pearls, and that many icons of saints be made of metal pieces, not only ancient saints, but also all the new Russian miracle-workers and enlighteners, venerable fathers and martyrs; and [the tsar] ordered all things required for the wedding be prepared."[98] These plans to marry the sister of Sigismund II Augustus did not, however, prevent Ivan IV from dispatching the other two delegations on their missions: Fedor Grigorev syn Beklemishev and the clerk (*pod'iachii*) Lasha Zinov'ev departed for Sweden to inquire after the sisters (who go unnamed in the text) of the new king, Erik XIV;[99] and Fedor Vasil'ev syn Voksherin and the clerk Semeika Miakinin departed for Karbarda to examine and bring back one of the daughters of the Circassian princes (neither the princes nor any of the daughters are named in the chronicle).[100]

Ivan IV and his advisors must have been sorely disappointed by the responses to their overtures. On February 19, 1561, an embassy from Sigismund II Augustus of Poland-Lithuania arrived in Moscow and proposed an absurdly high price for peace and for the hand of Catherine Jagiellon. The Poles required that, in exchange for a truce and dynastic alliance, Muscovy must turn over key border districts as well as title to cities the Muscovites had long considered part of their patrimony (Novgorod, Pskov, Toropets, Velikie Luki, Rzhev, Dorogobuzh, Smolensk, and "all the northern towns"). The Poles also demanded that any children born of the union between Ivan IV and the Polish princess would enjoy first rights of succession to the Muscovite throne over the children of Ivan IV's first marriage. And, perhaps the real deal-breaker, it was demanded that the Polish tsaritsa should be permitted to remain Catholic and have a church built inside the Terem for her personal use.[101] Ivan and his advisors rejected these demands. They insisted that "the marriage be celebrated in Moscow according to the ancient customs, as it has been done since times of old [*i svatovstvo po prezhnim obychaem na Moskve, kak izstari byvalo*]," but they tried to salvage the negotiations by attempting at least to agree on a truce. The Polish envoys were evidently not authorized to unlink the issues, and with that the matter ended.[102] An embassy from Sweden arrived in Moscow at about the same time as the Polish delegation, in February 1561, with a similar outcome. The envoys from Erik XIV reported that it was not the time to entertain any kind of offer for a dynastic marriage, because the recent death of King Gustav I had left "the entire Swedish kingdom in utter grief."[103]

The Muscovite embassy to Karbardia produced a happier outcome. The embassy returned to Moscow on June 15, 1561, with a cavalcade of Circassian princes and a young maiden many in the party thought might be suitable for the tsar—Kuchenei, the daughter of Temriuk Aidarovich.[104] Kuchenei would shortly be invited to reside in the Terem where Ivan IV "saw her and liked her [*smotrel ee i poliubil*]."[105] Evidently, there was a period of examination and viewing, perhaps even physical examinations, before the choice could be settled upon. This might explain why, despite all of the tsar's advance preparations for his wedding, three weeks elapsed between Kuchenei's arrival and her proclamation as Ivan IV's intended (*nevesta*) on July 7. On that day, Kuchenei was given the name Mariia, after St. Mary Magdalen, and on July 20, she was baptized by Metropolitan Makarii himself. The wedding took place the next month, on August 21, 1561, in the Kremlin's Dormition Cathedral and was officiated by Metropolitan Makarii.[106]

The marriage to Mariia Temriukovna was a safe, and in some ways traditional, choice. As a foreigner, her entry into the Terem did not disrupt the balance of forces already in place, however tenuously, in the court. In fact, it may have strengthened it. With no one following in her wake, she did not add a new group of royal in-laws to the boyar elite. According to Veselovskii:

> The second marriage of Tsar Ivan threatened to rattle the position of the Zakhar'ins most of all…And it seems to me that the decision of Tsar Ivan to find his second wife abroad, in the surrounding realms, should be seen in light of his kinship with the Zakhar'ins. We do not know if Ivan himself thought this, but it is certain that, in the struggle for influence over the tsar, the idea of searching for a bride abroad was for the Zakhar'ins the best of all possible options.[107]

Veselovskii's speculation is plausible: Ivan's marriage to Mariia Temriukovna fits the pattern of second marriages going back generations. Moreover, the link with the family of Ivan's first wife (the Iur'evs or, as Veselovskii called them, the Zakhar'ins) is clear from the subsequent marriage of Mariia Temriukovna's first cousin Boris (Khoroshai) Kambulotovich Cherkasskii to Anastasiia's niece Marfa Nikitichna, which probably reflects a still earlier association between Anastasiia's family and Mariia Temriukovna's, perhaps dating to as early as 1555.[108]

The marriage did not, however, solve the problem of heirs. Ivan IV's and Mariia Temriukovna's lone son, Vasilii, died on May 3, 1563, only six weeks after his birth, and the couple evidently had no other children.[109] Ivan IV remained married to Mariia Temriukovna until her death six years later, on September 1, 1569;[110] but he and his advisors may have been feeling the anxiety of what was clearly a failed match well before that. This anxiety may explain the odd events that took place between 1566 and 1569, when Ivan IV renewed his interest in marrying Catherine, the sister of King Sigismund II Augustus of Poland-Lithuania. This would be Ivan IV's third attempt to marry her. The first was, as we have seen, in 1543 (before he married Anastasiia Iur'eva), and the second was back in 1560 (after Anastasiia's death). In the intervening years, Catherine had married John, Duke of Finland and future King John III of Sweden (the brother of Erik XIV), on October 4, 1562. But the marriage was a scandal inside the Swedish royal family. The groom had failed to get the requisite permission from his brother for the marriage, and so John and his bride, Catherine, were placed in fairly strict, if comfortable, confinement in Gripsholm Castle in Sweden between 1563 and 1566. During their confinement, Catherine gave birth to two of her three children, including a son, the future Sigismund III of Poland-Lithuania (r. 1587–1632) and Sweden (r. 1592–1599).

Once again, dynastic marriage and diplomacy were intersecting. Between 1566 and 1569, Erik XIV of Sweden was desperate for an alliance with Ivan against his enemies in the Northern Seven Years War (1563–1570). Ivan IV made it a stipulation in his negotiations that Catherine, the king's sister-in-law, should be turned over to him as part of any peace settlement, even though they both were married at the time—Ivan IV to Mariia Temriukovna, and Catherine to John of Finland. Erik XIV initially rejected Ivan IV's request for Catherine's hand and offered his own daughter Virginia Eriksdotter to Ivan IV's son Tsarevich Ivan Ivanovich (the first appearance of any marriage plans for the tsar's son, who at the time was only 12 or 13 years old).[111] Erik XIV's diplomatic circumstances at the time were, to be sure, quite dire, but his willingness to consider the unseemly marriage proposal between the tsar and his sister-in-law may have been affected by more than just military and diplomatic advantage. The king suffered from bouts of severe mental illness, which, in these years was getting harder to conceal and is today often blamed for his erratic and sometimes tyrannical rule.

It was perhaps this illness that accounts for his sending an embassy to Moscow in October 1566 with all the terms Ivan IV had hoped for: the hand of Catherine in exchange for an alliance against Poland-Lithuania and Denmark as well as territorial concessions in Estonia.[112] The treaty was signed in February 1567, and the tsar immediately dispatched an embassy to retrieve Catherine. When they arrived, however, Erik XIV was in the throes of a bout of mental illness, and the Muscovite embassy waited in Stockholm for an entire year before they were finally told that the deal was off. Quoting Karamzin's account of this episode, the king's advisors eventually told the Muscovite visitors that "to hand over Catherine to the tsar, to separate a wife from her husband and a mother from her children, would offend both God and the law; that the tsar would forever be infamous for doing such an unchristian thing; that Sigismund had another sister [Anna], a virgin, whom Erik could obtain for the tsar, and that the Swedish embassy had entered the treaty concerning Catherine without the king's knowledge."[113] The Muscovites asked to discuss the matter with the king himself, but he was at that time so incapacitated by his illness that no rational communications were possible. The king was ousted in January 1569 (his willingness to consider Ivan IV's indecent proposal perhaps being the last straw for members of the king's council and the Swedish Estates) and was replaced by his brother, John III—Catherine Jagiellon's husband. The matter did not end there, however. Ivan IV's diplomatic correspondence with the new king continued to press the question of a marriage with Catherine, though they were firmly snubbed at every turn. The matter ended only with the convening of a bride-show in the summer of 1571, at which Ivan IV and his son Ivan Ivanovich selected their wives (Ivan IV's third and Ivan Ivanovich's first).[114]

Ivan IV's motives in pressing for the marriage with Catherine remain unknown, but most biographers of both the king and the tsar have argued that the reasons behind this odd episode were most likely diplomatic. Zimin believed that Ivan harbored ambitions for the Lithuanian and Polish thrones, and the marriage with a Polish princess improved his chances of obtaining them.[115] Madariaga rejected this speculation, pointing out that "[h]ad the purely dynastic question been the main issue…Ivan could well have applied for the hand of the remaining unmarried—and older—sister of Sigismund, Anna, when his wife Anastasiia died."[116] In other words, Ivan IV did not have to marry Catherine to make his bid for the throne; a marriage with Anna would have served his purposes just as well. Madariaga has a point. While Catherine would go on to become queen-consort of Sweden (1569–1583), Anna was the real kingmaker in Poland-Lithuania. On the death of Sigismund II Augustus in 1572, Anna helped to convince the Sejm to select Henry of Valois, the younger brother of Charles IX of France, as king, contingent on his marriage to her. Henry accepted the throne in 1573 and became the first elected king of Poland, but he reneged on his promise to marry Anna. The death of his older brother prompted Henry to return to France in the summer of 1574 to assume the French throne (as Henry III). In 1575, Anna again controlled the succession in Poland-Lithuania by agreeing to marry the nobleman Stephen Báthory, with whom she reigned as co-ruler. On Báthory's death in 1586, the childless Anna proposed her nephew Sigismund III Vasa (Catherine Jagiellon's son) as her husband's successor, and he became the third elected king of Poland. Anna Jagiellon was clearly one of the most extraordinary women of her day, which may be the reason the match with Ivan never happened. Anna's position as king-maker in Poland-Lithuania would hardly have continued if Ivan was her husband, and someone as politically able and cunning as Anna surely knew that. It may well be that Ivan IV did not so much prefer Catherine as he was denied by Anna.

Perhaps the most convincing case for Ivan's diplomatic motives was made by Bodil Nävdal-Larsen, who argued that, in marrying Catherine Jagiellon, the tsar hoped to obtain Livonia as a dowry, since it had proved impossible to seize it through force of arms during the first years of the Livonian War (1558–1583).[117] It would not, after all, be the only time Ivan would use dynastic marriage as an alternative to conquering Livonia. In 1573, he would marry the surviving daughter of Vladimir Staritskii to Magnus of Denmark in the hopes of converting this prized province into a puppet kingdom of Muscovy, with Magnus, now Ivan's in-law, enthroned as its loyal and subservient king. As the Habsburgs were proving at this very time in central Europe, marriage could be better than warfare as a tool of empire building.

Even if the match with Catherine Jagiellon offered some possible diplomatic advantages, it certainly made no sense dynastically. Beyond the fact that she was already married (no small obstacle, even for a tsar), Catherine's age must have raised concerns. By the end of 1566, when the idea of the marriage was brought up again, Catherine was already forty years old and therefore reaching the end of her reproductive life. Concerns over her age may have been allayed some by the fact that in 1567, at the height of the negotiations between Ivan IV and Erik XIV, Catherine was pregnant again with her last child (a daughter, Anna). But even with clear evidence of Catherine's health and fertility, could Ivan IV have reasonably assumed he could have more children with her? Perhaps the tsar was already beginning to think about marriage in the lackadaisical and flexible way he would later: that once Ivan's diplomatic objectives were met, he could quietly put Catherine away so he could get back to the business of securing the succession by marrying someone with better reproductive prospects. In the end, the tsar's motives in pursuing Catherine remain unknown and may ultimately lie in the psychology of the man—an inscrutable topic even more in dispute than his dynastic policy or the number and identity of his many wives.

The Jagiellon episode signaled the close of a period, from 1526 to the death of Ivan IV's second wife in 1569, when the place of the bride-show in Muscovite political culture was hammered out. In these years it was decided by Vasilii III, Ivan IV, and the boyars and relatives around them to continue the bride-show experiment that had first been tried in 1505 and, moreover, to apply the custom to second marriages (Vasilii III) and to collaterals (Iurii Vasil'evich and Vladimir Staritskii). It was in these decades that the bride-show became entrenched as a royal matrimonial custom in Muscovy, and when the links to the larger political culture solidified. The six bride-shows between 1505 and 1549 (and perhaps as many as seven, if Vladimir Staritskii had one in 1555) had established the procedure for finding a bride for the tsar (the tsardom-wide search), had identified the key players in the search (the boyars and their wives who vetted and physically examined the candidates), and had negotiated and defined the prescribed role the groom played in selecting his spouse. By 1571, when Ivan was arranging his second bride-show (for his third marriage), the custom had been around more than half a century and had become the default means for arranging marriages in the ruling dynasty and an essential element of the political system.

The Jagiellon episode also marks a turn in Ivan IV's thinking about heirs and successors. In the 1540s and 1550s, the confidence of a young and robust Ivan IV led him and his advisors to think of the dynasty as a whole: three young men (Ivan IV, Iurii Vasil'evich, and Vladimir Staritskii) who would repopulate the ranks of the dynasty, which had been decimated by the ruthless imposition of primogeniture. But by the 1560s, Ivan IV had seen three daughters and two sons die in their cribs. The two remaining sons from his first marriage (Ivan and Fedor) could not possibly be thought to be sufficient for securing the succession, especially when the younger of them, Fedor, displayed signs of frailty. Instead of being reassured by the fertility of Vladimir Staritskii's marriages, the old fears and suspicions of collaterals reemerged, and Vladimir Staritskii was deemed to be a threat. It is no coincidence, then, that the execution of the Staritskiis came only one month after the death of Ivan IV's second wife, Mariia Temriukovna. These executions were not so much the act of a madman out to destroy his family as a desperate attempt to gain control over the dynasty. The remainder of Ivan IV's reign would display that desperation even more, as the tsar donned the nuptial crown again and again in hopes of producing more heirs, and as he arranged marriages for his sons and other members of the dynasty. It is to the remainder of Ivan's reign that we now turn.

Chapter 4

"To Assuage the Melancholy"

The Many Wives of Ivan IV

> The Muscovite tsar, in order to assuage the melancholy that had mounted because of things that had gone badly for him, and after repudiating his former wife because of her character, which is permitted for him to do as often as he pleases, at this point having already married six times, married again after announcing a public gathering of girls; and at that time he also compelled many of his boyars and advisors to marry.[1]

The tsar's last bride-show and last marriage was described by Polish diplomat Reinhold Heidenstein, whose account of the Livonian wars was published 1584, the year of Ivan IV's death. The above short passage from that account pulls together many of the unresolved questions of Ivan IV's personal life: the number of his wives; the reasons for marrying so many times, the legitimacy of the later marriages "permitted to him," and his continuing use of the bride-show. Surely, one of the "things that had gone badly for him" was his family life and, more especially, his maniacal pursuit of male heirs. Heidenstein's text provides a road map for examining some of the less explored areas of the terrible tsar's biography.

Ivan IV is known to history as much for his multiple marriages as for his reforms, his conquests, or his atrocities. And rightly so. No influence has traditionally been deemed more significant to his personality and reign than his wives. Ivan IV is said to have loved his first wife so desperately that her death plunged him into a decades-long fit of melancholia, giving rise to the old and still largely prevailing notion of a reign divided into two parts: a "good Ivan" and a "bad Ivan."[2] Alternatively, or additionally, Ivan IV is said to have been influenced by his second wife to create the *oprichnina*—a term understood by some to indicate the division of the country into two parts and the creation of a secret mounted police force dressed in monastic black with severed dogs' heads and brooms hanging from their saddles, symbols of their mission to sweep Muscovy clean of the tsar's enemies.[3] Ivan IV was so taken with his third bride that he set all good sense aside and married her even though she was deathly ill at the time of the wedding and died shortly thereafter. As he sped through the next set of wives, Ivan IV turned his court upside down, alternately promoting then demoting (or executing) the bride's relatives and effectively turning the gates of the Kremlin into a revolving door for royal in-laws. Even Ivan IV's foreign policy was not immune to the impact of his matrimonial upheavals. His pursuit of a Jagiellon wife figured prominently in Muscovite relations with Poland and Sweden, as we have already seen, and in his final years, he sent repeated inquiries to Elizabeth I of England for the hand of the queen's distant kinswoman Lady Mary Hastings, and perhaps even the queen herself—even though, during all these overtures to Poland and England, the tsar was already married.[4]

It is a strange feature of the biographical literature on Ivan IV that, despite all the attention devoted to his family life, there have been few serious studies of the tsar's multiple marriages.[5] As a result, fundamental questions about the tsar's family remain unresolved: how many marriages did Ivan IV actually have—5? 6? 7? or perhaps even 8? What were the dates of his weddings, and how many were arranged by bride-shows? Were the later weddings performed traditionally, and were they canonically legitimate? This chapter continues the study of Ivan IV's marriages begun in Chapter 3, taking up the questions of Muscovite political culture, the bride-show, and Ivan IV's concerns over the succession in the context of the tsar's later marriages.

Marfa Sobakina and Anna Koltovskaia

The death of Mariia Temriukovna on September 1, 1569, only finalized what Ivan IV and his advisors must already have known: his second marriage had been a colossal failure. The marriage produced one son, Vasilii, who died in infancy, but no other pregnancies or births as far as the sources show. He had two sons when he entered the marriage in 1561, one healthy and one not, and the same two sons when Mariia Temriukovna died. Ivan IV must have felt a sense of unease about the future of the dynasty—a desire to assure that the direct line of the dynasty continued and inherited his throne, and a fear that the two sons he had might not be sufficient to do so. This unease explains the run of short-lived and unfruitful marriages Ivan entered into starting in 1571 and ending with his death fourteen years later. Ivan was also increasingly anxious to populate the dynasty with heirs he could control, which, as we have suggested, lay behind the executions of much of the Staritskii line just after Mariia Temriukovna's death. Ivan's desire to provide for and control the succession also lay behind other marriages in the dynasty that he and his advisors would organize in the second half of his reign. Much of the tsar's activities from his third marriage in 1571 on would relate, in one way or another, to the succession.

To be sure, it was not a given that Ivan IV would be permitted a third marriage. He had to appeal to church authorities for permission—a "blessing," in church parlance—to marry yet again, since in the Orthodox understanding of the sacrament, the three marriages canonically allowed a Christian are not hers or his by right but are permitted only through the blessing of a father-confessor, and even then only begrudgingly and with prescribed penance.[6] Even so, the tsar and his advisors pulled out all stops to justify the request. Ivan IV based his case on three arguments. First, he argued that remarriage was necessary "because of the needs of the body [*radi nuzhi telesnyia*]," evidently relying on St. Paul's injunction that "if they cannot exercise self-control, let them marry, since it is better to be married than to be burnt up" (1Cor 7:9). In other words, Ivan IV argued that his remarriage would save him from sinning. Second, Ivan IV reminded the clerics of the young ages of his sons (*radi svoikh sovershena vozrasta ne dostigshikh*), pointing out his obligation to continue rearing them and, perhaps also, their need for a stepmother. (Ivan Ivanovich was 15 years old and Fedor Ivanovich was 12 at the time of Mariia Temriukovna's death.) Third, for these reasons and probably others, Ivan concluded that monasticism was not an option for him (*togo radi vo inochestvo ot"iti ne vozmozhe*). He had to stay in the world, he decided, because his carnal cravings had not yet been extinguished and because his duties as a father were not finished. Of these, the first argument was probably the most persuasive to Metropolitan Kirill—the dangers to the soul posed by illicit sex always being the paramount spiritual danger—and so he blessed Ivan IV's remarriage because "to live in the world without a wife is a temptation [*blazneno*]."[7]

Showing not the slightest hint of stigma or shame, Ivan IV and his advisors arranged what may have been the largest bride-show in the nearly two-centuries-long history of the custom in Muscovy. According to Taube and Kruse—two Livonian nobles who had been captured at the beginning of the Livonian wars in 1559 (Taube) and 1560 (Kruse) and later became advisors to Ivan IV until their defections to Poland in 1571—the tsar gathered as many as 2,000 candidates at his *oprichnina* retreat, Alexandrovo Sloboda, over the course of a year.[8] The bride-show was so large because it was doing double duty: it was used to pick not only the tsar's third bride but also his son's first. Very little is known about this bride-show, except for the outcome. On June 26, 1571, Ivan IV announced his selection of Marfa Vasil'evna Sobakina, for himself, and of Evdokiia Bogdanovna Saburova for his son and heir, Tsarevich Ivan Ivanovich.[9] This is the same Saburov clan that had given Vasilii III his first wife in the first ever bride-show in 1505. (Evdokiia was the second cousin twice removed of Vasilii III's wife, Solomoniia.)[10] The weddings of Ivan IV and his son were a week apart. Ivan IV married Sobakina on October 28, 1571,[11] and Tsarevich Ivan Ivanovich married Saburova on November 4, 1571,[12] both evidently at Alexandrova Sloboda.

The Sobakins were an established servitor family in Moscow as early as the 1430s. Vasilii Ivanovich Sobakin is recorded as a boyar and a signatory of Vasilii II's will, but the boyar line of the clan had subsequently died out.[13] Members of other lines continued to serve in provincial centers: Sobakins are recorded in sixteenth-century service registers as holding the rank of *dvortsovyi syn boiarskii* in Kolomna, Tver', and the Novgorod lands (*Bezhetskii verkh*).[14] They were a branch of the same lineage to which the Nagoi clan belonged, which gave a bride to Prince Vladimir Staritskii (his first) and Ivan IV (his last).[15] The Sobakins may also have been distant relatives of Ivan IV's first wife, Anastasiia Iur'eva. At the end of the fifteenth century one of the members of the clan, a certain Timofei Sobakin, is in some sources reported as married to the daughter of Ivan Ivanovich Koshkin, the grandson of the boyar Fedor Koshka, the founder of the Iur'ev line.[16] Whatever the truth of the matter, the background of the tsar's third bride is known well enough to dispel the claims in some biographies of Ivan IV that Marfa came from a Novgorod merchant family.[17]

This was a remarkable moment in Muscovite history: for practical purposes, the double marriage of the tsar and his son. Not only did Ivan IV and Ivan Ivanovich find their wives in the same bride-show, not only were they betrothed on the same day and married at the same royal retreat, but their Sobakin and Saburov in-laws co-mingled in large numbers at Ivan IV's wedding. Sobakin kinsmen performed important honorific duties at the wedding. The bride's father and uncles were seated at the Side Table (*v Krivom stole*), her brother was the tsar's first best man and was with him in the baths, as were two of her first cousins and a second cousin. Other relatives made up the wedding bed (*u posteli*), arranged the traditional showering of hops (*s osypalom*), held the cap (*kolpak*), carried the wedding candles (*nesti obruchal'nye svechi*), walked in the procession in front of the tsar (*pered gosudarem khodit'*) or behind the bride's sleds (*za san'mi*), and heated the bath (*myl'niu topiti*). All together, twelve Sobakin kinsmen performed sixteen different duties at the wedding.[18]

The family of Ivan IV's future daughter-in-law—the Saburovs—was also prominently represented at Ivan IV's wedding. Ivan Ivanovich Men'shii Saburov, the bride's first cousin once removed, filled the role as the tsar's second best man, and his wife was one of the two matchmakers. Another cousin, Ivan Vasil'evich Saburov, performed part of the duties with the cap (*kolpak*), and still another, Grigorii Paninovich Saburov, was seated at the main banquet table (*za stolom*). Evdokiia Bogdanovna Saburova, Tsarevich Ivan Ivanovich's betrothed, is not mentioned in the wedding muster, but her sister, Domna, is recorded as having sat in the tsar's place (*na meste gosudareve*). It was a symbolically important post. This person sat in the banquet hall with the bride until the groom arrived in procession, which signaled the formal beginning of the set of rituals on the first day of the wedding.[19] Tallying it up, five Saburovs each filled a different honorific post at Ivan IV's wedding.

Alas, the son's wedding a week later is not as well documented as his father's. The only known description of it that survives are in two unpublished later copies of a preliminary version of the wedding ceremonial (*chin*), which describe fairly well the various elements of the wedding ritual (the decorations in the various Kremlin palaces where the wedding was to be held, precise directions for the processions, and instructions on many of the other rituals) but contain unfortunately very few names of those who filled honorific posts.[20] The few that are listed include the bride and groom, of course; the tsar and his new wife; the groom's brother, Tsarevich Fedor Ivanovich, who served as thousandman; a priest, Fr. Timofei, who is identified as the groom's father-confessor (*dukhovnik*) and who officiated at the wedding; and the bride's sister, the same Domna from Ivan IV's wedding the week before, who this time was to sit in the tsarevich's place (*na tsarevichevo mesto*).[21] That Domna occupied the same position at both the father's and the son's weddings only reinforces the conclusion that these weddings were linked events: planned simultaneously and using the same scribal staff to compose the wedding documents and assemble courtiers for their various honorific duties.[22]

The officiating priest, Fr. Timofei, is another link between the two weddings. The published versions of Ivan IV's wedding muster, all short redactions, omit the name of the clergy who served at the wedding, but unpublished long redactions of the text include them: "And the tsar's father-confessor, Fr. Timofei, officiated, and behind the tsar in the processions to and from the churches was Archpriest Semion Pokrovskii, and with the holy water was the priest Vasilii and the deacon Foma."[23] While Metropolitan Kirill gave his blessing for Ivan IV to remarry, he did not officiate. Ivan IV's marriage to Marfa Sobakina would be the first where a priest, not the first hierarch, would officiate at a tsar's or grand prince's wedding. Ivan IV had been married the first and second times by Metropolitan Makarii, as were his uncle (Andrei Staritskii), his brother (Iurii Vasil'evich), and his cousin (Vladimir Staritskii and Evdokiia Nagaia). His father and mother (Vasilii III and Elena Glinskaia) were married by Metropolitan Daniil.[24] The demotion in the rank of the officiating clergy was probably deliberate: a signal from the church that its permission of Ivan IV's remarriage was an act of *œconomia*, or a bending of the formal rules, which was allowed only in individual cases when concern for the salvation of a soul trumped the canons.

The rank of officiating clergy at these weddings is thus redolent of a controversy. Tsarevich Ivan Ivanovich should not have been under the same stricture as his father, since this was his first marriage. It is only a speculation, but it is easy to imagine that Fr. Timofei was conscripted to do both weddings so that the son's should not in any way outshine the father's by having the son married by the first hierarch of the church while the father was married only by a priest. The selection of the tsar's father-confessor (*dukhovnik*) further puts the spotlight on the penitential nature of the wedding, putting the ritual in the hands of the cleric who heard the tsar's confessions and, by Orthodox notions of pastoral care, was most responsible for his soul and salvation.[25] Whatever the case, the innovation of having the ruler married by his father-confessor (instead of the first hierarch) would subsequently become common practice.[26]

The composition of the Sobakina wedding roster reveals that the selection of Sobakina and Saburova at the 1571 bride-show was a part of a general reshuffling of factions at court. How this might have happened was suggested by Skrynnikov. He argued that the Sobakin wedding was the brainchild of Maliuta Skuratov, Ivan IV's favorite at the time and one of the most ruthless of the *oprichniki*. On the basis of commemorations made by Ivan IV on behalf of Skuratov, Skrynnikov argued that the Sobakins and the Skuratovs were distant kin, perhaps affines.[27] Maliuta Skuratov, furthermore, was linked to the Saburovs through his son-in-law Boris Godunov, since the Godunovs and Saburovs were agnates. Skuratov's other daughters were married to a Shuiskii (Prince Dmitrii Ivanovich, brother of the future tsar Vasilii Ivanovich Shuiskii) and to a Glinskii (Prince Ivan Mikhailovich, first cousin of Tsar Ivan IV).[28] In this way, the marriages of father and son created a kinship network that, it was hoped, would endure for two generations. It lasted less than a month.

For all the careful coordination in the two weddings, neither groom "lived happier ever after." Marfa Sobakina fell ill before the wedding and was ill even while the wedding was being celebrated. She was probably too sick to participate in Tsarevich Ivan Ivanovich's wedding to Evdokiia Saburova. She died on the night of November 13–14, 1571, just three weeks after her wedding, and just a little more than a week after Tsarevich Ivan Ivanovich's—the union never having been consummated, or so Ivan IV claimed.[29] Suspicions of foul play in her death arose immediately, and the tsar suspected persons close to him.[30] Zabelin, Karamzin, and others believed the tsar's assertion that Sobakina was murdered, perhaps poisoned, and laid the blame for it in the laps of the families of the tsar's first two wives—the Iur'evs and Cherkasskiis—who, it must be admitted, had a great deal to lose from Ivan IV's remarriage in terms of their station at court and the status of Ivan IV's sons by his first wife, should Sobakina give birth to healthy boys.[31]

As for the tsarevich's marriage, within a few years Saburova was repudiated, perhaps on Tsar Ivan IV's command. She was tonsured a nun with the name Aleksandra and then confined at the Our Lady of the Intercession Monastery in Suzdal' (*Pokrovskii monastyr'*), where in 1619 she died and was buried. When she was repudiated is unclear, though most historians have assumed it was in 1575, just before the tsar and the tsarevich remarried (Ivan IV for the fifth time, the tsarevich for the second).[32]

Shortly after Sobakina's death, Ivan IV convened a church council in the Dormition Cathedral to receive a blessing to marry a fourth time. The tsar was treading on new and canonically dangerous territory now. The Eastern Orthodox Church over time had embraced and sanctified the notion of marriage as symbolic of the mystical union between Christ and His Church (as found in Matt. 22:2–12; Matt. 24:10; Lk. 12:36; Eph. 5:22–33; and, of course, Christian interpretations of the Tanak's Song of Songs) and so gradually had insinuated itself into both the canonical regulation and ritualized certification of marriage from at least the time of Athenagoras of Athens (133–190) or, later, St. Basil the Great (330–379) and St. John Chrysostom (ca. 347–407). The final legal statement on the church's canonical stance on marriage came in the Tome of Union of the Council of Constantinople in 920, issued in the wake of the marital excesses of the tetragamist Byzantine emperor Leo VI (866–912). The Tome of Union (what Fr. John Meyendorff called "the most solemn set of rules accepted by both church and empire concerning the conditions of successive marriages")[33] permitted remarriage but placed restrictions on a third and strictly forbade a fourth. Those persons seeking a third marriage would receive the church's blessing only if they were under forty years old (with four years' penance), but persons over forty years old might marry a third time only if they had no surviving children from either of their previous marriages (again with a penance, this time of five years).[34] According to the Tome of Union, violators of the ban on a fourth marriage "shall be excluded from every religious congregation and even forbidden to enter the holy temple, as long as the union continues."[35]

Muscovite canonical ordinances likewise drew the line at three marriages, but the penalties varied. The 1551 Stoglav Council—convened just twenty years before Ivan IV's third marriage—devotes Chapters 18 through 24 to a range of topics touching on Orthodox Christian marriage; and in Chapter 23, the council comes down decidedly against fourth marriages. It recalls the tetragamist controversy of the Byzantine emperor Leo VI and quotes St. Gregory of Nazianzus's harsh condemnation of remarriage: "The first [marriage] is legal, the second is condoned, the third violates the law, and the fourth is dishonorable, like unto a swine's life."[36] In Chapter 24, St. Basil the Great is cited and the penalties for remarriage are prescribed, but the chapter nonetheless contemplates scenarios for fourth marriages. Men and women who contracted a fourth time were prohibited from entering a church for four years and kept away from the communion cup for eighteen years. Those marrying a third time were not to commune for five years.[37] Chapter 21 prohibits those marrying a second time from communing for two years (or just one year, if the digamist is "young").[38]

In his appeal to the council in the spring of 1572, Ivan IV recounted his matrimonial history for the assembled hierarchs: his first wife, Anastasiia Iur'eva, with whom he had lived for thirteen and a half years, was, he alleged, murdered by evil people around him; his second wife, Mariia Cherkasskaia, with whom he had lived for eight years, succumbed in the end to many and various illnesses; and his third, Marfa Sobakina, to whom he had been married for only two weeks, had been ill the entire time, the victim of a conspiracy, he claimed, of "those close to me [*blizhnikh*]," which prevented the union from ever being consummated.[39] In the previous year, the tsar had justified his appeal for a third marriage on the grounds of the "needs of the body," the young ages of his sons, and his own unsuitability for monasticism.[40] Now, in his appeal for a fourth marriage, he grasped for even more broadly significant justifications: the sorrowful state of the Christian polity he ruled, the continuing minority of his children, and his claim that the third marriage should not count because it was never consummated. No mention was made this time of any "needs of the body."

According to the official description of the council, which was composed later and therefore may not in every way accurately report the attitudes of the bishops and monastic fathers, what most persuaded them was Ivan IV's display of humility and remorse at having to seek permission to remarry at all, his tears, and his fervent pleas for forgiveness. (It is unlikely that the council would at all be persuaded that the third marriage did not "count," given the church's view that marriages were made through the grace-filled rituals of the nuptial service, not by consummation.)[41] But the tsar was asking for a lot this time; and no matter how many tears he shed or appeals to the welfare of the realm he made, the tsar would have to outlast the sturdy resistance of Metropolitan Kirill. It was only after the hierarch's death on February 8, 1572, that the remaining bishops and monastic fathers acquiesced to the tsar's request.[42]

In rendering their decision on a fourth marriage (and probably also when they had approved Ivan IV's appeal for a third the previous year), the assembled hierarchs and monastic authorities referred to many of the standard patristic sources for marriage: the "canons of the Holy Apostles and of the Holy Seven Ecumenical Councils," the "fourth and eighteenth rules of St. Basil the Great," and the "first title [*izbranie*] of the Nomocanon."[43] They must therefore also have known the prescribed penance for remarriage according to these ancient sources and the Stoglav but chose not to impose it. Instead, the council prohibited Ivan IV from entering a church until Easter, or Pascha (March 22 in the year 1573), when he would be permitted, with the blessing of his father-confessor, to take communion and partake of the lesser antidorum (*men'shaia dora*). For the next year, up until the next Pascha, Ivan was not permitted to enter the nave (*tserkov'*) of the church but was required to stand in the vestibule, where others under penance stood during divine services. At Pascha of his second year of penance (1574), he still had to stand outside the nave but was permitted to enter the church to take communion and partake of both the lesser antidorum and the greater (*bol'shaia*) antidorum.[44] During the third (and final) year of penance (1575), he was permitted to enter the church and "stand with the faithful," and to commune, with the blessing of his father-confessor, on the twelve Feasts of the Lord and Mother of God (*khoditi i priimati po Vladychnim prazdnikom i po Bogorodichnym*), and at Pascha.[45] All of these restrictions were waived, however, when the tsar was on campaign with his army. Severe as it may seem, it is clear that the tsar was dealt with lightly by his bishops. Ivan IV was over age forty at the time of his petition to the church council, and he had children (sons, moreover), which clearly disqualified him for remarriage; and the term of his penance (three years) was far less than that prescribed in the Tome of Union and by the other textual authorities that the council consulted.

The council issued its ruling, such as it was, on April 29, 1572, and Ivan IV married Anna Koltovskaia sometime before May 31.[46] Ivan IV accepted his punishment, and he probably lived under penance for the rest of his life, not just for the next three years.[47] Antonio Possevino noted in 1584 that Ivan IV was even then living under (apparently additional) penance. According to him, the tsar "can no longer receive the Eucharist because, in accordance with their laws, it is forbidden to anyone who has had more than three wives to have communion with the body of Christ our Lord."[48]

As for the bride, the Koltovskiis claimed in genealogical rosters (*rodoslovnie rospisi*) compiled in the seventeenth century that the family descended from the large Sorokoumov-Glebov clan, but Margarita Bychkova has raised doubts about this genealogy.[49] Even so, contemporary sources record the family's history of honorable service in the provinces and on diplomatic and other assignments reaching back to the late fifteenth century. Anna Koltovskaia, like Marfa Sobakina before her, was the daughter of a Kolomna *syn boiarskii*, but other members of her clan served also in Kashira and Tarusa.[50] The new tsaritsa's father had died by 1550 and many of her other male kin had died before her wedding with the tsar, prompting Bychkova to conclude that the match "harkens back to [Ivan's] father's second marriage: like Elena Glinskaia, Anna had no close relatives; they had all died before the marriage."[51] Unfortunately, no wedding description of any kind (ceremonial or muster) survives.[52]

It is often mentioned in the biographies of Ivan IV that Anna Koltovskaia participated in the bride-show in Alexandrovo Sloboda and had been a runner-up.[53] This conclusion appears to rest on the fact that Ivan IV married so quickly—within one month—after the church council gave its begrudging approval for this fourth marriage. Ivan IV could not possibly have found a new bride by means of a new bride-show in so short a time, it is thought, so Anna Koltovskaia must have been a finalist in the previous bride-show only a few months before. While this is a reasonable assumption, there is no direct evidence for it one way or the other. The interval between the public announcement of a bride-show, the selection of a winner, and a wedding could be remarkably short, as we have already seen. Therefore, the span of one month between the church council's approval (April 29) and the end of May (by which time Ivan and Anna were married) does not necessarily preclude a bride-show.

The selection of Anna Koltovskaia coincided with yet another shakeup at court. The first to go were the Sobakins, the relatives of Ivan's unfortunate third bride. Some Sobakins immediately suffered after Marfa Sobakina's death. In 1572, Marfa's uncle, Vasilii Stepanovich Men'shii, who had been made an okol'nichii about the time of Ivan IV's wedding to Marfa, was tonsured a monk (with the name Varlaam) at the Kirillo-Belozerskii monastery. Other demotions and executions followed, and no new Sobakins entered into the tsar's circle after Marfa's death. Over the course of the next year, Sobakins would gradually be replaced by the Koltovskiis and their allies. The passing of the torch from the Sobakins to the Koltovskiis was signaled in the summer of 1572, when Boris Davydovich Tulupov's cousin married the new tsaritsa's brother, Grigorii Alekseevich Koltovskii, during a visit by the tsar and his entourage to Novgorod. Witnessing (and no doubt lamenting) the wedding were Vasilii

Stepanovich Sobakin and Kallist Vasil'evich Sobakin who had accompanied the tsar's party on the expedition to Novgorod—the last sign of royal favor before their executions in the following year. In 1573, two Sobakins were present at the wedding, again in Novgorod, of Mariia Staritskaia and Magnus, the so-called king of Livonia, but that was the Sobakins' last moment in the sun. The abrupt, and ultimately tragic, rise and fall of the Sobakins presents perhaps the most extraordinary example of how royal marriage and court politics could combine to make or break a family's fortunes—sometimes with dizzying speed.[54]

A mere four months after her marriage to the tsar, Anna Koltovskaia was repudiated in September or October 1572, tonsured a nun (with the name Dar'ia), and sent away to spend the remainder of her life in a convent—first at the remote Vvedenskii-Tikhvinskii Convent, then for a time at the Voskresenskii Goritskii Convent (near the Kirillo-Belozerskii Monastery), then back at Tikhvin, where she died on April 5, 1626.[55] Why she was repudiated, and so rapidly, is nowhere explained in the sources, but her health was not the reason; she enjoyed a long and relatively active life given her circumstances. She lived through the upheavals of the Time of Troubles and long enough to see Mikhail Romanov crowned tsar and married twice, receiving on both occasions the same special wedding gifts that other members of the royal family received: an oblong ornamental cloth (*ubrusets*), richly made of taffeta with pearls sewn into the fabric; and an ornamental kerchief (*shirinka*), also of taffeta, with rich gold-thread embroidery and gold fringe along its edges.[56] Even fifty-three years after her brief marriage to Ivan IV, Anna was considered royalty. And she acted that way at times, even from her monastic cell. New biographical details of her life after the Terem have come to light recently and show her to have been an active defender and promoter of her own fiscal interests and status as a former tsaritsa, "exploit[ing]," as Thyrêt puts it, "royal prestige for the benefit of her own kin and her beloved fellow nuns."[57]

Five Weddings and the Succession

After Koltovskaia's repudiation, Ivan IV went without any wife for more than two years—from the fall of 1572 to, probably, January 1575, the longest interval of unmarried life he had as an adult. Despite the hiatus, marriage and succession remained on his mind. In fact, these years represent the most active period in dynastic marriage since 1547–1549, when Ivan and his brother and cousin had married in relatively quick succession for the same reason: to enlarge the dynasty and ensure the succession. This time, however, Ivan IV and his advisors looked beyond the male members of the dynasty to branches that descended from it in the female line.

The first marriage in these years was on April 12, 1573, when the tsar arranged the wedding in Novgorod of Vladimir Staritskii's daughter Mariia to Magnus, the younger brother of King Frederick II of Denmark (r. 1559–1588).[58] The marriage was a chapter in the Livonian War (1558–1578), Ivan IV's grand designs to expand Muscovy's Baltic frontiers at the expense of Sweden, Poland, and the Livonian knights. Ivan IV's campaigns up to 1559 had left him in possession of large tracts of territory in Livonia, but much of Estonia and southern Livonia remained outside his control. Magnus had originally inherited the duchy of Holstein from his father, King Christian III of Denmark (r., in Denmark, 1534–1559), part of the narrow isthmus connecting northern Jütland with the European continent. In 1560, however, Magnus's older brother, King Frederick II, exchanged Magnus's inheritance for the remote island bishopric of Ösel and other territories on the Livonian mainland. Ivan IV's fortunes in the war had been flagging since 1560, and as a way of recasting his territorial ambitions into a more feasible goal, he hatched a plan to add his own conquests to the Danish prince's patrimony and to transform the unified territory into the "Kingdom of Livonia." For Magnus, allying himself with Ivan IV was his best hope for a kingdom of his own. His brother Frederick II already had an heir, and Magnus therefore knew it was unlikely he would ever inherit the Danish throne. For Ivan IV, Magnus presented an ideal opportunity to further his objectives in the Livonian War: Magnus already had a footing in the territory he coveted, and placing Magnus on a puppet throne under Muscovite protection would have given Ivan IV nearly the same control of this space that he would have had if he had conquered and annexed the territories outright, without the costs of conquest and occupation.[59]

Part and parcel of the alliance between Magnus and Ivan IV was a dynastic union between their respective houses. Ivan IV offered Magnus one of the daughters of his first cousin Prince Vladimir Staritskii, Efimiia and Mariia, both of whom, along with their brother Vasilii, had been spared execution with their parents, sister, and grandmother in 1569. Ivan IV proposed in 1570 that Magnus marry the elder daughter, Efimiia, who was at the time only ten years old.[60] The marriage looks outwardly like a traditional diplomatic match, reinforcing a treaty and made in the interests of Muscovy's foreign policy; but it had as much to do with domestic politics, because it was intended from the beginning that Magnus and his Daniilovich bride should live in territory controlled by Muscovy, not in a distant foreign land. Ivan IV was not so much giving away the bride as he was adopting the groom.

On June 10, 1570, Magnus arrived in Moscow, was proclaimed king, and pledged loyalty to Ivan IV. But right from the start things did not go as planned. The bride Ivan IV had promised to Magnus, Efimiia Vladimirovna Staritskaia, died of the plague the following year.[61] Not discouraged, the tsar substituted the unfortunate girl's younger sister, Mariia, as Magnus's bride. The wedding took place two years later, presumably to give Mariia time to reach marriageable age, in the Church of St. Dmitrii on Proboinaia Street in Novgorod. According to the muster and ceremonial, Ivan IV himself attended, as did his son Tsarevich Ivan Ivanovich, the bride's brother Prince Vasilii Vladimirovich, and Vasilii's wife, Mariia. Much of the court was present as well. The Chinggisid tsarevich Mikhail Kaibulovich, perhaps the leading figure in Ivan IV's court at that moment, was the thousandman (*tysiatskii*), and numerous other boyars and high-ranking courtiers and their wives served as best men (*druzhki*), matchmakers (*svakhi*), and holders of the *kika*, the forty sables, the ceremonial loaves of bread and cheese, the candles, the torches, and so on. While the usual nuptial traditions were followed, it was a liturgically hybrid wedding service, officiated over by two sets of clergy and elements of two different rituals. As the *chin* puts it, the groom was married "according to his own rites [*po ego zakonu*]," and the bride "according to Christian rites [*po kristianskomu zakonu*]."[62]

The ruling dynasty issuing from Mariia and Magnus would be Oldenburg in the male line (the Danish ruling house) and Daniilovich in the female line, and it seems that Ivan IV had that dynastic configuration, as well as Baltic diplomacy, in mind in arranging this marriage. The Danish diplomat Hans Schultz reported that, at a reception held for Magnus in Moscow in June 1570, Ivan had unexpectedly proclaimed that "King" Magnus would succeed him on the throne after his death, not one of his two sons. "My dear brother," Ivan IV is reported to have said (addressing Magnus), "in view of your fidelity and that of the German people, and because of my devotion to the latter (for I am of German ancestry and Saxon blood), and despite the fact that I have two sons—one 17 and the other 13 years old: Your Grace, when I am dead, you will be my heir and the ruler of my kingdom."[63] Schultz interpreted the proclamation as a not-so-veiled threat against the boyars in attendance, not as a genuine announcement of Ivan's dynastic plans, but Skrynnikov, for example, may be right when he points out that this threat in 1570 comes five years before Ivan actually did skip over his sons and hand the crown to someone else, Simeon Bekbulatovich.[64] Why Ivan IV should wish to pass over his sons in 1570 (and later in 1575) remains unknown, but the speculation of some historians that he did not like or trust his eldest son and viewed his younger son as too sickly to reign may, if true, get us close to an explanation.[65] Passing the throne to a cognatic member of the dynasty—someone like Magnus, who was entirely beholden to Ivan for his status—may have looked like a very sensible move to a father who was unsatisfied with the likes of his own sons.

The fates of Mariia and Magnus were far from those planned for them in 1573. Despite some early successes at the front, Magnus proved himself to be incompetent as a general and untrustworthy as an ally. In 1577, Magnus betrayed Ivan IV in a desperate attempt to strike out on his own by rallying local nobles against both the Poles and the Muscovites. It was probably Magnus's marriage ties to Ivan IV that kept him from the gallows for his treachery, but he was compelled to renounce his royal title and accept confinement at his residence in Pilten, in Courland, dying in 1583, a reduced and bitter man.[66] His wife, Mariia, and daughter, Evdokiia, fared little better. Boris Godunov, Tsar Fedor Ivanovich's guardian and chief advisor, dispatched Jerome Horsey to Courland to entice the young widow and her daughter by Magnus back to Moscow with the promise of an appanage and a suitable new husband. "Instead of an appanage and a groom," Karamzin colorfully puts it, "Boris offered her a choice between the cloister and prison."[67] She chose the cloister, asking only not to be separated from her daughter—a plea that was cruelly ignored. Mariia lived out the remaining years of her life (she died on June 13, 1597) as the nun Marfa. Her daughter, Evdokiia, returned to Moscow with her mother but died soon after, on March 17, 1589.[68] This final pruning of the Staritskii branch of the dynasty was, like the first pruning in 1569, motivated by fears over the succession. But this time, they were Godunov's fears—and his ambitions to assume the throne himself—not Tsar Fedor Ivanovich's, that were in play. As Giles Fletcher put it, Mariia was lured back to Moscow "by some that love the succession better than herself."[69]

As for Mariia's brother Vasilii, he attended his sister's wedding to Magnus in 1573, and the wedding muster and the unpublished ceremonial both list a wife named Mariia.[70] The Piskarevskii Chronicle reports that Vasilii Vladimirovich married a Mezetskii princess (the first name is not given in the text, nor does it provide a date) at Alexandrovo Sloboda.[71] There has been some debate about the identity of Vasilii's wife, and whether he had even married at all,[72] but the evidence from the wedding texts leaves little doubt that he did, though her identification as a Mezetskaia still awaits corroboration. Whatever the case, there was evidently no issue from the union. The Staritskii clan was extinct.

Ivan IV's brief time as a bachelor came to an end at the turn of 1575 when he married his fifth wife, Anna Vasil'chikova, the daughter of a family of *deti boiarskie* in Kashira, as Koltovskaia had been. Vasil'chikova is repeatedly described in older biographies as a "mistress" or an "uncanonical" wife whose wedding to Ivan IV was celebrated without the usual rituals and without the church's blessing.[73] But the existence of manuscript (and published) copies of the Vasil'chikova wedding ceremonial and muster puts to rest all doubt about the historicity of the wedding: Vasil'chikova was as legitimate as any of Ivan's other wives.[74] And like Anastasiia Iur'eva and Marfa Sobakina (and possibly Anna Koltovskaia), Vasil'chikova probably participated in a bride-show. One is suggested in the report of the imperial diplomat Daniel Printz von Buchau from 1575, who wrote just a few weeks or months after Ivan IV's wedding had been celebrated. In this report, Printz counts Ivan IV's first five wives—correctly identifying the first, second, and fourth by name, and putting all five in the right order. Then he reports on the wedding that had just taken place: "Now he [i.e., Ivan IV] has taken another wife, the daughter of some or other boyar, blessed, as they say, with a beautiful figure; but because she is his fifth wife, the majority constantly shun her."[75] The passage then proceeds to a description of how bride-shows worked in Muscovy, suggesting that this fifth wife—Anna Vasil'chikova is unnamed in the text—had been selected that way. Besides the reference to the bride-show, this passage is important because it is one of the few places where any of the observers of Ivan IV's domestic life took the trouble to describe the socially awkward and isolated position in which the tsar's later brides found themselves through no fault of their own. Vasil'chikova was shunned by the women, and perhaps also the men, of the court who may have found it difficult to know how to treat a young woman whose marriage to the tsar violated so many cultural and religious norms. The Terem must have been a relentlessly lonely place for royal wives anyhow, but Ivan IV's marital capriciousness can only have made the situation for his later wives all the worse.

There is some disagreement among Ivan IV's biographers about the date of the Vasil'chikova wedding. The wedding description (a combined ceremonial and muster) provides only the year—7083, or 1574/75—but no month or day for the wedding. Skrynnikov argued that the wedding took place between September 1 and November 13, 1574, because it was probably then, just before the new year began (that is, before September 1, 1574), that a large estate (*pomest'e*) was given to the bride's brothers Nazarii and Grigorii—a sign of royal favor that far exceeded their prior status in the service hierarchy and therefore must have been related to the coming marriage between the tsar and their sister. (Just the year before, both brothers are recorded as having received a relatively meager *oklad*, or fiscal entitlement, of fifty rubles.) Skrynnikov knew that the marriage could not have occurred during the Nativity Fast, which starts every year on November 14 and lasts until December 25. Skrynnikov also knew that one servitor who attended the wedding (Mikhail Vasil'evich Kolychev) had departed for the Swedish border on January 30, proving that the event took place before then.[76] For some reason, Skrynnikov did not consider the available dates in January for the wedding, but Zimin argued on the basis of a detailed study of the Vasil'chikova wedding rosters that it was precisely during those January dates—between January 7 and January 30, 1575—that the wedding most likely took place.[77] Zimin's is the more plausible conclusion, fitting better what we know about the weddings of Ivan's sons in the same year (as we will see below).

The Vasil'chikova wedding followed all the customary rules for royal marriages in Muscovy, not just the liturgical rubrics on the timing of nuptials. The extant ceremonial describes a wedding that was celebrated in much the same way as Ivan IV's previous weddings had been celebrated. The venue where most of the gatherings took place was decorated, according to the text, "in the customary way [*nariazheno bylo po obychaiu*]."[78] The bride is referred to as "tsarevna" at the beginning of the text, before the wedding service (as we have seen, a traditional and fictive title given to the winners of bride-shows before their weddings), and routinely as "tsaritsa and grand princess" after the wedding ceremony.[79] At the wedding, the bride performed her traditional role of bestowing gifts (*shirinki*) through her first best man (*druzhka*).[80] And, perhaps the plainest proof that this was a royal wedding like any other, the text states that the couple was married (that is, "crowned"; *venchal*) by a priest, and that afterward the couple received the usual acclamations and greetings from Ivan IV's sons and from "all the boyars and scribes and *deti boiarskie*."[81]

Like the Sobakina wedding before it, the Vasil'chikova wedding was officiated by a priest, not the metropolitan, which was the way the church had chosen to handle Ivan IV's later marriages. The surviving wedding ceremonial and muster hint at some controversy over the appointment of clergy, however. The ceremonial oddly omits the names of the priests who served at the wedding (the priests who uttered a prayer over the couple before the wedding, and who "accompanied the tsar to all the churches," and who walked in the procession to and from the church with holy water), and the text explains that "the tsar so ordered that their names not be written down."[82] Happily, the muster supplies the names: Fr. Vasilii Borodatoi was to officiate, and Fr. Vasilii Molodoi and Deacon Pankratei were charged with attending to the holy water.[83] One is tempted to speculate on why the tsar specifically ordered that the names of the officiating clergy be omitted from the ceremonial. So far as we know, the tsar had not formally petitioned the church for permission to marry a fifth time (as he did before his third and fourth marriages), and so perhaps he was having trouble convincing a priest to accept the questionable honor of presiding over his nuptials. Perhaps Ivan IV was protecting the identity of the clergy he had cajoled into officiating at the wedding so they would not be reproved by their bishops or prohibited beforehand from serving. Perhaps the tsar did not know until the last minute whom the metropolitan would assign to perform the wedding. Whatever the case, the text of the wedding ceremonial preserves an undeniable whiff of scandal.

It is hard not to agree with Zimin that the Vasil'chkova wedding was, in at least one way, "peculiar" (*osobennoi*). Zimin's exhaustive study of the wedding ceremonial revealed that "absent [from it] were the flower of the titled Muscovite aristocracy from the old *zemshchina*," that part of the country that Ivan IV had not appropriated into his own personal "privy domain," or *oprichnina*.[84] Present instead was an entire cast of royal favorites. Most prominent were the Kolychevs, led by Vasilii Ivanovich Umnoi-Kolychev, the rising star in Ivan IV's inner circle, his wife, and eighteen other members of the Kolychev clan.[85] Also in attendance was the favorite Boris Davydovich Tulupov and three of his kinsmen;[86] a number of Godunovs;[87] several Shuiskiis;[88] eleven Vasil'chikovs,[89] and a few individuals personally close to the tsar, such as Afanasii Fedorovich Nagoi and Bogdan Iakovlevich Bel'skii.[90] Though celebrated with the customary rituals and clearly with the participation and blessing of the church, the honorific posts at the Vasil'chikova wedding were filled by those personally close to Ivan IV, not by representatives of all the great clans at court, as was usually the case.[91] Like the Sobakina wedding in 1571, this was an exclusive event.

Both of Ivan IV's sons, Ivan Ivanovich and Fedor Ivanovich, married in this same year, probably shortly after Ivan's wedding with Vasil'chikova. We know next to nothing about these marriages: there are no known wedding texts that describe the nuptials or the reasons for the choice of spouse. We do not know for sure if there were bride-shows, nor do we know the exact dates of the marriages or what order they fell in over the course of the year (1575). What we do know is that early in 1575, the tsar's son Ivan Ivanovich married his second wife, Pelageia/Feodosiia Mikhailovna Petrova-Solovaia, after repudiating his first wife. Born with the name Pelageia (she changed it to Feodosiia on her marriage to the tsarevich), she was the daughter of a middle-level servitor, Mikhail Timofeevich Petrov, who was appointed *okol'nichii* in 1577 (he served only until 1578), and whom Zimin identified as an *oprichnik*. Neither she nor any of her kin are mentioned in the descriptions of the Vasil'chikova wedding. Pelageia/Feodosiia was tonsured a nun with the name Praskov'ia, possibly on Ivan IV's orders, in or shortly after November 1579.[92] Why Petrova-Solovaia was repudiated remains unknown, but her failure to give the tsar a grandson after four years of marriage to the tsarevich is a likely explanation. In any case, her downfall was not linked to her health: she lived until 1620.[93]

Also in 1575, Ivan IV's younger son, Fedor Ivanovich, married Irina Fedorovna Godunova, the sister of Ivan IV's latest favorite, Boris Fedorovich Godunov. Some historians have dated the wedding to 1580, following Karamzin's (erroneous) speculation that the wedding took place at the same time as the appointment of the bride's brother Boris Fedorovich Godunov to boyar rank.[94] But the first signs of the Godunov clan's rising star are apparent well before 1580. Five Godunovs were present at Ivan IV's wedding to Vasil'chikova in 1575.[95] In that same year, Dmitrii Ivanovich Godunov was appointed an *okol'nichii*, and in the following year, his nephew Boris Fedorovich (Irina's brother) was appointed *kravchii*.[96]

In addition, embroidered altar shrouds (*peleny*) in the inventories at Borovsko-Pafnut'ev and Holy Trinity St. Sergius Monastery dated March 5, 1575, and May 3, 1575, contain inscriptions that identify Irina already as Fedor Ivanovich's wife.[97] That Tsarevich Fedor Ivanovich married in 1575, not 1580, is finally also supported by Daniel Printz von Buchau, who was in Muscovy from November 1575 to February 1576 and wrote his account of his visit to Muscovy in 1578. Printz notes that "both sons, the older one 20 years old and the younger one 18, both still without whiskers, entered into marriage with some or other daughters of boyars in the same year when we were there."[98] Printz's account is detailed enough to believe, even getting the ages for the brothers about right. Pulling this evidence together, it is safe to conclude that Ivan IV and both his sons were married by March 5, 1575, probably all three in close interval.

A fifth marriage in the dynasty took place in late 1575 (or early 1576)—between Simeon Bekbulatovich and Anastasiia Ivanovna Mstislavskaia.[99] Like the other four marriages in the early 1570s (the tsar's, the tsar's sons', and Mariia Staritskaia's), this one was aimed at repopulating the dynasty. It can and should be considered a dynastic event because, even though it did not involve a bride-show (the bride and groom were paired by the tsar and his advisors), Anastasiia Mstislavskaia was, for all intents and purposes, a member of the dynasty. The marriage was also a clear indication of Ivan's intention to repopulate the dynasty with heirs he could control, even if this meant bumping his sons from the line of succession to exert and maintain that contol.

Simeon Bekbulatovich—born Saín Bulat—had arrived in Muscovy in 1561 in Mariia/Kuchenei Temriukovna Cherkasskaia's retinue.[100] He was a descendant of Ghinggis Khan through his eldest son, Jochi, and Mariia/Kuchenei was Saín Bulat's maternal aunt. These connections probably gave him instant clout at Ivan's court. By 1570, Ivan IV had made him the khan of Kasimov, where he ruled as a faithful ally to Moscow—in the same way it was hoped Magnus would rule in Livonia. In 1573, Saín Bulat converted to Orthodox Christianity and was given the name Simeon upon his baptism; and two years later, Ivan IV abdicated his throne in his favor and became merely "Ivan Moskovskii."[101] Ivan IV's new bride, Anna Vasil'chikova, who had been tsaritsa for only a few months, presumably surrendered her title, too. Bekbulatovich's reign was brief. In the fall of 1576, "Ivan Moskovskii" resumed his throne; and Bekbulatovich, the former "grand prince of all Rus'," received in compensation a large appanage made up of Tver' and Torzhok.[102]

As illustrious as Simeon's background was, it was Anastasiia Ivanovna Mstislavskaia's ancestry, not Bekbulatovich's, that made this a dynastic wedding.[103] Mstislavskaia was the great-granddaughter of Ivan III's daughter Evdokiia, who had married Tsarevich Peter (Kudai Kul—another converted Ghinggisid tsarevich) on January 25, 1506.[104] Tsarevich Peter and Evdokiia in turn had two daughters, both evidently named Anastasiia.[105] One daughter married Prince Fedor Mikhailovich Mstislavskii in 1529, and it was their granddaughter Anastasiia Ivanovna Mstislavskaia who married Tsar Simeon Bekbulatovich in 1575 or 1576.[106] Tsarevich Peter and Evdokiia's other daughter married Prince Vasilii Vasil'evich Shuiskii in 1538.[107] Their daughter Marfa Vasil'evna Shuiskaia in turn married Prince Ivan Dmitrievich Bel'skii in 1554, but the marriage was childless.[108] Thus, by 1575, when Ivan IV placed Simeon Bekbulatovich on the throne as grand prince of all Rus', only Ivan IV, his two sons, the Mstislavskii princes, and the surviving members of the cadet Staritskii line could claim descent from Ivan III (see Appendix D.2).

Surviving wedding documentation shows that Tsarevich Peter's descendants via his two daughters had long been regarded as a branch of the Daniilovich dynasty.[109] The 1554 wedding of Princess Marfa Shuiskaia (Tsarevich Peter and Evdokiia Ivanovna's granddaughter) and Prince Ivan Dmitrievich Bel'skii was clearly an event in the dynasty. A ceremonial was compiled, evidently by the same scribes of the Foreign Office who managed the documentation for all royal nuptials, and two copies of it were kept in the royal archive.[110] The ceremonial includes a brief genealogical notice identifying the bride as a descendant of the ruling house: "In the year 1554, the 8th day of November, Tsar and Grand Prince Ivan Vasil'evich of all Russia married Prince Ivan Dmitrievich Bel'skii to Princess Marfa, the daughter of Vasilii Vasil'evich Shuiskii, and a maternal granddaughter of Tsarevich Peter; and the sovereign himself gave her away in marriage."[111] The wedding of Anastasiia Ivanovna Mstislavskaia (Tsarevich Peter and Evdokiia's great-granddaughter) and Tsar Simeon Bekbulatovich in 1575 or 1576 was similarly treated as a dynastic affair. Copies of the wedding texts again were kept in the royal archive,[112] and a brief snippet of the muster that is imbedded in a later chronicle reveals that Ivan IV, his son, and his courtiers had participated in the wedding.[113]

Very likely, the weddings of the descendants of Tsarevich Peter and Evdokiia (including those for which no sources survive) were all treated as dynastic affairs. The chancellery apparatus was mobilized, members of the dynasty were present and performed prominent roles, and the documentation for the weddings was deposited in the tsar's archive, something that was never done for the weddings of even the most powerful boyars. So prominent was this branch of the dynasty that, according to Zimin, Vasilii III's 1509 will, which was deliberately destroyed in 1533 just before his death, nominated Tsarevich Peter as his successor—not one of his younger brothers Iurii, Dmitrii, Simeon, or Andrei.[114] When Tsarevich Peter died in March 1523 and after his daughter had married Prince Fedor Mikhailovich Mstislavskii in 1529, Vasilii III's younger brothers, according to Zimin, were still being passed over as heirs to the throne, now in favor of the Mstislavskii princes.[115]

From 1570 to 1575 or 1576, Ivan IV married off every available member of his dynasty—himself, his sons, and his Staritskaia and Mstislavskaia cousins. These five marriages were part of a deliberate and ongoing policy to repopulate the dynasty and secure the succession, a policy that Ivan and his boyar advisors had been pursuing as far back as the spate of royal marriages in 1547–1549. In other words, Ivan and his advisors were doing the same thing in the 1570s as Vasilii III was doing in the 1520s: treating the cognatic members of the dynasty (Efimiia Staritskaia and Anastasiia Mstislavskaia) as if they were agnates, and perhaps even privileging their succession rights over male members of the family (Vasilii III's brothers and Ivan IV's sons). Thinking of these five marriages as linked events reveals both how consistent dynastic marriage policy was over the sixteenth century and how desperate Ivan IV had become to provide for and control the succession.

Vasilisa

When Ivan IV's marriage to Anna Vasil'chikova ended is unknown, but we do know when she probably died. Ivan IV donated 300 rubles on January 12, 1577, to Holy Trinity-St. Sergius Monastery for commemorative prayers, and another 300 rubles on the same day the following year. The tsar also made a gift of 100 rubles to Iosifo-Volokolamskii Monastery for an annual *korm* (commemorative meal) on January 7 of each year for the commemoration of Anna Vasil'chikova's soul.[116] Putting these two sources together, we have the likely date of Vasil'chikova's death: January 7, 1577.[117] She was buried at the Convent of the Intercession (*Pokrovskii devichii monastyr'*) in Suzdal', presumably having first been tonsured a nun.[118] When the tsar sent her away is unclear. Most biographers of Ivan IV have suggested that Anna was dispatched to a monastery in 1576, but this is largely a guess. What is known for sure, however, is that Ivan IV was free to remarry by no later than early January 1577. Which is exactly what he did.

If Ivan IV's biographers have had some doubts about the legitimacy of his marriage to Anna Vasil'chikova, they have had even more doubts about his marriage to his sixth wife, Vasilisa Melent'eva. She remains a shadowy figure for a number of reasons. First, all the sources that speak of Vasilisa as one of Ivan IV's wives are, in Zimin's words, "vague and late."[119] No muster or ceremonial has yet been discovered for this wedding, which would provide the best possible proof that a wedding took place. In fact, Ivan IV's wedding to Vasilisa is the only one of his purported seven weddings for which not even at least a fragment of a wedding description in one form or another has survived. Second, Vasilisa is a biographical anomaly. She was married before her nuptials with Ivan IV, the only consort of a Muscovite ruler ever to have been previously married; and her social background is unusual for a royal bride. Vasilisa's first husband, Melentii Ivanov, was a scribe, suggesting that she too may have come from a family of scribes, not from the middle ranks of the service aristocracy—that thin layer of servitors that produced nearly every royal bride in the sixteenth and seventeenth century.[120] Even the name by which she is known to us is problematical. Melent'eva is not her surname but, rather, the Christian name of her first husband, Melentii. Still, the name Melent'eva has carelessly been used as if it were her surname in biography after biography. In fact, Vasilisa should properly be called by the Russian formulation of her name: *Vasilisa zhena Melent'eva* (that is, Vasilisa, the wife of Melentii).

What is the evidence that Ivan IV actually married Vasilisa? First, there is the *Excerpts from the Chronograph of the Marriages of Tsar Ivan Vasil'evich*—almost certainly a concoction of the forger Alexander Ivanovich Sulakadzev (see Appendix A). The passage on Vasilisa reports that

> in the year 7085/1577, on January 23, in the evening after the sermon, and after an inspection with the tsar's own eyes, the tsar married the widow Vasilisa Melent'evna [*sic*], whose husband had been stabbed to death by an *oprichnik*, who was very well-formed and beautiful, such as was not found

> among those maidens who had been brought in for the tsar to see and were not selected; and on May 1, in Novgorod, he confined her permanently for having paid too much attention to the master of arms Prince Ivan Devtelev, whom he had executed.[121]

The *Chronograph* thus provides a date for the marriage (January 23, 1577—just two weeks after Anna Vasil'chikova's death), a date for her confinement (May 1, presumably that same year), the reasons for her confinement (her illicit interest in another man), and a fairly clear statement that Vasilisa was a contestant in a bride-show. The *Chronograph* thus provides the most detailed biographical information available on Vasilisa, but none of it is reliable. The *Chronograph*'s problems as a source are so numerous and irresolvable that it should be set aside entirely in favor of clues from other sources that, while not as rich in detail and dates, are nonetheless far more trustworthy.

As for authentic sources, we can turn first to the Elagin Miscellany (*Elaginskaia smes'*), a source, cited and trusted by Karamzin, that includes Vasilisa among Ivan IV's seven wives. Even so, the *Elaginskaia smes'* isolates Vasilisa from all Ivan IV's other wives by reporting that Ivan IV joined with Vasilisa not through the usual Orthodox rites of marriage. Instead, the text says that Ivan IV "received a blessing to be with the widow Vasilisa Melent'eva, that is to say, to live with the woman [*imal molitvu so vdovoiu Vasilisoiu Melent'evoiu, sirech' s zhenshchinem*]."[122] The phrase *imal molitvu* has been the sole basis for historians and biographers since Karamzin to suggest that either Ivan IV had somehow obtained a priest's blessing (and, therefore, the church's permission) to live with Vasilisa—who, in this passage, is scurrilously referred to as "that woman [*s zhenshchinem*]"—without the benefit of marriage, or that Ivan IV had obtained a kind of "civil marriage."[123]

Neither speculation is plausible, but they do show the lengths to which some historians over the centuries have gone to try to make sense of this truly confounding mystery. The colloquial term for "getting married" was, of course, "crowning" (*venchanie*—noun; *venchati*—verb), taken after the signature ritual of Orthodox wedding services where the bride and the groom wore crowns (or had them held over their heads). Inasmuch as Ivan IV and Vasilisa had both been previously married, the "crowning" ritual was prohibited. Chapter 23 of the Stoglav prohibits the crowning ceremony for second marriages: "For those marrying a second time, there is no crowning, but only a prayer is read from the service [*molitva po pravilom*]."[124] As Eve Levin put it, generally for cases like this, instead of the crowning service, "prayers over the newlyweds were recited at vespers."[125] Moreover, the prayers recited (at vespers or whenever it was done in the case of Ivan IV and Vasilisa) would not have been the same celebratory prayers typical of the Orthodox wedding but, rather, would be more penitential in nature, acknowledging the weakness of the flesh and the church's reluctant bending to human carnal needs. To be sure, the Russian church was flexible on the rules about crowning—allowing it for Ivan IV's later weddings (Ivan IV was "crowned" at his fifth wedding with Vasil'chikova), probably because in those cases the bride had not previously been married.[126] But in the case of the marriage to Vasilisa, where both the bride and groom had been married previously (and in the groom's case, of course, more than once previously), there could be no compromising on the liturgical rites. If Ivan IV married Vasilisa in a church wedding, it was probably without a crowning, and what is more, with scolding prayers: a ritual that would not, therefore, be described as a "crowning" and might very well be called, for lack of a better euphemism, "*imal molitvu*."[127]

The best evidence yet offered that Ivan IV married Vasilisa derives from Vladimir Borisovich Pavlov-Sil'vanskii's pioneering study of land cadastres from Viaz'ma. Pavlov-Sil'vanskii found that Ivan IV had given enormous estates (both *pomest'ia* and *votchiny*—service tenure and inherited estates) to Fedor and Mariia, the children of Melentii Ivanov (*Melent'evy deti Ivanova*) and his wife Vasilisa, in 1578/79 (7087), and that these estates were inordinately large given Melentii's relatively low social status and unnoteworthy record of service.[128] In Skrynnikov's words, "few of even the most prominent boyars were ever rewarded so generously for even the most distinguished service to the sovereign." The only thing that could account for this kind of royal favor, according to Skrynnikov, is that "not long before the granting of this land, their mother—the widow Vasilisa Melent'eva—had become the sixth wife of Tsar Ivan."[129] Though this is hardly direct evidence, Skrynnikov is right that this gift of huge tracts of land strongly suggests a marriage, supporting Karamzin's *Elaginskaia smes'* that Vasilisa was Ivan IV's sixth wife.

Another new and important piece of evidence for the marriage to Vasilisa takes us back again to a consideration of her name. A rare inscription in a seventeenth-century Muster Book includes an enumeration of Ivan

IV's wives with an entirely new surname for Vasilisa: The inscription reads that "the sovereign was married 6 [corrected over 4] times," then lists them: Anastasiia Iur'eva, Mariia Cherskasskaia, Mariia Sobakina, Anna Koltovskaia, Mariia Nagaia, and Vasilisa Radilova (*da Vasilisa Radilovykh*).[130] According to this unique inscription, then, Vasilisa was from the Radilov clan, a middle-level servitor family that is well-known and mentioned in Muster Books, the Book of Thousands (*Tysiachnaia kniga*) and the other usual registers of honorable service by courtier clans.[131] If this inscription is right, some of the mysteries about Ivan IV's sixth wife are resolved. We would, for a start, finally have a surname for her: Radilova. Putting this inscription together with the other scraps of evidence of her life, we can conclude that Vasilisa married Melentii Ivanov and had two children, Fedor and Mariia, before marrying Ivan IV.[132] Moreover, Vasilisa's social background now comes into focus: she should no longer be seen as originating in the same class of scribes to which her first husband belonged, but in the provincial gentry—the same social layer that produced many of Ivan IV's other wives.

The dates of Ivan IV's marriage to Vasilisa and of her repudiation and death are, of all Ivan IV's wives, the least certain. Her first husband, Melentii Ivanov, disappears from the sources in 1573/74, and Skrynnikov reasonably supposed that the wedding took place shortly before the granting of the huge estates to Vasilisa's children in 1578/79.[133] If he is right, then there may have only been a few months between Anna Vasil'chikova's death (January 7, 1577) and Ivan IV's remarriage to Vasilisa, perhaps later that same year. Vasilisa's fate after the marriage is equally blurry. Our only source for her fate is Sulakadzev's *Chronograph*, which reads that Vasilisa was confined (*zatochi*) in Novgorod on May 1, 1577, because Ivan IV had noticed she was paying too much attention to his master of arms (*oruzhnichii*), "Ivan Devetelev."[134] The word "confined" in this text has often been taken to mean "imprisoned," and this may be so. Certainly, many historians have alleged this fate for her, probably relying on Zimin's hope that Sulakadzev's *Chronograph*, despite its obvious textual problems, may be reflecting sources that no longer survive.[135] But if we discount the *Chronograph* (as we should), we are left with no evidence at all of what happened to her.

Whatever happened to Vasilisa Radilova (and it may be time to begin calling her by this name), we now have at hand a preponderance of evidence that she was Ivan IV's sixth wife. The *Elaginskaia smes'* that

Karamzin so much trusted, the gift of the estate to the two Ivanov children that Skrynnikov so much emphasized, the inscription in the Muster Book, the phrase *imal molitvu* and the Orthodox Church's views on the crowning service and remarriage—this scattered but compelling evidence cannot be easily dismissed.

If we are to believe the traces of evidence that Ivan IV married Vasilisa, then we must accept that the couple had a wedding. The matter calls for some interpretive backbone. It is time to abandon once and for all the odd notion that Ivan IV had something approaching a "civil union" or otherwise received from the church permission to live in a conjugal union with Vasilisa without the benefit of the normal and accepted nuptial blessing. The mysteries of what the phrase "*imal molitvu*" means and the lack of any wedding *chin* do not trump the simple fact that the church defined and regulated what marriage was, even during the reign of a tsar as capricious as Ivan IV. The notion that the church would have sanctioned Ivan IV's conjugal cohabitation with Vasilisa is utterly dismissible; and there simply was no category then in place for anything like a "civil union."

The Seven Wives of Ivan IV

Ivan IV married for the last time on September 6, 1580.[136] His bride was Mariia Nagaia, a young woman from the same family that had given Ivan IV's cousin Vladimir Staritskii his first wife back in 1549. The marriage is documented not only by manuscript and published wedding musters;[137] it is attested, of course, by the lives and subsequent careers during the Time of Troubles of his wife, Mariia (the nun Marfa) Nagaia, and their son, Dmitrii of Uglich (and the impostors who pretended to be him). The Nagaia wedding followed the usual set of nuptial customs and rituals. Nagaia was chosen at Ivan IV's last bride-show. The 1584 report from Reinhold Heidenstein, quoted at the beginning of this chapter, states that the tsar married "after announcing a public gathering of girls"—presumably, a bride-show from which he selected Mariia Nagaia. The wedding ceremony was also performed in the traditional way: in church and with processions, banquets, speeches, and all the usual honorific posts.[138] As Daniel Kaiser put it, "The record of this last wedding is fairly extensive, and provides substantial parallels with Ivan IV's earlier marriages."[139]

In this way, the Nagoi wedding was very much like the other later weddings of Ivan IV's reign. Like the Sobakina and Vasil'chikova weddings before it, the Nagaia wedding was celebrated traditionally but was attended by a narrow circle of guests. The bride's relatives appear in large numbers in the wedding muster. Both her uncle Afanasii Fedorovich Nagoi, who was one of the tsar's closest confidants and had been made a boyar in 1574, and her father, Fedor Fedorovich Nagoi, who had been appointed an *okol'nichii* in 1576 sat at the *okol'nichii* table.[140] Besides these two, eight other Nagoi relatives had honorific positions at the wedding.[141] Even so, the Nagaia wedding was really a showcase for the Godunovs, who placed fourteen members of the clan in fifteen different honorific posts at the wedding.[142] The Nagaia wedding and the Sobakina and Vasil'chikova weddings before it show plainly how the tsar's nuptials had gradually become, in Bychkova's words, more "'familial' [*semeinyi*] than public [*gosudarstvennyi*]."[143] Ivan's later weddings, quoting Bychkova again, "do not display the signs of a state function, which undoubtedly had been the case [with the weddings] in the first half and middle of the sixteenth century."[144]

Thus it is possible to talk about a change in the way royal weddings were performed over Ivan IV's reign. While the rituals remained intact, the composition of the participants came to be dominated in the later marriages by his new in-laws and his trusted favorites and their kin. The change was introduced in 1571—at the Sobakina wedding. How dramatic this change was can be seen in a comparison of the number of in-laws at royal weddings before, during, and after Ivan's reign. It will be remembered that 12 Sobakins and 5 Saburovs appeared on the muster at the 1571 Sobakina wedding: the highest number of in-laws at any Muscovite royal wedding. The Vasil'chikova wedding roster includes 11 of the bride's relatives, and the Nagaia wedding roster included 10. These numbers are extraordinarily high compared to the representation of in-laws at previous royal weddings: 4 Iur'evs and 3 Iakovlevs at Ivan IV's wedding with Anastasiia Iur'eva (1547); 3 Nagois at Vladimir Staritskii's wedding with Evdokiia Nagaia (1549); and no in-laws at all at Iurii Vasil'evich's wedding (1547) or at Vladimir Staritskii's second wedding (1555). Moving into the seventeenth century, Mikhail Romanov's first wedding (1624) had 5 in-laws, Aleksei Mikhailovich's first wedding (1648) had 7, and Aleksei' Mikhailovich's second wedding (1671) had none. The only seventeenth-century wedding that compares with the number of in-laws at Ivan's later weddings is Mikhail Fedorovich's second (1626), which had 12 Streshnev in-laws. Why Ivan IV's later weddings should be so highly populated with in-laws and favorites is explained by the tsar's volatile relations with many of his boyars during the *oprichnina* and later. Certainly, the increase in the number of in-laws was deliberate and occurred in the context of a fairly stable set of nuptial rituals. As Daniel Printz von Buchau put it at the time (1575): "In celebrating the wedding, he summons only the relatives of the bride and a few trusted courtiers."[145]

At about the same time that Ivan IV married Nagaia, his son Tsarevich Ivan Ivanovich took a new wife, Elena Ivanovna Sheremeteva (his third). Sources do not indicate if father and son held a joint bride-show or if the weddings were celebrated in close proximity to each other, as in 1571 (and possibly also 1575). Nor are there any hints in the sources that this remarriage for the tsarevich spawned any objections from churchmen based on canon law, or what penance the groom had to perform (this was, after all, his third marriage), or even how the choice of bride was made. The tsarevich's bride, Elena Ivanovna Sheremeteva, came from one of the most important families in Muscovy: a scion of the clan that produced the Iur'evs (Ivan IV's first wife's family) and many other prominent boyar and courtier families.[146] The bride's father, Ivan Vasil'evich Bol'shoi Sheremetev, had been a boyar (1549–1570), as were two of her uncles, Ivan Vasil'evich Men'shoi (1558–1577) and Nikita Vasil'evich (1557/58–1563/64). Two other uncles, Semen and Fedor, were *okol'nichie*.[147] The marriage between Tsarevich Ivan Ivanovich and Elena Sheremeteva represents a rare instance when the daughter of a boyar married into the dynasty. The only other case in the sixteenth century was Iulianiia Paletskaia, the wife of Ivan IV's brother Prince Iurii Vasil'evich, whose father, Dmitrii Fedorovich, was made an *okol'nichii* and then a boyar (by July 1547), and whose uncle Ivan Fedorovich was the first of his clan with Duma rank (*okol'nichii*, by 1531).[148] The Sheremetev line was, to be sure, new to these titles. Although the bride's ancestors enjoyed a long history of prominence, this was the first generation that members of this clan had reached such high rank. Even so, it is hard not to see the Sheremetev match as anything but an outlier among royal marriages, harking back to the 1418 marriage between the dynasty and the Patrikeevs, a union that for nearly a century positioned the descendants of that marriage in close proximity to the ruler.

Elena Sheremeteva's marriage to the tsarevich did not, however, lead to good things for the bride or the groom. The death of Tsarevich Ivan Ivanovich on November 19, 1581, possibly at his father's hand, consigned

Elena to a common fate for royal women: forced tonsuring as the nun Leonida at Novodevichii Convent in Moscow.[149] Like Anna Koltovskaia before her, she maintained an active relationship with her birth family and with tsars that followed Ivan IV on the throne—with her brother-in-law Tsar Fedor Ivanovich (1584–1598) and his wife, Tsaritsa Irina Fedorovna Godunova.[150] As Thyrêt summarized, "Although the forced tonsure of royal wives was aimed at undercutting the influence of these tsaritsy and their kin at the Muscovite court, their retirement to a monastery did little to curtail their personal engagement in economic and administrative matters."[151] Elena's clan, the Sheremetevs, would not be ruined by the failed marriage: the family would, in Robert Crummey's summation, be "among the richest and most prominent noble clans until the end of the last [i.e., nineteenth] century."[152]

The Nagaia and Sheremeteva weddings in 1580 would be the last of Ivan IV's reign. The number of marriages Ivan IV's sons contracted is well-known (Ivan—three; Fedor—one), even if many of the details of these unions remain a mystery, as we have seen. The number of Ivan IV's wives has not been so easily ascertained, however. The evidence presented here shows that he married seven times (see table 4.1). But chronicles (all dating from well after Ivan's reign), foreign travelers' accounts (dating from late in Ivan's reign and after) and biographies and historical treatments of Ivan's reign offer varying enumerations of Ivan's wives.

As for primary sources, the Piskarev Chronicle, which dates from the first third of the seventeenth century, reports under the entry for the year 7092 (1583/84) that Ivan IV had six wives—and gets the order wrong: Anastasiia Iur'eva, Mariia Cherkasskaia, Marfa Sobakina, Anna Vasil'chikova, Anna Koltovskaia, and Mariia Nagaia (Anna Vasil'chikova should be listed after Anna Koltovskaia and Vasilisa Radilova is omitted).[153] The Moscow Chronicle, which dates from the second quarter of the seventeenth century, also lists Ivan's wives under the year 7089 (1580/81), reporting that Ivan IV "was married seven times" but strangely lists only six (though it puts them in the correct order): Anastasiia Iur'eva, Mariia Cherkasskaia, Marfa Sobakina, Anna Koltovskaia, Anna Vasil'chikova, and Mariia Nagaia.[154] Karamzin's *Elaginskaia smes'* lists seven wives: Anastasiia Romanovna Iur'eva, Mariia (Kochenei) Temriukovna Cherkasskaia, Marfa Vasil'evna Sobakina, Anna Alekseevna Koltovskaia (the nun Dar'ia), Anna Grigor'evna Vasil'chikova, Vasilisa Melent'eva, and Mariia Fedorovna Nagaia (the nun Marfa).[155]

TABLE 4.1.

The Wives of Ivan IV and His Sons

Ivan IV	Ivan Ivanovich	Fedor Ivanovich
1. Anastasiia Romanovna Iur'eva Married: February 3, 1547 Ivan IV's age: 16 Died: August 7, 1560		
2. Mariia Temriukovna Cherkasskaia Married: August 21, 1561 Ivan IV's age: 30 Died: September 1, 1569		
3. Marfa Vasil'evna Sobakina Married: October 28, 1571 Ivan IV's age: 41 Died: November 13, 1571	1. Evdokiia Bogdanovna Saburova Married: November 4, 1571 Repudiated: by 1575 Died: November 28, 1620	
4. Anna Alekseevna Koltovskaia Married: between April 29 and May 31, 1572 Ivan IV's age: 41 Sent to monastery, tonsured the nun Dar'ia: September or October, 1572 Died: April 5, 1626		
5. Anna Grigor'evna Vasil'chikova Married: between January 7 and January 30, 1575 (Zimin); or in September–October 1574 (Skrynnikov) Ivan IV's age: 44 Repudiated: August–September, 1576? Died: January 7, 1577	2. Pelageia Solovaia Married: 1575 Repudiated: after November 12, 1579 Sent to monastery as nun Praskov'ia Died: 1620	1. Irina Godunova Married: 1575
6. Vasilisa Radilova Married: 1577? Ivan IV's age: 44 or 45? Imprisoned: ? Died: ?		
7. Mariia Fedorovna Nagia Married: September 6, 1580 Ivan IV's age: 50	3. Elena Sheremeteva Married: 1580 Sent to monastery 1581 as nun Leonida	

Seven is the consensus among foreign travelers to Muscovy in the late sixteenth and seventeenth centuries. While Jerome Horsey, who was in Russia from 1573 to 1591, thought Ivan IV had married only five times, others put the number at seven.[156] Possevino, the papal emissary who described events in Muscovy during his diplomatic mission there in 1581–1582, mentions seven wives, though he names only two: Ivan IV's first wife, Anastasiia, and his "seventh wife, Mariia, the daughter of Fedor Nagoi, with whom the Prince contracted his special kind of marriage last year."[157] At about the same time, the Livonian pastor Paul Oderborn, who never actually traveled to Muscovy, counted seven wives;[158] as did Reinhold Heidenstein in 1580.[159] Foreigners' accounts dating from after Ivan IV's death and into the seventeenth century all agree the number is seven. The French mercenary Jacques Margeret wrote in his 1607 account of his experiences in Muscovy that Ivan IV "had seven wives (which is against their religion, which does not permit the taking of more than three)."[160] The Swedish diplomat Peter Petreius also numbered Ivan IV's wives at seven, as did the Dutch merchant Isaac Massa.[161] Clearly, if only among foreign observers, there was an early consensus that Ivan IV had taken seven wives.[162]

There is less of a consensus among historians. Karamzin based his enumeration of Ivan's wives on the *Elaginskaia smes'*, as we have seen, counting seven. Solov'ev, however, believed that Ivan IV only had five (Iur'eva, Cherkasskaia, Sobakina, Koltovskaia, and Nagaia) and relegated Anna Vasil'chikova and Vasilisa Melent'eva to the status of mistresses.[163] Most historians today adopt one or the other of these two numbers (five or seven), even if some do not quite know what to do with Vasil'chikova and Melent'eva.[164]

An eighth wife, Mariia Ivanovna Dolgorukova, who is sometimes mentioned in the biographies of Ivan IV, is totally unhistorical.[165] The only source for her existence is Sulakadzev's *Chronograph*, which reports that "in the year 7080/1572, on November 11, [the tsar] received a blessing [*priia molitvu*] and secretly married [*sochetasia otai*] Mariia Ivanovna Dolgorukova."[166] The source reports that Ivan IV married Dolgorukova in November 1572, about a month after sending his fourth wife, Anna Koltovskaia, away to a convent. Ivan IV repudiated Dolgorukova on the morning after his wedding because he had discovered that she was not a virgin. Enraged, he put her to death in the most cruel and inhumane manner: by lashing her to a carriage and driving the horses attached to it into the Sera river, drowning her. She was, according to the text, of unrivaled beauty—likened to a graceful bird—and Ivan IV later regretted the entire episode. According to the *Chronograph*, Ivan, filled with remorse, adorned the church domes at Alexandrovo Sloboda to propitiate for his enormous sin. While this is a colorful story, it is entirely uncorroborated, directly or indirectly, and therefore should be treated with far more skepticism than that which Ivan IV's biographers have previously seen fit to show it.

The Canonicity of Ivan IV's Later Marriages

While there is good evidence in hand for numbering Ivan IV's marriages at seven, there remains the question of the canonical legitimacy of the last four. Nearly all of Ivan IV's biographers who have commented on the tsar's private life have repeated the refrain that all of his marriages beyond the third one (to Sobakina) were uncanonical because of the Orthodox Church's prohibition against tetragamy.[167] Is this a fair reading of the Orthodox Church's treatment of Ivan IV's later marriages?

A good place to go for insight into this question is the church's own sources, including, mainly, sinodikons (*sinodiki*)—liturgical books containing lists of names of the dead to be read at appointed times of the day or year (depending on the kind of sinodikon and the amount of the donation), beseeching God for the salvation of the souls of departed relatives.[168] By the turn of the seventeenth century, it had become customary to insert a formulaic listing of the leaders of Muscovy's church and state at or near the first folios of the text: all patriarchs, all tsars, all metropolitans, all grand princes, all tsaritsas, all grand princesses, and so on, after which usually followed lists of other donors to the monastery or church, arranged by family (*rod*).[169] The arrangement could, in fact, vary from text to text, but there is nonetheless enough uniformity to examine how the lists of tsaritsas compare across monasteries and convents: to identify who gets prayed for where, and who gets omitted.

Sinodikons treat the first four wives and the last as fully legitimate tsaritsas. The sinodikons from Holy Trinity–St. Sergius Monastery provide a typical example. Five of these sinodikons list Ivan IV's first three wives, and one sinodikon also includes his seventh.[170] Three sinodikons from the mid-seventeenth century list Ivan IV's first four wives, but place the fourth—Anna Koltovskaia—out of place, at the beginning of the list.[171] Other sinodikons from other monasteries do the same thing: wives one through four, plus seven, with wife number four (Koltovskaia) listed first.[172] The set of sinodikons from Dormition Cathedral in the Kremlin also usually lists tsaritsas in their first folios. The earliest of these sinodikons, from the late sixteenth century, lists the first four wives of Ivan IV (with Anna Koltovskaia placed first), while another from the mid-seventeenth century lists the first three wives and the last (omitting Anna Koltovskaia entirely), and yet another from the eighteenth century lists Ivan IV's first four wives in their proper order, then his last.[173] The inconsistent placement of Anna Koltovskaia in the list of Ivan's brides (sometimes fourth, sometimes first) is probably explained by the fact that she was the last of Ivan IV's tsaritsas to die—within living memory of the seventeenth-century copyists of some of these sinodikons—and therefore was placed at the top of new lists of royal wives as they were composed or copied. In any case, the fact that Mariia Nagaia is included in the lists at all is proof that a wife beyond three could be regarded as legitimate and worthy of commemorative prayers as a tsaritsa.

However, Anna Vasil'chikova (Ivan IV's fifth wife) and Vasilisa Radilova (his sixth) are omitted from all these sinodikons. As we have seen, Anna Vasil'chikova was a thoroughly authentic wife, and Ivan IV did commission prayers and commemorative meals for the sake of her soul. Vasil'chikova's omission from the list of tsaritsas in sinodikons is therefore odd, since we know from surviving wedding descriptions, among other sources, that she bore the title of tsaritsa. On the other hand, her marriage with Ivan IV in January 1575 fell just a few months before her husband abdicated his throne to Simeon Bekbulatovich, sometime before October 30, 1575.[174] When, exactly, Simeon Bekbulatovich was removed from the throne is disputed, with views ranging from August to mid-September 1576.[175] Is Anna Vasil'chikova's name omitted from the list of tsaritsas in sinodikons because she had been repudiated during the time Ivan IV was not on the throne, and so the marriage ended when Vasil'chikova was not a tsaritsa? Since we only know when she died (January 7, 1577) and not when she was repudiated, this explanation is plausible, though entirely speculative.

As for Vasilisa Radilova, her omission from sinodikons and the lack of any known separate commemorative donations from Ivan IV on her behalf contribute to the enigma of the tsar's sixth marriage. Vasilisa disappeared from history, and her fate is a complete mystery. Perhaps she was, as the *Chronograph* alleges, "confined" (*zatochi*) in prison. The *Chronograph* is, it bears repeating, an extremely suspect source; but if Vasilisa was thrown in prison, as Zimin, Kobrin, and others have concluded, she would be the only one of Ivan IV's brides who had not died while still married to the tsar (as his first, second, and third wives did) or been forced into a convent (as his fourth and fifth wives were). (His seventh wife outlived him.) Vasilisa alone among Ivan IV's wives would have ended her life in prison, the victim of the tsar whose wrath knew no boundaries who, unlike some of his other victims, garnered no forgiveness.

Regardless of whether he was married five, six or seven times, Ivan IV violated the canons on Christian marriage. And the church clearly knew it. But given the church's blessing of his third and fourth marriages (and probably the others, as well), to see Ivan IV's later marriages merely as flagrant violations of canon law (and to leave it at that) misses the point. As Fr. John Meyendorff put it in his seminal study of church law on marriage, "marital and sexual problems were approached by church authority on the level of pastoral, sacramental, and penitential discipline, not civil law"; and "the historical study of such norms"—that is, the marriage norms emanating from "Christian Scriptures and the theology of the Church"—"cannot be separated from social realities.... A medieval society, like that of Byzantium, took seriously not only the rules and regulations, imposed by state and church authority, but also the spiritual and 'eschatological' dimension of human relations. The Christian ideal of marriage—unique and eternal—was the norm by which social realities were judged, even when they were very far from reflecting the ideal."[176] In other words, there are rules, and then there is the application of those rules. Ivan IV, who was "very far from reflecting the ideal," violated the rules on Christian marriage up and down; but the Eastern Orthodox Church saw remarriage first and foremost as a pastoral and penitential issue, not a legal one—despite all the canon law that had accumulated on the subject over the centuries. Ivan IV's fourth, fifth, sixth, and seventh weddings were thus canonical inasmuch as they were clearly permitted, however reluctantly, by the church and officiated over by a priest. Ivan IV had to endure consequences for these marriages in the form of penance and prohibition from the communion cup, but as far as we can tell from this distance, all of Ivan IV's weddings were legitimate, despite what the canons said.

Why did Ivan IV continue to use the bride-show through most of his marriages, down to his last in 1580? Was this merely another display of the tsar's "total disregard for the bonds of Christian matrimony," as

Madariaga put it?[177] Was he acting out a pathology rooted in his own troubled childhood in remarrying so often and in so openly celebrating the rites of marriage, including the summoning of young women to the Kremlin time and time again? Or, was there a method to the madness—a deliberate attempt to exploit marriage rituals for his own dynastic and political goals?

Ivan IV's use of the bride-show after his first marriage would have made even a Byzantine emperor blush, but he might have had a good reason to continue to use the custom. While it may be that the tsar's remarriages were viewed in a penitential way by the church, as we have suggested, observers at the time must nonetheless have regarded them as scandalous affairs. In an environment of scandal and shock, Ivan IV and his advisors might have been very keen to make everything else about the wedding follow the rubrics and customs precisely. Ivan IV continued to use the bride-show for his third, fifth, and seventh (and probably fourth and sixth) weddings precisely because that is what tsars did when they married. Bride-shows were the custom, and for Ivan IV to arrange them for his later marriages helped to establish and project the appearance of tradition and legitimacy that can only have been more and more necessary the more he married. This concern for legitimacy may also be why Ivan IV seems to have performed all the other usual nuptial rituals—the banquets, processions, speeches, showering with hops, and so on—every time he married anew. The rank of the clergy may have changed, and the roster of attendants performing honorific duties may have narrowed to include favorites and in-laws more than ever before, but the wedding ritual itself remained remarkably stable and, therefore, projected an image of legitimacy and continuity with the past. The usual nuptial rituals would also help to establish the legitimacy of any children that might issue from the tsar's later marriages.

Ivan IV was married for a total of 27 to 29 years between the time of his first marriage (at age 16) in 1547 and his death in 1584. Of his 7 marriages, 5 occurred during the last 13 years of his life (1571–1584). His longest marriage was his first (13.5 years), his shortest, his third (17 days). The longest interval between marriages that we can confirm (not knowing the dates for the marriage to Vasilisa) is between his fourth marriage (to Koltovskaia) and fifth (to Vasil'chikova): 2 years, 4 months. The shortest interval is 6 months (between numbers three and four, Sobakina and Koltovskaia). These figures dramatically confirm Daniel Kaiser's grim assessment that the "tsar did not have a very enviable domestic life. Not only was his childhood lost in the intrigues which surrounded the throne during the years of his minority, but he reached maturity only to engage in numerous, largely unhappy matches."[178] More than "unhappy," these serial marriages were dynastic disasters. Muscovy endured its own version of "the King's Great Matter"; and Ivan IV was just as single-minded, just as willing to thwart or bend religious rules, and just as fixated on the birth of sons and heirs as was Henry VIII. For all their marriages, however, neither man could prevent the eventual extinctions of their houses.

Chapter 5

"Scheming to Be Rid of the Chosen Tsarevna"

Conflict and Conspiracy in the Romanov Bride-Shows

> The tsar took counsel with the patriarch and spoke with the hierarchs and boyars and Duma men about entering into lawful wedlock; and the patriarch and hierarchs gave their blessing to such a goodly act as joining together in lawful love, and the boyars and Duma men gave their assent. And the tsar learned that one of his closest men had a daughter, a maiden of worthy stature and beauty and of excellent reason, and ordered her to be taken to his palace and placed in the care of his sisters, the tsarevnas, and given the same honors as his sisters the tsarevnas, until such time as the celebration and festivities take place. But from time immemorial the wily devil has sowed his tares in the Russian land: so that once a man has attained even a small degree of glory and honor and riches he is sure to be hated. Some of the [other] boyars and closest men [also] had daughters, but the tsar did not think of marrying any one of them. And those maidens' mothers and sisters, who lived in the tsarevnas' apartments, were jealous of this and schemed to do something to be rid of the chosen tsarevna, in the hope that the tsar would then take to himself the daughter of some other great boyar or closest man; and soon they accomplished this by poisoning her.[1]

Grigorii Karpovich Kotoshikhin captured in the above passage a contemporary picture of the high stakes involved in royal marriage in mid-seventeenth-century Muscovy in his *On Russia in the Reign of Aleksei*

Mikhailovich (*O Rossii v tsarstvovanii tsaria Alekseia Mikhailovicha*). Kotoshikhin was well-placed to paint such a vivid picture of the high politics surrounding royal marriage. In the 1660s, he was a middle-ranking scribe in the Foreign Office, whose scriptorium had been responsible for compiling and preserving the documents generated for Muscovite royal marriages since the middle of the sixteenth century. He had access to the ceremonials and musters in the royal archive, which he must have had occasion to consult, since his description of royal weddings is detailed and accurate. When in the summer of 1664 he fled Muscovy (perhaps out of fear that his treasonous conveyance of secret diplomatic dispatches to the Swedes would be found out, or out of fear of demotion or arrest at the hands of his immediate superiors whom he had repeatedly antagonized), Kotoshikhin had a lot of firsthand knowledge to offer anyone who would give him safe haven. Kotoshikhin variously found refuge in Poland, Prussia, and Lübeck, and in the summer of 1665 he petitioned the king of Sweden and the regency council (the king, Charles XI, was in his minority at the time) for entry into royal service as an advisor on military or diplomatic matters pertaining to Muscovy. His offer was accepted, and he was commissioned to compose a "description of the whole Muscovite state," arranged in thematic chapters and treating the broadest possible range of political, social, economic, and cultural dimensions of his homeland. His "description" is the debriefing of a traitor, displaying time and again an eagerness to please his new masters by revealing to them some of the lesser known aspects—the dirty laundry—of court culture and life inside the thick, impenetrable walls of the Kremlin. It is telling that Chapter 1 of his *On Russia* is devoted to the personal life of the ruler, and that the first part of that opening chapter describes how the tsar married.[2]

Kotoshikhin conveys an image of a political system that hinged on the choice of bride for the tsar. Even with the active role that the boyars and their wives played in the careful selection and vetting of candidates and their families, some boyars would not be satisfied with the choice the tsar made. This dissatisfaction was sometimes enough to throw off the delicate balance of court factions that a carefully organized bride-show was designed to create. The conspiracies hatched by some boyar clans against the matrimonial choices of the first two Romanov tsars are among the most revealing episodes of devious politicking and kinship-motivated intrigue in Muscovite history. This chapter charts the bride-show in the seventeenth century and focuses on three wedding scandals—involving Tsar Mikhail Fedorovich and Mariia Khlopova, and Tsar Aleksei Mikhailovich and Efimiia Vsevolozhskaia and Ovdot'ia Beliaeva—that together illustrate the centrality of kinship in the political system and reveal dramatically the lengths to which seventeenth-century courtiers could go to play and win the "game" of marriage politics.

The Khlopova Affair

The extinction of the Daniilovich dynasty that followed the death in 1598 of Ivan IV's son Tsar Fedor Ivanovich plunged Muscovy into a period of dynastic and social turmoil called the Time of Troubles (1598–1613). With his death, there were no more male heirs to the throne, although the lineage continued in the female line through Prince Fedor Ivanovich Mstislavskii and his children, and Simeon Bekbulatovich was still alive, even if his royal charisma (as a Chingisid and former grand prince) had become for him more of a burden than an asset. The Troubles have been interpreted variously by historians—as a social revolution against the impositions of serfdom, as a class-based peasant war, as a factional civil war between boyars—but it is hard not to agree with Chester Dunning's conclusion that, in the end, this conflict was essentially political and fundamentally about succession to the throne.[3]

The men that came to the throne during the Troubles had no need for the bride-show. Tsar Fedor Ivanovich's successor, Tsar Boris Godunov (1598–1605), came to the throne in 1598 already married; and his son, the sixteen-year-old Fedor Borisovich (r. April–June 1605), did not live long enough after his father to marry. Even so, Boris did attempt during his brief reign to arrange marriages for his son and his daughter: Fedor Borisovich with the Georgian house of Bagration and Kseniia Borisovna with the Swedes, the English, the Danes, and the Bagrations. All of these failed marriage projects were with foreigners.[4] As far as our sources indicate, no domestic matches for either Godunov child were seriously contemplated. The next tsar, the First False Dmitrii (1605–1606), invaded Muscovy with a prospective bride already at his side—Marina Mniszech, the Catholic daughter of Jerzy Mniszech, one of the imposter's chief Ruthenian supporters. He married Marina on May 8, 1606, less than a year after his entry into Moscow the previous June. A little more than a week later, on May 17, he was assassinated by boyar-led conspirators.[5] One of those conspirators, Vasilii Shuiskii, came to the throne immediately afterward, late in May 1606, already betrothed to Princess Ekaterina/Mariia Petrovna Buinosova-Rostovskaia.[6] The wedding itself was not performed until January 17, 1608, twenty months after he became tsar—a delay probably explained by the constant level of crisis, defection, and insurrection that largely characterized Vasilii Shuiskii's reign (1606–1610).[7]

Even though there were no bride-shows during the Troubles, royal marriage remained at the forefront of the various efforts to stabilize and establish the new regimes—Godunov's, the First False Dmitrii's, and Shuiskii's. Each of the tsars of the Troubles moved with resolve and caution to arrange marriages that would help to bolster the legitimacy of their fledgling dynasties, either by forging links to established foreign royal houses (Boris Godunov's children), with a regional strongman (the First False Dmitrii), or with powerful and well-connected clans at court (Vasilii Shuiskii). Marriage was clearly a part of the common strategy used by successive regimes during the Troubles to solidify and legitimize their hold on power.

By contrast, the marriage of the first Romanov tsar, Mikhail Fedorovich (1613–1645), was a matter that the boyars who put him on the throne were not eager to take up. Three years passed after his election to the throne by an Assembly of the Land in 1613 before the new tsar began the search for a bride.[8] It could be argued that the delay was due to the new tsar's age. Mikhail had ascended the throne at the age of only 16, and was aged 19–20 in 1616. But then, tsars married young as a rule. Most Muscovite rulers or heirs apparent in the previous dynasty had married at about the age of 17.[9] The tsar's youth was not, therefore, a factor in holding off his marriage. Alternatively, the delay might be explained by the absence of Mikhail's father, Filaret, who had been a captive in a Polish prison since 1610. There may have been some reluctance to make such an important dynastic decision while the family's real leader was not available to participate in the deliberations over the choice of bride. This explanation, however, is belied by the fact that the first attempt to marry off the young tsar—in 1616—took place while Filaret was still a captive in Poland. Moreover, even after his return to Moscow in 1619, Filaret's role in the bride search was overshadowed by that of Mikhail's mother, Filaret's former wife, the nun Marfa (née Kseniia Ivanovna Shestova), who had been with Mikhail at the time of his election to the throne in 1613.[10]

The delay is best explained by the highly political and potentially explosive nature of royal bride selection, as shown by the conspiracies and intrigues that came about when the question of Mikhail's marriage was finally taken up by his relatives. Nothing could reignite the blood feuds of the previous fifteen years of Troubles more easily than a bride who was not universally acceptable to all the court's factions. It is conceivable that the Romanovs—Mikhail's mother and uncles, as well as their affines and allies—remembered the tragic fates of the First False Dmitrii (murdered a week after his wedding) and Tsar Vasilii Shuiskii (shoved off the throne in 1610, he died in a Polish prison in 1612), both of whom had married relatively soon after their ascensions to the throne. Thus, the delay was deliberate: to give the new tsar and his circle a chance to consolidate power and build a record of stable rule. To begin a bride search right after the election to the throne would only have transformed the feuding over the succession to the throne, which had dominated politics during the Troubles, into feuding over the choice of a bride (which itself had direct implications for the succession).[11] After fifteen years of vendettas, foreign interventions, and peasant and Cossack uprisings, it might have been thought best to put off for a time the new tsar's marriage (even with the obvious risks to the continuation of the fledgling dynasty that this entailed) for the sake of establishing peace between the boyar clans at court.

The biostatistics of Muscovy being what they were (twenty years was a little less than half the lifespan of most Russian rulers),[12] the matter of Tsar Mikhail Fedorovich's marriage could not be put off forever. Zabelin speculated that the young tsar picked Mariia Ivanovna Khlopova, his first prospective bride, in a bride-show, and he was right.[13] The summary report of the investigation into the disgrace of Mariia Khlopova, written in September 1623, begins by pointing out that "Mariia Khlopova was brought to the Terem [*v Verkh*] to the bride-show [*obiran'ia*] for the tsar's wedding."[14] Preparations for the bride-show had begun at the end of 1615, and by Christmas the choice of Khlopova had been made.[15] The Khlopovs had a long, if not especially distinguished, career in Muscovite service and are mentioned in numerous military muster rolls (*Razriadnye knigi*), the Book of Thousands of 1550 (*Tysiachnaia kniga*), the Court Notebook (*Dvorovaia tetrad'*), and Boyar Lists (*Boiarskie spiski*) from the late sixteenth and early seventeenth centuries.[16] They were not by any means a family of the first tier, but they had a respectable record of honorable service. They were, in a word, not unlike the families of other tsaritsas of the sixteenth and seventeenth centuries.

The choice having been made, plans for the wedding proceeded, but at a snail's pace. The precise chronology of events remains unclear from the extant sources, but we know that Khlopova was included in a bride-show that was held in the Terem before Christmas 1615 (*k rozhdestvu*), and that she and her family were ejected from the Kremlin probably in late June or early July 1616.[17] Thus, as the sources put it, she lived "in the upper chambers [*v Verkhu*] for a long time." How long, however, is unclear. According to an investigative report of September 1623, she resided with her relatives in the upper chambers for six weeks total (not six months), which would mean that she did not immediately move into the Kremlin after her selection at Christmas.[18] However long she resided in the Kremlin, it was longer than usual and therefore worthy of comment in the sources. While in the Terem, she underwent various rituals. She participated in the religious rites that designated her as the tsar's consort (*i molitva narecheniiu ei byla*).[19] She was given the fictive title tsaritsa (not the usual title, tsarevna). Her name was changed from Mariia to Anastasiia, modifying her identity in the way that was customary for royal brides. And she began to be treated with the deferential etiquette and outward respect one normally pays to royalty (*chiny u nei byli po Gosudarskomu chinu*).[20]

Consistent with her modified identity, Mariia/Anastasiia Khlopova began more and more to assume the role of a royal consort. In mid-May 1616, she and the tsar made a pilgrimage together to Holy Trinity–St. Sergius Monastery to pray before the relics of the saint for a blessing of their marriage; and on June 9 Khlopova gave her future mother-in-law, the nun Marfa Ivanovna, a gift of "two forties of sables, one worth 30 rubles, the other 25 rubles"—gifts that were part of, or in anticipation of, the usual ritual exchange of gifts that took place before, during, and after Muscovite royal weddings in these centuries.[21] Litanies in the Orthodox liturgy, which beseech God for a blessing on the ruler and his family, had been amended so as to include Mariia's name, and the court elite had ceremoniously pledged their fidelity to her as their tsaritsa, kissing the cross ritually to solemnize their oath.[22] In the second half of June, skilled workers in the palace workshops produced the costumes to be worn at appointed moments during the three days of wedding celebrations, and craftsmen built the sleds for the processions that formed such a vital part of the wedding ritual. Zabelin is therefore right in suggesting that the wedding was planned for sometime at the very end of June or early July 1616.[23]

Khlopova's treatment in the Terem was both remarkable and unusual. It was not the common custom to bestow upon the bride the title tsaritsa, but rather the title tsarevna; and it may have also have been rare to commemorate her in the litanies at divine services, to have the court elite kiss the cross to her, or to apply to her the official royal etiquette—all this being fitting for a royal consort, of course, but perhaps premature for a bridal candidate. The explanation may lie in the fact that, according to one source at least, Tsar Mikhail Fedorovich and Mariia/Anastasiia had already been formally betrothed (*obruchena*).[24] Orthodox wedding services consisted of two elements, the betrothal (*obruchenie*) and the crowning (*venchanie*) services, which could either be performed separately months or years apart or be combined and performed one right after the other. As Eve Levin put it, "Byzantine custom generally included a betrothal months or even years in advance of the wedding, but Slavic custom was more mixed. Many of the manuscripts of the betrothal and wedding rites reveal the two ceremonies as entirely separate, the betrothal ending with a benediction and dismissal of the congregation. Many other manuscripts end the betrothal ceremony with the order to continue with the wedding service, if it was to take place the same day."[25]

The Muscovite practice for royal weddings in the sixteenth and seventeenth centuries was to link the two services. Of the nine weddings between 1526 and 1648 that report the location of the betrothal, only two (Vasilii III in 1526 and the First False Dmitrii in 1606) have them separate from the crowning, and both were located in the palace, just before the couple and their cortège moved in procession to the church for the nuptials.[26] In 1616, they were evidently not linked in time or place: Tsar Mikhail Fedorovich and Mariia/Anastasiia Khlopova were betrothed sometime during her stay in the Terem, prompting the kissing of the cross to her, the formalized etiquette, and the title tsaritsa over tsarevna.[27] This is consistent with Orthodox sensibilities, since a couple formally betrothed in this way was to be treated as married, even to the point that, quoting Eve Levin again, "Once a betrothal was made in church, it was almost as difficult to break as a marriage... Under canon law, a man or woman who was betrothed to one person but married another was guilty of adultery. If a couple managed to break their betrothal after a church ceremony, they were considered previously married, and suffered the disabilities attached to that position."[28] The betrothal alone served as a strong enough, albeit preliminary, bond between the couple to justify treating Mariia/Anastasiia Khlopova as if she already were a tsaritsa.

Weeks stretched into months between her selection in the bride-show and the planned wedding. The reason for this lengthy pause in events remains unknown, but it may be connected to the marriages of the two men who were the closest advisors to the young tsar and close relatives of his mother—the brothers Boris Mikhailovich and Mikhail Mikhailovich Saltykov. Boris Saltykov married in early November 1615—around the time the tsar's bride-show was being organized—and his brother Mikhail was married in July 1616, right around the time that the tsar's marriage with Khlopova was planned.[29] The identity of Boris's bride is unknown (we know her only as Mariia Ivanovna), but Mikhail's wife is Praskov'ia Ivanovna Poleva.[30] The Polevs enjoyed a long history of service and are included in many of the important court registers in the sixteenth and seventeenth centuries.[31] Praskov'ia's uncle Grigorii Osipov syn Polev had carried the wine in a large cup (*sklianitsa*) to the church at the wedding of Tsar Ivan IV and Marfa Sobakina in 1571;[32] and another kinswoman (her second cousin) was married to the boyar Vasilii Petrovich Sheremetev.[33] The Polevs would therefore be linked with many of the most important boyar clans in Muscovy in the seventeenth century and, as we have seen, would put a candidate in the 1680 bride-show for Tsar Fedor Alekseevich. How these connections and service history might have figured into the politics surrounding Tsar Mikhail's choice of Khlopova in 1616 remains unknown because the Polev genealogy is not well elucidated, but it can hardly be coincidence that the tsar and his two intimate advisors and relatives were marrying within so short an interval. Thus, it may be the case that the tsar's wedding was delayed as much by the search for an appropriate wife for Mikhail Saltykov as by factors relating to Mariia/Anastasiia Khlopova herself.

The choice of a bride for the Romanov tsar appeared to have been resolved, but in point of fact, matters were hardly settled. Six weeks after her installation in the Terem, Mariia/Anastasiia was suddenly and unexpectedly struck with horrifying convulsions and fits of vomiting. The illness immediately raised doubts about the young girl's fitness for meeting the chief duty of a tsaritsa, giving birth to healthy children. Foreign doctors were summoned, and the tsar's kinsman, the cupbearer (*kravchii*) Mikhail Mikhailovich Saltykov, was evidently put in charge of investigating Mariia/Anastasiia's situation and recovery. Saltykov discussed her condition with the doctor (*doktor*) Valentine Bills, then had Bills and a pharmacist (*lekar'*) named Balthser examine the young girl in turn. Saltykov reported to the tsar that the consensus of the two men was that Mariia/Anastasiia was seriously ill, that the problem was likely not curable, and that her prospects for a long life of child-bearing were remote.[34]

The illness put the tsar in a very difficult position. How could he marry a young girl who had such a grave sickness, and whose family conspired to conceal it from the tsar and his advisors? The tsar, his father the patriarch, and three boyars who were also royal relatives (the tsar's uncle Ivan Nikitich Romanov, his first cousin Prince Ivan Borisovich Cherkasskii, and Cherkasskii's brother-in-law Fedor Ivanovich Sheremetev)[35] conducted interviews of Mariia/Anastasiia, her father, and her uncle. They consulted with Mikhail Saltykov, who presented the medical opinions. In the end, the group decided that Mariia/Anastasiia's illness was not an isolated or minor episode but, rather, an indication of fragile health. The tsar, evidently with sincere regret, expelled Mariia/Anastasiia from the Terem (*soslat' s Verkhu*), along with her relatives. She departed about two weeks after the onset of her illness—in late June or early July, right about the time when the wedding was supposed to take place.[36]

The family was sent away in disgrace. Mariia/Anastasiia was sent directly from the Terem to the estate of her grandmother Fedora Zheliabuzhkaia. Within two days of her departure from the Kremlin, all signs of the illness disappeared. Within ten days, Mariia/Anastasiia, her maternal grandmother, an aunt, and her two maternal uncles, Ivan and Aleksandr Zheliabuzhkii, were sent in exile to Tobol'sk. Her father, Ivan Khlopov, was given a military governorship (*voevodstvo*) in Vologda. In August 1619—less than two months after Mikhail Romanov's father, Filaret, returned from Polish captivity (June 14, 1619) and was installed as patriarch (June 24, 1619)—the Khlopovs were moved again. Mariia/Anastasiia and her kin were transferred from Tobol'sk to Verkhotur'e, and from there to Nizhnii Novgorod in December 1620, occupying the house once owned by Kuz'ma Minin, the hero of the Time of Troubles. Ivan Khlopov was transferred in 1619 from his post in Vologda to his estate near Kolomna.[37] The Khlopovs and their kin, who had stood at the threshold of exalted power and status, were ruined.

Mariia/Anastasiia Khlopova's disgrace put an end to any immediate plans to marry Mikhail Romanov. For a time, Tsar Mikhail Fedorovich resolutely refused to consider other candidates, perhaps in hopes that Khlopova might be returned to him. But he was eventually convinced to take up the question of marriage again, and he did so by first exploring foreign candidates. First proposed to him was the daughter of the Lithuanian ruler, a union that, it was suggested, might lead to a return of lost territories and a stable peace on the western frontier. According to a chronicle account, this proposal originated with Mikhail's father, Patriarch Filaret, but was dropped almost immediately without any overtures being made to the Lithuanian court.[38] In September 1621, a delegation was dispatched from Moscow to Copenhagen to inquire about the daughters of Duke Johann-Adolph of Holstein-Gottorp, the second cousin (once removed) and brother-in-law of King Christian IV of Denmark. The king himself, however, refused to meet with the Muscovite ambassadors, feigning illness, and left the matter in his courtiers' hands. He was, in truth, unwilling to consider the match in part because of the need for the prospective bride to convert to Orthodoxy. The Russians refused, in turn, to discuss the matter with anyone but the king himself, and there the matter ended.[39] A second delegation was sent abroad in January 1623, this time to Sweden. Muscovite envoys were dispatched with the proposal to wed the Romanov tsar to Catherine, sister-in-law of King Gustav II Adolph and younger sister of the Hohenzollern elector of Brandenburg, Georg Wilhelm.[40] This match had also been urged on the tsar by his father; but once again, neither the candidate nor her family was willing to consider conversion, and the matter was dropped.[41]

Mikhail's search for a suitable and willing foreign match having failed, his attention focused again on a native-born candidate, and Mariia Khlopova's name reentered the discussions. Why this was so may in part be explained by Mikhail's unfailing affection for Mariia—even seven years after her disgrace and exile. But the discussion of the bride search above provides an additional plausible explanation for the reemergence of the Khlopova name in Mikhail's matrimonial dilemma. The Khlopovs had already passed a very rigorous screening. It is safe to assume that they, like all bridal candidates, had their genealogies and medical histories investigated. If, indeed, Mariia Khlopova was not gravely ill (and the fact that she recovered quickly and remained healthy enough to survive exile for seven years suggested she was not), then her candidacy deserved reconsideration, if only to avoid another extensive and lengthy bride search. Thus, while Mikhail's emotions played some role, it is hard not to see far more practical motivations as well behind the revival of the Khlopova candidacy.

On September 15, 1623, after the Swedish match had fallen through, the investigation of the Khlopov affair was reopened. The investigators are identified in the narrative report produced at the time as consisting of the same men who investigated the affair back in 1616: the tsar, his father, and three boyars (Romanov, Cherkasskii, and Sheremetev). The first witnesses to be summoned before this group, on the next day, September 16, were the two foreigners who had examined Khlopova shortly after her illness set in—Bills (a physician) and Balthser (a pharmacist). These two conjured up slightly different diagnoses: Bills reported that Khlopova had been afflicted with a gastrointestinal disorder that, in his opinion, should have passed quickly and without lasting complications. Bills claimed he had seen and successfully treated illnesses like this before and, most important, that the illness would "not affect fertility or the ability to bear children."[42] Balthser, who was consulted next, diagnosed jaundice (*zheltaia bolezn'*) but agreed with Bills that the illness was not serious. Either diagnosis would have controverted the report made by Mikhail Mikhailovich Saltykov, who, it will be remembered, told the tsar right after the event that the two doctors had determined Khlopova's illness to be chronic and incurable. Balthser also reported a strange question posed by Saltykov. As the 1623 investigative report puts it, "Mikhailo asked him: 'Will she ever be tsaritsa [*budet li ona im gosudarynia*]?' And [Balthser] replied: 'How would I know that; it was none of my business.'"[43]

Mikhail Saltykov, who was now an *okol'nichii*, was summoned in next.[44] He attempted in every way to distance himself from events. Saltykov claimed that he had never actually given Mariia/Anastasiia any medicine. Any medicine that either Bills or Balthser had prescribed was administered either by them or by her father, Ivan Khlopov. He also admitted that he had asked Balthser if the illness was treatable but contradicted the testimony of both foreigners by claiming that Balthser had told him that he could not cure the illness, but that Bills, as a doctor, might be able to. At that point, Bills and Balthser were brought in and asked to repeat their testimony in front of Saltykov—eye-to-eye, as the text put it (*s ochei na ochi*)—and both repeated their former testimony without alteration. Saltykov, for his part, denied in front of the two men that he had ever asked if Mariia/Anastasiia would be the tsaritsa, but he did say that, on instruction from the nun Marfa Ivanovna, the tsar's mother, he had asked Balthser if Khlopova had any sort of physical defect (*kakie porchi*). According to Saltykov, Balthser replied that he could not say for sure and that only a doctor was capable of determining that. Balthser then interjected that Saltykov had indeed asked if Khlopova could be tsaritsa, a claim that Saltykov denied again. The interview ended with Tsar Mikhail Fedorovich asking Saltykov if something he had told the tsar in 1616 was true: that a woman in Uglich once had this same illness and had lived for about a year but then had died. Saltykov replied that he did not remember saying any such thing to the tsar.[45]

These first inquiries raised enough questions to require further investigation. Mariia's father (Ivan) and uncle (Gavrilo) were recalled to Moscow and interviewed on September 19. Her father attested to his daughter's good health since childhood. On the next day, Mariia's father-confessor, Fr. Gavrilo—who had heard her confessions before she came to the Terem, while she lived there, in the days just after her expulsion, and before she was dispatched to exile in Siberia—testified that he had never seen the slightest hint of deception on her part and that Mariia had been a healthy young girl for as long as he had known her. Her uncle Gavrilo testified on the same day and reported that Mariia had been in perfect health up to and since her sudden illness in the Kremlin. Gavrilo added that Mariia's illness appeared only shortly after he had had a heated argument with Mikhail Saltykov.

According to Gavrilo, about two weeks before the onset of Mariia's illness, Tsar Mikhail Fedorovich had toured the Armory (*Oruzheinaia palata*) with Gavrilo Khlopov. They were met there by Mikhail Saltykov, who, in addition to being the cupbearer (*kravchii*), served at that time as the royal arms bearer (*oruzhnichii*). In the course of the tour, the tsar came upon a finely made Turkish saber, the workmanship of which very much impressed him. Noticing the tsar's interest in the saber, Saltykov confidently announced that his smiths in the Armory could produce equally fine specimens. The tsar, evidently already valuing the opinions of his soon-to-be in-law, handed the saber over to Gavrilo and asked if he thought the Armory could fashion such fine arms. Gavrilo looked over the saber and announced that he doubted that sabers of such high quality could be produced in the Armory. Insulted and enraged, Saltykov snatched the saber from Khlopov's hands and the two began to argue. It is from this moment, said Gavrilo, that the Saltykovs began to see the Khlopovs as enemies. Not only had the upstart Gavrilo contradicted Saltykov in front of the tsar, he had evidently raised doubts about the ability of the Armory to produce quality arms under his direction. In the end, Gavrilo attributed

Mariia/Anastasiia's illness to her eating too many sweets, but he also noted that things only got worse once the Saltykov brothers—Mikhail and Boris—got involved in handling the case.[46]

On September 21, the tsar, his father, and the small circle of boyars leading the investigation dispatched a delegation to Nizhnii Novgorod where Mariia/Anastasiia was living. The delegation included Sheremetev, Archimandrite Iosif of the Chudov monastery in the Kremlin, the court groom (*iasel'nichii*) Bogdan Matveevich Glebov, the scribe (*d'iak*) Ivan Mikhailov, Mariia's father, Ivan, the doctor Artemii Dii, and Bills and Balthser. Their mission was to question Mariia herself and those around her about her health and to record any information she offered about the cause of her sudden illness seven years before. The composition of this delegation was designed to assure that the tsar and his father received a wholly independent report on Khlopova's health. Whereas in 1616 the young tsar had relied on Mikhail Mikhailovich Saltykov for all the reports on Khlopova's health (as cupbearer [*kravchii*], he was responsible for the dispensing of all medications), this new inquiry was deliberately organized so as to avoid any chance of conspiracy by any one person or clan. The delegation included a variety of court officials and specialists: one of the tsar's boyar in-laws (Sheremetev); a trusted Orthodox cleric; a scribe to record the interviews; Mariia's father, presumably to look after Khlopov clan interests; and a team of doctors, including the original examining physicians and a third (Dii) who probably could lend a fresh perspective on Mariia's health. There was to be no repeat of the Saltykov deception.

The first news from Nizhnii Novgorod came on October 11, when Mariia's father-confessor in exile, Fr. Gerasim, arrived in Moscow. He presented himself before the patriarch and reported that he had heard her confession many times in the years she had been in Nizhnii Novgorod and had become very well acquainted with the young girl. Never had he himself noticed nor heard from any other source of any illness whatsoever. In his opinion, Mariia/Anastasiia was a completely healthy young woman.[47]

The priest's conclusions were bolstered by the findings of Sheremetev's delegation. On October 16, Sheremetev's report arrived in Moscow, declaring that Khlopova was healthy. Interviews with Mariia/Anastasiia and her relatives had revealed that the young girl had been enjoying excellent health all the years of her confinement. There had been no Khlopov conspiracy to hide any illness since there was no previous illness to hide. But these investigations in Moscow and Nizhnii Novgorod did reveal a different conspiracy—one aimed at derailing the marriage of the tsar to Khlopova. The conspirators were easy to identify. Mikhail Saltykov had handled the medical examinations of Mariia Khlopova at the time of the incident. He had falsely reported the doctors' diagnosis. There were bad feelings between the Saltykovs and Mariia's uncle Gavrilo. And Saltykov was unable to explain why, except for the one isolated episode in 1616, Mariia had enjoyed perfect health. That it had been Mikhail Saltykov—along with his brother Boris, whose name also popped up in the investigation—who together conspired to ruin the Khlopova match only confirmed the early suspicions of Mariia's father, who reported that all through the initial investigations back in 1616, "they were whispering to each other."[48]

Reprisals against the guilty Saltykov brothers were swift. On October 24, 1623, even while the tsar's delegation was still in Nizhnii Novgorod awaiting word from Moscow on what to do next, both Mikhail and Boris Saltykov were disgraced and exiled for causing Mariia's illness and then lying to the tsar about it.[49] Now, it was the Saltykovs' turn to be ruined by the whole affair. As for Mariia/Anastasiia, despite her clean bill of health, her position as the tsar's consort was never restored. On November 1, Sheremetev received instructions to return to Moscow, leaving Khlopova in Nizhnii Novgorod, her pension doubled. Her father, Ivan, was to be sent to his estates near Kolomna.[50] By the end of September of the following year, Tsar Mikhail and the entire court celebrated his marriage to Mariia Vladimirovna Dolgorukova.

Historians have explored this episode before, but fundamental questions remain. Was the plot hatched by the two Saltykov brothers solely motivated by the argument with Gavrilo? If Khlopova was proved to be healthy, and the victim of a vicious conspiracy, why was she not restored to her position as the tsar's bride-to-be once the truth had been exposed?

The first attempts to explain the Saltykovs' behavior focused on the personal animus that is said to have developed between them and Khlopova's family. Solov'ev pointed to the Armory incident as the spark that ignited the conspiracy.[51] Mikhail Saltykov's treachery was an act of revenge for having been slighted in the tsar's presence. The argument at the Armory plays an important role in Zabelin's treatment of the Khlopova affair, as well. The Saltykovs were the first family of Tsar Mikhail's court. Mikhail and Boris had been with Mikhail and his mother in Kostroma in 1613 when a delegation from the Assembly of the Land came to announce Mikhail's election to the throne. With Mikhail's father in a Polish prison, Mikhail's mother consulted with these two brothers about the risks and opportunities in accepting the throne. After his coronation Mikhail elevated them to high office, and they proved to be among the new tsar's closest and most trusted advisors. The Armory incident was important because, according to Zabelin, it revealed very plainly the risks that Mikhail's marriage could pose to the status the Saltykovs had enjoyed these first few years of the reign. Among the Khlopovs there was a very able man—Gavrilo—who just might supplant Mikhail and Boris in the positions they had, up until then, occupied so close to the person of the tsar.[52] Zabelin also introduced kinship into his analysis, emphasizing the fact that the Saltykovs were relatives of Mikhail's mother, who had opposed the match from the start. Zabelin, however, did not venture further into the genealogies. He apparently knew that there was some kind of connection between the Shestovs (nun Marfa Ivanovna's family) and the Saltykovs, since he made use of a chronicle that contains an entry identifying the brothers as "nephews of the tsar's mother" (*tsarevy materi plemianniki*).[53] Zabelin's treatment, however, placed the Armory incident at the center of the Saltykov brothers' motivation, and their kinship ties with the nun Marfa are mentioned only to explain how they became, in effect, agents of Mikhail's mother in the conspiracy.

It is here that genealogists entered the fray. In the "Queries" section of the second issue of the *Proceedings of the Russian Genealogical Society* (*Izvestiia Russkogo genealogicheskogo obshchestva*), the genealogist D. F. Kobevo explored the precise genealogical relationship between the two Saltykov brothers and the nun Marfa Ivanovna. How were Mikhail and Boris Saltykov "nephews" of the tsar's mother, as the chronicle reported?[54] The question sparked research and publishing activity among some of Russia's top archivists and genealogists of the day.[55] One of them, N. V. Miatlev, used a dismayingly vast number of disparate sources to establish that the Saltykov brothers were, indeed, nephews of the nun Marfa and cousins of the young tsar by virtue of marriage ties between the Saltykovs and Shestovs through the Mikhalkov clan.[56] But Miatlev, in his typically meticulous fashion, went farther, exploring the relationship between the Saltykovs and the woman Tsar Mikhail ended up marrying instead of Khlopova, Mariia Vladimirovna Dolgorukova. He claimed to have found a link between the two families via the Zvenigorodskii clan, the family of the woman Miatlev believed was Mariia's mother. Miatlev was the first to examine the Khlopov affair from a purely genealogical perspective and, along the way, devalued the importance of the Armory incident as a motive for the conspiracy. The Saltykovs were not mere agents of the tsar's mother—eager to be avenged for a slight and out to preserve their individual honor and clan's status at court. Rather, Miatlev portrays them as acting in the interests of their own clan and their affines.

Miatlev's conclusions were recently scrutinized by Russian genealogist O. V. Shcherbachev, who tied up many of the loose ends.[57] Shcherbachev points out that, although Miatlev was right about the genealogical ties linking the Saltykovs and Shestovs, the link between the Dolgorukovs and the Saltykovs proceeded not through the Zvenigorodskiis but through the Barbashins. His revised genealogy displays the links between Tsar Mikhail's mother, the Saltykovs, and the Dolgorukovs (see chart 5.1).

CHART 5.1. KINSHIP TIES OF THE SALTYKOVS*

(Source: Shcherbachev, "O rodstve," 65)

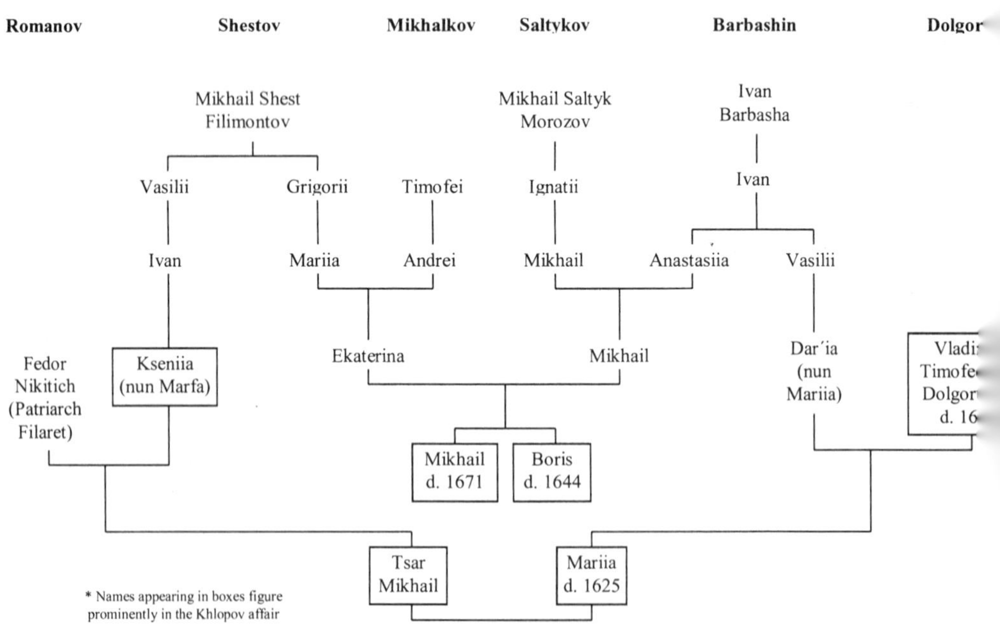

* Names appearing in boxes figure prominently in the Khlopov affair

Furthermore, Shcherbachev offered evidence that demonstrates these ties were regarded as important to the persons who figured in the Khlopov affair. Shcherbachev examined entries for the Saltykov clan in various sinodikons (*sinodiki*), or monastic and church commemoration books. These entries had been commissioned by Mikhail or Boris (or both) and contained the names of their relatives who were to be remembered in prayer at several monasteries across Russia.[58] What is noteworthy is that the nun Marfa, Mariia Dolgorukova, and Mariia's parents are listed in and among the ancestors and close kin of the Saltykov brothers. In effect, the entries trace, by means of prayers for the dead, the genealogical links that united the Shestovs, Saltykovs, and Dolgorukovs.[59] To the Saltykov commemorations that Shcherbachev found can be added an entry in the sinodikon for the family of Prince Vladimir Timofeevich Dolgorukov, Tsaritsa Mariia's father, in St. Catherine's Monastery on Mt. Sinai. This very interesting entry begins with Mariia, the young bride of the tsar; then the nun Marfa, Tsar Mikhail's mother; and then Prince Vladimir himself and his third wife, Dariia/Mariia (Barbashina)—Mariia's mother. The rest of Prince Vladimir's family follows.[60] Given the events of 1616 and 1623, this pattern can hardly be random. Marfa was an important Dolgorukov ally and a relative who deserved commemoration. The evidence from these commemorations supports the view put forward by Zabelin and others that it was the nun Marfa who preferred Dolgorukova over Khlopova in 1623 and 1624.[61] Only her role in the selection of Dolgorukov's daughter explains her presence at the very top of Prince Vladimir's commemoration list; certainly, it is not explained by Marfa's genealogical relation to the donor, Prince Vladimir, which was, in point of fact, quite distant.

The sinodikons and genealogies pinpoint a cluster of families, horizontally linked by marriage, which acted in concert in court politics. A Dolgorukov tsaritsa was a victory for the Saltykovs precisely because they were in-laws. Had the tsar's planned wedding with Khlopova materialized, the Saltykovs' intimate position at court might very well have been jeopardized. Surely these considerations operated on the mind of Mikhail Saltykov at least as much as the insult he reportedly suffered at the hands of Gavrilo Khlopova at the Armory. To consent to Mariia Khlopova as tsaritsa was to allow room for her kinsmen in the inner circle at court. Among these kinsmen was first and foremost Gavrilo, who was evidently as abrasive as he was able. It would have also brought the Zheliabuzhskiis, Mariia's mother's family, to court. The fact that one of them shared

Mariia's Kremlin apartment and the Khlopovs' disgrace suggests that they may also have shared in the glory had the marriage plans succeeded. What other families may have had a stake in the Khlopov candidacy is hard to determine. The Khlopov genealogy is, sadly, very obscure. They had distant ties to the Nagoi clan;[62] and through Mariia's mother's clan (the Zheliabuzhskiis), the Khlopovs had a complex web of kinship links that joined them with a number of important families, including the Golitsyns, and, ironically enough, even with their enemies, the Saltykovs.[63]

It remains for us to consider why Khlopova was not reembraced as the tsar's bride-to-be once her good health had been established. Here, the role of Mikhail's mother was paramount. According to the chronicle account for these events, the nun Marfa remained throughout these events adamantly against the proposed union. When Khlopova's health was declared to be sound by the delegation sent to Nizhnii Novgorod, Marfa said she would sooner exile herself from the court—sharing voluntarily, as it were, the punishment meted out on her Saltykov kinsmen—than see her son marry Khlopova.[64] Zabelin attributed Marfa's stubborn opposition to the match to the personal loathing she felt toward her would-be daughter-in-law. Marfa shared the hatred that the Saltykovs felt for the Khlopovs, and the exile of the former only embittered her all the more against the girl.[65] It cannot be an accident that the new bridal candidate to whom Marfa directed her son was Mariia Dolgorukova, a kinswoman of the Shestov and Saltykov clans.

That the young tsar heeded his mother's objections has often been attributed either to his inability to stand up to his mother's stronger personality or to his affection for his mother. The matter of the tsar's character flaws can be left in the realm of speculation—if anything, the Khlopova affair shows as much the tsar's resolution as it does his compliant character. But it is clear that the tsar was attached to, perhaps even dependent upon, his mother. That Tsar Mikhail's father played no, or at best a peripheral, role in the selection of a bride is revealed directly by a report by a Dutch diplomatic mission to Moscow in 1624, recently published and analyzed by Paul Bushkovitch.[66] In it, the young tsar's relationship with his father is characterized as distant and unaffectionate: "the natural affections of the son [i.e., Tsar Mikhail] being more directed toward his mother than toward his father, on account of the long separation between father and son."[67] According to this same report, the tsar's mother also strongly objected to the proposed match with the Brandenburg princess in 1623.

"Day and night," the text reads, "she protested and swore not to give her blessing to her son."[68]

The nun Marfa—one of the most formidable and fascinating women of her time—was a member of a faction that endured the disgrace and exile of two of its leading members. She continued to battle for the interests of the kinship bloc to which she belonged. If Marfa resented the Saltykov exile, it was because it represented a blow to the strength of her faction at court, not because she shared the injured pride of the royal arms bearer. In their conspiracy against Mariia/Anastasiia Khlopova, the Saltykov brothers did not act alone.

Mariia Dolgorukova and Evdokiia Streshneva

Having been spurned by foreign royal houses and having had his preferred domestic choice ruled out by the bullying influences of his mother, Tsar Mikhail Romanov married Princess Mariia Vladimirovna Dolgorukova on September 19, 1624. Was there a bride-show in 1624? Was the selection of Mariia Dolgorukova entirely the nun Marfa Ivanovna's doing, "secretly prepared for him according to her own preferences," as Zabelin put it?[69] Or did Marfa Ivanovna's influence on her son's matrimonial choice play out within the context of a bride-show organized, however perfunctorily, in 1624?

Were one to look at the chronicle account of the Khlopova affair and the marriage to Dolgorukova, one would see no hint of a bride-show whatsoever.[70] In fact, the chronicle reports that the tsar entered the marriage with Dolgorukova against his will—something that was not supposed to happen when there was a bride-show. The entire point of the bride-show was to pick a candidate pleasing to the tsar, even if, as was usually the case, the list of candidates was carefully crafted for political rather than physical or moral reasons. The tsar married Dolgorukova, the chronicle account says, out of obedience to his mother, not out of love nor even in preference over other candidates. Therefore most historians who have looked at the tsar's marriage have concluded that there was no bride-show and that the choice was made in private, between father, mother, son, and close relatives.[71] Tsar Mikhail was doing what he was told.

On the other hand, there is good reason to believe that a bride-show was organized in 1624. A little-known genealogical notice, written in a seventeenth-century hand on a loose, single *stolbets*, or manuscript roll, contains the genealogies for Mariia Vladimirovna Dolgorukova and a distant cousin, Ogrofena Vladimirovna Dolgorukova. The purpose of this small artifact remains unknown; it was found among the personal papers of the famed Russian historian Gerhard Friedrich Müller and was published for the first time by Oleg Shcherbachev.[72] It is evidently not a fragment of a typical genealogy like those found in Genealogical Books (*Rodoslovnye knigi*), because it includes the names of spouses and concentrates exclusively on the genealogies of Mariia and Ogrofena, not the clan as a whole. This small text is almost certainly one of the genealogical investigative reports of prospective bridal candidates that were compiled in advance of a bride-show, like the one that survives for Ovdot'ia Gundorova, a prospective candidate in January 1547 for Ivan IV's first marriage (discussed in Chapter 2). To be sure, the inventory of the Foreign Office archive refers to a Dolgorukov genealogy in and among those of other families that appear to have been investigated.[73] Ogrofena, like Mariia, might very well have been a bridal candidate in 1624 since her Dolgorukov roots would have made her just as acceptable to Mikhail's mother as Mariia.[74] That Marfa Ivanovna's goal all along was to marry her son to any suitable Dolgorukova kinswoman, rather than to Mariia Dolgorukova specifically, is clear from the simple fact that in 1616, when the conspiracy against Khlopova was launched, Mariia was too young to be considered for marriage. She was evidently born in 1608, making her eight years old in 1616.[75] This small genealogical notice is therefore probably a remnant of a bride-show that was organized and performed so as to lend the stamp of tradition to the prearranged Dolgorukova match.

That a bride-show was held in 1624 is confirmed and plainly recorded in the Dutch diplomatic report published by Bushkovitch, retiring any doubts. It mentions that "from hundreds of young girls from the entire country none was found more suitable for this calling than the daughter of Prince Vladimir Dolgorukii, and on September 19, 1624, the wedding with her was promptly celebrated."[76] Thus, the obvious and deliberate manipulation of Tsar Mikhail's choice of bride by his domineering mother took place within the context of a bride-show.

As masterful as the nun Marfa Ivanovna's handling of the affair was, her plans were nonetheless foiled in the end. Mikhail's bride took ill during the wedding and slowly withered away until her pitiful death on January 6, 1625.[77] Zabelin suggested that Mariia Dolgorukova, like

Mariia Khlopova before her, had been the victim of court conspiracy, and this may have been the case.[78] Whatever the truth of the matter, Dolgorukova's death marked the end of Marfa's control over her son's marital arrangements.

Tsar Mikhail Fedorovich did not long mourn the bride his mother had chosen. He and his handlers almost immediately began considering a new marriage for the tsar. He would marry his second wife, Evdokiia Streshneva, on February 5, 1626—just a year and a month after Dolgorukova's death.[79] The bride-show in advance of this wedding is well established in the sources. The inventory for the archive of the Foreign Office includes a reference to a genealogy of the Streshnev family, showing that they were investigated along with a number of other families that may have supplied candidates for a bride-show in 1626. Historical tales composed after Mikhail Romanov's second wedding state directly that he selected Evdokiia Streshneva by means of a bride-show.[80] One such tale reports that sixty young maidens were brought to Moscow, selected for their "age, beauty, and intellect."[81] Another reports that Evdokiia was not actually one of the bridal contestants but, rather, an attendant (*prisluzhnitsa*) for one of the contestants.[82]

The Swedish prisoner-of-war Philip John von Strahlenberg, evidently using these tales and other sources, provided a detailed description of the bride-show for Tsar Mikhail's second wedding: "The Czar having declared his Intension of marrying, to the Senate, the Bojars look'd out for the most beautiful Ladies that were to be found, and sent them to Court."[83] Strahlenberg continues:

> As soon as the Czar was determin'd in his Choice, the Grande Gouvernante only was made acquainted with it, and order'd to get Cloaths made for them all, and for the Bride a Wedding-Suit.
>
> In the mean Time, A Day for the Solemnization of the Nuptials was appointed, tho' none of them knew who was to be the Bride; And that Day being come, the new Cloaths were distributed, and the Bride then receiv'd her Nuptial Robes. Which made it known on whom the choice was fallen. They then all paid their congratulatory Compliments to the Bride, and as soon as she was proclaim'd, the Rest were sent home.
>
> Eudocia, Czar Michael's Consort, was Maid of Honor at the Senator Scheremetow's Court. Her father was a poor Nobleman, who living

> privately upon his small estate, about 200 Wersts from the City of Muscow, was not so soon inform'd of his Daughter's good Fortune.
>
> Soon after the Nuptials were celebrated, the Czar sent one of the Lords of his Bedchamber to him, with suitable wearing Apparel, Servants, Coaches and Horses, and every Thing necessary to convey him and his whole Family to Muscow.
>
> When this Lord came to his Seat, he found Streschnew in the Fields, where he himself, with others, were at the Plough; And after he had saluted him, in the Name of the Czar and the Czarina, his Daughter, he acquainted him it was their Desire he should come to Muscow.
>
> This compliment very much surprised honest Streschnew, who thought the Lord only jested with him; His Answer, therefore, was: My Lord, I do not know you; however, I see you are one of our Great Czar's Court; I am but a poor Nobleman, and think it no Shame to maintain myself and Family in the Manner you see; Therefore I beg you not hinder me from taking the Advantage of the fair Weather.
>
> But the Lord delivering him a Letter from his Daughter, the Czarina, which he desired him to read, and to go home, and accept of the Presents he had left for him there, he was, at Length, convinc'd it was no jest: Upon which he set out for Muscow, where he was created Bojar before his Arrival, and his Family is to this Day of good Esteem.[84]

Strahlenberg's colorful story gets some of the details wrong, of course. Evdokiia's father not only knew about his daughter's selection as tsaritsa, he, his wife, and nine other members of his family were present at the wedding celebrations, serving in honorific positions: holding the bride's wedding candle, marching in the wedding train, attending to the wedding bed, and attending the bride in her private apartments.[85] Moreover, the *chin* for Tsar Mikhail's wedding makes it clear that the bride ritually "entered" into the Terem three days before the wedding, not immediately upon her selection.[86] And Luk'ian Streshnev, Evdokiia's father, was not promoted to boyar rank while still en route to Moscow. He was elevated to *okol'nichii* in 1630, and to boyar only in 1634.[87] Still, Strahlenberg's account, written more than a century after these events, can be forgiven these errors and accepted merely as confirmation of the other sources that describe a bride-show in 1626.

Evdokiia Streshneva, like Mariia Khlopova before her, met with the disapproval of the tsar's mother. According to a later literary source, the nun Marfa Ivanovna was persuaded to consent to the marriage only by a determined speech delivered to her by her (no doubt by this time thoroughly frustrated) son.[88] A more likely factor in the Streshneva choice was the obscurity of the Streshnev clan. John LeDonne called the Streshneva match (as well as royal matches with other seventeenth-century brides) "misalliances by the standards of French and English royalty," and Robert Crummey called the Streshnevs (and the other seventeenth-century in-laws) "undistinguished," "obscure," and "upstarts."[89] If Marfa Ivanovna and her Saltykov kin found Mariia/Anastasiia Khlopova objectionable because they lacked kinship ties with her and because the kin she did have proved to be able and popular with the tsar, then Evdokiia Streshneva's obscure origins may have made her a benign choice for all factions at court. The Streshnevs were, as Strahlenberg put it, "poor Noblemen," but they were nonetheless rich in children who were or soon would be of marriageable age. All factions at court could therefore hope to marry into the clan of the new royal in-laws, becoming in-laws of the royal in-laws—a very enviable place to be in this political system. And it appears that the Streshnevs capitalized on their biostatistical advantage. As Crummey put it, "the Streshnevs managed, between Mikhail's marriage to Evdokiia and the end of the century, to forge ties with the Golitsyns, Lykovs, Vorotynskiis, Troekurovs, and Saltykovs, among others."[90] However, the Streshneva match can best be explained by the simple fact that Tsar Mikhail Fedorovich was now twenty-eight years old, and the need for him to produce an heir for the fledgling Romanov dynasty had become the paramount concern for anyone invested in the success of the new dynasty. For ten years, the tsar and his handlers had been trying to secure the new dynastic regime with the birth of heirs. After two foiled attempts, it was time to let the tsar marry the woman everyone found the least objectionable.

Whatever the reason for the selection of Streshneva, the marriage was fruitful but not entirely lucky. Tsar Mikhail and Tsaritsa Evdokiia had ten children together, although only four of them would live to adulthood. When the couple died—as it turns out, within a month of each other (Tsar Mikhail on July 12, 1645, on his birthday and Tsaritsa Evdokiia on August 18, 1645)—the whole of the Romanov dynasty consisted only of one 16-year old boy (Aleksei, who would succeed him on the throne), and three young girls (Irina, Anna, and Tat'iana), aged 18, 15, and 9 years.[91] In the middle of the seventeenth century, Muscovy's ruling house consisted of a gaggle of orphaned teenagers.[92]

The Vsevolozhskaia Affair

Not twenty-five years after Tsar Mikhail Fedorovich had finally married, the plotting we observed in the Khlopova incident happened again when the tsar's son Tsar Aleksei Mikhailovich attempted to marry for the first time. There are uncanny parallels in these episodes; but whereas the Saltykovs' treachery was revealed and the conspirators punished, the plot against Aleksei's betrothed succeeded and the conspirator got away with it.

There are apparent inconsistencies in the sources that describe how Tsar Aleksei Mikhailovich met his first betrothed, Efimiia Fedorovna Vsevolozhskaia, in 1647, and his first wife, Mariia Ilichna Miloslavskaia, in 1648; but a partial narrative can nonetheless be reconstructed. According to Kotoshikhin, the tsar picked Efimiia because he "learned that one of his closest men had a daughter, a maiden of worthy stature and beauty and of excellent reason, and ordered her to be taken to his palace and placed in the care of his sisters, the tsarevnas, and given the same honors as his sisters the tsarevnas, until such time as the celebration and festivities take place."[93] Kotoshikhin here does not mention a bride-show. In fact, the text could be read to mean that the tsar had not even laid eyes on the young woman before she was whisked away to the Terem, which can hardly have been the case. To be sure, Kotoshikhin's account is not inconsistent with there having been a bride-show, though why he would not mention it here, in his discussion—however brief—of the Vsevolozhskaia affair, is peculiar. But then, Kotoshikhin never discusses bride-shows at all in his account, despite the lengthy passages he devotes to marriage in Muscovy.[94] Nor, in this instance, does he even mention Efimiia's name.

Other sources do directly mention a bride-show. Samuel Collins, the personal doctor to the tsar, twice mentions a bride-show for Tsar Aleksei Mikhailovich in his account of his years at the Muscovite court: "His Imperial Majesty intending to marry, had divers young Ladies brought before him,"[95] and "the Czar being to take a Wife, all the choice beauties in the Country are brought before him, one he fancies, and gives her a Handkerchief and Ring, she appears again in a Royal dress."[96] Collins's proximity to the tsar renders his account broadly reliable, especially when set beside the account of a Swedish traveler named Ferber, who wrote in the midst of the episode and before the final determination of Efimiia's fate. Ferber's account provides useful details about the bride-show in 1647: "On February 14, His Imperial Majesty had installed in the palace, in the Great Hall, 6 maidens, selected from 200 others, and designated for that purpose by the great lords [*vel'mozhi*], and the tsar selected for himself as wife the daughter of an undistinguished boyar Fedor Vsevolozhskii." This valuable passage renders the date of the bride-show according to the Gregorian calendar, which was ten days different from the Julian calendar then in use in Muscovy (so the bride-show actually took place on February 4), and claims—rightly, as we have seen—that the tsar picked his bride from a small number of candidates handpicked for him by the great clans. Ferber does, however, misidentify Raf/Fedor Vsevolozhskii as an "undistinguished boyar," a rank he did not (and never would) hold.

The apparent contradiction in these accounts is mended by remembering that Kotoshikhin was actually reporting and emphasizing the underlying calculations that brought the winning bridal candidate into the Terem, not the bride-show, which, to him, may not have been worth noting; whereas Collins and Ferber may have been emphasizing the mechanisms of the bride-show, which to them were the far more exotic and fascinating aspects of the tsar's marriage. The fact that Collins and Ferber then go on to provide details about the scandal that ensued upon Tsar Aleksei's choice—details glossed over in Kotoshikhin—shows that, at the very least, these authorities were interested in different things when relating this episode.

On February 4, 1647, Tsar Aleksei Mikhailovich participated in the final stage of a bride-show, inspecting six young women who had been, as Ferber put it, selected for him by the boyars. From these six, Aleksei chose Efimiia Rafovna Vsevolozhskaia, the daughter of a middle-level courtier.[97] (Her father, Raf, then changed his name to Fedor.) Unlike Mariia Khlopova, who had been moved into her Kremlin apartments and had resided in them for at least six weeks, or longer, before being poisoned, Efimiia was to have no prolonged engagement. Efimiia was selected on February 4, and the wedding was scheduled for Sunday, February 14.[98]

Sources conflict again about what happened next. According to Ferber, "when the maiden heard the news of her selection, she fainted out of great fear and joy. The grand prince and his lords concluded from this that she had a fainting disease; they sent her away to a location three versts away from Moscow, to a certain boyar, to determine what to do with her. In the meantime, her parents, who swore that she had previously been entirely healthy, were taken into custody. If this maiden again falls ill with the same sickness, then her parents will be sent into exile. Many here think that the grand prince will marry another after Easter."[99] Ferber evidently wrote before any whiff of a conspiracy emerged, and so his account—evidently repeating what he had been told—focuses on Efimiia's health. Was she ill with some sort of fainting disease and had her family concealed this fact? The notion that someone else, a boyar in the court, was responsible had not yet been openly considered. At least, no rumors about boyar involvement had yet filtered out for Ferber to report.[100]

Other sources, by contrast, attributed Efimiia's collapse to a conspiracy. Kotoshikhin reported that Tsar Aleksei's first intended had been poisoned by the wives of the great boyars, who wanted the tsar to marry one of their daughters.[101] Collins also reported a conspiracy. He discusses the episode in two places in his account. In one place, Collins reports that the match with Vsevolozhskaia was foiled by a conspiracy between the tsar's father-confessor and the *boiaryni*. Soon after the tsar had picked Vsevolozhskaia, Collins says:

> his chief Confessor had a mind to perswade him to another, who had an younger Sister, so when this fair Lady was brought, they found his Majesties inclinations so strong for her, as they fear'd she would get the Crown, and indeed so she did, it being a Ceremony, upon his liking, to tye the Crown upon her head, but the plot was so laid, that the Women should tye up her hair so hard as to put her into a Swoon, which they did, crying out she had the Falling-sickness: Upon this her Father was accused of Treason for proposing his Daughter, whip't, and sent with disgrace into *Syberia*, where he died. The Maid remains still a Virgin, and never had any fit since.[102]

In another place, however, Collins names a different mastermind of the plot: boyar Boris Ivanovich Morozov, the chief magnate of the realm, the tsar's trusted tutor and de facto foster father, and like the Saltykov brothers before him, the person with the most to lose by the wrong choice of bride:

> Boris ordered the crown to be tyed so hard about her head, that she fell into a swoon, this was presently construed an Epileptick fit; her Father being examined with torments, was, alas poor old Gentleman, sent into Syberia, and died by the way with grief, and left his Family in disgrace. The maid is still alive, but never known to have had any more fits. She has been offer'd many Noblemen, but refuses all, and keeps the Handkerchief and Ring. The Czar allows her a pension to expiate the injury done to her Father and Family.[103]

Whether she was poisoned or somehow otherwise caused to faint, and whether the culprits were the boyars' wives, the tsar's priest, or his favored tutor, there is little doubt that Vsevolozhskaia's collapse was interpreted by the tsar and his inner circle as a disqualifying illness. When the betrothal was actually broken off is unclear. Scribes in the Foreign Office began composing the draft wedding ceremonials and musters before the tsar selected her on February 4 since some copies of the texts leave spaces where the bride's name was to appear, which were later filled in with Efimiia's name. Other copies have her name as part of the base text, suggesting that the editing of the texts continued right up until the tsar renounced her.[104] We know that on February 12, two days before the wedding was to have taken place, Efimiia was given all the fine linens that had been prepared for use at the wedding as a kind of parting gift.[105] It was therefore sometime between these dates—February 4 and February 12—that Efimiia was expelled from the Terem and shortly sent in exile to Tiumen' along with her father, Raf, her mother, Nastas'ia, and her brother Andrei.[106] Tsar Aleksei, so distraught over the incident that he refused food, was convinced to forget Efimiia by going bear hunting.

Many historians have accepted Collins's indictment of Morozov as the mastermind of the plot, but Solov'ev dissented. While he agreed that Efimiia had been the victim of some kind of plot, Solov'ev rejected the view that Morozov was the brains behind it all, leaving the mystery of who was guilty unsolved for lack of corroborating evidence. Zabelin, however, accepted Collins's testimony about Morozov's guilt. The evidence against Morozov is, Zabelin admits, post factum and circumstantial but, nonetheless, overwhelming: "Morozov acted very subtly [*tonko*] and skillfully [*iskusno*]" to ruin the Vsevolozhskaia match.[107] Morozov saw Tsar Aleksei's wedding either as an opportunity to shore up his own position at court or as a sure way to lose it, depending on whom the tsar married. In this, Zabelin relied on the account of these events by Adam Olearius: "To maintain the favor of His Tsarist Majesty, [Morozov] strove to enter into a close kinship with him. He advised him to marry soon, and so that the choice should fall on a person of the middling nobility, to which Morozov himself belonged, he proposed a nobleman's daughter whose sister Morozov himself thought of marrying." Olearius further explained: "At the time there was a certain nobleman named Il'ia Danilovich Miloslavskii, who had two beautiful daughters but no sons. This Il'ia frequently came to Morozov, who then was factotum at the court, as they say, and assiduously wooed him, so that Morozov came to admire him not only for the sake of his lovely daughters but also for his complaisance." Just as Kotoshikhin also reported, Olearius says that the two daughters were brought to the court "ostensibly to visit the Tsar's sisters. When His Tsarist Majesty glimpsed them, he fell in love with the older [*sic*] one."[108] Well before there had been a bride-show, Morozov had a bride in mind for the young tsar—one of the two daughters of Il'ia Daniilovich Miloslavskii, Mariia or Anna. Morozov's opportunity was to have Aleksei marry one of the two girls so that he might, with their father's acquiescence, marry the other one himself. The fact that Morozov and the girl were probably separated by decades in age was hardly a deterrent either to him or to the girl's father.

Miloslavskii had long been Morozov's *créature*, and over time, a bond of friendship and a political alliance had been forged between the two.[109] While not important in its own right, the Miloslavskii clan had kinship ties with the Dolgorukovs, the family of Tsar Mikhail's first wife, as well as the Sokovnins, the Khitrovos, and Rtishchevs.[110] Thus, Il'ia Daniilovich Miloslavskii's faithful clientage, his clan's useful kinship ties to other clans, and his two unwed daughters presented Morozov with the perfect chance to link himself even more closely to the young tsar and, at the same time, to eliminate any chance that he might be eclipsed by in-laws to whom he might not (and, in the case of the Vsevolozhskiis, apparently did not) have ties. It was the Khlopova affair all over again.

But Aleksei (probably unwittingly) foiled Morozov's masterfully crafted plan by picking Vsevolozhskaia in the bride-show. How and when Miloslavskaia came to the tsar's attention is unclear, however. Zabelin believed that Morozov had one or both of the Miloslavskii girls included in the bride-show on February 4, and so Tsar Aleksei had already seen at least one of the Miloslavskii candidates.[111] Olearius, however, reports that Morozov arranged to have the tsar meet both Miloslavskii girls for the first time in the Kremlin apartments of the tsar's sisters, where he took a fancy to the older Miloslavskaia, Mariia (a meeting that could have occurred either before or after the bride-show).[112] Kotoshikhin, by contrast, reports that Aleksei "happened to be in the church where he was crowned [the Cathedral of the Dormition of the Mother of God—Uspenskii sobor] and saw the two daughters of a certain Moscow *dvorianin*, Il'ia Miloslavskii, standing in church at prayer, and sent to his palace for some maidens and ordered them to take the younger [*sic*] daughter of that *dvorianin* to his upper chambers; and when the service was over the tsar came to his chambers, looked at her and became enamored."[113] Whatever the case, Collins and Kotoshikhin agree that, when Efimiia fainted in everyone's presence, Morozov acted swiftly to discredit her, which, as Zabelin convincingly argued, amounted to a solid indictment of Morozov. Whether Archpriest Stefan Vonafant'ev and the *boiaryni* were involved cannot be known, but it is hard to imagine how any conspiracy so firmly located within the Terem as this one was could be feasible without the collusion of the elite women who lived there. As for the archpriest's involvement, it is entirely possible that Aleksei, who heeded the archpriest's advice in so many areas, would also have given his opinions in his choice of spouse due consideration. The fact that the tsar heeded Archpriest Stefan's admonitions to alter the traditional and ancient wedding ritual so as to omit the pagan fertility rites and many of the secular games and entertainments that were customary at royal weddings only goes to show the length of the archpriest's reach. Collins's account rings true in many ways.

Morozov's plan worked without a hitch. However he met her, Aleksei found Mariia Miloslavskaia to be satisfactory, and he married her on January 16, 1648. At the wedding ceremony, Morozov served as the "proxy father" of the groom.[114] Eleven days later, on January 27, Morozov married Mariia's sister, Anna.[115] The pact was complete when Il'ia Daniilovich, the father of the bride, was made an *okol'nichii* one day after the tsar's wedding, and a boyar less than a week after Morozov's.[116]

As was the case among the conspirators in the Khlopova affair, the bonds of familial and political alliance between Boris Morozov and Il'ia Miloslavskii were inscribed in sinodikons. In fact, the association between these two men and their two clans is remarkably intimate. Several extant sinodikons contain prayer lists for Il'ia Miloslavskii and Boris Morozov positioned directly next to each other, indicating that the commemorations were requested by both men (or their families) at the same time.[117] Moreover, the two men often included each other at the very top of each other's prayer lists. Boris Morozov (who is frequently listed by his baptismal name, which, ironically enough, was Il'ia)[118] appears directly next to his father-in-law, Il'ia Miloslavskii, in many Morozov commemoration lists.[119] Similarly, Il'ia Miloslavskii's commemoration lists frequently include Morozov and his kin at or near the very top, sometimes even before Il'ia's own blood kin appear.[120] Interestingly, the sinodikon entries for a number of other members of the Morozov and

Miloslavskii clans also include both Boris and Il'ia, showing that other members of their clans valued the bond between them as well.[121]

Morozov's conspiracy succeeded in establishing a bloc of clans at court that linked him by ties of kinship not only to the tsar and to the Miloslavskiis but also to their up-and-coming relatives (the Rtishchevs, Khitrovos, and Sokovnins). This bloc produced some of the most prominent political figures of the later seventeenth century and governed Muscovy, albeit with some very bloody interruptions, until the family of Tsar Aleksei's second wife, Natal'ia Kirillovna Naryshkina, challenged their political hegemony in the 1690s.

The Beliaeva Affair

The death of Mariia Miloslavskaia on March 3, 1669, evidently left the tsar shattered. She had been his consort for more than twenty years and had given him thirteen children, nine of whom had survived childhood—six daughters (Evdokiia, Marfa [the nun Margarita], Sofiia [the nun Susanna], Ekaterina, Mariia, and Feodosiia) and four sons (Aleksei, Fedor, Simeon, and Ivan).[122] The tsar's affection for Mariia has been noted by others variously[123] but is best attested, oddly enough, in the wedding *chin* for his second marriage. In this text, the tsar justifies his remarriage in terms of his children, pointing out that "already another year has passed in great sadness seeing the incessant tears of our royal children at the loss of their birth mother the most pious tsaritsa, whose wailing and sobbing I can no longer endure." The text also reveals the tsar's somber and mournful mood after Mariia's death, reporting that at the tsar's wedding, "they did not play upon the drums or play the flutes [*siposhi*] because, after the death of the pious tsaritsa and grand princess Mariia Il'ichna, such music was not played."[124]

However affected he may have been by the death of his consort, Tsar Aleksei Mikhailovich and his entire court must have been thrown into a panic by the death of the four-year-old Tsarevich Simeon Alekseevich, on June 14, 1669, followed on January 17, 1670, by the death of the tsar's eldest son and heir, the sixteen-year-old Tsarevich Aleksei Alekseevich, leaving him with only two sons to serve as heir—the frail Fedor, age eight, and the mentally disabled Ivan, age two. Finding a new bride to bear him more sons became imperative. In November 1669, the tsar began searching for a new bride by summoning candidates to appear before him in small groups of two to eight: he saw thirty-three maidens in eight sessions before Aleksei Alekseevich's death in January. Afterward, he saw thirty-eight more candidates in ten sessions between February and April 1670 (see table 5.1).[125] After several months of bride-shows, Aleksei settled in mid-April 1670 on two finalists: Ovdot'ia Ivanovna Beliaeva, who had been escorted to the bride-show by her uncle Ivan Shikhirev and grandmother, the nun Iraida; and Natal'ia Kirillovna Naryshkina, a relative of Artemon Sergeevich Matveev, one of Tsar Aleksei's favorites. (Matveev's wife's niece Evdokiia Petrovna Khomutova was married to Natal'ia's uncle Fedor Poluekhtovich Naryshkin.)[126] But, as it had the

TABLE 5.1.

THE BRIDE-SHOWS FOR TSAR ALEKSEI MIKHAILOVICH, 1669–1670

Year	Day	Number of Candidates	Year	Day	Number of Candidates
7178/1669	November 28	6	7178/ 1670	January 3	2
	November 30	6		February 1	4
	December 4	4		February 11	2
	December 12	5		February 27	6
	December 14	2		March 11	2
	December 20	6		March 12	3
	December 29	1		March 17	2
				April 5	8[1]
				April 10	4[2]
				April 13	4
				April 17	2

1—Of the 8, 3 are listed as being from Novgorod, 1 from Suzdal', 2 from Kostroma, and 2 from Riazan'.

2—Of the 4, 1 is listed as being from Vladimir, 1 from Novgorod, and 1 from Kostroma. (The fourth was likely from Moscow.)

first time he married, Tsar Aleksei Mikhailovich's choice of bride again spawned a conspiracy.

Just as it seemed that the tsar was about to decide, perhaps in favor of Beliaeva, two letters were found, one lying on the ground in the vestibule of the Hall of Facets (*Granovitaia palata*), the other in the vestibule to the Tower Hall (*Shaternaia palata*). The letters were turned over to Bogdan Khitrovo, another of the tsar's favorites and perhaps the leading figure in Aleksei's court. Khitrovo immediately took the letters to the tsar. The letters do not survive, and their exact contents remain unknown. Zabelin speculated that the letters were written by enemies of the Naryshkin match and contained some sort of allegation against Natal'ia Naryshkina.[127] Suspicion quickly fell on Ivan Shikhirev, Ovdot'ia Beliaeva's uncle, who was probably too outspoken an advocate of his niece's candidacy for his own good. Earlier during the vetting of bridal candidates, Shikhirev became alarmed at Khitrovo's suggestion that his niece was unsuitable because of her "skinny arms," and he attempted to convince the foreign doctor who was evaluating candidates to attest to Beliaeva's health and normal proportions. In the course of the investigation into the letters, the doctor, Stefan von Haden, now reported his conversation with Shikhirev, who was immediately arrested. Under interrogation and merciless torture, Shikhirev confessed to doing all he could to advocate for his niece, including soliciting von Haden and the archimandrite of the Chudov monastery (the future Patriarch Ioakim) to intervene on his niece's behalf, but he strenuously denied any part in writing the letters.

When Shikhirev provided no answers, the investigation, led by the tsar himself, moved in a different direction. On April 24, 1670, every scribe serving in the chancelleries was asked to provide handwriting samples for comparison to two phrases that appeared in the letters.[128] Not finding any perfect matches, the entire court was assembled two days later below the porch of the tsar's residence (*Postel'noe kryl'tso*) and shown the letters. All those gathered were ordered to divulge anything they knew about the letters or suffer disgrace. There the story ends. Sources are silent on the outcome of the investigations, and the author of the letters may never have been discovered. But if the plotters went unpunished (except, of course, for Shikhirev who, according to Zabelin, was probably innocent of any crime), their scheme to control the tsar's choice of bride failed. Aleksei married Natal'ia Naryshkina nine months later, on January 22, 1671.

Fresh insights into the Beliaeva affair have recently been made by

Paul Bushkovitch, who introduced a vital new set of sources to the matter: the dispatches of Nicolas Heinsius, the Dutch envoy in Moscow at the time.[129] These dispatches show that the investigation into the matter had continued into the summer months of 1670, and that the torturing had continued too, including now a number of women who had been implicated in one way or another. They also suggest the content of one or both of the mysterious letters found earlier in April. Heinsius reported the allegation that Natal'ia Naryshkina had had a dalliance with a Polish nobleman while her father had been serving in Smolensk. The dispatches also name the chief opponent of Natal'ia's candidacy: not Shikhirev, whose opposition to Natal'ia we might expect, given that Ovdot'ia was his niece, but, rather, the tsar's older sister, Tsarevna Irina Mikhailovna. Both Tsarevna Irina and Ovdot'ia Beliaeva had a connection to Ascension (*Voznesenskii*) Convent in the Kremlin. Ovdot'ia was a ward of the convent and lived on its grounds, and her mother, the nun Iraida, may have resided there as well. Tsarevna Irina, as the senior female member of the dynasty, also had close ties to the convent—the "house convent of the women of the ruling dynasty, the place where the tsaritsas were buried."[130] However they were connected, Heinsius's dispatches make it clear that Tsarevna Irina was plotting against Natal'ia Naryshkina in favor of Ovdot'ia Beliaeva. Tsar Mikhail had his mother meddling in his wedding plans; Tsar Aleksei had his sister Irina.

But who was making the case for Natal'ia that overcame the allegations against her? Historians who have looked into this scandal have convinced themselves that Natal'ia's candidacy was promoted by her kinsman Matveev. Bushkovitch, however, has challenged this traditional view, arguing that Matveev's advocacy for Natal'ia postdates the bride-show: "The list compiled by the Privy Chancellery of the girls brought to the palace for the viewing, the *smotriny*, note in a number of cases that the girl lived with a relative or someone other than her parents, but there is no such notation after Natalia's name. The most likely explanation is that she lived in Matveev's house (if at all) only after the viewing."[131] Bushkovitch attributes any association between Matveev and the Narshyshkins solely to Matveev's opportunism: "When Matveev was on the rise, Natal'ia appeared in the list of girls chosen for inspection, but we do not actually know that he put her on that list. What we do know is that once she emerged as one of the more serious contenders in spring 1670, Matveev was believed by [Natal'ia's] opponents to be her supporter."[132]

Pavel Sedov, however, has provided new and convincing documentary support for the traditional view. According to Sedov, Natal'ia certainly did live in Matveev's house in Moscow before the bride-show. He points to a gift Natal'ia made on March 19, 1671 (two months after her marriage with Tsar Aleksei), of fabric to her former spiritual father, Fr. Aleksei Iakovlev, of the Church of St. Nicholas the Wonderworker, located directly next door to Matveev's house in Moscow—the church Matveev attended. This gift, for Sedov, proves a prior connection between Natal'ia and Matveev's house.[133]

That Natal'ia lived with Matveev is also mentioned in Reutenfels's account of the bride-shows in 1669 and 1670, which he says were held at Matveev's house. Reutenfels's account points out that, after the tsar had set his heart on Natal'ia, "a few weeks later, early in the morning, [the tsar] sent to Artamon's house several boyars with carriages from the court accompanied by a troop of cavalrymen and trumpeters." He continues:

> The newly selected bride lived there, completely unaware of what lay before her, and was peacefully and deeply sleeping. The best men [*shafera*], having informed Artamon of the honorable commission that had been bestowed upon them by the tsar, zealously asked to be allowed, in accordance with their mission, to take the bride together with them to the palace. Artamon could not, of course, defy the tsar's command, which was anyway quite agreeable, and, having awakened Natal'ia from her deep sleep, announced to her the tsar's intentions, which she wisely agreed to immediately, finding this inevitable. Then they quickly dressed her in royal clothing, which was brought with them from the court, so that the people could see her richly adorned, and they took just a few of her attendants to the royal palace. Her attire, encrusted with so many gems, was so heavy on account of them that she for several days complained that it nearly broke all her bones. After her arrival, she immediately went to church with the tsar, where, in the presence of only a few people, the wedding was performed by the royal father-confessor, and only the most notable [*znatnyia*] persons were in the course of several days treated to magnificent feasts, and the Kremlin during this whole time was closed all around.[134]

Matveev—like Saltykov and Morozov before him—was a skillful manipulator of events and was careful not to reveal his cards too soon. He did not immediately present his niece and ward to Tsar Aleksei when the bride-shows began back in November of the previous year, even though he had been plotting his niece's marriage to the tsar from the very start. Only after Tsarevich Aleksei Alekseevich's death on January 17, 1670, when, presumably, the tsar's seriousness of purpose about his second marriage was infused with new urgency, did Matveev have Natal'ia appear before the tsar: at the very first bride-show convened after the tsarevich's death (February 10). Matveev appears not to have been in a hurry. Clearly, rushing to secure the tsar's bed was a sure-fire way to make powerful enemies. And pitted against him was the most powerful opponent one could have, the tsar's influential sister.

What is perhaps ironic about this conspiracy is that Ovdot'ia Beliaeva probably had been Aleksei's preferred choice from the moment he met her, and so Tsarevna Irina should not have had much to worry about. Beliaeva had appeared before the tsar on April 17, 1670, along with one other candidate, whereupon the bride-shows ended, probably because Aleksei had found in Beliaeva the girl he wanted. However, Natal'ia still had powerful advocates who were keeping her candidacy alive—Matveev, first and foremost—even after the tsar had passed over her and had met with other prospects. Otherwise, the plot to sabotage Natal'ia Naryshkina makes no sense: Beliaeva was clearly the tsar's favorite, and so the letters attacking Natal'ia were unnecessary unless someone powerful and well-placed was still advocating for her. That someone was clearly Matveev; and the letters against Naryshkina were designed not only to be the last nail in the coffin of the Naryshkina candidacy but also an early blow to Matveev's influence at court, which was sure to plummet once the tsar married Beliaeva. The plot backfired, however. Once suspicions were raised against Shikhirev, it was Beliaeva's candidacy that was ruined, not Naryshkina's.

The choice between Naryshkina, backed by Matveev, and Beliaeva, backed by Tsarevna Irina, was, in fact, a struggle between two opposing figures at court, played out behind the fiction of the tsar's free choice to pick which of the two he wanted for a bride. Of course, a tsar could pick freely at a bride-show, but only from among the small number of finalists presented him. Control of the list of finalists was, with few exceptions, out of his hands. In some ways, then, the trick of the bride-show was in the careful screening of candidates and in getting the right list of finalists presented to the tsar. But as the Khlopova, Vsevolozhskaia, and Beliaeva affairs demonstrate, free choice did not always translate into the full and free acceptance of that choice by the boyars, especially those who occupied their intimate positions on account of their own kinship ties to the dynasty established a generation earlier, when the previous tsar married. The overlay of kinship politics and the tsar's free choice in the bride-show generated a ritual that, by the end of the seventeenth century, was as rigged as it was necessary to the political system. It may always have been so. Trakhaniotov's role in the first bride-show in 1505 comes readily to mind as an early example of influence over ritual. But over time, the bride-show progressively failed to conceal and moderate the rough-and-tumble politics underlying the choice of a bride for the ruler, which was its original purpose.

By the time Tsar Aleksei's sons married in the 1680s, the size and structure of the Muscovite court had begun to change fundamentally through the inflation of honors, the abolishment of precedence (*mestnichestvo*), and the gradual adoption of foreign manners and tastes at court. The cultural expressions of monarchical power changed, too. The bride-show, like so many other court rituals, appeared more and more foreign and antiquated to the Muscovites themselves, and so any effort in the last decades of the century to maintain the façade of a free and open choice in a bride-show appeared hollow and contrived. In fact, the behind-the-scenes manipulations so eclipsed the outward rituals of the bride-show that documentation—and memory—of them in the last decades of the century become extremely thin. It is a testament to how fundamental the bride-show was in old Muscovy that, once the cultural forms of the court began to change, the bride-show was among the first of the old rituals to become obsolete. The fictive and staged elements of the bride-show now served no purpose but to expose the entire ritual as obsolete, less and less tethered to any cultural meaning or political arrangement in the tsar's court. It is to the marriages of the sons of Tsar Aleksei—for whom the last bride-shows were organized—and to the fading role and gradual obsolescence of the bride-show, that we now turn.

Chapter 6

"Worthy Because the Tsar Adores You"

The Last Bride-Shows and the Return of Foreign-Born Brides

> Great monarch, doesn't thworde whole world heed your word? Who doesn't stand in awe of your words and actions? And where is the man who dares cross your pleasure? You have the power to raise high all that lives. A single word from you will make your people take up arms; a single word and they must go put them down. When at times you brandish your scepter, you cause strife or glory. Your word can raze cities, topple mountains, and shatter strong walls. Is it right for you, because of a mere woman, to feel slighted for a long time and to be so very sad? Are your kingdoms not teeming with beautiful women, equal in beauty even to goddesses? Who can insult you by slighting your authority, if you order that beautiful women in your kingdom be found and brought before you? Have them brought here to your royal palace. Let the most beautiful and noble one with whom you fall in love be your beloved wife, instead of Vashti.[1]

These lines are taken from the first secular play ever performed in Russia, *The Comedy of Artaxerxes*, staged for Tsar Aleksei Mikhailovich on October 17, 1672. Composed by Johann Gottfried Gregorius, a Lutheran pastor resident in Moscow, the ten-hour-long production is said to have left the tsar "rapt and filled with wonder."[2]

The play follows the narrative structure of the biblical book of Esther, which, in Chapter 2 (Acts 1 and 2 in the play), includes a bride-show from which the Persian King Artaxerxes picks Esther to be his new queen.[3] Act 1, Scene 1, finds the king together with his nobles—referred to in the play as "boyars"—who are extolling the king as a "powerful monarch" and as a "god on earth." Artaxerxes, however, has been away hosting a banquet and is in "profound grief" because he has not seen his "marvelous vision," his "splendid tsarina." The king sends for her: "Let all the nobles, gazing on her beauty, see the loveliest, the chosen among women."[4] Vashti, Artaxerxes's queen, is meanwhile hosting her own banquet for the women of the palace when she receives the king's summons. She objects to being paraded in front of a "gathering of those drunken princes of so many lands" and refuses to obey the command.[5] The queen's refusal is interpreted by the king's "boyars" as not only a slight against the king but a slight by all wives against their husbands. The king asks his chamberlains what he should do, and one of them, Memucan, proposes a harsh and unforgiving remedy: "Let Vashti for her pride and disobedience be cast out by you for as long as she lives; let her never again behold your countenance; and choose another in her place, oh tzar." King Artaxerxes takes his "boyar's" advice and banishes Vashti.[6] The next scene—some three or four years later in the biblical text, but only one day later in the play—is quoted above, with another of the king's "boyars," Harbonah, advising the king to "order that beautiful women in your kingdom be found and brought before you." "Good!" declares Artaxerxes. "Dispatch with speed messengers to all parts of my realm to order all beautiful women be brought before me so that we may conclude this matter before morning."[7]

Among the women gathered for Artaxerxes to inspect is Esther. Esther is introduced to the king, who has evidently been told in advance of her stunning beauty and virtue. He is instantly mesmerized by her, even before speaking to her: "How much this lovely girl already stirs my heart from afar." "Arise, goddess," Artaxerxes tells her, "and kiss this hand. All are afraid of it, but you need no longer fear it." After one last consultation with his advisors, all of whom approve and applaud the choice, Artaxerxes proclaims Esther queen: "Take her [Vashti's] throne, oh most beautiful woman!"[8] Esther is proclaimed worthy: "worthy of the crown, worthy because the tzar adores you."[9] The play then moves on to the other plots in the story—Haman's diabolical plot to exterminate the Jews of Media and Persia, the wise counsel of Esther's uncle Mordecai, and Queen Esther's role in saving her people and exposing Haman's evil manipulations of the king—all of which confirms Artaxerxes's wisdom in selecting Esther as his bride.

The tsar, his tsaritsa, and the other members of the audience viewing this performance in the fall of 1672 could not have missed the obvious parallels between the plot and characters in the Esther play and the events and personalities in the Muscovite court. The play was staged just two-and-a-half years after the completion of the bride-show, which ran in fits and starts between November 1669 and April 1670, and about twenty-one months after Tsar Aleksei Mikhailovich had married his second wife, Natal'ia Naryshkina, having settled on her as his bride after the Beliaeva controversy. I. M. Kudriavtsev, the major Soviet scholar of the play, thought the topic of this drama and the situation in the court were linked, even pairing the characters in the play with some of the figures around the tsar. "It is very likely," he writes, "that the concrete situation in the court at that time played a role in the choice of subject matter for the play. The tsar had just married the ward of Artemon Sergeevich Matveev, Natal'ia Kirillovna Naryshkina—the Muscovite Esther."[10] The parallels between the tsar and Artaxerxes were apparent to many even before the play dramatized them on the stage. The wedding ceremonial for Tsar Aleksei and Natal'ia Kirillovna contains a speech given by Metropolitan Pavel of Sarskii and Podonskii (Krutitskii), which admonished the groom to "rejoice unto God, o most noble autocrat, in your noble spouse, as once did Abraham rejoice in Sarah, Isaac in Rebecca, Jacob in the beautiful and the fruitful Rachel, David in the most wise Abigail, and as did Artaxerxes in the noble Esther; and may the Lord God bring you happiness in your royal nuptial bedchamber."[11]

In adapting the biblical story for the stage, the playwright Gregorius put on display many of the traditional elements of the bride-show custom in Muscovy. Esther's virtue and beauty are emphasized as the determining factors behind Artaxerxes's choice. She is called "this beautiful girl, unblemished and glorious," and "the true moon," while other women were "mere stars."[12] Esther expresses pious disregard for the riches of this world, declaring that she is "not at all drawn to greatness. I have only one wish: to live abundantly in poverty rather than in riches."[13] Esther rehearses what most Muscovite courtiers must have thought was the only appropriate reaction to her selection at the bride-show, saying, "I accept this high rank in meekness and will be obedient out of duty rather than because of the honor you have bestowed on me today."[14] Perhaps Gregorius's most significant alteration of the biblical Esther for the Muscovite audience was her social background. The biblical text clearly portrays Esther as a descendant of the Saulide dynasty, but the playwright identifies her as a commoner—"I am of common lineage," says Esther, humbly declaring herself to be unworthy to be queen.[15] This alteration made the biblical story into something much more familiar to those in the audience, and in fact the play may have in some ways served as a set of instructions for Natal'ia Naryshkina—Tsar Aleksei's Esther—about what a Muscovite tsaritsa was supposed to be: beautiful, wise, pious, loyal, and obedient.[16]

The play and its idealized bride-show appeared on the stage just at the moment when the custom was sliding into obsolescence and desuetude. Precisely as the bride-show was making its first appearance as a story-motif in Muscovy, it was simultaneously being drained of any useful cultural meaning in the Muscovite court by changes in the underlying political culture. This chapter examines the bride-show in the last decades of the seventeenth century, situating the custom in and among the general trends of reform at court and in elite culture. In this chapter we also explore how royal marriage under Peter I again became a tool of Muscovite diplomacy and how the Romanovs reentered the European royal marriage market. The bride-show, conjured as a response to the obstacles presented by inter-dynastic marriage, was discarded when it no longer reflected or facilitated the political culture of the court at home, and when the Russians ceased to subordinate their diplomatic interests to the strictest possible readings of canon law.

A Bride without a Bride-Show

Tsar Aleksei Mikhailovich's death on January 29, 1676, thrust his eldest surviving son, the fourteen-year-old Fedor, onto the throne. It also "unleashed a struggle of unparalleled ferocity among the boyars," according to Bushkovitch. "Not since the end of the Time of Troubles," he continues, "had the Russian aristocracy fought among themselves with such ruthlessness."[17] Between Tsar Aleksei's death and his son's marriage in July 1680, the political situation at court was thoroughly unsettled, with old favorites exiting and new favorites yet to be entrenched in power, and with the young tsar's marriage hanging in the balance.

The first target of these struggles was Artamon Sergeevich Matveev, Tsar Aleksei Mikhailovich's favorite and the chief advocate of Natal'ia Naryshkina's candidacy back in 1671. His fall from grace came quickly after Tsar Aleksei's death. Never popular with the majority of the boyars for his "control of the main Chancelleries and his personal influence on Tsar Aleksei," Matveev's hold on power began to slip within days of the tsar's death.[18] A reshuffling of the chancelleries left Matveev with fewer of them in his own hands or those of his clients, and new appointments to the rank of boyar brought new men into the Duma who tilted the balance against him. Opposition to Matveev also presented itself in charges of sorcery and magic leveled against him and others linked to him—a common enough way to disparage a political opponent. In this case, however, the charges may have been rooted in the changes in custom, manners, and dress that were associated with Matveev and were increasingly common in Tsar Aleksei's court after his marriage to Natal'ia Naryshkina, including the staging of plays like *The Comedy of Artaxerxes*.[19] Matveev, whose ability to discern which way the winds of fortune at court were blowing had helped him rise to power in the first place, must have known he was doomed well before early June 1676, when he was stripped of his boyar rank and sent into exile in Pustozersk.[20] The sorcery charges against Matveev's clients continued to be investigated until the summer of 1679, but by this point the struggle among boyars and factions at court had moved on to the main event: the back-and-forth contest between the families and allies of Tsar Aleksei's first wife, the Miloslavskiis, and those of his second, the Naryshkins—a struggle that would only be settled when Peter I won final victory over his half sister Sophia in 1698.[21]

The new tsar, Fedor III Alekseevich, was alert and intelligent, credited with the composition of church hymns and tutored by Simeon Polotskii in languages and literature, but he had suffered from physical disabilities and poor health since childhood.[22] There may have been little hope of his presiding at court or leading an army on horseback (near the end of his life, his health deteriorated to the point that he had to be carted about in a portable bed), but early in his reign there was some hope that he could at least father a son to succeed him. While he was somewhat young to marry at the time he succeeded his father in 1676 (he was fourteen years old), Fedor Alekseevich did not marry until four years later, on July 18, 1680 (at age nineteen), by which time he was relatively old by Muscovite standards. It is easy to imagine several reasons why the tsar's nuptials might have been delayed, even with the risk to the succession that a delay might pose: the tsar's ongoing illnesses; a reasonable fear that his marriage might spawn new conspiracies, as had happened with his father and grandfather; or the general instability that the ouster of Matveev and the ensuing sorcery investigations had produced at court.[23] When he did finally marry, Fedor's bride, Agafiia Simeonovna Grushetskaia, was not unlike the winners of most other Muscovite bride-shows: a daughter, as Bushkovitch puts it, of a "middling noble family." Her great-great-grandfather, Karp Evstafievich Grushetskii, had immigrated to Muscovy from Poland at the end of the sixteenth century, and his descendants had hovered in the provincial gentry and at the rank of Moscow courtier (*dvorianin moskovskii*) until Agafiia's marriage with the tsar.[24]

That a bride-show was organized for the young tsar is apparent from a manuscript that lists the gifts distributed to 18 candidates who had participated in bridal inspections in June and July 1680 (the text is discussed in Chapter 2 and presented in full in Appendix C).[25] The text provides a list of runners-up: eighteen names are arranged in the text into three groups (4, 7, and 7). The bottom two groups of the candidates, totaling fourteen, received identical gifts (bolts of moiré, each 5 *arshin*, or about 11.5 feet in length; and bolts of damask, each 23 feet in length). The best gifts (bolts of silver brocade, satin, and damask, each 10 *arshin*, or about 23.3 feet in length) were given only to the first four candidates listed. It may be to these four candidates that the Dutch diplomat Johan Willem van Keller was referring in a letter of June 28, 1680, when he reported that four candidates had been presented to the tsar, all from prominent families (he calls them "grandees").[26] Two of these finalists, Anna Fedorovna and Marfa Fedorovna, were the daughters of Prince Fedor Fedorovich Kurakin, Tsar Fedor III's former tutor, who had been a boyar since 1660 and came from one of the richest families of the seventeenth century. The third, Vasilisa Ivanovna, was the daughter of Ivan Bogdanovich Khitrovo, who was the son of the royal favorite Bogdan Matveevich Khitrovo, an ally of the Miloslavskiis, who had been a boyar since 1676. The last of the finalists was the unnamed daughter of the deceased (d. 1675) *okol'nichii* Prince Daniil Stepanovich Velikogo-Gagin.[27] Instead of any of these four finalists, however, Tsar Fedor III married Agafiia Grushetskaia, who, in the words of van Keller's report, was from "*een mediocre Familie*."[28]

Did the high-born candidates lose out in the bride-show to Grushetskaia? Did Grushetskaia even participate in the bride-show? The Russian historian Vasilii Nikitich Tatishchev conveyed an account that provides important details about Tsar Fedor III's bride search. He reports that the tsar spotted Agafiia Grushetskaia while participating in a religious procession, not in a bride-show, and identifies two of the tsar's favorites, Ivan Maksimovich Iazykov and Mikhail Timofeevich Likhachev, as closely involved in the choice:

It happened that the tsar was in a procession with holy icons, and among the many onlookers was a certain maiden whom the tsar liked. He ordered that information about her be obtained. Iazykov immediately obeyed the command and learned that the girl was the daughter of a Polish noble [*shliakhetskaia doch'*] and was living with her aunt, the wife of the *dumnyi d'iak* Zaborovskii, and immediately passed this information on to the tsar. And on that same day, Iazykov went to Zaborovskii's residence and inquired after the girl and saw her, and again informed the tsar of all he learned. Soon afterward, this same Zaborovskii was told to preserve his niece and not to give her away in marriage. This matter was for a short time kept entirely secret. But when the tsar first informed [Ivan Mikhailovich] Miloslavskii of his intentions to marry Grushetskaia, Miloslavskii urged caution, and requested time to investigate the girl. And learning that Likhachev and Iayzkov were behind everything, he set himself in a ruinous conspiracy against it, suggesting to the tsar something that would provoke the tsar's abhorrence, having him believe that the girl and her mother were involved in certain immoral activities. And so instead of her, he presented to the tsar other girls, who he hoped would be grateful to him.

All this plunged the tsar into a deep melancholy, so much so that he did not even want to eat.... Iazykov, discerning that this was all the work of Miloslavskii, and with the tsar's permission, immediately went with Likhachev to the residence of Zaborovskii; and they [i.e., Iazykov and Likhachev] told him [Grushetskaia's uncle?] what had been said about Grushetskaia and asked him, under penalty of death, to tell them the truth. Inasmuch as her uncle and cousin were filled with fear, and since it was improper to have the girl herself speak to these charges, her being a maiden, they [i.e., Iazykov and Likhachev] learned little from the men of the household, though it was easy enough to imagine the truth. However, the girl, having learned of these unexpected charges against her, said to her uncle that she was not ashamed even to speak the truth to the tsar herself. And they requested that she come out to them and tell them the truth, and she told them. And they had no doubts whatsoever of her virtue and she assured them of her honor on pain of death.[29]

As Sedov has shown, much of what Tatishchev reports is corroborated in other sources.[30] The tsar made a rare public appearance on Palm Sunday, April 4, 1680—undoubtedly the occasion during which he caught sight of Grushetskaia in the crowd.[31] Sedov plausibly argued that the tsar's infatuation with Grushetskaia started in April and accounts for the promotion of her cousin Vasilii Fokin syn Grushetskii to *striapchii* on May 2 and for Matveev's release from exile in Pustozersk to the somewhat more comfortable Mezen' on May 11.[32] The opposition of Ivan Mikhailovich Miloslavskii and others to the match that Tatishchev reports is also corroborated. The Danish diplomat Heinrich Butenant von Rosenbusch pointed to dissatisfaction with the choice in some quarters, reporting that "the great men set themselves strongly against the marriage."[33] Tatishchev also assigns to Iazykov and Likhachev, two of the young tsar's favorites, the primary responsibility for the match. Not that they knew the girl beforehand or steered the tsar her way over other candidates; rather, Tatishchev's account suggests that the two royal favorites quickly seized upon the tsar's expressed fascination for Grushetskaia because she represented a safe (from their point of view) alternative to any of the daughters of the boyars, like the daughters of Khitrovo, Kurakin, or the other daughters of boyars and courtiers who are listed as having received gifts after the bride-shows in June–July 1680. Grushetskaia was a good choice for Iazykov and Likhachev because she would pose less risk to their favored positions at court than would the daughter of an already highly placed courtier. In some ways, then, Iazykov and Likhachev had the same fears as the Saltykov brothers did in the case of Mariia Khlopova in 1616, though in this case they had the tsar on their side.

Finally, Tatishchev confirms that there was a bride-show, but he offers a striking new detail about it. He writes that the bride-show was organized by Miloslavskii in response to Tsar Fedor III's infatuation with Grushetskaia. The timing of events supports this conclusion: the tsar encounters Grushetskaia in early April, promotes her kinsman in early May, and the bride-show takes place only in late June (van Keller's letter mentioning the four finalists is dated June 28) or early July (the inventory of gifts reports that the bride-shows took place in July). Was Grushetskaia omitted from the bride-show altogether, or was she placed in it as a kind of inside candidate? The fact that Grushetskaia's name is omitted from the inventory of gifts says nothing of course about her participation since she was the winner and the inventory is, in effect, a list of runners-up. Clearer indications come from van Keller, who reports two days after the wedding (on July 20) that the tsar's wife "was not one of the princesses (about whom I wrote in the postscript to my previous letter) who were brought into the court so that His Majesty could pick his wife from among them."[34] It is also interesting to note that Grushetskaia's kinsman Vasilii

Fokin syn Grushetskii—who had just been promoted in rank—is listed on the inventory as the servitor charged in August 1680 with conveying gifts to one of the losing candidates, which tends to confirm van Keller's testimony that Grushetskaia had not originally been a candidate since her relative's presence in the environs of the bride-show smacks of partiality or, at least, unfair access or involvement of one candidate's family in the process.[35] Thus, even though a bride-show was organized in 1680 (the evidence for one is clear enough), the tsar's bride had not been a candidate in it or, in any case, certainly was not one of the finalists.

The bride-show for Fedor III in 1680 displays both a fundamental fact, true probably of all bride-shows over this period, and the new depths to which the bride-show custom had sunk by the end of the seventeenth century: royal favorites or relatives frequently exploited the bride-show custom to channel preferred candidates to the royal groom. This is what Trakhaniotov, Skuratov, Umnoi-Kolychev, Boris Godunov, the Saltykov brothers, Boris Morozov, Irina Mikhailovna, and Miloslavskii were all doing. But in Fedor III's case, perhaps for the first time, the bride-show was set up primarily to steer the tsar away from, not toward, a candidate—to offer alternatives to the tsar's preferred candidate, whom he had met in a different way, on his own, outside the bride-show ritual. In a sense, then, the bride-show replaced the administering of poisons (to Khlopova and perhaps Sobakina and Dolgorukova), replaced the overly tight braiding of hair (Vsevolozhskaia), and replaced the spreading of malicious rumors about preferred or chosen candidates (Naryshkina)—all the instruments of ruined nuptial plans. Even more to the point, the selection of Grushetskaia did not need the imprimatur of the bride-show: her status as the tsar's betrothed did not require her participation in a bride-show—even an openly rigged bride-show—to lend it legitimacy. The tsar's preferences in this instance played out in the open contest between favorites and royal in-laws at court, not behind the decorous and structured rituals of the bride-show. The laud offered Esther in *The Comedy of Artaxerxes* applies perfectly to Agafiia: she truly was "worthy because the tzar adores you." Times had changed.

A Wedding without the Wedding Ritual

These changes in the uses of the bride-show were accompanied by changes in the wedding ritual itself. The original plans for Fedor III's wedding are known from a fragmentary draft of the ceremonial (*chin*), the larger part of which had been consumed in one of the fires that struck the royal archive.[36] From what survives, we can see that Fedor III's was to have been a fully traditional Muscovite royal wedding. In fact, a close inspection of the charred fragments reveals that Fedor III's draft ceremonial was little more than a modified copy of the ceremonial composed for the second wedding of Aleksei Mikhailovich in 1671. As the text itself states, "all was done in advance, conforming to the previous royal ritual."[37]

While only fragmentary, the text nonetheless tells us a great deal about the plans for the wedding. We learn, for example, that Patriarch Ioakim was to be present and to offer a blessing on the union.[38] A reference to rosters (*rospisi*) suggests the scriptoria of the royal chancelleries had started working on the lengthy lists of courtiers who would fill the various honorific positions at the wedding celebrations.[39] The council secretary (*dumnyi d'iak*) of the Muster Chancellery, Vasilii Semenov, is mentioned in the fragments and may have been the compiler of these musters and the chief organizer of the wedding.[40] We know that the boyar Prince Nikita Ivanovich Odoevskii was to play a prominent role at the wedding.[41] And the text hints that Fedor III's wedding was to be as sober as Aleksei Mikhailovich's second wedding had been, omitting the usual and raucous entertainments that punctuated previous royal nuptial celebrations.[42] Fedor III's draft ceremonial duplicates the passage in the speech delivered by Patriarch Ioasaf to Tsar Aleksei—which in 1680 was going to be delivered by Patriarch Ioakim to Tsar Fedor Alekseevich—promising the tsar that "tomorrow, on Sunday, we will celebrate with psalms and hymns and spiritual songs."[43] Perhaps most significant, the document shows that the date of the wedding was moved. The original plans called for the wedding to take place in June, probably on June 13,[44] but in fact it took place more than a month later, on July 18.[45]

Between June 13 and July 18, plans changed. What was to have been a grand and glittering spectacle—with the entire court in attendance over the course of three days of banquets, processions, speeches, and various fertility and bonding rituals—was abandoned and the tsar and Grushetskaia were married in a much smaller and private wedding.[46] Instead of a long and detailed manuscript roll (*stolbets*) or wedding album, as were compiled for previous Romanov weddings, Fedor III's official wedding description is a small booklet of eleven trimmed folios;[47] and the wedding described in these folios was very different from what had originally been planned.[48]

The text of the official wedding description begins with events on the eve of the wedding—Saturday, July 17. According to the text, the tsar announced his intention to marry Grushetskaia to his most intimate courtiers, his inner circle of "boyars, *okol'nichie*, and Duma and closest [*blizhnie*] advisors."[49] Then he summoned the patriarch to inform him of his plans and asked for a blessing. The patriarch blessed him, offered prayers of thanksgiving, and delivered a brief congratulatory speech.[50] The wedding was then announced to the other courtiers, "boyars and *okol'nichie* and advisors in Duma ranks [*dumnye liudi*]."[51] Playing their prescribed role, the assembled courtiers are depicted as hearing the news for the first time, though with all of the activity surrounding the creation of the ceremonial draft a month before, it is unlikely anyone at court could have been caught unaware of Fedor III's plans: "Having heard these words [the wedding announcement] from the sovereign's holy lips, they were filled with inexpressible joy, and thanked God who is glorified in the Trinity, that in His inexpressible mercy to the holy pious sovereign tsar, He has deigned to begin such a right and good affair."[52] Also on Saturday, Agafiia Semenovna was installed in her Kremlin apartments (*tsaritsyny khoromy*) and given the fictive title "tsarevna," which, as we have seen, was customary in the sixteenth and seventeenth centuries.[53] Fedor III next

> walked privately [*taino*] to the cathedral and apostolic church of the Honorable and Glorious Dormition of the Most Pure Mother of God to pray; and in contrast to previous weddings, His Holiness the patriarch did not go out to the cathedral for the blessing because the great sovereign wished to enter it privately; and having completed his prayers in the cathedral, prayers concerning his intentions to marry, he walked from the church to his palace [*gosudarskie khoromy*].[54]

The day ends with the guards who manned the Kremlin's walls, gates, and trellisworks taking their stations in the evening, "one hour before the ringing of the bells for vespers."[55]

The wedding ceremony itself, on Sunday, July 18, was conducted very quietly, without the banquets, grand processions, speeches, and sea of courtiers typical of the traditional Muscovite wedding day. The only roster of courtiers in the official description of the wedding lists those who had been appointed to the small entourage that walked in procession to the church for the wedding:

> And in contrast to previous royal weddings, there was not the usual royal ritual, and after the great sovereign there walked in procession only the boyars Prince Nikita Ivanovich and Prince Iakov Nikitich Odoevskii, Prince Iurii Alekseevich and Mikhailo Iur'evich Dolgorukov, Prince Fedor Fedorovich Kurakin, Ivan Bogdanovich Khitrovo, *okol'nichii* Ivan Timofeevich Kondyrev, the *postel'nichii* [master of the bed] Ivan Maksimovich Iazykov, and the *striapchii s kliuchom* [chamber butler] Mikhailo Timofeevich Likhachev[56]

—a list that includes the fathers of two of the candidates in the July bride-show organized by I. M. Miloslavskii (Kurakin and Khitrovo), and the tsar's favorites (Iazykov and Lichachev). The patriarch's entourage was about as small. The text lists two archpriests, two sacrists (*kliucharia*), a deacon, and two church singers (*gosudarevy pevchie*).[57] At this point, the narrative of the text is interrupted by what amounts to an explanation for the unusually small retinues: "And besides those written above, no other persons of rank were present [*nikogo chinovykh liudei ne bylo*] because the great sovereign wished to go [*itit' perekhodami*] to the blessing of his marriage only with his closest advisors."[58] This was a striking reduction, even when compared to the tsar's father's wedding in 1671—which was in many ways more solemn than celebratory: with Tsar Aleksei in procession (*za gosudarem*) were ten boyars, eight *okol'nichie*, the *kaznachei* (treasurer), the *postel'nichii* (master of the bed), and nine *dumnye dvoriane*, plus a wedding entourage (*poezd*) made up of forty-two *stol'niki* (table-men) and eighteen *dvoriane* (courtiers).[59] It was therefore perhaps some compensation for the smallness of the affair that Tsar Fedor III's wedding service was performed by the patriarch, not his father-confessor—the first time since Ivan IV's second wedding in 1560 that the first hierarch had performed a royal wedding (with the exception of the First False Dmitrii).[60]

Only on the next day (Monday, July 19) did the entire court assemble. But here again there was no banquet, no exchange of gifts, no further meeting with church hierarchs—none of the ceremonies and rituals customary for the second day of the wedding. The tsar and his new tsaritsa merely received the boyars and courtiers one by one, each offering his congratulations to the couple.[61] And here the official record of the wedding ends.

Fedor III's first wedding represents a substantial break with the royal wedding traditions of the past, but questions about the ritual remain. Just how many servitors were present, and did the ones there fill the traditional honorific posts (thousandman, proxy father and proxy mother, best men, matchmakers, and so on)? On the one hand, chronicle excerpts from the end of the seventeenth century commenting on Fedor III's second marriage (with Marfa Matveevna Apraksina in 1682) report that "at the wedding were the same people serving as thousandman, and as best men, and as matchmakers, and in all the ranks, as served in ranks at the tsar's last wedding."[62] "This evidence," Sedov proposes, "permits one to propose that, in the way they were performed, both weddings of Fedor Alekseevich utilized all the traditional ranks."[63] On the other hand, the list of names in the official version of the wedding description (the shorter booklet) simply is not large enough to cover all the honorific posts at a traditional royal wedding, nor does it include any women (except for the bride), who would have filled some of the most visible positions at the wedding. Who were the matchmakers? Who were the bride's attendants in her bedchamber? Who held the *kika*? It is therefore hard to dismiss the plain and straightforward words in the official description: "In contrast to previous royal weddings, there was no usual royal wedding ritual [*a protiv prezhniago ikh tsarskogo china, nikakikh chinov ne bylo*]."[64] As Sedov himself conceded, the tsar's first wedding was "unusual [*neobychnyi*]."[65] It is possible, of course, that the handful of courtiers named in the *chin* filled the traditional honorific posts at the wedding (and that their unnamed wives filled some of the other duties traditionally assigned to women); but even if so, the number of posts was greatly reduced, and many were probably eliminated entirely. It is hard not to see the two extant ceremonials—the charred draft *stolbets* and the terse booklet—as reflecting two very different versions of the wedding. The reasons for the change can only be imagined, but the tsar's poor health and reduced stamina may be the simplest and best explanation.

But Tsar Fedor III's marriage was traditional in at least one way: it was recognized by all, even foreigners, as the key moment in the political life of the court, as all Muscovite weddings in these centuries were. As the Danish ambassador, Friedrich von Gabel, put it in his description of the weeks and months before Tsar Fedor III's wedding: "Everything here is now full of mistrust and everyone is waiting for the time that his majesty the tsar will choose a spouse in order to see what planets will rise with her."[66] Clearly, Iazykov and Likhachev were two planets that rose fast and high. Butenant von Rosenbusch noted the other big winners: the bride's family. "Some of the great men have fallen in importance," he writes, "and the tsaritsa has put her party into a game which will now see some changes."[67] As Sedov put it, "the Grushetskiis and Zaborovskiis, and also their close and distant relatives, entered the upper echelons of the aristocracy in the capital as a single large clan. In the last quarter of the seventeenth century, events in the court constituted a major factor in the inflation of honors."[68] Between July 17 and August 1, 1680, the tsaritsa's kin were promoted in large numbers, though mostly to the middle court ranks: to *stol'nik* (20 appointments), *striapchii* (7 appointments), and *spal'nik* (3 appointments). There were also two appointments to Duma ranks: one to boyar (S. I. Zaborovskii, the bride's maternal uncle, on July 20) and one to *dumnyi dvorianin* (N. I. Akinfov, a relative of Iazykov, on July 23).[69] The rituals may have been in flux, but marriage politics clearly was still alive and well in the last decades of the seventeenth century.

The Last Bride-Shows

Agafiia Grushetskaia died in July 18, 1681, shortly after giving birth to a son, Il'ia, who promptly followed his mother to the grave three days later.[70] Fedor III was himself not far from the grave either; but with no heir, he was prevailed upon by his advisors to consider marrying again, very probably in late November 1681, if not before.[71] Fedor III's second marriage could be held out as one of the best examples of the decisive influence of a royal favorite in the selection of a bride for the tsar. The sources point to Fedor III's favorite, Iazykov, as steering the tsar to Marfa Matveevna Apraksina, the daughter of a provincial nobleman who, like Grushetskaia, also had Polish roots and, more important, had links to the two most important players at court: Iazykov, who was her kinsman, and Artamon Matveev, who was her godfather.[72]

But Apraksina had competition. According to Tatishchev, Apraksina and Iazykov had many powerful figures arrayed against them, including the tsar's aunt, sisters, and I. M. Miloslavskii. Some around the tsar proposed that he marry one of the two daughters of Aleksandr Petrovich Saltykov (Tatishchev does not tell us which one). Others around the tsar had other candidates in mind. A bride-show, or a series of bride-shows, was held sometime between late November 1681 and mid-February 1682. No list of bridal candidates survives, but entries dated April 9, 1682, in the ledger book (*Prikhodno-razkhodnaia kniga*) of the tsaritsa's Master's Office

(*Tsaritsyna Masterskaia palata*) lists the gifts given to bridal candidates who participated in it. Sedov has compared the gifts in this ledger with the inventory of gifts given at Fedor III's first wedding (discussed above and in Chapter 2, published in full in Appendix C) and deduced, very plausibly, that there were twelve candidates.[73] We know that one of the two Saltykova sisters was a candidate, and the tsar's choice, Apraksina, had probably been in the bride-show as well. A third candidate is mentioned in the correspondence of the Old Believer leader Archpriest Avvakum: Princess Anastasiia Urusova, the daughter of Princess Evdokiia Urusova. "Let Nastas'ia, who wants to become ts[aritsa], pray for me," he writes in one of his letters.[74] The identities of the other nine candidates are not known.

The tsar was also not at first inclined toward Iazykov's candidate. He preferred Praskov'ia Saltykova, who two years later would marry Fedor III's younger and physically and mentally disabled brother, Ivan V. In passages describing Praskov'ia's selection in 1684 for Ivan V, Strahlenberg says that Praskov'ia "had been chosen before, for the deceased Brother Theodore, or Feodor, but the Match was prevented by the above-mentioned Jasikow, for his private interest, who persuaded the Czar to marry the Lady Apraxin, and managed Matters, so, that Soltikow was sent to Jeniseiski, in Siberia, as Governour and Weywode, whither his beautiful Daughter was obliged to follow him."[75] With Saltykova out of the way, the tsar went along with his favorite's recommendation.

The tsar's poor health played a role in the choice of spouse. It had been up and down over the course of the previous year, even to the point that doctors strongly urged him to put off any thought of marrying until he was stronger.[76] "But," Tatishchev writes, "Iazykov's influence prevailed in the matter." He used his proximity to the tsar to steer him toward the candidate whose selection best protected Iazykov's station at court. The bride-show was a risk, of course: anything could happen when the tsar had the last word. But Fedor III was physically too weak to assert himself against the forceful impositions of his trusted favorite. How he exerted that influence can only be imagined, but it may be that Iazykov simply overwhelmed the tsar with a flood of advice all pointing toward Apraksina. One source of this advice was Metropolitan Illarion of Suzdal', an ally of Iazykov who in December 1681—right in the midst of the bride-show—was appointed to the episcopal see in Suzdal' and spent the winter of 1681–1682 in Moscow advocating Apraksina to the tsar.[77] As Strahlenberg summarizes: "Notwithstanding His weak Constitution, His chief Favorite, the Privy

Counsellour, Jasykow, persuaded Him to marry one Martha or Marvea Matweowna, almost on his Death's-Bed, merely to hinder the Succession of His half Brother, Peter. Her Father was a new created Nobleman, the son of a Scrivener, Mathias Apraxin, by Name."[78]

The selection of Marfa Apraksina was publicly announced on February 12, 1682.[79] As the "Muster Without Precedence (*Razriad bez mest*)" for the year 7190/1682 reports, the bride performed the typical prenuptial rituals:

> On February 12, the sovereign picked for himself a wife [*vibrot' sebe v suprugi*] the maiden Marfa Matveevna, the daughter of Matvei Vasil'evich Apraksin. And on that same day, the patriarch bestowed the title [*narekli*] of tsarevna and grand princess on Marfa Matveevna. And on that same day, the patriarch emerged from his apartments into the Front Hall [*v perednei*] and informed the boyars and *okol'nichie* and people of Duma ranks [*dumnye liudi*] that Marfa Matveevna had been proclaimed tsarevna and grand princess [*narekli tsarevnu i velikoiu kniazhnu*]. On February 15 of the same year, the wedding took place, and the sovereign contracted his second marriage. And the great sovereign was pleased to marry the daughter of Matvei Vasil'evich Apraksin, Marfa Matveevna.[80]

The selection was probably made before February 12, of course; it was merely on that day that the formal announcement was made and the preliminary rituals were set in motion, including giving the bride a new, fictive title (tsarevna). Following prior custom, it was almost certainly on that day that the bride was ritually entered into the apartments of the tsaritsa in the Terem. The "Muster Without Precedence" goes on to hint that the wedding ritual was like the scaled-down version used for Fedor III's first wedding—that "there was no wedding ritual whatsoever [*a svadebnogo chinu nikakova nebyla*]."[81]

This same line is repeated in the draft muster for the wedding.[82] The muster describes a wedding that was as private and small as the tsar's first wedding two years before. On the morning of the wedding, the bride and groom attended the Divine Liturgy together at the Church of the Resurrection, a private chapel in the tsar's residence (*v verkhu*). The wedding itself was performed at this same chapel by Archpriest Mikita Vasil'evich of the Annuciation (*Blagoveshchenskii*) cathedral, the traditional chapel for the members of the royal family, though the editing of the draft suggests that originally Patriarch Ioakim was supposed to officiate.[83] The text lists twenty-four servitors who were to attend the tsar,[84] and it mentions audiences and banquets (*stoly*) that were originally planned but were cancelled, probably because of the tsar's lack of stamina for even these reduced celebrations.[85] The text mentions no traditional wedding ranks—proxy father, proxy mother, best men, and so on—nor the names of any women beside the bride. As with Fedor III's first wedding, it may be that those courtiers mentioned in the surviving texts (and their unnamed wives) held these posts, but the sources do not indicate it one way or the other.

All the fuss and bother of finding a bride and marrying her to the dying tsar came to nothing. The tsar's health had never been good, but his condition was generally declining and seemed to have taken a steep downward turn after the death of his infant son and first wife. He died of his still undiagnosed illness on April 27, 1682, perhaps never consummating the marriage. According to Strahlenberg, "it seems the Czar was already reduced to so weak a Condition, that He never touched Her, and soon after died without Heirs."[86]

On Fedor's death, Ivan V and his half brother Peter I became co-tsars, and the last bride-shows in Muscovy were assembled for them. Having two tsars on the throne was a compromise solution to a potentially violent feud that could have easily erupted over the succession. Ivan V was Fedor III's full brother (the son of Tsar Aleksei Mikhailovich's first marriage) while Peter was Fedor III's half brother (the son of Aleksei's second marriage). Fedor III's death would normally have made his next oldest sibling the successor, but Ivan V was plainly unfit to rule. He was physically disabled and severely mentally handicapped, which markedly affected his speech and other basic cognitive abilities. Peter, on the other hand, was the very picture of health. Both boys were young—Ivan was fifteen and Peter only nine, turning ten, and so, no matter who succeeded, there was going to be a regency.

For almost exactly a month after Fedor III's death in April 1682, the succession remained undecided. On April 27, just after the tsar expired, Patriarch Ioakim gathered church hierarchs, monastic elders, boyars, and other high-ranking courtiers to discuss the succession. It was decided then that the throne should pass over Ivan because of his incapacities and go instead to Peter. This was of course not just a choice of one tsar over another—though the determining factor must have been Ivan's utter unfitness for the throne—but also a choice of the Naryshkin faction over the Miloslavskii faction. That shift is plainly shown by the return to Moscow on May 11 or 12 of Artamon Matveev, who had been exiled from the city and court politics since 1676. But Tsarevna Sofiia Alekseevna, Ivan V's full sister, managed to salvage her brother's candidacy. She turned the underlying anger and grievances of the musketeers (*strel'tsy*) against their unit commanders to the advantage of the Miloslavskii faction by encouraging rumors that Ivan V had been strangled by members of the Naryshkin clan. The *strel'tsy* broke into the Kremlin on May 11 (murdering Naryshkin allies and military commanders, including Artamon Matveev), and again on May 17 (murdering even more Naryshkin allies, including Kirill and Ivan Naryshkin, the former tsaritsa's kinsmen). The rebellion forced a reconsideration of the succession; and by May 26, just before Peter turned ten years old, both boys had been proclaimed tsar. Within a few days of that, Sofiia was acknowledged as regent over them.[87] Sofiia Alekseevna had turned catastrophe for the Miloslavskii faction into utter victory.

For the Miloslavskii's victory over the Naryshkins to have any longevity, Sofiia had to secure the succession in Ivan V's line, and so one of her first goals as regent was to arrange a bride-show for her helpless brother. Most of our sources point to the collusion between the Regent Sofiia and her lover, Vasilii Vasil'evich Golitsyn, one of the most remarkable men of his time.[88] In his early biography of Peter the Great (published in 1772), Zaharija Orfelin reports that Golitsyn had persuaded Sofiia that Ivan V should marry so that "when he has a son, he will naturally be the successor of his father, at which time it will not be too difficult to arrange for Peter to be sent off to a monastery and she, Sofiia, would continue as regent for Ivan's young son."[89] Orfelin then briefly describes the bride-show for Ivan V, reporting that Sofiia "presented to him, among other Russian maidens, the daughter of Fedor Saltykov, Praskov'ia, who was regarded at that time as the most beautiful woman in Russia, and whom the tsar married on January 9, 1684, in the usual ceremonies."[90] Orfelin's version seems to have relied on foreign travelers' accounts available then and now. Among them may have been Strahlenberg's description of Ivan V's marriage, which mentions a bride-show (as well as the underlying animosity between Sofiia and her half brother Peter). "Her love for her Brother John," he writes, "and Hatred to Peter, made her spare no Pains to procure a Wife for the former. Among others she proposed Praskowia, Daughter to Alexander Soltikow, who was counted the most beautiful Woman in the whole Empire."[91] Foy de la Neuville has a similar account, though he identifies

Golitsyn, not Sofiia, as the mastermind behind Ivan V's choice of bride:

> He [i.e., Golitsyn] therefore began by marrying off Ivan. The tsars never ally themselves with foreign countries, but order the most beautiful girls from all over Russia to be brought to the court. The girls are visited by the tsars' mothers, sisters, and relations together with doctors and surgeons, after which they select from among the chosen the one they prefer. It was not difficult for Golitsyn to find one who would do and was suitable for his plans. He gave her an Italian surgeon as a lover. The lover soon gave her a child, but unfortunately it was a girl. They had to console themselves and wait for better luck.[92]

It will be remembered that the winner of Ivan V's bride-show, Praskov'ia Saltykova, and her father, Aleksandr (who, according to Strahlenberg, "was afterwards named Theodore, because the Czare [Fedor III] did not like the Name Alexander"),[93] had been sent to Siberia by Iazykov at about the time of Fedor III's second marriage in 1682, in order to prevent her from marrying the tsar. Sofiia now summoned Praskov'ia back to Moscow to marry Ivan V. Strahlenberg continues, "the Princess Sophia order'd Soltikow to send his Daughter immediately to Muscow, and himself to come soon after: Accordingly, he sent her in a disguis'd Habit, with one of his Relations, and another Woman with her, so privately, from Siberia to Muscow, that no Body knew any Thing of it; And three Days after her Arrival, she was declared Czarina, and the Nuptials consummated."[94]

Neuville and Strahlenberg agree that this bride-show served only to cloak the controlling influence of Sofiia and Golitsyn, not actually to identify a bride for the tsar—the same way the bride-shows for Fedor III concealed the backroom politicking by Miloslavskii and Iazykov. Of course, being so severely disabled, Ivan V did, in fact, need the advice of his kin. It is unlikely the man could dress himself, let alone handle the selection of his own consort. Nonetheless, the charade of the bride-show went on, even though no one could have believed any longer that these were fair and genuinely open searches for the most beautiful, virtuous, and pious maidens in Muscovy. The bride-show had always concealed and enabled behind-the-scenes maneuvering and politicking by boyars, their wives, and their in-laws, as we have seen. But by the time the co-rulers were marrying in the 1680s, the maneuvering and politicking was in plain view. No one now was bothering to pretend to accept the fiction of an open contest, so much so that these last bride-shows are actually less well documented than bride-shows done a century or more earlier.

Ivan V's bride was from a prominent old Muscovite family, but from a branch that did not enjoy high status at court. Her great-grandfather had left Muscovy for Poland in 1611, during the upheavals of the Time of Troubles, and the family returned to Muscovy only at mid-century. Praskov'ia's father was made a *stol'nik* in 1676 and was elevated to boyar rank only on February 2, 1684, clearly because of his daughter's selection as Ivan V's bride.[95] The allegation raised by Neuville that Praskov'ia's children by Ivan V were illegitimate has sometimes been dismissed, but there is reason to look again at his claim. Five years elapsed before the birth of Ivan V and Saltykova's first child, Mariia, on March 12, 1689, with the next four children, all daughters, following in rapid succession (four births in five years).[96] It is not out of the realm of possibility that Sofiia, Golitsyn, and their allies in the Miloslavskii faction could have taken action to arrange for heirs for Ivan V after it became clear that the couple could not manage to produce them on their own. The timing of births and marriages is here very suggestive of the kind of chicanery that Neuville describes. Ivan V's first child was conceived in the summer of 1688, just after Peter I turned sixteen (in May 1688) and his marriage was already in discussion and fast approaching (he married in January 1689). If the point in having the disabled Ivan V marry at all was the succession in the Miloslavskii branch of the Romanov dynasty, then Peter's reaching marriageable age was the worst possible nightmare for the regent. It could, of course, be coincidence; but Ivan V begins having children at precisely the moment, not any time during the five years before, when Peter himself is about to marry. Clearly, there was a race going on among the handlers of the two tsars as to who would have the first (and the most) children. Whether the father of Saltykova's children was Ivan V or some "Italian doctor" will not be known until forensic and genetic studies of the remains are done (a project that is long overdue), but Neuville's speculation is fully plausible, and perhaps even likely.[97]

Peter I married Evdokiia Fedorovna Lopukhina on January 27, 1689, on the urging of his mother, Tsaritsa Natal'ia Naryshkina.[98] That is, at least, what the many biographies of the first Russian emperor say. Lindsey Hughes summarizes this view, declaring plainly that the match "was arranged by Peter's mother and her relatives to emphasize the fact that Peter was now a man, and in the hope of getting a male heir before his half brother Ivan did."[99] The Lopukhins had been part of the Naryshkin and Matveev faction since the last years of Tsar Aleksei Mikhailovich's reign. Evdokiia's grandfather Avram Nikitich Lopukhin had served as the head of Tsaritsa Natal'ia's workshop (*Masterskaia palata*), and her father had been a *stol'nik* until he was promoted to *okol'nichii* on the day after his daughter married Peter, and to boyar on Peter's name day, June 29, five months later.[100] As Bushkovitch put it: "The Lopukhins were not only closely connected with the Naryshkins before Peter's wedding, but they had no reason to love Sofia's allies the musketeers."[101] In choosing Lopukhina, Peter's mother and relatives were picking someone from a family that was decidedly safe and politically trusted.

Peter's Naryshkin relatives had had marriage on the mind for quite some time. Christoph von Kochen, a Swedish diplomat in Moscow, reported as early as December 16, 1687, that "they say that in the course of the coming January, his tsarist majesty will marry," meaning January 1688,[102] but Von Kochen does not name a candidate. A letter dated a year later—January 18, 1689—finally does: Peter is reported then as being betrothed to "the daughter of a *stol'nik* named Lopukhin, of whose family it is said that they are of good wit and have a great following." In another letter dated February 1, 1689, just days after the wedding, Von Kochen shares some insights on the bride: that she was of "average beauty but good understanding."[103] Lopukhina had therefore been selected for Peter only by the turn of 1689, not two years before—though it is clear that the young tsar's marriage was a topic of concern and discussion for some time before he (or his mother) selected her.[104]

Was Lopukhina picked out of a bride-show? The evidence is thin but convincing. In his *History of Tsar Peter Alekseevich*, Prince Boris Ivanovich Kurakin states plainly that a bride-show was organized in 1689; and he was in a position to know. Kurakin married Aksiniia Fedorovna Lopukhina, the sister of Peter I's first wife, and so surely was privy to, and willing to report, family matters.[105] Kurakin wrote:

> In 7197 [1689], Tsaritsa Natal'ia Kirillovna, seeing her son, Tsar Petr Alekseevich, having reached his majority, decided to marry him off. And for the bride-show, many maidens from prominent families were assembled, especially a Princess Trubetskaia, who was a relative of Prince Boris Alekseevich Golitsyn, who in every way tried to arrange it that he marry her. But the Naryshkin party and Tikhon Streshnev were dead set against

> it, and did not allow it, fearing that by means of this marriage this Prince Golitsyn, along with the Trubetskois and their relatives, would seize power and oppress everyone else. Therefore Tikhon Streshnev looked among the lesser gentry for a bride and found a maiden from the Lopukhin family, the daughter of Fedor Lopukhin, whom he married.[106]

Kurakin's writings can be highly polemical and biased, but scholars have not called this passage into doubt, and probably for good reason.[107] That Peter I's first wedding was arranged, at least ostensibly, by a bride-show is further supported by the fact that the bride's father, Illarion Avramovich Lopukhin, changed his name to Fedor, which was (as we saw in Chapter 2) a custom that, however irregularly observed, was associated with bride-shows and the need to remake the identities of brides.

Kurakin's account of a bride-show therefore rings true and is more revealing than perhaps even he intended. Kurakin attributed the selection of Lopukhina to both the bride-show ritual and the back-room politicking of Peter I's relatives, which is consistent with the way bride-shows were working in the 1680s, and before that, Strahlenberg's reflection about bride-shows—that "Recommendation has usually had no small share in this Matter; Because, in so short a Time, it was impossible for the Czar perfectly to judge of their Humours and Passions"[108]—leaps to mind here. Surely, the "recommendation" of boyars, in-laws, and other relatives had played a decisive part in bride-shows from the very beginning, since Trakhaniotov in 1505, through the run of favorites (and the wives they supported) in Ivan IV's reign and the wedding projects of the first Romanovs that ran afoul of royal favorites and royal relatives. But something was different at the end of the seventeenth century. No longer did bride selection play out behind the concealing rituals of the bride-show. No longer were the chancelleries mobilized to canvass the country, far and wide, for prospective bridal candidates, leaving traces of the episode in the archives today. No longer were the weddings of the tsar extravagant and dazzling displays of monarchical power, dynastic continuity, and virile fertility. Instead, it was the bride-show that was concealed behind the decisive role played out more or less in public by royal favorites and relatives. The bride-show survived to 1689—but we still must attribute Fedor III's choice of Apraksina to his favorite, I. M. Iazykov; Ivan V's choice of Saltykova to his sister, the regent Sofiia; and Peter I's choice of Lopukhina to his mother and other Naryshkin relatives. Rather than agreeing with, for example, Zabelin, who believed that bride-shows "collapsed, so to say, under their own weight" after Tsar Fedor's first wedding in 1680, the case can be made that the role played by family and favorites so overshadowed the bride-show ritual in 1682, 1684, and 1689, that the bride-show began to look at best unnecessary and at worst farcical.[109]

As a result, the bride-shows of the late seventeenth century were not as well reported in surviving sources as in the previous century. The account of Peter I's marriage by the Austrian diplomat Johann-Georg Korb says as much:

> It may, indeed, have formerly been the practice in Russia to assemble all the maidens of Muscovy that were of comely form and remarkable beauty when the Czar was thinking of marrying, in order that he might select whichever pleased him best. But the custom is become obsolete; and the marriages of the Czars have of late been mostly decided by the advice of those who by official rank or favour were raised to the honour of standing beside the throne.[110]

To whom Korb was referring precisely by rulers "of late"—Fedor Alekseevich? Ivan V? Peter I?—goes unstated in the text; but Korb was right that the bride-show "is become obsolete" and that the selection of royal consorts had, especially recently, "been mostly decided by the advice" of those "standing beside the throne." The bride-show ritual had become so perfunctory and pointless that no one was even noticing it: not the foreigners who scribbled down everything they saw or were told, and not even the scribes in the chancelleries whose job it once was to make the bride-show happen.

Times were, after all, changing. The system of precedence (*mestnichestvo*) had been abolished in 1682, which had the effect of greatly reducing or eliminating many of the elaborate and lavish court ceremonies that provided the members of the court the opportunity to display and contest their relative location in the system of place-honor.[111] The demise of the Palm Sunday ritual—which was very much like a royal wedding in that it was at once a religious and political court happening—illustrates the point. Once involving a large segment of the court elite, the Palm Sunday procession was restricted to Moscow in 1678 and entirely abolished by the turn of the eighteenth century.[112] These changes occurred in the context of a general "inflation of honors," to use Crummey's phrase—a dramatic increase in the number of men holding Duma ranks from the 1670s on.[113] The court was flooded with "new men," which diluted the significance of many rituals and reduced the clout courtiers received from participating in them.[114]

The royal wedding ritual changed in the 1680s, too, but nonetheless remained a powerful symbolic moment in the life of the court. How this was so is demonstrated by a comparison of the wedding rituals for the co-tsars, Ivan V and Peter I. The wedding ritual employed for Ivan V and Praskov'ia Saltykova in 1684 represents something of a throwback to the days of the sumptuous weddings before Tsar Fedor Alekseevich in 1680. The wedding was celebrated not in a private chapel, as with the two weddings of Fedor III, but in the Dormition Cathedral, the traditional location for royal weddings—the first royal wedding to be held at that church since 1671. Moreover, the wedding was officiated by Patriarch Ioakim, and it appears that many of the traditional banquets, processions, and ritual baths were performed.[115] It was not a full revival of the large and glittering spectacles of earlier in the century. The Scottish mercenary Patrick Gordon recorded in his diary that "the Emperor Johan Alexevitz was privately (as usuall) marryed to Praskovia Feodorovna Sultikov [in] 1684," a reference probably to the handful of attendants who were with the couple in the church.[116] Even so, the wedding of the hapless Ivan V outshone the previous two weddings (of Fedor III in 1680 and 1682), which may have been the only ones that many in the court would have remembered. Peter I's wedding, by comparison, ranks perhaps with Fedor III's weddings as one of the most modest of the sixteenth and seventeenth centuries. No ceremonial (*chin*) survives; and the only descriptions of it come from brief notices in chronicles and foreigners' accounts. The wedding was solemnized not in the Dormition Cathedral but in the palace chapel (*v verkhu*) of the Holy Apostles Peter and Paul, and not by the patriarch but by Archpriest Merkurii Gavrilovich of the Annunciation Cathedral, Peter I's (and Fedor III's) father-confessor.[117] It also appears that the celebrations of the wedding—the banquets and other gatherings of courtiers—took place at another time, not on the days surrounding the wedding. Patrick Gordon reports that "on the twentieth [*sic*] of January, the Czar Peter, now in his seventeenth year, was married to Eudoxia Feodorovna Laouchin. The marriage festivities were held at court on the seventh of February."[118]

Why should the wedding rituals of the co-tsars be so very different? First, these weddings represented vital moments in the ongoing political struggle between the Miloslavskiis and Naryshkins, the two factions at court that formed around the in-laws of Tsar Aleksei Mikhailovich's two marriages. Ivan V's wedding was to be the Miloslavskii's day in the sun—an unmistakable declaration to all of the clan's restored position after the death of Matveev and the demotion of his Naryshkin allies, and a symbolic demonstration of Sofiia's grasp on power. To have Ivan V marry with many of the elements of a traditional Muscovite royal wedding was, in a sense, a flexing of the muscles. Peter I's wedding, on the other hand, sacrificed symbolism for practicality. The unexpected pregnancy of Ivan V's wife after so many years of barrenness had to come as a blow to Naryshkin hopes for their restoration to the Kremlin. The manner and form of the wedding must have been far less important to Peter I's mother and her allies than simply accomplishing the marriage. Now that Praskov'ia and Ivan V (perhaps with the aid of the "Italian doctor") had demonstrated that they could conceive children, a stripped-down ritual would suffice.

Sofiia's plans to continue the Miloslavskii branch of the Romanov dynasty ultimately failed. Praskov'ia gave birth to five daughters between March 1689 and September 1694, and three survived to adulthood, all of them marrying. The line continued through Ivan V's daughter Ekaterina Ioannovna, who married Karl Leopold, the duke of Mecklenburg-Schwerin, in 1717. Their daughter Elisabeth-Katharina-Christine (Anna Leopoldovna) married Anton Ulrich, duke of Braunschweig-Wolfenbüttel, and had five children, the eldest of whom was titular emperor as Ivan VI (1740–1741). The other four—Ekaterina, Elisaveta, Peter, and Aleksei—lived out their lives, unmarried, in comfortable exile in Horsens, Denmark.[119] Peter I, on the other hand, quickly fathered three sons, Aleksei (born February 23, 1690), Aleksandr (born October 4, 1691), and Paul (born in 1693).[120] Aleksandr and Paul died in infancy,[121] but Aleksei reached adulthood, married, and fathered a son (the future Peter II). Aleksei later met a tragic end at the hands of his father, but only after the struggle with the Miloslavskiis had long been won, and after Peter I had made other arrangements for the succession. Sofiia would end her days as the nun Sossana in the Novodevichii Convent, sent there by her half brother in September 1689 and tonsured a nun after the revolt of the *strel'tsy* in June 1698.[122] But even without Peter's final, clear victory over the Miloslavskii faction, it is hard to imagine that Sofiia's hold on power could have survived Ivan V's failure to father a son or, for that matter, his death in 1696. Ultimately, Sofiia and her faction were defeated by the unlucky pairing of chromosomes, which repeatedly yielded daughters over sons—double-crossed, as it were, by the family gene pool.

Dynastic Marriage in Petrine Russia

The two-centuries-long period that began with the first bride-show in 1505 came to an end the same way it began: with a new pattern in Muscovite royal marriage brought on by new attitudes toward marrying the Heterodox. It was argued above that the bride-show was introduced as a response to the challenges of finding a bride for the ruler. The usual pool of brides (the daughters of Rus' appanage princes) gradually shrank and eventually disappeared as Muscovy expanded; the cost of marrying a foreigner was exorbitant and ultimately excessive; and the risks to soul and body were deemed too great in marrying a Catholic or, later, a Protestant. From 1505 to 1689, foreign brides were largely eschewed in favor of domestic candidates selected out of a pool of candidates in a bride-show, most of whom were from middle-ranking aristocratic families. These brides functioned as fictive foreigners—strangers brought in from the regions with few connections to the powerful boyars at court, just as a foreign-born bride would be. The practice initially worked well for the Muscovite dynasty: providing fertile and healthy brides for tsars, introducing new blood into the court aristocracy, and regulating the competition between factions at court. But this coherent and deliberate policy was, as we have seen, beginning to break down as the seventeenth century entered its last decades, and was abolished entirely by the time Peter I repudiated his wife Evdokiia Lopukhina, the winner of the last bride-show.

Peter sent Evdokiia away in 1698, shortly after his return from the Grand Embassy (1697–1698). As Lindsey Hughes put it, Peter I's first visit to the west "proved crucial for the fate of Evdokiia." Hughes continues, "Evdokiia was consigned to a nunnery, a decision influenced by a combination of Peter's boredom with a wife who compared unfavourably with women he had met abroad and Evdokiia's association with conservative groups, including her own kinsmen who opposed reform."[123] The dissolution of this marriage is attributable to the insurmountable personality differences between Peter and Evdokiia and to the resulting animus that developed between them. Peter was interested in all things western and more at home with the foreigners of the German Quarter of Moscow than with his boyars or with Orthodox churchmen. Evdokiia was, by contrast, the model of Muscovite womanhood—demure, pious, perfectly at home in the routines of the Terem, and highly suspicious of all foreigners. For many of Peter I's biographers, the stark differences that separated Peter and Evdokiia mirrored, in a way, the differences between Old Russia and the Russia Peter was struggling to create.[124]

Peter abandoned his first wife, Evdokiia, and shortly thereafter the centuries-old bride-show custom. In 1711, Peter secretly married Marfa Skavronska, his mistress (probably since 1704), who took the name Ekaterina Alekseevna in Orthodox baptism and is best known as Catherine I (r. 1725–1727).[125] Peter's wedding would not be celebrated publicly until February 19, 1712.[126] A match based entirely on Peter I's attraction to, and emotional dependence on, Catherine, this marriage was far more rooted in the bonds of love and affection than those arranged by bride-shows during the previous two centuries. She truly was one royal bride who was "worthy because the tsar adored her." It was a marriage unlike any other in the dynasty: the bride was a foreigner whose "lowly" origins were, as Hughes puts it, "notorious."[127] In marrying her without a bride-show, Peter arguably did more to change the political culture of Muscovy than any of his administrative, military, or cultural reforms. He removed his own marriage and those of his successors from the traditional struggles and maneuverings that underlay all court politics.

The marriages Peter I arranged for his Romanov relatives had the same effect on the political culture. Peter arranged for his nieces to marry into foreign ruling houses in the hope that these unions would further his diplomatic and strategic goals in the Great Northern War. In 1710 he married Anna Ioannovna (the daughter of Ivan V and the future Empress Anna) to Friedrich Wilhelm of Courland; and in 1711 he married his son Aleksei Petrovich to Charlotte Christine Sophie of Braunschweig-Wolffenbüttel in Torgau, Saxony. In 1716, he sent Ekaterina Ioannovna (another daughter of Ivan V) off to Danzig to marry Karl Leopold of Mecklenburg-Schwerin, and before his death he arranged for his daughter Anna Petrovna to marry Karl Friedrich of Holstein-Gottorp.[128] (There is some evidence that Peter I also permitted another niece, Praskov'ia Ioannovna, to marry Ivan Dmitriev-Mamonov in or around 1723, and if so, this is the only marriage by a Russian dynast to a domestic spouse in the whole of the eighteenth century.)[129] As Ernest Zitser put it:

> Peter's intention to marry members of his family to foreign royalty... flew in the face of the "traditional" structures of political authority, which were maintained by controlling the marital choices of the new (and still relatively insecure) Russian royal house. By reinstituting the practice of equal marriage between heads of state, the tsar was able to establish tactical diplomatic alliances for his ambitions in the Baltic and at the same time demonstrate the power of the Romanov dynasty over the boyar clans that had once brought it to the throne.[130]

Before these marriages by Peter and his nieces and children, there had not been a marriage between a prince of the Muscovite dynasty and a foreigner since Ivan IV's marriage to Mariia Cherkasskaia in 1561, and no marriage between a princess and a foreigner since Elena Ivanovna in 1495.[131] Peter I had clearly reclaimed royal marriage as a tool for Muscovite diplomacy.

But in reclaiming marriage as a diplomatic tool, Peter I ran up against the hard lessons learned from the debacle of Elena Ivanovna's mixed marriage—lessons that were only confirmed and compounded by the further stiffening of confessional lines and the rise of Russian national consciousness that occurred after the Time of Troubles.[132] As we have seen, the question of mixed-faith marriages had long been problematic for the Muscovites. Elena Ivanovna's husband, Alexander of Lithuania, objected to many of the Orthodox nuptial rituals in 1495 and afterward persistently hounded his wife to convert.[133] Magnus, the fictive "king of Livonia," agreed to marry Mariia Vladimirovna Staritskaia in 1573 in an Orthodox church, with the usual nuptial rituals, including drinking from a common cup and being showered with hops (*osypalo*). But the couple was actually married in parallel services—the groom "according to his own rites (*po ego zakonu*)" and by his own clergy (*popu rimskomu*) and the bride "according to Christian rites (*po kristianskomu zakonu*)"—and were physically separated during the services: Magnus, not being Orthodox, was not allowed to enter the nave of the church (St. Dmitrii on Proboinaia Street, in Novgorod) but had to stand at the portico (*v paperti*) during the entire service.[134] Boris Godunov's plans in 1599 to marry his daughter Kseniia to Gustav, the son of King Erik XIV of Sweden (and the half brother of Viriginia Eriksdotter, whom Ivan IV briefly considered as a bride for his son Tsarevich Ivan Ivanovich), were foiled by the prospective groom's unwillingness to convert to Orthodoxy (he had already converted once—from Lutheranism to Catholicism) and by his profligate lifestyle after his arrival in Moscow. Tsar Boris broke off all wedding plans—Gustav's reluctance to drop his mistress, whom he brought with him to Moscow, perhaps being the last straw.[135] Boris's other prospective groom for Kseniia, Hans of Denmark, the brother of King Christian IV (r. 1588–1648), was willing to adopt Orthodoxy but fell ill shortly after his arrival in Moscow in 1602 and tragically died before he could convert.[136]

Perhaps the most wrenching episode in which religion collided with dynastic marriage was in 1644–1645, when Tsar Mikhail Fedorovich sought to marry his daughter Irina Mikhailovna to Valdemar of Denmark, the son of King Christian IV. For months, negotiators in Copenhagen and Moscow had been hammering out the details of the union, and it was at length agreed that Valdemar would come to Moscow, receive an appanage for his maintenance, and reside thereafter in Muscovy. He was permitted to remain Lutheran but was enjoined to respect Irina's Orthodoxy and to be faithful and loyal to his father-in-law, the tsar. The deal having been made, the young Danish prince arrived in Moscow in January 1644 ready to marry Irina and expecting none of the uproar his proposed marriage was about to unleash.[137]

The problem was Valdemar's religion. The agreement that prince Valdemar could keep his Lutheran faith was met with stiff opposition in certain circles of the Russian Orthodox Church. The early seventeenth century was generally a period of hardening of confessional lines between Orthodox and non-Orthodox—Catholics, Protestants, and Uniates.[138] Part of the conflict revealed itself in sacramental theology, that is, the variant understanding of the "validity" of each other's sacraments. Baptism was, in this context, the main battleground, since it determined who was a member of which faith and reflected each church's view of the "validity" of the other's sacraments. How were converts to be received: by rebaptism and chrismation (as one does a newborn), by chrismation alone, or just by a renunciation and confession of past heretical beliefs?[139] A church council had been called back in 1620 by Patriarch Filaret in order to resolve the dispute in the Russian church over the form and rules for requiring the baptism of converts and spouses of Orthodox.[140] One side in the debate made the case that Orthodox could, indeed, marry non-Orthodox persons and that, should the non-Orthodox spouse choose to convert, rebaptism would not be required: Catholic and Protestant baptisms were "valid" or could be rendered so ex post facto. Since there was only "one baptism" (Eph. 4:4–5), performance of the Orthodox sacrament of chrismation should be enough to effect the conversion. The other side insisted that no mixed marriage ought to be permitted, as a rule, and that in any case conversions to Orthodoxy must always take the appropriate form of triple immersion, in the name of the Father, Son, and Holy Spirit. It was the second view that was adopted by the council, and it was this ruling that set the stage for the clergy's resistance to Irina Mikhailovna's marriage with Valdemar.

The Valdemar affair revived the same debates that had arisen at the council in the 1620s. Insisting on Valdemar's conversion, for example, was the priest Ivan Nasedka, who figured prominently in the Valdemar affair and had experience with royal marriage matters.[141] In 1621, he was sent to Denmark in the embassy that explored the possibility of a marriage between the young Tsar Mikhail Fedorovich and one of the daughters of Duke Johann-Adolph of Holstein-Gottorp. His experience on this embassy prompted him to write a treatise against Lutheranism called "Exposition against the Lutherans" (*Izlozhenie na liutory*), in which he itemized the theological errors he found in its creed. He also worked on the *Kirillova kniga*, a compilation of patristic, historical, and other theological writings that was created as a source book for the theological dispute over Irina's marriage to Valdemar. For Nasedka, the marriage could not possibly be performed unless Valdemar first converted and was (re)baptized in the Orthodox manner. A more practical view was offered by Prince Semen Shakhovskoi, who has been called "the first *intelligent*" in Russian history.[142] Shakhovskoi used both historical precedents and the church fathers to argue in a memorandum to Tsar Mikhail Fedorovich that the good of the state, not the burdensome biases of clerics, ought to determine what is permissible in this matter; and since the Valdemar marriage project was a diplomatic venture, it ought to be the tsar who decided whether the marriage could be performed or not.[143] Stuck in the middle of this theological rancor was Valdemar, who insisted on the original marriage agreement, which had allowed him to keep his religion.

It eventually became clear that the marriage would never take place; and what had been an unfortunate turn of events now turned ugly. Valdemar was virtually imprisoned in his Kremlin compound and forbidden to leave Russia. Desperate to escape, he once attempted a breakout of his house arrest but was discovered and reconfined, this time under heavy guard. Valdemar may have followed the course of Gustav of Sweden, living and eventually dying in Russian exile, had not fate stepped in. On the night of July 12–13, 1645, Tsar Mikhail Romanov died after suddenly and unexpectedly taking ill during an evening church service. His death put a final end to the wedding project, and within just a few months Valdemar was on his way back to Denmark.

The failure of the marriage project was not accepted without recriminations. Punishments were meted out by the new tsar on those who had worked vigorously for the doomed marriage project. The emissaries to Denmark who negotiated the marriage agreement to which Valdemar so tenaciously clung were exiled; Prince Semen Shakhovskoi was sentenced to death by burning for blasphemy and apostasy but ended up only exiled to the remote northern town of Sol' Vychegodskaia; Semen Luk'ianovich Streshnev, the royal cupbearer (*kravchii*) and a royal in-law, was exiled along with his wife for allegedly having employed sorcery and magic to try to sway Valdemar to convert; and Prince Ivan Nikitich Khovanskii was exiled for having provided Tsar Mikhail with false assurances of Valdemar's eventual acquiescence to Orthodox baptism and the bad advice to keep the young prince in Moscow, even against his will, if necessary.[144] Few episodes in the seventeenth century show as clearly as the bungled Valdemar affair the enduring complexities of using dynastic marriage as a tool in foreign policy.

These impractical attitudes toward religion and marriage collided head-on with Peter I's plans to use the weddings of his relatives as opportunities to advance his diplomatic goals. The liturgical and confessional compromises Peter I made in order to marry off three of his kin—his son Aleksei Petrovich and his nieces Ekaterina Ivanovna and Anna Ivanovna—stand in stark contrast to Muscovite precedent but also reveal his staunch defense of confessional Orthodox identity. The foreign spouses of all three were permitted to remain Lutheran. That Ekaterina Ivanovna's husband, Karl Leopold, and Anna Ivanovna's husband, Friedrich Wilhelm, both remained Lutheran after their marriages to Muscovite princesses is not surprising. They were both the rulers of their realms (Mecklenburg-Schwerin and Courland), and so their confessional identity was naturally linked to their status as sovereigns. Both Ekaterina and Anna remained Orthodox, so these were mixed marriages—not unlike the marriage of

Elena Ivanovna and Alexander in 1495. Any sons born to Ekaterina Ivanovna and Anna Ivanovna were to be raised in the religion of their foreign fathers since they would have succession rights in their respective realms. Their daughters, however, were to be raised in the Orthodox Church. But it was a remarkable concession to practical politics that Tsarevich Aleksei's wife, Charlotte-Christine-Sophia of Braunschweig-Wolfenbüttel, was permitted to remain Lutheran given the fact that she was expected to become the next tsaritsa. It is hard to imagine how this bride could have filled the traditional role that Thyrêt identified for a tsaritsa as the "intercessor for the realm" and "spiritual helpmate" when she was not Orthodox.[145] Inasmuch as he was the heir to the throne, all of Aleksei Petrovich's children, irrespective of their sex, were to be baptized and raised Orthodox.[146] All three weddings were, on Peter I's insistence, performed by an Orthodox priest, despite their scattered locations (Torgau, Danzig, and St. Petersburg).

Peter I's willingness to accommodate his foreign in-laws reached even into the rubrics of the Orthodox wedding service itself, as the wedding of Anna Ivanovna and Duke Friedrich Wilhelm of Courland in 1710 demonstrates. No formal description of the wedding survives, but the detailed account by the Danish diplomat Joost Jules provides a good substitute for one. Having stipulated that the wedding be performed in an Orthodox church by an Orthodox priest, Peter I nonetheless attempted to make the service seem less exotic to the duke, who had expressed his discomfort with the Orthodox rites. First, Peter I agreed to have those portions of the service that required the priest to address the duke translated from Slavonic into Latin. Jules was well placed to report this modification in the service because it was his own secretary who did the translations and helped prepare the officiating priest for the wedding by working on his pronunciation of the Latin passages.[147] Second, Peter eliminated whole parts of the wedding service itself. According to Jules's account:

> Other customary (wedding) rituals were not performed: thus they (the bride and groom) did not drink to each other's health, they did not process around the lectern (*analoi*), and they did not hold candles in their hands. It is possible that the tsar arranged things this way deliberately, so that these ancient, foreign customs did not too much consternate the duke, who (even with these adjustments) agreed only very reluctantly to be married in a Russian service.[148]

These elements of the service—all from the crowning ceremony (*venchanie*)—were prescribed for weddings in the Euchologion (*Trebnik*) and each symbolized aspects of the Orthodox understanding of the sacrament of marriage. The common cup, which was a substitute for communion in the ancient wedding service, now symbolized the joining of man and woman "as one flesh." The flames of the candles held by the couple represented the life of virtue and godliness that the couple was to lead. As the light of Christ illumined the dark world of sin, the godly life of the married couple would likewise shine as a model of piety to the world and become a vehicle for the salvation of the couple. The procession around the lectern is perhaps the signature ritual of Orthodox weddings. Sometimes called the "Dance of Isaiah" after the troparia that are sung at this point in the service, this ceremony has the officiating priest join the hands of the couple with his stole (*epitrakhil'*) and lead them three times in a circle around the lectern located in the center of the nave of the church—the circle symbolizing the eternity of marriage.[149]

Word of these concessions got around the higher ranks of the Orthodox clergy, and Peter I had a surprisingly hard time finding someone to perform the modified rites. According to Jules, Peter I first wrote to Metropolitan Stefan (Iavorskii) of Riazan' in Moscow, the *locum tenens* of the vacant patriarchal throne, ordering him to come to Petersburg and officiate at the wedding, but the hierarch feigned illness, writing back to Peter that he was too weak to make the long trip to St. Petersburg.[150] Peter next summoned hieromonk Stefan (Pribylovich), the assistant director of the Russian Patriarchal School in Moscow. Fr. Stefan complied with the order to come to St. Petersburg but refused to marry the couple. In defense of his position, the monk boldly presented arguments from the canons, from the Hebrew and Greek Scriptures, and from history to justify his view that marriages between the Orthodox and non-Orthodox were not permissible. Peter I was not eager to take on the church over the matter, especially since the duke, who was already very reluctant to marry in the Russian church, might be tempted by any hint of trouble to rethink the terms of the proposed union. As Jules put it: "In order to avoid a feud with the clergy at a time of war, a clergy which in Russia is obstinate and ignorant, and, in addition, could easily attract to its cause the simple people, the tsar no longer pressed the issue, and ordered his father-confessor Fr. Feodosii (Ianovskii) to perform the wedding."[151] Peter found himself having to walk a fine line between accommodating a fussy groom and cajoling churchmen far too determined, from Peter's vantage point anyway, to uphold inconvenient canons.

That Peter I was willing to modify the ancient wedding ritual demonstrates the lengths to which he was willing to go to address the concerns and objections of his new in-law. Peter was not willing to let his diplomatic initiatives be impeded by ancient liturgical texts. On the other hand, the wedding agreements he negotiated for his kin in a sense show that he was hardly indifferent to Orthodox sensibilities about intermarriage. Just like Ivan III, Peter I was unwilling to permit conversion from Orthodoxy for any of his royal relatives, and he insisted as much as he could that children born of these unions be Orthodox. Peter's dynastic marriage policies have been construed by some as evidence of his disenchantment and disaffection with the rites and doctrines of the Orthodox Church, but that view is, to borrow James Cracraft's words, "the outcome either of misunderstanding or wishful thinking or of both." "So far as Peter was concerned," Cracraft continues, "he remained, as he himself declared in a letter of September 1721 to the eastern patriarchs, a 'devoted son of our most Beloved Mother the Orthodox Church.'"[152] Peter's compromises, then, were directed at accomplishing his diplomatic objectives, not at eroding Orthodox belief or liturgical practice. These are motives that Semen Shakhovskoi would have understood very well.

The contrast between Peter I's accommodations and Ivan III's staunch insistence on Orthodox nuptial customs could not be more striking, nor could the two provide better bookends for this study of Muscovite bride-shows and the underlying political culture dependent on them. Muscovite bride-shows and the political culture of the court evolved together over the course of the sixteenth century, and they likewise together fell into desuetude at the end of the seventeenth century. Bride-shows were called into being by the needs of the political culture and were later circumvented, then ignored, then quietly done away with, as the underlying political system underwent fundamental transformations. Like so many dimensions of elite culture and society, the bride-show ritual was already shedding its symbolic meaning and losing its political importance at court by the time Peter I appeared on the scene; so Peter I did not so much abolish the ritual as find it already to be in something of a shambles. In reclaiming dynastic marriage as a usable tool for diplomacy, Peter I achieved something that his predecessors had failed to do since Elena Ivanovna and Grand Duke Alexander married in 1495. If, then, Peter I was "revolutionary" in anything, it was in undoing the divorce between dynastic marriage and diplomacy. It may be that Peter I's dynastic policy was the most fundamental and enduring change one can credit to him.

Epilogue

The full story of the bride-show does not end with Peter I. The dynastic and marriage politics analyzed above took on new shapes and meanings in the eighteenth century, and the bride-show itself eventually assumed the role of a cultural artifact of a Russia that was fading fast in memory and trailing off into the past. How did the demise of the bride-show affect royal marriage in the eighteenth and nineteenth centuries? How did the bride-show in Muscovy, as in Byzantium, transition from a historical and fundamental political ritual to a story-motif?

Peter I's policies on the marriages of his relatives and children constituted only the first steps toward a new paradigm in dynastic marriage. The eighteenth century was a turbulent and transitional time for the Romanov dynasty—with the marriage of the ruler continuing to play a prominent role in court politics, and with the succession bouncing from one branch of the dynasty to the other and back again. Dynastic marriage and royal succession settled into a new and firm pattern only at the turn of the eighteenth century, when Paul I (r. 1796–1801) issued a new law of succession, which regulated both.

Royal marriage remained an important matter in the dynasty in the eighteenth century even though the five rulers immediately following Peter I's death did not wed while on the throne. Peter I's second wife and successor, Catherine I (r. 1725–1727), did not remarry, while his grandson by his first wife, Peter II (r. 1727–1730), was twice betrothed—first to Mariia, the daughter of Peter I's favorite, Alexander Menshikov, and then, after his disgrace, to Ekaterina Alekseevna Dolgorukova, the niece of Vasilii Lukich Dolgorukov, the new favorite at court. As it happened, Peter II died on the very day he was to wed Dolgorukova. He was succeeded by two empresses and an infant titular emperor: Anna Ioannovna (r. 1730–1740), the daughter of Ivan V; Elizaveta Petrovna (r. 1741–1762), Peter I's daughter; and Ivan VI (r. 1740–1741), Ivan V's great-grandson—none of whom married (at least officially) while on the throne.[1] Thus the marriage of Peter I's grandson (Anna Petrovna's son), Karl Pieter Ulrich (the future Peter III), to Sophie-Friederike-Auguste of

Anhalt-Zerbst (the future Catherine II) in August 1745 was the first marriage in the dynasty in twenty years—since Anna Petrovna's marriage in 1725. Catherine II's son Paul I married twice, both times to foreigners. In September 1773, he married Wilhemina-Louisa of Hesse-Darmstadt (who took the name Natal'ia Alekseevna), who died in childbirth on April 15, 1776. Some five months later, Paul I married Sophie-Dorothea-Auguste-Luise of Württemberg (Mariia Feodorovna), who was the mother of all his children.[2] It was Paul I who essentially reestablished the Romanov dynasty, with nine of his ten children marrying into some of the most important ruling houses in Europe (Habsburg, Hohenzollern, Baden, Saxe-Coburg-Saalfeld, Orange-Nassau, Oldenburg, Württemberg, and Mecklenburg-Schwerin) between 1793 and 1824.[3] From Paul I on, the now prolific House of Romanov was as actively immersed in the European royal marriage market as any other dynasty.[4]

Despite—or, rather, because of—the fact that Romanov rulers were either not marrying at all or were taking their spouses from abroad, royal marriage remained the focus of politics in the eighteenth century, just as it had in the sixteenth and seventeenth centuries. John LeDonne has shown how the royal in-laws of the seventeenth century—the Dolgorukovs, the Streshnevs, the Miloslavskiis, the Naryshkins, the Apraksins, the Grushetskiis, the Saltykovs, and the Lopukhins—continued to comprise the foundations of the court groupings in the eighteenth century and that these kinship-based groupings best explain the patterns of assignments to important administrative postings in the central and provincial governments.[5] In a sense, the marriage-based political order was frozen in time during and after Peter I's reign. The advantages the royal in-laws enjoyed in the seventeenth century became, as LeDonne says, even more important in the following century when these were the only ties that anyone at all had to the royal family.[6] The persistence of traditional notions of marriage politics that Le Donne sees in the post-Petrine court is also demonstrated by a document compiled by, or on the orders of, Alexander Menshikov in June 1727, shortly after Catherine I's death, containing a list of all the former empress's relatives.[7] The purpose of this document was to have at hand a list of names of royal relatives who might now play a role at court or in the marriage market—not unlike the lists of royal relatives that were compiled of bridal candidates during the era of bride-shows. It was still possible, or at least feared, that one could ride on the coattails of royal in-laws. Despite Peter I's far-ranging governmental reforms, his closing of the Terem, and his preference for foreign spouses, the central place that royal in-laws occupied at court and the centrality of marriage politics remained largely as before.[8]

The return of foreign-born brides in the eighteenth century does not therefore signal a change in the role royal marriage played in the political culture of the court. Rather, dynastic marriage, no longer tethered to the panoply of traditional Muscovite nuptial rituals (the bride-show, the renaming of prospective brides or their fathers, the formal entry of the winner of the bride-show into the Terem), was now again a tool of diplomacy. But royal marriage remained a politically charged matter, leading often to the calculated decision simply to abstain from marriage altogether: an outcome that occurred not only by chance (the death of Peter II, the age and poor luck of Ivan VI) but also by choice, as in the case of three empresses (Anna Ioannovna, Elizaveta Petrovna, Catherine II). The politicking over the marriages of eighteenth-century rulers was as weighty and potentially politically divisive as it had been in the previous two centuries, but it did not produce a single, coherent new pattern in royal marriage. The eighteenth century was transitional, and a new pattern took shape only at the very end of it, under Paul I.

The new pattern in dynastic marriage was a direct consequence of Paul I's new law of succession. It will be remembered that in 1722 Peter I had issued the very first written law of succession that Muscovy had ever known.[9] According to the law, Peter I and his successors chose the next emperor according to their own wishes. The old and flimsy custom, never inscribed into a law code, that a father should be succeeded on the throne by his eldest son was swept aside. Instead, the law provided that whoever the ruler chose—a daughter, a granddaughter, a cousin, a niece or nephew, or even someone from another family entirely—would be the heir. And as anyone at the time might have easily predicted, the succession subsequently bounced between two distantly related branches of the Romanov dynasty (the descendants of Ivan V and of Peter I) until the end of the century. This untenable situation in the dynasty ceased only with the promulgation of a new law of succession by Paul I on April 5, 1797, the day he was crowned. The Pauline law established that the law itself would be the instrument that determined the succession, not the will of the emperor. The law also established succession by male primogeniture in the dynasty, though succession could fall to a woman in the event of the failure of all male lines of descent. And it established the monarch as the head of the imperial family and assigned to him the right to approve all marriages within the dynasty.[10] Paul I's successor, Alexander I, added the requirement that all Romanovs had to marry equally (that is, someone from a reigning or formerly reigning royal family) and that those who did not do so sacrificed their children's rights of succession.[11] Thus, the law provided a clearly defined order of succession within the Romanov dynasty and established the rules for membership in the dynasty—and therefore, eligibility for the succession—by maintaining a strict control of marriage. In essence, Paul I's law, with Alexander I's addendum, meant that no member of the imperial family could ever again marry a Russian maiden. The last five emperors all married foreigners, as did most of their brothers and sisters. The few (though growing number of) Romanovs who married morganatically did so fully aware of the consequences these unions had for the children that issued from them.[12]

As for the bride-show itself, while it was as defunct as the Terem or the *terlik* (caftan), it lived on, even thrived, as a story-motif in literature, music, and art—a transition from life to art that also occurred with Byzantine bride-shows. Lying dormant for most of the eighteenth century, the bride-show was remembered in the nineteenth century during the nostalgic revival in arts and letters of all things pre-Petrine. The bride-show was one of the features of Old Russia that the Romantic-era writers and artists identified as most characteristic of the distinctiveness of Russia and its monarchy.

Brides, bride-shows, and the private lives of tsars and tsaritsas were subjects that many historical novelists found to be tempting themes for fiction. A genre of literature that in Russia was, according to Dan Ungurianu, "by far the most important genre of Romantic prose," historical novels recast in fictional form many of the episodes reconstructed in this book.[13] Naturally enough, the many marriages of Ivan IV attracted the attention of many writers, but his third and seventh marriages (to Marfa Sobakina and Mariia Nagaia) contained dramatic elements that seem to have especially invited attention and embellishment. The bride-shows of the first Romanovs also provided many good plots for the historical novelist, particularly the first marriages of Mikhail Fedorovich and Aleksei Mikhailovich. The failed marriage projects with foreigners, fictionalized biographies of brides, and the imagined private lives of the tsars all were choice topics for writers of varying quality.[14] In all these works, and in varying degrees, authors relied on available primary sources and published historical works; but the goal of telling a good tale sometimes—perhaps necessarily—interfered with historical accuracy. These fictional works tended to distort as much as they helped to establish the popular image of the Muscovite royal bride, royal marriage, the bride-show ritual, and the relationships between members of the royal family over time.

The playwright Lev Mei took up the topic of Ivan IV's third marriage, to Marfa Sobakina, in his 1849 play *Tsarskaia nevesta* (*The Tsar's Bride*).[15] The play is forgettable, but it was early on thought of as a good subject for an opera.[16] In 1898, Nikolai Andreevich Rimskii-Korsakov adapted the play into an opera that was one of the "most popular and most frequently staged in Russia and around the Soviet Union,"[17] with several memorable and significant musical compositions (the overture, Griaznoi's recitative and aria in Act 1, Liubasha's song in Act 1, Marfa's aria in Act 2).[18] Very loosely based on historical events, the work nonetheless draws upon many of the popular notions of bride-shows from foreigners' accounts and official wedding descriptions. The beautiful Marfa, who in the play is the daughter of a merchant (as in the *Chronograph of the Marriages of Ivan Vasil'evich*), is the object of desire of both Grigorii Griaznoi, an *oprichnik*, and Prince Ivan Sergeevich Lykov, a boyar. As both conspire to win her love (Griaznoi even resorting to the use of a magic potion), it is announced that the tsar, Ivan IV, has selected Marfa as his bride, which does not deter Griaznoi. At the wedding, he slips into Marfa's drink what he thought was a love potion, but in reality was poison (switched by Griaznoi's jilted ex-lover), plunging Marfa into an illness that will take her life. Predictably, everyone else dies in the end—except the tsar, who will soldier on without the ravishing Marfa at his side, to marry again and again. The opera's continuing popularity was aided and demonstrated by its adaptation to film by the Soviet director Vladimir Gorikker in 1965—an example of the Soviet dramatized "film-opera" genre, which aimed to enhance the appeal of famous operatic works by filming them on location, rather than on stage.[19]

Perhaps no art form displays the bride-show more vividly, and with its full panoply of fictive and mythic elements, than the handful of paintings made by some of Russia's most important artists. Mikhail Nestorov's *Pervaia vstrecha tsaria Alekseia Mikhailovich s boiaryshneiu Mariei Il'inichny Miloslavskoi* (*The First Meeting of Tsar Aleksei Mikhailovich with Mariia Il'inichna Miloslavskaia*, 1887) depicts not a grand gathering of many candidates but, rather, the private meeting that, according to Olearius, the boyar Boris Morozov had arranged for the young tsar to meet the favored candidate. Konstantine Egorovich Makovskii's *Vybor nevest* (*Bride-Show*, 1887) portrays the opposite end of the range, with Tsar Aleksei Mikhailovich standing before his throne in the Palace of Facets with a throng of young women in two lines emanating out from him—an image that ignores the fact that, according to foreigners' accounts (Collins and Ferber), the tsar was presented with only six finalists. The famous artist Il'ia Efimovich Repin's painting *Vybor nevest* (*Bride-Show*, 1886) similarly depicts Tsar Aleksei's bride-show as a formal ritual in a grand, palatial space (not the Palace of Facets) but appears to get the number of finalists right. And Grigorii Sedov's 1882 *Vybor nevesty tsarem Alekseem Mikhailovichem* (*Tsar Aleksei Mikhailovich Selects His Bride*, 1882) is perhaps worth special note. Sedov, like Repin, evidently knew Collins's account: there are six finalists. The setting is clearly inside the Terem, a room with decorated walls lined with benches. Each young woman is dressed lavishly, with a fur-trimmed collar and ornamented head covering, and each one piously and modestly avoids direct eye contact with the tsar. Aleksei is young and beardless, holding, as Collins had described, a ring and kerchief in his fingers, ready to be given to his choice. And in the shadows behind the tsar looms a boyar, probably Boris Morozov—bearded, attentive, with his arm poised ready to lunge forward to pull back the tsar should he make a motion toward the "wrong" candidate. Few images pull together the facts and fictions of the bride-show that have been the focus of this study better than Sedov's: the role of beauty, virtue, and the tsar's ostensible free choice, on the one hand, and the manipulative, potentially disruptive, and kinship-based influence of the tsar's boyar handlers, on the other.[20]

What conclusons can we now draw about Muscovite bride-shows? Reaching beyond the specific findings about how candidates were found for the bride-show, or the number of Ivan IV's wives, or the changes over time to the traditional royal wedding ritual, what larger questions of Muscovite political culture has this study elaborated? How do the compelling and colorful stories of brides and royal grooms fit into the narrative of Muscovite history?

First, this study reveals that the bride-show was not a purely ornamental feature of the ruler's court but, rather, a central and essential component of the early modern Russian political system. Bride-shows make their appearance precisely when Muscovite political culture was coalescing into its final form—between the victory of the Muscovite (Daniilovich) line of the Riurikovich dynasty in the civil wars (1425–1453) and the annexation of the last stray principalities of northeastern Rus' in the first decades of the sixteenth century (by 1521). Specifically, the bride-show was adopted at the turn of the sixteenth century because of the convergence of three insights: that the traditional and favored pool of spouses for Muscovite dynasts had dried up, as Muscovy succeeded in consolidating under its control the principalities of northeastern Rus'; that marriages with foreigners were costly and problematical on religious grounds, as the marriage of Elena Ivanovna and Grand Duke Alexander of 1495 had proved; and that marriages with the daughters of prominent boyars disrupted the balance of factions at court, as was amply demonstrated by the the succession crisis of 1497–1502. The bride-show avoided all these problems by providing a mechanism for identifying a new pool of bridal candidates: Muscovite women who were Orthodox but not from prominent families and, therefore, not a threat to the stability of the court.

Second, the bride-show was a borrowing and belongs alongside the many other customs that Muscovy was taking from the Byzantine tradition at the end of the fifteenth and early sixteenth centuries (and, for that matter, from there and elsewhere before that). The new rituals, titles, costumes, and court etiquette helped to project the image of Muscovy as the true and valid successor of Orthodox Byzantium. The Byzantine-style bride-show was adopted in 1505 for Vasilii III—the first in its nearly two-centuries-long run—for the same reasons that the Byzantine-style coronation ritual was re-created in 1498 for Ivan III's grandson Dmitrii Vnuk. Both siphoned off the clout that all things Byzantine were enjoying at the court in Ivan III's reign. More to the point, Vasilii III's bride-show in some measure compensated for the fact that he was never crowned by his father—the performance of one ancient royal Byzantine ritual making up for the absence of the other.

Third, bride-shows and the political culture underlying them changed substantially over time. Once adopted, the bride-show would evolve in ways that would further entrench it in the political culture of the court and move it away from the Byzantine model. The custom would continue for nearly two centuries, being arranged for second marriages and for collateral members of the dynasty and becoming an important controlling device regulating the sometimes fractious relationships between boyar clans and court groupings by effectively excluding these clans from the marriage pool. The multiple marriages of Ivan IV, the change in dynasty, the hardening of confessional lines between Orthodox and Heterodox, the inflation of honors—all these events generated adjustments to the underlying political culture. And the bride-show likewise underwent adjustments. These adjustments over time may be why foreigners' accounts provide such varying descriptions of how the bride-show worked: it is difficult to sketch a picture of a moving object.

Fourth, this study of bride-shows provides new insights into the continuing debate over the nature of monarchical power in Muscovy. It is hard to reconcile the findings that have emerged from this study of the bride-show with the long-held and received view of the grand prince or tsar as an autocrat. Neither the patrimonial model of Richard Pipes nor the despotism model of Marshall Poe, nor the autocracy model of Richard Hellie—which all contemplate a monarch who owns the land and people of Muscovy without legal infringement from the aristocracy or mitigating comment from society—can account for the sources that emerged from bride-shows. Were we to believe most foreigners' accounts or uncritically accept the claims of official documentation, then we might be persuaded to follow these models, or Zabelin's conclusion that the bride-show was an instrument of state-building and a signature feature of the Muscovite autocratic system.

But a fresh reading of these sources and, more important, a careful study of the chancellery documents generated around bride-shows suggest something else altogether. The focus on kinship in the investigations of potential bridal candidates, the role of the boyars and their wives in these investigations, the willingness of boyars to foil the tsar's selection, and the frequent and decisive influence of favorites in the selection all point to a collaborative selection of royal spouses that is far more consistent with the consensus model of limited monarchical power that has been advocated by Kollmann, Kivelson, Rowland, Keenan, and others and that traces its roots back to Veselovskii. The bride-show therefore represents an example of the gaping gulf between the image and reality of monarchical power in Muscovy—of what has hazily been called the "façade of autocracy." While the bride-show clearly projected an image of power and majesty that extended far and wide across the tsardom (here Zabelin is wholly believable), the reality of the matter is that no court happening exposes the collaborative nature of decision-making at the highest levels better than the bride-show. Tsars picked their brides from a limited pool almost always composed of women from middling servitor families. The pool of candidates were hand-picked for them by means of preliminary bride-shows. Only the boyars and other courtiers, not the royal grooms, participated in the preliminary bride-shows. Kinship trumped virtue and perhaps even beauty as a selection criterion. These are not features of a despotism.

Bride-shows were spectacles that were staged, choreographed, and largely rigged. The details of how each bride-show was manipulated by relatives or by favorites varied from case to case, but the choice of bride always played out against the underlying context of kinship politics. In other words, the many episodes described above where the ruler's choice of bride was controlled or interfered with were not merely a string of isolated plots by overly ambitious servitors but, rather, an articulation of the very purpose of Muscovite court politics. The selection of a bride for the tsar so benefited the new royal in-laws (and their in-laws) and so determined a large part of the composition of the boyar elite and inner circle of royal advisors that controlling this selection became a fixation of politics. Fretting over the tsar's choice of bride was a normal part of political life among the great families of Muscovy.

Finally, this study has shown that bride-shows were a common, if not ubiquitous, feature across the Eurasian space, found in locations stretching from the Bosporus to the Yellow Sea and in periods ranging from the ancient world to the turn of the twentieth century. In each place and time, the bride-show was closely linked with the political system, alternately controlling or facilitating the access of in-laws to the court, regulating or defining the power of nobles, projecting or manipulating images of monarchical authority, and augmenting or limiting the power of the ruler. This is not to say that all or even most of the bride-shows in this space are related: the only real evidence of borrowing that can be established is from the Byzantines to Muscovy and, perhaps, to the Carolingian empire. Rather, the bride-show was a flexible ritual that served many purposes, in different cultural spaces, and in different ways elucidated the features of the underlying political culture. Clearly, the bride-show needs to be foregrounded not only in the historical literature of early Russian history but elsewhere as well.

If Muscovy was in any way distinct, it was surely in the isolating role of religion. One of the principal motivations for introducing the bride-show in 1505 was to avoid the real diplomatic complexities and perceived spiritual dangers of marriage to the Heterodox. It was evidently deemed worth the losses that might be incurred to Muscovy's diplomatic interests abroad to withdraw from the European royal marriage market. And it was these same interests abroad, two centuries later, that lured Peter I into reintroducing Russia to the marriage market. Clearly, religious attitudes helped to shape dynastic and foreign policy.[21] The bride-show was thus a response to, and a blinkered expression of, confessional chauvinism. Only when the interests of the state began finally to compete successfully with the interests of God did Russia reemerge from its nuptial isolation. The "window on the West" offered a view out onto a wedding.

When Mikhail Mikhailovich Shcherbatov wrote his essay "On the Marriage of Russian Tsars," he chose to structure it as a fictional dialog because, as he put it, "The topic on which I have decided to write is so subject to diverging views, that I could not hope to explain it all in essay form; and so as to provide a better elaboration of it, I decided to write a dialog, where both sides could fully express their views."[22] In the end his two interlocutors—the minister and the "citizen"—fail to agree whether it is best for the Russian heir, Pavel Petrovich (the future Paul I) to marry a foreign princess or a native-born daughter of one of his own subjects. "I can see that you can defend your ideas very well," the minister says, "but as I predicted at the outset, I remain unmoved from my previous position."[23] Shcherbatov may not have realized it, as we do now, but in writing this essay he was providing an updated defense of the bride-show. His arguments are nearly identical to those put to Vasilii III by Iurii Trakhaniotov back in 1505 when the bride-show was adopted. His back-and-forth dialog reflected the uncertainty in Romanov dynastic marriage policy during the liminal eighteenth century, after the aged and infirm bride-show met its final demise but before a new law of succession would bring order to the nuptial chaos. Nor, finally, could he have imagined that it would be Paul I—about whose remarriage his dialog was written—who would settle the unresolved questions about royal marriage once and for all.

Appendix A

EXCERPTS FROM THE CHRONOGRAPH OF THE MARRIAGES OF TSAR IVAN VASIL'EVICH

The *Excerpts from the Chronograph of the Marriages of Tsar Ivan Vasil'evich* appears on three folios in a manuscript miscellany presently housed in the Russian National Library (Rossiiskaia natsional'naia biblioteka) in St. Petersburg, Russia. The manuscript once belonged to Alexander Ivanovich Sulakadzev, a noted collector and forger of medieval Slavic manuscripts.[1] Although the text is widely (and probably correctly) regarded as a concoction of Sulakadzev's imagination, there appears to have been no effort on his part to further the deception by imitating the handwriting from earlier centuries. Dates are given (inconsistently) in both Slavic and Arabic numerals, and the passage includes none of the letters from Church Slavonic that were commonly used in Ivan IV's time (except for numerals). The text on each folio is framed in a box drawn with the same writing instrument and ink as the main text, using a straight edge, though the title of the text (Iz Khronografa o brakakh Ioanna Vasil.) appears above and outside the frame on the first folio (fol. 156v).

The edition below is the first publication of the *Chronograph* in its entirety, though some fragments from the *Chronograph* have been quoted in secondary biographical literature on Ivan IV (usually in the footnotes).[2] The publication below observes the usual rules for text editions and preserves all of the orthographical features of the original, except that dates have all been converted into Arabic numerals.[3] Paragraph breaks, folio breaks, and all punctuation in the text, however idiosyncratic, have been preserved.

(л. 156 об.)

Изъ Хронографа о бракахъ царя Иоанна Васил.

Въ лѣто 7055. 1547. ѳевраля 13 сочетася бракомъ царь Иванъ Васил: на Анастасіи Романовне Захаріиной, иже нужне умре 7 августа 7068-е.

Въ лѣто 7068. 1560 августъ 21 обрачися царь вторичьно на Маріи Ѳеодоровнѣ Черкаской, а съ тучи нравныя и зѣло лютые терпи умре. сентября 1 лѣта 7078-е. 1570.

Въ лѣто 7079. 1571. октобрія 28, соборнѣ поял царь дѣву Ноугороцкую гостїю Марфу Васильевну Собакину, но пожи съ нею больнѣ, отъя животъ и умре ноября 13 дня.

Въ лѣто 7080-е. 1572. априлія 29. забы законъ царь и поязася устраши церковныя власти, Анну Алексеевну Колтовскую, но пожи в тугѣ и мученіи съ нею, и насильнѣ постриже ю на Тихфинт. умре априлія 5, 7134 лѣта. //

(л. 157) Въ лѣто 7081 1572. ноембрія 11 дня прія молитву, и сочетася отай на княжнѣ Маріи Ивановне Долгорукая кою утопи въ рецѣ Серѣ въ колымагѣ за тисну ю крепцѣ, на ярыхъ конехъ, и воскручинися за неже въ ней не обрете дѣвства, а погуби ю на утре ноембрія 12. дня, но вельми бысть добра и красоты юныя колпицы, и восплакася повелѣ злато полосную главу церкви Слободы Александровой, очернити чрезъ полосу злату.

Въ лѣто 7083-е.[4] 1574. іюлія 5. на день Офонасія опять царь о здравѣ дыша яростію благословися у попа духовнаго сво[е]го[5] и обничася на Аннѣ Василіевне Васильчиковой, и заточи ю нужне августа 14. на канунѣ Успенія. //

(л. 157 об.) Въ лѣто 7085-е 1577. января въ 23. на канунъ по слова, и яко ведѣнья очей царскихъ, царь обрачися со вдовою Василисою Мелентьевною, юже мужа ея опричникъ закла, зѣло урядна и красна, таковые не бысть въ дѣвахъ кіихъ возяше на зреніе царю, и не взлюбися и 1. мая в Новѣградѣ и неотдохну заточи ю, чтя ю зрящу яро на оружничаго Ивана Девтелева князя коего и казни.

Въ лѣто 7088. 1580. сентембія. 2 оженися царь въ восьмые на Маріи Ѳеодоровнѣ Нагово, отъ ея же родися 19. октобря 7091. лѣта царьевичь Димитріи, по крещенью, а на молитвѣ Уаръ, кой претерпѣ много скитаясь, ю на Московскомъ царствѣ закланъ, а она умре юля 20 лѣта 7116-е. //

РНБ, Q.XVII.17, лл. 156 об. – 157 об.

Notes

1. For a description of the text, see M. N. Speranskii, "Russkie poddelki rukopisei v nachale XIX veka (Bardin i Sulakadzev)," in *Problemy istochnikovedeniia* 5 (1956), 44–101 (at 100); and *Otchet Imperatorskoi publichnoi biblioteki za 1863 god* (St. Petersburg, 1864), 60–61.

2. Excerpts, with modernized orthography and grammar, appear in Solov'ev, *Istoriia Rossii s drevneishikh vremen*, 3:739, n. 136 (on Mariia Dolgorukova and Vasilisa Melent'eva); Zimin, *V kanun groznykh potriasenii*, 85 (on Vasilisa Melent'eva); Skrynnikov, *Rossiia posle oprichniny*, 99 (on Vasilisa Melent'eva); de Madariaga, *Ivan the Terrible*, 327 (in English translation, on Vasilisa Melent'eva); and Pushkareva, *Women in Russian History*, 73 (in English translation, on Mariia Dolgorukova and Vasilisa Melent'eva).

3. On these rules, see I. A. Bulygin, ed., *Pravila izdaniia "Aktov Russkogo gosudarstva XVI–XVII vv."*; and *Pravila izdaniia istoricheskikh dokumentov Instituta istorii AN SSSR i Moskovskogo Istoriko-arkhivnogo instituta.*

4. The Cyrillic date is corrected over another date.

5. The letter «e» is missing in the manuscript.

Appendix B

Candidates in the Bride-Shows for Tsar Aleksei Mikhailovich, 1670–1671

The following document, "A List of Women at the Bride-Shows for Tsar Aleksei Mikhailovich," has been previously published: P. P. Pekarskii, "Spisok devits, iz kotorykh v 1670 i 1671 godakh vybiral sebe suprugu tsar' Aleksei Mikhailovich," 469–72; and Zabelin, *Domashnii byt russkikh tsarits*, 252–53. The edition below corrects these publications on the basis of the manuscript original in RGADA.

Список девиц на смотринах у царя Алексея Михайловича

(л. 2) 178 год ноября в 28 день по государеву цареву и великого князя Алексея Михайловича всеа великыя и малыя и белыя Росии самодержца указу, девиц которые были в приѣзде в выборе и в котором месяце и числе и им роспись.

Того же числа Иевлева дочь Голохвастова Оксинья,

Смирнова дочь Демского Марфа, //

(л. 2 об.) Васильева дочь Векентьева Каптелина живет у головы Московских стрельцов у Ивана Жидовинова,

Анна Кабылина живет у головы Московских стрельцов Ивана Мещеринова,

Марфа Апрѣлева живет у головы Московских стрельцов Юрья Лутохина,

Лвова дочь Ляпунова Овдотья. //

(л. 3) ноября в 30 день

князь Григорьева дочь Долгорукого княжна Анна,

Иванова дочь Полева Аграфѣна,

Печатника Алмаза Ивановича внуки Анна да Настасья,

Григорьева дочь Вердеревского Анна,[1]

Тимофеева дочь Дубровского Анна.

(л. 3 об.) декабря в 4 день

княж Михаиловы дочери Гагарина княжна Анна, княжна Марфа,

Аверкиева дочь Больтина Аграфена,

Тихонова дочь Зыкова Овдотья.

декабря в 12 день

князь Юрьева дочь Сонцова княжна Марья,

Павлова дочь Леонтьева Парасковья, //

(л. 4) Викулина дочь Изволского Татьяна,

Михаилова дочь Карамышева Василиса,

Матвеева дочь Мусина Пушкина Парасковья.

декабря в 14 день

Андреева дочь Дашкова Соломонида Редрикова,

Захарьева дочь Красникова. //

(л. 4 об.) декабря в 20 день

Алексеева дочь Еропкина Настасья,

Елизарьевы дочери Уварова Домна да Овдотья,

Истопничева Иванова дочь Протопопова Федора,

Романовы дочери Бунина Олга да Овдотья.

декабря в [2]9 день

Тимофеева дочь Клокочова Овдотья. //

(л. 5) генваря в 3 день

Лаврентьева дочь Капустина Анисья

Андреева дочь Коренева Анна живет у вотчима своего у Якима Жолобова.

февраля в 10 день

Думного дворянина Замятни Федоровича Леонтьева дочь Овдотья,

Ивана Федорова сына Нащокина дочь Марья, //

(л. 5 об.) Кирилова дочь Нарышкина Наталья,[2]

Андреева дочь Незнанова Дарья.

февраля в 11 день

Федорова дочь Еропкина Анна,

Иванова дочь Мотовилова Марфа.

февраля в 27 день

Васильева дочь Колычова Марфа,

Ильина дочь Полованова Марья,

Иванова дочь Ростопчина Офимья, //

(л. 6) Ильина дочь Морева Ирина,

Васильевы дочери Толстого Настасья да Агафья.

марта в 11 день

Фролова дочь Синявина Федосья,

Федорова дочь Смердова Варвара.

марта в 12 день

Борисовы дочери Толстого Матрена да Марья, //

(л. 6 об.) Елизарьева дочь Чевкина Анна.

марта в 17 день

Богданова дочь Жедринского Анна,

Васильева дочь Загряскoво Марфа.

апреля в 5 день

Из Великого Новагорода:Никитина дочь Овцына Анна живет у гологы Московских стрельцов Юрья Лутохина,

Петрова дочь Одинцова Пелагѣя живет у Григорья Аладьина, //

(л. 7) Тимофеева дочь Сатина Феодосья живет у Григорья Баяшева.

Из Суздаля:

Петрова дочь Полтева Дарья.

Из Костромы:

Богданова дочь (Поздеева) Офимья живет у дяди своево Матвея Поздеева,

Васильева дочь Апраксина Марья.

С Резани:

Борисова дочь Колемина Овдотья,

Назарьева дочь Колемина Оксинья. //

(л. 7 об.) апреля в 10[3] день

Елисѣева дочь Житова Овдотья.

Из Володимера:

Нестерова дочь Языкова Хомякова Марья живет у путного клюшника у Михаила Лихачева.

Из Новагорода:

Петрова дочь Скобелцына Офимья.

С Костромы:

Пантелеева дочь Симонова Марья живет у Володимера Басланова.[4] //

(л. 8) апреля в 13 день

Артемьева дочь Рчинова Дарья,

княж Степановы дочери Хотетовского, княжна Настасья, княжна Ульяна, княжна Анисья.

апреля в 17 день

Из Вознесенского девича монастыря Иванова дочь Беляева Овдотья, привез дядя ее родной Иван Шехирев[5] да бабка ее Ивановская посестрия Еганова[6] старица Ираида,

Артемьева дочь Линева Овдотья. //

РГАДА, ф. 27, оп. 1, д. 287, лл. 2–8.
Подлинник

Notes

1. The name «Анна» is corrected over another name.

2. A small line or check mark, in pencil or faded black ink, appears in the left margin next to this name.

3. In Zabelin, mistakenly «апреля в 1 день».

4. The first letter is uncertain: «Б» or «В». «Б» is most likely. Zabelin has «Асланова».

5. The first two letters of the name «Шехирев» are corrected.

6. In Pekarskii and Zabelin: «Егакова».

Appendix C

Gifts Given to Candidates in the Bride-Show for Tsar Fedor Alekseevich, 1680

The following document was published previously by Zabelin (*Domashnii byt russkikh tsarits*, 259), but there are variations between his edition and the archival original.[1] The text below is based on the manuscript, with the variant readings in the publication presented in the notes. The text is initialed by the scribe on the rectos of folios 9–13: Фе // дор // Ка // зан // цов.

(л. 8 об.) Того ж числа[2] великого г[о]с[у]д[а]ря и великог[о] кн[я]зя Феодора Алексѣевича всеа великия и малыя и бѣлыя Росиі самодержца жалованья дано девицамъ, которые были в[ъ] выборе в[ъ] прошлом во 188-м году въ юле м[е]с[я]це.[3]

По зарбаву серебреном да по[4] отласу да по камке мѣрою по десяти аршин:

боярина княз Федора Федоровича Куракина двум дочерямъ княжнѣ Анне Федоровне да княжнѣ Марфе Федоровне, //

(л. 9) боярина Ивана Богдановича Хитрово дочери Василисе Ивановне,

околничего кн[я]зя Данила Степановича Великого Гагина.

Отвозил думной дворянин Никито Ивановичь Акинфовъ.

По об[ъ]яри мѣрою по пяти аршинъ по камке мѣрою по десяти аршинъ: //

(л. 9 об.) столников:

кн[я]зь Никиты княж Иванова с[ы]на Ростовского взял Василеи Фокин Грушецкой,

князь Семена княж Юрьева с[ы]на Великогороцкого[5] дочери,

Федорова Иванова с[ы]на Головленкова дочери,
Петра Андрѣева с[ы]на Измаилова дочери, //
(л. 10) Ивана Поликарпова с[ы]на Полтева дочери,
Михаила Тимофѣева с[ы]на Измаилова,
Онодрея[6] Денисьева дочери.
Отвозил к[ъ] ним диакъ Корнила Петров. //
(л. 10 об.) Об[ъ]яри по пяти ж аршин камки по десяти аршинъ:
княз Алексѣя княж Юрьева с[ы]на Звенигородцкого дочери ево княжнѣ,
Викулы Федорова с[ы]на Изволского дочери ево,
Исая...[7] Квашнина дочери ево,
Петра Иванова с[ы]на Вердеревского дочери ево, //
(л. 11) князь Семена княж Иванова с[ы]на Львова дочери ево княжнѣ,
князь Володимера княж ... с[ы]на Волконского дочери ево княжнѣ,
Алексѣя ... Кирѣевского дочери ево.
Отвозил дьякъ Федоръ Казанцовъ. //
(л. 11 об.) И всего имъ г[о]с[у]д[а]р[е]ва жалованья дано:
четыре зарбава цена имъ сто адин рубль, отласомъ сорокъ аршин,
об[ъ]ярей семьдесят аршин,
камокъ сто восмьдесять аршин. //

РГАДА, ф. 396, оп. 2, д. 873, лл. 8 об – 11 об.
Подлинник

Notes

1. Sedov noticed these variations, as well (*Zakat Moskovskogo tsarstva*, 353 and n. 17).

2. The word «числа» is added above the line.

3. The beginning of the text published by Zabelin varies from the manuscript: «14 августъ 1680 г. Великаго государя жалованья дано девицамъ, которыя были въ выборе въ прошломъ въ 188 г. въ июлѣ месяцѣ».

4. The letter «п» in «по» is corrected over «о».

5. Zabelin's edition has «Звенигородскаго» here.

6. This is a mistake in the original manuscript. It should read «Ондрея».

7. Here and below, where marked by ellipses, the original has a blank space, presumably for the insertion of a name. The blank space is also noted in Zabelin's edition.

Appendix D

GENEALOGIES

APPENDIX D.1. SELECT GENEALOGY OF THE DANIILOVICH DYNASTY TO IVAN III

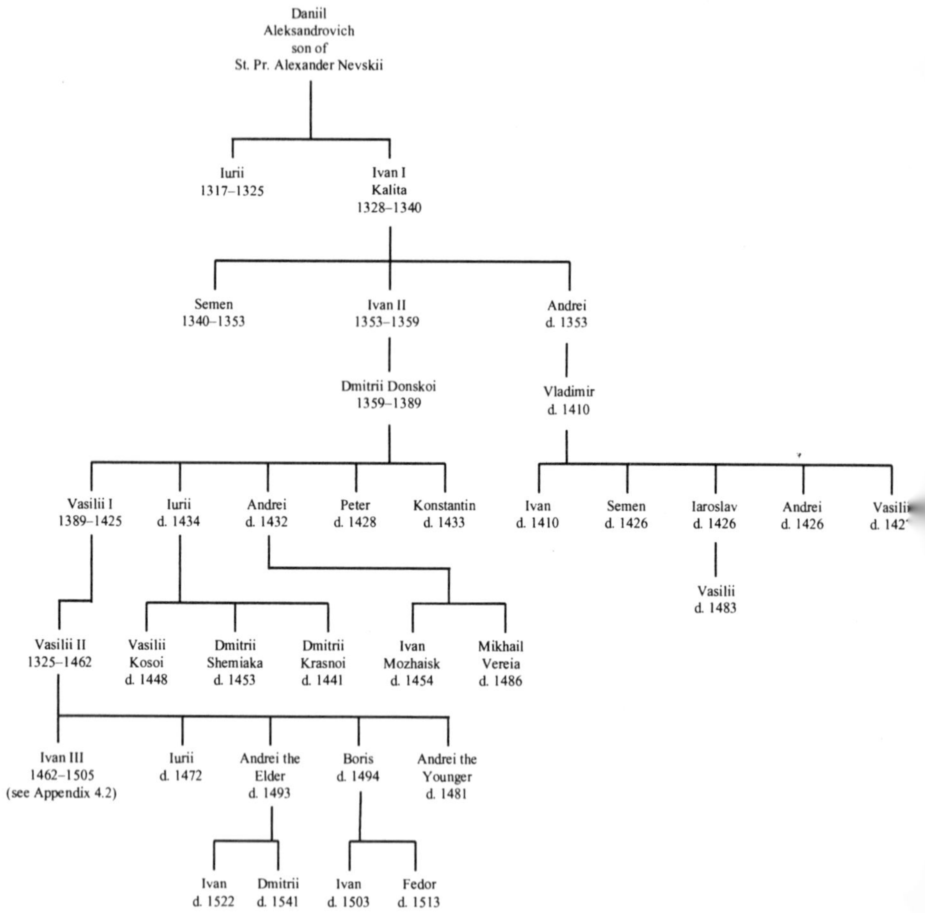

APPENDIX D.2. SELECT GENEALOGY OF THE DANIILOVICH DYNASTY FROM IVAN III, SHOWING MARRIAGES AND LINES OF DESCENT.

(Frames around names indicate those marriages for which bride-shows were organized or seem likely.)

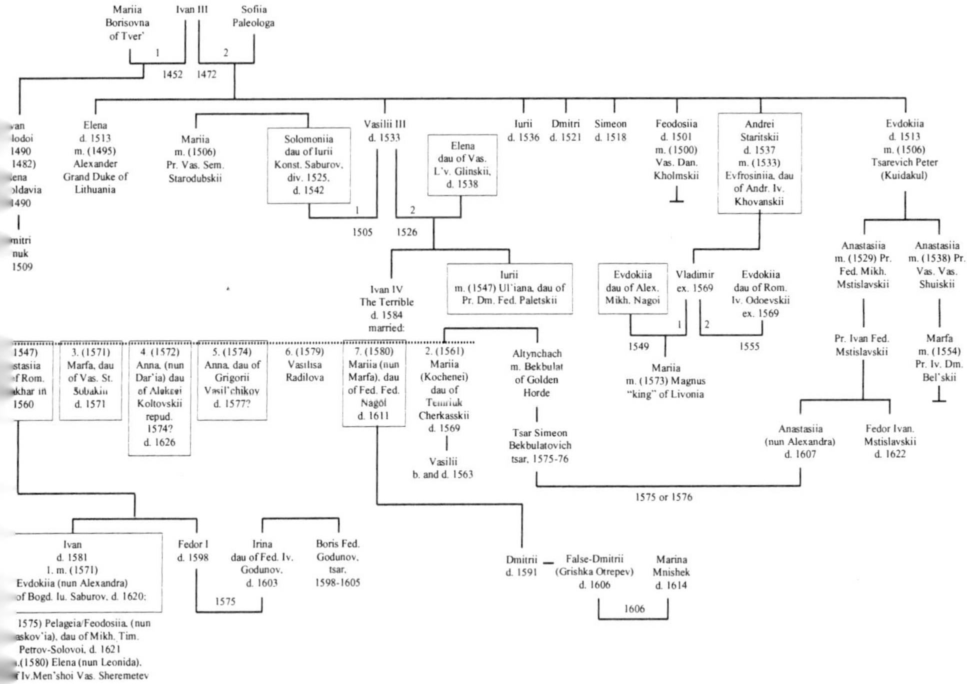

APPENDIX D.3. Select Genealogy of the Romanov Dynasty from Mikhail Fedorovich to Paul I, Showing Marriages and Lines of Descent.

(Frames around names indicate those marriages for which bride-shows were organized or seem likely.)

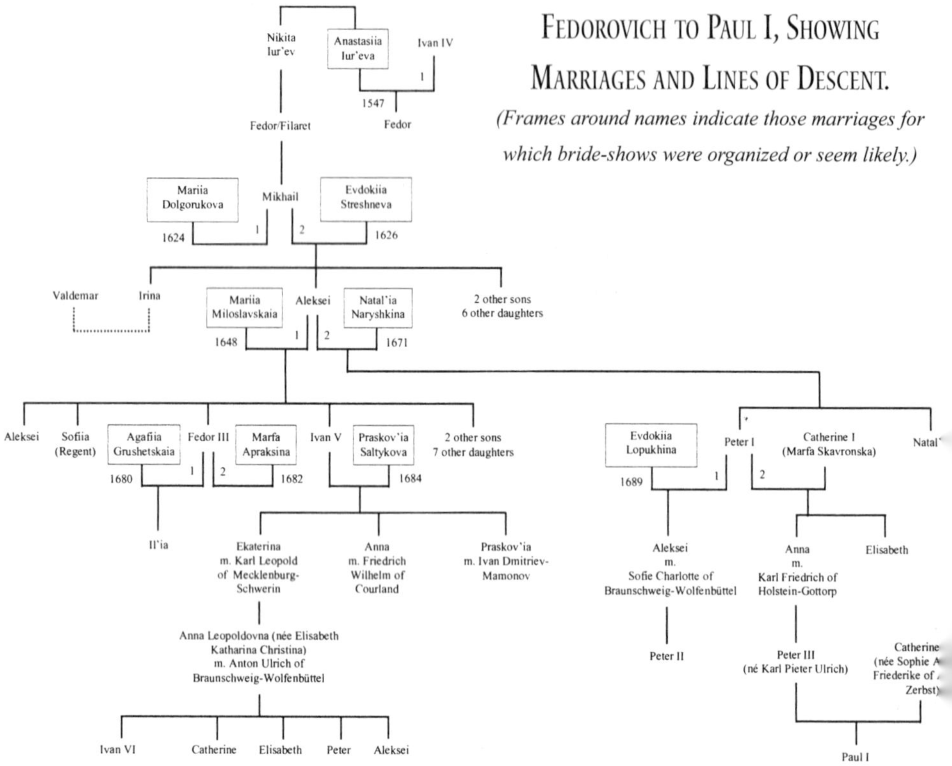

Abbreviations

AAE	*Akty, sobrannye v bibliotekakh i arkhivakh Rossiiskoi Imperii Arkheograficheskoiu ekspeditsieiu Imperatorskoi Akademii nauk.* 4 vols. St. Petersburg: Tipografiia II Otdeleniia Sobstvennoi E. I. V. Kantselariii, 1836.
AI	*Akty istoricheskie, sobrannye i izdannye Arkheograficheskoiu kommissieiu.* 5 vols. St. Petersburg: Tipografiia Ekspeditsii zagotovleniia gosudarstvennykh bumag, 1841–1842.
ASEI	*Akty sotsial'no-ekonomicheskoi istorii severo-vostochnoi Rusi.* 3 vols. Moscow: Akademii nauk SSSR, 1952–1964.
BAN	Biblioteka Rossiiskoi Akademii nauk [Library of the Russian Academy of Sciences], St. Petersburg.
ChIOIDR	*Chteniia v Imperatorskom obshchestve istorii i drevnostei Rossiiskikh pri Moskovskom universitete.* Moscow: Universitetskaia tipografiia, 1846–1918.
DAI	*Dopolneniia k Aktam istoricheskim, sobrannyie i izdannye Arkheografeskoiu kommissieiu.* 12 vols. St. Petersburg: Arkheograficheskaia kommissiia, 1846–1872.
DDG	*Dukhovnye i dogovornye gramoty velikikh i udel'nykh kniazei XIV–XVII vv.* Edited by Lev Vladimirovich Cherepnin. Moscow: Akademii nauk SSSR, 1950.
DR	*Dvortsovye razriady, po vysochaishemu poveleniiu, izdannye II-m otdeleniem sobstvennoi Ego Imperatorskogo Velichestva kantseliarii.* 4 vols. St. Petersburg: Tipografiia II otdeleniia Sobstvennoi E. I. V. Kantseliarii, 1850–1855.
DRV	*Drevniaia rossiiskaia vivliofika. Soderzhashchaia v sebe sobranie drevnostei rossiiskikh, do istorii geografii, i genealogii rossiiskoi kasaiushchikhsia.* Edited by Nikolai [Ivanovich] Novikov. 2d ed. 20 vols. Moscow: V tipografii Kompanii tipograficheskoi, 1788–1791.
fol., fols.	folio, folios (Russ.: *list, listy*)
GIM	Gosudarstvennyi istoricheskii muzei [State Historical Museum], Moscow.

IA — *Istoricheskii arkhiv*. 10 vols. Moscow: Izdatel'stvo Akademii nauk SSSR, 1936–1954.

IaOB — Iaroslavskaia oblastnaia biblioteka [Yaroslavl' Regional Library].

Izvestiia RGO — *Izvestiia Russkogo genealogicheskogo obshchestva*. Old Series. 4 vols. 1900–1911.

MGAMID — Moskovskii glavnyi arkhiv ministerstva inostrannykh del [Moscow Main Archive of the Ministry of Foreign Affairs]

op. — *opis'* (a subdivision of an archival collection)

PiB — *Pis'ma i bumagi imperatora Petra Velikogo*. 13 vols. to date. St. Petersburg, 1887–.

PSRL — *Polnoe sobranie russkikh letopisei*. 42 vols. to date. St. Petersburg-Petrograd-Leningrad-Moscow: Arkheograficheskaia komissiia, Nauka, Arkheograficheskii tsentr, and Iazyki slavianskoi kul'tury, 1841–2005.

PSZ — *Polnoe sobranie zakonov Rossiiskoi Imperii*. Series 1: 1649–1825. 45 vols., with 3 vols. of plates. St. Petersburg: Tipografiia II Otdeleniia Sobstvennoi Ego Imperatorskogo Velicheskogo Kantseliarii, 1830. Series 2: 1825–1881. 55 vols. St. Petersburg: Tipografiia II Otdeleniia Sobstvennoi Ego Imperatorskogo Velicheskogo Kantseliarii, 1830–1884. Series 3: 1881–1913. 33 vols. St. Petersburg: Gosudarstvennaia tipografiia, 1885–1916.

pt., pts. — part, parts (in a multi-volume work or collection)

RGADA — Rossiiskii gosudarstvennyi arkhiv drevnykh aktov [Russian State Archive of Ancient Acts], Moscow.

RBS — *Russkii biograficheskii slovar'*. 27 vols. St. Petersburg, Petrograd, Moscow: Izdanie Imperatorskogo Russkogo istoricheskogo obshchestva, 1896–1918; vols. 3A and 20A, 1991.

RGB — Rossiiskaia gosudarstvennaia biblioteka [Russian State Library], Moscow

RIB — *Russkaia Istoricheskaia Biblioteka*. 39 vols. St. Petersburg, Petrograd, Leningrad: various publishers, 1872–1927.

RNB — Rossiikaia natsional'naia biblioteka [Russian National Library], St. Petersburg.

RRK — *Rossiiskaia rodoslovnaia kniga*. Edited by Petr Dolgorukov. 4 vols. St. Petersburg: Tipografiia Karla Vingebera, Tipografiia Eduarda Veimara, Tipografiia III Otdeleniia Sobstvennoi E. I. V. Kantseliarii, 1854–1857.

rub. rubric (Russ.: *rubrik*, a subdivision of RGADA's *fond* 135)

SbIRIO *Sbornik Imperatorskogo russkogo istoricheskogo obshchestva*. 148 vols. St. Petersburg: various publishers, 1867–1916.

sec. section (Russ.: *otdel'*, a division of RGADA's *fond* 135)

SGGD *Sobranie gosudarstvennykh gramot i dogovorov, khraniashchikhsia v gosudarstvennoi kollegii inostrannykh del*. 5 vols. Moscow: Tipografiia N. S. Vsevolozhskogo, 1813–1894.

TODRL *Trudy Otdela drevnerusskoi literatury, Instituta russkoi literatury*.

VIMAIViVS Voenno-istoricheskii muzei artillerii, inzhenernykh voisk i voisk sviazi [The Military-Historical Museum of Artillery, Engineers, and Communications Forces], St. Petersburg.

ZhMNP *Zhurnal Ministerstva narodnogo prosveshcheniia*. 362 vols. (Old Series, 1834–1905). 72 vols. (New Series, 1906–1917). St. Petersburg and Petrograd: Ministerstva narodnogo prosveshcheniia, 1834–1917.

Notes

Introduction

1. Mikhail Mikhailovich Shcherbatov, *On the Corruption of Morals in Russia*, 97.

2. Shcherbatov, "O brakakh rossiiskikh tsarei," in *Neizdannye sochineniia*, 100–111.

3. Shcherbatov, "O brakakh rossiiskikh tsarei," 100–101.

4. Shcherbatov, "O brakakh rossiiskikh tsarei," 102.

5. Shcherbatov, "O brakakh rossiiskikh tsarei," 102–3.

6. Shcherbatov, "O brakakh rossiiskikh tsarei," 103.

7. Shcherbatov, "O brakakh rossiiskikh tsarei," 104.

8. Shcherbatov, "O brakakh rossiiskikh tsarei," 105.

9. Shcherbatov, "O brakakh rossiiskikh tsarei," 105–6.

10. Shcherbatov, "O brakakh rossiiskikh tsarei," 106.

11. Shcherbatov, "O brakakh rossiiskikh tsarei," 106–7.

12. See Shcherbatov, *On the Corruption of Morals in Russia*, 16–54, 133–34; and Hans Rogger, *National Consciousness in Eighteenth-Century Russia*, 40–41.

13. Paul I's two eldest sons similarly chose their brides from among German-born princesses presented to them: Alexander I chose his wife from among the two daughters of the Duke of Baden, and his younger brother, Constantine Pavlovich, chose his from among the three daughters of the duke of Sachsen-Coburg-Saalfeld. See Evgenii Petrovich Karnovich, *Tsetsarevich Konstantin Pavlovich*, 38–48; and Nikolai Karlovich Shil'der, *Imperator Aleksandr Pervyi: Ego zhizn' i tsarstvovanie*, 1:63–90.

14. Before the birth of Paul's children, the dynasty consisted only of Paul; his mother, Catherine II; and four disinherited and imprisoned distant cousins, the siblings of Ivan VI (1740–1741) who had been murdered in Shlüsselburg Fortress in 1762. The four siblings—Catherine, Elisabeth, Peter, and Alexis—had lived in exile since 1742 and were moved to Horsens, Denmark, in 1780 to live out their lives under the protective care of their aunt Queen Juliana Mary of Denmark (wife of Frederick V). None of them ever married. See M[odest Andreevich] Korf, *Braunshveigskoe semeistvo*; and Russell E. Martin, "'For the Firm Maintenance of the Dignity and Tranquility of the Imperial Family': Law and Familial Order in the Romanov Dynasty."

15. See the Epilogue.

16. See Vasilii Nikitich Tatishchev, *Istoriia Rossiiskaia*, 7:172–83. Nikolai Mikhailovich Karamzin, *Istoriia gosudarstva Rossiiskogo*, vol. 7, cols. 132–34 (and n. 402); vol. 8, cols. 58–59 (and n. 164); vol. 9, cols. 110–18, 161–62 (and nn. 367, 494, and 554); vol. 10, cols. 45–46. Sergei Mikhailovich Solov'ev, *Istoriia Rossii s drevneishikh vremen*, 3:151–53, 431–33, 701; 5:125, 481–82; 7:130–31, 196–97, 258, 449, 574–75. Stepan Borisovich Veselovskii, *Issledovaniia po istorii oprichniny,* 231, 300–301, 397; idem, *Issledovaniia po istorii klassa sluzhilykh zemlevladel'tsev*. Aleksander Aleksandrovich Zimin, *Oprichnina Ivana Groznogo*, 466; idem, *V kanun groznykh potriasenii*, 14–30, 85–88; idem, *Rossiia na poroge novogo vremeni (Ocherki politicheskoi istorii Rossii pervoi treti XVI v.)*, 67–70, 298–99. Ruslan Grigor'evich Skrynnikov, *Tsarstvo terrora*, 140, 435, 457, 479; idem, *Ivan Groznyi*, 206–14.

17. Ivan [Egorovich] Zabelin, *Domashnii byt russkikh tsarei v XVI i XVII st.*, vol. 1, pts. 1 and 2 of *Domashnii byt russkogo naroda v XVI i XVII st.*; idem, *Domashnii byt russkikh tsarits v XVI i XVII st.*, vol. 2 of *Domashnii byt russkogo naroda v XVI i XVII st.*; idem, *Materialy* [accompanying *Domashnii byt russkogo naroda v XVI i XVII st.* and *Domashnii byt russkikh tsarits v XVI i XVII st.*].

18. Zabelin, *Domashnii byt russkikh tsarits*, 207–8.

19. The literature is large and growing. See the following titles and their bibliographies: Natalia Pushkareva, *Women in Russian History from the Tenth to the Twentieth Century*; idem, "Women in the Medieval Russian Family of the Tenth through Fifteenth Centuries"; Nancy Shields Kollmann, "Women's Honor in Early Modern Russia"; idem, "The Seclusion of Elite Muscovite Women"; Eve Levin, *Sex and Society in the World of the Orthodox Slavs, 900–1700*; Daniel Kaiser, "Property among Elite Women in 17th-Century Russia"; idem, "'Whose Wife Will She Be at the Resurrection?' Marriage and Remarriage in Early Modern Russia"; Christine D. Worobec, "Accommodation and Resistance"; Isolde Thyrêt, "The Royal Women of Ivan IV's Family and the Meaning of Forced Tonsure"; idem, "Marfa Ivanovna and the Expansion of the Role of the Tsar's Mother in the Seventeenth Century"; idem, "The Cultural Politics of the Grand Princes of Muscovy"; idem, *Between God and the Tsar: Religious Symbolism and the Royal Women of Muscovite Russia*; Ann Kleimola, "'In accordance with the canons of the Holy Apostles': Muscovite Dowries and Women's Property Rights"; Donald Ostrowski; *Muscovy and the Mongols: Cross-Cultural Influences on the Steppe Frontier, 1304–1589,* 64–84; and Edward L. Keenan, "Ivan the Terrible and His Women." See also, for comparison, Abby E. Zanger, *Scenes from the Marriage of Louis XIV: Nuptial Fictions and the Making of Absolutist Power*; Trevor Dean and K. J. P. Lowe, *Marriage in Italy, 1300–1650*; and John Carmi Parsons, ed., *Medieval Queenship*.

20. See, for example, the list of candidates in Tsar Aleksei Mikhailovich's bride-shows in 1669–1670, and the list of gifts given to candidates in the bride-show in 1682 for Tsar Fedor Alekseevich. Zabelin, *Domashnii byt russkikh tsarits*, 252–53, 259.

21. Vladislav Dmitreevich Nazarov, "O strukture 'Gosudareva dvora' v seredine XVI v."; idem, "Svadebnye dela XVI v."

22. Margarita Evgen'evna Bychkova, *Sostav klassa feodalov Rossii v XVI v.*

23. R. Martin, "Muscovite Royal Weddings: A Descriptive Inventory of Manuscript Holdings in the Treasure Room of the Russian State Archive of Ancient Acts, Moscow"; idem, "Archival Sleuths and Documentary Transpositions: Notes on the Typology and Textology of Muscovite Royal Wedding Descriptions in the Sixteenth and Seventeenth Centuries"; and idem, "Royal Weddings and Crimean Diplomacy: New Sources on Muscovite Chancellery Practice during the reign of Vasilii III."

24. Kollmann, *Kinship and Politics: The Making of the Muscovite Political System, 1345–1547*, 8–18 (at 9). Kollmann here is borrowing categories and terminology from Max Weber (see p. 9, and 245 n. 14).

25. See works cited in Kollmann, *Kinship and Politics*, 9–18.

26. Classic statements of the "Patrimonial" approach include Marshall Poe, "The Truth about Muscovy"; and Richard Pipes, *Russia under the Old Regime*.

27. Edward L. Keenan, "Muscovite Political Folkways"; Kollmann, *Kinship and Politics*; Valerie A. Kivelson, "Culture and Politics, or the Curious Absence of Muscovite State Building in Current American Historical Writing"; idem, "Muscovite 'Citizenship': Rights without Freedom"; idem, *Autocracy in the Provinces: The Muscovite Gentry and Political Culture in the Seventeenth Century*; Daniel Rowland, "Architecture, Image, and Ritual in the Throne Rooms of Muscovy, 1550–1650: A Preliminary Survey"; idem, "Did Muscovite Literary Ideology Place Limits on the Power of the Tsar (1540s–1660s)"; idem, "The Problem of Advice in Muscovite Tales about the Time of Troubles"; Ostrowski, "The Façade of Legitimacy: Exchange of Power and Authority in Early Modern Russia"; George G. Weickhardt, "The Pre-Petrine Law of Property"; idem, "Was There Private Property in Muscovite Russia?" (compare with Pipes, "Was There Private Property in Muscovite Russia?"). See also Cornelia Soldat, "The Limits of Muscovite Autocracy: The Relations between the Grand Prince and the Boyars in the Light of Iosif Volotskii's *Prosvetitel*"; and Michael Flier, "Breaking the Code: The Image of the Tsar in the Muscovite Palm Sunday Ritual." On the so-called Harvard School, see Poe's review of Kollmann, *By Honor Bound: State and Society in Early Modern Russia*; and idem, "The Truth about Muscovy." On the preferred terms "structural" and "anthropological," see Kollmann, *Kinship and Politics*, 18.

28. Kivelson embraces the term "Harvard School." See her "On Words, Sources, and Historical Method: Which Truth about Muscovy?"

29. The term "Keenan's Cambridge Clones" was most recently discussed at a panel at the annual conference of the American Association for the Advancement of Slavic Studies (AAASS) in Toronto in November 2003. See R. Martin, "Introduction: Edward Keenan's Influence on Early Russian Studies."

30. See Richard Hellie, "Thoughts on the Absence of Elite Resistance in

Muscovy"; idem, "Edward Keenan's Scholarly Ways." For works influenced by the anthropological model, see, for a start, Hartmut Rüß, *Adel und Adelsoppositionen im Moskauer Staat*; Gustav Alef, *Rulers and Nobles in Fifteenth-Century Muscovy*; and Sergei Bogatyrev, *The Sovereign and His Counsellors: Ritualised Consultations in Muscovite Political Culture, 1350s–1570s*, and Kollmann's review of it in *Slavic Review*. Charles J. Halperin has purposefully pitted himself against the Harvard School—in particular, against the works of Edward Keenan. See his "Muscovy as a Hypertrophic State: A Critique"; idem, "The 'Russian' and 'Slavonic' Languages in Sixteenth-Century Muscovy"; idem, "The Culture of Ivan IV's Court: The Religious Beliefs of Bureaucrats"; and idem, "Edward Keenan and the Kurbskii-Groznyi Correspondence in Hindsight."

31. Arnold van Gennep, *The Rites of Passage*, 139.

32. On the composition and organization of wedding-related documents in the Treasure Room (*Drevlekhranilishche*) at RGADA, see Lev Vladimirovich Cherepnin, ed., *Gosudarstvennoe drevlekhranilishche khartii i rukopisei: Opis' dokumental'nykh materialov fonda 135*, 3–5; and R. Martin, "Muscovite Royal Weddings."

33. Shcherbatov, *On the Corruption of Morals in Russia*, 155.

34. Shcherbatov, *On the Corruption of Morals in Russia*, 155, 157.

Chapter 1

1. Sigismund von Herberstein, *Rerum Moscoviticarum Commentarii*, 47–48. See also Sigismund Herberstein [Sigizmund Gerbershtein], *Zapiski o Moskovii*, 86–88.

2. Isabel de Madariaga suggests that Ivan III's poor health may have been due to a stroke. See her *Ivan the Terrible: First Tsar of Russia*, 23 and 390 n. 2. See also Zimin, *Rossiia na poroge novogo vremeni*, 66.

3. On Trakhaniotov and Greeks in Muscovy at the turn of the sixteenth century, see Robert Croskey, "Byzantine Greeks in Late Fifteenth- and Early Sixteenth-Century Russia," 35–56; Boris Nikolaevich Floria, "Greki-emigranty v Russkom gosudarstve vtoroi poloviny XV–nachala XVI v. Politicheskaia i kul'turnaia deiatel'nost'," 123–43; Zimin, *Rossiia na rubezhe XV–XVI stoletii (Ocherki sotsial'no-politicheskoi istorii)*, 247–48; idem, *Rossiia na poroge novogo vremeni*, 67; Anna Leonidovna Khoroshkevich, *Russkoe gosudarstvo v sisteme mezhdunarodnykh otnoshenii kontsa XV–nachala XVI v.*; Zabelin, *Domashnii byt russkikh tsarits*, 207; Karamzin, *Istoriia gosudarstva Rossiiskogo*, vol. 7, n. 402; and *DDG*, 362–63 (no. 89).

4. See Gerbershtein, *Zapiski o moskovitskikh delakh*, 38–39, 71–73; and idem, *Zapiski o Moskovii*, 86–88, 110–11, 306–7 n. 223. See also Zimin, *Rossiia na poroge novogo vremeni*, 67.

5. On Iurii Konstantinovich Saburov, see Kollmann, *Kinship and Politics*, 142–43, 233, who cautiously concludes that he became a boyar between October

1506 and September 1509. Other sources seem firm that he was a boyar as early as 1506. See Zimin, "Sostav boiarskoi dumy XV–XVI vekakh," 49; Ann M. Kleimola, "Patterns of Duma Recruitment, 1505–1550," 255; and *ASEI*, 3:68–72 (no. 48). Compare with Zimin, *Formirovanie boiarskoi aristokratii v Rossii vo vtoroi polovine XV–pervoi treti XVI v.*, 195, which has him only as an *okol'nichii* from 1509 until his death in 1511/12.

6. See the commentary (written by Andrei Pliguzov) in Gerbershtein, *Zapiski o Moskovii*, 306 n. 223.

7. For a recent and rounded assessment of Herberstein's account, see Frank Kämpfer and Reinhard Frötschner, eds., *450 Jahre Sigismund von Herbersteins Rerum Moscoviticarum Commentarii, 1549–1999. Jubiläumvorträge herausgegeben von Frank Kämpfer und Reinhard Frötschner.*

8. See Zimin, *Formirovanie boiarskoi aristokratii v Rossii*, 273.

9. Warren T. Treadgold, "Bride-Shows of the Byzantine Emperors," also his earlier work "The Problem of the Marriage of the Emperor Theophilus." His five bride-shows were Constantine VI and Maria of Amnia (788); Stauracius and Theophano (807); Theophilos and Theodora (830); Michael III and Eudokia Dekapolitissa (855); and Leo VI and Theophano (882). Treadgold rejects the bride-shows identified by other scholars. For Leo IV and Irene (768), see J[ohn] B[agnell] Bury, *A History of the Eastern Roman Empire from the Fall of Irene to the Accession of Basil I*, 81; Steven Runciman, "Some Notes on the Role of the Empress," 120–21. For Leo VI and his third wife, Eudokia Baïana (900), see Photeine P. Bourboulis, *Studies in the History of Modern Greek Story-Motives*, 37; Romilly Jenkins, *Byzantium: The Imperial Centuries, A.D. 610–1071*, 215. See also Ostrowski, *Muscovy and the Mongols*, 83, who follows Runciman.

10. Lennart Rydén, "The Bride-Shows at the Byzantine Court—History or Fiction?"

11. Defenders of Treadgold's argument include L.-M. Hans, "Der Kaiser als Märchenprinz: Brautschau und Heiratspolitik in Konstantinopel 395–882"; and Gilbert Dagron, "Nés dans la pourpre."

12. Paul Speck, "Eine Brautschau für Staurakios?"; Claudia Ludwig, *Sonderformen byzantinischer Hagiographie und ihr literarisches Vorbild*, 104–45; Ralph-Johannes Lilie, *Byzanz unter Eirene und Konstantin VI. (780–802)*, 42–43; Dmitrii Afinogenov, "The Bride-Show of Theophilos: Some Notes on the Sources"; Martha Vinson, "Romance and Reality in the Byzantine Bride-Show," 102–20 (esp. 106); idem, "Rhetoric and Writing Strategies in the Ninth Century"; idem, "The Life of Theodora and the Rhetoric of the Byzantine Bride-Show"; and Judith Herrin, *Women in Purple: Rulers of Medieval Byzantium*, 132–38, 170–72, 185, 190–91, 222–25, 237, 292 n. 84. Herrin vexingly waivers on the historicity of Byzantine bride-shows, calling them in different places a "rhetorical exercise," which "may be no more than a literary fiction," and also "a parade of suitable young women" that "may well have been arranged" (134, 137, 172).

13. Treadgold, "The Historicity of Imperial Bride-Shows," 39–52.

14. Jenkins, *Byzantium: The Imperial Centuries*, 98; Runciman, "Some Notes on the Role of the Empress," 120–21. See also Bourboulis, *Studies in the History of Modern Greek Story-Motives*, 35. On Rus'-Khazar relations, see Omeljian Pritsak, *The Origin of Rus'*, vol. 1: *Old Scandinavian Sources other than the Sagas*, 3–33, 84.

15. See D[ouglas] M. Dunlop, *The History of the Jewish Khazars*, 100, 109–10; and *Ibn Fadlan's Journey to Russia: A Tenth-Century Traveller from Baghdad to the Volga River*, 76.

16. Treadgold, "Bride-Shows of the Byzantine Emperors," 398.

17. Treadgold, "Bride-Shows of the Byzantine Emperors," 397. See also the introduction in Marie-Henriette Fourmy and Maurice Leroy, "La Vie de S. Philarete," 103.

18. Treadgold, "Bride-Shows of the Byzantine Emperors," 398.

19. See *The Chronicle of John Malalas*, Book 14, paragraphs 3–4 (pp. 191–93); and *Constantinople in the Early Eighth Century: The Parastaseis syntomoi chronikai*, 141 (Eng. trans.).

20. Herrin, *Women in Purple*, 135.

21. For the Judgment of Paris myth, see, for a start, The *Cypria* Fragments (Fragment 1) (Greek, 7th–6th centuries B.C.E,) in Hesiod, *Hesiod, the Homeric Hymns, and Homerica*, 239; Ovid's *Heriodes (*Latin, 1st century B.C.E. to 1st C.E.) in Ovid, *Heriodes and Amores*, 201–3; Pseudo-Hyginus's *Fabulae* (Latin, 2nd century C.E.) in Hyginus, *The Myths of Hyginus*, 82–83; Pseudo-Apollodorus's *Biblioteca* (Greek, 2nd century C.E.) in Apollodorus, *The Library of Greek Mythology*, 94; and Lucian's *Dialogues of the Gods* (Greek, 2nd century) in Lucian, *Lucian's Dialogues*, 38–48.

22. Herrin, *Women in Purple*, 137.

23. See Treadgold, "Bride-Shows of the Byzantine Emperors," 402–3; idem, "The Problem of the Marriage of the Emperor Theophilus," 327; and Anna M. Silvas, "Kassia the Nun ca. 810–865: An Appreciation," who calls bride-shows, euphemistically, a "Judgment of Paris" (at pp. 20–21).

24. Jacob Reutenfels, "Skazanie sviatleishemu gertsogu toskanskomu Koz'me Tret'emu o Moskovii," in *ChIOIDR*, vol. 214 (1905, bk. 3), 1–137 (quotation at 81) (Inostrannye materialy). The remainder of the account is in *ChIOIDR*, vol. 218 (1906, bk. 3): 129–228.

25. Gilbert Dagron, *Emperor and Priest: The Imperial Office in Byzantium*, 47–48.

26. On the literary "yarns," see Bourboulis, *Studies in the History of Modern Greek Story-Motives*, 40–52. On the related Cinderella story-motif, see Alan Dundes, ed., *Cinderella: A Casebook*; Marian Roalfe Cox, *Cinderella: Three Hundred and Forty-Five Variants of Cinderella, Catskin, and Cap o' Rushes, Abstracted and Tabulated, with a Discussion of Mediæval Analogues, and Notes*; Anna Birgitta Rooth, *The Cinderella Cycle*; and Stith Thompson, *Motif-Index of Folk Literature: A Classification of Narrative Elements in Folk-Tales, Ballads,*

Myths, Fables, Mediæval Romances, Exempla, Fabliaux, Jest-Books, and Local Legends, 3:389–90 (H1301.1, H1301.1.1), 396 (H1381.3.1, H1381.3.2); 5:14 (L162).

27. The text reads: "inspectis plerisque nobilium filiabus." See *Annales Regni Francorum, inde ab a. 741. usque ad a. 829., qui dicuntur Annales Laurissenses Maiores et Einhardi*, ed. Friedrich Kurze, 150 (s.a. 819). For the English translation used here, see *Carolingian Chronicles: Royal Frankish Annals and Nithard's Histories*, 105.

28. The text reads: "undecumque adductus procerum filias inspitiens, Iudith filiam Uuelponis nobilissimi comitis in matrimonium iunxit." See Thegan, *Die Taten Ludwigs (Gesta Hludowici imperatoris),* and Astronomus, *Das Leben Kaiser Ludwigs (Vita Hludowici imperatoris)*, ed. Ernst Tremp, 392.

29. For a skeptical view of a Carolingian bride-show in 819, see Mayke de Jong, "Bride Shows Revisited: Praise, Slander and Exegesis in the Reign of the Empress Judith," 257–77. On Byzantine influences in the Carolingian west, see Michael McCormick, *Eternal Victory: Triumphal Rulership in Late Antiquity, Byzantium, and the Early Medieval West*, 362–84; idem, "Byzantium and the Early Medieval West: Problems and Opportunities," 1–17; idem, "Byzantium and the West, A.D. 700–900," 349–80; and idem, "Diplomacy and the Carolingian Encounter with Byzantium down to the Accession of Charles the Bald," 15–48.

30. See Patricia Buckley Ebrey, *Women and the Family in Chinese History*, 177–93; Jennifer Holmgren, "Imperial Marriage in the Native Chinese and Non-Han State, Han to Ming," 58–96; and Ellen Soullière, "The Imperial Marriages of the Ming Dynasty," 15.

31. Marco Polo, *The Travels of Marco Polo: The Marsden Translation*, 143–45.

32. Soullière, "The Imperial Marriages of the Ming Dynasty," 23–24.

33. Juan González de Mendoza, *The History of the Great and Mighty Kingdom of China and the Situation Thereof*, 1:65–66.

34. Soullière, "The Imperial Marriages of the Ming Dynasty," 23–24.

35. Álvaro Semedo, *The History of the Great and Renowned Monarchy of China*, 120–21. See also Soullière, "The Imperial Marriages of the Ming Dynasty," 21–22.

36. See Ebrey, "Introduction," in *Marriage and Inequity in Chinese Society*, 2–6, 8–11.

37. Shuo Wang, "Qing Imperial Women: Empresses, Concubines, and Aisin Gioro Daughters," 152.

38. On the *xiunŭ* draft, see Wang, "The Selection of Women for the Qing Imperial Harem," 212–22.

39. See contemporary newspaper reports of Qing Imperial weddings: "An Imperial Wedding. The Emperor of China has taken unto himself several wives," *New York Times*, December 26, 1872; and "Imperial Nuptials. How the Wife of the Chinese Emperor Has Been Chosen," *New York Times*, July 11, 1887.

40. Evelyn Rawski, "Ch'ing Imperial Marriage and Problems of Rulership," in *Marriage and Inequity in Chinese Society*, 187; and idem, *The Last Emperors: A Social History of Qing Imperial Institutions*, 131.

41. See Wang, "Qing Imperial Women."

42. Holmgren, "Imperial Marriage," 75; Soullière, "Reflections on Chinese Despotism and the Power of the Inner Court," 132–34.

43. Bourboulis, *Studies*, 15–39 (quote at 15).

44. Bourboulis, *Studies*, 30.

45. Ostrowski, *Muscovy and the Mongols*, 83.

46. Ševčenko's comments were made during a session of the Early Slavic Seminar at the Davis Center at Harvard University on April 10, 2009. The literature on Muscovite borrowing from Byzantium is substantial and touches a range of cultural and political topics. See the following and their bibliographies: Ostrowski, *Muscovy and the Mongols*; Michael Cherniavsky, "Khan or Basileus: An Aspect of Russian Mediaeval Political Theory"; D. [N.] Dubakin, "O vliianii Vizantii na semeinyi byt russkogo obshchestva." See also the brief but elegant treatment of kingship in Muscovy and Byzantium in Francis Oakley, *Kingship*, 83–86.

47. See the bibliography in *Slovar' knizhnikov i knizhnosti drevnei Rusi*, vol. 1: *XI–pervaia polovina XIV v.*, 471–74.

48. The literature on Esther and the Gennadii Bible is substantial. See the following and their bibliographies: Horace G. Lunt and Moshé Taube, *The Slavonic Book of Esther: Text, Lexicon, Linguistic Analysis, Problems of Translation*; *Slovar' knizhnikov i knizhnosti drevnei Rusi*, vol. 2: *Vtoraia polovina XIV–XVI v.*, pt. 1:145–46 (entry for "Gennadii"); Moshé Altbauer and Moshé Taube, "The Slavonic Book of Esther: When, Where, and from What Language Was It Translated?"; A. V. Gorskii and K. I. Nevostruev, *Opisanie slavianskikh rukopisei Moskovskoi sinodal'noi biblioteki*.

49. See Ostrowski, *Muscovy and the Mongols*, 231; A. I. Pliguzov and I. A. Tikhoniuk, "Poslanie Dmitriia Trakhaniota novgorodskomu arkhiepiskopu Gennadiiu Gonzovu o sedmerichnosti schisleniia let"; and Zabelin, *Domashnii byt russkikh tsarits*, 208–11.

50. Another Greek name also appears in proximity to the Esther text: Maksim Grek (ca. 1475–1556), the translator of biblical and liturgical texts and a prominent figure in the grand princely court. Moshé Taube and Hugh Olmsted have very persuasively argued that Maksim Grek was the likely translator of a new Slavonic version of the so-called *Tale of Esther* (*Povest' o Esfiri*). See Moshé Taube and Hugh M. Olmsted, "'Povest' o Esfiri': The Ostroh Bible and Maksim Grek's Translation of the Book of Esther."

51. See Carol B. Stevens, *Russia's Wars of Emergence, 1460–1730*; John Lister Illingworth Fennell, *Ivan the Great of Moscow*, 132–59; Konstantin Vasil'evich Bazilevich, *Vneshniaia politika tsentralizovannogo gosudarstva (vtoraia polovina XV veka)*, 239–81; *Pamiatniki diplomaticheskikh snoshenii*

drevnei Rusi s derzhavami inostrannymi, vol. 1, cols. 1–154.

52. See "Pamiatniki diplomatichskikh snoshenii Moskovskogo gosudarstva s Pol'sko-Litovskim gosudarstvom," vol. 3: "1560–1671 gg.," *SbIRIO*, vol. 35, nos. 17–35 (pp. 71–188); Robert M. Croskey, *Muscovite Diplomatic Practice in the Reign of Ivan III*, 251–66; and M. N. Berezhkov, "Elena Ivanovna, velikaia kniaginia litovskaia i koroleva pol'skaia."

53. See Alef, "Was Grand Prince Dmitrii Ivanovich Ivan III's 'King of the Romans'?" in *Essays in Honor of A. A. Zimin*, 94–96; Marc Szeftel, "The Title of the Muscovite Monarch up to the End of the Seventeenth Century"; Khoroshkevich, "Ob odnom iz epizodov dinasticheskoi bor'by v Rossii v kontse XV veka," 134–36.

54. See A. I. Kozachenko, "K istorii velikorusskogo svadebnogo obriada," 62; and *SbIRIO*, vol. 35, no. 24 (sections XI–XV, pp. 120–24).

55. Fennell, *Ivan the Great*, 162–63; *SbIRIO*, vol. 35, no. 25 (pp. 138–44), and no. 31 (sections I–VI, pp. 160–63).

56. The written assurance (*gramota*) from Alexander to Ivan III was preserved in the royal archive and appears in subsequent inventories. *Opisi Tsarskogo arkiva XVI v. i Arkhiva Posol'skogo prikaza 1614 g.*, 36 (box 183), 61 (fols. 48–48v), 65 (fols. 63v–64); *Opis' arkhiva Posol'skogo prikaza 1626 goda*, 1:85 (fols. 93v–94); 1:255 (fol. 420); and *Opis' arkhiva Posol'skogo prikaza 1673 goda*, 1:150–52 (fols. 286v–290v). The quote is taken from the 1626 inventory.

57. *DRV*, 14:5–15.

58. *DRV*, 14:2; *SbIRIO*, vol. 35, no. 31 (section VII, pp. 163–64).

59. *DRV*, 14:5–11.

60. The inventories include a fragmentary original and two complete later copies. The original: RGADA, *fond* 135, section IV, rubric II, no. 1; published in Khoroshkevich, "Iz istorii dvortsovogo deloproizvodstva kontsa XV v." The copies: BAN, 16.15.15, fols. 1–26v; BAN, 32.4.21, fols. 6–23v. On these inventories, see R. Martin, "Muscovite Royal Weddings," 77–189 (esp. 81–86); and idem, "Gifts for the Bride: Dowries, Diplomacy, and Marriage Politics in Muscovy." Diplomatic reports and related correspondence about the marriage are in *DRV*, 14:1–4; *Razriadnaia kniga 1475–1605 gg.*, ed. V. I. Buganov, 1:40–42; and *SbIRIO*, vol. 35, nos. 30–31 (pp. 157–71).

61. This rare icon, named after the first lines of Psalm 148, depicts all creation praising the Lord, with saints arranged in multiple tiers around the central figure of Christ enthroned.

62. BAN, 16.15.15, fols. 3v–5, 15–15v, 17v–18.

63. BAN, 16.15.15, fols. 1–3; BAN, 32.4.21, fols. 6–7v.

64. For examples of processions and of the groom on horseback at Muscovite royal weddings, see *DRV*, 13:2–3, 28, 38, 56–57, 95, and elsewhere.

65. *DRV*, 14:11.

66. On the Priest Foma, see S. Mirnov, *Drevne-russkii dukhovnik*, 250. All of these customary elements are repeated in descriptions of other Muscovite royal

weddings. *DRV*, 13:8, 11, 12 and elsewhere. See also *Domostroi: Rules for Russian Households in the Time of Ivan the Terrible*, ed. and trans. Carolyn Pouncy, 204–39.

67. See [Fr.] John Meyendorff, *Marriage: An Orthodox Perspective*, 29–42.

68. Kozachenko, "K istorii velikorusskogo svadebnogo obriada," 64–65.

69. Meyendorff, *Marriage: An Orthodox Perspective*, 20–29.

70. *DRV*, 13:10 (Vasilii III, 1526), 13:24 (Andrei Staritskii, 1533), 13:42 (Iurii Vasil'evich, 1547). Starting from the first wedding of Tsar Mikhail Romanov in 1624, the practice was changed so that the common cup was not smashed but taken by clergy into the altar after the couple had drunk from it. See RGADA, *fond* 135, sec. IV, rub. II, no. 14, fol. 13 (Tsar Mikhail's first wedding, 1624); *DRV*, 13:164 (his second wedding, 1626); and *DRV*, 13:206 (Tsar Aleksei Mikhailovich's first wedding, 1648).

71. Kozachenko, "K istorii velikorusskogo svadebnogo obriada," 64–65; *SbIRIO*, vol. 35, no. 35 (pp. 184–88); *DRV*, 14:13–15.

72. Kozachenko, "K istorii velikorusskogo svadebnogo obriada," 65.

73. *SbIRIO*, vol. 35, no. 36 (section III, pp. 191–92).

74. *SbIRIO*, vol. 35, no. 17 (sections I–VI, pp. 68–72); no. 24 (sections XIV–XV, pp. 123–24); no. 25 (section III, pp. 139–40); no. 25 (section V, pp. 141–44); no. 28 (sections I–XIII, pp. 145–56); no. 30 (sections I–V, pp. 157–59); no. 31 (sections I–XVII, pp. 159–71); no. 35 (sections I–II, pp. 182–88); no. 36 (sections I–VI, pp. 188–96); no. 40 (sections I–III, pp. 204–11); no. 49 (sections I–III, pp. 239–42); no. 56 (sections III–IV, pp. 269–73); no. 57 (sections I–II, pp. 273–74); no. 58 (sections I–V, pp. 274–77); no. 60 (sections I–IV, pp. 278–80); no. 61 (section IV, p. 288); no. 62 (section III, pp. 292–93); no. 63 (sections I–III, pp. 294–95); no. 64 (sections I–III, pp. 295–300); no. 76 (section I, pp. 425–26).

75. BAN, 32.4.21, fol. 23v.

76. For Evdokiia and Tsarevich Peter, see BAN, 32.4.21, fol. 37v; for Mariia Saburova and Starodubskii, see BAN, 32.4.21, fol. 48.

77. On Ivan III's first marriage, see *PSRL*, 12:77 (6960, Patriarshaia ili Nikonovskaia Chronicle). On the birth of Ivan Molodoi, see *PSRL*, 4:131 (6960, Fourth Novgorodskaia Chronicle); 8:147 (6966, Voskresenskaia Chronicle); 12:112 (6966). On Ivan Molodoi's marriage, see *PSRL*, 4:134 (6991); 6:36 (6991, First Sofiiskaia Chronicle), 6:234–35 (6991, Second Sofiiskaia Chronicle); 8:214 (6991); 12:214 (6991).

78. On his birth, see *PSRL*, 4:155 (6990); 6:235 (6992); 12:215 (6992).

79. On Ivan's second marriage, see *PSRL*, 4:133, 246; 6:196–97 (6980), 6:278 (6981, otryvok russkoi letopisi); 8:175–76 (6981); 12:151 (6981). On Vasilii's birth, see *PSRL*, 4:133 (6981); 6:19 (6987, First Sofiiskaia Chronicle), 6:33 (6987), 6:222 (6987); 8:200 (6987); 12:190–91 (6987). On Elena's birth, see *PSRL*, 8:182 (6984); 12:168 (6984).

80. On his death, see *PSRL*, 4:135 (6997), 157 (6998); 8:219 (6998); 12:222 (6998).

81. Sources report her name differently. For Anna, see *PSRL*, 24:232

(n.d., Tipografskaia Chronicle). For Mariia, see Karamzin, *Istoriia gosudarstva Rossiiskogo*, vol. 5, n. 254; and N. de Baumgarten, "Généalogies des branches régnantes de Rurikides du XIIIe au XVIe siècle," 17 (table III), 20 (n. 8).

82. On the Patrikeevs and their kinship ties to the dynasty, see Kollmann, *Kinship and Politics*, 133–40.

83. Kollmann, "Consensus Politics: The Dynastic Crisis of the 1490s Reconsidered," 250–51; and Gerberstein, *Zapiski o Moskovii*, 111, and 318 n. 312.

84. *PSRL*, 12:263 (7000); 24:214 (7006).

85. *PSRL*, 12:263 (7000); 20:366–68 (7006, L'vovskaia Chronicle); 24:213 (7006). See also Bychkova, "Obriady venchaniia na prestol 1498 i 1547 godov: Voploshchenie idei vlasti gosudaria"; and George P. Majeska, "The Moscow Coronation of 1498 Reconsidered." On the coronation of heirs during the lifetimes of their fathers, see Nazarov, "O sopravitel'stve v Moskovskom velikom kniazhestve (konets XIV–nachalo XVI veka)," 112–15. See also Andrew W. Lewis, *Royal Succession in Capetian France: Studies in Familial Order and the State*; and idem, "Anticipatory Association of the Heir in Early Capetian France."

86. *PSRL*, 24:213 (7003), 24:214 (7007); 26:291 (7006, Vologodsko-Permskaia Chronicle); 30:139 (7007, Vladimirskii Chronicle).

87. *PSRL*, 20:368 (March 7007); 4:531 (7001 [sic]); 26:291 (June 7007); Ia. S. Lur'e, "Kratkii letopisets pogodinskogo sobraniia," *Arkheograficheskii ezhegodnik za 1962 g.*, 443 (July 7007); Shmidt, "Prodolzhenie khronografa redaktsii 1512," *IA* (1951, no. 7): 273 (January 7007); Kollmann, "Consensus Politics," 254.

88. See, e.g., Cherepnin, *Russkie feodal'nye arkhivy XIV–XVI vekov*, 2:289–320; Bazilevich, *Vneshniaia politika*, 360–76; Fennell, *Ivan the Great*, 315–52; and John V. A. Fine, Jr., "The Muscovite Dynastic Crisis of 1497–1502."

89. Kollmann, "Consensus Politics," 253; Alef, "Aristocratic Politics and Royal Policy in Muscovy in the Late Fifteenth and Early Sixteenth Centuries." Crummey adopted Kollmann's and Alef's conclusions. See his *The Formation of Muscovy, 1304–1613*, 104–5, 110–13.

90. See R. Martin, "Archival Sleuths and Documentary Transpositions," 271–81, 291.

91. BAN, 16.15.15, fols. 27v–28; *DRV*, 13:2. See also Zimin, *Formirovanie*, 38–42.

92. BAN, 16.15.15, fols. 27v–28; *DRV*, 13:2. See also Zimin, *Formirovanie*, 30, 34; Kollmann, "Consensus Politics," 260; and idem, *Kinship and Politics*, 79.

93. BAN, 16.15.15, fol. 28; *DRV*, 13:2. See also Zimin, *Formirovanie*, 38, 40; Kollmann, "Consensus Politics," 253, 259.

94. BAN, 16.15.15, fol. 28; *DRV*, 13:2; Zimin, *Formirovanie*, 38, 42–43.

95. BAN, 16.15.15, fol. 29v; *DRV*, 13:4; Zimin, *Formirovanie*, 229.

96. BAN, 16.15.15, fol. 29v; *DRV*, 13:4; Zimin, *Formirovanie*, 233.

97. See BAN, 16.15.15, fol. 30v; *DRV*, 13:5.

98. Kollmann, "Consensus Politics," 255.

99. Kollmann, "Consensus Politics," 257.

100. *PSRL*, 26:295 (7010); 28:337 (7013, Letopisnyi svod 1518 g.).

101. *PSRL*, 26:294 (7009).

102. *PSRL*, 23:198 (7017, Ermolinskaia Chronicle); Kollmann, *Kinship and Politics*, 209.

103. On the ages of marriage for members of the Daniilovich dynasty, see Kollmann, Appendix 1, "The Calculation of Boyars' Ages," table A1.1 "Vital Statistics of Daniilovich Males," in *Kinship and Politics*, 192.

104. Iu. N. Shcherbachev, "Datskii arkhiv," *ChIOIDR*, vol. 184 (1893, bk. 1), 3; N. N. Bantysh-Kamenskii, *Obzor vneshnykh snoshenii Rossii (do 1800)*, vol. 1, addendum (p. 298).

105. *SbIRIO*, vol. 35, no. 76 (section I, pp. 426–27).

106. *SbIRIO*, vol. 35, no. 76 (section I, p. 427).

107. *SbIRIO*, vol. 35, no. 77 (section V, pp. 442–43).

108. "Margrave" refers to the Hohenzollern margrave of Brandenburg-Ansbach, Friedrich, who was married to Alexander's sister Sophia. Wilhelm Karl Prinz von Isenburg, ed., *Europäische Stammtafeln: Stammtafeln zur Geschichte der europäischen Staaten*, vol. 1, table 61; vol. 2, table 85.

109. The Bavarian prince is Georg von Bayern-Landshut, son of Ludwig IX of Bavaria and the husband of Hedwig, Alexander's sister. Isenburg, *Europäische Stammtafeln*, vol. 1, table 27; vol. 2, table 85.

110. The "Stettin prince" is Bogislav X of Pomerania, who was married to Alexander's sister Anna. Isenburg, *Europäische Stammtafeln*, vol. 1, tables 126 and 127; vol. 2, table 85.

111. The French king is Francis I. Tsereteli suggested that the sister described in the text is Margarete. See E. Tsereteli, *Elena Ioannovna. Velikaia kniaginia litovskaia, russkaia, koroleva pol'skaia*, 282–84. See also Isenburg, *Europäische Stammtafeln*, vol. 2, table 17. The Hungarian king is Ladislaus II, brother of Alexander and Jan Albrecht, the previous king of Poland (r. 1492–1501). Hungary and Poland were, in 1503–1504, both ruled by the Jagiellon dynasty, which had succeeded to these thrones after the extinction of the Neapolitan (Anjou) branch of the Capetian dynasty of France (descended from Charles d'Anjou, son of King Louis VIII). Isenburg, *Europäische Stammtafeln*, vol. 2, tables 105 and 118.

112. The Danish king referred to here is Hans (r. 1481–1513). His daughter Elisabeth was the first objective of Vasilii's efforts to find a foreign bride. Isenburg, *Europäische Stammtafeln*, vol. 2, table 72. The document is published in *SbIRIO*, vol. 35, no. 77 (section XVI, pp. 452–53). See also Croskey, *Muscovite Diplomatic Practice*, 266–68.

113. *SbIRIO*, vol. 35, no. 77 (section XVI, p. 453).

114. Bazilevich, *Vneshniaia politika*, 325, 330–31, 332–37; Zimin, *Rossiia na rubezhe*, 102–4; Tsereteli, *Elena Ioannovna*, 57–81.

115. Isolde Thyrêt, *Between God and Tsar: Religious Symbolism and the Royal Women of Muscovite Russia*; and idem, "'Blessed Is the Tsaritsa's Womb':

The Myth of Miraculous Birth and Royal Motherhood in Muscovite Russia."

116. See Marie Tanner, *The Last Descendant of Æneas: The Habsburgs and the Mythic Image of the Emperor*.

117. On Giovio, see T. C. Price Zimmermann, *Paolo Giovio: The Historian and the Crisis of the Sixteenth Century*.

118. On Dmitrii Gerasimov, see Natal'ia A. Kazakova, "Dmitrii Gerasimov i russko-evropeiskie kul'turnye sviazi v pervoi treti XVI v."; and Ostrowski, "Ironies of the Tale of the White Cowl."

119. On the royal scriptorium and archive of the Foreign Office, see Martin, "Royal Weddings and Crimean Diplomacy," 402–6.

120. Karamzin believed that Giovio must have been describing one of the two weddings of Vasilii Ivanovich (in 1505 and 1526), but it must in fact be the first that he describes, since the second wedding took place after the writing of Giovio's book and its publication in Rome. See Karamzin, *Istoriia gosudarstva Rossiiskogo*, vol. 7, col. 132.

121. Pavel Iovii Novokomskii, "Kniga o moskovitskom posol'stve," 273–74.

122. Peter Petreius [Petr Petrei], "Istoriia o velikom kniazhstve Moskovskom," 235–36.

123. Philip John von Strahlenberg, *An Historico-Geographical Description of the North and Eastern Parts of Europe and Asia; But more particularly of Russia, Siberia, and Great Tartary; Both in their Ancient and Modern State*, 217–18.

124. Johann Georg Korb, *Diary of an Austrian Secretary of Legation at the Court of Czar Peter the Great*, 2:131.

125. Reutenfels, "Skazanie sviatleishemu gertsogu toskanskomu Koz'me Tret'emu o Moskovii," 80–81.

126. On the date of the wedding, for September 4, see *PSRL*, 6:50 (7014); 8:245 (7014); 12:259 (7014); 20:3756 (7014); 26:297 (7014); 34:8 (7014, Postnikovskii Chronicle); 37:173 (7014, Vologodskaia Chronicle); 39:176–77 (7014, First Sofiiskaia Chronicle, I. N. Tsarskii Copy); also Shmidt, "Prodolzhenie khronografa redaktsii 1512 g.," 276. Other sources give September 5, see *PSRL*, 5:261 (7014, First Sofiiskaia Chronicle); or September 8, see *PSRL*, 30:140 (7014); Lur'e, "Kratkii letopisets pogodinskogo sobraniia, 444 (7015); or September 14, see *PSRL*, 31:124 (7014, Mazurinskii Chronicle); or even October 18, see *PSRL*, 37:99 (7015, Arkhangelogorodskii Chronicle).

127. Lur'e, "Kratkii letopisets," 444 (7014, 7015 [*sic*], should be 7013 and 7014).

128. That the bride-show happened no later than August 1505 is deduced from the placement in the "Kratkii letopisets" of the notation about the bride-show at the end of 7013 (in the source 7014, incorrectly) and the notation of the wedding at the very beginning—that is, in September—of 7014 (in the source 7015, again incorrectly). On these dates, see Zimin, *Rossiia na poroge novogo vremeni*, 67.

129. Kollmann, *Kinship and Politics*, 143.

130. Kollmann, *Kinship and Politics*, 143. See also Crummey, *Aristocrats*

and Servitors: The Boyar Elite in Russia, 1613–1689, 70–71, 76–81.

131. Statistics represent weddings where the spouse is known and the date is known or can be approximated for the fourteenth, fifteenth, and sixteenth centuries (n=70). See Baumgarten, "Généalogies des branches régnantes de Rurikides, XIII–XVI s.," 10–35 (tables II, III, IV, and V).

132. Harmut Rüß, "Elena Vasil'evna Glinskaja."

133. On Tsarevich Peter, see Ostrowski, "The Extraordinary Career of Tsarevich Kudai Kul/Peter in the Context of Relations between Muscovy and Kazan'." On the Glinskiis, see Zimin, *Formirovanie*, 142–43, and Kollmann, *Kinship and Politics*, 207. On Mariia Temriukovna, see RNB, Titov Collection, no. 891, fol. 326v (fragment of wedding muster). On Magnus, see *DRV*, 13:97–103; BAN, 16.15.15, fols. 175–78v; BAN, 32.4.21, fols. 129v–132; RGADA, *fond* 135, sec. IV, rub. II, no. 10, fols. 1–3.

134. Martin, "Ritual and Religion in the Foreign Marriages of Three Muscovite Princesses," 371–78.

CHAPTER 2

1. Grigorii Georgievskii, *Prazdnichnye sluzhby i tserkovnye torzhestva v staroi Moskve*, 347–56.

2. W. F. Ryan, *Russian Magic at the British Library: Books, Manuscripts, Scholars, Travellers*, 76–77.

3. On the Palm Sunday ritual, see, for a start, Michael Flier, "Breaking the Code: The Image of the Tsar in the Muscovite Palm Sunday Ritual," 213–42; idem, "The Iconography of Royal Procession: Ivan the Terrible and the Palm Sunday Ritual," 109–25. On the Epiphany ritual, see Paul Bushkovitch, "The Epiphany Ceremony of the Russian Court in the Sixteenth and Seventeenth Centuries." On religious processions, see Kollmann, "Pilgrimage, Procession, and Symbolic Space in Sixteenth-Century Russian Politics."

4. Paul Kléber Monod, *The Power of Kings: Monarchy and Religion in Europe, 1589–1715*, 81–86 (quote at 83).

5. Monod, *The Power of Kings*, 83; Michèle Fogel, *Les Cérémonies de l'information dans la France du XVIe au milieu du XVIIIe siècle*, 11–19.

6. Petreius, "Istoriia o velikom kniazhestve Moskovskom," 235–26.

7. Karamzin, *Istoriia gosudarstva Rossiiskogo*, vol. 7, n. 402; and Francesco da Collo [Franchesko da Kollo], *Ital'ianets v Rossii XVI veka, Franchesko da Kollo. Donoshenie o Moskovii*, 53, 66.

8. Jerome Horsey, "The Travels of Jerome Horsey," 277–78.

9. Johann Taube and Elbert Kruse, "Poslanie Ioganna Taube i Elberta Kruze kak istoricheskii istochnik," 55.

10. Strahlenberg, *An Historico-Geographical Description*, 218; and idem, *Zapiski kapitana Filippa Ioganna Stralenberga ob istorii i geografii Rossiiskoi imperii Petra Velikogo. Servernaia i vostochnaia chast' Evropy i Azii*, 83.

11. Samuel Collins, *The present State of Russia*, 11–12; idem, "Nyneshnee sostoianie Rossii," trans. P. Kireevskii, *ChIOIDR* (1846, bk. 1), 4–5 (Materialy inostrannye).

12. Foy de la Neuville, *A Curious and New Account of Muscovy in the Year 1689*, ed. Lindsey Hughes, 50.

13. For the first document, dated by Nazarov to mid December 1547, see RGADA, *fond* 135, sec. IV, rub. II, no. 2, fols. 6–7; and Nazarov, "Svadebnye dela XVI v.," 117–18 (document 4). The second document has the date "January 9" inscribed on it, see RGADA, *fond* 135, sec. IV, rub. II, no. 2, fol. 8; and Nazarov, "Svadebnye dela XVI v.," 121 (document 12).

14. A third list of scribes (compiled, according to Nazarov, at the end of January 1547) also appears to be related to Ivan IV's bride-show: RGADA, *fond* 135, sec. IV, rub. II, no. 2, fol. 14; Nazarov, "Svadebnye dela XVI v.," 121–22 (document 15).

15. RGADA, *fond* 135, sec. IV, rub. II, no. 2, fol. 6; and Nazarov, "Svadebnye dela XVI v.," 117 (document 4).

16. RGADA, *fond* 135, sec. IV, rub. II, no. 2, fol. 8; and Nazarov, "Svadebnye dela XVI v.," 117 (document 12). Prince P. A. Bulgakov is called by the surname Kurakin in RGADA, *fond* 135, sec. IV, rub. II, no. 2, fol. 6–7; and Nazarov, "Svadebnye dela XVI v.," 117 (document 4). The Bulgakov and Kurakin princes were scions of the Patrikeev princely line, which itself was a scion of the Lithuanian Gedyminid Dynasty. See Zimin, *Formirovanie*, 29–35 (esp. table 1 on p. 30); and Kollmann, *Kinship and Politics*, 225–26.

17. In addition to the courtier and scribe in each of the thirteen groups recorded in the December 1546 list, the January 1547 list adds the names of *pod'iachie* who were also sent (*po nikh poslan*). RGADA, *fond* 135, sec. IV, rub. II, no. 2, fol. 8; and Nazarov, "Svadebnye dela XVI v.," 121 (document 12).

18. Nazarov, "Svadebnye dela XVI v.," 114–15.

19. The identification is Nazarov's ("Svadebnye dela XVI v.," 115).

20. RGADA, *fond* 135, sec. IV, rub. II, no. 5, fol. 1; Nazarov, "Svadebnye dela XVI v.," 118 (document 5).

21. RGADA, *fond* 135, sec. IV, rub. II, no. 5, fol. 8; Nazarov, "Svadebnye dela XVI v.," 121 (document 12).

22. *DRV*, 13:36.

23. BAN, 16.15.15, fols. 103–4; BAN, 32.4.21, fols. 79–79v; *DRV*, 13:46.

24. RGADA, *fond* 27, *op.* 1, no. 287, fols. 7–8. See Appendix 2.

25. Nazarov suggested that (in the sixteenth century, at least) there were two methods for assembling a pool of bridal candidates: dispatching courtiers to form "commissions" and hold preliminary bride-shows in provincial towns and summoning candidates directly to Moscow. Nazarov, "Svadebnye dela XVI v.," 114–15. Zabelin, however, saw the dispatching of courtiers and the summons to Moscow as part of a single process. Zabelin, *Domashnii byt russkikh tsarits*, 212–15. This study largely follows Zabelin.

26. Karamzin, *Istoriia gosudarstva Rossiiskogo*, vol. 7, n. 402; and Da

Collo, *Ital'ianets v Rossii XVI veka*, 53, 66.

27. RGADA, *fond* 135, sec. IV, rub. II, no. 5, fol. 1 (Novgorod), fols. 5, 6 (Viaz'ma and Dorogobuzh), fol. 55 (Rostov), fol. 56 (Viaz'ma).

28. Valerie Kivelson, *Autocracy in the Provinces*, 26.

29. Quoted above. RGADA, *fond* 135, sec. IV, rub. II, no. 5, fol. 1; Nazarov, "Svadebnye dela XVI v.," 118 (document 5).

30. RGADA, *fond* 135, sec. IV, rub. II, no. 5, fol. 55; and no. 2, fols. 6–7.

31. RGADA, *fond* 135, sec. IV, rub. II, no. 5, fol. 55; Nazarov, "Svadebnye dela XVI v.," 118–19 (document 6).

32. RGADA, *fond* 135, sec. IV, rub. II, no. 5, fol. 56; Nazarov, "Svadebnye dela XVI v.," 119 (document 7).

33. RGADA, *fond* 135, sec. IV, rub. II, no. 5, fol. 3; Nazarov, "Svadebnye dela XVI v.," 123 (document 19).

34. Nazarov, "Svadebnye dela XVI v.," 114.

35. Nazarov, "Svadebnye dela XVI v.," 115.

36. RGADA, *fond* 135, sec. IV, rub. II, no. 5, fol. 6; Nazarov, "Svadebnye dela XVI v.," 120 (document 11).

37. RGADA, *fond* 135, sec. IV, rub. II, no. 5, fol. 5; Nazarov, "Svadebnye dela XVI v.," 120 (document 10).

38. Quoted in Zabelin, *Domashnii byt russkikh tsarits*, 257.

39. See Kollmann, *By Honor Bound*, 72–82; idem, "The Seclusion of Elite Muscovite Women"; and Ostrowski, *Muscovy and the Mongols*, 64–84.

40. Kivelson, *Autocracy in the Provinces*, 103–5, 267.

41. Treadgold found some of the same hesitancy among Byzantine fathers to produce their daughters for bride-shows, which he also attributed to the custom of seclusion of elite women. See his "Bride-Shows of the Byzantine Emperors," 398.

42. Herberstein, *Rerum Moscoviticarum Commentarii*, 47–48; idem, *Zapiski o Moskovii*, 86–88.

43. Petreius, "Istoriia o velikom kniazhestve Moskovskom," 235–36. On Herberstein as a source for other foreigners' accounts, see Poe, *"A People Born to Slavery": Russia in Early Modern European Ethnography, 1476–1748*, 128–44; and idem, "Herberstein and the Origin of the European Image of Muscovite Government."

44. On the number of boyars and *okol'nichie* in 1505, see Kleimola, "Patterns of Duma Recruitment, 1505–1550," 251–58.

45. Karamzin, *Istoriia gosudarstva Rossiiskogo*, vol. 7, n. 402; and Da Collo, *Ital'ianets v Rossii XVI veka*, 53, 66.

46. Taube and Kruse, "Poslanie Ioganna Taube i Elberta Kruze kak istoricheskii istochnik," 55.

47. Daniel Printz von Buchau, "Nachalo i vozvyshenie Moskovii," *ChIOIDR*, vol. 99 (1876, bk. 3), 1–46 (at 28).

48. "Pis'ma odnogo Shveda iz Moskvy v 1647 godu pisannye," *Severnyi*

arkhiv (January 1822, no. 3): 151–54 (at 153). On this letter, see V[asilii Nikolaevich] Berkh, *Tsarstvovanie Tsaria Alekseia Mikhailovicha*, 2:43–47 and n. 33.

49. Karamzin, *Istoriia gosudarstva Rossiiskogo*, vol. 7, n. 402; and Da Collo, *Ital'ianets v Rossii XVI veka*, 53, 66.

50. Pavel Iovii Novokomskii, "Kniga o moskovitskom posol'stve," 273–74.

51. Reutenfels, "Skazanie sviatleishemu gertsogu toskanskomu Koz'me Tret'emu o Moskovii," 81–82.

52. Neuville, *A Curious and New Account of Muscovy*, 50.

53. See Zabelin, *Domashnii byt russkikh tsarits*, 386–96; and, generally, Keenan, "Ivan the Terrible and His Women."

54. See, for example, the key role played by foreign doctors in Taube and Kruse's account of Ivan IV's marriage in 1571, and in the Khlopova affair in 1616 (see Chapter 5).

55. Taube and Kruse, "Poslanie Ioganna Taube i Elberta Kruze kak istoricheskii istochnik," 55.

56. Strahlenberg, *An Historico-Geographical Description*, 218; and idem, *Zapiski kapitana Filippa Ioganna Stralenberga*, 83–84.

57. Reutenfels, "Skazanie sviatleishemu gertsogu toskanskomu Koz'me Tret'emu o Moskovii," pt. 1, 81–82.

58. Heidenstein, "Zapiski o Moskovskoi voine (1578–1582)," 194–95.

59. Shmidt, "Pozdnyi letopischik so svedeniiami po istorii Rossii XVI v.," *Letopisi i khroniki: sbornik stat'ei, 1973 g.*, 347.

60. Shmidt, "Pozdnyi letopischik," 351–52.

61. Shmidt, "Pozdnyi letopischik," 348.

62. The account in Heidenstein evidently also influenced the *Histoire universelle* by de Thou, which includes a version of this bride-show that is very close to it and to Shmidt's chronicle. See Jacques-Auguste de Thou, *Histoire universelle de Jacques-Auguste de Thou. Depuis 1543. jusqu'en 1607. Traduite sur l'édition Latine de Londres*, 8:430.

63. Collins, *The present State of Russia*, 11–12.

64. Reinhold Heidenstein, "Zapiski o Moskovskoi voine (1578–1582)," in *Reingol'd Geidenshtein. Zapiski o Moskovskoi voine (1578–1582). Al'bert Shlikhting. Novoe izvestie o Rossii vremeni Ivana Groznogo. Genrikh Shtaden. O Moskve Ivana Groznogo*, ed. Aleksandr Ivanovich Tsepkov, 194–95.

65. Heidenstein, "Zapiski o Moskovskoi voine"; see also Pavel Iovii Novokomskii, "Kniga o moskovitskom posol'stve," 273–74.

66. Strahlenberg, *An Historico-Geographical Description*, 84.

67. This line ("*ne vedakh podlinno istorii, lzhivye raznye o tom spletali na gosudarei rosiiskikh po zlobe k rosiiskomu narodu*") is inserted in the *letopischik* but absent from Heidenstein and de Thou. Shmidt, "Pozdnyi letopischik," 352.

68. Madariaga, *Ivan the Terrible*, 442 n. 38.

69. Kollmann, *Kinship and Politics*, xiv, 9, 19, 43, 126, 146–51; and Kivelson, *Autocracy in the Provinces*, 215.

70. Nazarov, "Svadebnye dela XVI v.," 115.

71. RGADA, *fond* 135, sec. IV, rub. II, no. 5, fol. 58. Nazarov, "Svadebnye dela XVI v.," 116 (document 1).

72. The disqualification of the Pleshcheev women from Vasilii III's bride-show has been interpreted variously. Zimin believed that the Pleshcheevs were avoided because of their ties to Prince Iurii Ivanovich of Dmitrov, Vasilii III's younger brother, and because of their presumed support for Dmitrii's succession to the throne after Vasilii. Zimin, *Rossiia na poroge novogo vremeni*, 276–77. Nazarov questioned this view, pointing out that prominent Pleshcheevs (and Shcheniatevs) disappear from the service rolls no later than 1522—far too early to connect their disappearance with the conflict in 1525 over Vasilii's second marriage. Instead, Nazarov argues that the exclusion of Pleshcheev and Shcheniatev kinswomen from Vasilii's bride-show was connected to the defection in 1510/11 of I. T. Iurlov-Pleshcheev and to the capture by the Lithuanians of prominent members of both clans (D. A. Basman-Pleshcheev and Princes M. I. and D. I. Bulgakov, agnatic cousins of the Shcheniatevs) in 1514 in the battle of Orsha. Nazarov, "Svadebnye dela XVI v.," 115–16. Zimin countered by pointing out that the disgraced Pleshcheevs were forgiven in 1530, right after the birth of Vasilii III's son, Ivan Vasil'evich (the future Ivan IV), and so the entire matter most likely had to do with Vasilii's second marriage. Zimin, *Formirovanie*, 200. Zimin also noted that the Pleshcheevs were linked to the Kirillo-Belozerskii monastery, where Vassian Patrikeev had been interred and which had served as a bastion of support for the Patrikeev faction—further suggesting a link in the political interests of these two clans at court. Zimin, *Rossiia na poroge novogo vremeni*, 276.

73. Taube and Kruse suggest that the reason for the written reports with physical descriptions of potential bridal candidates was to prevent deception on the part of fathers—so that substitutes could not be sent to Moscow in place of their daughters; see their "Poslanie Ioganna Taube i Elberta Kruze kak istoricheskii istochnik," 55. But as the Gundorova description, cited below, shows, physical descriptions were rudimentary (hardly sufficient to reveal impostors) and focused more on medical histories and kinship ties than anything else.

74. RGADA, *fond* 135, sec. IV, rub. II, no. 5, fol. 57; Nazarov, "Svadebnye dela XVI v.," 117 (document 8).

75. On Genealogical Books as historical sources, see Bychkova, *Rodoslovnye knigi XVI–XVII vv. kak istoricheskii istochnik*, 122–76; and Bychkova and Maksim Igorevich Smirnov, *Genealogiia v Rossii: istoriia i perspektivy*, 3–109.

76. Afanasii Andreevich Godunov was a second cousin once removed of Tsar Boris Godunov. A. B. Lobanov-Rostovskii, ed., *Russkaia rodoslovnaia kniga*, 2:39–45.

77. Grigorij K. Kotošixin, *O Rossii v carstvovanie Alekseja Mixajloviča*, 29; Collins, *The present State of Russia*, 11–12, 103; Adam Olearius, *The Travels of Olearius in Seventeenth-Century Russia*, 203–5. See also Crummey, *Aristocrats and Servitors*, 71, 76–78.

78. On Gramotin's role in these two weddings, see Martin, "Choreographing the 'Tsar's Happy Occasion': Tradition, Change, and Dynastic Continuity in the Weddings of Tsar Mikhail Romanov," 797–805.

79. Gal'tsov, *Opis' arkhiva Posol'skogo prikaza 1626 goda*, 1:367–68.

80. Mariia Dolgorukova's father, Prince Vladimir Timofeevich, had married both a Barbashina and an Eletskaia. See Oleg Viacheslavovich Shcherbachev, "O rodstve Saltykovykh s Mikhailom Fedorovichem Romanovym," 62–67; Gennadii Aleksandrovich Vlas'ev, ed., *Potomstvo Riurika*, pt. 3, 10–12; P[etr] V. Dolgorukov, ed., *Skazaniia o rode kniazei Dolgorukovykh*, 16.

81. RGADA, *fond* 27, *op*. 1, no. 287. The text is published in P. P. Pekarskii, "Spisok devits, iz kotorykh v 1670 i 1671 godakh vybiral sebe suprugu tsar' Aleksei Mikhailovich"; and in Zabelin, *Domashnii byt russkikh tsarits*, 252–53.

82. RGADA, *fond* 396, *op*. 2, no. 873, fols. 8v–11v. The text is published in Zabelin, *Domashnii byt russkikh tsarits*, 259.

83. The thirty-nine families were Demskii, Vekent'ev, Kobykin, Aprelev, Polev, Gagarin, Boltin, Sontsov, Karamyshev, Redrikov, Krasnikov, Uvarov, Protopopov, Bunin, Klokochev, Kapustin, Korenev, Neznanov, Motovilov, Polivanov, Rostopchin, Morev, Siniavin, Smerdov, Chevkin, Zhedrinskii, Zagriaskii, Ovtsyn, Odintsov, Satin, Pozdeev, Kolemin, Zhitov, Khomiakov, Skobeltsyn, Simonov, Rchinov, Beliaev, and Linev.

84. The ten families were Liapunov, Dolgorukov, Ivanov, Dubrovskii, Leont'ev, Eropkin, Nashchokin, Kolychev, Tolskoi, and Poltev. The remaining nine families, representing eleven women on the list, had members who reached Duma ranks after 1671: Golokhvastov, Verderevskii, Zykov, Izvol'skii, Musin-Pushkin, Dashkov, Narshykin (the winning contestant), Apraksin, Khotetovskii.

85. Lobanov-Rostovskii, *Russkaia rodoslovnaia kniga*, 1:121; Crummey, *Aristocrats and Servitors*, 190.

86. *RRK*, 4:395–96; Leonid Mikhailovich Savelov, *Rodoslovnye zapisi: Opyt rodoslovnogo slovaria russkogo drevnego dvorianstva*, 3:121; Crummey, *Aristocrats and Servitors*, 186.

87. Anna was the fourth cousin once removed of Mariia Vladimirovna Dolgorukova, the first wife of Mikhail Romanov. Both were descended from Prince Vladimir Ivanovich Dolgorukov, Anna through his son Semen and Mariia through his son Timofei. See Vlas'ev, *Potomstvo Riurika*, pt. 3, 36.

88. The first Dolgorukov boyar was Vladimir Timofeevich Dolgorukov, the father of Tsaritsa Mariia. He obtained boyar rank in 1605. Crummey, *Aristocrats and Servitors*, 179.

89. See Crummey, *Aristocrats and Servitors*, 188, 190.

90. The eight families were Kurakin, Khitrovo, Veliko-Gagin, Lobanov-Rostovskii, Izmailov, Poltev, L'vov, and Volkonskii.

91. The four families were Dinis'ev, Kvashnin, Verderevskii, and Kireevskii.

92. The three families were Zvenigorodskii, Golovlenkov, and Izvol'skii.

93. RGADA, *fond* 181, no. 115, fol. 74v.

94. As the winner, Grushetskaia is not, naturally, mentioned in the list of those who received parting gifts.

95. The genealogical sources consulted include the following: Vlas'ev, *Potomstvo Riurika*; *RRK*; Lobanov-Rostovskii, *Russkaia rodoslovnaia kniga*; Savelov, *Rodoslovnye zapisi*; Vitol'd Vladislavovich Rummel' and Vladimir Vladimirovich Golubtsov, eds., *Rodoslovnyi sbornik russkikh dvorianskikh familii*.

96. On the Khotetovskiis, see Vlas'ev, *Potomstvo Riurika*, pt. 1, 255; *RRK*, 2:191. On the Boltins, see *RRK*, 4:303; Savelov, *Rodoslovnye zapisi*, 1:199. On the Kolychevs, see *RRK*, 4:136–41. On the Zvenigorodskiis: *RRK*, 1:71. On the Sheremetevs, see *RRK*, 3:499. On the Cherkasskiis, see *RRK*, 2:37.

97. Vasilii Timofeevich Satin (the brother of Feodosiia Timofeevna Satina, a candidate in 1669–1670) married Anna Romanovna Koreneva around 1660. Anna's kinswoman Anna Andreevna was also a candidate in 1669–1670. See Vlas'ev, *Potomstvo Riurika*, pt. 1, 403; *RRK*, 4:35–36.

98. On the Polevs: *RRK*, 1:278. On the Izmailovs: ibid., 174. On the Saltykovs: Shcherbachev, "O rodstve Saltykovykh s Mikhailom Fedorovichem Romanovym," 62–67; *RRK*, 2:71. On the Buturlins: *RRK*, 2:158.

99. On the Naryshkins and Matveevs: Lobanov-Rostovskii, *Russkaia rodoslovnaia kniga*, 1:239–40; Crummey, *Aristocrats and Servitors*, 101–2. Paul Bushkovitch argues, contrary to the traditional view, that Artamon Matveev probably was not instrumental in Tsar Aleksei's selection of Natal'ia Naryshkina in 1670. Bushkovitch, *Peter the Great: The Struggle for Power*, 57–63, 112–13, 123–24, 143, 156–57; and idem, "Aristocratic Faction and the Opposition to Peter the Great: The 1690s," 89–90. Compare with Lindsey Hughes, *Sofia: Regent of Russia 1657–1704*, 20, 36–37, 50–51, 96, 223; idem, *Russia in the Age of Peter the Great*, 393; and Pavel V. Sedov, *Zakat Moskovskogo tsarstva: Tsarskii dvor kontsa XVII veka*, 114–15 n. 9. See also Chapter 5.

100. Crummey, *Aristocrats and Servitors*, 8.

101. On these other rituals, see Flier, "Court Ceremony in an Age of Reform: Patriarch Nikon and the Palm Sunday Ritual," 73–95; idem, "Breaking the Code: The Image of the Tsar in the Muscovite Palm Sunday Ritual"; Crummey, "Court Spectacles in Seventeenth-Century Russia: Illusion and Reality," 130–58; Martin, "Ritual and Religion in the Foreign Marriages of Three Muscovite Princesses"; idem, "Choreographing the 'Tsar's Happy Occasion'"; and Sedov, *Zakat Moskovskogo tsarstva*, 397–556.

102. Four of the 12 courtiers named in the source (RGADA, *fond* 135, sec. IV, rub. II, no. 2, fols. 6–7, 8; see table 2.1) eventually were promoted to boyar rank: Prince Fedor Andreevich Kurakin (in May 1548; see Kollmann, *Kinship and Politics*, 226); Prince Petr Andreevich Kurakin/Bulgakov (between 1555/56 and March 1559; see Kollmann, *Kinship and Politics*, 226); Vladimir Vasil'evich Morozov (between 1559 and 1561/62; see Kollmann, *Kinship and Politics*, 220); and *okol'nichii* Ivan Dmitreevich Shein (about 1551/52; see Kollmann, *Kinship*

and Politics, 221). *Okol'nichii* Ivan Ivanovich Bezzubtsev disappears from the sources in 1547 before promotion to boyar (Kleimola, "Patterns of Duma Recruitment, 1505–1550," 251; Zimin, *Formirovanie*, 188, 210 n. 218). Five of the others (Prince Semen Fedorovich Alabyshev, Princes Boris and Dmitrii Dmitreevich Shchepin, and Prince Petr Semenovich Ianov-Rostovskii) did not get promoted but had relatives that were. Zimin, "Sostav boiarskoi dumy v XV–XVI vekakh," *Arkheograficheskii ezhegodnik za 1957 g.*, 41–87; Kleimola, "Reliance on the Tried and True: Ivan IV and Appointments to the Boyar Duma, 1565–1584"; and idem, "Kto Kogo: Patterns of Duma Recruitment, 1547–1564." Two princes (Ivan and Fedor Mezetskii) enjoyed privileged service careers but did not hold Duma ranks (on the Mezetskii princes, see Kollmann, *Kinship and Politics*, 75).

103. The ceremonial (*chin*) for the wedding of Tsarevich Ivan Ivanovich and Evdokiia Saburova refers to the bride throughout as "tsarevna" or "tsarevna kniazhna." BAN, 16.15.15, fols. 161v, 162, 162v, 163, 163–63v, 164v, and elsewhere.

104. The formal entry of the bride-to-be and the bestowal of the title tsarevna are attested for the following seventeenth-century weddings. For Tsar Mikhail Fedorovich and Evdokiia Streshneva (1626): RGADA, *fond* 135, sec. IV, rub. II, no. 16, fols. 5v; *DRV*, 13:145. For Tsar Aleksei Mikhailovich and Mariia Miloslavskaia (1648): RGADA, *fond* 135, sec. IV, rub. II, no. 24, fol. 7; *DRV*, 13:181; Kotošixin, *O Rossii*, 20; Phillip Benjamin Uroff, *Grigorii Karpovich Kotoshikhin, On Russia in the Reign of Alexis Mikhailovich*, 37; 320–21 n. 42. For Tsar Aleksei Mikhailovich and Natal'ia Naryshkina (1671): RGADA, *fond* 135, sec. IV, rub. II, no. 28, fol. 26; no. 29, fol. 12v; no. 30, fols. 12v–13. For Tsar Fedor Alekseevich and Agafiia Grushetskaia (1680): RGADA, *fond* 135, sec. IV, rub. II, no. 32, fol. 5v. For Mariia Khlopova, Tsar Mikhail Fedorovich's first bridal candidate who is referred to as "tsaritsa": *SGGD*, vol. 3, no. 63 (September 15, 1623), 257–66 (at 261); Zabelin, *Domashnii byt russkikh tsarits*, 221. No reference to either ritual can be found for the first marriage of Mikhail Fedorovich, but that may be because no *chin*—the source most likely to report it—survives for the wedding. Efimiia Vsevolozhskaia, Tsar Aleksei Mikhailovich's first bridal candidate, was to be given the title tsarevna before her disqualification: RGADA, *fond* 135, sec. IV, rub. II, no. 21, fols. 5 and 78; and Zabelin *Domashnii byt russkikh tsarits*, 247.

105. RGADA, *fond* 135, sec. IV, rub. II, no. 24, fol. 7.

106. RGADA, *fond* 135, sec. IV, rub. II, no. 2, fols. 1, 2, 3v (*kniazhna*); and fols. 3, 4, 4v, 5 (*velikaia kniaginia*). The folios in this text are out of order. The order should be 2, 3, 4, 5, [a missing folio], 1. See R. Martin, "Muscovite Royal Weddings," 98–102.

107. RGADA, *fond* 135, sec. IV, rub. II, no. 5, fols. 18–31, 31–42, 43–54; Bychkova, *Sostav klassa feodalov*, 139–43.

108. *DRV*, 13:105; Zabelin, *Domashnii byt russkikh tsarits*, 218–19; Karamzin, *Istoriia gosudarstva Rossiiskogo*, vol. 9, n. 379.

109. For Pelageia/Feodosiia Petrova-Solovaia: *Materialy po istorii SSSR*,

vol. 2, "Piskarevskii letopisets," ed. by O. A. Iakovleva, commentary by L. N. Pushkarev, 165 n. 98. For Ekaterina/Mariia Buinosova-Rostovskaia: S. A. Belokurov, ed., *Razriadnye zapisi za Smutnoe vremia (7113–7121 gg.)*, 248. For Mariia/Nastas'ia Khlopova: *PSRL*, vol. 5, 65 (n.d., Addendum to Second Pskovskaia Chronicle); *AI*, vol. 3, no. 91 (December 30, 1620), 89–90; *SGGD*, vol. 3, no. 63 (p. 261). Zabelin speculated that the new names may have been a means of further associating the new in-laws with the dynasty. Khlopova chose Nastas'ia (i.e., Anastasiia) as her royal name because, he suggested, it was reminiscent of Anastasiia, the wife of Tsar Ivan IV. Zabelin, *Domashnii byt russkikh tsarits*, 221. One popular source claims that Peter I's first wife may also have changed her name, from Praskov'ia to Evdokiia. P. Kh. Grebel'skii and A. B. Mirvis, *Dom Romanovykh. Bibliograficheskie svedeniia o chlenakh tsarstvovavshego doma, ikh predkakh i rodstvennikakh*, 123. Foy de la Neuville calls Lopukhina "Mafia or Martha." See Neuville, *A Curious and New Account of Muscovy*, 41.

110. Vsevolozhskii is referred to as both Raf and Fedor. For Raf: RGADA, *fond* 135, sec. IV, rub. II, no. 21, fol. 1; no. 22, fol. 66; *AI*, vol. 4, no. 59, 165–66; *SGGD*, vol. 3, no. 155. For Fedor: "Pis'ma odnogo shveda iz Moskvy v 1647 godu pisannye," 152; Zabelin, *Domashnii byt russkikh tsarits*, 245–49. For Aleksandr Saltykov: RGADA, *fond* 180, *op*. 1, no. 3, fol. 37; Mikhail Ivanovich Semevskii, *Tsaritsa Praskov'ia, 1664–1723. Ocherk iz Russkoi istorii XVIII veka*, 11 (Semevskii believed the name was selected to honor the recently deceased Tsar Fedor III). For Illarion Lopukhin: *RBS*, 10:692.

111. Zabelin, *Domashnii byt russkikh tsarits*, 216 (see also 221, 243, 245).

112. "Fedor" is, like Anastasiia, a "Romanov name." The clan's founder (Fedor Koshka) and the father of the first Romanov tsar (Fedor Nikitich/Patriarch Filaret) both bore the name. Adoptive patronymics are also found among the foreign brides of eighteenth- and nineteenth-century rulers. The name Fedorovna was adopted by the wives of Emperor Paul I (second wife), Nicholas I, Alexander III, and Nicholas II. "Alekseevna" was adopted by Catherine I, Catherine II the Great, Paul I's first wife, and Alexander I's wife. Alexander II's wife took the patronymic "Alexandrovna." Emperor Peter III, son of Karl-Friedrich of Holstein-Gottorp, was styled "Peter Fedorovich," his patronymic similar to that adopted by many royal women who came from abroad, as he did. See Richard S. Wortman, *Scenarios of Power: Myth and Ceremony in Russian Monarchy*, 1:57–58.

113. RGADA, *fond* 135, sec. IV, rub. II, no. 21, fols. 5 and 78.

114. For early drafts (3 days): RGADA, *fond* 135, sec. IV, rub. II, no. 21, fol. 78; no. 23, fol. 46. For later versions (2 days): RGADA, *fond* 135, sec. IV, rub. II, no. 24, fol. 7; no. 23, fol. 78; *DRV*, 13:181.

115. For Naryshkina: RGADA, *fond* 135, sec. IV, rub. II, no. 30, fols. 12v–13. For Grushetskaia: RGADA, *fond* 135, sec. IV, rub. II, no. 32, fol. 5v.

116. Chester S. L. Dunning, *Russia's First Civil War: The Time of Troubles and the Founding of the Romanov Dynasty*, 33.

117. Keenan, "Muscovite Political Folkways," 144.

Chapter 3

1. Zimin, "Vypis' o vtorom brake Vasiliia III," in *TODRL* 30 (1976): 144 (fols. 95–95v). The *Extract* contains a number of odd words and phrases that have remained undeciphered, including *Sarapadasiistii* in the quote, and elsewhere the oddities *Ur'diukeliami* and *ialdarilom*. See Shmidt, "O vremeni sostavlenia 'Vypisi' o vtorom brake Vasiliia III," 114. See also "Vypis' iz gosudarevy gramoty, chto prislana k velikomu kniaziu Vasiliiu Ivanovichu o sochetanii vtorago braku i o razluchenii pervago braka chadorodiia radi. Tvorenie Paiseino startsa Ferapontova monasteryia," ed. O. M. Bodianskii, *ChIOIDR* (1847, bk. 12 [on title page: 8]), 1–8 (Smes').

2. Karamzin, *Istoriia gosudarstva Rossiiskogo*, vol. 7, n. 277.

3. The passage in the *Extract* is attributed to Patriarch Mark III, who ruled only briefly in 1503—well before Vasilii III had even married Solomoniia.

4. Zimin, "Vypis' o vtorom brake Vasiliia III," 135.

5. On the dating of the "Vypis' o vtorom brake Vasiliia III," see Mikhail Nikolaevich Tikhomirov, *Istoricheskie sviazi Rossii so slavianskimi stranami i Vizantiei*, 82; idem, "Stranitsa iz zhizni Ivana Peresvetova," 73; and idem, "K voprosu o Vypisi o vtorom brake Vasiliia III"; Shmidt, "O vremeni sostavlenia 'Vypisi' o vtorom brake Vasiliia III"; idem, "K izucheniiu 'Istorii' kniazia Kurbskogo (O pouchenii popa Sil'vestra)," *Slaviane i Rus': Sbornik stat'ei k shestidesiatiletiiu Akademika B. A. Rybakova*, 366–74 (esp. 369); Sergei Alekseevich Belokurov, *O biblioteke moskovskikh gosudarei v XVI stoletii*, appendix, L–LXV; Evgenii Evstigneevich Golubinskii, *Istoriia russkoi tserkvi,* 2 (part 1): 732–33; Natal'ia Aleksandrovna Kazakova, *Vassian Patrikeev i ego sochineniia*, 68–71; idem, *Ocherki po istorii russkoi obshchestvennoi mysli: pervaia tret' XVI veka*, 117–18, 182; idem, "Vopros o prichinakh osuzhdeniia Maksima Greka," 113; Zimin, "Vypis' o vtorom brake Vasiliia III"; and M. D. Kagan, "Povest' o vtorom brake Vasiliia III," *Slovar' knizhnikov i knizhnosti drevnei Rusi*, vol. 2, pt. 2:232. A recent study of the text explores its connections with other compositions produced in the scriptoria of the Pskov Snetogorskii Monastery (or another nearby monastery) by, or under the direction of, Hegumen Kornilii and proposes a date for the archetype between 1565 and 1570. See Ia. G. Solodkin, "K datirovke 'Vypisi' o vtorom brake Vasiliia III."

6. See Zimin, "Vypis' o vtorom brake Vasiliia III"; Kazakova, *Vassian Patrikeev i ego sochineniia*; and Solodkin, "K datirovke 'Vypisi' o vtorom brake Vasiliia III."

7. *PSRL*, 34:15 (7034, Postnikovskii Chronicle); Tikhomirov, "Zapiski o regentstve Eleny Glinskoi i boiarskom pravlenii 1533–1547 gg.," 278–88 (esp. 280). Solomoniia was repudiated on November 28, 1525, and on the next day she was tonsured with the name Sofiia at the Convent of the Nativity of the Mother of God "*na Rve*" in Moscow. She was then sent to Kargopol' for five years, living in a "cell in the woods," then was dispatched to the Pokrov Convent

in Suzdal', where she lived until her death on December 18, 1542. Her remains were buried at the Pokrov Convent. See *PSRL*, 4:295–96 (7031 and 7032, First Pskovskaia Chronicle); 6:264 (7034, Second Sofiiskaia Chronicle); 8:271 (7034, Voskresenskaia Chronicle); 24:222–23 (7034, Tipografskaia Chronicle); "Istoriia o velikom kniaze Moskovskom," *RIB*, 31:161–354 (at 162–63); Gerberstein, *Zapiski o Moskovii*, 38; Karamzin, *Istoriia gosudarstva Rossiiskogo*, vol. 7, cols. 82–84, and n. 280; Zimin, *Rossiia na poroge novogo vremeni*, 293–97. See also the excellent treatment of Solomoniia and the myth of the "tsaritsa's blessed womb" in Thyrêt, *Between God and Tsar*, 34–39.

8. See the bibliography in Dmitrii Mikhailovich Bulanin, "Maksim Grek," *Slovar' knizhnikov i knizhnosti drevnei Rusi*, vol. 2, pt. 2:89–98.

9. *DDG*, 415 (no. 100). See also Skrynnikov, *Sviatiteli i vlasti*, 142; and Madariaga, *Ivan the Terrible*, 27–30.

10. Treadgold, "Bride-Shows of the Byzantine Emperors," 402 (see also 409).

11. RGADA, *fond* 135, sec. IV, rub. II, no. 5, fol. 58; Nazarov, "Svadebnye dela XVI v.," 114, 116 (document 1).

12. See Begunov, "Povest' o vtorom brake Vasiliia III," 105–18 (at 109). On the "Tale," see M. N. Tikhomirov, "Novyi pamiatnik Moskovskoi politicheskoi literatury XVI v.," 112–14; A. N. Nasonov, "Materialy i issledovaniia po istorii russkogo letopisaniia," in *Problemy istochnikovedeniia*, vol. 6, 248–52; Kazakova, *Vassian Patrikeev i ego sochineniia*, 68–71; Zimin, *Russkie letopisi i khronografy kontsa XV–XVI v.*, 13.

13. Begunov, "Povest' o vtorom brake Vasiliia III," 117.

14. Begunov, "Povest' o vtorom brake Vasiliia III," 118. See also Kagan, "Povest' o vtorom brake Vasiliia III," *Slovar' knizhnikov i knizhnosti drevnei Rusi*, vol. 2, pt. 2:230–33; and Solodkin, "K datirovke 'Vypisi' o vtorom brake Vasiliia III."

15. Begunov, "Povest' o vtorom brake Vasiliia III," 118. The titles raise doubts about Begunov's dating of the *Tale*.

16. On the date of the wedding, see *PSRL*, 8:271 (7034); BAN, 16.15.15, fol. 64; BAN, 32.4.21, fol. 49; BAN, 21.10.25, fol. 2; and the Kirillo-Belozerskii Chronicle (1580s), in Zimin, "Kratkie letopistsy XV–XVI vv.," 29. Several sources have the date as January 28: Begunov, "Povest' o vtorom brake Vasiliia III," 118; *DRV*, 13:5; BAN, 31.6.40, fol. 4; BAN, 32.5.11, fol. 4v; BAN, 31.7.20, fol. 3v; IaOB, RK319031V, fol. 2; *DAI*, 1:21–22. Others report January 24: *PSRL*, 6:264 (7034); or February 21: *PSRL*, 24:222–23 (7034).

17. On the four brothers arriving in Muscovy in 1508, see Bychkova, "Rodoslovie kniazei Glinskikh," which includes the text of a Glinskii genealogy: "1686 g., marta 4. Rospis' kniazei Glinskikh, podannaia v Razriad" (a publication of RGADA, *fond* 210, *op.* 18, no. 87, fols. 1–2). See also *PSRL*, 26:299 (7016).

18. See *PSRL*, 8:257 (7022).

19. On Elena's brothers' ages, see Kollmann, *Kinship and Politcs*, 144, 207, and 275 n. 121.

20. The best recent genealogical study of the Glinskiis is Bychkova, "Rodoslovie kniazei Glinskikh," which revised and expanded her previous study, "Rodoslovie Glinskikh iz Rumiantsevskogo sobraniia." See also Zimin, *Formirovanie*, 142–43; Rüß, "Elena Vasil'evna Glinskaja"; Jósef Wolff, *Kniaziowie Litewsko-ruscy od końca czternastego wieku*, 77–86; Władysław Pociecha, "Gliński, Michał Lwowicz"; N. P. Chulkov, "Glinskii, Kn. Vasilii L'vovich," *RBS* 5 (1916): 318–19; and V. Korsakov, "Glinskii, Kn. Mikhail L'vovich," *RBS* 5 (1916): 324–30.

21. On Elena's mother, see *PSRL*, 4:296 (7032, First Pskovskaia Chronicle).

22. On Glinskii claims to Tatar and Chinggisid ancestry, see Bushkovitch, "Princes Cherkasskii or Circassian Murzas: The Kabardians in the Russian Boyar Elite, 1560–1700," 11 and n. 7.

23. Kollmann, *Kinship and Politics*, 144.

24. Herberstein, *Rerum Moscoviticarum Commentarii*, 47–48; and Gerbershtein, *Zapiski o Moskovii*, 86–88.

25. On Elena's western upbringing and Vasilii III's shaving his beard, see Karamzin, *Istoriia gosudarstva Rossiiskogo*, vol. 7, cols. 84–85 and nn. 282 and 285; Gerbershtein, *Zapiski o Moskovii*, 39; Zabelin, *Domashnii byt russkikh tsarits*, 269; Pushkareva, *Women in Russian History*, 65. On Vasilii III's affection for Elena, see also *PSRL*, 4:296 (7032, First Pskovskaia Chronicle). On Elena's beauty, see the discussion of the forensic reconstruction of her features in T. D. Panova, *Kremlevskie usypal'nitsy: istoriia, sud'ba, taina*, 146–48 (including an image on plate 47).

26. Baumgarten, "Généalogies des branches régnantes de Rurikides," 18–19 (table III), 22–23.

27. The average lifespan of grand princes born in the thirteenth through sixteenth centuries was only 46.6 years. Kollmann, *Kinship and Politics*, 191–93. Only four males in the dynasty for whom data survives had longer lives than Vasilii III.

28. J. Martin, *Medieval Russia, 980–1584*, 248. See also Kollmann, "Collateral Succession in Kievan Rus'."

29. Iurii died in 1472 at the age of 31. On his death, see *PSRL*, 4:244 (6981, First Pskovskaia Chronicle); 8:175 (6981); and 12:150 (6981). Andrei "the Younger" was 29 when he died in 1493. On his death, see *PSRL*, 4:154 (6989, Fourth Novgorodskaia Chronicle); 5:261 (6989); 8:213 (6989); 12:212 (6989).

30. On his marriage (to Princess Elena Romanovna Mezetskaia), see *PSRL*, 4:149 (6977, Fourth Novgorodskaia Chronicle); 5:274 (6977); 8:158 (6978); 12:123–24 (6978). Prince Andrei "the Elder" had two sons, Ivan and Dmitrii, and two daughters. Prince Andrei and his sons were arrested in 1491 in a plot against Ivan III. Prince Andrei died in prison in November 1493. *PSRL*, 8:227 (7002); 12:237 (7002); 15:501 (7001). His son Prince Ivan was permitted to take monastic vows under the name Ignatii and died in 1522 in Vologda, later being canonized by the church for his life of "passion-bearing." On the arrest

of Ivan, see *PSRL*, 4:160 (7000, Fourth Novgorodskaia Chronicle); 8:4, 223 (7000); 12:231 (7000). On Ivan's tonsuring, see *PSRL*, 3:198 (7031, Otryvok iz razriada Novgorodskikh letopisei); 7:239 (n.d.). On his canonization, see E. E. Golubinskii, *Istoriia kanonizatsii sviatykh v russkoi tserkvi*, in *ChOIDR*, vol. 204 (1903, no. 1), 1–600 (at 153). The other son, Dmitrii, was eventually released from prison in 1540 and promptly died. On his arrest, see *PSRL*, 4:160 (7000, Fourth Novgorodskaia Chronicle); 8:4, 223; 12:231 (7000). On his release, see Karamzin, *Istoriia gosudarstva Rossiiskogo*, vol. 8, col. 37 and nn. 93 and 94. On his death, see *PSRL*, 29:39 (7049, Letopisets nachala tsarstva; but compare with Baumgarten, "Généalogies des branches régnantes de Rurikides," 23 n. 29).

31. On Prince Boris's marriage, see *PSRL*, 4:150 (6979, Fourth Novgorodskaia Chronicle); 5:275 (6979); 6:191 (6979). Boris had two sons and a daughter. The elder son, Fedor (prince of Volok) married in 1504 but had no issue. The other son, Ivan (prince of Ruza), never married and the line died out. On Fedor's marriage, see *PSRL*, 6:49 (7012); 8:244 (7012). On his death, see *PSRL*, 6:253 (7021); 8:253 (7021). On Ivan's death, see *PSRL*, 8:244 (7012); 12:258 (7012). Prince Boris's daughter, Anna, married. See *SGGD*, vol. 1, no. 131 (pp. 339–40); and Baumgarten, "Généalogies des branches régnantes de Rurikides," 18, 23–24.

32. Counting only those sons that lived to age fifteen.

33. J. Martin, *Medieval Russia*, 178–201, 219–22, 236–48; Ostrowski, "Systems of Succession in Rus' and Steppe Societies." Genealogical sources for the Daniilovichi include Julius Forssman, *Die Beziehungen altrussischer Fürstengeschlechter zu Westeuropa. Ein Beitrag zur Geschichte Ost- und Noreuropas im Mittelalter*; Dworzaczek, *Genealogia*; Baumgarten, "Généalogies des branches régnantes de Rurikides"; A. V. Ekzempliarskii, *Velikie i udel'nye kniaz'ia severnoi Rusi v tatarskii period, s 1238 po 1505 g.*

34. On the incident over the golden belt at Vasilii II's wedding, see, most recently, C. K. Woodworth, "Sophia and the Golden Belt: What Caused Moscow's Civil Wars of 1425–1450?" See also Kollmann, *Kinship and Politics*, 134; Veselovskii, *Issledovaniia po istorii klassa sluzhilykh zemlevladel'tsev*, 341; and *PSRL*, 26:189 (6941).

35. On the dynastic wars, see Halperin, *The Tatar Yoke: The Image of the Mongols in Medieval Russia*, 157–69; Iakov Solomonovich Lur'e, *Dve istorii Rossii XV-ogo veka rannie i pozdnie nezavisimye i ofitsial'nye letopisi po obrazovanii Moskovskogo gosudarstva* (especially chapter 2); Zimin, *Vitiaz' na rasput'e: feodal'naia voina v XV v.*; Keenan, "Muscovite Political Folkways"; Kollmann, *Kinship and Politics*, 108, 133–36, 153–59; Alef, "The Crisis of the Muscovite Aristocracy: A Factor in the Growth of Monarchical Power"; and idem, "A History of the Muscovite Civil War: The Reign of Vasilii II (1425–1462)."

36. Keenan, "Muscovite Political Folkways," 135.

37. Keenan, "Muscovite Political Folkways," 141.

38. One (Mikhail Andreevich, prince of Vereia) had been loyal to Vasilii II in the civil war and had married, though his issue moved to Lithuania; and the

other (Vasilii Iaroslavovich, prince of Borovsk and Serpukhov), although an ally of Vasilii II, was arrested in 1456 with three of his four sons, all of whom had died in prison by 1483, the fourth son escaping to Lithuania. See Kollmann, *Kinship and Politics*, 156–57; J. Martin, *Medieval Russia*, 237–48.

39. Baumgarten, "Généalogies des branches régnantes de Rurikides," 6.

40. The identity of Prince Iurii Patrikeev's bride is reported inconsistently in the sources. Some refer to her as Mariia, others (probably with more authority) as Anna. For Mariia: Karamzin, *Istoriia gosudarstva Rossiiskogo*, vol. 5, col. 109 and n. 254; Baumgarten, "Généalogies des branches régnantes de Rurikides," 18, 20, and n. 8. For Anna: *PSRL*, 24:232; *Vremennik Imperatorskogo moskovskogo obshchestva istorii i drevnostei rossiiskikh*, 10:80, 136, 225 ("Rodoslovnaia kniga" in *Materialy*); Kollmann, *Kinship and Politics*, 131. Baumgarten (op. cit.) refers to the bride as the daughter not of Vasilii I but of Dmitrii Donskoi.

41. Kollmann, Appendix 1, "The Calculation of Boyars' Ages," table A1.1 "Vital Statistics of Daniilovich Males," in *Kinship and Politics*, 192.

42. The original draft wedding *chin* does not report the day or month of the wedding, only that in January 7041/1533, Andrei Staritskii had petitioned Vasilii III to marry. RGADA, *fond* 135, sec. IV, rub. II, no. 4, fol. 1v. Some chronicles report that the wedding took place on February 22, but this is clearly a scribal error since these chronicles also state, by way of providing additional detail, that the wedding took place on the Sunday of the Publican and the Pharisee, a church feast that moves in accordance with the paschal cycle and fell in the year 7041 (1532/1533) on February 2. See *PSRL*, 8:282 n. 1 (7041); 13:68, and n. 1 (7041); 20:415. This date for the wedding is confirmed by the Extended Version (*Prostrannaia redaktsiia*) of the Muster Books (*Razriadnye knigi*), which puts the wedding on the Feast of the Presentation of the Lord (*Sretenie*), a feast that is canonically fixed to February 2. See *Razriadnaia kniga 1475–1605*, 1:233.

43. RGADA, *fond* 135, sec. IV, rub. II, no. 4, fol. 1v; R. Martin, "Royal Marriages and Crimean Diplomacy," 392–98, 414. *DRV* has the verb "preferred" in the singular (*poliubil*), as do other later copies of this text: *DRV*, 13:19; BAN, 16.15.15, fol. 78; BAN, 21.10.25, fol. 15v; BAN, 31.6.40, fol. 11v; BAN, 32.5.11; fol. 13v; BAN, 31.7.20, fol. 10. But see also BAN, 32.4.21, fol. 60, which has the plural (*poliubili*).

44. On the Khovanskii clan, see Zimin, *Formirovanie*, 29–35.

45. See Carol Belkin Stevens, *Russia's Wars of Emergence, 1460–1730*.

46. "Posol'stvo ot velikogo kniazia Ivana Vasil'evicha k koroliu Sigizmundu Kazimirovichu s blizhnim boiarinom Borisom Ivanovichem Sukinym" (September 16, 1543–June 1544)," *SbIRIO*, vol. 59, no. 15 (section III, pp. 221–33, at 228).

47. *PSRL*, 13:450 (7055).

48. *Pis'ma russkikh gosudarei i drugikh osob tsarskogo semeistva*, 3–5.

49. See RGADA, *fond* 135, sec. IV, rub. II, no. 2, fols. 6–7, 8; no. 5, fols. 1, 5, 6, 8, 55, 57; Nazarov, "Svadebnye dela XVI v.," 117–18, 119, 120, 121; *PSRL*,

13:450, 453 (7055). See also Karamzin, *Istoriia gosudarstva Rossiiskogo*, vol. 8, col. 58 and n. 164; and Zabelin, *Domashnii byt russkikh tsarits*, 212–13.

50. On the ancestors of Anastasiia, see Kollmann, *Kinship and Politics*, 100–103, 211–16; and Savelov, "Boiare Romanovykh i ikh rodstvennyia sviazi."

51. Kollmann, *Kinship and Politics*, 102, 175, 215.

52. Karamzin, *Istoriia gosudarstva Rossiiskogo*, vol. 8, col. 58. The "contemporaries" that Karamzin cites include unidentified chronicles and the speech of Metropolitan Makarii at the wedding in February 1547 (see n. 164).

53. Solov'ev, *Istorii Rossii s drevneishikh vremen*, 3:432–33.

54. Skrynnikov, *Ivan Groznyi*, 207.

55. Madariaga, *Ivan the Terrible*, 54. See also Liudmilla Evgen'evna Morozova and Boris Nikolaevich Morozov, *Ivan Groznyi i ego zheny*, 66–67, who split the difference, attributing Ivan IV's choice both to the "beauty, humility, and spiritual qualities of the bride" and to "her distinguished ancestry and her proximity to the grand princely court."

56. On the regency and Ivan IV's minority, see Mikhail Markovich Krom, *"Vdovstvuiushchee tsarstvo": politicheskii krizis v Rossii 30–40-kh godov XVI veka*; Halperin, "The Minority of Ivan IV"; Kollmann, "The Grand Prince in Muscovite Politics: The Problem of Genre in Sources of Ivan's Minority," 292–313.

57. Kollmann, *Kinship and Politics*, 167.

58. Kollmann, *Kinship and Politics*, 169–70. On Prince Vasilii Vasil'evich Shuiskii's marriage to Anastasiia Petrovna, see *PSRL*, 29:32 (7046).

59. Kollmann, *Kinship and Politics*, 174.

60. On these executions and exiles, see Kollmann, *Kinship and Politics*, 174.

61. Kollmann, *Kinship and Politics*, 127.

62. See Halperin, "The Minority of Ivan IV," 41.

63. For Paul I's law of succession (with Alexander I's addenda), see *PSZ*, series 1, 24:587–89, no. 17.910 (April 5, 1797); and 37:129–30, no. 28.208 (March 20, 1820).

64. *PSRL*, 8:119 (6955), 125 (6960). See also Levin, *Sex and Society*, 93–94.

65. The average age at first marriage for heirs apparent was 18.5 years (19.5 if we eliminate those who married younger than Ivan IV did; the mode was 17), and the average age for non–heirs apparent was 22.3 years (23.7 if, again, we eliminate marriages at ages younger than Ivan IV's; the modes were 18 and 22). See Kollmann, "The Calculation of Boyars' Ages," in *Kinship and Politics*, 192.

66. *DRV*, 13:36.

67. On Prince Ivan Fedorovich Paletskii, see Kollmann, *Kinship and Politics*, 224; Kleimola, "Kto Kogo: Patterns of Duma Recruitment, 1547–1564," 217; idem, "Patterns of Duma Recruitment, 1505–1550," 254; Zimin, "Sostav," 60; idem, *Formirovanie*, 43.

68. RGADA, *fond* 135, sec. IV, rub. II, no. 5, fol. 57; Nazarov, "Svadebnye dela XVI veka," 117 (document 8). On the links between the Gundorovs and Paletskiis, see Zimin, *Formirovanie*, 35–43.

69. *PSRL*, 13:325 (7068).

70. See Baumgarten, "Généalogies des branches régnantes de Rurikides," 12 (table II) and 18–19 (table III).

71. On this date, see BAN, 32.4.21, fols. 79–79v; and BAN, 16.15.15, fols. 103v–104. *DRV* 13:46 has the wedding on May 31, 7058/1550. Some sources report the date when Ivan IV commanded (*prigovoril*) Prince Vladimir to marry (September 10) incorrectly (as September 1). Compare BAN, 16.15.15, fol. 79; and BAN, 32.4.21, fol. 103; BAN, 21.10.25, fol. 40v, with BAN, 31.6.40, fol. 26; BAN, 32.5.11, fol. 31; BAN, 31.7.20, fol. 27; IaOB, RK319031V, fol. 55; and *DRV*, 13:46.

72. *DRV*, 13:46. The surviving wedding description for Vladimir Staritskii's second wedding, a *razriad*, does not report whether a bride-show was held or not.

73. These lines do not appear in *DRV*, 13:46, but do in BAN, 32.4.21, fols. 79–79v; and BAN, 16.15.15, fols. 103–103v.

74. RGADA, *fond* 135, sec. IV, rub. II, no. 5, fol. 26; Bychkova, *Sostav klassa feodalov*, 142; *DRV*, 13:33.

75. Fedor Mikhailovich Nagoi's rank as a boyar is inconsistently reported in the sources. See Kollmann, *Kinship and Politics*, 222.

76. Sources indicate that the wedding took place on April 21, the Sunday after Easter, which in 1555 fell on April 14 (BAN, 16.15.15, fol. 146v; BAN, 32.4.21, fol. 109). Other sources report the date variously: for April 22, see BAN, 21.10.25, fol. 69; BAN, 31.6.40, fol. 43; BAN, 31.7.20, fol. 45v; BAN, 32.5.11, fol. 54; IaOB, RK319031V, fol. 102; *DRV*, 13:80. For April 28, see Baumgarten, "Généalogies des branches régnantes de Rurikides," 19 (table III), 25. Some sources also misidentify the year (7063/1555): BAN, 31.7.20, fol. 45v (7066); BAN, 32.5.11, fol. 54 (7066); IaOB, RK319031V, fol. 102 (7066); *DRV*, 13:80 (7066/1558). On Evdokiia Nagaia's death, see sources cited in Baumgarten, "Généalogies des branches régnantes de Rurikides," 25.

77. On the sources for Vladimir Staritskii's second wedding, see R. Martin, "Archival Sleuths and Documentary Transpositions," 294–95; and idem, "Muscovite Royal Weddings," 122–23. For Ivan IV's musters, see *DRV*, 13:29, 86.

78. Kleimola, "Reliance on the Tried and True," 59, 62; Zimin, "Sostav," 75, 77.

79. Crummey, *Aristocrats and Servitors*, 120. In the seventeenth century, the Odoevskiis would place numerous members in Duma ranks and be among the wealthiest aristocratic families in Russia (see pp. 30, 72–74, 113–21, and elsewhere).

80. Baumgarten, "Généalogies des branches régnantes de Rurikides," 19 (table III), 27.

81. Sergei Bogatyrev, "Reinventing the Russian Monarchy in the 1550s: Ivan the Terrible, the Dynasty, and the Church," 292.

82. Bogatyrev, "Reinventing the Russian Monarchy," 279.

83. Bogatyrev, "Reinventing the Russian Monarchy," 292.

84. Bogatyrev, "Reinventing the Russian Monarchy," 279, 280, 283, 292. See also idem, "Micro-Periodization and Dynasticism: Was There a Divide in the Reign of Ivan the Terrible?"

85. Kollmann, *Kinship and Politics*, 158; idem, "Divides and Ends: The Problem of Periodization"; and Bogatyrev, "Micro-Periodization and Dynasticism," 402–3.

86. On the date of Vladimir's execution, see Skrynnikov, *Tsarstvo terrora*, 355–56, 387 n. 78. The number of children who died with Vladimir Staritskii and his second wife has been reported variously. See Kollmann, *Kinship and Politics*, 158; Piskarevskii Chronicle, in *Materialy po istorii SSSR*, vol. 2: *Dokumenty po istorii XV–XVII vv.*, 76–78, 160–62 (nn. 62–65 and 67–69); Baumgarten, "Généalogies des branches régnantes de Rurikides," 18 (table III), 27; Włodzimierz Dworzaczek, *Genealogia. Tablice*, 23; Forssman, *Die Beziehungen altrussischer Fürstengeschlechter zu Westeuropa*, Tafel X.

87. The date of Efrosiniia's execution varies in sources, some reporting October 9, others October 11, still another October 20. See Skrynnikov, *Tsarstvo terrora*, 387 n. 79.

88. On Anastasiia's death, see *PSRL*, 4:312 (7069); and *Letopisets russkii (Moskovskaia letopis' 1552–1562 gg. Po rukopisi, prinadlezhashchei A. N. Lebedevu)*, in *ChIOIDR*, vol. 174 (1895, bk. 3), 140 (Materialy istoricheskie).

89. On Ivan IV's and Anastasiia's children: for Anna, *PSRL*, 13:158 (7058), 20:475 (7057), 20:478 (7058); for Mariia, *PSRL*, 20:478 (7059); for Dmitrii, *PSRL*, 13:222–23, 232 (7061); 20:533, 541 (7061); *ChIOIDR*, vol. 174 (1895, bk. 3), 6 (Materialy istoricheskie); for Ivan, *PSRL*, 13:239 (7062); 20:547 (7062); for Evdokiia, *PSRL*, 13:265 (7064), 299–300 (7066); 20:547 (7062); for Fedor, *PSRL*, 13:283 (7065); 20:583 (7065); *ChIOIDR*, vol. 174 (1895, bk. 3), 74 (Materialy istoricheskie). See also Baumgarten, "Généalogies des branches régnantes de Rurikides," 19–18 (table III), and 26–27.

90. *PSRL* 13:329 (7068); and *ChIOIDR*, vol. 174 (1895, bk. 3), 142 (Materialy istoricheskie).

91. See Karamzin, *Istoriia gosudarstva Rossiiskogo*, vol. 9, cols. 1–30, and nn. 22 and 28; Madariaga, *Ivan the Terrible*, 143–44; Skrynnikov, *Tsarstvo terrora*, 139–40; Veselovskii, *Issledovaniia po istorii oprichniny*, 95; *Perepiska Ivana Groznogo s Andreem Kurbskim*, Ia. S. Lur'e and Iu. D. Rykov, eds., 8 (and 379 n. 14), 46 (and 403 n. 122), and 104 (and 406 n. 11); Horsey, "Travels," 304.

92. The narrative evidence from the "Tale of the Marriage of Ivan the Terrible with Mariia Temriukovna" is late and unreliable, though interesting as a literary monument of the late seventeenth century. See S. K. Rosovetskii, "Povest' o zhenit'be Ivana Groznogo na Marii Temriukovne."

93. See Madariaga, *Ivan the Terrible*, 144.

94. See Alexander Filjushkin, *Ivan the Terrible: A Military History*, 172;

Madariaga, *Ivan the Terrible*, 192; "Pamiatniki diplomatichskikh snoshenii Moskovskogo gosudarstva s Pol'sko-Litovskim gosudarstvom," vol. 3: "1560–1671 gg.," *SbIRIO*, vol. 71, no. 3 (pp. 23–46, at 31), nos. 8–9 (pp. 131–63, at 143–56).

95. Karamzin, *Istoriia gosudarstva Rossiiskogo*, vol. 9, n. 24.

96. See Isenburg, *Europäische Stammtafeln*, vol. 2, Tafeln 85, 87, and 98.

97. Karamzin, *Istoriia gosudarstva Rossiiskogo*, vol. 9, col. 9.

98. *PSRL*, 13:330 (7068).

99. Erik XIV had two sisters that may have been considered in 1560: Katharina (born 1539) and Caecilie (born 1540). See Isenburg, *Europäische Stammtafeln*, vol. 2, Tafel 79.

100. *PSRL*, 13:329–30 (7068). See also Bushkovitch, "Princes Cherkasskii or Circassian Murzas," 11–14.

101. *PSRL*, 13:331 (7069); *ChIOIDR*, vol. 174 (1895, bk. 3), 145 (Materialy istoricheskie).

102. *PSRL*, 13:331 (7069).

103. *PSRL*, 13:331 (7069).

104. Ekaterina Nikolaevna Kusheva, *Narody severnogo Kavkaza i ikh sviazi s Rossiei: vtoraia polovina XVI—30-gody XVII veka*, 179–256. *Kabardino-russkie otnosheniia v XVI–XVIII vv.: dokumenty i materialy*, vol. 1.

105. *PSRL*, 13:333 (7069); *ChIOIDR*, vol. 174 (1895, bk. 3), 147–48 (Materialy istoricheskie).

106. *PSRL*, 13:333 (7069); *ChIOIDR*, vol. 174 (1895, bk. 3), 147–48 (Materialy istoricheskie). A fragment of the wedding muster survives (RNB, Titov Collection, no. 891, fol. 326v).

107. Veselovskii, *Issledovaniia po istorii oprichniny,* 295–96. Bogatyrev doubts Veselovskii's speculation. "Micro-Periodization and Dynasticism," 406 n. 36.

108. In addition to Veselovskii, *op. cit.*, see Bushkovitch, "Princes Cherkasskii or Circassian Murzas," 15; Zimin, *V kanun groznykh potriasenii*, 52; Savelov, "Boiare Romanovykh i ikh rodstvennyia sviazi," 238, 240.

109. *PSRL*, 13:365, 366 (7071).

110. On Mariia Temriukovna's death, see Karamzin, *Istoriia gosudarstva Rossiiskogo*, vol. 9, col. 81 and n. 269; and Baumgarten, "Généalogies des branches régnantes de Rurikides," 18–19 (table III) and 24 (note 36). Madariaga has her death on September 9, 1569. Madariaga, *Ivan the Terrible*, 242.

111. On Tsarevich Ivan Ivanovich and Virginia Eriksdotter, see Karamzin, *Istoriia gosudarstva Rossiiskogo*, vol. 9, col. 72, and n. 239; "Pamiatniki diplomaticheskikh snoshenii Moskovskogo gosudarstva s Shvedskim gosudarstvom," vol. 1: "1556–1586 gg.," *SbIRIO*, vol. 129, nos. 11–16 (pp. 123, 127, 136–37, 138–44, 149–61, 163–67, 171, 178–79, 183–85, 190, 192, 196, 206–7, 216–19).

112. On Erik XIV's willingness to hand over his sister-in-law, Catherine, see *SbIRIO*, vol. 71, nos. 1, 2, 3, 12, 18, 19, 25 (pp. 8–9, 10–20, 31–46, 187–89, 220, 262–63, 447–51, 469–71, 506–18, 800–807).

113. Karamzin, *Istoriia gosudarstva Rossiiskogo*, vol. 9, cols. 72–73.

114. Bodil Nävdal-Larsen, *Erik XIV, Ivan Groznyj og Katarina Jagellonica*, 54–85.

115. Zimin, *Oprichnina Ivana Groznogo*, 261.

116. Madariaga, *Ivan the Terrible*, 212–14.

117. Nävdal-Larsen, *Erik XIV, Ivan Groznyj og Katarina Jagellonica*, 4–17.

Chapter 4

1. Reinoldi Heidensteini, *De Bello Moscovitico quod Stephanus rex Poloniæ gessit Commentariorum libri VI*, 100; Geidenshtein, "Zapiski o Moskovskoi voine," 194–95. The passage also appears in Karamzin, *Istoriia gosudarstva Rossiiskogo*, vol. 9, n. 554.

2. See Karamzin, *Istoriia gosudarstva Rossiiskogo*, vols. 8 and 9. See also Viacheslav Valentinovich Shaposhnik, *Ivan Groznyi. Pervyi russkii tsar'*, 80–203; Madariaga, *Ivan the Terrible*, 60–159; Andrei Pavlov and Maureen Perrie, *Ivan the Terrible*, 55–106, esp. 94–95; Floria, *Ivan Groznyi*, 28–136; Zimin, *Reformy Ivana Groznogo. Ocherki sotsial'no-ekonomicheskoi i politicheskoi istorii Rossii serediny XVI v.*; and idem, *Oprichnina Ivana Groznogo*. The "good Ivan" and "bad Ivan" can also be found in *Prince A. M. Kurbsky's History of Ivan IV*, ed. J. L. I. Fennell, 152–58. The influence of the text of the *History of Ivan IV* on Karamzin and subsequent authors is independent of any considerations of the text's authenticity, which has been called into question. See Keenan, "Putting Kurbskii in His Place, or: Observations and Suggestions concerning the Place of the *History of the Grand Prince of Moscow* in the History of Muscovite Literary Culture"; and Brian Boeck, "Eyewitness or False Witness? Two Lives of Metropolitan Filipp of Moscow."

3. See Heinrich von Staden, *Aufzeichungen über den Moskauer Staat*, 19–20; idem, *The Land and Government of Muscovy*, 17–18; and Ostrowski, *Muscovy and the Mongols*, 193.

4. This representation of Ivan IV's matrimonial woes can be found in different measures in the biographical works cited below, and in popular biographies like Robert Payne and Nikita Romanov, *Ivan the Terrible*. The lone source for Ivan IV's purported proposal to the queen herself is Horsey, in "Travels," 279–80. See also Pavlov and Perrie, *Ivan the Terrible*, 195–96; and "Pamiatniki diplomaticheskikh snoshenii Moskovskogo gosudarstva s Anglieiu," vol. 2: "(s 1581–1604 god)," *SbIRIO*, vol. 38 (pp. 3–9, 65–70).

5. Serious studies of Ivan's family life include Kaiser, "Symbol and Ritual in the Marriages of Ivan IV"; Veselovskii, *Issledovaniia po istorii oprichniny*, 292–301; Keenan, "Ivan the Terrible and His Women." See also Keenan, "Vita: Ivan Vasil'evich. Terrible Czar: 1530–1584." For the wedding descriptions in the *Domostroi*, see Pouncy, *Domostroi*, 204–39. Some of the more popular works include S. Gorskii, *Zheny Ioanna Groznogo*; Nikolai Aleksandrovich Vasetskii,

Zhenshchiny: vo vlasti i bezvlastii, 26–54; Daniil Lukich Mordovtsev, *Russkie istoricheskie zhenshchiny. Populiarnye raskazy iz russkoi istorii: zhenshchiny do-petrovskoi Rusi*, 110–27; and Sergei Nechaev, *Ivan Groznyi: Zheny i nalozhnitsy "Sinei Borody."* The best by far among the popular works is Morozova and Morozov, *Ivan Groznyi i ego zheny*.

6. See the condemnation of third marriages in Theophanes, *Chronographia*, 1:442–43; and Meyendorff, *Marriage: An Orthodox Perspective*, 44–57.

7. *DRV*, 13:105; *AAE*, vol. 1, no. 284 (at 329). Grand Prince Simeon (ruled 1341–1353) also married three times (in 1333, 1345, and 1347), the second and third of which were in their own ways also controversial. See *PSRL*, 7:209 (6853, Voskresenskaia Chronicle); 23:107 (6853); 24:118 (6853) (first marriage); 7:209 (6853), 210 (6854); 10:216 (6853); 23:107 (6853); 24:118 (6853) (second marriage); 7:210 (6855); 8:72 (6907); 10:218 (6855); 23:108 (6855), 137 (6907); 24:119 (6855) (third marriage). See also N. S. Borisov, "Moskovskie kniaz'ia i russkie mitropolity XIV veka," 36–37; Karamzin, *Istoriia gosudarstvo Rossiiskogo*, vol. 4, cols. 169, 145–46, and nn. 364 and 365.

8. *Poslanie Ioganna Taube i Elberta Kruze*, ed. and trans. M. G. Roginskii, 55; *AAE*, vol. 1, no. 284 (at 329). Staden, *O Moskve Ivana Groznogo. Zapiski nemtsa-oprichnika*, 95. See also Ostrowski, *Muscovy and the Mongols*, 83; Skrynnikov, *Oprichnyi terror*, 141; Zabelin, *Domashnii byt russkikh tsarits*, 214–15; Karamzin, *Istoriia gosudarstva Rossiiskogo*, vol. 9, col. 110, and n. 354; Zimin, *Oprichnina Ivana Groznogo*, 348–49; and Veselovskii, *Issledovaniia po istorii oprichniny*, 308.

9. See Taube and Kruse, *Poslanie*, 55. See also Skrynnikov, *Oprichnyi terror*, 141; Zimin, *Oprichnina Ivana Groznogo*, 348–49.

10. *RRK*, 4:197–204.

11. On the date of Ivan IV's wedding, see *PSRL*, 3:167 (7080, Second Novgorodskaia Chronicle); *DRV*, 13:86 (lists month, not day); and *Novgorodskie letopisi (tak nazyvaemye Novgorodskaia vtoraia i Novgorodskaia tret'ia letopisi)*, 107–8 (has 28 October). See also Morozova and Morozov, *Ivan Groznyi i ego zheny*, 168; Skrynnikov, *Tsarstvo terrora*, 435; idem, *Oprichnyi terror*, 142 and n. 2; and Baumgarten, "Généalogies des branches régnantes de Rurikides," 18–19 (table III) and 24 (note 36).

12. The extant ceremonial for Tsarevich Ivan Ivanovich reports only November 1571 for the date of the wedding, but *Novgorodskie letopisi* (107–8) reports November 4. See also Skrynnikov, *Oprichnyi terror*, 142; Zimin *Oprichnina Ivana Groznogo*, 466; Veselovskii, *Issledovaniia po istorii oprichniny*, 300; Karamzin, *Istoriia gosudarstva Rossiiskogo*, vol. 9, cols. 110, 111, and nn. 364 and 367. Taube and Kruse say that the tsarevich's wedding took place on St. Mikhail's day, or November 8 (*Poslanie*, 55).

13. *PSRL*, 13:24 (6946: Nikonovskaia Chronicle); *DDG*, no. 61 (p. 198). See also Morozova and Morozov, *Ivan Groznyi i ego zheny*, 166–67; Kollmann, *Kinship and Politics*, 111, 136, 207, 211; and, by contrast, Robert Craig Howes,

trans. and ed., *The Testaments of the Grand Princes of Moscow*, 261.

14. *Tysiachnaia kniga 1550 g. i Dvorovaia tetrad' 50-x godov XVI v.*, ed. A. A. Zimin, 158–59 (fol. 118v), 195–96 (fol. 146), 201 (fol. 151) (Dvorovaia tetrad').

15. "Rodoslovnaia kniga po spisku kniazia M. A. Obolenskogo," in A. V. Antonov, ed., *Pamiatniki istorii russkogo sluzhilogo sosloviia*, 10–170 (at 112); Veselovskii, *Issledovaniia po istorii oprichniny*, 445–46; S. D. Sheremetev, "Po povodu rodosloviia Nagikh," *Izvestiia RGO*, vol. 1 (1900): 3–6 (otdel I); G. V. Meshcherinov, "K rodosloviiu Nagikh," *Izvestiia RGO*, vol. 2 (1903): 10–12 (otdel I); I. S. Beliaev, "K rodosloviiu Nagikh," *Izvestiia RGO*, vol. 3 (1909): 88–92 (otdel I) (see also D. F. Kobeko's "Primechanie," on pp. 92–93); N. V. Miatlev, "K rodosloviiu Nagikh," *Izvestiia RGO*, vol. 4 (1911): 71–91 (otdel I); Lobanov-Rostovskii, *Russkaia rodoslovnaia kniga*, 1:236–38, 296–99.

16. *Sbornik materialov po istorii predkov tsaria Mikhaila Feodorovicha Romanova*, ed. N. N. Selifontov, pt. 1, 235–36; Morozova and Morozov, *Ivan Groznyi i ego zheny*, 166–67.

17. See, for example, Pushkareva, *Women in Russian History*, 72; Howes, *Testaments of the Grand Princes of Moscow*, 324 n. 57; Zabelin, *Domashnii byt russkikh tsarits*, 214; Solov'ev, *Istoriia Rossii s drevneishikh vremen*, 3:702. These claims appear to have derived from the *Chronograph of the Weddings of Ivan Vasil'evich*, a probable forgery that is published in Appendix 1.

18. *DRV*, 13:86–97. The 12 Sobakins were Kallist Vasil'evich (groom's best man, *druzhka*); Kallist's wife, Sofiia (matchmaker, *svakha*); Ivan Dmitreevich (carried the showering, *osypalo*); boyar Vasilii Stepanovich (seated at the side table, *v Krivom stole*); *okol'nichii* Grigorii Vasil'evich (seated at the side table); *okol'nichii* Vasilii Stepanovich (seated at the side table); Boris Vasil'ev syn (processed in front of groom and was with the groom in the baths); Parfenii Ivanov syn (processed in front of groom, was with the groom in the baths, and carried the bolster, *zgolov'e*, to the church); Stepan Vasil'ev syn (processed in front of groom and carried the bolster to the church); Nikita Dmitriev syn (processed behind the sled and attended to nuptial bed); Semen Vasil'ev syn (held the cap, *kolpak*, carried the betrothal candles to the banquet hall and to the church); Petr Vasil'ev syn (held the 40 sables, heated and tended the baths). Morozova and Morozov claimed there were 14 Sobakins at the wedding (*Ivan Groznyi i ego zheny*, 167); Zimin says 11 but was probably omitting Sofiia, the wife of Kallist Sobakin (*Oprichnina Ivana Groznogo*, 350 n. 4).

19. *DRV*, 13:88.

20. BAN, 16.15.15, fols. 161–174v; and BAN, 32.4.21, fols. 119v–127.

21. BAN, 16.15.15, fols. 161–161v. Tsar Ivan IV sat "*na Bol'shom meste*" (see fol. 163v). On Tsarevich Fedor Ivanovich, see fol. 161v; on Fr. Timofei, see fols. 166v–167; on Domna, see fols. 163–64.

22. On these posts, see Ivan Petrovich Sakharov, ed., *Skazaniia russkogo naroda*, 1–25. On the chancellery staff's work on wedding documentation, see R.

Martin, "Choreographing the 'Tsar's Happy Occasion'," "Archival Sleuths," and "Royal Weddings and Crimean Diplomacy."

23. BAN, 16.15.15, fol. 155; BAN, 32.4.21, fol. 115v; and RGADA, *fond* 181, no. 123, fol. 3.

24. On Metropolitan Makarii at Ivan IV's first wedding, see RGADA, *fond* 135, sec. IV, rub. II, no. 5, fol. 10; *PSRL*, 20:470 (7055, L'vovskaia Chronicle); and Bogatyrev, "Reinventing the Russian Monarchy in the 1550s," 273–82. On Makarii at Ivan IV's second wedding, see *Letopisets russkii (Moskovskaia letopis' 1552–1562 gg.), ChIOIDR*, vol. 185 (1895, bk. 3), 148. See also *DRV*, 13:9 (Vasilii III), 13:42 (Iurii Vasil'evich), 13:24 (Andrei Staritskii), and 13:51 (Vladimir Staritskii).

25. Fr. Timofei is identified as both the tsar's and the tsarevich's *dukhovnik* (BAN, 16.15.15, fol. 166v; BAN, 32.4.21, fol. 120). Fr. Timofei is not, however, listed among Ivan IV's confessors according to S. Smirnov, *Drevne-russkii dukhovnik*, 251–52.

26. The exceptions being the First False Dmitrii's marriage to Marina Mniszek in 1606 (*DRV*, 13:116; Dunning, *Russia's First Civil War*, 214); Fedor III Alekseevich's to Agafiia Simeonovna Grushetskaia in 1680 (*DRV*, 11:192); and Tsar Ivan V Alekseevich's to Praskov'ia Fedorovna Saltykova in 1684 (*DRV*, 11:196). In each of these cases the marriage ritual was being exploited to serve immediate dynastic goals (the First False Dmitrii asserting his legitimacy and identity through links to Patriarch Ignatii; Fedor III compensating for the entirely new, and greatly reduced, wedding ritual; and Ivan V, or his sister, Sofiia Alekseevna, putting on a glittering wedding to show up their rival half brother, Peter I). As for Tsar Vasilii Shuiskii in 1608, the wedding muster does not identify who officiated at the wedding and reports only that the tsar's father-confessor, Archpriest Kondratii of the Cathedral of the Annunciation, carried the holy water in the procession to the Granovitaia Palata. Patriarch Hermogen, a staunch supporter of Shuiskii, was involved in the early consultations on the marriage and gave his blessing on the union. RGADA, *fond* 135, sec. IV, rub. II, no. 13, fol 6; and Belokurov, *Razriadnye zapisi za Smutnoe vremia*, 270.

27. Skrynnikov, *Oprichnyi terror*, 141 and n. 4.

28. *RRK,* 1:235; 4:319–20; Lobanov-Rostovskii, *Russkaia rodoslovnaia kniga*, 2:99–100; Veselovskii, *Issledovaniia po istorii oprichniny*, 298.

29. On Sobakina's death, see *PSRL*, 3:167 (7080, Second Novgorodskaia Chronicle); and *Novgorodskie letopisi,* 108.

30. *DRV*, 13:104–5.

31. Zabelin, *Domashnii byt russkikh tsarits*, 218–19; Karamzin, *Istoriia gosudarstva Rossiiskogo*, vol. 9, col. 110; Veselovskii, *Issledovaniia po istorii oprichniny*, 300; idem, "Dukhovnoe zaveshchanie Ivana Groznogo kak istoricheskii istochnik," *Izvestiia AN SSSR* 4, no. 6 (1947): 505–20.

32. *AAE*, vol. 1, no. 333 (p. 402); *AI*, vol. 1, no. 218 (414–15); *RIB*, 32:644–45; V. Georgievskii, "Ikony Ioanna Groznogo i ego sem'i v Suzdale,"

3–21 (which has 1619 as her date of death); Karamzin, *Istoriia gosudarstva Rossiiskogo*, vol. 9, cols. 210–11 and nn. 364, 367, and 609 (has 1620 for her death); *RRK*, 4:204 (has 1619 for her death); Thyrêt, "Royal Women of Ivan IV's Family," 161–62 (has 1619 for her death); *Vremennik Ivana Timofeeva*, 19–23, 459 nn. 33–35.

33. Meyendorff, "Christian Marriage in Byzantium: The Canonical and Liturgical Tradition," 102.

34. L. G. Westerink, *Nicholas I, Patriarch of Constantinople: Miscellaneous Writings*, vol. 6 of *Dumbarton Oaks Texts*, xiv–xix, 57–85; and Meyendorff, "Christian Marriage in Byzantium," 102.

35. Westerink, *Nicholas I*, 63.

36. E. B. Emchenko, *Stoglav: Issledovanie i tekst*, 284.

37. Emchenko, *Stoglav*, 284–85.

38. Emchenko, *Stoglav*, 283.

39. *DRV*, 13:104; *AAE*, vol. 1, no. 284 (at 329–31); Solov'ev, *Istoriia Rossii s drevneishikh vremen*, 3:702.

40. *DRV*, 13:105; *AAE*, vol. 1, no. 284 (at 329).

41. Levin, *Sex and Society*, 109, 111–13.

42. *DRV*, 13:105; Karamzin, *Istoriia gosudarstva Rossiiskogo*, vol. 9, n. 380; Skrynnikov, *Tsarstvo terrora*, 257.

43. *DRV*, 13:106–7; *AAE*, vol. 1, no. 284 (at 330).

44. The precise meaning of the lesser and greater antidora is not entirely clear. The lesser antidorum probably refers to the small particle of unconsecrated bread distributed to the faithful by the bishop or priest after one communes, but it may also refer to bread given the faithful during the vigil service (*vsenoshchnoe bdenie*) on the eves of feast days. The greater antidorum may refer to the consecrated bread used during Proskomedia—the preparatory service just before the Eucharistic liturgy.

45. *DRV*, 13:108–9; *AAE*, vol. 1, no. 284 (at 330–31).

46. On the date of the Koltovskaia wedding, see Morozova and Morozov, *Ivan Groznyi i ego zheny*, 176–78; and Karamzin, *Istoriia gosudarstva Rossiiskogo*, vol. 9, cols. 114–15, and n. 380.

47. Alterations to the southern end of the portico of the Church of the Annunciation (*Blagoveshchenskii sobor*), the private chapel of the royal family, have often been attributed to Ivan IV's penance for his marriage to Koltovskaia, but archeological studies of the church date the renovations to an earlier time. See I. A. Sterligova and L. A. Shchennikova, eds., *Tsarskii khram: Blagoveshchenskii sobor Moskovskogo kremlia v istorii Russkoi kul'tury*; I. Ia. Kachalova, N. A. Maiasova, and L. A. Shchennikova, *Blagoveshchenskii Sobor Moskovskogo kremlia: k 500-letiiu unikal'nogo pamiatnika russkoi kul'tury*, 6–97.

48. Antonio Possevino, *The Moscovia of Antonio Possevino, S. J.*, 48.

49. Morozova and Morozov, *Ivan Groznyi i ego zheny*, 178. See also the genealogy in Bychkova, *Sostav klassa feodalov*, 135 (based on RGADA, *fond*

210, *op.* 18, nos. 18 and 46). See also N. P. Likhachev, *"Gosudarev rodoslovets" i rod Adashevykh*, 94.

50. *Tysiachnaia kniga 1550 g. i Dvorovaia tetrad' 50-x godov XVI v.*, 159, 160, 162, 164, 164; *Razriadnaia Kniga 1475–1598 gg.*, ed. V. I. Buganov, 187, 238, 244, 285, 292, 323, and elsewhere; Zimin, *Oprichnina Ivana Groznogo*, 470; Morozova and Morozov, *Ivan Groznyi i ego zheny*, 178; Bychkova, *Sostav klassa feodalov*, 134–37.

51. Bychkova, *Sostav klassa feodalov*, 134–37 (quote at 137).

52. The recent claim that a muster for this wedding exists is erroneous. See Iurii Vladimirovich Ankhimiuk, *Chastnye Razriadnye knigi s zapisami za posledniuiu chetvert' XV–nachalo XVII vekov*, 239–41. Compare with Viktor Ivanovich Buganov, *Razriadnye knigi poslednei chetverti XV–nachale XVII v.*, 62–63. The manuscript in question (RNB, Q.IV.86, fols. 269v–276v) includes a previously unknown copy of the ceremonial (*chin*) joined with a complete version of the muster (*razriad*) for Ivan IV's wedding with Anna Vasil'chikova. Other known copies of the muster are incomplete. See RGADA, *fond* 135, sec. IV, rub. II, no. 3, fols. 9–10; no. 11, fols. 1–28; RGADA, *fond* 156, *op.* 1, no. 1, fols. 6–7; no. 5, fols. 1–17, 18–41; and A. A. Vasil'chikov, ed., "Chin brakosochetaniia tsaria Ivana Vasil'evicha s tsaritseiu Annoiu Vasil'chikovykh (7083/1575 g.)."

53. See, for example, Madariaga, *Ivan the Terrible*, 276; and Pushkareva, *Women in Russian History*, 73.

54. Bychkova, *Sostav klassa feodalov*, 134–37; Veselovskii, *Issledovaniia po istorii oprichniny*, 299–300; Morozova and Morozov, *Ivan Groznyi i ego zheny*, 181–82; *DRV*, 13:97–103.

55. On the date of Koltovskaia's repudiation by Ivan IV, see Morozova and Morozov, *Ivan Groznyi i ego zheny*, 193; Pavlov and Perrie, *Ivan the Terrible*, 192; and Madariaga, *Ivan the Terrible*, 281 (who cites Horsey as her source, though he had nothing to say about Koltovskaia). Skrynnikov and some others have suggested that Koltovskaia was repudiated in 1574. See Skrynnikov, *Tsarstvo terrora*, 471; Thyrêt, "Royal Women of Ivan IV's Family," 163; and Baumgarten, "Généalogies des branches régnantes de Rurikides," 18–19 (table III) and 24 (note 36). The later date for Koltovskaia's tonsure is based, evidently, on a speculative note in Karamzin, *Istoriia gosudarstva Rossiiskogo*, vol. 9, n. 393. In an early study, Skrynnikov had the view that the marriage lasted less than one year. Skrynnikov, *Ivan Groznyi*, 210.

56. See R. Martin, "Gifts for Kith and Kin: Gift Exchanges and Social Integration in Muscovite Royal Weddings"; and RGADA, *fond* 135, sec. IV, rub. II, nos. 14, 15, and 19.

57. Thyrêt, "The Royal Women of Ivan IV's Family," 163–68 (quote at 166–67). On Anna Koltovskaia's life after her tonsuring, see A. V. Mashtafarov, "Dariia," in *Pravoslavnaia entsiklopediia*, 14:199–201.

58. *DRV*, 97–103; D. Tsvetaev, "Mariia Vladimirovna i Magnus Datskii," *ZhMNP* 196 (March 1879): 57–85; Karamzin, *Istoriia gosudarstva Rossiiskogo*, vol.

9, cols. 104, 130. See also Isenburg, *Europäische Stammtafeln*, vol. 2, table 72.

59. Filjushkin, *Ivan the Terrible: A Military History*, 166–74; Stevens, *Russia's Wars of Emergence*, 85–92.

60. The name of the elder daughter is reported variously. Most sources call her Efimiia. Karamzin, *Istoriia gosudarstva Rossiiskogo*, vol. 9, cols. 101, 104, and nn. 335, 344; Tsvetaev, "Mariia Vladimirovna i Magnus Datskii," 61; Skrynnikov, *Tsarstvo terrora,* 478; Baumgarten, "Généalogies des branches regnantes de Rurikides," 19. Others prefer Evdokiia. Zimin, *Oprichnina Ivana Groznogo*, 433 n. 5, presumably on the basis of a grave inscription. See V. B. Girshberg, "Materialy dlia svoda nadpisei na kamennykh plitakh Moskvy" (no. 133, pp. 60–61). Tsvetaev considered the inscription, which was a later addition to the grave site, to be wrong (*op. cit*., 85).

61. On her death, see Karamzin, *Istoriia gosudarstva Rossiiskogo*, vol. 9, cols. 101, 105, and nn. 335 and 344.

62. On the marriage rites, see R. Martin, "Ritual and Religion," 366–71.

63. Iu. N. Shcherbachev, "Kopengagenskie akty, otnosiashchiesia do russkoi istorii (1326–1569)," pt. 2, *ChIOIDR*, vol. 257 (1916, bk. 2), 34.

64. Skrynnikov, "Samoderzhavie i Oprichnina," in N. E. Nosov, ed., *Vnutrenniaia politika tsarizma (seredina XVI–nachalo XX vv.)*, 69–99; and idem, *Tsarstvo terrora*, 430, 494.

65. See Madariaga, *Ivan the Terrible*, 267, 300–301; Skrynnikov, *Rossiia posle oprichniny*, 20–36; idem, *Tsarstvo terrora*, 494, 508; Zimin, *Oprichnina Ivana Groznogo*, 432.

66. See Magnus's own account of his Muscovite odyssey: Frede P. Jensen, ed., "Hertug Magnus af Holstens forsvarsskift af 1579 om hans forhold til tsar Ivan den Grusomme." See also Madariaga, *Ivan the Terrible*, 254–55; and Skrynnikov, *Oprichnyi terror*, 399.

67. Karamzin, *Istoriia gosudarstva Rossiiskogo*, vol. 10, col. 48. Horsey, "Travels," 315–17.

68. See Tsvetaev, "Mariia Vladimirovna i Magnus Datskii," *ZhMNP*, 57–85 (at 77–85); Karamzin, *Istoriia gosudarstva Rossiiskogo*, vol. 9, n. 506; vol. 10, col. 48, and n. 152; Baumgarten, "Généalogies des branches régnantes de Rurikides," 27; *PSRL*, 34:572 (7077, Piskarevskii Chronicle); and *Materialy po istorii SSSR*, vol. 2 (Piskarevskii Chronicle), 78 and 161 n. 66. The family of Mariia Staritskaia is included in the entry for the family of Prince Andrei Staritskii (Mariia's grandfather) in a seventeenth-century sinodikon from the Holy Trinity–St. Sergius Monastery, see RGB, *fond* 304, *op*. 1, no. 814, fols. 126v–127.

69. Fletcher, "Of the Russe Commonwealth," 129.

70. Muster: BAN, 16.15.15, fols. 178v–183; BAN, 32.4.21, fols. 133–37; BAN, 21.10.25, fols. 81–87; BAN, 31.7.20, fols. 50v–53; BAN, 31.6.40, fols. 49–52v; BAN, 32.5.11, fols. 61–65v; RGADA, *fond* 135, sec. IV, rub. II, no. 10, fols. 1–3; and *DRV*, 13:97–103; *Razriadnaia kniga 1475–1605 gg*., 2:329–35. For the ceremonial: BAN, 16.15.15, fols. 175–78v; BAN, 32.4.21, fols. 129v–132.

71. *PSRL*, 34:572 (7077); *Materialy po istorii SSSR*, vol. 2 (Piskarevskii Chronicle), 78.

72. S. I. Khazanova, "Oprichnina v Piskarevskom letopistse i letopisanie XVII veka," 58; Tikhomirov, "Piskarevskii letopisets kak istoricheskii istochnik o sobytiiakh XVI–nachala XVII v.," 238; *Materialy po istorii SSSR*, vol. 2 (Piskarevskii Chronicle), 161 nn. 64, 67 (commentary by O. A. Iakovleva).

73. See, for example, A. E., "Vasil'chikova (Anna)," *Entsiklopedicheskii slovar'*, 5:620. On the Vasil'chikovs, see Zimin, *V kanun groznykh potriasenii*, 14.

74. RGADA, *fond* 135, sec. IV, rub. II, no. 11, fols. 1–28, published in Vasil'chikov, "Chin brakosochetaniia tsaria Ivana Vasil'evicha s tsaritseiu Annoiu Vasil'chikovykh." For other manuscript copies, see RGADA, *fond* 135, sec. IV, rub. II, no. 3, fols. 9–10; RGADA, *fond* 156, *op*. 1, no. 1, fols. 6–7; and no. 5, fols. 1–17v, 18–41. On these manuscripts, see R. Martin, "Muscovite Royal Weddings," 102–9, 124–26. See also RNB, Q.IV.86, fols. 269v–276v.

75. Daniel Printz von Buchau, "Nachalo i vozvyshenie Moskovii," 28 (Materialy innostrannye). For the original, see Buchau, *Scriptores rerum Livonicarum*, 2:687–728. On Printz, see Poe, *"A People Born to Slavery"*, 42; and idem, *Foreign Descriptions of Muscovy: An Analytic Bibliography of Primary and Secondary Sources*, 102.

76. See Skrynnikov, *Rossiia posle oprichniny*, 10 n. 26.

77. See Zimin, *V kanun groznykh potriasenii*, 14 (and the sources listed in n. 36, which also argue for the January date).

78. RGADA, *fond* 135, sec. IV, rub. II, no. 11, fol. 2.

79. For Anna Vasil'chikova as "*tsarevna*", see RGADA, *fond* 135, sec. IV, rub. II, no. 11, fols. 4, 5, 8, 9, 10, 11; as "tsaritsa and grand princess," see fols. 3, 10, 13, 14, 17, and elsewhere.

80. RGADA, *fond* 135, sec. IV, rub. II, no. 11, fol. 9. On the bride giving gifts on the first day of royal weddings, see R. Martin, "Gifts for Kith and Kin."

81. RGADA, *fond* 135, sec. IV, rub. II, no. 11, fols. 11–13.

82. RGADA, *fond* 135, sec. IV, rub. II, no. 11, fol. 7.

83. RGADA, *fond* 135, sec. IV, rub. II, no. 11, fol. 25.

84. Zimin, *V kanun groznykh potriasenii*, 14–21. On the *oprichnina* as Ivan IV's "privy domain," see Keenan, "The Privy Domain of Ivan Vasil'evich," 73–88.

85. The other Kolychevs were Ignatei Vasil'evich (bride's first best man, *druzhka*); his wife, Agafiia (bride's first matchmaker, *svakha*); Vasilii Ivanovich Umnoi (sat with boyars, "opposite *boiaryni*"); Timofei Danilov syn (sat with boyars); Matvei Tret'iakov syn Loshakov (with the bolster, *zgolov'e*); Ivan Fedorov syn (carried the foot pillow to the church, *podnozh'e*, and set the banquet table); Aleksei Zhdanov syn (set the table and prepared the foot pillow); Venedikht Borisov syn (carried the groom's candle); Ivan Afanas'ev syn (carried the bride's ceremonial loaf, served at the banquet table, and tended the

wedding costumes); Vasilii Grigor'evich (organized and led the wedding procession); Mikhail Vasil'evich, Zhdan Tret'iakov syn, Peter Fedorov syn, Mikhailo Fedorov syn, Grigorii Fedorov syn, Vasilii Zhdanov syn, Bogdan Vasil'ev syn, Fedor Vasil'ev syn, Stepan Nikitin syn, Oleksei Nikitin syn (all in the wedding procession). See Vasil'chikov, "Chin brakosochetaniia tsaria Ivana Vasil'evicha s tsaritseiu Annoiu Vasil'chikovykh," 8–13; Zimin, *V kanun groznykh potriasenii*, 15, 248 n. 38; and idem, "Kolychevy i russkoe boiarstvo XIV–XVI vv.," 5–71.

86. Tulupovs: Anna, the wife of Prince Davyd Ivanovich (sat with *boiaryni*); Boris Davydovich (sat with boyars "opposite the *boiaryni*"); Andrei Vladimirovich and Nikita Vladimirovich (tended the costumes and served the tsareviches at the banquet table); Ivan Vladimirovich (in the wedding procession). See Vasil'chikov, "Chin brakosochetaniia tsaria Ivana Vasil'evicha s tsaritseiu Annoiu Vasil'chikovykh," 8–13; Zimin, *V kanun groznykh potriasenii*, 15.

87. Godunovs: Boris Fedorovich (groom's first best man); Boris's (unnamed) wife (groom's first matchmaker); Dmitrii Ivanovich (sat at the side table, *v Krivom stole*); Nikita Fedorov syn (wedding procession); and Fedor Ivanov syn (wedding procession). See Vasil'chikov, "Chin brakosochetaniia tsaria Ivana Vasil'evicha s tsaritseiu Annoiu Vasil'chikovykh," 8–13; Zimin, *V kanun groznykh potriasenii*, 15.

88. Shuiskiis: Ivan Petrovich Shuiskii (sat at the side table); Dmitrii Ivanov syn (tended the foot pillow and served the groom's banquet table); Vasilii Ivanov syn (served the groom's banquet table); Andrei Ivanov syn (served the groom's banquet table). See Vasil'chikov, "Chin brakosochetaniia tsaria Ivana Vasil'evicha s tsaritseiu Annoiu Vasil'chikovykh," 8–13; Zimin, *V kanun groznykh potriasenii*, 20.

89. Vasil'chikovs: Nazarii (bride's second best man); his wife (bride's second matchmaker); Anna Andreeva zhena (sat with the *boiaryni*); Orina Grigor'eva zhena Andreeva syn (sat with the *boiaryni*); Grigorii Andreev syn (sat opposite the *boiaryni*); Il'ia Andreev syn (sat opposite the *boiaryni*); Grigorii Borisov syn (walked beside the groom's horse in the procession); Mikita Grigor'ev syn (held the cap, *kolpak*; served food, with the groom in the baths); Ivanko Alekseev syn (held the foot pillow, *podnozh'e*; served food); Andriushka Grigor'ev syn (served food); and Mikita (same as Mikita Grigor'ev syn?) (prepared the white garments, *s plat'em striapali*). See Vasil'chikov, "Chin brakosochetaniia tsaria Ivana Vasil'evicha s tsaritseiu Annoiu Vasil'chikovykh," 8–13.

90. Zimin, *V kanun groznykh potriasenii*, 19–20.

91. Zimin, *V kanun groznykh potriasenii*, 14–21; Bychkova, *Sostav klassa feodalov*, 131–33.

92. Zimin concluded that Pelageia/Feodosiia's tonsuring took place after November 12, 1579, because that is the last mention of the bride's father in the sources (Zimin, *V kanun groznykh potriasenii*, 91).

93. See *Materialy po istorii SSSR*, vol. 2 (Piskarevskii Chronicle), 85, 165 n. 98; Kleimola, "Reliance on the Tried and True," 60; Zimin, "Sostav boiar-

skoi dumy," 78; Lobanov-Rostovskii, *Russkaia rodoslovnaia kniga*, 2:135–36; Karamzin, *Istoriia gosudarstva Rossiiskogo*, vol. 9, col. 208, and n. 609.

94. For the dating of Fedor Ivanovich's wedding in 1575, see Karamzin, *Istoriia gosudarstva Rossiiskogo*, vol. 9, col. 187, and n. 554; Zimin, "Sostav boiarskoi dumy," 78 and n. 436; *Materialy po istorii SSSR*, vol. 2 (Piskarevskii Chronicle), 163 n. 88; Madariaga, *Ivan the Terrible*, 292; Skrynnikov, *Tsarstvo terrora*, 489–90. For the dating of the wedding in 1580, see Payne and Romanov, *Ivan the Terrible*, 376. Morozova and Morozov, *Ivan Groznyi i ego zheny*, 223, have 1577. See also Berry and Crummey, *Rude and Barbarous Kingdom*, 294 n. 8. On Boris Fedorovich Godunov's appointment to boyar in 1580, see, in addition to Karamzin: Kleimola, "Reliance on the Tried and True," 59, 62; and Zimin, "Sostav Boiarskoi dumy," 78.

95. There were five Godunovs at the Vasil'chikova wedding: Boris Fedorovich (groom's first best man, and with the groom in the baths); Boris's wife (the groom's first *svakha*); Dmitrii Ivanovich (sat at the side table); Nikita Fedorov syn and Fedor Ivanov syn (wedding procession). See Vasil'chikov, "Chin brakosochetaniia tsaria Ivana Vasil'evicha s tsaritseiu Annoiu Vasil'chikovykh," 8–13; Zimin, *V kanun groznykh potriasenii*, 18.

96. On Boris Fedorovich Godunov's appointment as *kravchii* in 1576, see Zimin, *V kanun groznykh potriasenii*, 40, and 255 n. 161. On Dmitrii Ivanovich Godunov's appointment as *okol'nichii* that same year, see Kleimola, "Reliance on the Tried and True," 59; and Zimin, "Sostav Boiarskoi dumy," 78.

97. Archimandrite Leonid [Kavelin], *Istoriko-arkheologicheskoe i statisticheskoe opisanie Borovskogo Pafnut'eva monastyria Kaluzhkoi guberni*, 98–99 (March 5, 1575); idem, *Nadpisi Troitskoi Sergievoi Lavry*, 32 (May 3, 1575).

98. Printz, "Nachalo i vozvyshenie Moskovii," 28 (Materialy innostrannye).

99. On the marriage, see *PSRL*, 34:192 (7081, Piskarevskii Chronicle), 226 (n.d., Moskovskii Chronicle).

100. *PSRL*, 13:333 (his name here is given as Saíl). See also A. V. Beliakov, "Chingisidy v Rossii v XV–XVI vekakh," 42; V. V. Vel'iaminov-Zernov, *Issledovaniia o kasimovskikh tsariakh i tsarevichakh*, 2:9–11.

101. The possible reasons for Ivan IV's abdication are summarized in Ostrowski, "Simeon Bekbulatovich's Remarkable Career as Tatar Khan, Grand Prince of Rus', and Monastic Elder"; and Shaposhnik, *Tserkovno-gosudarstvennye otnosheniia v Rossii v 30–80-e gody XVI veka*, 363–74.

102. Several documents from the court of Simeon Bekbulatovich's appanage are extant, including a list of servitors in his court and petitions to him as "grand prince." See RGADA, *fond* 210, *Moskovskii stol*, no. 1131 (22), fols. 17–23.

103. Anastasiia Mstislavskaia may have previously been married to Tsarevich Mikhail Kaibulich, born Murtaza-Ali, a converted Tatar prince who had come to Muscovy and served in Ivan's court. See *PSRL*, 34:226 (n.d., Moskovskii Chronicle); RGB, *fond* 304, no. 838, fols. 95–96 (sinodikon for Holy Trinity

Monastery). Beliakov, "Chingisidy v Rossii," 42, doubts the marriage to Mikhail Kaibulich but does not explain why. Mikhail Kaibulich, a second cousin once removed of Simeon Bekbulatovich, had accepted Orthodox baptism, sometime in or before January 1570, and quickly became a prominent figure in Ivan IV's court. During the *oprichnina*, he was recognized as the head of the *zemshchina*—that part of Muscovy's land and resources left outside Ivan's personal domain. Mikhail Kaibulich died, however, in 1575. Kaibulich may himself have been previously married—to the daughter of I. V. Sheremetev. Zimin, *V kanun groznykh potriasenii*, 27. On Kaibulich's place at court, see Zimin, *V kanun groznykh potriasenii*, 27; idem, *Oprichnina Ivana Groznogo*, 351, 465 n. 1; Skrynnikov, *Oprichnyi terror*, 212. See also *SbIRIO*, vol. 129 (pp. 219, 221, 224, 226).

104. Kuidai Kul had converted to Orthodoxy on December 21, 1505. *PSRL*, 4:136 (7014, Fourth Novgorodskaia Chronicle); 6:51 (7014, First Sofiiskaia Chronicle), 244–45 (7014, Second Sofiiskaia Chronicle); 8:245–46 (7014).

105. Kollmann, *Kinship and Politics*, 282 n. 113; Miatlev, "K rodoslovniiu kniazei Mstislavskikh," 304; R. Martin, "Gifts for the Dead," 190. See also the Piskarevskii Chronicle, which names one of the two daughters Anna. *PSRL*, 34:178 (7046, Piskarevskii Chronicle); *Materialy po istorii SSSR*, vol. 2 (Piskarevskii Chronicle), 21, and 157 n. 21.

106. There has been some debate about the date of the marriage of Anastasiia Mstislavskaia and Tsar Simeon. Kashtanov believed that the marriage took place sometime very shortly after Simeon's conversion in 1572. S. M. Kashtanov, "O vnutrennei politike Ivana Groznogo v period 'velikogo kniazheniia' Simeona Bekbulatovicha," 458. Zimin, on the other hand, insisted that the wedding took place in 1575 or 1576, during Simeon's brief reign. Zimin, "Ivan Groznyi i Simeon Bekbulatovich v 1574 g.," 148, 160 n. 94.

107. The identity of these two daughters has sometimes been confused. Some noted genealogists believed that Tsarevich Peter and Evdokiia Ivanovna had only one daughter, named Anastasiia, who married both Prince Fedor Mikhailovich Mstislavskii and Prince Vasilii Vasil'evich Shuiskii. See Lobanov-Rostovskii, *Russkaia rodoslovnaia kniga*, 1:42; *RRK*, 1:234.

108. For the marriage, see *DRV*, 13:73–79.

109. See Zimin, "Ivan Groznyi i Simeon Bekbulatovich v 1575 g.," 141–63; idem, *V kanun groznykh potriasenii*, 24–28; and idem, *Rossiia na poroge novogo vremeni*, 98–99, 294–99.

110. Shmidt, ed., *Opisi Tsarskogo arkhiva XVI v. i Arkhiva Posol'skogo prikaza 1614 g.*, 41. These documents are no longer extant.

111. See, e.g., BAN, 16.15.15, fol. 134; and *DRV*, 13:73. See also a chronicle entry for this wedding, which similarly traces the bride's genealogical ties with the Muscovite dynasty, in *PSRL*, 13:253 (7063).

112. Shmidt, *Opisi Tsarskogo arkhiva*, 60. These documents are also no longer extant.

113. *PSRL*, 34:226 (n.d., Moskovskii Chronicle).

114. Zimin, *V kanun groznykh potriasenii*, 25; Solov'ev, *Istoriia Rossii s drevneishikh vremen*, 3:187–293.

115. Zimin suggests this on the basis of the loyalty charter (*krestotseloval'naia zapis'*) signed by Prince Fedor Mikhailovich, pledging his loyalty to Vasilii III and promising not to flee to Lithuania or Poland. See Zimin, "Ivan Groznyi i Simeon Bekbulatovich," 147–48; idem, *V kanun groznykh potriasenii*, 26. For the charter, see RGADA, *fond* 135, sec. III, rub. II, no. 12; *DRV*, 3:63–68 (no. 136); and *SGGD*, pt. 1, no. 157 (pp. 433–35).

116. *Vkladnaia kniga Troitse-Sergieva monastyria*, ed. E. N. Klitina, T. N. Manushina, and T. V. Nikolaeva, 121 (fol. 451); and *Das Speisungsbuch von Volokolamsk: Eine Quelle zur Sozialgeschechte russischer Klöster im 16. Jahrhundert*, ed. Ludwig Steindorff, 99 (fol. 71v), and 342.

117. Zimin believed that Isaac Massa was referring to Vasil'chikova when he reported that Ivan IV "married several women whom he threw into a convent when, after three years, they had given him no children." *V kanun groznykh potriasenii*, 27, and 263 n. 8. See also Isaac Massa, *A Short History of the Beginnings and Origins of These Present Wars in Moscow*, 16. According to Morozova and Morozov (*Ivan Groznyi i ego zheny*, 216), Vasil'chikova died at the end of 1576. Madariaga has her death sometime in 1575 or 1576 (*Ivan the Terrible*, 311). Baumgarten has her repudiated in 1574 and dying on January 7 in "Généalogies des branches régnantes de Rurikides," 18–19 (table III) and 24–25 (n. 36). Andrei Ivanovich Iurganov puts Vasil'chikova's death "no later than October 20, 1579," but this date is based on a misidentification of a certain "Anna Vasil'chikova" for whom Tsar Ivan IV made commemorative donations to Holy Trinity–St. Sergius Monastery (according to Iurganov, the tsaritsa's aunt, Anna Petrovna Vasil'chikova, not the tsaritsa herself). See his "O date napisaniia zaveshchaniia Ivana Groznogo," 135–36. The *Chronograph of the Marriages of Tsar Ivan Vasil'evich* has Ivan IV marrying Vasil'chikova in July 5, 1574, and sending her to a convent (*zatochi*) that same year, on August 14—dates that obviously cannot be correct (see Appendix 1).

118. Karamzin, *Istorii gosudarstva Rossiiskogo*, vol. 9, n. 494; Zimin, *V kanun groznykh potriasenii*, 85.

119. Zimin, *V kanun groznykh potriasenii*, 85.

120. See R. Martin, "Gifts for the Bride"; Crummey, *Aristocrats and Servitors*, 76–78, 80–81, 164. On Melentii Ivanov as a scribe, see Zimin, *V kanun groznykh potriasenii*, 86.

121. RNB, Q.XVII.17, fol. 157v.

122. Karamzin, *Istoriia gosudarstva Rossiiskogo*, vol. 9, col. 162, and n. 494.

123. Madariaga, *Ivan the Terrible*, 292, 311, 327, 442, note 38; Vladimir Borisovich Kobrin, *Ivan Groznyi*, 133–34; Pushkareva, *Women in Russian History*, 73; K[azimierz] Waliszewski, *Ivan the Terrible*, 372–74; Jules Koslow, *Ivan the Terrible*, 200.

124. Emchenko, *Stoglav*, 284.

125. Levin, *Sex and Society*, 107.

126. *RIB*, 6:867–68; Levin, *Sex and Society*, 107–8.

127. See also Meyendorff, "Christian Marriage in Byzantium," 106. The fact that no *chin* or *razriad* survives for the wedding with Vasilisa does not at all mean, of course, that there never was one. No wedding text survives for Ivan IV's Cherkasskaia wedding (only a fragment from it in a later chronicle), for the first wedding of Vasilii III (in 1505), for the second and third weddings of Tsarevich Ivan Ivanovich (Ivan IV's son, in 1575 and 1580), or for the wedding of Ivan IV's son Tsar Fedor Ivanovich (1575).

128. Vladimir Borisovich Pavlov-Sil'vanskii, "Novye svedeniia v pistsovykh knigakh Viazemskogo uezda kontsa XVI v.," 93; and idem, *Pistsovye knigi Rossii XVI v.*, 76. Skrynnikov quotes from the source, RGADA, *fond* 1209, book 619, fols. 89–89v, in his *Ivan Groznyi*, 212. See also Zimin, *V kanun groznykh potriasenii*, 86.

129. Skrynnikov, *Ivan Groznyi*, 212; idem, *Rossiia posle oprichniny*, 99–100.

130. RGADA, *fond* 181, no. 119, fol. 215. Originally, the text listed only Anastasiia Iur'eva, Mariia Cherkasskaia, Anna Koltovskaia, and Mariia Nagaia. Mariia Sobakina and Vasilisa "Radilovykh" are inserted, and Anna Vasil'chikova is entirely omitted.

131. *Razriadnaia kniga 1475–1598 g.*, 323. *Tysiachnaia kniga 1550 g. i Dvorovaia tetrad' 50-x godov XVI v.*, 185 (fol. 138v), 186 (fol. 139) (Dvorovaia tetrad'); 220 (fol. 158v) (Spisok streltskikh golov i sotnikov, Spisok 100-go goda). *Boiarskie spiski poslednei chetverti XVI–nachala XVII vv. i Rospis' russkogo voiska 1604 g.*, 1:135, 170, 201, 241, 324; 2:80.

132. Mariia would go on to marry Gavrilo Grigor'evich Pushkin. See Morozova and Morozov, *Ivan Groznyi i ego zheny*, 219.

133. Zimin, *V kanun groznykh potriasenii*, 86, and 264 n. 10. Skrynnikov, *Ivan Groznyi*, 212.

134. On Ivan Tevekelev (note corrected spelling) as Ivan IV's *oruzhnichii* (from 1572/73 to 1576/77), see the *Chronograph* (RNB, Q.XVII.17, fols. 157–157v); and the so-called "Sheremetev spisok" in *DRV*, 20:53 (7081: Ivan Devetelevich becomes *oruzhnichii*), 20:55 (7085: Ivan Devetelevich removed as *oruzhnichii*); and Kobrin, "Sostav Oprichnogo dvora Ivana Groznogo," 75.

135. Zimin, *V kanun groznykh potriasenii*, 85–86; Morozova and Morozov, *Ivan Groznyi i ego zheny*, 218–19; Kobrin, *Ivan Groznyi*, 134. Madariaga speculated that her death may have been in childbirth (*Ivan the Terrible*, 311, 327, 436 n. 39, and 439 n. 54).

136. There is disagreement on the date of Ivan IV's wedding with Mariia Nagaia. The day and month are known, but some have put the wedding in 1581. See Bychkova, *Sostav klassa feodalov*, 131, 133, 134. Others have put it in 1580. See *DRV*, 13:112; Morozova and Morozov, *Ivan Groznyi i ego zheny*, 234; Madariaga, *Ivan the Terrible*, 327. Baumgarten lists only the year 1580. "Géné-

alogies des branches régnantes de Rurikides," 18–19 (table III) and 25 (note 36).

137. BAN, 21.10.25, fols. 88–91v; BAN, 31.7.30, fols. 53v–55v; BAN, 31.6.40, fols. 53–55v; BAN, 32.5.11, fols. 65v–69; *Razriadnaia kniga 1475–1605 gg.*, 3:169–75; *DRV*, 13:112–16, 83–85. The edition in Novikov's *DRV* is faulty, placing the list of courtiers in the Nagaia wedding cortège (*poezd*) together with the muster (*razriad*) for Prince Vladimir Staritskii and Evdokiia Odoevskaia (on pp. 80–83, 83, 83–85).

138. The wedding took place at Alexandrovo Sloboda. RGADA, *fond* 188, no. 468, fols. 332v–333.

139. Kaiser, "Symbol and Ritual," 250.

140. On their ranks, see Skrynnikov, *Rossiia posle oprchininy*, 100; Kleimola, "Reliance on the Tried and True," 60, 62.

141. Nagois: Mikhail Aleksandrovich (bride's second best man); his wife (bride's second matchmaker); Semen Fedorovich (sat in the *okol'nichii*'s place); Andrei Fedorovich (sat in the *okol'nichii*'s place); Mikhail Fedorovich (held the cap, *kolpak*); Petr Afanas'evich (held the cap); Andrei Aleksandrovich (carried the groom's bolster to church, *zgolov'e*); Afanasii Aleksandrovich (patrolled on the groom's stallion during the banquet). See *DRV*, 13:112–16.

142. Godunovs at the Nagaia wedding: Boris Fedorovich (bride's first best man); Boris's wife (bride's first matchmaker); Agrafena, wife of Dmitrii Ivanovich (sat with *boiaryni*); Efimiia, wife of Vasilii Osipovich Asanov-Godunov (sat with *boiaryni*); Pelageia, wife of Stepan Vasil'evich (sat with *boiaryni*); Dmitrii Ivanovich (sat with boyars); Stepan Vasil'evich (sat with boyars); Ivan Vasil'evich (sat with boyars); Iakov Mikhailovich (carried the ceremonial loaf); Konstantin Mikhailovich (carried the groom's ceremonial loaf); Nikita Vasil'evich (carried the groom's ceremonial loaf); Petr Vasil'evich (carried the groom's ceremonial loaf); Andrei Nikitin syn (carried the bride's ceremonial loaf); and Ivan Vasil'evich (tended the bride's sled). See *DRV*, 13:112–16.

143. Bychkova, *Sostav klassa feodalov*, 134.

144. Bychkova, *Sostav klassa feodalov*, 131.

145. Printz, "Nachalo i vozvyshenie Moskovii," 28.

146. On the Sheremetevs, see Kollmann, *Kinship and Politics*, 216; Zimin, *Formirovanie*, 180, 188–89, 295; Kleimola, "Reliance on the Tried and True," 63; idem, "Patterns of Duma Recruitment," 254; *RRK*, 3:494–507.

147. Kleimola, "Kto Kogo," 217.

148. Kollmann, *Kinship and Politics*, 224–25.

149. See the summary of views on Ivan Ivanovich's death in Pavlov and Perrie, *Ivan the Terrible*, 192–93; and Shaposhnik, *Tserkovno-gosudarstvennye otnosheniia v Rossii*, 400–402. On Elena/Leonida at the Novodevichii Convent, see V. I. Koretskii, ed., *Istochniki po sotsial'no-ekonomicheskoi istorii Rossii XVI–XVII vv.: Iz Arkhiva Moskovskogo Novodevichego monastyria*, 195.

150. Thyrêt, "The Royal Women of Ivan IV's Family," 162–63; *AI*, vol. 4, no. 166 (pp. 316–21); N. A. Maiasova, "Tri shitykh pokrova XVI v sobranii mu-

zeev Kremlia," *Materialy i issledovaniia: Gosudarstvennye muzei Moskovskogo Kremlia*, 1:133–47.

151. Thyrêt, "The Royal Women of Ivan IV's Family," 163.

152. Crummey, *Aristocrats and Servitors*, 117 (see also pp. 70, 81, 113–23, 149).

153. *PSRL*, 34:194 (7092, Piskarevskii Chronicle).

154. *PSRL*, 34:229 (7089, Moskovskii Chronicle).

155. Karamzin, *Istoriia gosudarstva Rossiiskogo*, vol. 9, n. 494.

156. Horsey, "Travels," 286.

157. *The Muscovia of Antonio Possevino*, 48.

158. Ivan Ivanovich Polosin, *Sotsial'no-politicheskaia istoriia Rossii XVI–nachale XVII v. Sbornik statei*, 206.

159. Madariaga read Heidenstein's report as pertaining to Ivan IV's sixth wedding, not the seventh wedding. Madariaga, *Ivan the Terrible*, 327 and 442, n. 38.

160. Jacques Margeret, *The Russian Empire and Grand Duchy of Muscovy: A 17th-Century French Account*, 15.

161. Petreius, *Istoriia o velikom kniazhestve Moskovskom*, 270. Isaac Massa, *A Short History of the Beginnings and Origins of These Present Wars in Moscow under the Reign of Various Sovereigns down to the Year 1610*, 20. See also Zimin, *V kanun groznykh potriasenii*, 86.

162. On these foreigners' accounts, see Poe, *Foreign Descriptions of Muscovy*, 110, 118, 120, 143, 146, 151, 152. The author of Kurbskii's third letter to Ivan IV mentions "five or six wives," which, alas, the editors of the text edition take as accurate. See *Perepiska Ivana Groznogo s Andreem Kurskim*, 179 and 413 n. 56.

163. Solov'ev, *Istoriia Rossii s drevneishikh vremen*, 3:432, 433, 702, 703.

164. Madariaga, *Ivan the Terrible*, 53–55, 144–47, 186–87, 242–43, 268–70, 276, 281, 285, 292, 311, 327–28, 340–41, 343–44, 429 n. 17, 431 n. 2; Pavlov and Perrie, *Ivan the Terrible*, 191–92; Skrynnikov, *Ivan Groznyi*, 208–12; Kobrin, *Ivan Groznyi*, 134; and Zimin, *V kanun groznykh potriasenii*, 85. But see also Morozova and Morozov, *Ivan Groznyi i ego zheny*, which asserts only six (pp. 6–8).

165. See, for example, Pushkareva, *Women in Russian History*, 73 (who lists Dolgorukova as Ivan IV's fifth of eight wives); and Waliszewski, *Ivan the Terrible*, 374 (who lists Dolgorukova as seventh of eight).

166. RNB, Q.XVII.17, fol. 157v. See Appendix 1. See also Solov'ev, *Istoriia Rossii s drevneishikh vremen*, 3:739 n. 136.

167. The claim is widespread, but see, for a start, Morozova and Morozov, *Ivan Groznyi i ego zheny*, 176; Bychkova, *Sostav klassa feodalov*, 131; Zimin, *V kanun groznykh potriasenii*, 86; Skrynnikov, *Rossiia posle oprinchniny*, 13–14.

168. On sinodikons, see R. Martin, "Death and Dying: The Early Period (up to Peter I)," 7:210–14; Jennifer B. Spock, "Community Building and Social Identity: Donations to the Solovki Monastery 1460–1645"; Ludwig Steindorff,

"Memorial Practice as a Means of Integrating the Muscovite State"; idem, "Commemoration and Administrative Techniques in Muscovite Monasteries"; idem, "Princess Mariia Golenina: Perpetuating Identity through Care for the Deceased"; idem, *Memoria in Altrußland: Untersuchungen zu den Formen christlicher Totensorge*; and S. V. Konev, "Sinodikologiia. Chast' I-aia: Klassifikatskiia istochnikov."

169. On these royal commemorations, see R. Martin, "Praying for the Dead in Muscovy: Kinship Awareness and Orthodox Belief in the Commemorations of Muscovite Royalty"; and idem, "Gifts and Commemoration: Donations to Monasteries, Legitimacy, and Remembering the Royal Dead in Muscovy (7159/1651)."

170. RGB, *fond* 304, nos. 40, 42, 813, 814, 818; but no. 43 omits the last wife (Nagaia).

171. RGB, *fond* 304, nos. 813, 814, and 818.

172. GIM, Muzeinoe sobranie (Museum Collection), no. 3652; and GIM, Eparkhial'noe sobranie (Eparchy Collection), no. 413. One sinodikon lists Koltovskaia in the correct place (fourth): RGADA, *fond* 396, *op.* 2, no. 3714.

173. GIM, Sobranie Uspenskogo sobora (Dormition Cathedral Collection), nos. 64 (sixteenth century), 69 (mid-seventeenth century), and 70 (eighteenth century).

174. See the 1575 petition by Ivan IV to Bekbulatovich: RGADA, *fond* 27, no. 12. See also *Poslanie Ivana Groznogo*, eds. D. S. Likhachev and Ia. S. Lur'e, 195–96 (see also photos of parts of the petition on photo plates between p. 196 and p. 197); and *RIB*, 22.2:76–77.

175. For August 1576, see Zimin, *V kanun groznykh potriasenii*, 41; for mid-September 1576, see Koretskii, "Zemskii sobor 1575 g. i postavlenie Simeona Bekbulatovicha 'velikim kniazem vseia Rusi'." Zimin cites sources that report Simeon Bekbulatovich as having sat on the throne "for one year" (*V kanun groznykh potriasenii*, 255 n. 166), "for more than one year" (*PSRL*:34:192 [7081, Piskarevskii Chronicle]); and "for two whole years" (Margeret, *The Russian Empire and Grand Duchy of Muscovy*, 16).

176. Meyendorff, "Christian Marriage in Byzantium," 101 and 106–7.

177. Madariaga, *Ivan the Terrible*, 212.

178. Kaiser, "Symbol and Ritual," 249.

Chapter 5

1. Uroff, *On Russia*, 36; Kotošixin, *O Rossii*, 19.

2. On Kotoshikhin's account and life, see George Weickhardt, "Kotoshikhin: An Evaluation and Interpretation"; Pennington's "Introduction" in Kotošixin, *O Rossii*, 1–7; and A. I. Markevich, *Grigorii Karpovich Kotoshikhin i ego sochinenie o Moskovskom gosudarstve v polovine XVII veka,* 6–56.

3. Dunning, *Russia's First Civil War*, 109–22, 254, 260. We can agree with

him here without accepting his views on the False Dmitrii as "one of the only truly enlightened rulers Russia ever had" (p. 82) or that the Troubles were a "civil war carried out in Tsar Dmitrii's name" (p. 480). The literature on the Time of Troubles is substantial (see Dunning, *Russia's First Civil War*, 1–27), but the classic treatment by Platonov still merits consideration: *Ocherki po istorii Smuty v Moskovskom gosudarstve XVI–XVII vv.* .

4. See W. E. D. Allen, "The Georgian Marriage Projects of Boris Godunov"; idem, *Russian Embassies to the Georgian Kings (1589–1603)*; and N. E. Evans, "The Anglo-Russian Royal Marriage Negotiations of 1600–1603."

5. For more on the First False Dmitrii, see V. I. Ul'ianovskii, *Smutnoe vremia*, 232, 238–69; Dunning, *Russia's First Civil War*, 214, 221–22, 224–34; idem, "Who Was Tsar Dmitrii?"; B. A. Uspenskii, "Svad'ba Lzhedmitriia"; and Maureen Perrie, *Pretenders and Popular Monarchism in Early Modern Russia.*

6. Dunning, *Russia's First Civil War*, 211.

7. Solov'ev, *Istoriia Rossii s drevneishikh vremen*, 4:449, 484; G. V. Abramovich, *Kniaz'ia Shuiskie i Rossiiskii tron*, 149.

8. On the election of Mikhail Romanov as tsar in 1613, see, for a start, Liudmila Evgen'evna Morozova, *Rossiia na puti iz Smuty: Izbranie na tsarstvo Mikhaila Fedorovicha*; Dunning, *Russia's First Civil War*; Edward G. Orchard, "The Election of Michael Romanov"; and the little-known honors thesis by Craig Gayen Kennedy, "The Romanov Relations: A Kinship-Based Analysis of the 1613 Election of Mikhail Romanov to the Muscovite Throne."

9. Kollmann, *Kinship and Politics*, 192–93.

10. On the extraordinary role of Marfa in Tsar Mikhail Fedorovich's court, see Thyrêt, *Between God and Tsar*, 44, 120–21; and idem, "Marfa Ivanovna and the Expansion of the Role of the Tsar's Mother in the Seventeenth Century."

11. On the role of succession in the Time of Troubles, see Dunning, *Russia's First Civil War*, 2–12.

12. Kollmann, *Kinship and Politics*, 192–93.

13. Zabelin's narrative of events remains the most complete treatment to date: *Domashnii byt russkikh tsarits*, 219–41, which relies principally on *SGGD*, vol. 3, no. 63 (pp. 257–66). See also *PSRL*, 5:65–66 (n.d., Addendum to Second Pskovskaia Chronicle); Solov'ev, *Istoriia Rossii s drevneishikh vremen*, 5:127–28; and *RBS*, 21:338–39.

14. *SGGD*, vol. 3, no. 63 (pp. 257–66, at 257).

15. On Khlopova's selection just before Christmas ("*k rozhdestvu*"), see *SGGD*, vol. 3, no. 63 (p. 261).

16. See *Razriadnaia kniga, 1475–1598 gg.*, 44, 68, 260, 359, 373, 412, 422, 436, 485, 491, 501, 505, 514, 534; *Tysiachnaia kniga 1550 g. Dvorovaia tetrad'*, 90, 160, 241; *Boiarskie spiski poslednei chetverti XVI–nachale XVI vv. i Rospis' russkogo voiska 1604 g.*, 1:41, 62, 116, 136, 137, 138, 159, 160, 202, 203, 204, 210, 226, 271, 282, 294, 295, 309, 310, 311; 2:21, 22.

17. See Zabelin, *Domashnii byt russkikh tsarits*, 229.

18. *SGGD*, vol. 3, no. 63 (p. 264); and Zabelin, *Domashnii byt russkikh tsarits*, 228.

19. *SGGD*, vol. 3, no. 64 (p. 266).

20. See *SGGD*, vol. 3, no. 63 (pp. 257, 261, 264); no. 64 (p. 266). One source, cited by Zabelin, calls her "tsarevna," which is more typical of prospective brides after their selection in the bride-show. See Zabelin, *domashnii byt russkikh tsarits*, 221–22.

21. See *SGGD*, vol. 3, no. 63 (p. 261); and the source cited in Zabelin, *Domashnii byt russkikh tsarits*, 221–22. On gift exchanges at Muscovite royal weddings, see R. Martin, "Gifts for Kith and Kin."

22. *SGGD*, vol. 3, no. 63 (p. 261); no. 64 (p. 266); Zabelin, *Domashnii byt russkikh tsarits*, 220–22.

23. Zabelin, *Domashnii byt russkikh tsarits*, 229.

24. *PSRL*, 5:65 (n.d., Addendum to Second Pskovskaia Chronicle).

25. Levin, *Sex and Society*, 89.

26. For betrothal in church, linked to crowning service, see Andrei Staritskii (*DRV*, 24); Iurii Vasil'evich (*DRV*, 13:42); Vladimir Staritskii (*DRV*, 13:51); Tsar Simeon (*DRV*, 13:65); Mikhail Romanov, first wedding (RGADA, *fond* 135, sec. IV, rub. II, no. 14, fols. 4 and 7); Mikhail Romanov, second wedding (*DRV*, 13:164); Aleksei Mikhailovich, first wedding (*DRV*, 13:205). For betrothal in palace, separate from crowning service, see Vasilii III (*DRV*, 13:7); First False Dmitrii (RGADA, *fond* 135, sec. IV, rub. II, no. 12, fol. 2).

27. That the tsar and Khlopova were betrothed in 1616 may have caused some confusion later, when the tsar actually did marry for the first time in 1624. A very early draft of the 1624 wedding *chin* includes several questions (and answers subsequently inscribed next to them) about wedding choreography, including one about the location of the betrothal (*obruchenie*) service: whether it should take place in the tsar's palace or in the church, immediately before the crowning (*venchanie*) service. The answer, inscribed nearby, advises to "look in the *Book of Needs* [*Potrebnik*], as the sovereign patriarch has ordered." The *Potrebnik* they consulted evidently contained a joint betrothal and crowning, which is how the tsar's wedding in 1624 was performed. RGADA, *fond* 135, sec. IV, rub. II, no. 14, fols. 4 and 7; R. Martin, "Choreographing the 'Tsar's Happy Occasion,'" 802–3.

28. Levin, *Sex and Society*, 89–90. See also Kotošixin, *O Rossii*, 160–64.

29. Zabelin, *Domashnii byt russkikh tsarits*, 229–30; and Zabelin, *Materialy* [accompanying *Domashnii byt russkikh tsarei i tsarits v XVI i XVII st.*], "Materialy k tomu II," 572–74.

30. See Shcherbachev, "O rodstve," 64.

31. *Razriadnaia kniga, 1475–1598 gg.*, 152, 172, 192, 196, 228, 236, 360, 361, 362, 381, 384, 386, 399, 416, 438, 439, 441, 445, 449, 450, 468, 472–74, 478, 484, 488, 490, 501, 506, 509, 510, 514, 518, 519, 531, 532, 533; *Tysiachnaia kniga 1550 g. Dvorovaia tetrad' piatidesiatykh godov XVI veka*, 148, 179 (Dvorovaia tetriad'); *Boiarskie spiski poslednei chetverti XVI–nachale XVI vv. i*

Rospis' russkogo voiska 1604 g., 1:15, 89, 90, 127, 128, 181, 185, 251, 255; 2:44, 57; *Boiarskaia kniga 1658 goda*, 27, 155.

32. *DRV*, 13:90.

33. Lobanov-Rostovskii, *Russkaia rodoslovnaia kniga*, 1:278; Kobeko, "Sheremetevy i Polevy," *Izvestiia RGO*, vol. 1 (1900): 7–30 (at 13–14).

34. *SGGD*, vol. 3, no. 63.

35. *SGGD*, vol. 3, no. 63 (pp. 259–60). Filaret's sister Marfa had married Boris Kambulatovich Cherkasskii. Among Marfa and Prince Boris's children were Prince Ivan, who took part in these investigations, and Irina, who married Fedor Sheremetev, who also participated. See *RRK*, 2:37–38; Lobanov-Rostovskii, *Russkaia rodoslovnaia kniga*, 3:13.

36. *SGGD*, vol. 3, nos. 63 and 64; Zabelin, *Domashnii byt russkikh tsarits*, 229.

37. See *AI*, vol. 3, nos. 80 and 91 (pp. 77–78 and 90, respectively); and *AAE*, vol. 3, no. 218 (pp. 322–23).

38. *PSRL*, 5:65 (n.d., Addendum to Second Pskovskaia Chronicle); Zabelin, *Domashnii byt russkikh tsarits*, 233. The identity of the prospective bride is unclear. Poland-Lithuania was ruled at the time by King Sigismund III of the Swedish House of Vasa (the father of Wladislav, a onetime candidate for the Muscovite throne during the Troubles). Sigismund had no eligible daughters or sisters. Isenburg, *Europäische Stammtafeln*, vol. 2, table 79.

39. *PSRL*, 5:65 (n.d., Addendum to Second Pskovskaia Chronicle); *DR*, 1:488; Bantysh-Kamenskii, *Obzor vneshnikh snoshenii Rossii*, 1:217; Zabelin, *Domashnii byt russkikh tsarits*, 233–34.

40. Bantysh-Kamenskii, *Obzor vneshnikh snoshenii Rossii*, 4:153; Isenburg, *Europäische Stammtafeln*, vol. 1, table 62; vol. 2, table 79.

41. Bushkovitch, "Shvedskie istochniki o Rossii 1624–1626 gg.," 370.

42. *SGGD*, vol. 3, no. 62 (p. 258).

43. *SGGD*, vol. 3, no. 62 (pp. 258–59).

44. Mikhail Saltykov was promoted to *okol'nichii* in January 1623, just nine months before this investigation began. See Crummey, *Aristocrats and Servitors*, 183.

45. *SGGD*, vol. 3, no. 63 (pp. 258–59).

46. It appears that Saltykov, in order to prove Gavrilo Khlopov wrong, later commissioned a saber in the Armory that was to be as fine as the Turkish specimen examined and praised by the tsar. See Zabelin, *Domashnii byt russkikh tsarits*, 222 n. 1. For Gavrilo's account, see *SGGD*, vol. 3, no. 63 (pp. 261–62).

47. *SGGD*, vol. 3, no. 63 (p. 264); Zabelin, *Domashnii byt russkikh tsarits*, 236–37.

48. *SGGD*, vol. 3, no. 63 (p. 265); Zabelin, *Domashnii byt russkikh tsarits*, 237.

49. *SGGD*, vol. 3, no. 64 (pp. 266–67).

50. *SGGD*, vol. 3, no. 65 (p. 268).

51. Solov'ev, *Istoriia Rossii s drevneishikh vremen*, 5:127–28.

52. Zabelin, *Domashnii byt russkikh tsarits*, 220–42.

53. *PSRL*, 5:66 (n.d., Addendum to Second Pskovskaia Chronicle); Zabelin, *Domashnii byt russkikh tsarits*, 219.

54. *Izvestiia RGO*, vol. 2 (1903), IV: 1.

55. N. P. Chulkov, "Zametka," *Letopis' Istoriko-Rodoslovnogo Obshchestva v Moskve* (1907, no. 4): 47; Shcherbachev, "O rodstve," 62.

56. Miatlev, "Rodoslovnye zametki," *Letopis' Istoriko-Rodoslovnogo Obshchestva v Moskve* (1907, no. 4): 10–16.

57. Shcherbachev, "O rodstve," 62–67.

58. See R. Martin, "Gifts for the Dead: Kinship and Commemoration in Muscovy (The Case of the Mstislavskii Princes)"; and Steindorff, "Commemoration and Administrative Techniques in Muscovite Monasteries."

59. Shcherbachev, "O rodstve," 63–64. One additional manuscript sinodikon closely parallels the contents of the sources cited by Shcherbachev (see p. 63 nn. 9 and 10): GIM, Barsov Collection, no. 966.

60. The entry further confirms Shcherbachev's conclusion that Mariia was the daughter of Prince Vladimir's third wife (Dariia/Mariia Vasil'evna Barbashina), not his first (Mariia Dmitrievna Eletskaia, née Zvenigorodskaia, as Miatlev proposed). The remainder of the entry includes Prince Vladimir's other daughter, Elena, and three unidentified names, two of which are almost certainly Vladimir's children who had died very young. See Moshé Altbauer, ed., *Saint Catherine's Monastery, Mount Sinai: An Orthodox Pomjanyk of the Seventeenth–Eighteenth Centuries*, 20.

61. Zabelin, *Domashnii byt russkikh tsarits*, 241.

62. Mariia's father's first cousin Mamelfa Il'ichna married Ivan Semenovich Nagoi, the first cousin of Mariia/Marfa Nagaia, Ivan IV's seventh wife. See Miatlev, "K rodosloviiu Nagikh."

63. Mariia Khlopova's great aunt Solomoniia married twice. Her first husband was Fedor Alekseevich Basmanov (d. 1570/71). Their son, Ivan, married Anna Vasil'evna Saltykova, the daughter of Vasilii L'vovich Saltykov and the second cousin of Mikhail and Boris Saltykov, the conspirators in 1616. Their grandchild Fetin'ia Basmanova married Prince Vasilii Iansheevich Suleshev, whose brother Prince Iurii was married to the sister of Mikhail and Boris Saltykov. See *RRK*, 2:70–71. See also Andrei Pavlovich Pavlov, *Gosudarev dvor i politicheskaia bor'ba pri Borise Godunove, 1584–1605*, 194. Solominiia's second marriage was to the boyar Prince Vasilii Iur'evich Golitsyn (d. 1584), whose niece (Evdokiia) was married to Alexander Iur'ev, Tsar Mikhail's uncle. See *RRK*, 1:285.

64. *PSRL*, 5:66 (n.d., Addendum to Second Pskovskaia Chronicle).

65. Zabelin, *Domashnii byt russkikh tsarits*, 240–41.

66. Bushkovitch, "Shvedskie istochniki o Rossii," 359–81.

67. The diplomatic report is preserved, oddly, in the Swedish archives: the Dutch mission to Muscovy made its way back to the Netherlands via Stockholm,

and the diplomatic materials at length found their way into a Swedish archival collection including materials on relations with Moscow. See Bushkovitch, "Shvedskie istochniki o Rossii," 362–63 (quote on p. 370).

68. Bushkovitch, "Shvedskie istochniki o Rossii," 370.

69. Zabelin, *Domashnii byt russkikh tsarits*, 241.

70. *PSRL*, 5:66 (n.d., Addendum to Second Pskovskaia Chronicle).

71. Grigorii A. Miloradovich, "Tsaritsa Mariia Dolgorukova," 9.

72. RGADA, *fond* 199, portfel' 284, pt. 2, no. 8; Shcherbachev, "O rodstve," 66 (see also the table on p. 65).

73. *Opis' arkhiva Posol'skogo prikaza 1626 goda*, 1:367–68.

74. Zabelin, *Domashnii byt russkikh tsarits*, 241; Miloradovich, "Tsaritsa Mariia Dolgorukova," 9.

75. Miloradovich, "Tsaritsa Mariia Dolgorukova," 5–6.

76. Bushkovitch, "Shvedskie istochniki o Rossii," 370.

77. *DR*, 1:633. See also Miloradovich, "Tsaritsa Mariia Dolgorukova," 27. The source published by Bushkovitch ("Shvedskie istochniki o Rossii," 370) reports that Tsaritsa Mariia fell ill "four days after the wedding."

78. See Zabelin, *Domashnii byt russkikh tsarits*, 241–42. The genealogist Petr Dolgorukov agreed that Mariia was poisoned (see his *Skazaniie o rode Dolgorukovykh*, 15). See also Miloradovich, "Tsaritsa Mariia Dolgorukova," 31.

79. RGADA, *fond* 135, sec. IV, rub. II, nos. 17, 18, 19; RGADA *fond* 135, sec. V, rub. III, no. 16.

80. Arkhimandrit Leonid, "Luk'ian Stepanovich Streshnev: Starinnoe istoricheskoe predanie," *ChIOIDR* (1872, bk. 2), 1–9 (v: smes'); *Izbornik Slavianskikh i Russkikh sochinenii i statei, vnesennykh v khronografy Russkoi redaktsii*, comp. A. Popov, 208; *Russkii Vestnik* (1811, no. 1), 8; A. V. Barsukov, *Rod Sheremetevykh*, 3:54, 55.

81. *Izbornik Slavianskikh i Russkikh sochinenii i statei*, 208; *Rod Sheremetevykh*, 3:54.

82. See *Rod Sheremetevykh*, 3:55.

83. Strahlenberg, *An Historico-Geographical Description*, 218.

84. Strahlenberg, *An Historico-Geographical Description*, 218–19.

85. *DRV*, 13:151, 161, 162, 168, 170.

86. *DRV*, 13:145.

87. Crummey, *Aristocrats and Servitors*, 183.

88. Archimandrite Leonid, "Luk'ian Stepanovich Streshnev," 1–3.

89. John P. LeDonne, *Absolutism and Ruling Class: The Formation of the Russian Political Order, 1700–1825*, 9; Crummey, *Aristocrats and Servitors*, 77.

90. Crummey, *Aristocrats and Servitors*, 77–78.

91. On the children, see Arkhimandrit Leonid, "Luk'ian Stepanovich Streshnev," 10 (list of Tsar Mikhail's children omits Evdokiia Mikhailovna, who died on the day she was born); and G. I. Studenkin, "Romanovy: tsarstvuiushchii dom Rossiiskoi imperii s 1613 g.," viii–ix.

92. On the death of Mikhail Romanov, see Ol'ga Evgen'evna Kosheleva, "Leto 1645 goda: smena lits na rossiiskom prestole"; and R. Martin, "Gifts and Commemoration."

93. Kotošixin, *O Rossii*, 19; Uroff, *On Russia*, 36.

94. See Kotošixin, *O Rossii*, 18–29, 159–71.

95. Collins, *The present State of Russia*, 11–12.

96. Collins, *The present State of Russia*, 103.

97. For this date, see Zabelin, *Domashnii byt russkikh tsarits*, 245.

98. The date of the planned nuptials was inscribed on a draft of the wedding ceremonial (*chin*). See RGADA, *fond* 135, sec. IV, rub. II, no. 21, fol. 1.

99. See "Pis'ma odnogo shveda iz Moskvy v 1647 godu pisannye," 151–54.

100. See Berkh, *Tsarstvovanie Tsaria Alekseia Mikhailovicha*, 1:45–47; Zabelin, *Domashnii byt russkikh tsarits*, 244–50; and Phillip Longworth, *Alexis, Tsar of All the Russias*, 32–36.

101. Kotošixin, *O Rossii*, 19.

102. Collins, *The present State of Russia*, 11–12.

103. Collins, *The present State of Russia*, 103. See also Zabelin, *Domashnii byt russkikh tsarits*, 246. On Collins's account, see L. Loewenson, "The work of Robert Boyle and 'The present State of Russia.'"

104. RGADA, *fond* 135, sec. IV, rub. II, no. 21, fols. 1–71; no. 22, fols. 1–8, 9–13, 14–19, 20, 62, 63–77; RGADA, *fond* 156, *op*. 1, no. 8.

105. Zabelin, *Domashnii byt russkikh tsarits*, 247.

106. In 1649, the family was transferred to Verkhotur'e—where the Khlopovs spent part of their time in exile—and Efimiia's father was made the military governor, or *voevoda*. From there, the family was bounced around between Tobol'sk, Tiumen', and Verkhotur'e. Raf Vsevolozhskii died in 1652. The next year, Efimiia along with her mother and brother were sent to the family's estate in the Kasimov district, where she lived out her life as a spinster despite an abundance of suitors. See *AI*, vol. 4 (St. Petersburg, 1842), no. 59 (p. 165); *SGGD*, pt. 3, no. 155 (pp. 479–80); *AAE*, vol. 4, no. 18 (p. 31); Zabelin, *Domashnii byt russkikh tsarits*, 248–50.

107. Zabelin, *Domashnii byt russkikh tsarits*, 245. It is a curious bibliographical fact that one of the earliest biographies of Aleksei Mikhailovich, by Berkh, is the first to bring the Vsevolozhskii incident to light. Berkh notes he first encountered word of it in a French work (André Guillaume Contant d'Orville, *Les fastes de la Pologne et de la Russe*, 2:95–96), which says that Efimiia fainted because her hair was tied too tightly, echoing (or borrowing from?) one of Collins's explanations. Unable to find any references in the secondary literature available at the time, Berkh began to look for clues of the incident in Russian sources. His first success was his discovery of the published *gramota* from Aleksei to Ivan Litvinov, the *voevoda* in Kasimov, which treats the return of the Vsevolozhskiis from exile on their estates there (*SGGD*, vol. 3 [p. 479]). The second discovery was Ferber's letter, which provided a narrative of the incident.

See Berkh, *Tsarstvovanie tsaria Alekseia Mikhailovicha* (1:42–46; 2:43 n. 33), which contains the text of the letter.

108. Adam Olearius, *The Travels of Olearius in Seventeenth-Century Russia*, 204.

109. On the Miloslavskiis, see Crummey, *Aristocrats and Servitors*, 87; Solov'ev, *Istoriia Rossii s drevneiskhikh vremen*, 5:482–84; Zabelin, *Domashnii byt russkikh tsarits*, 250–51.

110. See Sedov, *Zakat Moskovskogo tsarstva*, 98; Crummey, *Aristocrats and Servitors*, 78–79; Vlas'ev, *Potomstvo Riurika*, vol. 1, pt. 3, 31.

111. Zabelin, *Domashnii byt russkikh tsarits*, 244–45.

112. Olearius, *Travels*, 204.

113. Kotošixin, *O Rossii*, 19–20; Uroff, *On Russia*, 36, 37.

114. See RGADA, *fond* 135, sec. IV, rub. II, no. 24, fol. 2v; *DRV*, 13:175 (as, mistakenly, "Boris Petrovich Morozov").

115. Morozov's union with Anna Miloslavskaia was not a happy one. Collins reports that Anna became embittered and resentful about being compelled to marry a man so much older than she (Collins, *The present State of Russia*, 103–4). The couple had no children. Zabelin, *Domashnii byt russkikh tsarits*, 251, 575; *PSRL*, 37:202 (7156, Letopisets Ivana Slobodskogo).

116. Crummey, *Aristocrats and Servitors*, 188.

117. See, e.g., RGADA, *fond* 188, *op*. 1, no. 46, fol. 12 (Morozov), and fols. 12–12v (Miloslavskii); GIM, Eparchial'noe sobranie, no. 706, fol. 36v; and B. S. Pushkin, ed., "Novyi genealogicheskii material. Sinodik Vozdvizhenskogo monastyria (v Moskve)," 246. See also R. Martin, "Political Folkways and Praying for the Dead in Muscovy: Reconsidering Edward Keenan's 'Slight' against the Church," 269–90.

118. On this identification, see RGB, *fond* 304, no. 818, fols. 241v–242; GIM, Sobranie Uspenskogo sobora, no. 66, fols. 50v–51; GIM, Sobranie Simonovkogo monastyria, no. 2, fols. 33v–34; Lobanov-Rostovskii, *Russkaia rodoslovnaia kniga*, 2:128.

119. RGADA, *fond* 188, *op*. 1, no. 49, fol. 107; and GIM, Eparchial'noe sobranie, no. 710, fols. 117–117v; GIM, Sobranie Simonovkogo monastyria, no. 2, fol. 46; GIM, Sobranie Barsova, no. 954, fol. 7v.

120. RGADA, *fond* 188, *op*. 1, no. 46, fols. 12–12v; GIM, Sobranie Uspenskogo sobora, no. 66, fol. 62; GIM, Eparchial'noe sobranie., no. 706, fol. 36v.

121. Boyar Ivan Glebovich Morozov, Boris's nephew, included both his uncle and Il'ia Miloslavskii in his list of kin to be commemorated in the sinodikon of the hermitage of the Protection of the Virgin (*Pokrovskaia pustyn'*) in Vologda district. The same document includes a separate entry for a certain *boiarynia* Kseniia Ivanovna Miloslavskaia, which also includes both men. See GIM, Muzeinoe sobranie, no. 265, fols. 93 and 95 (respectively). Boyar Ivan Mikhailovich Miloslavskii, Il'ia's second cousin once removed, also included both men in his

entry in the sinodikon for the Monastery of the Ascension (*Voznesenie*): GIM, Eparkhial'noe sobranie, no. 667, fol. 140.

122. See Studenkin, "Romanovy, tsarstvuiushchii dom Rossiiskogo imperii s 1613 g.," ix–xii.

123. See, for example, Sedov, *Zakat Moskovskogo tsarstva*, 113; Lindsey Hughes, *The Romanovs: Ruling Russia, 1613–1917*, 45; Longworth, *Alexis*, 197–99; W. Bruce Lincoln, *The Romanovs: Autocrats of All the Russias*, 54–55.

124. RGADA, *fond* 135, sec. IV, rub. II, no. 29, fols. 2v and 15; and no. 30, fols. 3v and 15.

125. RGADA, *fond* 27, *op.* 1, no. 287. See Paul Bushkovitch, *Peter the Great*, 57–63; Longworth, *Alexis*, 198–99; Zabelin, *Domashnii byt russkikh tsarits*, 252–59.

126. See Lobanov-Rostovskii, *Russkaia rodoslovnaia kniga*, 1:240–41; Aleksandr A. Vasil'chikov, "Rod Naryshkinykh," col. 1498; Bushkovitch, *Peter the Great*, 112–13, 123–24, 143, 156–57; and idem, "Aristocratic Faction and the Opposition to Peter the Great," 89–90. Claims that Matveev's wife was from the Scottish Hamiltons have, according to Sedov, "firmly entered the historical and reference literature and become generally accepted." Sedov, however, convincingly shows that the Khomutovs, Matveev's wife's family, had actually fairly recently entered service near Novgorod. See Sedov, *Zakat Moskovskogo tsarstva*, 83–84; Hughes, *Sofia: Regent of Russia*, 20, 36–37, 50–51, 96, 223; and idem, *Russia in the Age of Peter the Great*, 393.

127. Zabelin, *Domashnii byt russkikh tsarits*, 252–58. See also Longworth, *Alexis*, 199–200; and Solov'ev, *Istoriia Rossii s drevneishikh vremen*, 7:130–31.

128. Handwriting samples from the investigation survive: RGADA, *fond* 27, nos. 52 and 299.

129. Bushkovitch, *Peter the Great*, 61–63.

130. Bushkovitch, *Peter the Great*, 63.

131. Bushkovitch, *Peter the Great*, 60.

132. Bushkovitch, *Peter the Great*, 60–61.

133. Sedov, *Zakat Moskovskogo tsarstva*, 114 n. 9.

134. Reutenfels, "Skazanie sviatleishemu gertsogu toskanskomu Koz'me Tret'emu o Moskovii," pt. 1, 81–82.

Chapter 6

1. Johann Gottfried Gregorii, "*The Comedy of Artaxerxes* (1672)," 155. Louria's translation is based on I. M. Kudriavtsev, ed., *Artakserksovo Deistvo: Pervaia p'esa Russkogo teatra XVII v.*, 149–50.

2. Laurent Rinhuber, *Relation du voyage en Russie fait en 1684 par Laurent Rinhuber, publié pour la première fois d'après les manuscrits qui se conservent à la Bibliothèque ducale publique de Gotha*, 29; and Kudriavtsev, *Artakserksovo Deistvo*, 19.

3. On the play, see R. Martin, "Muscovite Esther: Bride-Shows, Queenship, and Power in *The Comedy of Artaxerxes*," 21–42; Claudia R. Jensen, *Musical Cultures in Seventeenth-Century Russia*, 179–209; Crummey, "Court Spectacles," 139–41; John A. Stone, "The Pastor and the Tzar: A Comment on *The Comedy of Artaxerxes*," 215–51; Kudriavtsev, *Artakserksovo Deistvo*, 3–122; André Mazon and Frédéric Cocron, *La Comédie d'Artaxerxès, présentée en 1672 au Tsar Alexis par Gregorii Le Pasteur: Texte allemande et texte russe*; Kudriavtsev, comp., "Novye postupleniia," 138–39.

4. "*The Comedy of Artaxerxes* (1672)," 148 (Act 1, Scene 1). According to the biblical text, King Artaxerxes has just ended a banquet for all the chief officials of his kingdom in the capital city of Susa that lasted 180 days. He then holds another banquet lasting seven days "for all the people living in the citadel of Susa, to high and low alike" (Est. 1:1–5), while Artaxerxes's queen, Vashti, hosts a banquet "for the women in the royal palace" (Est. 1:9).

5. "*The Comedy of Artaxerxes* (1672)," 149–51 (Act 1, Scene 2). The biblical text of Esther tells much the same story: that Vashti had "wronged not only the king but also all the officers-of-state and all the peoples inhabiting the provinces of King Ahasuerus" (Est. 1:17). Josephus provides an alternative reason for Vashti's refusal to come to Artaxerxes's banquet when summoned. According to him, Vashti's refusal was rooted in "the laws of the Persians, which forbid the wives to be seen by strangers." Flavius Josephus, *The Complete Works of Flavius Josephus*, 175.

6. "*The Comedy of Artaxerxes* (1672)," 151–53 (Act 1, Scene 3). The play agrees with the biblical text. Vashti was disgraced, "never to appear again before King Ahasuerus," so that "all the women will henceforth bow to the authority of their husbands, both high and low alike" (Est. 1:19, 20).

7. "*The Comedy of Artaxerxes* (1672)," 154–56 (Act 2, Scene 1). According to the book of Esther: "A search should be made on the king's behalf for beautiful young virgins, and the king appoint commissioners throughout the provinces of his realm to bring all these beautiful young virgins to the citadel of Susa, to the harem under the authority of Hegai, the king's eunuch, custodian of the women" (Est. 2:1–3).

8. The inspection in the biblical text included a twelve-month "preparatory period": six months with "oil of myrrh," presumably for ritualized purification, and another six months with "spices and lotions commonly used for feminine beauty treatment" (Est. 2:12). At the completion of this year-long preparatory period, each candidate was presented to the king "in the evening, and the following morning returned to another harem entrusted to the care of Shaashgaz, the king's officer, custodian of concubines," and the candidate did not return to the king "unless he was particularly pleased with her and had her summoned by name" (Est. 2:13–14). When it was Esther's turn, "the king liked Esther better than any of the other women; none of the other girls found so much favour and approval with him. So he set the royal diadem on her head and proclaimed her

queen instead of Vashti" (Est. 2:17). In the play, however, there is no night spent with the king, but only an inspection of her appearance and a brief interview. "*The Comedy of Artaxerxes* (1672)," 162–64 (Act 2, Scene 6).

9. "*The Comedy of Artaxerxes* (1672)," 160.

10. Kudriavtsev, *Artakserksovo Deistvo*, 40.

11. RGADA, *fond* 135, sec. IV, rub. II, no. 29, fol. 53v; no. 30, fols. 53v–54.

12. "*The Comedy of Artaxerxes* (1672)," 162, 163.

13. "*The Comedy of Artaxerxes* (1672)," 157.

14. "*The Comedy of Artaxerxes* (1672)," 163.

15. "*The Comedy of Artaxerxes* (1672)," 160. Esther's royal ancestry is suggested in the biblical text by the brief genealogy of Mordecai, Esther's uncle, at the beginning of Chapter 2, which calls to mind King Saul: Mordecai's great-grandfather Kish has the same name as Saul's father (1 Sam. 9:1); Shimei, Mordecai's grandfather, is a name found in the Saulide dynasty (2 Sam. 16:5–8); and both Mordecai and Saul are identified as Benjaminites (1 Sam. 9:1–2). It is likely on the bases of these onomastic similarities that Josephus declares plainly that Esther was "herself of the royal family." Josephus, *The Complete Works*, Book XI, Chapter VI (at pp. 174–75). See also Jon D. Levenson, *Esther: A Commentary*, 56–58.

16. See R. Martin, "Muscovite Esther," 36–42.

17. Bushkovitch, *Peter the Great*, 80.

18. Bushkovitch, *Peter the Great*, 86–87.

19. Bushkovitch, *Peter the Great*, 86–90 and n. 18; Sedov, *Zakat Moskovskogo tsarstva*, 351. See also, generally, W. F. Ryan, "The Witchcraft Hysteria in Early Modern Europe: Was Russia an Exception?"; Kivelson, "What Was *Chernoknizhestvo*? Black Books and Foreign Writings in Muscovite Magic"; idem, "Political Sorcery in Sixteenth-Century Muscovy."

20. Bushkovitch, *Peter the Great*, 90–95; T. V. Starostina, "Ob opale A. S. Matveeva v sviazi s sysknym delom 1676–1677 gg. o khranenii zagovornykh pisem."

21. On the Miloslavskii-Naryshkin struggle of the 1670s and 1680s, see Sedov, *Zakat Moskovskogo tsarstva*; Bushkovitch, *Peter the Great*, 12–169; and LeDonne, "Ruling Families in the Russian Political Order, 1689–1825."

22. See Jensen, *Musical Cultures*, 30, 63, 71; Hughes, *Sophia: Regent of Russia*, 33, 45, 63; and, generally, Bushkovitch, *Religion and Society: The Sixteenth and Seventeenth Centuries*, 163–74.

23. Sedov believes that these investigations were the reason for the delay in taking up the tsar's marriage. Sedov, *Zakat Moskovskogo tsarstva*, 350 and n. 2. On the tsar's illness from childhood, see idem, "Detskie gody tsaria Fedora Alekseevicha."

24. See Bushkovitch, *Peter the Great*, 112–13; and Lobanov-Rostovskii, *Russkaia rodoslovnaia kniga*, 1:153–54.

25. RGADA, *fond* 396, *op*. 2, no. 873; Zabelin *Domashnii byt russkikh tsarits*, 259. On this document, see Sedov, *Zakat Moskovskogo tsartsva*, 353;

Bushkovitch, *Peter the Great*, 112–15; A. P. Bogdanov, "Fedor Alekseevich," *Voprosy istorii* (1994, no. 7): 74; Solov'ev, *Istoriia Rossii s drevneishikh vremen*, 7:197–98.

26. Van Keller's report is published in Bushkovitch, *Peter the Great*, 113 n. 63. See also Sedov, *Zakat Moskovskogo tsarstva*, 353, which also quotes the relevant passages of the letter.

27. Crummey, *Aristocrats and Servitors*, 30, 113–15, 191, 193, 195; Bushkovitch, *Peter the Great*, 95.

28. See Sedov, *Zakat Moskovskogo tsarstva*, 353.

29. Tatishchev, *Istoriia Rossiiskaia*, 7:174.

30. Sedov, *Zakat Moskovskogo tsarstva*, 350–53.

31. *DR*, 4:144; *Vykhody gosudarei tsarei i velikikh kniazei Mikhaila Fedorovicha, Alekseia Mikhailovicha, Fedora Alekseevicha, vsea Rusi samoderzhtsev (s 1632 po 1682)*, 683; Sedov, *Zakat Moskovskogo tsarstva*, 353; and Bogdanov, "Fedor Alekseevich," 74.

32. Sedov, *Zakat Moskovskogo tsarstva*, 352, 354.

33. See Bushkovitch, *Peter the Great*, 113 and n. 63.

34. Bushkovitch, *Peter the Great*, 113 n. 63; Sedov, *Zakat Moskovskogo tsarstva*, 355.

35. The gift went to the unnamed daughter of the *stol'nik* Prince Nikita Ivanov syn Rostovskii. RGADA, *fond* 396, *op*. 2, no. 873, fol. 8, has no day or month, but the version in Zabelin, *Domashnii byt russkikh tsarits*, 259, has "14 August 1680."

36. RGADA, *fond* 135, sec. IV, rub. II, no. 31. The text is formatted for later revision, as was typical of early drafts. Spaces were left for names of courtiers to be inserted later (fols. 3r, 10r, 15r, 17r), and the full title of the tsar is sometimes omitted, replaced by the letter "P" (probably for "*pisat'*")—evidently a marker indicating that the full title should be written in later (fols. 7r, 11r). On this source, see R. Martin, "Muscovite Royal Weddings," 184–86; and V. N. Shumilov's description of the manuscript in L. V. Cherepnin, ed., *Gosudarstvennoe drevlekhranilishche khartii i rukopisei*, 139 (no. 335).

37. The passage pertains to the tsar's banquet table and how it was to be arranged in grand fashion (*nariady velikie*). Compare RGADA, *fond* 135, sec. IV, rub. II, no. 31, fol. 5 (Fedor Alekseevich); and RGADA, *fond* 135, sec. IV, rub. II, no. 30, fol. 25 (Aleksei Mikhailovich).

38. RGADA, *fond* 135, sec. IV, rub. II, no. 31, fol. 13.

39. RGADA, *fond* 135, sec. IV, rub. II, no. 31, fol. 11.

40. RGADA, *fond* 135, sec. IV, rub. II, no. 31, fol. 3. In point of fact, the text contains only the truncated line "Council Secretary of the Muster Chancellery Vasilii…," which likely refers to Semenov since there were no other council secretaries of the Muster Chancellery named Vasilii at the time of the wedding. See Veselovskii, *D'iaki i pod'iachie v XV–XVII vv.*, 468–69.

41. RGADA, *fond* 135, sec. IV, rub. II, no. 31, fol. 32.

42. See R. Martin, "Choreographing the 'Tsar's Happy Occasion'," 806; and Jensen, *Musical Cultures*, 87–88.

43. RGADA, *fond* 135, sec. IV, rub. II, no. 31, fol. 13. Compare with RGADA, *fond* 135, sec. IV, rub. II, no. 30, fols. 14–14v.

44. June is mentioned twice in the charred fragments of the draft ceremonial—once without any day indicated (RGADA, *fond* 135, sec. IV, rub. II, no. 31, fol. 20) and once with the date "June 21" (fol. 17r). Events that were to take place on June 21 according to the fragmentary draft are the same as those that occurred on the fourth day of Aleksei Mikhailovich's wedding (Aleksei was married on a Sunday, so day 4 was a Wednesday), which would suggest that Fedor Alekseevich's wedding was planned for June 18, a Sunday. But this cannot be the case since June 21, 1680, was a Monday, not a Wednesday; and, counting back, June 18, 1680, was not a Sunday, but a Friday, when marriages were not to be celebrated (see Levin, *Sex and Society*, 163–67). A solution to this contradiction might be provided on the archival folder surrounding this manuscript. Here, in an eighteenth-century hand, is inscribed "13 June 1680: The Wedding of Tsar Fedor Alekseevich with Agafiia Semenovna Grushetskaia." This date may be correct since June 13 was a Sunday in 1680, and since the archivist who wrote this inscription may have had more of this tattered text available to him in the eighteenth century than survives today. Thus it may be that events that took place on the fourth day after the wedding of Aleksei Mikhailovich had been scheduled for the eighth day after Fedor Alekseevich's—June 21, a Monday.

45. For the official description, see RGADA, *fond* 135, sec. IV, rub. II, no. 32, fol. 1v (July 18). See also *PSRL*, 31:173 (7188, Mazurinskii Chronicle); 37:184 (7188, Vologodskaia Chronicle), which has July 19; and *DRV*, 11:192 (July 18).

46. Zabelin, *Domashnii byt russkikh tsarits*, 259; Berkh, *Tsarstvovanie tsaria Feodora Alekseevicha i istoriia pervogo Streletskogo bunta*, 1:83–84.

47. RGADA, *fond* 135, sec. IV, rub. II, no. 32.

48. Sedov believes that the two documents—the charred stolbets reflecting a traditional Muscovite royal wedding and the official wedding booklet—may not reflect different ceremonies: "It is unclear which of these 'ceremonials' more accurately describes the royal wedding or, perhaps, if they both portray the way things occurred." Sedov, *Zakat Moskovskogo Tsarstva*, 355.

49. RGADA, *fond* 135, sec. IV, rub. II, no. 32, fol. 2v.

50. RGADA, *fond* 135, sec. IV, rub. II, no. 32, fols. 2v–5.

51. RGADA, *fond* 135, sec. IV, rub. II, no. 32, fol. 5v.

52. RGADA, *fond* 135, sec. IV, rub. II, no. 32, fols. 3v–4.

53. RGADA, *fond* 135, sec. IV, rub. II, no. 32, fol. 5v.

54. RGADA, *fond* 135, sec. IV, rub. II, no. 32, fols. 6–6v. Compare with RGADA, *fond* 135, sec. IV, rub. II, no. 30, fol. 13v (ceremonial for Tsar Aleksei Mikhailovich). On this procession at previous weddings on the wedding day, see R. Martin, "Choreographing the 'Tsar's Happy Occasion'," 814–15.

55. RGADA, *fond* 135, sec. IV, rub. II, no. 32, fols 7–7v.

56. RGADA, *fond* 135, sec. IV, rub. II, no. 32, fols. 8–8v.

57. RGADA, *fond* 135, sec. IV, rub. II, no. 32, fols. 9–9v; *DRV*, 11:192.

58. RGADA, *fond* 135, sec. IV, rub. II, no. 32, fol. 10.

59. Archimandrite Leonid, "Razriadnye zapiski o likhakh byvshikh na vtorykh svad'bakh tsaria i velikogo kniazia Mikhaila Fedorovicha," 17–18, 20–22.

60. *DRV*, 11:192. While the charred fragments of the original ceremonial (RGADA, *fond* 135, sec. IV, rub. II, no. 31) omit the relevant passages that identify the serving priest, the parallels with Aleksei Mikhailovich's second wedding ceremonial are so close as to suggest that Fedor Alekseevich was originally to be married by his father-confessor, as his father was.

61. RGADA, *fond* 135, sec. IV, rub. II, no. 32, fols. 10v–11.

62. Tikhomirov, "Zapiski prikaznykh liudei kontsa XVII v.," *TODRL* 12 (1956): 448. The text also appears in *PSRL*, 31:173 (7190, Mazurinskii Chronicle).

63. Sedov, *Zakat Moskovskogo tsarstva*, 388.

64. RGADA, *fond* 135, sec. IV, rub. II, no. 32, fol 8.

65. Sedov, *Zakat Moskovskogo tsarstva*, 354. See also O. A. Kniaz'kina, "Obriadnost' kak raznovidnost' kul'turnoi zhizni obshchestva (na primere istoricheskoi traditsii svadebnogo obriada rossiiskikh tsarei XVI–XVII vv.)," esp. 151–52.

66. Von Gabel's report is presented in full in Bushkovitch, *Peter the Great*, 96–97, n. 29.

67. Bushkovitch, *Peter the Great*, 113 and n. 63.

68. Sedov, *Zakat Moskovskogo tsarstva*, 356.

69. On these appointments, see Sedov, *Zakat Moskovskogo tsarstva*, 356.

70. *PSZ*, series 1 (1649–1825), 45 vols. (St. Petersburg, 1830), 2:279, no. 829 (July 18, 1680), 2:331, no. 877 (July 11, 1681), 2:351–52, no. 878 (July 14, 1681), 2:341, no. 881 (July 21, 1681); *SGGD*, vol. 4, no. 121 (p. 376); *DAI*, vol. 8, nos. 78 (p. 102). See also Sedov, *Zakat Moskovskogo Tsarstva*, 368; Bushkovitch, *Peter the Great*, 117; Solov'ev, *Istorii Rossii s drevneishikh vremen*, 7:258.

71. The date is based on reports from foreign diplomats in Moscow. See Sedov, *Zakat Moskovskogo tsarstva*, 384.

72. Sedov, *Zakat Moskovskogo tsarstva*, 386; "Dnevnik zverskogo izbieniia moskovskikh boiar v stolitse v 1682 godu i izbranie dvukh tsarei Petra i Ioanna," 397; Hughes, *Sophia*, 47.

73. See Sedov, *Zakat Moskovskogo tsarstva*, 386 (who cites RGADA, *fond* 396, *op*. 2, no. 876, fols. 10v, 13, 15).

74. See quoted passages in Sedov, *Zakat Moskovskogo tsarstva*, 387.

75. Strahlenberg, *An Historico-Geographical Description*, 226.

76. Sedov, *Zakat Moskovskogo tsarstva*, 383–94; Bushkovich, *Peter the Great*, 123; Bogdanov, "Fedor Alekseevich," 74–75.

77. Sedov, *Zakat Moskovskogo tsarstva*, 387.

78. Strahlenberg, *An Historico-Geographical Description*, 226.

79. *PSZ*, series 1, 2:379, no. 907 (February 15, 1682); *DAI*, vol. 9, no. 93 (pp. 201–3); Solov'ev, *Istoriia Rossii s drevneiskhikh vremen*, 7:303.

80. Solov'ev, *Istoriia Rossii s drevneiskhikh vremen*, 7:314.

81. Solov'ev, *Istoriia Rossiia s drevneiskhikh vremen*, 7:314.

82. RGADA, *fond* 210, *Moskovskii stol*, no. 621, fols. 238–43 (at fol. 241).

83. RGADA, *fond* 210, *Moskovskii stol*, no. 621, fol. 242.

84. RGADA, *fond* 210, *Moskovskii stol*, no. 621, fols. 239–41. These 24 attendants were boyar Prince Fedor Fedorovich Kurakin, boyar Rodion Matveevich Streshnev, boyar Ivan Mikhailovich Miloslavskii, boyar Prince Petr Ivanovich Prozorovskii, boyar Ivan Bogdanovich Khitrovo, boyar and *dvoretskii* Prince Vasilii Fedorovich Odoevskii, boyar and *oruzheinichii* Ivan Maksimovich Iazykov, *kravchii* Prince Ivan Grigorevich Kurakin, *okol'nichii* Petr Ivanovich Matiushkin, *okol'nichii* Boris Gavrilovich Iushkov, *okol'nichii* Ivan Timofeevich Kondyrev, *postel'nichii* Aleksei Timofeevich Likhachev, *kaznachei* Mikhail Timofeevich Likhachev, *chashnik* Semen Ivanovich Iazykov, *dumnyi dvorianin* Mikita Ivanovich Akinfov, *dumnyi dvorianin* Vasilii Savich Narbekov, and the *stol'niki komnatnye* Prince Mikhail Prince Iakovlev syn Cherkasskii, Prince Boris Prince Alekseev syn Golitsyn, Ivan Andreev syn Iazykov, Ivan Vasil'ev syn Dashkov, Stepan Bogdanov syn Lovchikov, Petr Matveev syn Apraksin, Fedor Matveev syn Apraksin, and Andrei Matveev syn Apraksin.

85. RGADA, *fond* 210, *Moskovskii stol*, no. 621, fols. 242, 243.

86. Strahlenberg, *An Historico-Geographical Description*, 226.

87. On these events, see Hughes, *Sofia*, 52–88; and *Vosstanie v Moskve, 1682 g. Sbornik dokumentov*, esp. 254–67 (no. 204).

88. On Golitsyn, see Hughes, *Sophia*, 48; and Abby Smith, "The Brilliant Career of Prince Golitsyn."

89. Zaharija Orfelin, *Petar Veliki*, 1:194; and idem, *Zhitie i slavnyia dela Petra Velikago Samoderzhitsa Vserossiiskago s predpolozheniem kratkoi geograficheskoi i politicheskoi istorii o Rossiiskom tsarstve*, 153–54. See also Semevskii, *Tsaritsa Praskov'ia*, 7–8.

90. Orfelin, *Petar Veliki*, 1:194; *Zhitie i slavnyia dela Petra Velikago*, 154. On the date of the wedding of Ivan V and Saltykova, see *PSRL*, 33:188 (7192, Dvinskoi Chronicle); *PSRL*, 37;184 (7192, Vologodskaia Chronicle); *PSRL*, 31:203 (7192, Letopisets 1619–1691 gg.) has February, but no day indicated.

91. Strahlenberg, *An Historico-Geographical Description*, 230.

92. Neuville, *A Curious and New Account of Muscovy*, 50.

93. Strahlenberg, *An Historico-Geographical Description*, 230 n. 43.

94. Strahlenberg, *An Historico-Geographical Description*, 230.

95. Crummey, *Aristocrats and Servitors*, 206; *RRK*, 2:71–73; Poe (with Ol'ga E. Kosheleva, Russell E. Martin, and Boris N. Morozov), *The Russian Elite in the Seventeenth Century: The Çonsular and Ceremonial Ranks of the Russian "Sovereign's Court," 1613–1713*, 445.

96. The other children were Feodosiia, born on June 4, 1690; Ekaterina, born on October 29, 1691; Anna (January 28, 1693); and Praskov'ia (September 24, 1694). See Studenkin, "Romanovy: tsarstvuiushchii dom Rossiiskoi imperii," i–xxxii (at xi–xiii). For a dismissal of Neuville's claim, see Hughes's comment in Neuville, *A Curious and New Account*, 50 n. 149.

97. Full panel, 37-marker Y chromosome DNA tests for all royals would resolve many lingering genealogical questions about Russia's dynasties, including the one raised by Catherine the Great about the paternity of her son Paul I, whom the empress alleged was the son of another Saltykov—Sergei Vasil'evich (her first lover). See Catherine II, *The Memoirs of Catherine the Great*, 301; Madariaga, *Russia in the Age of Catherine the Great*, 10; Herbert H. Kaplan, *Russia and the Outbreak of the Seven Years' War*, 103 and 106 n. 13.

98. For the date of the wedding of Peter I and Lopukhina, see *PSRL*, 31:204 (7197, Letopisets 1619–1691 gg.); *PSRL*, 33:189 (7197, Dvinskoi Chronicle); *PSRL*, 37:187 (7197, Vologodskaia Chronicle); and *PSZ*, 3:10–11, no. 1333 (January 1689).

99. Hughes, *Russia in the Age of Peter the Great*, 393. See also idem, "Peter the Great's Two Weddings: Changing Images of Women in a Transitional Age," 32; S. V. Efimov, "Evdokiia Lopukhina—posledniaia russkaia tsaritsa XVII veka," 137; Mikhail Mikhailovich Bogoslovskii, *Peter I: Materialy dlia biografii*, 1:66; I. I. Golikov, *Deianiia Petra Velikogo*, 49.

100. Bushkovitch, *Peter the Great*, 156–57; Crummey, *Aristocrats and Servitors*, 197, 209; Sergei Konstantinovich Bogoiavlenskii, *Prikaznye sud'i XVII veka*, 211; [Archimandrite Leonid], "Pamiat' o tsaritse Evdokiia na eia rodine."

101. Bushkovitch, *Peter the Great*, 156–57.

102. Christoph von Kochen, "Moskva v 1687–1688 gg.," ed. K. A. Viskovatov, *Russkaia starina* 9 (September 1878): 123–24.

103. For the letters dated January 18, 1689, and February 1, 1689, see Bushkovitch, "Aristocratic Faction," 90 n. 23; and idem, *Peter the Great*, 156.

104. Compare Bushkovitch, *Peter the Great*, 156. There may have been some discussion of Peter's marriage as early as 1685 or 1686, to the daughter of the deposed Georgian king of Imeretia, Archil, who arrived in Moscow and eventually retired there, dying in 1713. See Eugene Schuyler, *Peter the Great, Emperor of Russia*, 1:118.

105. *RRK*, 1:316.

106. Boris Ivanovich Kurakin, "Gistoriia o tsare Petre Alekseeviche," 1:55; also published as "'Gistoriia' o tsare Petre Alekseeviche' B. I. Kurakina," 1:369.

107. See Efimov, "Evdokiia Lopukhina," 138. On the problems with Kurakin's writings as sources generally, see Ernest Zitser, "The *Vita* of Prince Boris Ivanovich 'Korybut'-Kurakin: Personal Life-Writing and Aristocratic Self-Fashioning at the Court of Peter the Great."

108. Strahlenberg, *An Historico-Geographical Description*, 218.

109. Zabelin, *Domashnii byt russkikh tsarits*, 259–60.

110. Korb, *Diary of an Austrian Secretary of Legation at the Court of Czar Peter the Great*, 1:132.

111. On the abolition of *mestnichestvo*, see Kollmann, *By Honor Bound*, 138–39, 203, 226–31, 233–35, and 250; Crummey, "Reflections on Mestnichestvo in the 17th Century," 269–81; Markevich, *Istoriia mestnichestvo v Moskovskom gosudarstve XV–XVII veke*, 497–611; and, generally, idem, *O mestnichestve*.

112. On the Palm Sunday ritual, see Michael Flier, "Court Ceremony in an Age of Reform," 73–95; idem, "Breaking the Code," 213–42; and idem, "The Iconography of Royal Procession," 118.

113. Crummey, *Aristocrats and Servitors*, 31.

114. "New men" is a phrase used by Crummey (*Aristocrats and Servitors*, 26). See also Poe, "Tsar Aleksei Mikhailovich and the Demise of the Romanov Political Settlement," 537–64.

115. *DRV*, 11:196–97; Semevskii, *Tsaritsa Praskov'ia*, 7–10.

116. This quotation is taken from a 1724 copy of the diary: RGADA, *fond* 180, *op*. 1, no. 3, fol. 37.

117. *DRV*, 11:196; Hughes, "Peter the Great's Two Weddings," 32; G. V. Esipov, "Tsaritsa Evdokiia Feodorovna," 3; Smirnov, *Drevne-russkii dukhovnik*, 253–54.

118. Patrick Gordon, *Passages from the Diary of General Patrick Gordon of Auchleuchries in the years 1635–1699*, 165.

119. See M. A. Korf, *Braunshveigskoe semeistvo*, 373–414.

120. *DRV*, 11:183–85, 187–88.

121. *DRV*, 11:213, 227.

122. Hughes, *Sophia*, 221–61.

123. Hughes, "Peter the Great's Two Weddings," 34. See also her *Russia in the Age of Peter the Great*, 393–94.

124. See James Cracraft, *The Revolution of Peter the Great*, 10, 120; Bogoslovskii, *Materialy*, vol. 1; Solov'ev, *Istoriia Rossii s drevneiskhikh vremen*, 7:449–50, 574–75; Semevskii, *Tsaritsa Katerina Alekseevna, Anna i Villim Mons*, 11–17.

125. On 1711 as the date for Peter's private wedding with Ekaterina Alekseevna, see G. A. Mikhailov, "Graviura A. Zubova 'Svad'ba Petra I': real'nost' i vysysel," 42–44; and Zitser, *The Transfigured Kingdom: Sacred Parody and Charismatic Authority at the Court of Peter the Great*, 119. Others put the date of the secret wedding in 1707. See Hughes, *Russia in the Age of Peter the Great*, 396.

126. *PiB*, 12(i): 86, 361; Charles Whitworth [Ch. Vitvort], "Ch. Whitworth to the right honourable m. secretary S-t John," *SbIRIO*, vol. 61 (1888), no. 41 (p. 143).

127. As Hughes briefly notes, opinions on her origins range. She was either "the illegitimate daughter of a serf or the orphaned daughter of a Swedish officer." Hughes, *Russia in the Age of Peter the Great*, 395.

128. Anna Petrovna's wedding to Karl Friedrich of Holstein-Gottorp took

place just months after Peter I's death, but the marriage alliance was negotiated by Peter I in the last years of his life. See R. Martin, "Ritual and Religion." A brief historical composition dating from the early eighteenth century praises Peter's preference for foreign brides: "For previous all-Russian sovereign tsars and autocrats did not permit their daughters to marry, neither to foreigners nor to Russians. But this most wise monarch [i.e., Peter I], laying aside all these ancient ways, instead followed the example of the blessed accounts of the ancient Greek emperors, namely emperors Constantine and Michael Paleologus and other great Christian rulers, such as Grand Prince Yaroslav, who is known as Georgii in Holy Baptism, and others. And he [Peter] allowed his daughter Tsarevna Anna Petrovna to marry Duke Karl Friedrich of Holstein Gottorp." VIMAIViVS, *fond* 52, *op*. 114, no. 1, fol. 400v. I thank Irina Aleksandrovna Voznesenskaia for making me aware of this document.

129. See Hughes, *Russia in the Age of Peter the Great*, 51, 261–62, 405–6, 411–15.

130. Zitser, *Transfigured Kingdom*, 117–18.

131. Omitting, as we should, the marriage of the First False Dmitrii with Marina Mnishek.

132. The best treatment of these processes in Russia remains Rogger, *National Consciousness in Eighteenth-Century Russia*, 1–7, 39–41, and elsewhere. See also Dunning, *Russia's First Civil War*, 404–23, 461–80.

133. See R. Martin, "Dowries and Diplomacy."

134. See R. Martin, "Ritual and Religion." For the description of the wedding, see, preferably, BAN, 16.15.15, fols. 175–78v; and BAN, 32.4.21, fols. 129v–132, but also *DRV*, 13:97–103.

135. Gustav did not leave Russia but was given Uglich as an appanage. The First False Dmitrii would arrest and exile him to Iaroslav, but he would be released by Tsar Vasilii Shuiskii and sent to live in Kashin, where he died in 1607. Solov'ev, *Istoriia Rossii s drevneiskhikh vremen*, 4:366, 693 n. 24; Konrad Brussov, *Moskovskaia khronika, 1584–1613*, 84–85, 209–10, and 340 n. 17.

136. The actual conditions established by the Russians for Hans are not known because of the loss of the documentation that stipulated them. They can be deduced, however, on the basis of Hans's actions upon arriving in Moscow, and perhaps also the stipulations and conditions placed on Phillip of Schleswig, Hans's kinsman and potential replacement as Kseniia's groom. See Karamzin, *Istoriia gosudarstva Rossiiskogo*, vol. 11, col. 28, and nn. 59 and 77; and "Dva svatovstva inozemnykh printsev k russkim velikim kniazhnam v XVII stoletii," trans. A. Shliapkin, in *ChIOIDR* (1867, bk. 4): 1–72 (at 1–56, Materialy inostrannye).

137. The best treatment of the episode remains A. P. Golubtsov, *Preniia o vere, vyzvannyia delom korolevicha Val'demara i tsarevny Iriny Mikhailovny*. See also Iu. N. Shcherbachev, "Materialy po istorii drevnei Rossii, khraniashchiesia v Kopengagene (1326–1690)," *ChIOIDR* (1893, bk. 1), 221, 224 and elsewhere; and G. V. Forsten, "Snosheniia Danii s Rossiei v tsartvovanie Khristiana IV," 331–34 (otdel nauk).

138. See Barbara Skinner, *On the Western Front of the Eastern Church: Uniate and Orthodox Conflict in 18th-Century Poland, Ukraine, Belarus, and Russia*, chapter 1; and M. V. Dmitriev, V. N. Floria, and S. G. Iakovenko, eds., *Brestskaia uniia 1596 g. i obshchestvenno-politicheskaia bor'ba na Ukraine i v Belorussii v kontse XVI–nachale XVII v.*

139. On this debate, see, for example, A. Serafimov, *Pravila i praktika tserkvi otnositel'no prisoedineniia k pravoslaviiu nepravoslavnykh khristian*; and Andrei V. Psarev, "The 19th Canonical Answer of Timothy of Alexandria: On the History of Sacramental *Oikonomia*."

140. On the council, see Bushkovitch, *Religion and Society in Russia*, 52–53; and A. A. Bulychev, "O publikatsii postanovlenii tserkovnogo sobora 1620 g. v mirskom i inocheskom 'Trebnikakh' (M., 1639)," *Germenevtika drevnerusskoi literatury*, 2:35–62.

141. On Nasedka, see Bushkovich, *Religion and Society in Russia*, 134–36; A. Shilov, "Ivan Nasedka," *RBS*, [vol. 11] (1914), 105–10.

142. On Shakhovskoi, see Keenan, "Semen Shakhovskoi and the Condition of Orthodoxy," 795; idem, *The Kurbskii-Groznyi Apocrypha: The Seventeenth-Century Genesis of the "Correspondence" Attributed to Prince A. M. Kurbskii and Tsar Ivan IV*, 33–35, 75, 180–86; V. I. Gal'tsov, "Svedeniia o S. I. Shakhovskom v opisi arkhiva Posol'skogo prikaza 1673 g."

143. For the memorandum, see A. P. Golubtsov, "Pamiatniki prenii o vere, voznikshikh po delu korolevicha Val'demara i tsarevny Iriny Mikhailovny" (pp. 164–65, Materialy istoriko-literaturnye).

144. On these punishments, see Kosheleva, "Prigovor kniaziu Ivanu Nikitichu Khovanskomu."

145. Thyrêt, *Between God and Tsar*, chapter 2.

146. See *PSZ*, series 1, 4:494–97, no. 2272 (June 10, 1710), 4:669–73, no. 2354 (April 19 /May 10, 1711); and 5:453–54, no. 3007 (April, 7/18 1716). Wedding contracts survive for Aleksei Petrovich and Anna Petrovna (RGADA, *fond* 156, *op*. 1, nos. 14 and 15). See also O. G. Ageeva, "Novye iavleniia v obshchestvennoi zhizni i bytu Peterburga pervoi cheterti XVIII veka: na premere tsarskikh svadeb," 89–103 (at 92); Semevskii, *Tsaritsa Praskov'ia,* 46 n. 1; and Solov'ev, *Istoriia Rossii s drevneishikh vremen*, 8:356.

147. Joost Jules [Iust Iul'], "Zapiski Iusta Iulia," 33–38.

148. Jules, "Zapiski," 36.

149. On the symbolism of these rituals and the crowning ceremony generally, see Meyendorff, *Marriage*, 33–42; and Levin, *Sex and Society*, 83–95.

150. His illness did not prevent him from setting off for Riazan' immediately after responding to Peter. See Jules, "Zapiski," 33–34; and Solov'ev, *Istoriia Rossii s drevneishikh vremen*, 8:338.

151. Jules, "Zapiski," 33.

152. Cracraft, *The Church Reform of Peter the Great*, 27–28.

Epilogue

1. The literature abounds with accounts of Empress Elizabeth's secret marriage to Aleksei Razumovskii, but, as Anisimov has put it, "We still have no direct evidence of this marriage." See Evgenii V. Anisimov, *Five Empresses: Court Life in Eighteenth-Century Russia*, 214–18 (quote at 215); and Douglas Smith, "Did Catherine the Great and Grigorii Potemkin Wed? Some Myths, Facts, and Observations on Secret Royal Marriages," 84.

2. On these marriages, see Studenkin, "Rodoslovie tsarstsvuiushchago v Rossii doma Romanovykh," xix.

3. On these marriages, see Studenkin, "Rodoslovie tsarstsvuiushchago v Rossii doma Romanovykh," xx–xxii.

4. See Hughes, *The Romanovs*, 86.

5. John P. LeDonne, "Ruling Families in the Russian Political Order."

6. This argument is elaborated in R. Martin, "The Petrine Divide and the Periodization of Early Modern Russia."

7. RGADA, *fond* 156, *op.* 1, no. 197.

8. This is the thesis of Brenda Meehan Waters, *Autocracy and Aristocracy: The Russian Service Elite of 1730.*

9. For the Petrine Law of Succession, see *PSZ*, series 1, 6:496–97, no. 3893 (February 5, 1722). On prior systems of succession in Kievan and Muscovite Rus', see the following (and the sources they cite): Ostrowski, "Systems of Kinship Succession in Rus' and Steppe Societies"; J. Martin, *Medieval Russia*; Kollmann, "Collateral Succession in Kievan Rus'"; and Nitsche, *Grossfürst und Thronfolger*.

10. *PSZ*, series 1, 24:587–89, no. 17.910 (April 5, 1797).

11. *PSZ*, series 1, 37:129–30, no. 28.208 (March 20, 1820). On the Pauline Law and Alexander I's amendment, see Wortman, "The 'Fundamental State Laws' of 1832 as Symbolic Act"; idem, *The Formation of a Russian Legal Consciousness*; idem, "Russian Monarchy and the Rule of Law: New Considerations of the Court Reform of 1864," 1:176–78.

12. The requirement for equal marriage (or *Ebenbürtigkeit*) under the Pauline Law was interpreted so strictly that even Alexander II's second marriage, to Ekaterina Mikhailovna Dolgorukova, who was a princess of the Riurikid dynasty and of the same family as Tsar Mikhail Romanov's first wife, was deemed morganatic, with their children having no rights of succession, though they were granted the titles of Counts Romanovskii-Iur'evskii. See Hughes, *The Romanovs*, 185, 186, 188, 189; and R. Martin, "The Petrine Divide."

13. Dan Ungurianu, *Plotting History: The Russian Historical Novel in the Imperial Age*, 5.

14. See Ungurianu's useful inventory of historical novels in *Plotting History*, 209–62.

15. Lev Aleksandrovich Mei, *Izbrannye proizvedeniia*, 329–422.

16. Both Milii Alekseevich Balakirev and Alexander Porfir'evich Borodin considered using the play as the basis for an operatic work before Rimskii-Korsakov.

17. Harlow Loomis Robinson, "Nikolai Rimsky-Korsakov. *The Tsar's Bride*," 112.

18. The opera has been recorded numerous times, but perhaps the preferred recording remains Nicolai Rimsky-Korsakov, *The Tsar's Bride*, audio CD (2008). See also Nikolay Rimsky-Korsakov, *The Tsar's Bride: Opera in Four Acts*.

19. Nikolai Rimskii-Korsakov, *Tsarskaia nevesta*, DVD (1965), which is based on the play by Lev Mei.

20. Other depictions of bride-shows include A. Abramov, *Vybor nevesty tsaria Alekseia Mikhailovicha* (*Tsar Aleksei Mikhailovich Picks a Bride*; 1882), and various engravings and plates that have appeared in books. For example, N. P. Lambin, *Istoriia Petra Velikogo*, 32 (engraving by El'van); or the engraving in Georgievskii's *Prazdnichnye sluzhby i tserkovnye torzhestva*, 354–55, which is based on Makovskii's painting.

21. See R. Martin, "Religion and Ritual."

22. Shcherbatov, "O brakakh rossiiskikh tsarei," 100.

23. Shcherbatov, "O brakakh rossiiskikh tsarei," 111.

Bibliography

Manuscript Sources

Russian State Archive of Ancient Acts [Russkii gosudarstvennyi arkhiv drevnikh aktov], Moscow.

Fond 27. Privy Chancellery [Prikaz tainykh del]

Opis' 1, no. 12: Petition from Ivan IV to Bekbulatovich, 1575

Opis' 1, no. 287: List of virgins from which in 1670 and 1671 Tsar Aleksei Mikhailovich selected his bride

Opis' 1, nos. 52 and 299: Materials relating to Beliaeva Affair

Fond 135. Treasure Room [Drevlekhranilishche]

Section III, rubric II, no. 12: Loyalty Oath of Fedor Mikhailovich Mstislavskii

Section IV, rubric II, nos. 1, 2, 3, 4, 5, 7, 8, 9, 10, 11, 12, 13, 14, 15, 16, 17, 18, 19, 21, 22, 23, 24, 25, 26, 27, 28, 29, 30, 31, 32: Descriptions of royal weddings

Section V, rubric III, no. 16. Illuminated description of the wedding of Tsar Mikhail Romanov (1626).

Fond 156. Historical and Ceremonial Collection [Istoricheskoe i tseremonal'noe sobranie]

Opis' 1, nos. 1, 3, 4, 5, 6, 7, 8, 9, 10: Descriptions of royal weddings

Opis' 1, nos. 14, 15: Royal wedding contracts

Opis' 1, no. 197: List of Catherine I's relatives

Fond 180. Chancellery of the Moscow Main Archive of the Ministry of Foreign Affairs [Kantseliariia MGAMID]

Opis' 1, no. 3: Diary of Patrick Gordon

Fond 181. Manuscript Division of the Library of the Moscow Main Archive of the Ministry of Foreign Affairs [Rukopisnyi otdel Biblioteki MGAMID]

No. 115: List of tutors and other privy servitors for Tsar Aleksei Mikhailovich

No. 119: Muster book

No. 123: Wedding Muster (long redaction) for Ivan IV and Marfa Sobakina

Fond 188. Manuscript Collection of RGADA [Rukopisnoe sobranie RGADA]

Opis' 1, no. 468: Muster book

Opis' 1, nos. 46, 49: Sinodikons

Fond 199. Papers of G.-F. Müller [Portfeli G.-F. Millera]

Opis' 284, pt. 2, no. 8: Dolgorukov genealogies

Fond 210. Muster Chancellery [Razriadnyi prikaz]
Moskovskii stol, no. 621: Royal wedding description
Moskovskii stol, no. 1131: Documents relating to Simeon Bekbulatovich
Opis' 18, no. 87: Genealogy of Glinskiis
Opis' 18, nos. 18 and 46: Koltovskii genealogies
Fond 396. Archive of the Armory [Arkhiv Oruzheinoi palaty]
Opis' 2, no. 873: Manuscript miscellany with list of gifts to prospective brides
Opis' 2, no. 3714: Sinodikon

Russian State Library [Rossiiskaia gosudarstvennaia biblioteka], Manuscript Division, Moscow.
Fond 304 [Sobranie Troitse-Sergeeva Monastyria]
Opis' 1, nos. 40, 42, 43, 813, 814, 818, 838: Sinodikons

State Historical Museum [Gosudarstvennyi istoricheskii muzei], Moscow.
Eparkhial'noe sobranie (Eparchy Collection), no. 413, 667, 706, 710: Sinodikons
Muzeinoe sobranie (Museum Collection), nos. 265, 3652: Sinodikons
Sobranie Simonovskogo monastyria (Simonov Monastery Collection), no.2: Sinodikon
Sobranie Barsova (Barsov Collection), nos. 954, 966: Sinodikons
Sobranie Uspenskogo sobora (Dormition Cathedral Collection), nos. 64, 66, 69, 70: Sinodikons

Russian National Library [Rossiiskaia national'naia biblioteka], St. Petersburg.
Titov Collection,
No. 891: Royal wedding muster (fragment)
Q.IV.86: Manuscript miscellany, including royal wedding descriptions
Q.XVII.17: Manuscript miscellany, including the *Chronograph of the Marriages of Ivan Vasil'evich*

Library of the Russian Academy of Sciences, BAN [Biblioteka Rossiiskoi Akademii nauk], Manuscript Division, St. Petersburg.
Nos. 16.15.15; 32.4.21; 21.10.25; 31.6.40; 32.5.11; and 31.7.20: Royal wedding descriptions (compilatory manuscript books).

The Military-Historical Museum of Artillery, Engineers, and Communications Forces [Voenno-istoricheskii muzei artillerii, inzhenernykh voisk i voisk sviazi], St. Petersburg.
Fond 52, *op.* 114, no. 1: Manuscript miscellanea containing an early history of Russia in the eighteenth century

Iaroslav Regional Library [Iaroslavskaia oblastnaia biblioteka], Manuscript Divi No. RK319031V

Published Primary and Secondary Sources

Abramovich, G. V. *Kniaz'ia Shuiskie i Rossiiskii tron.* Leningrad: Izdatel'stvo Leningradskogo universiteta, 1991.

Afinogenov, Dmitrii. "The Bride-Show of Theophilos: Some Notes on the Sources." *Eranos* 95 (1997): 10–18.

Ageeva, O. G. "Novye iavleniia v obshchestvennoi zhizni i bytu Peterburga pervoi chetverti XVIII veka: na primere tsarskikh svadeb." In *Russkaia kul'tura v perekhodnyi period ot srednevekov'ia k novomu vremeni. Sbornik statei*. Edited by A. N. Kopylov, 89–103. Moscow: Institut Rossiiskoi istorii RAN, 1992.

Akty, sobrannye v bibliotekakh i arkhivakh Rossiiskoi imperii Arkheograficheskoiu ekspeditsieiu Imperatorskoi Akademii nauk. 4 vols. St. Petersburg: Tipografiia II Otdeleniia Sobstvennoi E. I. V. Kantselariii, 1836.

Akty istoricheskie, sobrannye i izdannye Arkheograficheskoiu kommissieiu. 5 vols. St. Petersburg: Tipografiia Ekspeditsii zagotovleniia gosudarstvennykh bumag, 1841–1842.

Akty sotsial'no-ekonomicheskoi istorii severo-vostochnoi Rusi. 3 vols. Moscow: Akademiia nauk SSSR, 1952–1964.

Alef, Gustav. "Aristocratic Politics and Royal Policy in Muscovy in the Late Fifteenth and Early Sixteenth Centuries." *Forschungen zur osteuropäischen Geschichte* 27 (1980): 77–109.

———. "The Crisis of the Muscovite Aristocracy: A Factor in the Growth of Monarchical Power." *Forschungen zur osteuropäischen Geschichte* 15 (1970): 15–58.

———. "A History of the Muscovite Civil War: The Reign of Vasilii II (1425–1462)." Ph.D. diss., Princeton University, 1956.

———. *Rulers and Nobles in Fifteenth-Century Muscovy*. London: Variorum Reprints, 1983.

———. "Was Grand Prince Dmitrii Ivanovich Ivan III's 'King of the Romans'?" In *Essays in Honor of A. A. Zimin*. Edited by Daniel Clarke Waugh, 89–101. Columbus: Slavica, 1985.

Allen, W. E. D. "The Georgian Marriage Projects of Boris Godunov." *Oxford Slavonic Papers* 12 (1965): 69–79.

———. *Russian Embassies to the Georgian Kings (1589–1603)*. 2 vols. Cambridge, UK: Published by the Haklyut Society for the University Press, 1970.

Altbauer, Moshé, ed. *Saint Catherine's Monastery, Mount Sinai: An Orthodox Pomjanyk of the Seventeenth–Eighteenth Centuries*. Cambridge, Mass.: Harvard University Press, 1989.

Altbauer, Moshé, and Moshé Taube. "The Slavonic Book of Esther: When, Where, and from What Language Was It Translated?" *Harvard Ukrainian Studies* 8 (1984): 304–20.

Anisimov, Evgenii V. *Five Empresses: Court Life in Eighteenth-Century Russia*. Translated by Kathleen Carroll. Westport, Conn.: Praeger, 2004.

Ankhimiuk, Iurii Vladimirovich. *Chastnye Razriadnye knigi s zapisami za posledniuiu chetvert' XV–nachalo XVII vekov*. Moscow: Drevlekhranilishche, 2005.

Annales Regni Francorum, inde ab a. 741. usque ad a. 829., qui dicuntur Annales Laurissenses Maiores et Einhardi. Edited by Friedrich Kurze. In the series

Monumenta Germaniae historica. Scriptores rerum Germanicarum in usum scholarum separatism editi, 6. Hanover: Impensis Bibliopolii Hahniani, 1895.

Antonov, A. V., ed. "Rodoslovnaia kniga po spisku kniazia M. A. Obolenskogo." In *Pamiatniki istorii russkogo sluzhilogo sosloviia*. Moscow: Drevlekhranilishche, 2011.

Apollodorus. *The Library of Greek Mythology*. Translated by Keith Aldrich. Lawrence, Kans.: Coronado Press, 1975.

Bantysh-Kamenskii, N. N. *Obzor vneshnykh snoshenii Rossii (do 1800)*. 4 vols. Moscow: Izdatel'stvo Komissii pechetaniia gos. gramot i dogovorov pri Moskovskom glavnom arkhive Ministerstva inostrannykh del, 1894–1902.

Baron, Samuel H., and Nancy Shields Kollmann, eds. *Religion and Culture in Early Modern Russia and Ukraine*. DeKalb: Northern Illinois University Press, 1997.

Barsukov, A. V. *Rod Sheremetevykh*. 8 vols. St. Petersburg: [n.p.], 1881–1904.

Baumgarten, N. de. "Généalogies des branches régnantes de Rurikides du XIIIe au XVIe siècle." *Orientalia Christiana* 35, no. 94 (June 1934): 1–152.

Bazilevich, Konstantin Vasil'evich. *Vneshniaia politika tsentralizovannogo gosudarstva (vtoraia polovina XV veka)*. Moscow: Izdatel'stvo Moskovskogo universiteta, 1952.

Begunov, Iu. K. "Povest' o vtorom brake Vasiliia III," *TODRL* 25 (1970): 105–18. Beliaev, I. S. "K rodosloviiu Nagikh." *Izvestiia RGO*. Vol. 3 (1909): 88–92 (otdel I).

Beliakov, A. V. "Chingisidy v Rossii v XV–XVI vekakh." *Arkhiv russkoi istorii* 8 (2007): 9–59.

Belokurov, Sergei Alekseevich. *O biblioteke moskovskikh gosudarei v XVI stoletii*. Moscow: Tipografiia G. Lissnera i A. Geshelia, 1898.

———, ed. *Razriadnye zapisi za Smutnoe vremia (7113–7121 gg.)*. Moscow: Tipografiia Shtaba Moskovskogo voennogo Okruga, 1907.

Berezhkov, M. N. "Elena Ivanovna, velikaia kniaginia litovskaia i koroleva pol'skaia." *Trudy Deviatogo arkheologicheskogo s"ezda v Vil'ne, 1893*. Vol. 2. Moscow: Tipografiia Imperatorskoi Akademii nauk, 1897.

Berkh, V[asilii Nikolaevich]. *Tsarstvovanie Tsaria Alekseia Mikhailovicha*. 2 vols. St. Petersburg: Tipografiia Kh. Gintse, 1831.

———. *Tsarstvovanie tsaria Feodora Alekseevicha i istoriia pervogo Streletskogo bunta*. 2 vols. St. Petersburg: Tipografiia Kh. Gintse, 1834–1835.

Berry, Lloyd E., and Robert O. Crummey. *Rude and Barbarous Kingdom: Russia in the Accounts of Sixteenth-Century English Voyagers*. Madison: University of Wisconsin Press, 1968.

Boeck, Brian. "Eyewitness or False Witness? Two Lives of Metropolitan Filipp of Moscow." *Jahrbücher für Geschichte Osteuropas* 55, no. 2 (2007): 161–77.

Bogatyrev, Sergei. "Micro-Periodization and Dynasticism: Was There a Divide in the Reign of Ivan the Terrible?" *Slavic Review* 69, no. 2 (Summer 2010): 398–409.

———. "Reinventing the Russian Monarchy in the 1550s: Ivan the Terrible, the Dynasty, and the Church." *Slavonic and East European Review* 85, no. 2 (April 2007): 271–93.

———. *The Sovereign and His Counsellors: Ritualised Consultations in Muscovite Political Culture, 1350s–1570s*. Helsinki: Finnish Academy of Sciences, 2000.

Bogdanov, A. P. "Fedor Alekseevich." *Voprosy istorii* (1994, no. 7): 59–77.

Bogoiavlenskii, Sergei Konstantinovich. *Prikaznye sud'i XVII veka*. Moscow: Izdatel'stvo Akademii nauk, 1946.

Bogoslovskii, Mikhail Mikhailovich. *Peter I: Materialy dlia biografii*. 5 vols. Moscow: OGIZ, Gosudarstvennoe sotsial'no-ekonomicheskoe izdatel'stvo, 1940–1948.

Boiarskaia kniga 1658 goda. Edited by N. M. Rogozhin. Moscow: Rossiiskii institut istorii RAN, 2004.

Boiarskie spiski poslednei chetverti XVI–nachala XVII vv. i Rospis' russkogo voiska 1604 g. Ukazatel' sostava gosudareva dvora po fondu razriadnogo prikaza. Edited by V. I. Buganov. Compiled by S. P. Mordovina and A. L. Stanislavskii. 2 vols. Moscow: TsGADA, 1979.

Borisov, N. S. "Moskovskie kniaz'ia i russkie mitropolity XIV veka." *Voprosy istorii* (1986, no. 8): 30–43.

Bourboulis, Photeine P. *Studies in the History of Modern Greek Story-Motives*. In the series Hellenikā periodikon suggramma Hetaipeias Makedonikōn Spoudōn, suppl. 2. Thessalonike: n.p., 1953.

Brussov, Konrad. *Moskovskaia khronika 1584–1613*. Edited by I. I. Smirnov. Moscow-Leningrad: Izdatel'stvo Akademii nauk SSSR, 1961.

Buchau, Daniel Printz von [Daniil Prints iz Bukhova]. "Nachalo i vozvyshenie Moskovii." *ChIOIDR*. Vol. 99 (1876, bk. 3), 1–46 (Materialy inostrannye).

———. *Scriptores rerum Livonicarum*. 2 vols. Riga and Leipzig: Eduard Frantzen Verlags-Comptoir, 1853.

Buganov, Viktor Ivanovich. *Razriadnye knigi poslednei chetverti XV–nachale XVII v*. Moscow: Izdatel'stvo Akademii nauk SSSR, 1962.

Bulanin, Dmitrii Mikhailovich. "Maksim Grek." In *Slovar' knizhnikov i knizhnosti drevnei Rusi*. Edited by D. S. Likhachev. Vol. 2: Vtoraia polovina XIV–XVI v. (part 2): 89–98. Leningrad: Nauka, 1987–2003.

Bulychev, A. A. "O publikatsii postanovlenii tserkovnogo sobora 1620 g. v mirskom i inocheskom 'Trebnikakh' (M., 1639)." In *Germenevtika drevnerusskoi literatury*. Vol. 2:35–62. Moscow: Rossiiskaia Akademiia nauk, Institute mirovoi literatury im. A. M. Gor'kogo, 1989.

Bulygin, I. A., ed. *Pravila izdaniia "Aktov Russkogo gosudarstva XVI–XVII vv."* Moscow: Institut istorii, Akademiia nauk SSSR, 1984.

Bury, J[ohn] B[agnell]. *A History of the Eastern Roman Empire from the Fall of Irene to the Accession of Basil I*. London: Macmillan, 1912.

Bushkovitch, Paul. "Aristocratic Faction and the Opposition to Peter the Great:

The 1690s." *Forschungen zur osteuropäischen Geschichte* 50 (1995): 80–120.

———. "The Epiphany Ceremony of the Russian Court in the Sixteenth and Seventeenth Centuries." *Russian Review* 49, no. 1 (January 1990): 1–17.

———. *Peter the Great: The Struggle for Power*. Cambridge: Cambridge University Press, 2001.

———. "Princes Cherkasskii or Circassian Murzas: The Kabardians in the Russian Boyar Elite, 1560–1700." *Cahiers du Monde russe* 45, nos. 1–2 (January–June 2004): 9–30.

———. *Religion and Society in Russia: The Sixteenth and Seventeenth Centuries*. New York: Oxford University Press, 1992.

———. "Shvedskie istochniki o Rossii 1624–1626 gg." *Arkhiv russkoi istorii* 8 (2007): 359–81.

Bychkova, Margarita Evgen'evna. "Obriady venchaniia na prestol 1498 i 1547 godov: Voploshchenie idei vlasti gosudaria." *Cahiers du Monde russe et soviétique* 34, nos. 1–2 (1993): 245–55.

———. "Rodoslovie Glinskikh iz Rumiantsevskogo sobraniia." In *Zapiski Otdela rukopisei GBL* 38 (1977): 104–25.

———. "Rodoslovie kniazei Glinskikh." In *Istoricheskaia genealogiia/Historical Genealogy* 3 (1994): 25–27.

———. *Rodoslovnye knigi XVI–XVII vv. kak istoricheskii istochnik*. Moscow: Nauka, 1975.

———. *Sostav klassa feodalov Rossii XVI veka: istoriko-genealogicheskoe issledovanie*. Moscow: Nauka, 1986.

Bychkova, Margarita Evgen'evna, and Maksim Igorevich Smirnov. *Genealogiia v Rossii: istoriia i perspektivy*. Moscow: Territoriia, 2004.

Carolingian Chronicles: Royal Frankish Annals and Nithard's Histories. Translated by Bernhard Walter Scholz and Barbara Rogers. Ann Arbor, Mich.: Ann Arbor Paperbacks for the University of Michigan Press, 1972.

Catherine II. *The Memoirs of Catherine the Great*. Edited by Dominique Maroger. Translated by Moura Budberg. New York: Macmillan, 1955.

Cherepnin, Lev Vladimirovich, ed. *Gosudarstvennoe drevlekhranilishche khartii i rukopisei. Opis' dokumental'nykh materialov fonda 135*. Compiled by V. N. Shumilov. Moscow: [Vneshtorizdat], 1971.

———. *Russkie feodal'nye arkhivy XIV–XVI vekov*. 2 vols. Moscow-Leningrad: Akademiia nauk SSSR, 1948–1951.

Cherniavsky, Michael. "Khan or Basileus: An Aspect of Russian Mediaeval Political Theory." *Journal of the History of Ideas* 20, no. 4 (October–December 1959): 459–76.

The Chronicle of John Malalas. Translated by Elizabeth Jeffreys, Michael Jeffreys, and Roger Scott. In the series Byzantina Australiensia, 4. Melbourne: Australian Association of Byzantine Studies, 1986.

Chteniia v Imperatorskom obshchestve istorii i drevnostei Rossiiskikh pri Mos-

kovskom universitete. 264 vols. Moscow: Universitetskaia tipografiia, 1846–1918.

Chulkov, N. P. "Glinskii, Kn. Vasilii L'vovich." *RBS* 5 (1916): 318–19.

———. "Zametka." *Letopis' Istoriko-Rodoslovnogo Obshchestva v Moskve* (1907, no. 4): 47.

Collins, Samuel [Samuil Kollins]. "Nyneshnee sostoianie Rossii." Translated by Petr Kireevskii. *ChIOIDR*. Vol. 1 (1846, bk. 1), 1–47 (Materialy inostrannye).

Collins, Samuel. *The present State of Russia*. London: John Winter, 1667.

Collo, Francesco da [Franchesko da Kollo]. *Ital'ianets v Rossii XVI veka. Franchesko da Kollo. Donoshenie o Moskovii*. Edited and translated by Olga Simchich. Moscow: Nasledie, 1996.

Constantinople in the Early Eighth Century: The Parastaseis syntomoi chronikai. Edited by Averil Cameron and Judith Herrin. Leiden: Brill, 1984.

Cox, Marian Roalfe. *Cinderella: Three Hundred and Forty-Five Variants of Cinderella, Catskin, and Cap o' Rushes, Abstracted and Tabulated, with a Discussion of Mediæval Analogues, and Notes*. Vol. 31 of *Publications of the Folk-Lore Society*. Nendeln/Liechtenstein: Kraus Reprint Limited, 1967.

Cracraft, James. *The Church Reform of Peter the Great*. Stanford: Stanford University Press, 1971.

———. *The Revolution of Peter the Great*. Cambridge, Mass.: Harvard University Press, 2003.

Croskey, Robert. "Byzantine Greeks in Late Fifteenth- and Early Sixteenth-Century Russia." In *The Byzantine Legacy in Eastern Europe*. Edited by Lowell Clucas. Boulder, Colo.: East European Monographs, 1988.

———. *Muscovite Diplomatic Practice in the Reign of Ivan III*. New York: Garland, 1987.

Crummey, Robert O. *Aristocrats and Servitors: The Boyar Elite in Russia, 1613–1689*. Princeton: Princeton University Press, 1983.

———. "Court Spectacles in Seventeenth-Century Russia: Illusion and Reality." In *Essays in Honor of A. A. Zimin*. Edited by Daniel Clarke Waugh, 130–58. Columbus, Ohio: Slavica, 1983.

———. *The Formation of Muscovy, 1304–1613*. London: Longman, 1987.

———. "Reflections on Mestnichestvo in the 17th Century." *Forschungen zur osteuropäischen Geschichte* 27 (1980): 269–81.

Dagron, Gilbert. *Emperor and Priest: The Imperial Office in Byzantium*. Translated by Jean Birrell. Cambridge: Cambridge University Press, 2003.

———. "Nés dans la pourpre." *Travaux et Mémoires du Centre de Recherche d'Histoire et Civilisation byzantines* 12 (1994): 105–42.

Dean, Trevor, and K. J. P. Lowe. *Marriage in Italy, 1300–1650*. Cambridge: Cambridge University Press, 1998.

Dmitriev, M. V., V. N. Floria, and S. G. Iakovenko, eds. *Brestskaia uniia 1596 g.*

i obshchestvenno-politicheskaia bor'ba na Ukraine i v Belorussii v kontse XVI–nachale XVII v. 2 vols. Moscow: Indrik, 1996.

"Dnevnik zverskogo izbieniia moskovskikh boiar v stolitse v 1682 godu i izbranie dvukh tsarei Petra i Ioanna." *Starina i Novizna* 4 (1901): 395–406.

Dolgorukov, P[etr] V., ed. *Rossiiskaia rodoslovnaia kniga*. 4 vols. St. Petersburg: Tipografiia Karla Vingebera, Tipografiia Eduarda Veimara, Tipografiia III Otdeleniia Sob. E. I. V. Kantselarii, 1854–1857.

———. *Skazaniia o rode kniazei Dolgorukovykh*. St. Petersburg: Tipografiia E. Pratsa, 1840.

Domostroi: Rules for Russian Households in the Time of Ivan the Terrible. Edited and translated by Carolyn Pouncy. Ithaca: Cornell University Press, 1994.

Dubakin, D. [N]. "O vliianii Vizantii na semeinyi byt russkogo obshchestva." *Khristianskoe chtenie* (1881, nos. 3–4): 354–62.

Dukhovnye i dogovornye gramoty velikikh i udel'nykh kniazei XIV–XVII vv. Edited by Lev Vladimirovich Cherepnin. Moscow: Akademiia nauk SSSR, 1950.

Dundes, Alan, ed. *Cinderella: A Casebook*. New York: Wildman, 1983.

Dunlop, D[ouglas] M. *The History of the Jewish Khazars*. Princeton: Princeton University Press, 1954.

Dunning, Chester S. L. *Russia's First Civil War: The Time of Troubles and the Founding of the Romanov Dynasty*. University Park: Pennsylvania State University Press, 2001.

———. "Who Was Tsar Dmitrii?" *Slavic Review* 60, no. 4 (Winter 2001): 705–29.

Dunning, Chester S. L., Russell E. Martin, and Daniel Rowland, eds. *Rude and Barbarous Kingdom Revisited: Essays in Russian History and Culture in Honor of Robert O. Crummey*. Bloomington, Ind.: Slavica, 2008.

"Dva svatovstva inozemnykh printsev k russkim velikim kniazhnam v XVII stoletii." Translated by A. Shliapkin. *ChIOIDR*. Vol. 63 (1867, bk. 4): 1–72 (Materialy inostrannye).

Dvortsovye razriady, po vysochaishemu poveleniiu, izdannye II-m otdeleniem sobstvennoi Ego Imperatorskogo Velikchestva kantseliarii. 4 vols. St. Petersburg: Tipografiia II otdeleniia Sobstvennoi E. I. V. kantseliarii, 1850–1855.

Dworzaczek, Włodzimierz. *Genealogia. Tablice*. Warsaw: Państwowe Wydawn. Naukowe, 1959.

E., A. "Vasil'chikova (Anna)." *Entsiklopedicheskii slovar'*. 43 vols. Edited by I. E. Andreevskii. Leipzig and St. Petersburg: F. A. Brokgauz (Leipzig) and I. A. Efron (St. Petersburg), 1890–1907. Vol. 5 (1891), 620.

Ebrey, Patricia Buckley. *Women and the Family in Chinese History*. London: Routledge, 2003.

Efimov, S. V. "Evdokiia Lopukhina—posledniaia russkaia tsaritsa XVII veka." In *Srednevekovaia Rus'. Sbornik nauchnykh statei k 65-letiiu so dnia rozhdeniia professor R. G. Skrynnikova*. Edited by S. V. Lobachev and

A. S. Lavrov, 136–65. St. Petersburg: Izdatel'stvo Sankt-Peterburgskogo universiteta, 1995.

Ekzempliarskii, A. V. *Velikie i udel'nye kniaz'ia severnoi Rusi v tatarskii period, s 1238 po 1505 g.* 2 vols., plus addenda. St. Petersburg: Izdatel'stvo I. I. Tolstogo, 1889–1891.

Emchenko, E. B. *Stoglav. Issledovanie i tekst*. Moscow: Indrik, 2000.

Entsiklopedicheskii slovar'. 43 vols. Edited by I. E. Andreevskii. Leipzig and St. Petersburg: F. A. Brokgauz (Leipzig) and I. A. Efron (St. Petersburg), 1890–1907.

Esipov, G. V. "Tsaritsa Evdokiia Feodorovna." *Russkiia dostopamiatnosti*. Vol. 1, VI, 1–38. Moscow: R. Ris, 1883.

Evans, N. E. "The Anglo-Russian Royal Marriage Negotiations of 1600–1603." *Slavonic and East European Review* 61, no. 3 (July 1983): 363–87.

Fennell, John Lister Illingworth. *Ivan the Great of Moscow*. London: Macmillan, 1963.

Filjushkin, Alexander. *Ivan the Terrible: A Military History*. London: Frontline Books, 2008.

Fine, John V. A., Jr. "The Muscovite Dynastic Crisis of 1497–1502." *Canadian Slavonic Papers* 7 (1966): 198–215.

Fletcher, Giles. "Of the Russe Commonwealth." In *Rude and Barbarous Kingdom: Russia in the Accounts of Sixteenth-Century English Voyagers*. Edited by Lloyd E. Berry and Robert O. Crummey, 85–246. Madison: University of Wisconsin Press, 1968.

Flier, Michael S. "Breaking the Code: The Image of the Tsar in the Muscovite Palm Sunday Ritual." In *Medieval Russian Culture*. Vol. 2. In the series California Slavic Studies, 19. Edited by Michael S. Flier and Daniel Rowland, 213–42. Berkeley and Los Angeles: University of California Press, 1994.

———. "Court Ceremony in an Age of Reform: Patriarch Nikon and the Palm Sunday Ritual." In *Religion and Culture in Early Modern Russia and Ukraine*. Edited by Samuel H. Baron and Nancy Shields Kollmann, 73–95. Dekalb: Northern Illinois University Press, 1997.

———. "The Iconography of Royal Procession: Ivan the Terrible and the Palm Sunday Ritual." In *European Monarchy: Its Evolution and Practice from Roman Antiquity to Modern Times*. Edited by Heinz Duchhardt, Richard A. Jackson, and David Sturdy, 109–25. Stuttgart: F. Steiner, 1992.

Flier, Michael S., and Daniel Rowland, eds. *Medieval Russian Culture*. Vol. 2. In the series California Slavic Studies, 19. Berkeley and Los Angeles: University of California Press, 1994.

Floria, Boris Nikolaevich. "Greki-emigranty v Russkom gosudarstve vtoroi poloviny XV–nachala XVI v. Politicheskaia i kul'turnaia deiatel'nost'." *Rusko-Balkanski kulturni vruzki prez srednovekovieto*. Sofia: Izdatelstvo na Bulgarskata Akademiiana naukite, 1982.

———. *Ivan Groznyi*. 2d ed. Moscow: Molodaia gvardiia, 2002.

Fogel, Michèle. *Les cérémonies de l'information dans la France du XVIe au milieu du XVIIIe siècle*. Paris: Fayard, 1989.

Forssman, Julius. *Die Beziehungen altrussischer Fürstengeschlechter zu Westeuropa. Ein Beitrag zur Geschichte Ost- und Noreuropas im Mittelalter*. 2 vols. Bern: Herbert Lang, 1970.

Forsten, G. V. "Snosheniia Danii s Rossiei v tsartvovanie Khristiana IV." *ZhMNP* 280 (April 1892): 281–335 (otdel nauk).

Fourmy, Marie-Henriette, and Maurice Leroy. "La Vie de S. Philarete." *Byzantion* 9 (1934): 85–170.

Gal'tsov, V. I. "Svedeniia o S. I. Shakhovskom v opisi arkhiva Posol'skogo prikaza 1673 g." *Arkheograficheskii ezhegodnik za 1976 g.*, 79–81. Moscow: Izdatel'stvo Akademii nauk SSSR, 1977.

Gennep, Arnold van. *The Rites of Passage*. Translated by Monika B. Vizedom and Gabrielle L. Caffee. Chicago: Phoenix Books of the University of Chicago Press, 1961.

Georgievskii, Grigorii. *Prazdnichnye sluzhby i tserkovnye torzhestva v staroi Moskve*. Moscow: Tipografiia I. D. Sytina, 1896. Reprint, Moscow: Mezhdunarodnye izdatel'skii tsentr Pravoslavnoi literatury, 1995.

Georgievskii, V. "Ikony Ioanna Groznogo i ego sem'i v Suzdale." *Starye gody* (November 1910): 3–21.

Girshberg, V. B. "Materialy dlia svoda nadpisei na kamennykh plitakh Moskvy." Pt. 1. In *Numizmatika i epigrafika* 1 (1960): 3–77.

Golikov, I. I. *Deianiia Petra Velikogo*. 2d ed. Vol. 2. Moscow, Tip. Nikolaia Stepanova, 1837.

Golubinskii, Evgenii Evstigneevich. *Istoriia kanonizatsii sviatykh v russkoi tserkvi*. In *ChIOIDR*, Vol. 204 (1903, bk. 1), 1–600.

———. *Istoriia russkoi tserkvi*. 2 vols., each in two parts. Moscow: Napechatannoe Imperatorskim obshchestvom istorii i drevnostei rossiiskikh, 1901–1911.

Golubtsov, A. P. "Pamiatniki prenii o vere, voznikshikh po delu korolevicha Val'demara i tsarevny Iriny Mikhailovny." *ChIOIDR*. Vol. 161 (1892, bk. 2), i–xxvi, 1–349.

———. *Preniia o vere, vyzvannyia delom korolevicha Val'demara i tsarevny Iriny Mikhailovny*. Moscow: [n.p.], 1891.

Gordon, Patrick. *Passages from the Diary of General Patrick Gordon of Auchleuchries in the Years 1635–1699*. New York: Da Capo Press, 1968.

Gorskii, A. V., and K. I. Nevostruev. *Opisanie slavianskikh rukopisei Moskovskoi sinodal'noi biblioteki*. Pt. 1. Moscow: V Sinodal'noi tipografii, 1855.

Gorskii, S. *Zheny Ioanna Groznogo*. Moscow: Knigoizdatel'stvo "Delo," 1912.

Grebel'skii, P. Kh., and A. B. Mirvis. *Dom Romanovykh. Bibliograficheskie svedeniia o chlenakh tsarstvovavshego doma, ikh predkakh i rodstvennikakh*. 2d ed. St. Petersburg, n.p.: 1992.

Gregorii, Johann Gottfried. "*The Comedy of Artaxerxes* (1672)." Translated by Yvette Louria, with the editorial assistance of John A. Stone. *Bulletin of the New York Public Library* 72, no. 3 (March 1968): 139–210.

Halperin, Charles J. "The Culture of Ivan IV's Court: The Religious Beliefs of Bureaucrats." In *The New Muscovite Cultural History: A Collection in Honor of Daniel B. Rowland*. Edited by Valerie Kivelson, Karen Petrone, Nancy Shields Kollmann, and Michael S. Flier, 93–105. Bloomington, Ind.: Slavica, 2009.

———. "Edward Keenan and the Kurbskii-Groznyi Correspondence in Hindsight." *Jahrbücher für Geschichte osteuropäische* 46 (1998): 376–403.

———. "The Minority of Ivan IV." In *Rude and Barbarous Kingdom Revisited*. Edited by Chester S. L. Dunning et al., 41–52. Bloomington, Ind.: Slavica, 2008.

———. "Muscovy as a Hypertrophic State: A Critique." *Kritika* 3, no. 3 (Summer 2002): 501–7.

———. "The 'Russian' and 'Slavonic' Languages in Sixteenth-Century Muscovy." *Slavonic and East European Review* 85, no. 1 (January 2007): 1–24.

———. *The Tatar Yoke: The Image of the Mongols in Medieval Russia*. Corrected edition. Bloomington, Ind.: Slavica, 2009.

Hans, L.-M. "Der Kaiser als Märchenprinz: Brautschau und Heiratspolitik in Konstantinopel 395–882." *Jahrbuch der Österreichischen Byzantinistik* 38 (1988): 46–52.

Heidenstein, Reinhold [Reinoldi Heidensteini]. *De Bello Moscovitico quod Stephanus rex Poloniæ gessit Commentariorum libri VI*. Basel: Conrad. Valdkirchium, 1588.

———. "Zapiski o Moskovskoi voine (1578–1582)." In *Reingol'd Geidenshtein. Zapiski o Moskovskoi voine (1578–1582). Al'bert Shlikhting. Novoe izvestie o Rossii vremeni Ivana Groznogo. Genrikh Shtaden. O Moskve Ivana Groznogo*. Edited by Aleksandr Ivanovich Tsepkov. In the series Istochniki istorii. Riazan': Aleksandriia, 2005.

Hellie, Richard. "Edward Keenan's Scholarly Ways." *Russian Review* 46 (1987): 177–90.

———. "Thoughts on the Absence of Elite Resistance in Muscovy." *Kritika* 1, no. 1 (Winter 2000): 5–20.

Herberstein, Sigismund von. *Rerum Moscoviticarum Commentarii*. Basileae: Ex officina Oporiniana, 1571.

———. [Gerbershtein, Sigizmund]. *Zapiski o Moskovii*. Edited by V. L. Ianin. Translated by A. I. Malein and A. V. Nazarenko. Moscow: Izdatel'stvo Moskovskogo universiteta, 1988.

———. [Gerbershtein, Sigizmund]. *Zapiski o moskovitskikh delakh*. Edited and translated by A. I. Malein. St. Petersburg: Izdatel'stvo A. S. Suvorina, 1908.

Herrin, Judith. *Women in Purple: Rulers of Medieval Byzantium*. Princeton: Princeton University Press, 2001.

Hesiod. *Hesiod, the Homeric Hymns, and Homerica*. Translated by Hugh G. Evelyn-White. Charleston, S.C.: BiblioBazaar, 2007.

Holmgren, Jennifer. "Imperial Marriage in the Native Chinese and Non-Han State, Han to Ming." In *Marriage and Inequity in Chinese Society*. Edited by Rubie S. Watson and Patricia Buckley Ebrey, 58–96. Berkeley and Los Angeles: University of California Press, 1991.

Horsey, Jerome. "The Travels of Jerome Horsey." In *Rude and Barbarous Kingdom: Russia in the Accounts of Sixteenth-Century English Voyagers*. Edited by Lloyd E. Berry and Robert O. Crummey, 247–369. Madison: University of Wisconsin Press, 1968.

Howes, Robert Craig, trans. and ed. *The Testaments of the Grand Princes of Moscow*. Ithaca and New York: Cornell University Press, 1967.

Hughes, Lindsey. "Peter the Great's Two Weddings: Changing Images of Women in a Transitional Age." In *Women in Russia and Ukraine*. Edited by Rosalind Marsh, 31–44. Cambridge: Cambridge University Press, 1996.

———. *The Romanovs: Ruling Russia, 1613–1917*. New York: Continuum, 2008.

———. *Russia in the Age of Peter the Great*. New Haven: Yale University Press, 1998.

———. *Sofia: Regent of Russia, 1657–1704*. New Haven: Yale University Press, 1990.

Hyginus, *The Myths of Hyginus*. Translated by Mary Amelia Grant. Lawrence: University of Kansas Publications, 1960.

Ibn Fadlan's Journey to Russia: A Tenth-Century Traveller from Baghdad to the Volga River. Translated by Richard Frye. Princeton: Markus Weiner Publishers, 2005.

Isenburg, Wilhelm Karl, Prinz von, ed. *Europäische Stammtafeln: Stammtafeln zur Geschichte der europäischen Staaten*. 4 vols. Marburg: Verlag von J. A. Stargardt, 1975.

"Istoriia o velikom kniaze Moskovskom." In *RIB*, 31:162–63.

Iurganov, Andrei Ivanovich. "O date napisaniia zaveshchaniia Ivana Groznogo." *Otechestvennaia istoriia* 6 (1993): 125–41.

Izbornik Slavianskikh i Russkikh sochinenii i statei, vnesennykh v khronografy Russkoi redaktsii. Compiled by A. Popov. Moscow: Tipografiia A. I. Mamontova, 1869.

Izvestiia Russkogo genealogicheskogo obshchestva. Old Series. 4 vols. 1900–1911.

Jenkins, Romilly. *Byzantium: The Imperial Centuries, A.D. 610–1071*. New York: Random House, 1966.

Jensen, Claudia R. *Musical Cultures in Seventeenth-Century Russia*. Bloomington: Indiana University Press, 2009.

Jensen, Frede P., ed. "Hertug Magnus af Holstens forsvarsskift af 1579 om hans forhold til tsar Ivan den Grusomme." *Danske Magazin*. Series 8, vol. 4, pt. 1 (1976): 54–83.

Jong, Mayke de. "Bride Shows Revisited: Praise, Slander and Exegesis in the Reign of the Empress Judith." In *Gender in the Early Medieval World: East and West, 300–900*. Edited by Leslie Brubaker and Julia M. H. Smith, 257–77. Cambridge: Cambridge University Press, 2004.

Josephus, Flavius. *The Complete Works of Flavius Josephus*. Translated by William Whiston. Chicago: Thompson and Thomas, 1901.

Jules, Joost [Iust Iul']. "Zapiski Iusta Iulia." *Russkii arkhiv* (1892, bk. 3): 5–48.

Kabardino-russkie otnosheniia v XVI–XVIII vv.: dokumenty i materialy. K 400-letiiu prisoedineniia Kabardy k Rossii. 2 vols. Edited by T. Kh. Kumykov and E. N. Kusheva. Moscow: Izdatel'stvo Akademii nauk SSSR, 1957.

Kachalova, I. Ia., N. A. Maiasova, and L. A. Shchennikova. *Blagoveshchenskii Sobor Moskovskogo kremlia: k 500-letiiu unikal'nogo pamiatnika russkoi kul'tury*. Moscow: Iskusstvo, 1990.

Kagan, M. D. "Povest' o vtorom brake Vasiliia III." In *Slovar' knizhnikov i knizhnosti Drevnei Rusi*. Edited by D. S. Likhachev, 230–33. Vol. 2: *Vtoraia polovina XIV–XVI v*. (part 2). Leningrad: Nauka, 1989.

Kaiser, Daniel H. "Property among Elite Women in 17th-Century Russia." In *Rude and Barbarous Kingdom Revisited*. Edited by Chester S. L. Dunning et al., 427–40. Bloomington, Ind.: Slavica, 2008.

———. "Symbol and Ritual in the Marriages of Ivan IV." *Russian History* 14, nos. 1–4 (1987): 247–62.

———. "'Whose Wife Will She Be at the Resurrection?' Marriage and Remarriage in Early Modern Russia." *Slavic Review* 62, no. 2 (Summer 2003): 302–23.

Kämpfer, Frank, and Reinhard Frötschner, eds. *450 Jahre Sigismund von Herbersteins Rerum Moscoviticarum Commentarii, 1549–1999: Jubiläumvorträge herausgegeben von Frank Kämpfer und Reinhard Frötschner*. In the series Schriften zur Geistesgeschichte des östlichen Europa, 24. Wiesbaden: Harrassowitz, 2002.

Karamzin, Nikolai Mikhailovich. *Istoriia gosudarstva Rossiiskogo*. Reprint, from 1842–1844 edition. 12 vols. in 4 books. Moscow: Kniga, 1988.

Karnovich, Evgenii Petrovich. *Tsetsarevich Konstantin Pavlovich*. St. Petersburg: A. S. Suvorin, 1899.

Kaplan, Herbert H. *Russia and the Outbreak of the Seven Years' War*. Berkeley and Los Angeles: University of California Press, 1968.

Kashtanov, Sergei Mikhailovich. "O vnutrennei politike Ivana Groznogo v period 'velikogo kniazheniia' Simeona Bekbulatovicha." In *Trudy Moskovskogo gosudarstvennogo istoriko-arkhivnogo instituta* 16 (1961): 427–62.

Kazakova, Natal'ia Aleksandrovna. "Dmitrii Gerasimov i russko-evropeiskie kul'turnye sviazi v pervoi treti XVI v." In *Problemy istorii mezhdunarodnykh otnoshenii (sbornik statei pamiati akademika E. V. Tarle)*. Edited by V. I. Rutenberg et al., 248–66. Leningrad: Institute istorii AN SSSR,

Leningradskoe otdelenie, 1972.

———. *Ocherki po istorii russkoi obshchestvennoi mysli: pervaia tret' XVI veka.* Leningrad: Nauka, 1970.

———. *Vassian Patrikeev i ego sochineniia.* Moscow-Leningrad: Izdatel'stvo Akademii Nauk SSSR, Leningradskoe otdelenie, 1960.

———. "Vopros o prichinakh osuzhdeniia Maksima Greka." *Vizantiiskii vremennik* 28 (1968): 109–126.

Keenan, Edward L. "Ivan the Terrible and His Women." *Russian History* 37, no. 4 (Winter 2010): 322–59.

———. *The Kurbskii-Groznyi Apocrypha: The Seventeenth-Century Genesis of the "Correspondence" Attributed to Prince A. M. Kurbskii and Tsar Ivan IV.* Cambridge, Mass.: Harvard University Press, 1971.

———. "Muscovite Political Folkways." *Russian Review* 45 (1986): 115–81.

———. "The Privy Domain of Ivan Vasil'evich." In *Rude and Barbarous Kingdom Revisited.* Edited by Chester S. L. Dunning et al., 73–88. Bloomington, Ind.: Slavica, 2008.

———. "Putting Kurbskii in His Place, or: Observations and Suggestions Concerning the Place of the *History of the Grand Prince of Moscow* in the History of Muscovite Literary Culture." *Forschungen zur osteuropäischen Geschichte* 24 (1978): 131–61.

———. "Semen Shakhovskoi and the Condition of Orthodoxy." *Harvard Ukrainian Studies* 12/13 (1988/1989): 795–815.

———. "Vita: Ivan Vasil'evich. Terrible Czar: 1530–1584." *Harvard Magazine* 80, no. 3 (January–February 1978): 48–49.

Kennedy, Craig Gayen. "The Romanov Relations: A Kinship-Based Analysis of the 1613 Election of Mikhail Romanov to the Muscovite Throne." A.B. thesis, Harvard University, 1984.

Khazanova, S. I. "Oprichnina v Piskarevskom letopistse i letopisanie XVII veka." *Arkhiv russkoi istorii* 8 (2007): 49–59.

Khoroshkevich, Anna Leonidovna. "Iz istorii dvortsovogo deloproizvodstva kontsa XV v." *Sovetskie arkhivy* 5 (1980): 29–34.

———. "Ob odnom iz epizodov dinasticheskoi bor'by v Rossii v kontse XV veka." *Istoriia SSSR* (September–October 1974, no. 5): 129–39.

———. *Russkoe gosudarstvo v sisteme mezhdunarodnykh otnoshenii kontsa XV–nachala XVI v.* Moscow: Nauka, 1980.

Kivelson, Valerie A. *Autocracy in the Provinces: The Muscovite Gentry and Political Culture in the Seventeenth Century.* Stanford: Stanford University Press, 1996.

———. "Culture and Politics, or the Curious Absence of Muscovite State Building in Current American Historical Writing." *Cahiers du Monde russe* 46, nos. 1–2 (2005): 19–28.

———. "Muscovite 'Citizenship': Rights without Freedom." *Journal of Modern History* 74 (September 2002): 465–89.

———. "On Words, Sources, and Historical Method: Which Truth about Muscovy?" *Kritika* 3, no. 3 (Summer 2002): 487–99.

———. "Political Sorcery in Sixteenth-Century Muscovy." In *Culture and Identity in Muscovy, 1359–1584*. Edited by A. M. Kleimola and G. D. Lenhoff, 267–83. Moscow: "ITZ-Garant," 1997.

———. "What Was *Chernoknizhestvo*? Black Books and Foreign Writings in Muscovite Magic." In *Rude and Barbarous Kingdom Revisited*. Edited by Chester S. L. Dunning et al., 459–72. Bloomington, Ind.: Slavica, 2008.

Kleimola, Ann M. "In Accordance with the Canons of the Holy Apostles": Muscovite Dowries and Women's Property Rights." *Russian Review* 51, no. 3 (April 1992): 204–29.

———. "Kto Kogo: Patterns of Duma Recruitment, 1547–1564." *Forschungen zur osteuropäischen Geschichte* 38 (1986): 205–20.

———. "Patterns of Duma Recruitment, 1505–1550." In *Essays in Honor of A. A. Zimin*. Edited by Daniel Clarke Waugh, 232–58. Bloomington, Ind.: Slavica, 1983.

———. "Reliance on the Tried and True: Ivan IV and Appointments to the Boyar Duma, 1565–1584." *Forschungen zur osteuropäischen Geschichte* 46 (1992): 51–63.

Kniaz'kina, O. A. "Obriadnost' kak raznovidnost' kul'turnoi zhizni obshchestva (na primere istoricheskoi traditsii svadebnogo obriada rossiiskikh tsarei XVI–XVII vv.)." Ph.D. diss., Moscow, 1987.

Kobeko, D. F. "Primechanie." *Izvestiia RGO*. Vol. 3 (1909): 92–93 (otdel I).

———. "Sheremetevy i Polevy." *Izvestiia RGO*. Vol. 1 (1900): 7–30 (otdel I).

Kobrin, Vladimir Borisovich. *Ivan Groznyi*. Moscow: Moskovskii rabochii, 1989.

———. "Sostav Oprichnogo dvora Ivana Groznogo." *Arkheograficheskii ezhegodnik za 1959 g.*, 16–91. Moscow: Izdatel'stvo Akademii nauk SSSR, 1960.

Kochen, Christoph von. "Moskva v 1687–1688 gg." Edited by K. A. Viskovatov. *Russkaia starina* 9 (September 1878): 121–29.

Kollmann, Nancy Shields. *By Honor Bound: State and Society in Early Modern Russia*. Ithaca: Cornell University Press, 1999.

———. "Collateral Succession in Kievan Rus'." *Harvard Ukrainian Studies* 14, nos. 3–4 (1990): 377–87.

———. "Consensus Politics: The Dynastic Crisis of the 1490s Reconsidered." *Russian Review* 45, no. 3 (July 1986): 235–67.

———. "Divides and Ends: The Problem of Periodization." *Slavic Review* 69, no. 2 (Summer 2010): 439–47.

———. "The Grand Prince in Muscovite Politics: The Problem of Genre in Sources of Ivan's Minority." *Russian History* 14, nos. 1–4 (1987): 292–313.

———. *Kinship and Politics: The Making of the Muscovite Political System, 1345–1547*. Stanford: Stanford University Press, 1987.

———. "Pilgrimage, Procession, and Symbolic Space in Sixteenth-Century

Russian Politics." In *Medieval Russian Culture*. Vol. 2. In the series California Slavic Studies, 19. Edited by Michael S. Flier and Daniel Rowland, 163–81. Berkeley and Los Angeles: University of California Press, 1994.

———. "The Seclusion of Elite Muscovite Women." *Russian History* 10, pt. 2 (1983): 170–87.

———. Review of *The Sovereign and His Counsellors: Ritualised Consultations in Muscovite Political Culture, 1350s–1570s*, by Sergei Bogatyrev. *Slavic Review* 60, no. 3 (Autumn 2001): 645–46.

———. "Women's Honor in Early Modern Russia." In *Russia's Women: Accommodation, Resistance, Transformation*. Edited by Barbara Evans Clements, Barbara Alpern Engel, and Christine D. Worobec, 60–73. Berkeley and Los Angeles: University of California Press, 1991.

Konev, S. V. "Sinodikologiia. Chast' I-aia: Klassifikatskiia istochnikov." *Istoricheskaia genealogiia/Historical Genealogy* 1 (1993): 7–15.

Korb, Johann-Georg. *Diary of an Austrian Secretary of Legation at the Court of Czar Peter the Great*. 2 vols. Translated and edited by Count MacDonnell. London: Bradbury & Evans, 1863; Reprint, London: Cass, 1968.

Koretskii, V. I., ed. *Istochniki po sotsial'no-ekonomicheskoi istorii Rossii XVI–XVII vv.: Iz Arkhiva Moskovskogo Novodevichego monastyria*. Moscow: Akademii Nauk SSSR, 1985.

———. "Zemskii sobor 1575 g. i postavlenie Simeona Bekbulatovicha 'velikim kniazem vseia Rusi'." *Istoricheskii Arkhiv* (1959, no. 2): 148–56.

Korf, M[odest Andreevich]. *Braunshveigskoe semestvo*. Moscow: Prometei, 1993.

Korsakov, V. "Glinskii, Kn. Mikhail L'vovich." *RBS* 5 (1916): 324–30.

Kosheleva, Ol'ga Evgen'evna. "Leto 1645 goda: smena lits na rossiiskom prestole." In *Kazus 1999*. Edited by Iu. L. Bessmertnogo, 148–70. Moscow: Izdatel'skii tsentr Rossiiskogo gosudarstvennogo gumanitarnogo universiteta, 1999.

———. "Prigovor kniaziu Ivanu Nikitichu Khovanskomu." *Arkhiv russkoi istorii* 5 (1994): 139–44.

Koslow, Jules. *Ivan the Terrible*. New York: Hill and Wang, 1962.

Kotošixin, Grigorij K. *O Rossii v carstvovanie Alekseja Mixajloviča*. Edited by A. E. Pennington. Oxford: Oxford University Press, 1980.

Kozachenko, A. I. "K istorii velikorusskogo svadebnogo obriada." *Sovetskaia etnografiia* 1 (1957): 57–71.

"Kratkii letopisets pogodinskogo sobraniia." *Arkheograficheskii ezhegodnik za 1962 g.*, 431–44. Moscow: Akademiia nauk SSSR, 1963.

Krom, Mikhail Markovich. *"Vdovstvuiushchee tsarstvo": politicheskii krizis v Rossii 30–40-kh godov XVI veka*. St. Petersburg: Novoe literaturnoe obozrenie, 2010.

Kudriavtsev, I. M., ed. *Artakserksovo Deistvo: Pervaia p'esa Russkogo teatra XVII v*. Moscow-Leningrad: Izdatel'stvo Akademii nauk SSSR, 1957.

———, comp. "Novye postupleniia." In *Zapiski Otdela rukopisei Gosudarstvennoi Biblioteki SSSR imeni V. I. Lenina*, 98–177. Vol. 16. Moscow: Gosudarstvennaia biblioteka im. V. I. Lenina, 1954.

Kurakin, Boris Ivanovich. "Gistoriia o tsare Petre Alekseeviche." In *Arkhiv kn. F. A. Kurakina*. Edited by M. I. Semevskii. St. Petersburg: Tipografiia V. S. Valasheva, 1890.

———. "'Gistoriia o tsare Petre Alekseeviche' B. I. Kurakina." In *Rossiiu podnial na dyby....* Moscow: Molodaia gvardiia, 1987.

Kusheva, Ekaterina Nikolaevna. *Narody severnogo Kavkaza i ikh sviazi s Rossiei: vtoraia polovina XVI–30-gody XVII veka*. Moscow: Izdatel'stvo Akademii nauk SSSR, 1963.

Lambin, N. P. *Istoriia Petra Velikogo*. St. Petersburg: Tipografiia F. I. El'snera, 1844.

LeDonne, John P. *Absolutism and Ruling Class: The Formation of the Russian Political Order, 1700–1825*. New York: Oxford University Press, 1991.

———. "Ruling Families in the Russian Political Order, 1689–1825." *Cahiers du Monde russe et soviétique* 28 (1987): 233–322.

Leonid, Archimandrite [Kavelin]. *Istoriko-arkheologicheskoe i statisticheskoe opisanie Borovskogo Pafnut'eva monastyria Kaluzhkoi guberni v sviazi s istoricheskom skazaniem o prepodobnom Pafnutii, Borovskom chudotvortse, osnovatele onogo, s prilozheniem sviatitel'stv o blagodatnykh znameniiakh, iavlennykh im strazhdushchemu chelovechestvu*. 2d ed. Edited by I. Tokmakov. Kaluga: Tip. Gub. pravleniia, 1894.

———. "Luk'ian Stepanovich Streshnev: starinnoe istoricheskoe predanie." *ChIOIDR*. Vol. 81 (1872, bk. 2), 1–9 (Smes').

———. *Nadpisi Troitskoi Sergievoi Lavry*. St. Petersburg: Tipografiia Imperatorskoi Akademii nauk, 1881.

———. "Pamiat' o tsaritse Evdokiia na eia rodine." *Russkii arkhiv* 11, no. 4 (1873): cols. 648–53.

———. "Razriadnye zapiski o likhakh byvshikh na vtorykh svad'bakh tsaria i velikogo kniazia Mikhaila Fedorovicha v 1622 godu i tsaria i velikogo kniazia Alekseia Mikhailovicha v 1671 godu." In *Pamiatniki drevnei pis'mennosti i iskusstva*. St. Petersburg: Tipografiia V. S. Valasheva, 1885.

Letopisets russkii (Moskovskaia letopis' 1552–1562 gg. Po rukopisi, prinadlezhashchei A. N. Lebedevu). In *ChIOIDR*. Vol. 185 (1895, bk. 3), 1–190 (Materialy istoricheskie).

Levenson, Jon D. *Esther: A Commentary*. Louisville, Ky.: Westminster John Knox Press, 1997.

Levin, Eve. *Sex and Society in the World of the Orthodox Slavs, 900–1700*. Ithaca: Cornell University Press, 1989.

Lewis, Andrew W. "Anticipatory Association of the Heir in Early Capetian France." *American Historical Review* 83 (1978): 906–27.

———. *Royal Succession in Capetian France: Studies in Familial Order and the*

State. Cambridge, Mass.: Harvard University Press, 1981.

Likhachev, N. P. *"Gosudarev rodoslovets" i rod Adashevykh*. St. Petersburg: Tipografiia V. S. Balasheva, 1897.

Lilie, Ralph-Johannes. *Byzanz unter Eirene und Konstantin VI (780–802)*. Frankfurt am Main: Peter Lang, 1996.

Lincoln, W. Bruce. *The Romanovs: Autocrats of All the Russias*. New York: Anchor, 1981.

Lobanov-Rostovskii, A. B., ed. *Russkaia rodoslovnaia kniga*. 3 vols. A publication of *Russkaia starina*. St. Petersburg: Tipografiia Ministerstva Putei Soobshcheniia, Tipografiia V. S. Balasheva, 1873–1878.

Loewenson, L. "The work of Robert Boyle and 'The present State of Russia.'" *Slavic and East European Review* 33 (1954/1955): 470–85.

Longworth, Phillip. *Alexis, Tsar of All the Russias*. New York: Franklin Watts, 1984.

Lucian. *Lucian's Dialogues*. Translated by Howard Williams. London: George Bell and Sons, 1907.

Ludwig, Claudia. *Sonderformen byzantinischer Hagiographie und ihr literarisches Vorbild*. Frankfurt am Main: Peter Lang, 1997.

Lunt, Horace G., and Moshé Taube. *The Slavonic Book of Esther: Text, Lexicon, Linguistic Analysis, Problems of Translation*. Cambridge, Mass.: Harvard University Press and Harvard Ukrainian Research Institute, 1998.

Lur'e, Iakov Solomonovich. *Dve istorii Rossii XV-ogo veka rannie i pozdnie nezavisimye i ofitsial'nye letopisi po obrazovanii Moskovskogo gosudarstva*. St. Petersburg: Dmitrii Bulanin, 1994.

Madariaga, Isabel de. *Ivan the Terrible: First Tsar of Russia*. New Haven and London: Yale University Press, 2005.

———. *Russia in the Age of Catherine the Great*. New Haven and London: Yale University Press, 1981.

Maiasova, N. A. "Tri shitykh pokrova XVI v sobranii muzeev Kremlia." In *Materialy i issledovaniia: Gosudarstvennye muzei Moskovskogo Kremlia*, 133–47. Vol. 1. Moscow: Iskusstvo, 1973.

Majeska, George P. "The Moscow Coronation of 1498 Reconsidered." *Jahrbücher für Geschichte Osteuropas* 26 (1978): 353–61.

Margeret, Jacques. *The Russian Empire and Grand Duchy of Muscovy. A 17th-Century French Account*. Translated and edited by Chester S. L. Dunning. Pittsburgh: University of Pittsburgh Press, 1983.

Markevich, Aleksei Ivanovich. *Grigorii Karpovich Kotoshikhin i ego sochinenie o Moskovskom gosudarstve v polovine XVII veka*. Odessa: Tipografiia shtaba okruga, 1895.

———. *Istoriia mestnichestvo v Moskovskom gosudarstve XV–XVII veke*. Odessa: Tipografiia Odesskogo vestnika, 1888.

———. *O mestnichestve*. Kiev: Tipografiia M. P. Fritsa, 1879.

Martin, Janet. *Medieval Russia, 980–1584*. 2d ed. Cambridge: Cambridge University Press, 2008.

Martin, Russell E. "Archival Sleuths and Documentary Transpositions: Notes on the Typology and Textology of Muscovite Royal Wedding Descriptions in the Sixteenth and Seventeenth Centuries." *Russian History* 30, no. 3 (Fall 2003): 253–300.

———. "Choreographing the 'Tsar's Happy Occasion': Tradition, Change, and Dynastic Continuity in the Weddings of Tsar Mikhail Romanov." *Slavic Review* 63, no. 4 (Winter 2004): 794–817.

———. "Death and Dying: The Early Period (up to Peter I)." In *Supplement to the Modern Encyclopedia of Russian and Soviet History*. 9 vols. to date. Gulf Breeze, Fla.: Academic International Press, 1995–2008), 7:210–14.

———. "'For the Firm Maintenance of the Dignity and Tranquility of the Imperial Family': Law and Familial Order in the Romanov Dynasty." *Russian History* 37, no. 4 (Winter 2010): 389–411.

———. "Gifts and Commemoration: Donations to Monasteries, Legitimacy, and Remembering the Royal Dead in Muscovy (7159/1651)." *Forschungen zur osteuropäischen Geschichte* 76 (2010): 499–525.

———. "Gifts for Kith and Kin: Gift Exchanges and Social Integration in Muscovite Royal Weddings." In *Rude and Barbarous Kingdom Revisited*. Edited by Chester S. L. Dunning et al., 89–108. Bloomington, Ind.: Slavica, 2008.

———. "Gifts for the Bride: Dowries, Diplomacy, and Marriage Politics in Muscovy." *Journal of Medieval and Early Modern Studies* 38, no. 1 (Winter 2008): 119–45.

———. "Gifts for the Dead: Kinship and Commemoration in Muscovy (The Case of the Mstislavskii Princes)." *Russian History* 26, no. 2 (Summer 1999): 171–202.

———. "Introduction: Edward Keenan's Influence on Early Russian Studies." *Canadian Slavonic Papers* 48, nos. 3–4 (September–December 2006): 233–34.

———. "Muscovite Esther: Bride-Shows, Queenship, and Power in *The Comedy of Artaxerxes*." In *The New Muscovite Cultural History: A Collection in Honor of Daniel B. Rowland*. Edited by Valerie Kivelson, Karen Petrone, Nancy Shields Kollmann, and Michael S. Flier, 21–42. Bloomington, Ind.: Slavica, 2009.

———. "Muscovite Royal Weddings: A Descriptive Inventory of Manuscript Holdings in the Treasure Room of the Russian State Archive of Ancient Acts, Moscow." *Manuscripta* 50, no. 1 (June 2006): 77–189.

———. "The Petrine Divide and the Periodization of Early Modern Russia." *Slavic Review* 69, no. 2 (Summer 2010): 410–25.

———. "Political Folkways and Praying for the Dead in Muscovy: Reconsidering Edward Keenan's 'Slight' against the Church." *Canadian Slavonic Papers* XLVIII, nos. 3–4 (September–December 2006): 269–90.

———. "Praying for the Dead in Muscovy: Kinship Awareness and Orthodox Belief in the Commemorations of Muscovite Royalty." In *The Tapestry of the Russian Church* (forthcoming in 2012).

———. "Ritual and Religion in the Foreign Marriages of Three Muscovite Princesses." *Russian History* 35, nos. 3–4 (Fall–Winter 2008): 357–81.

———. "Royal Weddings and Crimean Diplomacy: New Sources on Muscovite Chancellery Practice during the reign of Vasilii III." *Harvard Ukrainian Studies* 19 (1995): 389–427.

Mashtafarov, A. V. "Dariia." In *Pravoslavnaia entsiklopediia.* 14 vols. to date. Vol. 14:199–201. Moscow: Tserkovno-nauchnyi tsentr "Pravoslavnaia entsiklopediia," 2000–2006.

Massa, Isaac. *A Short History of the Beginnings and Origins of These Present Wars in Moscow under the Reign of Various Sovereigns down to the Year 1610.* Translated by G. Edward Orchard. Toronto: University of Toronto Press, 1982.

Materialy po istorii SSSR. Vol. 2: *Dokumenty po istorii XV–XVII vv.* Moscow: Izdatel'stvo Akademii nauk SSSR, 1955.

Mazon, André, and Frédéric Cocron. *La Comédie d'Artaxerxès, présentée en 1672 au Tsar Alexis par Gregorii Le Pasteur: Texte allemande et texte russe.* Paris: Institut d'études slaves de l'université de Paris, 1954.

McCormick, Michael. "Byzantium and the Early Medieval West: Problems and Opportunities." In *Europa medievale e mondo bizantino: contatti effettivi e possibilità di studi comparati.* Edited by G. Arnaldi and G. Cavallo, 1–17. Rome: Istituto storico italiano per il medio evo, 1997.

———. "Byzantium and the West, A.D. 700–900." *New Cambridge Medieval History.* Vol. 2. Edited by Rosamond McKitterick, 349–80. Cambridge: Cambridge University Press, 1995.

———. "Diplomacy and the Carolingian Encounter with Byzantium down to the Accession of Charles the Bald." In *Eriugena: East and West. Papers of the Eighth International Symposium of the Society for the Promotion of Eriugenean Studies.* Edited by Bernard McGinn and Willemien Otten, 15–48. Notre Dame, Ind.: Notre Dame University Press, 1994.

———. *Eternal Victory: Triumphal Rulership in Late Antiquity, Byzantium, and the Early Medieval West.* In the series Past and Present Publications. Cambridge: Cambridge University Press, 1986.

Meehan Waters, Brenda. *Autocracy and Aristocracy: The Russian Service Elite of 1730.* New Brunswick, N.J.: Rutgers University Press, 1982.

Mei, Lev Aleksandrovich. *Izbrannye proizvedeniia.* Edited by K. K. Bukhmeier. Leningrad: Sovetskii pisatel', Leningradskoe otdelenie, 1972.

Mendoza, Juan González de. *The History of the Great and Mighty Kingdom of China and the Situation Thereof.* Translated by R. Parke. Edited by Sir George T. Staunton. 2 vols. London: Hakluyt Society, 1853–1854.

Meshcherinov, G. V. "K rodosloviiu Nagikh." *Izvestiia RGO.* Vol. 2 (1903): 10–12 (otdel I).

Meyendorff, John [Fr.]. "Christian Marriage in Byzantium: The Canonical and Liturgical Tradition." *Dumbarton Oaks Papers* 44 (1990): 99–107.

———. *Marriage: An Orthodox Perspective*. Crestwood, N.Y.: St. Vladimir's Seminar Press, 1984.

Miatlev, N. V. "K rodoslovniiu kniazei Mstislavskikh." *Letopis' Istoriko-rodoslovnogo obshchestva v Moskve*, nos. 1–4 (41–44) (1915): 300–317.

———. "K rodosloviiu Nagikh." *Izvestiia RGO*. Vol. 4 (1911): 71–91 (otdel I).

———. "Rodoslovnye zametki." *Letopis' Istoriko-Rodoslovnogo Obshchstva v Moskve* (1907, no. 4): 10–16.

Mikhailov, G. A. "Graviura A. Zubova 'Svad'ba Petra I': real'nost' i vysysel." In *Panorama iskusstv*. Vol. 11, 20–52. Moscow: Sovetskii khudozhnik, 1988.

Miloradovich, Grigorii A. "Tsaritsa Mariia Dolgorukova." *Russkii Arkhiv* (1897, bk. 3): 5–32.

Mirnov, S. *Drevne-russkii dukhovnik*. Moscow: Sinodal'naia tipografiia, 1913.

Monod, Paul Kléber. *The Power of Kings: Monarchy and Religion in Europe, 1589–1715*. New Haven: Yale University Press, 1999.

Mordovtsev, Daniil Lukich. *Russkie istoricheskie zhenshchiny. Populiarnye raskazy iz russkoi istorii: zhenshchiny do-petrovskoi Rusi*. St. Petersburg: K. N. Plotnikov, 1874. Reprint, Moscow: "Otechestvo," 1996.

Morozova, Liudmila Evgen'evna. *Rossiia na puti iz Smuty: Izbranie na tsarstvo Mikhaila Fedorovicha*. Moscow: Nauka, 2005.

Morozova, Liudmilla Evgen'evna, and Boris Nikolaevich Morozov. *Ivan Groznyi i ego zheny*. Moscow: Drofa-Plius, 2005.

Nasonov, A. N. "Materialy i issledovaniia po istorii russkogo letopisaniia." In *Problemy istochnikovedeniia*. Vol. 6. Moscow-Leningrad: Izdatel'stvo Akademii Nauk SSSR, 1958.

Nävdal-Larsen, Bodil. *Erik XIV, Ivan Groznyi og Katarina Jagellonica*. Uppsala: Uppsala Universitet, 1983.

Nazarov, Vladislav Dmitreevich. "O sopravitel'stve v Moskovskom velikom kniazhestve (konets XIV–nachalo XVI veka)." In *Verkhovnaia vlast', elita i obshchestvo v Rossii XIV–pervoi poloviny XIX veka: Rossiiskaia monarkhiia v kontekste evropeiskikh i aziatskikh monarkhii i imperii*, 112–15. Moscow: Museum of the Moscow Kremlin, 2009.

———. "O strukture 'Gosudareva dvora' v seredine XVI v." In *Obshchestvo i gosudarstvo feodal'noi Rossii. Sbornik statei posviashchennyi 70-letiiu akademika L'va Vladimirovicha Cherepnina*. Edited by V. T. Pashuto, 40–54. Moscow: Nauka, 1975.

———. "Svadebnye dela XVI v." *Voprosy istorii* (1976, no. 10): 110–23.

Nechaev, Sergei. *Ivan Groznyi: Zheny i nalozhnitsy "Sinei Borody."* Moscow: AST, 2010.

Neuville, Foy de la. *A Curious and New Account of Muscovy in the Year 1689*. Edited by Lindsey Hughes. Translated by J. A. Cutshall. In the series Occasional Papers of the School of Slavonic and East European Studies, 23. London: School of Slavonic and East European Studies, 1994.

New York Times. "Imperial Nuptials. How the Wife of the Chinese Emperor has been chosen." July 11, 1887.

———. "An Imperial Wedding. The Emperor of China has taken unto himself several wives." December 26, 1872.

Nitsche, Peter. *Grossfürst und Thronfolger: die Nachfolgepolitik der Moskauer Herrscher bis zum Ende der Rjurikenhauses*. Köln: Böhlau Verlag, 1972.

Novgorodskie letopisi (tak nazyvaemye Novgorodskaia vtoraia i Novgorodskaia tret'ia letopisi). St. Petersburg: Izdatel'stvo Arkheograficheskoi kommissii, 1879.

Novikov, Nikolai [Ivanovich], ed. *Drevniaia rossiiskaia vivliofika. Soderzhashchaia v sebe sobranie drevnostei rossiiskikh, do istorii geografii, i genealogii rossiiskoi kasaiushchikhsia*. 2d ed. 20 vols. Moscow: V tipografii Kompanii tipograficheskoi, 1788–1791.

Novokomskii, Pavel Iovii. "Kniga o moskovitskom posol'stve." In Sigizmund Gerbershtein. *Zapiski o moskovitskikh delakh*. Edited and translated by A. I. Malein, 251–75. St. Petersburg: Izdatel'stvo A. S. Suvorina, 1908.

Oakley, Francis. *Kingship: The Politics of Enchantment*. In the series New Perspectives on the Past. Malden, Mass., and Oxford: Blackwell, 2006.

Olearius, Adam. *The Travels of Olearius in Seventeenth-Century Russia*. Edited and translated by Samuel H. Baron. Stanford: Stanford University Press, 1967.

Opis' arkhiva Posol'skogo prikaza 1626 goda. 2 pts. Edited by V. I. Gal'tsov. Moscow: Glavnoe arkhivnoe upravlenie pri SM SSSR, 1977.

Opis' arkhiva Posol'skogo prikaza 1673 goda. 2 pts. Edited by V. I. Gal'tsov. Moscow: Glavnoe arkhivnoe upravlenie pri SM SSSR, 1990.

Opisi Tsarskogo arkhiva XVI v. i Arkhiva Posol'skogo prikaza 1614 g. Edited by Sigurd Ottovich Shmidt. Moscow: Izdatel'stvo vostochnoi literatury, 1960.

Orchard, Edward G. "The Election of Michael Romanov." *Slavonic and East European Review* 67, no. 3 (1989): 379–402.

Orfelin, Zaharija. *Petar Veliki*. 2 vols. Belgrade: Prosveta, 1970.

———. *Zhitie i slavnyia dela Petra Velikago Samoderzhitsa Vserossiiskago s predpolozheniem kratkoi geograficheskoi i politicheskoi istorii o Rossiiskom tsarstve, nyne pervee na Slavenskom iazyke spisana i izdana*. Venice: Tipografiia Dmitriia Feodozii, 1772.

Orville, André Guillaume Contant d'. *Les fastes de la Pologne et de la Russe*. 2 vols. Paris: J. P. Costard, 1769–1770.

Ostrowski, Donald. "The Extraordinary Career of Tsarevich Kudai Kul/Peter in the Context of Relations between Muscovy and Kazan'." In *States, Societies, Cultures East and West: Essays in Honor of Jaroslaw Pelenski*. Edited by Janusz Duzinkiewicz, 697–719. New York: Ross Publishing, 2004.

———. "The Façade of Legitimacy: Exchange of Power and Authority in Early Modern Russia." *Comparative Studies in Society and History* 44 (2002): 534–63.

———. "Ironies of the Tale of the White Cowl." *Paleoslavica* 10, no. 2 (2002): 28–32.

———. *Muscovy and the Mongols: Cross-Cultural Influences on the Steppe Frontier, 1304–1589*. Cambridge: Cambridge University Press, 1998.

———. "Simeon Bekbulatovich's Remarkable Career as Tatar Khan, Grand Prince of Rus', and Monastic Elder." *Russian History*. Forthcoming.

———. "Systems of Succession in Rus' and Steppe Societies." In *Family and the State in Chingissid and Post-Chingissid Central Asia*. Edited by Christopher P. Atwood and Edward Lazzarini. Forthcoming.

Otchet Imperatorskoi publichnoi biblioteki za 1863 god, 60–61. St. Petersburg, 1864.

Ovid. *Heriodes and Amores*. Translated by Grant Showerman. Cambridge, Mass.: Harvard University Press, 1958.

Pamiatniki diplomaticheskikh snoshenii drevnei Rusi s derzhavami inostrannymi. 10 vols. St. Petersburg: V Tipografii II Otdeleniia Sobstvennoi E.I.V. kantseliarii, 1851–1871.

Panova, T. D. *Kremlevskie usypal'nitsy: istoriia, sud'ba, taina*. Moscow: Indrik, 2003.

Parsons, John Carmi, ed. *Medieval Queenship*. New York: St. Martin's Press, 1993.

Pavlov, Andrei Pavlovich. *Gosudarev dvor i politicheskaia bor'ba pri Borise Godunove, 1584–1605*. St. Petersburg: Nauka 1992.

Pavlov, Andrei, and Maureen Perrie. *Ivan the Terrible*. London: Pearson Education, 2003.

Pavlov-Sil'vanskii, Vladimir Borisovich. "Novye svedeniia v pistsovykh knigakh Viazemskogo uezda kontsa XVI v." *Arkheograficheskii ezhegodnik za 1959 g.*, 92–102. Moscow: Izdatel'stvo Akademii nauk SSSR, 1960.

———. *Pistsovye knigi Rossii XVI v.* Moscow: Nauka, 1991.

Payne, Robert, and Nikita Romanov. *Ivan the Terrible*. New York: Thomas Y. Crowell, 1975.

Pekarskii, P. P. "Spisok devits, iz kotorykh v 1670 i 1671 godakh vybiral sebe suprugu tsar' Aleksei Mikhailovich." In *Izvestiia imperatorskogo Arkheologicheskogo obshchestva*. Vol. 5, no. 6 (St. Petersburg, 1865): 469–72.

Perepiska Ivana Groznogo s Andreem Kurbskim. Edited by Ia. S. Lur'e and Iu. D. Rykov. Leningrad: Nauka, 1979.

Perrie, Maureen. *Pretenders and Popular Monarchism in Early Modern Russia*. Cambridge: Cambridge University Press, 1995.

Petreius, Peter [Petr Petrei]. "Istoriia o velikom kniazhestve Moskovskom." In *O nachale voin i smut v Moskovii*. Edited by A. Liberman and S. Shokarev, 151–464. Moscow: Fond Sergeia Dubova Rita-Print, 1997.

Pipes, Richard. *Russia under the Old Regime*. New York: Schribner, 1974.

———. "Was There Private Property in Muscovite Russia?" *Slavic Review* 54, no. 2 (Summer 1994): 524–30.

Pis'ma i bumagi imperatora Petra Velikogo. 13 vols. to date. St. Petersburg, 1887–.

"Pis'ma odnogo Shveda iz Moskvy v 1647 godu pisannye." *Severnyi arkhiv* (January 1822, no. 3): 151–54.

Pis'ma russkikh gosudarei i drugikh osob tsarskogo semeistva. Moscow: Universitetskaia tipografiia, 1848.

Platonov, Sergei Fedorovich. *Ocherki po istorii Smuty v Moskovskom gosudarstve XVI–XVII vv. (Opyt izucheniia obshchestvennogo stroia i soslovnykh otnoshenii v Smutnoe vremia)*. St. Petersburg: Tipografiia I. N. Skorokhodova, 1899.

Pliguzov, A. I., and I. A. Tikhoniuk. "Poslanie Dmitriia Trakhaniota novgorodskomu arkhiepiskopu Gennadiiu Gonzovu o sedmerichnosti schisleniia let." In *Estestvenno-nauchnye predstavleniia Drevnei Rusi*. Edited by R. A. Simonov, 51–71. Moscow: Nauka, 1988.

Pociecha, Władysław. "Gliński, Michał Łwowicz." *Polskii słownik biograficzny* 8 (1959–1960): 65–69.

Poe, Marshall T. *Foreign Descriptions of Muscovy: An Analytic Bibliography of Primary and Secondary Sources*. Columbus: Slavica, 1995.

———. "Herberstein and the Origin of the European Image of Muscovite Government." In *450 Jahre Sigismund von Herbersteins Rerum Moscoviticarum Commentarii, 1549–1999: Jubiläumvorträge herausgegeben von Frank Kämpfer und Reinhard Frötschner*. Edited by Frank Kämpfer and Reinhard Frötschner, 131–71. In the series Schriften zur Geistesgeschichte des östlichen Europa, 24. Wiesbaden: Harrassowitz, 2002.

———. *A People Born to Slavery: Russia in Early Modern European Ethnography, 1476–1748*. Ithaca: Cornell University Press, 2000.

———. Review of *By Honor Bound: State and Society in Early Modern Russia*, by Nancy Shields Kollmann. *Russian Review* 59, no. 2 (April 2000): 299–300.

———. "The Truth about Muscovy." *Kritika* 3, no. 3 (Summer 2002): 1–14.

———. "Tsar Aleksei Mikhailovich and the Demise of the Romanov Political Settlement." *Russian Review* 62 (October 2003): 537–64.

Poe, Marshall T., with Ol'ga E. Kosheleva, Russell E. Martin, and Boris N. Morozov. *The Russian Elite in the Seventeenth Century: The Consular and Ceremonial Ranks of the Russian "Sovereign's Court," 1613–1713*. Vol. 1. Helsinki: Finnish Academy of Sciences and Letters, 2004.

Polnoe sobranie russkikh letopisei. 42 vols. St. Petersburg-Petrograd-Leningrad-Moscow: Arkheograficheskaia komissiia, Nauka, Arkheograficheskii tsentr, and Iazyki slavianskoi kul'tury, 1841–2005.

Polnoe sobranie zakonov Rossiiskoi Imperii. Series 1: 1649–1825. 45 vols., with 3 vols. of plates. St. Petersburg: Tipografiia II Otdeleniia Sobstvennoi Ego Imperatorskogo Velicheskogo Kantseliarii, 1830. Series 2: 1825–1881. 55 vols. St. Petersburg: Tipografiia II Otdeleniia Sobstvennoi Ego Imperatorskogo Velicheskogo Kantseliarii, 1830–1884. Series 3: 1881–1913. 33 vols. St. Petersburg: Gosudarstvennaia tipografiia, 1885–1916.

Polo, Marco. *The Travels of Marco Polo: The Marsden Translation*. Revised and edited by Manuel Komroff. Rochester, N.Y.: Leo Hart, 1933.

Polosin, Ivan Ivanovich. *Sotsial'no-politicheskaia istoriia Rossii XVI–nachale XVII v. Sbornik statei*. Moscow: Izdatel'stvo Akademii nauk SSSR, 1963.

Poslanie Ivana Groznogo. Edited by D. S. Likhachev and Ia. S. Lur'e. Moscow: Akademiia nauk SSSR, 1951.

Possevino, Antonio. *The Moscovia of Antonio Possevino, S.J.* Edited and translated by Hugh F. Graham. Pittsburgh: University Center for International Studies, 1977.

Pravila izdaniia istoricheskikh dokumentov Instituta istorii AN SSSR i Moskovskogo Istoriko-arkhivnogo institute. Moscow: Izdatel'stvo Akademii nauk SSSR, 1955.

Prince A. M. Kurbsky's History of Ivan IV. Edited by J. L. I. Fennell. Cambridge: Cambridge University Press, 1963.

Pritsak, Omeljian. *The Origin of Rus'*. Vol. 1: *Old Scandinavian Sources Other than the Sagas*. Cambridge, Mass.: Harvard Ukrainian Research Institute, 1981.

Psarev, Andrei V. "The 19th Canonical Answer of Timothy of Alexandria: On the History of Sacramental *Oikonomia*." *St. Vladimir's Theological Quarterly* 51, no. 2/3 (2007): 297–320.

Pushkareva, Natalia."Women in the Medieval Russian Family of the Tenth through Fifteenth Centuries." In *Russia's Women: Accommodation, Resistance, Transformation*. Edited by Barbara Evans Clements, Barbara Alpern Engel, and Christine D. Worobec, 29–43. Berkeley and Los Angeles: University of California Press, 1991.

———. *Women in Russian History from the Tenth to the Twentieth Century*. Translated by Eve Levin. Armonk, N.Y.: M. E. Sharpe, 1997.

Pushkin, B. S., ed. "Novyi genealogicheskii material. Sinodik Vozdvizhenskogo monastyria (v Moskve)." In *Sbornik statei posveshchennykh L. M. Savelovu*, 234–80. Moscow: Istoriko-rodoslovnoe obshchestvo v Moskve, 1915.

Rawski, Evelyn. "Ch'ing Imperial Marriage and Problems of Rulership." In *Marriage and Inequity in Chinese Society*. Edited by Rubie S. Watson and Patricia Buckley Ebrey, 170–203. Berkeley and Los Angeles: University of California Press, 1991.

———. *The Last Emperors: A Social History of Qing Imperial Institutions*. Berkeley and Los Angeles: University of California Press, 1998.

Razriadnaia kniga 1475–1598 gg. Edited by V. I. Buganov. Moscow: Nauka, 1966.

Razriadnaia kniga 1475–1605 gg. Edited by V.I. Buganov. 3 vols. Moscow: Institut istorii AN SSSR, 1977–1989.

Reutenfels, Jacob. "Skazanie sviatleishemu gertsogu toskanskomu Koz'me Tret'emu o Moskovii." In *ChIOIDR*. Part 1: vol. 214 (1905, bk. 3), 1–137 (Inostrannye materialy). Part 2: vol. 218 (1906, bk. 3), 129–228 (Inostrannye materialy).

Rimskii-Korsakov, Nikolai. *Tsarskaia nevesta*. DVD. Directed by Vladimir Gorikker. Moscow: Bolshoi Opera and Theater, 1965.

Rimsky-Korsakov, Nicolai. *The Tsar's Bride*. Audio CD (2008). Conductor, Fouat Mansourian. Moscow: Bolshoi Theater Orchestra, 1973.

Rimsky-Korsakov, Nikolay. *The Tsar's Bride: Opera in Four Acts*. Text by the composer and Ilia Fedorovich Tyumenev. New York: Opera Orchestra of New York, 1995.

Rinhuber, Laurent. *Relation du voyage en Russie fait en 1684 par Laurent Rinhuber, publié pour la première fois d'après les manuscrits qui se conservent à la Bibliothèque ducale publique de Gotha*. Berlin: A. Cohn, 1883.

Robinson, Harlow Loomis. "Nikolai Rimsky-Korsakov. *The Tsar's Bride*." *Opera Quarterly* 8, no. 4 (Winter 1991): 112–14.

Rogger, Hans. *National Consciousness in Eighteenth-Century Russia*. Cambridge, Mass.: Harvard University Press, 1960.

Rooth, Anna Birgitta. *The Cinderella Cycle*. Lund: C. W. K. Gleerup, 1951.

Rosovetskii, S. K. "Povest' o zhenit'be Ivana Groznogo na Marii Temriukovne." In *Pamiatniki kul'tury. Novye otkrytiia. Ezhegodnik 1975*, 27–37. Moscow: Nauka, 1976.

Rossiiskaia rodoslovnaia kniga. Edited by Petr Dolgorukov. 4 vols. St. Petersburg: Tipografiia Karla Vingebera, Tipografiia Eduarda Veimara, Tipografiia III Otdeleniia Sobstvennoi E. I. V. Kantseliarii, 1854–1857.

Rowland, Daniel. "Architecture, Image, and Ritual in the Throne Rooms of Muscovy, 1550–1650: A Preliminary Survey." In *Rude and Barbarous Kingdom Revisited*. Edited by Chester S. L. Dunning et al., 53–71. Bloomington: Slavica, 2008.

———. "Did Muscovite Literary Ideology Place Limits on the Power of the Tsar (1540s–1660s)." *Russian Review* 49 (1990): 125–55.

———. "The Problem of Advice in Muscovite Tales about the Time of Troubles." *Russian History* 6, pt. 2 (1979): 259–83.

Rummel', Vitol'd Vladislavovich, and Vladimir Vladimirovich Golubtsov, eds. *Rodoslovnyi sbornik russkikh dvorianskikh familii*. 2 vols. St. Petersburg: A. S. Suvorin, 1886–1887.

Runciman, Steven. "Some Notes on the Role of the Empress." *Eastern Churches Review* 4 (1972): 119–24.

Rüß, Hartmut. *Adel und Adelsoppositionen im Moskauer Staat*. Wiesbaden: Steiner, 1975.

———. "Elena Vasil'evna Glinskaja." *Jahrbücher für Geschichte Osteuropas* 19 (1971): 481–98.

Russkaia Istoricheskaia Biblioteka. 39 vols. St. Petersburg, Petrograd, Leningrad: various publishers, 1872–1927.

Russkii biograficheskii slovar'. 27 vols. St. Petersburg, Petrograd, Moscow: Izdanie Imperatorskogo Russkogo istoricheskogo obshchestva, 1896–1918; vols. 3A and 20A, 1991.

Ryan, W. F. *Russian Magic at the British Library: Books, Manuscripts, Scholars, Travellers*. In the British Library's series Panizzi Lectures for the year 2005. London: The British Library, 2006.

———. "The Witchcraft Hysteria in Early Modern Europe: Was Russia an Exception?" *Slavonic and East European Review* 76, no. 1 (1998): 49–84.

Rydén, Lennart. "The Bride-Shows at the Byzantine Court—History or Fiction?" *Eranos* 83 (1985): 175–91.

Sakharov, Ivan Petrovich, ed. *Skazaniia russkogo naroda*. Vol. 2, Book 6. St. Petersburg: Guttenburgovaia Tipografiia, 1849.

Savelov, Leonid Mikhailovich. "Boiare Romanovykh i ikh rodstvennyia sviazi." *Drevnosti. Trudy Imperatorskogo Moskovskogo arkheologicheskogo obshchestva* 24 (1914): 233–42.

———. *Rodoslovnye zapisi: Opyt rodoslovnogo slovaria russkogo drevnego dvorianstva*. 3 vols. Moscow: Istoriko-rodoslovnoe obshchestvo, 1906–1909.

Sbornik Imperatorskogo russkogo istoricheskogo obshchestva. 148 vols. St. Petersburg: various publishers, 1867–1916.

Sbornik materialov po istorii predkov tsaria Mikhaila Feodorovicha Romanova. Edited by N. N. Selifontov. 2 parts. St. Petersburg, n.p., 1898–1901.

Schuyler, Eugene. *Peter the Great, Emperor of Russia*. 2 vols. New York: Charles Scribner & Sons, 1884.

Sedov, Pavel V. "Detskie gody tsaria Fedora Alekseevicha." In *Srednevekovaia Rus': Sbornik nauchnykh statei k 65-letiiu so dnia rozhdeniia professora R. G. Skrynnikova*. Edited by S. V. Lobachev and A. S. Lavrov, 77–93. St. Petersburg: Izdatel'stvo Sankt-Peterburgskogo universiteta, 1995.

———. *Zakat Moskovskogo tsarstva: Tsarskii dvor kontsa XVII veka*. St. Petersburg: Dmitrii Bulanin, 2007.

Semedo, Álvaro. *The History of the Great and Renowned Monarchy of China*. London: John Crook, 1655.

Semevskii, Mikhail Ivanovich. *Tsaritsa Katerina Alekseevna, Anna i Villim Mons*. St. Petersburg: Tipografiia V. S. Balasheva, 1884. Reprint, Leningrad: Khudozhestvennaia literatura, 1990.

———. *Tsaritsa Praskov'ia, 1664–1723. Ocherk iz Russkoi istorii XVIII veka*. St. Petersburg: Tipografiia M. M. Stasiulevicha, 1883.

Serafimov, A. *Pravila i praktika tserkvi otnositel'no prisoedineniia k pravoslaviiu nepravoslavnykh khristian*. Kostroma, 1882.

Shaposhnik, Viacheslav Valentinovich. *Ivan Groznyi. Pervyi russkii tsar'*. St. Petersburg: Vita Nova, 2006.

———. *Tserkovno-gosudarstvennye otnosheniia v Rossii v 30–80-e gody XVI veka*. St. Petersburg: Izdatel'stvo St.-Petersburgskogo universiteta, 2006.

Shcherbachev, Iu. N. "Datskii arkhiv. Materialy po istorii drevnei Rossii, khraniashchiesia v Kopengagene (1326–1690)." *ChIOIDR*. Vol. 184 (1893, bk. 1): i–viii, 1–340.

———. "Kopengagenskie akty, otnosiashchiesia do russkoi istorii (1326–

1569)." Part 1. *ChIOIDR*. Vol. 255 (1915, bk. 4). Part 2. *ChIOIDR*. Vol. 257 (1916, bk. 2).

Shcherbachev, Oleg Viacheslavovich. "O rodstve Saltykovykh s Mikhailom Fedorovichem Romanovym." *Letopis' Istoriko-Rodoslovnogo Obshchestva v Moskve* (1995, no. 3): 62–67.

Shcherbatov, Mikhail Mikhailovich. "O brakakh rossiiskikh tsarei." In *Neizdannye sochineniia*. Edited by N. Rubenshtein, 100–111. Moscow: OGIZ SOTsEKGIZ, 1935.

———. *On the Corruption of Morals in Russia*. Edited and translated by Anthony Lentin. Cambridge: Cambridge University Press, 1969.

Sheremetev, S. D. "Po povodu rodosloviia Nagikh." *Izvestiia RGO*. Vol. 1 (1900): 3–6 (otdel I).

Shil'der, Nikolai Karlovich. *Imperator Aleksandr Pervyi. Ego zhizn' i tsarstvovanie*. 2d ed. 4 vols. St. Petersburg: A. S. Suvorin, 1904–1905.

Shilov, A. "Ivan Nasedka," *RBS* [vol. 11] (1914): 105–110.

Shmidt, Segurt Ottovich. "O vremeni sostavlenia 'Vypisi' o vtorom brake Vasiliia III (O pouchenii popa Sil'vestra)." In *Novoe o proshlom nashei strany. Pamiati akademika M. N. Tikhomirova*. Edited by Aleksandrov, 110–22. Moscow: Nauka, 1967.

———, ed. *Opisi Tsarskogo arkhiva XVI v. i Arkhiva Posol'skogo prikaza 1614 g*. Moscow: Izdatel'stvo vostochnoi literatury, 1960.

———, ed. "Pozdnyi letopischik so svedeniiami po istorii Rossii XVI v." In *Letopisi i khroniki: sbornik stat'ei, 1973 g.*, 347–53. Moscow: Nauka, 1974.

———. "Prodolzhenie khronografa redaktsii 1512." *IA* (1951, no. 7): 254–99.

Silvas, Anna M. "Kassia the Nun c. 810–865: An Appreciation." In *Byzantine Women: Varieties of Experience, AD 800–1210*. Edited by Lynda Garland, 17–40. Aldershot, UK: Ashgate, 2006.

Skinner, Barbara. *On the Western Front of the Eastern Church: Uniate and Orthodox Conflict in 18th-Century Poland, Ukraine, Belarus, and Russia*. DeKalb: Northern Illinois University Press, 2009.

Skrynnikov, Ruslan Grigor'evich. *Ivan Groznyi*. Moscow: Nauka, 1983.

———. *Oprichnyi terror*. St. Petersburg: Izdatel'stvo Leningradskogo universiteta, 1969.

———. *Rossiia posle oprichniny*. Leningrad: Izdatel'stvo Leningradskogo universiteta, 1975.

———. "Samoderzhavie i Oprichnina." In *Vnutrenniaia politika tsarizma (seredina XVI–nachalo XX vv.)*. Edited by N. E. Nosov, 69–99. Leningrad: Nauka, 1967.

———. *Sviatiteli i vlasti*. Leningrad: Lenizdat, 1990.

———. *Tsarstvo terrora*. St. Petersburg: Nauka, 1992.

Slovar' knizhnikov i knizhnosti drevnei Rusi. Vol. 1: *XI–pervaia polovina XIV v.* Edited by D. S. Likhachev. Leningrad: Nauka, 1987.

Slovar' knizhnikov i knizhnosti drevnei Rusi. Vol. 2: *Vtoraia polovina XIV–XVI v.*

Edited by D. S. Likhachev. 2 parts. Leningrad: Nauka, 1988–1989.

Smirnov, S. *Drevne-russkii dukhovnik*. Moscow: Sinodal'naia tipografiia, 1913.

Smith, Abby. "The Brilliant Career of Prince Golitsyn." *Harvard Ukrainian Studies* 19 (1995): 639–54.

Smith, Douglas. "Did Catherine the Great and Grigorii Potemkin Wed? Some Myths, Facts, and Observations on Secret Royal Marriages." In *Russian History from the Time of Troubles to the Collapse of the Soviet Union*. Edited by Steven A. Usitalo and William Benton Whisenhunt, 79–89. Lanham, Md.: Rowman and Littlefield, 2008.

Sobranie gosudarstvennykh gramot i dogovorov, khraniashchikhsia v gosudarstvennoi kollegii inostrannykh del. 5 vols. Moscow: Tipografiia N. S. Vsevolozhskogo, 1813–1894.

Soldat, Cornelia. "The Limits of Muscovite Autocracy: The Relations between the Grand Prince and the Boyars in the Light of Iosif Volotskii's *Prosvetitel'*." *Cahiers du Monde russe* 46, nos. 1–2 (January–June 2005): 265–76.

Solodkin, Ia. G. "K datirovke 'Vypisi' o vtorom brake Vasiliia III." *Gumanitarnye nauki v Sibiri* 2 (1998). Accessed at http://www.philosophy.nsc.ru/journals/humscience/2_98/11-SOLOD.HTM (October 24, 2010).

Solov'ev, Sergei Mikhailovich. *Istoriia Rossii s drevneishikh vremen*. 15 vols. Moscow: Izdatel'stvo sotsial'no-ekonomicheskoi literatury, 1959–1966.

Soullière, Ellen. "The Imperial Marriages of the Ming Dynasty." *Papers on Far Eastern History* 37 (1988): 15–42.

———. "Reflections on Chinese Despotism and the Power of the Inner Court." *Asian Profile* 12, no. 2 (1984): 130–45.

Speck, Paul. "Eine Brautschau für Staurakios?" *Jahrbuch der Österreichischen Byzantinistik* 49 (1999): 26–30.

Das Speisungsbuch von Volokolamsk: Eine Quelle zur Sozialgeschichte russischer Klöster im 16. Jahrhundert. Edited by Ludwig Steindorff. Vol. 12 in the series Bausteine zur Slavischen Philologie und Kulturgeschichte. Reihe B: Editionen, Neue Folge. Cologne: Böhlau, 1998.

Speranskii, M. N. "Russkie poddelki rukopisei v nachale XIX veka (Bardin i Sulakadzev)." *Problemy istochnikovedeniia* 5 (1956): 44–101.

Spock, Jennifer B. "Community Building and Social Identity: Donations to the Solovki Monastery, 1460–1645." *Jahrbücher für Geschichte Osteuropas* 55 (2007): 534–65.

Staden, Heinrich von. *Aufzeichungen über den Moskauer Staat*. Edited by Fritz T. Epstein. Hamburg: Cram, de Gruyter, 1964.

———. *The Land and Government of Muscovy*. Translated by Thomas Esper. Stanford: Stanford University Press, 1967.

———. *O Moskve Ivana Groznogo. Zapiski nemtsa-oprichnika*. Translated by I. I. Polosin. Moscow: M. and S. Sabashnikov, 1925.

Starostina, T. V. "Ob opale A. S. Matveeva v sviazi s sysknym delom 1676–1677 gg. o khranenii zagovornykh pisem." In *Uchenye zapiski Karelo-finskogo universiteta*. Vol. 2, vyp. 1: Istoricheskie i filologicheskie nauki (1947): 44–89.

Steindorff, Ludwig. "Commemoration and Administrative Techniques in Muscovite Monasteries." *Russian History* 22, no. 4 (Winter 1995): 433–54.

———. *Memoria in Altrußland: Untersuchungen zu den Formen christlicher Totensorge*. In the series Quellen und Studien Geschichte des östlichen Europe, 38. Stuttgart: Franz Steiner Verlag, 1994.

———. "Memorial Practice as a Means of Integrating the Muscovite State." *Jahrbücher für Geschichte Osteuropas* 55 (2007): 517–33.

———. "Princess Mariia Golenina: Perpetuating Identity through Care for the Deceased." In *Culture and Identity in Muscovy, 1359–1584*. Edited by A. M. Kleimola and G. D. Lenhoff, 557–77. Moscow: "ITZ-Garant," 1997.

Sterligova, I. A., and L. A. Shchennikova, eds., *Tsarskii khram: Blagoveshchenskii sobor Moskovskogo kremlia v istorii Russkoi kul'tury*. Moscow, IPP Kuna, 2008.

Stevens, Carol Belkin. *Russia's Wars of Emergence, 1460–1730*. Harlow, UK: Pearson Longman, 2007.

Stone, John A. "The Pastor and the Tzar: A Comment on *The Comedy of Artaxerxes*." *Bulletin of the New York Public Library* 72, no. 4 (April 1968): 215–51.

Strahlenberg, Philip John von. *An Historico-Geographical Description of the North and Eastern Parts of Europe and Asia; But more particularly of Russia, Siberia, and Great Tartary; Both in their Ancient and Modern State*. London: Printed for W. Innys and R. Manby, at the West-End of St. Paul's, 1738.

———. *Zapiski kapitana Filippa Ioganna Stralenberga ob istorii i geografii Rossiiskoi imperii Petra Velikogo. Servernaia i vostochnaia chast' Evropy i Azii*. Edited by M. P. Iroshnikov. Compiled by E. A. Savel'eva, Iu. N. Bespiatykh, and V. E. Vozgrin. Moscow-Leningrad: Institute istorii SSSR, Leningradskoe otdelenie, 1985.

Studenkin, G. I. "Romanovy: tsarstvuiushchii dom Rossiiskoi imperii s 1613 g." *Russkaia starina* 9 (April 1878): i–xxxii.

Szeftel, Marc. "The Title of the Muscovite Monarch up to the End of the Seventeenth Century." *Canadian-American Slavic Studies* 13, nos. 1–2 (1979): 59–81.

Tanner, Marie. *The Last Descendant of Æneas: The Habsburgs and the Mythic Image of the Emperor*. New Haven: Yale University Press, 1993.

Tatishchev, Vasilii Nikitich. *Istoriia Rossiiskaia*. 7 vols. Leningrad: Nauka, 1962–1968.

Taube, Johann, and Elbert Kruse. "Poslanie Ioganna Taube i Elberta Kruze kak istoricheskii istochnik." Edited and translated by Mikhail G. Roginskii. *Russkii istoricheskii zhurnal* 8 (1922): 10–59.

Taube, Moshé, and Hugh M. Olmsted. "'Povest' o Esfiri': The Ostroh Bible and

Maksim Grek's Translation of the Book of Esther." *Harvard Ukrainian Studies* 11, nos. 1/2 (1987): 100–117.

Thegan, *Die Taten Ludwigs (Gesta Hludowici imperatoris)*, and Astronomus, *Das Leben Kaiser Ludwigs (Vita Hludowici imperatoris)*. Edited by Ernst Tremp. Published together in the series Monumenta Germaniae Historica, Scriptores Rerum Germanicarum in usum scholarum separatim editi, 64. Hanover: Hahnsche Buchhandlung, 1995.

Theophanes. *Chronographia*. 2 vols. Edited by Karl de Boor. Leipzig: B. G. Teubneri, 1883–1884.

Thompson, Stith. *Motif-Index of Folk Literature: A Classification of Narrative Elements in Folk-Tales, Ballads, Myths, Fables, Mediæval Romances, Exempla, Fabliaux, Jest-Books, and Local Legends*. In the series Indiana University Studies (nos. 96, 97, 100, 101, 105, 106, 108, 109, 110, 111, 112). 6 vols. Bloomington, Ind.: n.p., 1932–1936.

Thou, Jacques-Auguste de. *Histoire universelle de Jacques-Auguste de Thou. Depuis 1543. jusqu'en 1607. Traduite sur l'edition Latine de Londres*. 16 vols. Londres, 1734.

Thyrêt, Isolde. *Between God and Tsar: Religious Symbolism and the Royal Women of Muscovite Russia*. DeKalb: Northern Illinois University Press, 2001.

———. "'Blessed Is the Tsaritsa's Womb': The Myth of Miraculous Birth and Royal Motherhood in Muscovite Russia." *Russian Review* 53, no. 4 (October 1994): 479–96.

———. "The Cultural Politics of the Grand Princes of Muscovy." *Russian History* 33, nos. 2–4 (Summer–Winter 2006): 333–52.

———. "Marfa Ivanovna and the Expansion of the Role of the Tsar's Mother in the Seventeenth Century." In *Rude and Barbarous Kingdom Revisited*. Edited by Chester S. L. Dunning et al., 109–29. Bloomington, Ind.: Slavica, 2008.

———. "The Royal Women of Ivan IV's Family and the Meaning of Forced Tonsure." In *Servants of the Dynasty: Palace Women in World History*. Edited by Anne Walthall, 159–71. Berkeley and Los Angeles: University of California Press, 2008.

Tikhomirov, Mikhail Nikolaevich. *Istoricheskie sviazi Rossii so slavianskimi stranami i Vizantiei*. Moscow: Nauka, 1969.

———. "K voprosu o Vypisi o vtorom brake Vasiliia III." In *Sbornik statei v chest' akademika A. I. Sobolevskogo*. Edited by V. N. Perets, 91–94. Moscow: Akademiia nauk SSSR, 1928.

———. "Novyi pamiatnik Moskovskoi politicheskoi literatury XVI v." In *Moskovskii krai v ego proshlom*, 112–14. Vol. 2 of the series Trudy Obshchestva izucheniia Moskovskoi oblasti. Moscow: Moskovskii otdel narodnogo obrazovaniia, 1930.

———. "Piskarevskii letopisets kak istoricheskii istochnik o sobytiiakh XVI–nachala XVII v." *Russkoe letopisanie*, 232–47. Moscow: Nauka, 1979.

———. "Stranitsa iz zhizni Ivana Peresvetova." In *Rossiiskoe gosudarstvo XV–XVII vv*. Edited by A. V. Murav'ev, S. O. Shmidt, and V. B. Pavlov-Sil'vanskii, 70–73. Moscow: Nauka, 1973.

———. "Zapiski o regentstve Eleny Glinskoi i boiarskom pravlenii 1533–1547 gg." *Istoricheskie zapiski* 46 (1954): 278–88.

———. "Zapiski prikaznykh liudei kontsa XVII v." *TODRL* 12 (1956): 442–57.

Timofeev, Ivan. *Vremennik Ivana Timofeeva*. Edited by V. P. Adrianova-Peretts. Commentary by O. A. Derzhavina. Moscow-Leningrad: Akademiia Nauk SSSR, 1951.

Treadgold, Warren. "Bride-Shows of the Byzantine Emperors." *Byzantion* 49 (1979): 395–413.

———. "The Historicity of Imperial Bride-Shows." *Jahrbuch der Österreichischen Byzantinistik* 54 (2004): 39–52.

———. "The Problem of the Marriage of the Emperor Theophilus." *Greek, Roman and Byzantine Studies* 16 (1975): 325–41.

Tsereteli, E. *Elena Ioannovna. Velikaia kniaginia litovskaia, russkaia, koroleva pol'skaia*. St. Petersburg: Tipografiia I. N. Sorokhodova, 1898.

Tsvetaev, D. "Mariia Vladimirovna i Magnus Datskii." *ZhMNP* 196 (March 1879): 57–85.

Tysiachnaia kniga 1550 g. i Dvorovaia tetrad' 50-x godov XVI v. Edited by A. A. Zimin. Moscow-Leningrad: Akademiia nauk SSSR, 1950.

Ul'ianovskii, V. I. *Smutnoe vremia*. Moscow: Evropa, 2006.

Ungurianu, Dan. *Plotting History: The Russian Historical Novel in the Imperial Age*. Madison: University of Wisconsin Press, 2007.

Uroff, Phillip Benjamin. *Grigorii Karpovich Kotoshikhin, On Russia in the Reign of Alexis Mikhailovich*. Ph.D. diss., University of Illinois, 1970.

Uspenskii, B. A. "Svad'ba Lzhedmitriia," *TODRL* 50 (1997): 404–25.

Vasetskii, Nikolai Aleksandrovich. *Zhenshchiny: vo vlasti i bezvlastii*. Moscow: "Znanie," 1977.

Vasil'chikov, Aleksandr A., ed. "Chin brakosochetaniia tsaria Ivana Vasil'evicha s tsaritseiu Annoiu Vasil'chikovykh (7083/1575 g.)." *Izvestiia RGO*. Vol. 1 (1900): 1–13 (otdel 3).

———. "Rod Naryshkinykh." In *Russkii arkhiv, izdavaemyi pri Chertkovskoi biblioteke Petrom Bartenevym* 9 (1871): cols. 1487–1519.

Vel'iaminov-Zernov, V. V. *Issledovaniia o kasimovskikh tsariakh i tsarevichakh*. 2 vols. St. Petersburg: Imperatorskaia Akademiia nauk, 1863–1867.

Veselovskii, Stepan Borisovich. *D'iaki i pod'iachie v XV–XVII vv*. Moscow: Nauka, 1973.

———. "Dukhovnoe zaveshchanie Ivana Groznogo kak istoricheskii istochnik." *Izvestiia AN SSSR* 4, no. 6 (1947): 505–20.

———. *Issledovaniia po istorii klassa sluzhilykh zemlevladel'tsev*. Moscow: Nauka, 1969.

———. *Issledovaniia po istorii oprichniny*. Moscow: Izdatel'stvo Akademii nauk SSSR, 1963.

Vinson, Martha. "The Life of Theodora and the Rhetoric of the Byzantine Bride-Show." *Jahrbuch der Österreichischen Byzantinistik* 49 (1999): 31–60.

———. "Rhetoric and Writing Strategies in the Ninth Century." In *Rhetoric in Byzantium*. Edited by E. Jeffreys, 9–22. Aldershot, UK: Ashgate, 2003.

———. "Romance and Reality in the Byzantine Bride-Show." In *Gender in the Early Medieval World: East and West, 300–900*. Edited by Leslie Brubaker and Julia M. H. Smith, 102–20. Cambridge.: Cambridge University Press, 2004.

Vkladnaia kniga Troitse-Sergieva monastyria. Edited by E. N. Klitina, T. N. Manushina, and T. V. Nikolaeva. Moscow: Nauka, 1987.

Vlas'ev, Gennadii Aleksandrovich, ed. *Potomstvo Riurika*. 1 vol. in 3 pts. St. Petersburg: T-vo R. Golike i A. Vil'borg, 1906–1907.

Vosstanie v Moskve, 1682 g. Sbornik dokumentov. Edited by V. I. Buganov. Moscow: Nauka, 1976.

Vremennik Imperatorskogo Moskovskogo obshchestva istorii i drevnostei rossiiskikh. 25 vols. Moscow: Universitetskaia tipografiia, 1849–1857.

Vykhody gosudarei tsarei i velikikh kniazei Mikhaila Fedorovicha, Alekseia Mikhailovicha, Fedora Alekseevicha, vsea Rusi samoderzhtsev (s 1632 po 1682). Edited by P. Stroiev. Moscow: Tipografiia Avgusta Semena, 1844.

"Vypis' iz gosudarevy gramoty, chto prislana k velikomu kniaziu Vasiliiu Ivanovichu o sochetanii vtorago braku i o razluchenii pervago braka chadorodiia radi. Tvorenie Paiseino startsa Ferapontova monasteryia." Edited by O. M. Bodianskii. *ChIOIDR* (1847, no. 12 [on title page: 8]), 1–8 (*Smes'*).

Waliszewski, K[azimierz]. *Ivan the Terrible*. Translated by Mary Loyd. Philadelphia: J. P. Lippincott, 1904.

Walthall, Anne, ed. *Servants of the Dynasty: Palace Women in World History*. Berkeley and Los Angeles: University of California Press, 2008.

Wang, Shuo. "Qing Imperial Women: Empresses, Concubines, and Aisin Gioro Daughters." In *Servants of the Dynasty: Palace Women in World History*. Edited by Anne Walthall, 137–58. Berkeley and Los Angeles: University of California Press, 2008.

———. "The Selection of Women for the Qing Imperial Harem." *Chinese Historical Review* 11, no. 2 (fall 2004): 212–22.

Watson, Rubie S., and Patricia Buckley Ebrey, eds. *Marriage and Inequity in Chinese Society*. Berkeley and Los Angeles: University of California Press, 1991.

Waugh, Daniel Clarke, ed. *Essays in Honor of A. A. Zimin*. Bloomington, Ind.: Slavica Publishers, 1983.

Weickhardt, George G. "Kotoshikhin: An Evaluation and Interpretation." *Russian History* 17, no. 2 (1990): 127–54.

———. "The Pre-Petrine Law of Property." *Slavic Review* 53, no. 4 (Winter 1993): 663–79.

———. "Was There Private Property in Muscovite Russia?" *Slavic Review* 54, no. 2 (Summer 1994): 531–38.

Westerink, L. G. *Nicholas I, Patriarch of Constantinople: Miscellaneous Writings*. Vol. 6 of *Dumbarton Oaks Texts*. Washington, D.C.: Dumbarton Oaks, 1981.

Whitworth, Charles [Ch. Vitvort]. "Ch. Whitworth to the right honourable m. secretary S-t. John," *SbIRIO*. Vol. 61 (1888): 1–263.

Wolff, Jósef. *Kniaziowie Litewsko-ruscy od końca czternastego wieku*. Warsaw: Księgarnia Gebethnera i Wolffa, 1895.

Woodworth, C. K. "Sophia and the Golden Belt: What Caused Moscow's Civil Wars of 1425–1450?" *Russian Review* 68, no. 2 (April 2009): 187–98.

Worobec, Christine D. "Accommodation and Resistance." In *Russia's Women: Accommodation, Resistance, Transformation*. Edited by Barbara Evans Clements, Barbara Alpern Engel, and Christine D. Worobec, 17–28. Berkeley and Los Angeles: University of California Press, 1991.

Wortman, Richard S. *The Formation of a Russian Legal Consciousness*. Chicago: University of Chicago Press, 2010.

———. "The 'Fundamental State Laws' of 1832 as Symbolic Act." *Miscellanea Slavica: Sbornik statei k 70-letiiu Borisa Andreevicha Uspenskogo*. Edited by F. B. Uspenskii, 398–408. Moscow: Indrik, 2008.

———. "Russian Monarchy and the Rule of Law: New Considerations of the Court Reform of 1864." *Kritika* 6, no. 1 (Winter 2005): 145–70.

———. *Scenarios of Power: Myth and Ceremony in Russian Monarchy*. 2 vols. Princeton: Princeton University Press, 1995–2000.

Zabelin, Ivan [Egorovich]. *Domashnii byt russkikh tsarei v XVI i XVII st*. Vol. 1, pts. 1 and 2 of *Domashnii byt russkogo naroda v XVI i XVII st*. Reprint, from 1918 and 1915 editions. Moscow: Iazyki russkoi kul'tury, 2000–2003.

———. *Domashnii byt russkikh tsarits v XVI i XVII st*. Vol. 2 of *Domashnii byt russkogo naroda v XVI i XVII st*. Reprint, from 1901 edition (3rd ed., with additions). Moscow: Iazyki russkoi kul'tury, 2003.

———. *Materialy* [accompanying *Domashnii byt russkogo naroda v XVI i XVII st*. and *Domashnii byt russkikh tsarits v XVI i XVII st*.]. Reprint, from various editions, with overlapping pagination. Moscow: Iazyki russkoi kul'tury, 2003.

Zanger, Abby E. *Scenes from the Marriage of Louis XIV: Nuptial Fictions and the Making of Absolutist Power*. Stanford: Stanford University Press, 1997.

Zimin, Aleksandr Aleksandrovich. *Formirovanie boiarskoi aristokratii v Rossii vo vtoroi polovine XV–pervoi treti XVI v*. Moscow: Nauka, 1988.

———. "Ivan Groznyi i Simeon Bekbulatovich v 1574 g." *Uchenye zapiski Kazanskogo gosudarstvennogo pedagogicheskogo universiteta* 80: *Iz istorii Tatarii* 4 (1970): 141–63.

———. "Kolychevy i russkoe boiarstvo XIV–XVI vv." *Arkheograficheskii ezhegodnik za 1963 g.*, 5–71 Moscow: Izdatel'stvo Akademii nauk SSSR, 1964.

———. "Kratkie letopistsy XV–XVI vv." In *Istoricheskii arkhiv* 5 (1950): 3–39.

———. *Oprichnina Ivana Groznogo*. Moscow: Mysl', 1964.

———. *Reformy Ivana Groznogo. Ocherki sotsial'no-ekonomicheskoi i politicheskoi istorii Rossii serediny XVI v.* Moscow: Izdatel'stvo sotsial'no-ekonomicheskoi literatury, 1960.

———. *Rossiia na poroge novogo vremeni (Ocherki politicheskoi istorii Rossii pervoi treti XVI v.).* Moscow: Mysl', 1972.

———. *Rossiia na rubezhe XV–XVI stoletii (Ocherki sotsial'no-politicheskoi istorii).* Moscow: Mysl', 1982.

———. *Russkie letopisi i khronografy kontsa XV–XVI v.* Moscow: Moskovskii gosudarstvennyi istoriko-arkhivnyi institut, 1960.

———. "Sostav boiarskoi dumy XV–XVI vekakh." In *Arkheograficheskii ezhegodnik za 1957 g.*, 41–87. Moscow: Akademiia nauk SSSR, 1958.

———. *V kanun groznykh potriasenii.* Moscow: Mysl', 1986.

———. *Vitiaz' na rasput'e: feodal'naia voina v XV v.* Moscow: Mysl', 1991.

———. "Vypis' o vtorom brake Vasiliia III." *TODRL* 30 (1976): 132–48.

Zimmermann, T. C. Price. *Paolo Giovio: The Historian and the Crisis of the Sixteenth Century.* Princeton: Princeton University Press, 1995.

Zitser, Ernest. *The Transfigured Kingdom: Sacred Parody and Charismatic Authority at the Court of Peter the Great.* Ithaca: Cornell University Press, 2004.

———. "The *Vita* of Prince Boris Ivanovich 'Korybut'-Kurakin: Personal Life-Writing and Aristocratic Self-Fashioning at the Court of Peter the Great." *Jahrbücher für Geschichte Osteuropas* 59, no. 2 (2011): 163–94.

Index